STRINGED INSTRUMENTS OF ANCIENT GREECE

Stringed Instruments
of
Ancient Greece

Martha Maas and Jane McIntosh Snyder

Yale University Press
New Haven and London

This book was published with the generous
assistance of Nicholas E. Kulukundis and Elias N.
Kulukundis.

Designed by James J. Johnson
and set in Times Roman type by
Brevis Press, Bethany, Connecticut.
Printed in the United States of America by
Halliday Lithograph, West Hanover, Massachusetts.

Library of Congress Cataloging-in-Publication Data

Maas, Martha, 1934–
   Stringed instruments of ancient Greece.

   Bibliography: p.
   Includes index.
   1. Musical instruments, Ancient—Greece.
I. Snyder, Jane McIntosh.   II. Title.
ML169.M2   1989   787′.00938   87–2103
ISBN 0–300–03686–8 (alk. paper)

10 9 8 7 6 5 4 3 2 1

Contents

Illustrations

(r.f. = red-figured   b.f. = black-figured   w.g. = white-ground)

Acknowledgments

This book is the result of a long collaborative effort. The authors worked together as a team to collect the evidence on which it is based; each read and criticized what the other wrote; and both shared in the editorial tasks of combining the material for each chapter. We hope that the resulting study reflects a true blending of the philological and musicological approaches to our subject.

The authors gratefully acknowledge financial assistance from the American Council of Learned Societies and the Ohio State University Center for Medieval and Renaissance Studies. We are also grateful to the Ohio State University College of Humanities in particular for generous support toward the cost of obtaining photographs, and to Deans Arthur Adams, Diether Haenicke, and G. Micheal Riley, as well as to the Ohio State University College of the Arts and to Dean Andrew Broekema. In addition, we should like to thank Professor Herbert Livingston (Chair, Division of Music History), Professor Mark Morford (former Chair, Department of Classics), and Professor Charles Babcock (Chair, Department of Classics). The authors are particularly grateful for publication subsidies from Ohio State University's Office of Research and Graduate Studies (Jack M. Hollander, Vice-President), the College of Humanities (G. Micheal Riley, Dean), and the College of the Arts (Robert L. Arnold, Acting Dean).

The authors have benefited greatly from the cooperation and assistance of many colleagues and friends. In particular we should like to thank Professors Douglas Feaver and Darrell Amyx for friendly help as we began our project; the American School of Classical Studies in Athens for assistance in studying material in Greek museums; Jean Susorney Wellington, Librarian, University of Cincinnati Classics Library, for kind help far beyond the call of duty; Susan Wyngaard and the late Jacqueline Sisson, Librarians, the Ohio State University Fine Arts Library, for bibliographical assistance; Karen Givler and Madonna Alessandro for expert typing and word processing; and the staffs of the various museums that we visited for their cooperation in allowing us to make study photographs, especially the National Museum in Athens, the British Museum, the Boston Museum of Fine Arts, and the Metropolitan Museum of Art in New York.

Finally, we are deeply indebted to Dr. Ann M. Miller and Steven McGuire for assistance in collecting the data on which this book is based, and to Professors Thomas Mathiesen, Timothy McNiven, Margaret Downie Banks, and Jon Solomon for their helpful criticism of our work. For any imperfections that remain, the authors alone are responsible.

Introduction

No ancient culture has left us more tantalizing glimpses of its music than that of the Greeks, whose art and literature speak to us again and again of the role of music, its power, and its importance to their society.

The music itself is almost gone; and while we have a handful of fragments of musical notation, mostly of late date, and a number of treatises on music, mainly by Roman-period authors, such sources present difficulties for the study of stringed instruments from pre-Minoan times to the death of Alexander: there is all too often no satisfactory way to distinguish sufficiently between the musical systems and practices of the classical and earlier periods, and those belonging only to later centuries. But epic and lyric poetry and drama on the one hand, and vase paintings, sculptures, and archaeological remains on the other, can tell us a great deal about the rich and abundant musical life of classical and preclassical times, if we study them attentively and allow them to explain each other.

In order to learn as much as possible about Greek music itself from sources of these kinds, it is practical to focus upon the musical instruments described and depicted, with attention to the musicians who played them and the occasions on which they were played. The stringed instruments, for which there has been no comprehensive study, were the most important and frequently used instruments of the Greeks; they can tell us the most, through visual and literary detail, about the music of this ancient culture.

The ancient Greeks, and their forerunners and neighbors in the lands surrounding the Aegean Sea, knew three types of stringed instruments: the lyre, the harp, and the lute.[1] These instruments are usually found in certain shapes and sizes that can be identified with a particular culture and period. But only the lyre, in various forms, appears to have found favor with Greek-speaking people before the middle of the fifth century B.C. (hereafter B.C. is understood unless otherwise noted); and it was still their predominant stringed instrument long after that time. For this reason, most of this book is about lyres: the phorminx, kithara, lyra, and barbitos.

We cannot attribute the origin of any of these instrument types to peoples living in the Aegean area, for the evidence indicates that lyres, harps, and lutes all existed in Mesopotamia and Egypt even earlier than in the area that was to become Greece, though questions about how they came to be known in Greek lands have thus far proved unanswerable. But the Greeks and their predecessors did create their own distinctive varieties of instruments within these categories, and it is these specifically Greek forms of the instruments that will concern us here.

Although instruments of the lute type do not begin to appear in our Greek sources until the fourth century B.C., harps are known to us in Cycladic evidence that predates the Greek or even the Minoan civilization. But harps then seem to disappear, and there are none among Minoan representations and barely a rumor of them among Greek sources until the late fifth century B.C. The lyres, first found in Minoan times, are present in evidence from some part of the Greek world from that time on. For many centuries the lyre was the most important musical instrument in the ancient Greek world; it appeared in a variety of different shapes as time went on and changed its functions to suit new customs and social structures. But just as there seems to have been a certain continuity of civilization in the Aegean area at least from late Minoan times all the way to the time of Alexander, so there seems to have been a continuity of practice, if not in music itself, at least in the building of instruments of the lyre type, a continuity that the authors hope to make clear in the present work.

There are twin dangers inherent in the study of ancient Greek instruments, and, as with Odysseus' sailing between Scylla and Charybdis, one must be careful not to fall victim to one while trying to avoid the other. On the one hand one must not rely too much on literary evidence, particularly on the statements of very late authors (a tendency found, for example, in the work of Huchzermeyer, who makes almost no reference to the visual evidence).[2] But one must also not rely too heavily on the visual evidence or fall into the trap of interpreting it too literally, as authors who use both literary and visual evidence often do. In this book the authors have tried to steer a careful course that will lead to neither whirlpool nor rocks and have treated both kinds of evidence with care and cordial skepticism.

Overly literal interpretations have been especially common among writers who discuss the question of how many strings the lyre had in the earlier periods. In discussing this matter, the authors of this study have been careful to consider medium, available techniques, the style of the period, the artist's intentions, and above all, the size of the object in question. Especially in the earlier periods (Minoan, Mycenaean, and Iron Age), the size of a representation has a great deal to do with the number of strings shown on the instrument; large paintings such as frescoes show the most strings, while vase paintings, bronze figures, and seal stones have fewer (the seal stones the fewest)—and terra-cotta figures play instruments with no strings at all.

A related problem arises from the use of generalizations based on only a few visual representations, so that a rather unusual example may sometimes be taken as representative.

> There is a story, perhaps apocryphal, of a scientist who published an astounding and improbable generalization about the behaviour of rats. An incredulous colleague came into his laboratory and politely asked to see the records of the experiments on which the generalization was based. "Here they are," said the scientist, dragging a notebook from a pile of papers on his desk. And pointing to a cage in the corner, he added, "there's the rat."[3]

The odor of something akin to a lone rat sometimes clings to works about the culture of antiquity, works in which the author has drawn conclusions on the basis of a very few examples. The authors of the present study, having collected virtually all the extant literary references (more than seven hundred) and approximately two thousand visual representations, are confident, however, that insofar as it is possible to do so, they have avoided this pitfall too. As the illustrations show, and as the discrepancies between literary and visual testimony will also sometimes indicate, there is a great diversity in the size, ornamentation, and details of shape even among the examples of one instrument within, say, the lyre family. This is one of the joys, as well as one of the difficulties, of the study of musical instruments. We should not expect that *any* two of the Greek instruments within a single type will look exactly alike: that is a feature of modern factory-produced instruments. Making instruments by hand is an art, and the master craftsman who makes stringed instruments does not make any two exactly the same, particularly in matters of decoration. This variety is reflected in the visual representations of the instruments, which themselves are creative works and not entirely faithful to their models—thus making it imperative that any study of the instruments be based on as many examples as possible.

The evidence left to us from the earliest periods in the history of Greek stringed instruments, the Minoan, Mycenaean, and Iron Age civilizations, is meager in comparison with that of later eras; the only literary evidence from this intriguing millennium is Homer's *Iliad* and *Odyssey,* and scenes painted on pottery are much less abundant than in later times, leaving us to rely for visual evidence on a scattering of marble, terra-cotta, and bronze figurines, frescoes, a sarcophagus painting, small groups of vase paintings, and a few fragments of actual instruments that have been found and preserved. During the Archaic period (roughly 700–525 B.C. as defined here) vase paintings become gradually more abundant, and the works of Hesiod and the early lyric poets as well as the *Homeric Hymns* offer us fascinating bits of information about the stringed instruments. But it is not until the fifth and fourth centuries, when the Golden Age of Athens produced a great outpouring of dramatic works, poetry, and visual arts, that we are able to construct a detailed account of the instruments and their uses in a particular time and place.[4]

The soil of Greece, unlike the sands of Egypt, has preserved only a few tantalizing bits and pieces of actual stringed instruments from our period. Whereas Egyptologists can study a number of harps, lutes, and lyres (as well as instruments of other kinds), often preserved in excellent condition, Hellenists have almost nothing except some ivory ornaments and facings, a few *plektra,* and fragments of tortoiseshells. In one case, unfortunately, the ivory pieces were excavated and incorporated into a "reconstruction" at a time when knowledge of the musical instruments was considerably less sophisticated than it is today. Such reconstructions not only mislead us but also obscure or even obliterate the evidence that these fragments might have provided, had they been preserved according to modern practices and *separate* replicas (not incorporating the fragments) made. Dangers of a similar sort are further demonstrated by the fact that investigators have based their descriptions of a Mycenaean lyre in a fresco from Pylos not on the original fragment of the fresco, but on the imaginative recreation of the scene in a painting by Piet de Jong, which supplies the player with arms and the instrument with strings and a soundbox shape.

Some items of evidence cited by previous authors have been rejected in the present study. We believe that in order for an item to be usable as evidence we must be able to distinguish clearly whether the instrument is a harp or a lyre (or if it is actually a musical instrument at all), and dubious examples ought not to be included at all in constructing theories or generalizations. Moreover, when there are very few items from any one century or location (as is generally the case before the Archaic period), the existing evidence cannot be used, for example, to assign to any one locality details of the design of ornaments or the way in which the instruments were held, or to determine separate types within the family of lyres.

The continuity of types of Greek stringed instruments that will be explored in this book could be traced as well in the musical culture of the Hellenistic, Roman, and even Medieval periods. But the continuing influence of the musical instruments of Classical Greece is a subject for a separate study, and for the present volume the deaths of Alexander the Great in 323 B.C. and of his tutor, Aristotle, the following year provide a convenient stopping point with which to mark the end of an era.

Citations of Works of Art

Works of art are cited within the text and notes by museum location, followed by the number assigned the object by the museum; the name of the museum is ordinarily not given unless it is needed to avoid confusion.[5] Alphabetical lists of all objects mentioned in each chapter, with references where possible, appear on pp. 205–18. Abbreviations of titles are listed in the bibliography. The method of citing the *Corpus Vasorum Antiquorum (CVA)* is as follows: the name of the country does not appear except when necessary to avoid confusion, and the plate numbers given are the cumulative numbers that appear in most series in the lower left-hand corner of the page. For example, in the case of Athens 17497, the reference reads *CVA* 2, pl. 56, 1–4, indicating *CVA,* Greece, volume 2, cumulative plate no. 56, photographs 1–4.

Abbreviations of Classical Works

A.	Aeschylus	Eustathius	Eustathius, *Commentarii ad Homeri Iliadem et Odysseam*
A. *A.*	Aeschylus, *Agamemnon*		
Anth. Pal.	*Anthologia Palatina*	*FGrH*	*Fragmente der griechischen Historiker* (ed. F. Jacoby)
Ath.	Athenaeus		
Ar.	Aristophanes	Hdt.	Herodotus
Ar. *Av.*	Aristophanes, *Aves* (*Birds*)	Hesiod *Th.*	Hesiod, *Theogony*
Ar. *Ec.*	Aristophanes, *Ecclesiazusae*	*h. Hom.*	*Hymni Homerici* (*Homeric Hymns*)
Ar. *Eq.*	Aristophanes, *Equites* (*Knights*)	Hom. *Il.*	Homer, *Iliad*
Ar. *Nu.*	Aristophanes, *Nubes* (*Clouds*)	Hom. *Od.*	Homer, *Odyssey*
Ar. *Pl.*	Aristophanes, *Plutus*	Hor. *C.*	Horace, *Carmina* (*Odes*)
Ar. *Ra.*	Aristophanes, *Ranae* (*Frogs*)	Hsch.	Hesychius
Ar. *Th.*	Aristophanes, *Thesmophoriazusae*	Hyg. *Astr.*	Hyginus, *Astronomica*
Ar. *V.*	Aristophanes, *Vespae* (*Wasps*)	*IG*	*Inscriptiones Graecae*
Arist. *Ath. Pol.*	Aristotle, *Athenaion Politeia*	Luc. *DDeor.*	Lucian, *Dialogi Deorum*
Arist. *EE*	Aristotle, *Ethica Eudemia*	Men.	Menander
Arist. *EN*	Aristotle, *Ethica Nicomachea*	Ov. *Her.*	Ovid, *Heroides*
Arist. *Po.*	Aristotle, *Poetica*	Paus.	Pausanias
Arist. *Pol.*	Aristotle, *Politica*	Pherecr.	Pherecrates
B. *Epin.*	Bacchylides, *Epinician Odes*	Phld. *Mus.*	Philodemus, *De Musica*
Boëth. *Mus.*	Boethius, *De Musica*	Phryn. Com.	Phrynicus (Comicus)
Cic. *Leg.*	Cicero, *Leges*	Pi.	Pindar
Cicero *Sen.*	Cicero, *De Senectute*	Pi. *N.*	Pindar, *Nemean Odes*
Diog. Ath.	Diogenes Atheniensis	Pi. *O.*	Pindar, *Olympian Odes*
Et. Mag.	*Etymologicum Magnum*	Pi. *P.*	Pindar, *Pythian Odes*
Euph.	Euphorio	Pl.	Plato
Eur.	Euripides	Pl. *Alc.*	Plato, *Alcibiades*
Eur. *Al.*	Euripides, *Alcestis*	Pl. *Clit.*	Plato, *Clitopho*
Eur. *Cyc.*	Euripides, *Cyclops*	Pl. *Cra.*	Plato, *Cratylus*
Eur. *Hel.*	Euripides, *Helena*	Pl. *Euthd.*	Plato, *Euthydemus*
Eur. *HF*	Euripides, *Hercules Furens*	Pl. *Grg.*	Plato, *Gorgias*
Eur. *Hyps.*	Euripides, *Hypsipyle*	Pl. *Lg.*	Plato, *Leges*
Eur. *IA*	Euripides, *Iphigenia Aulidensis*	Pl. *Ly.*	Plato, *Lysis*
Eur. *IT*	Euripides, *Iphigenia Taurica*	Pl. *Mx.*	Plato, *Menexenus*
Eur. *Med.*	Euripides, *Medea*	Pl. *Phd.*	Plato, *Phaedo*
Eur. *Ph.*	Euripides, *Phoenissae*	Pl. *Phlb.*	Plato, *Philebus*
		Pl. *Plt.*	Plato, *Politicus*

Pl. *Prt.*	Plato, *Protagoras*
Pl. *R.*	Plato, *Republic*
Pl. *Symp.*	Plato, *Symposium*
Pl. Thg.	Plato, *Theages*
Pl. *Tht.*	Plato, *Theatetus*
Pl. *Ti.*	Plato, *Timaeus*
Pl. Com.	Plato (Comicus)
Plu.	Plutarch
Plu. *De Pyth. or.*	Plutarch, *De Pythiae oraculis*
Plu. *Per.*	Plutarch, *Pericles*
Plu. *Them.*	Plutarch, *Themistocles*
Poll.	Pollux
Ps.-Arist. *Ath.*	Pseudo-Aristotle, *Athenaion Politeia*
Ps.-Arist. *Pr.*	Pseudo-Aristotle, *Problemata*
Ps.-Plutarch, *de mus.*	Pseudo-Plutarch, *De Musica*
S.	Sophocles
S. *Ichn.*	Sophocles, *Ichneutai*

S. *OC*	Sophocles, *Oedipus Coloneus*
S. *Ph.*	Sophocles, *Philoctetes*
S. *Tr.*	Sophocles, *Trachiniae*
Sapph.	Sappho
Simon.	Simonides
Stesich.	Stesichorus
Strabo, *Geog.*	Strabo, *Geography*
TGF	*Tragicorum Graecorum Fragmenta* (ed. A. Nauck)
Theoc. *Ep.*	Theocritus, *Epigrammata*
Thgn.	Theognis
Thphr. *HP*	Theophrastus, *Historia Plantarum*
X. *An.*	Xenophon, *Anabasis*
X. *Mem.*	Xenophon, *Memorabilia*
X. *Oec.*	Xenophon, *Oeconomicus*
X. *Sym.*	Xenophon, *Symposium*

STRINGED INSTRUMENTS OF ANCIENT GREECE

CHAPTER ONE

Homer and Before

Cycladic Harps

If we begin our account of stringed instruments at the very beginning, with objects created by pre-Greek inhabitants of the Aegean area, we find that the earliest known stringed instrument in this part of the ancient world is a harp. At least seven small marble figures of seated harpists (fig. 1), approximately 15 to 30 cm (6–12 in.) high and belonging to the period between 2700 and 2100 B.C., have been discovered on islands in the Cyclades (Keros, Thera, and Naxos).[1]

The language and culture of the people who made these remarkable marble figures are unknown. It is thought that they were a people who had come from western Anatolia (modern Turkey) and that they brought their instruments with them, although no evidence has been found from this period in Anatolia confirming the existence of such instruments there.[2] We cannot know what meaning their music had for them or how closely it was bound to their religious practices, though we can assume that, since these musician-figures were found in graves, music probably had a religious significance, and musicians an important place in the culture. But we know nothing of the occasions on which their music was performed, and the marble figures cannot reveal to us what their music sounded like or even whether the musicians sang while they played.

The small male figures are remarkable, not only because they are so different from the usual "Cycladic idol," the stylized mother-goddess figure, but also because they show an instrument quite different in shape from the well-documented harps of even earlier date

from the Egyptian and Middle Eastern civilizations. The Cycladic harp represented in figure 1 is a triangular frame harp with its soundbox (the base of the triangle) resting on the player's lap. The side of the triangle nearest the player's chest rises almost vertically from the end of the soundbox. It bends down at the top, and where it is joined to the "post" it forms an ornament shaped like a bird's beak. The lower end of the post emerges horizontally from the end of the soundbox away from the player's body before curving upward. The fact that there is both neck and post, completing the triangle and making this a *frame* harp, sets this instrument apart from the bow harps and angle harps of Egypt and Mesopotamia, which, built without the reinforcing post, were open on one side.

Since the marble figures do not show the strings at all, we cannot know how many there were or how they were attached. Nor do the figures (some of them broken) reveal exactly how the strings were sounded, though their similarity of pose suggests that the fingers of both hands were used; and we may assume that, as with harps from other countries, the strings were plucked individually rather than strummed.

A lack of sources from about 2000 to 1500 B.C. conceals from us whatever cultural contacts there may have been between these Cycladic people and the Greek-speaking people who began to arrive in the Aegean area after 2000 B.C. The same lack of source material obscures the relationship, if indeed there was any, between Cycladic musical culture and that of another, racially similar pre-Greek people of the southern Aegean: the Minoans, inhabitants of the island of Crete and builders of the great and powerful civilization that is known to us not only through the excavated ruins of its palaces but also through legends such as the stories of King Minos, Daedalus and Icarus, and Theseus and the Minotaur.

Minoan Lyres

Minoan civilization itself, as it existed after about 1600 B.C., has left us a number of objects of various kinds that reveal much about the Minoan use of music and instruments. The Minoans evidently had only one kind of stringed instrument, the lyre.[3] The idea for such an instrument, with two arms surmounted by a crossbar or yoke, did not originate with them; but the Minoan lyre has a characteristic not found elsewhere until a later time, a soundbox with a rounded base. Its parallel arms are symmetrically constructed (fig. 2a), while those of contemporary Mesopotamian and Egyptian instruments are for the most part asymmetrical.

Our best information concerning this instrument comes from a painting on the side of the famous stone sarcophagus from Hagia Triada (Heraklion Museum); from two frescoes, one from Hagia Triada (Heraklion Museum) and one now at Khora from Pylos (mainland Greece, not Crete, but clearly showing the same Minoan characteristics); and from two vase paintings, on a *pyxis* (ceramic box) from Kalamion (Khania 2308, fig. 2b), and on an *amphora* (storage jar) from Sitia (Hagios Nikolaos Museum, fig. 2c). All these items belong to the period known as Late Minoan III (ca. 1400–1100 B.C.), except for the Hagia Triada fresco (ca. 1550 B.C.). There are two additional items: a terra-cotta group showing a female lyre player and dancers, from Palaikastro (Late Minoan III, Heraklion Museum), and a seal stone of unknown location from Knossos (fig. 2d, Middle Minoan II, ca. 1900–1700 B.C.).[4]

Nearly all these sources create essentially the same picture.[5] The Hagia Triada sarcophagus (fig. 2a), however, presents it in its most complete form: a male lyre player, dressed in a long robe, walks in a religious procession, playing an elaborately constructed instrument (the painter has put the player's left elbow on the wrong side of the instrument, an obvious mistake that need not cause concern). This is the only one of the three largest representations that shows the soundbox, for both frescoes are badly fragmented. The sarcophagus painting shows a very narrow, rim-like soundbox, whereas that of the instrument on the Kalamion pyxis has a broad crescent shape.[6]

The two symmetrical arms of the instrument in the sarcophagus painting seem to grow out of the soundbox and to be made of the same material. In the three largest representations, the arms first bend sharply toward each other and even more sharply out again; they then curve around more gently, making a ring by coming down to touch the bend below. At this point there are enlargements resembling animals' heads. Since the instrument is painted white on the two frescoes, these details are thought to represent swans' heads and curving necks.[7]

Birds, which have an association with a goddess or goddesses in Minoan religion, appear *near* the lyre player in three of the paintings: atop double-ax decorated columns in the sarcophagus painting and flying near or above the performer in the Pylos fresco and on the Kalamion pyxis (fig. 2b). As for the lyres themselves, those in the three largest representations suggest swans' or birds' necks and heads; but the two vase paintings (especially the one on the amphora from Sitia [fig. 2c]), the Knossos seal stone (fig. 2d), and the Palaikastro terra-cotta all suggest snakes, which also played an important role in Minoan religion.

The top sections of the arms rise vertically from the upper curve of these ring-shaped "necks," and the crossbar is attached to them, quite close above the ring on the frescoes, farther up in the case of the sarcophagus painting. The arms continue a short way above the crossbar in the three large paintings.[8] The crossbar itself, in the three large paintings, is somewhat wider in the center and at the ends, which extend out beyond the instrument's arms (but this is not true of the amphora from Sitia). The sarcophagus painting suggests that the crossbar rests in niches cut in the arms of the instrument. Only the Pylos fresco and the Kalamion pyxis offer any evidence of the way in which the strings are fastened to the crossbar: the wavy outline of the crossbar on the fresco and the small triangles below the crossbar on the pyxis probably indicate leather pads (called *kollopes* by the Greeks) around which the strings were made fast.

The instrument unmistakably has seven strings on both the Kalamion pyxis and the sarcophagus; in the other representations, the strings are not shown or can no longer be clearly seen. Only the pyxis gives an idea of how the strings were secured at the bottom, showing a semicircle at the top of the soundbox to which the strings run. This curved bar was probably actually situated at the *bottom* of the soundbox and would not actually have been visible above the upper edge.[9]

"Size is a matter of space available rather than proportion in Minoan/Mycenaean art," warns the author of a study of the Hagia Triada sarcophagus.[10] We cannot tell exactly how large the Minoan lyre was or whether some instruments were larger and more elaborately made than others. But in all the representations the instrument is held vertically, and the three large paintings seem to show one approximately tall enough to reach from the player's waist to the top of his head, and about two-thirds as wide as it is high. The player holds it in his left arm, assisted by a sling (visible in the sarcophagus painting in the same color as the instrument) around his wrist and around the outer arms of the instrument, so that his left-hand fingers are free to pluck or damp the strings (we do not know, of course, whether either of these was actually done, or both—but it stands to reason that the fingers were freed for a purpose). His right hand, again in the sarcophagus painting (fig. 2a), holds a *plektron* or pick (in the same color as the player's skin), which might conveniently be made of ivory or bone, with which to sound the strings. This makes a harder, brighter sound, as guitarists know, than plucking with the fingers. If we can trust the details of the seal stone as shown in the drawing published by Arthur Evans, the plektron was attached to the bottom center of the soundbox with a cord. If the date has been correctly assigned to this seal by Nicolas Platon (who first recognized it as a representation of a musical instrument on the basis of a drawing in Evans' *Palace of Minos*), the manner of playing that involves a wrist sling and plektron on a cord is centuries older than we could have guessed from our other evidence. Both wrist sling and plektron with cord are details found again much later in connection with lyre playing on the Greek mainland.

Musicians and Occasions

Since we know nothing whatever at the present time about the musical system and practices of these Minoan musicians, it is useless to speculate about what intervals were used in their melodies, whether two or more pitches were allowed to sound simultaneously, whether the lyre was tuned in scale steps, whether the plektron plucked individual strings or strummed across them all, and so on. It is tempting to think that, because the Minoan lyre appears to have seven strings, the number that predominates later in Classical Greece, its tuning or music must be somehow related to that of the later Greek lyre—but additional evidence is lacking.

What we do know, from our examination of the paintings, is something of the musicians and the occasions on which they played. The sarcophagus painting shows a lyre player taking part in a procession that seems to be part of the preparations for a funeral feast, the bringing of liquids (probably wine and water) to

be mixed. It is a religious occasion, for the mixing bowl sits between columns surmounted by double axes, on which birds are perched to represent the deity or deities. The musician is male in all three large paintings (men's skin is brown, women's white—a convention also used by the Egyptians and much later by the Greeks), and his connection with religious observances suggests that he might be a person of some status and importance.

Some elements of the sarcophagus scene are found in the other paintings. The pyxis scene also has religious elements: an altar with "horns of consecration," double axes, and birds flying above. The Hagia Triada fresco seems to be a procession similar to the one described above, and the Pylos fresco, although it shows a seated musician, repeats the bird motif (a large bird flies away to the left of the lyre player).

The Palaikastro terra-cotta group, on the other hand, consists of three female dancers in a semicircle, holding hands, and accompanied by a female lyre player. Since this instrument is only roughly depicted, we do not know if it is meant to be the same as those in the paintings; but it does confirm that women might also play the lyre.

Lyres in the Bronze and Early Iron Ages: The Homeric Epics

Most of the objects we have been discussing belong to the period from about 1400 to 1100 B.C., when the Mycenaeans, the earliest known group of Greek-speaking peoples in the Aegean, had already obtained control of the island of Crete. The mingling of the styles of mainland Greece with those of Minoan culture is apparent in the decoration of the sarcophagus; and Minoan or Minoan-inspired artifacts are found in Greece, while items of Mycenaean fabrication or design are found in Crete.[11] The lyre that has been described was, though created by Minoan culture, well known to the Mycenaean Greeks, as its presence on the wall painting from the Mycenaean palace at Pylos (southwestern Peloponnesos, now at the Khora Museum) and on a vase fragment from Nauplia (fig. 3a; below, Mycenaean Lyres) attests.

What is not certain, unfortunately, is to what extent the lyre used by the Mycenaeans was derived from, or influenced by, the Minoan lyre.[12] The items that provide evidence concerning it are less helpful than those of Minoan culture, and the conclusions that can be drawn on the basis of the artifacts about Mycenaean use of stringed instruments, and even about the construction of the instruments, are correspondingly more limited. But we do have, fortunately, an abundance of information of a different sort about the Mycenaean lyre, information that comes from the two great Homeric epics, the *Iliad* and the *Odyssey,* which are in many ways a reflection of Mycenaean culture.

Few scholars now question that the *Iliad* and *Odyssey* were written down sometime between 850 and 700 B.C. but center on an event that took place in Mycenaean times, some four or five hundred years earlier. It is now generally agreed that the stories of the Trojan War and its aftermath were handed down through an oral tradition for many generations before they were shaped into what we now know as the *Iliad* and *Odyssey* and preserved through the written word. This is how it happens that set phrases are used over and over again in the Homeric epics to describe the same or a similar situation. Milman Parry, whose work established the theory about the technique of formulaic composition in the two poems, discovered that "the bards found and kept expressions which could be used in a variety of sentences, either as they stood or with slight modifications, and which occupied fixed places in the hexameter line."[13] The importance of the Homeric lyre, the phorminx, is demonstrated by its appearance in a formula used to fill out the end of the hexameter line, showing that Homer, or rather the Homeric oral tradition, regularly needed to describe the activity of music making that involved this instrument.[14]

When Heinrich Schliemann, relying on Homer and Pausanias, dug up Troy and Mycenae and discovered the "jewels of Helen" and the "mask of Agamemnon," the tendency was to assume that everything in the *Iliad* and *Odyssey* described Mycenaean life (ca. 1600–1150 B.C.) rather than that of the Dark Ages (ca. 1150–800 B.C.) or of Homer's own times (ca. 850–700 B.C.). Today, however, most scholars subscribe to the "composite" theory, which holds that Homer's poems contain material from both the Mycenaean (or Bronze) Age and from later periods.[15]

No attempt is made in the present study to sort out "early" or "late" material in the poems, probably an impossible task with respect to musical instruments. Although much of what Homer says about musical events sounds more characteristic of the elaborate palaces of the Bronze Age than of the evidently simpler dwellings and social structures of the "Dark Ages," we cannot rule out the existence of less glorious, post-Mycenaean versions of such court singers as Phemios and Demodokos, or of aristocratic amateur players such as Achilles. Homer may sometimes be reporting a tradition that had survived intact from the Bronze Age down to the eighth century, at other times preserving memories of recent musical traditions no

longer practiced in his own era, and at still other times describing customs that belong only to his own period. In any case, the basically coherent picture in the Homeric poems of the bard and the instrument he used suggests that in most important respects, if not in every detail, there was a continuity of tradition.[16]

The origin of the most common Homeric name for lyre, *phorminx,* remains a mystery. A Byzantine commentator gives a silly etymology: he imagines "phorminx" to be derived from *phroimion,* a contraction of the Greek form of prooemium ("prelude").[17] More recent etymologists have proposed a connection with the Sanskrit word for "bee" (*bhramara-h*), but this view of the phorminx as an instrument that "buzzes" has been disputed by reputable authorities.[18] We are left with the conclusion that the word *phorminx* was borrowed by the Greeks from some other, possibly non-Indo-European language, a view consistent with the Greeks' own belief that most of their names for musical instruments were of foreign origins.[19] The word continues to appear in Greek literature long after other names for various types of lyres had been introduced, especially by authors who want to evoke its Homeric associations.

The other Homeric word for lyre, *kitharis,* which also appears to be of non-Greek origins, is only rarely used in the poems.[20] *Kitharis* occurs only five times in Homer, and, except in one instance (*Od.* 1.153, where the kitharis is placed in Phemios' hands), seems always to be used in the generalized sense of "lyre playing": the suitors are interested only in kitharis and song (*Od.* 1.159); kitharis and song are among the possible gifts given to men by the gods (*Il.* 13.731); the Phaiakians are especially fond of kitharis and dance, along with fresh changes of clothes and hot baths (*Od.* 8.248); and Paris will not be helped in battle by kitharis, gifts of Aphrodite, or his fine locks of hair (*Il.* 3.54).[21] *Phorminx,* on the other hand, occurs twenty-one times and is in all but two cases (*Od.* 8.99 and 21.430) concrete, referring to a specific instrument being played or picked up.

Any major distinction that may at one time have existed between the terms *phorminx* and *kitharis* is blurred in Homer's usage. When Phemios plays the kitharis, for example, the verb used to describe his activity is *phormizein* (*Od.* 1.155); elsewhere the instrument that he plays (presumably the same as the one in this passage) is always referred to as a phorminx.[22] Conversely, the verb formed from kitharis, *kitharizein,* can be used with the noun *phorminx* as its direct object (*Il.* 18.570). (A partial analogy to this kind of interchangeability can be found in the English nouns *violin* and *fiddle,* and in the expression "to fiddle on one's violin.") Since the Homeric poems represent the collected efforts of many generations and display a mixture of dialects, it is not surprising that two different names appear to be applied to one and the same instrument.

Despite its rarity in Homer (and later authors as well), the name *kitharis* is, in a way, of greater historical importance than the word *phorminx*, for it is the parent of an imposing array of later musical terms. The derived word *kithara* and the many terms related to it will be discussed in the following chapters.

Lyre Players in the Iliad *and* Odyssey

The tales in the *Iliad* and *Odyssey* indicate that in Homeric times music making was not given over to slaves. Apparently there were no slave musicians of the sort so often encountered in Classical Athens, including some of the so-called flute girls (*auletrides*, which really means female players of the reed pipe, or *aulos*) who performed for the pleasure of men at symposia. Aside from Apollo, all the players described in the Homeric poems are either respected professional *aoidoi* ("singers"), always male, who earn their living through their craft, or male amateur musicians such as Achilles or Paris. No women players are mentioned, but since women in Homer do sing for their own entertainment at home, it is perhaps likely that the lyre was not entirely unknown among women at the Mycenaean courts or their Dark Age counterparts.

The respected role of the instrument is reflected in the Homeric conception of Apollo as the lyre player for the rest of the Olympian deities. No mere slave or servant makes music for the gods. Appropriately, both the first and the last reference in the *Iliad* to the Homeric lyre are connected with the god of music, who plays his phorminx at the gods' feast (*Il.* 1.603) and weddings (*Il.* 24.63). Within this divine framework fits the lyre playing of Apollo's mortal followers, who enjoy an especially prominent role in the *Odyssey*.

The status of the professional *aoidos* in Homeric society is clarified through some remarks put in the mouth of Odysseus' faithful swineherd, Eumaios (*Od.* 17.383–85). Eumaios mentions the *demioergoi* ("workers for the people"), who are summoned to the palace at Ithaka from the outside world to perform some service and are thus welcomed for their expertise; included in this class are, he says, seers, doctors, carpenters, and aoidoi, who delight people with their singing.[23] The two chief bards of the *Odyssey*, Phemios and Demodokos, are clearly members of this class of professional experts.

Although Phemios, the bard at Odysseus' palace, is not a slave, he is compelled by Penelope's voracious suitors to stay at the palace and entertain them (*Od.* 1.154, 22.331). He must provide the finishing touches for the suitors' innumerable free dinners by striking up his phorminx for song and dance. Like his counterpart in the fairy-tale land of the Phaiakians, Demodokos, he is described as a *theios aoidos* ("divine singer") but is not characterized nearly as fully as Demodokos.

Demodokos, the blind singer at the Phaiakian court of Alkinöos, may be the prototype for the notion of Homer as a blind poet. Since blindness also figures in the story of another singer (Thamyris), it may be that many aoidoi, like the seers, were in fact sightless. Blindness would have been no particular handicap in a tradition of oral poetry, and indeed, might even have increased one's capacity for the concentration necessary for such an art.[24] The portrait of Demodokos is fully drawn in book 8 of the *Odyssey*, where he is described as an aoidos who is "divine" (*theios*), "faithful" (*erieros*), and "exceedingly famous" (*periklutos*). Alkinöos orders that the singer be summoned for a feast in honor of the as yet unidentified guest (Odysseus), and the herald goes off to look for him, presumably at Demodokos' own house in the town, since some time passes before he and the singer appear. The guests have assembled and the meat has been prepared by the time Demodokos is led in by the herald, who sets up a chair for him, hangs his phorminx on a peg within reach, and gives him a cup of wine. When the guests have finished eating, the Muse stirs Demodokos to begin his song.

The importance of Demodokos as a public figure is emphasized by his name, which literally means "esteemed by the people." Homer stresses the literal meaning when in *Od.* 8.472 he begins a line with the proper name, immediately followed by a phrase meaning "honored by the people." He is even called a "hero" (*Od.* 8.483), a term generally reserved for great warriors. As a public figure, he performs not only at the king's court but also in the *agore*, the place of public assembly (*Od.* 8.109, 254ff.). As befits his high professional standing, he commands a full repertory of songs based on both myth and saga, so that he is able to satisfy Odysseus' request for a song on a particular topic, the story of the Trojan horse (*Od.* 8.492).

Other, less developed versions of the aoidos can be found elsewhere in both the *Iliad* and the *Odyssey*. In the midst of the Catalogue of Ships (*Il.* 2.594ff.), Thamyris is mentioned in passing as a Thracian who traveled from his native land to Thessaly and from there to Dorion in the Peloponnesos, where he foolishly boasted that even if the Muses themselves should sing, he could sing better. As a result the Muses maimed him (by blinding him, according to later authors), took away his "divine song," and made him forget how to play his instrument. The story perhaps suggests that Thamyris was an itinerant aoidos who made his living by carrying his songs from place to place.

An unnamed aoidos plays for the wedding feast given at the court of Menelaos in Sparta (*Od.* 4.18); and another unnamed singer, apparently a trusted friend of Agamemnon, is left by the king to keep an eye on Klytemnestra while he is away at Troy (*Od.* 3.267, an assignment easily thwarted by her lover Aigisthos, who removes the singer to an island). Further references to the professional player are probably contained in the description of Odysseus stringing his bow like a man who is an "expert in the phorminx" (*Od.* 21.406) and in the mention of lyre and song as among the various possible gifts of expertise granted to various men by the gods (*Il.* 13.731). Phemios' description of himself as "self-taught" (*Od.* 22.347) implies that there were others who learned the art from established experts who, like doctors or carpenters, passed on their professional skills to younger men.

The professionals, however, are not the only players of the phorminx whom Homer mentions. A youth, specifically described as such rather than as an aoidos, plays his instrument and sings the Linos song for a procession of harvesters (*Il.* 18.569), and both Paris and Achilles are sufficiently knowledgeable in the art of lyre playing to play for their own entertainment. In *Il.* 3.54, Hector rebukes Paris, saying that his lyre playing and beautiful hair will be no use to him in battle. Readers of the *Iliad* will also remember Homer's vivid picture of Achilles playing a phorminx taken from the plunder of a city near Troy and delighting his heart in songs about heroes, as the envoys from Agamemnon arrive to attempt a reconciliation between the two Greek leaders (*Il.* 9.186ff.). The presence of the phorminx in the hands of a great hero such as Achilles may well—like a kind of Biblical endorsement—account in part for the persistence of the lyre as an essential element in the education of the Athenian aristocracy of later times.

Descriptions of the Lyre in Homer

Despite his elaborate descriptions of some objects, Homer is not at all helpful in providing a detailed picture of what the phorminx looked like or exactly how it was played. Nowhere does he mention the number of strings of the phorminx, although such information is frequently included (often as a kind of epithet) in later writers who mention lyres. Nor does he mention the plektron.[25] The poems do, however, contain some limited information about several of the functional elements of the phorminx as well as about its decoration.

One of the most useful passages is the one mentioned above describing Odysseus' stringing of his great bow, in which his expertise is compared to that of a lyre player putting a string around a new *kollops*. In that passage, Homer says that the strings of the phorminx were made of "well-twisted" sheepgut (*Od.* 21.408). The kollops over which the string is pulled was probably not actually a "peg" (as it is usually translated) but rather a roll of rough leather, its friction helping to hold the string in place at the crossbar. The wooden pins through the leather that aid in securing and tuning the strings are seen in examples from later periods, but not in early examples.

Eustathius, the Byzantine commentator on the poems of Homer, reports in connection with this passage that the kollops was a tuning device made from hide from the necks of oxen or sheep; he fancies that the device was so called because the ancients also boiled *kolla* ("glue") out of these same neck hides.[26] Eustathius' definition accords with the information in other lexicographers' works and with the use of the word by Aristophanes, who, in speaking of the toughness of Aeschylus, compared him to the hide (kollops) of an ox.[27] Commentators have sometimes been puzzled as to why the text speaks of putting a string on a new "peg" rather than of putting on a new string; if, however, the kollops was a rough piece of hide, it is reasonable to suppose that it would wear smooth after a time and would have to be replaced much more frequently than a peg on a modern stringed instrument.[28]

The only other term in Homer for a part of the instrument is the *zugon*, mentioned in connection with Achilles' phorminx (*Il.* 9.187). Although sometimes translated in this passage as "bridge," the basic meaning of the term, which is "yoke," surely implies that it refers to the crossbar which joins together the two arms of the instrument. The particular phorminx described, since it is of exceedingly elaborate workmanship, has a "silver" crossbar, probably meaning inlaid with silver decoration.

There is only a general hint about the shape of the phorminx in one of the traditional epithets used to describe the instrument: *glaphuros*, which can mean "curved" or "arched," in addition to "hollow." Homer often applies the adjective to caves (that is, meaning "hollow" in the strictest sense), but he also applies it to a harbor (*Od.* 12.305), a shoreline that curves to form a protected area, and to ships, which are both "hollow" and "curved." In the case of the phorminx, surely the exterior outline of the instrument was more conspicuous than the hollow space inside the soundbox needed for any type of lyre. The exact nature of the curvature noted in the epithet, however, can only be guessed at; it must have referred either to the rounded base of the soundbox so evident in the representations in Geometric art, or to the possibly bulging back of the soundbox (seen in the later kithara), or even to a bow-shaped curvature of the whole instrument as viewed from the side (a view that artists did not attempt until the fifth century).[29]

The phorminx of Mycenaean times, like other important objects, was probably often richly decorated. Achilles' instrument, with its silver-ornamented crossbar, is described as *daidaleos* (*Il.* 9.187), or "curiously wrought," a word used elsewhere of richly decorated war-gear and furniture and the like. Both Apollo and Phemios play lyres that are *perikalles,* "exceedingly beautiful" (*Il.* 1.603 and *Od.* 1.153).

The word *phorminx* occurs twenty-one times in Homer's poems. Nearly two-thirds of these instances involve one of two traditional epithets applied to the instrument: *glaphuros* (discussed above) or *ligus. Ligus* (or, in its feminine form, *ligeia*) is often misunderstood by translators to mean "loud," although it was shown many years ago that the term describes not the instrument's *volume* but its *timbre,* and should therefore be translated as "bright-sounding."[30] The adjective is used elsewhere in Greek literature to describe the singing of nightingales, Muses, and Sirens and must in such contexts refer not to the loudness of their song but to its bright, clear sound. (The seductive Siren-song that Odysseus had to resist was not in the nature of an air-raid warning.)

The interpretation of *ligeia phorminx* as "clear-toned phorminx" is not contradicted by any of the other words associated with the sound of the instrument. In *Od.* 17.262 the sound is called an *ioe* (literally, a "rush," or "sweep"), used elsewhere by Homer of the wind, of fire, and of the human voice (at normal levels) as it penetrates the consciousness of a sleeping Odysseus (*Il.* 10.139). Similarly, the verb *epuein* (*Od.* 17.270) can be used of the wind or of the human voice calling aloud to someone. The word *boe* ("cry") in *Il.* 18.495 does, to be sure, indicate a loud sound, but since this is the only place in the poems where a number of lyres and auloi are played at the same time, the description of the sound as a "cry" is probably due partly to the presence of the auloi and partly to the fact that several instruments are being played at once.

Mycenaean and Early Iron Age Lyres: Archaeological Evidence

To complement this limited picture that the epic poems present of the Homeric phorminx itself, we must turn to archaeological remains and to the representations of lyres in Bronze and Iron Age art.

Mycenaean Lyres

The only stringed instrument found among the available Mycenaean archaeological evidence is a lyre similar in general shape to that of the Minoans. Our information about it comes from seven Mycenaean sources (ca. 1550–1100 B.C.): the ivory remains of two actual instruments found in a Mycenaean *tholos* (beehive shaped) tomb at Menidi north of Athens (Athens 1972); a bronze votive offering, 8 cm high, in the shape of a lyre, from the Amyklaion sanctuary near Sparta (fig. 3d); fragments found at Mycenae (now at Athens?) that appear to include plektra and part of the arm of a lyre; and three Mycenaean vase sherds, one from Nauplia (fig. 3a) with a complete instrument, one from Tiryns (fig. 3b, Nauplia 14.376) that shows the upper part of a lyre, and one (fig. 3c, Athens 9063) found on the island of Skopelos, near Euboea, that includes the lower part of a lyre.

Even more than the fresco from the palace at Pylos (see above, Minoan Lyres), the recently discovered vase fragment from Nauplia (fig. 3a) indicates Mycenaean familiarity with lyres of the shape associated with Minoan Crete. Though its lyre is out of proportion to the player (it is as tall as he is), it is important because it shows the lyre being played. There is clearly a sling for the player's left wrist that is represented as a small loop attached near the middle of the outer arm of the lyre, the same arrangement found on Minoan lyres and those of much later periods. This lyre, held upright like the Minoan lyres, also has arms shaped in a way that is reminiscent of the Minoan instruments: the arms curve inward and immediately out again slightly more than halfway up, as though the graceful curve seen on those lyres had been rather squashed (the sling is looped through the inner part of this curve).[31] This lyre too has seven strings, kollopes, and a narrow soundbox with a rounded base. It appears to have originally been painted over in white (see comments below on ivory facings); and it has a pair of small loops below the soundbox in the center, probably to indicate the lower string fastener.

The small bronze from the Amyklaion (fig. 3d), which has a rounded base (as does the instrument on the vase from Skopelos [fig. 3c]), and a rather tall soundbox one-third the height of the instrument, is perhaps more typical of Mycenaean instruments.[32] The arms are a continuation of the soundbox, straight and parallel, and the crossbar was attached almost at their top, as the remaining ends of it show. The bronze was molded to represent seven or eight strings—five remain, but there is room for two or three more that have been broken away. The vase painting from Skopelos also represents a lyre with seven strings, fastened below to a semicircular fitting attached to the soundbox (it appears at the top of the soundbox but was in practice no doubt affixed to the bottom edge).

The ivory fragments of one of the lyres found at Menidi have been incorporated into a reconstruction that is on display at the National Archaeological Museum in Athens.[33] They seem to consist of ivory facings for the top of a lower section of the right arm, the section of the left arm that met the crossbar, a piece that may have been part of the lower string fastening, and a larger piece with holes bored in it that may have been the crossbar. Of the second lyre (unreconstructed) it appears that the only remains are two pieces of ivory facing for the arms, about 25 and 34 cm (9.8 and 13.4 in.) long, and a small additional fragment.

From these fragments we can get only a very rough idea of what the size of the instruments might be: Nicolas Platon has estimated the height of the Menidi lyres at 60 to 75 cm (23.6 to 29.5 in.).[34] We do learn from these remains that the arms of the Mycenaean lyre might be ornamented with ivory, elaborately carved in the case of the first Menidi lyre, or decorated with incised patterns in the case of the fragment from Mycenae (which appears to be for the arm of a lyre). The ivory fragments of the Menidi lyres taper to a pointed tip above the crossbar and curve at the bottom in a way that suggests a narrow, rim-like soundbox. This last, however, may be misleading, for the ivory pieces may simply have been set into the top of a much taller soundbox, in the manner suggested in vase paintings of a later era (compare chap. 6, fig. 7); the soundbox may have resembled that of the Amyklaion bronze (fig. 3d).[35]

Perhaps most interesting of all are the carved ivory objects found with these remains, approximately 6.5 cm (2.5 in.) long (at Mycenae) to 14 cm (5.5 in.) long (at Menidi) that must surely be plektra with handles; these confirm that despite Homer's silence on the matter, the Mycenaeans as well as the Minoans played the lyre in this way. The plektron from Menidi is shaped rather like a teaspoon, with a narrow handle that might have been wrapped with cloth or leather.

The only other archaeological evidence for lyres in the Mycenaean world comes not from mainland Greece or its neighboring islands but from Cyprus, the ancient crossroads of the Mediterranean world, where Mycenaean culture mingled with that of the Near East. The Cypriote style of vase painting of about 1100–1050 B.C. is Mycenaean in form and decoration but is also pictorial, in accordance with Cypriote preference.[36] This fortunate combination produced the vase now in the Cyprus Museum at Nicosia (fig. 4, Kouklia T. 9 no. 7), on which one panel of the interior shows a figure wearing what appears to be a tasseled sword and holding up at face level a lyre only slightly larger than his head.[37] The lyre appears small in relation to the human figure, but this is again a matter of available space in the design of the panel rather than of real proportions. The same may be said of the fact that the instrument has only three strings: in the painting, there is room for only three brush strokes, while in actual practice, an instrument of only three strings would not need to be nearly so wide. The lyre itself is painted with a few strokes that give us only its basic shape: rounded base, straight arms, the crossbar near the top of the arms and extending a little beyond them on either side, and a soundbox that is not very tall but drawn with thicker strokes than the arms. The instrument was probably taller in proportion to its width than it is shown.[38]

Post-Mycenaean Lyres

The three centuries after the end of the Mycenaean period, from about 1100 to 800 B.C., the centuries following the migration of tribes from northwestern Greece ("Dorians") to the south and of many of the previous Greek inhabitants to the eastern shores and islands of the Aegean, began as a time of turmoil; and trade with the lands to the east, which had been interrupted during this time, was only gradually resumed. No remains or representations of lyres from mainland Greece of this time have been found, in part because mainland pottery of this period is decorated with abstract geometric patterns rather than with human figures. For this reason, our knowledge of Greek stringed instruments during the "Dark Ages," before the second half of the eighth century, such as it is, comes from the fringes of the Greek world.

The most important sources are from Cyprus, where a few Cypriote-geometric vases continued to be decorated in pictorial style. There are two such vases that show human figures holding lyres, one an amphora in Nicosia from the ancient cemetery of Kaloriziki near Kurion that may date from around 900 B.C., the other the "Hubbard amphora" (also in Nicosia) from northeastern Cyprus, most recently dated to about 800 B.C. The earlier amphora, from Kaloriziki (fig. 5a), has its human figures on the neck of the vase in two panels that seem related. On one side a figure holds a pitcher over an enormous amphora (a panel interpreted as a libation scene), and on the other side there is a standing figure with a lyre, a figure that might be said to be openmouthed, that is, singing.

The fact that the lyre shown looks very large and is given only three strings must again be taken as a matter of style and medium rather than realistic portrayal. But its shape and decoration must reflect to some degree the actual construction of an instrument known in Cyprus at the time: an instrument with a narrow soundbox and with even narrower arms rising from it, with a base not rounded, perhaps, but somewhat pointed—though to be honest we must admit that the painting may mislead us in this. Certainly it was an instrument with much decoration. The tops of the arms above the crossbar are finished with knoblike ornaments, and the ends of the crossbar each have two small crosspieces or disks. Most interesting, however, is the zigzag pattern painted touching the inside edge of each arm. Because of this pattern, Bernard Aign (p. 352) sees the Kaloriziki lyre as a descendant of the Minoan lyre with its circular "swan" necks; but there is some evidence that the zigzag pattern may have come instead from Anatolia, for a twelfth-century B.C. cylinder seal from Mardin in southeastern Anatolia, on which there is a round-based lyre with parallel arms and six strings, shows the arms constructed in zigzag fashion.[39] In any case, the arms of the instrument on the second (Hubbard) amphora (fig. 5b) have zigzags as well—and as in the case of the Anatolian cylinder seal, the arms are apparently not decorated but actually made in zigzag shape.

The figure on this later amphora is part of a more complete scene, a procession of people taking part, according to Dikaios, in a "funeral rite in honour of an enthroned lady." The front side of the vase shows the "enthroned lady, drinking through a siphon from a jar placed in front"; before her is a "female attendant pouring liquid" into the jar and carrying a string of fish; a bull's head shows on the far left, and on the right, behind the throne-like chair, "a sphinx smells a flower." On the other side of the vase there is a "group of dancing women with a male lyre player in the middle."[40] The participants on either side of him carry plants, perhaps as funeral offerings.

The size of the lyre in relation to the human figure and the way it is held (high and away from the body) recall the eleventh-century Mycenaean-Cypriote vase described above. The general shape of the instrument is also similar, except that the arms, in the later representation, have the zigzag construction and do not continue above the crossbar. Although neither the size of the instrument nor its number of strings (four) can be taken literally, the shape and decoration, once again, probably reflect that of an instrument known in Cyprus around 800 B.C., an instrument with a crescent-shaped soundbox.

In the museum at Heraklion, Crete, there is a small bronze seated figure (fig. 6) playing a round-based lyre with a taller soundbox than the instruments just described, which he holds in playing position, not vertically but tipped out at about 45°. His right hand touches the strings just above the soundbox (no plektron shown). The four thick bronze strings (it would have been inconvenient, with this thickness, to have more than four) are attached at the bottom to a curved fitting similar to the ones seen on the Minoan pyxis from Kalamion, on the Mycenaean vase from Skopelos, and on a relief of the late eighth century from Karatepe (southern Anatolia) to be discussed below. This curved bar, probably customarily made of metal and hooked into the bottom of the soundbox, seems to have been for many centuries a customary device for securing the strings at the lower end.

The soundbox of the Heraklion bronze, rounded at the base and straight across the top, is tall enough to resemble that of the Mycenaean bronze from the Amyklaion (fig. 3d). The arms, straight and undecorated, do not extend beyond the crossbar, or the crossbar beyond the arms (also a characteristic of later representations in bronze). The shape of this ninth- or eighth-century bronze lyre, except for the lack of free ends for arms and crossbar, is like that of the lyres depicted on a number of seal stones of the ninth through seventh centuries found at Tarsus (Anatolia), on the island of Rhodes, and elsewhere, and made in either Rhodes or Euboea (the instruments usually have only three strings, as might be expected in view of their small size). The bronze figure at Heraklion, though possibly not made by a Greek artist, nevertheless shows an instrument shape that must have been widely known in the Greek world of the ninth and eighth centuries.

Lyres in the Bronze and Iron Ages: Occasions and Music

The lyre was used for several distinct kinds of songs, some associated with ceremonial or religious occasions, others intended primarily for entertainment, and all of them sung either by the aoidoi or by amateur

musicians. The information given us by Homer is un-
even, since sometimes we are told only the generic
name of the song (with no information about its content or musical accompaniment), while at other times
we have virtually the entire text of the song and many
details about the circumstances of its performance but
are not told the generic name of the song. Still, the
Iliad and *Odyssey* provide us with some understanding
of the basic functions of music in Homeric society.

Ceremonial and Religious Occasions

Homer mentions by name four different kinds of songs
of a ceremonial nature. Two of these, paean (*paieon*)
and threnody (*threnos*), are nowhere described by Homer as having musical accompaniment, although perhaps the accompaniment simply goes unmentioned.
The word *paieon* is best left translated by its vague
English equivalent, paean, since its exact nature in its
early stages of development is uncertain. In Homer, it
is used not only as the name of a song but also as the
name of a god of healing, who seems to be identified
with, if not identical to, Apollo.[41] It may be that the
paean was originally a type of song addressed specifically to Apollo-as-Healer which later took on a
broader range of use. The young men of the Achaeans,
after a feast and sacrifice to the god, sing the paean in
order to propitiate Apollo and persuade him to turn
aside the terrible plague that has struck the Greek
troops (*Il.* 1.473). But elsewhere in the *Iliad,* this kind
of song is again sung by the young men (*kouroi*) when
Achilles bids them sing the paean as he and his men
drag the body of Hector back to the Greek ships (*Il.*
22.391). Under these circumstances, the paean appears to be essentially a victory song, perhaps a kind
of thank-offering to the gods, without explicitly mentioning any of them.

The nature of the threnos is clearer, for it obviously
refers to a dirge sung as part of funeral lamentations.
When Hector's body is brought back to Troy and laid
out to be mourned by his people, professional aoidoi
lead the threnody, and the women of Troy join in (*Il.*
24.721). Similarly, the ghost of Agamemnon recounts
to Achilles' ghost how the Muses themselves sang the
threnody at the funeral of Achilles (*Od.* 24.60).

The other two types of song that are specifically
named both include mention of the phorminx as the
accompanying instrument, in one case together with
the aulos. The *hymenaios,* or wedding song, is named
in the description of a scene represented on Achilles'
shield, in which a town is celebrating weddings and
festivals (*Il.* 18.490ff.); the brides are led out in a
torch-lit procession while the hymenaios is sung and

young men whirl in a dance to the music of phorminx
and auloi. Although the song itself is not elsewhere
mentioned in Homer, three other scenes in the poems
point to the use of the phorminx at wedding celebrations. Apollo holds and presumably plays the instrument at the wedding feast of Peleus and Thetis (*Il.*
24.63); a "divine singer" plays and sings at the wedding feast of Hermione in Sparta (*Od.* 4.18); and at
Odysseus' instruction, Phemios plays the phorminx so
as to convey the impression that there is a wedding
going on in the palace and thus delay the discovery by
outsiders that the suitors have been killed (*Od.*
23.133). Appropriately, the final recognition scene between Penelope and Odysseus also takes place against
the background of Phemios' song.

In a further scene on the shield of Achilles, Homer
describes the singing of the *linos* song by a youth who
accompanies himself on the phorminx while leading a
procession of singing and dancing girls and boys, who
carry the fruits of a grape harvest. From the context
one can assume that the linos song was probably a kind
of fertility song associated with the cycle of planting
and harvesting (or birth and death), although the
Greeks generally supposed it was a lament over the
death of a youth named Linos, to whom various iden-
tities were assigned.[42]

Formal Entertainment

The music of song and lyre is an essential part of various feasts described by Homer, for it provides the
formal entertainment that concludes the festive occasion, sometimes in combination with dancing. We have
already noted that just as Apollo plays at the feast of
the gods (*Il.* 1.603), so Phemios plays for the after-
dinner entertainment of the suitors (*Od.* 1.155 and
17.262). The content of such songs is revealed in further descriptions of both Phemios and Demodokos,
who, for the most part, sing stories of the Trojan War.
An example is Phemios' song about the Achaians'
homecoming from Troy (*Od.* 1.326). Penelope objects
to this particular song because it makes her sad, but
Telemachos says there is nothing wrong with the topic,
and anyway the audience always likes the latest song
circulating the best.[43]

Demodokos, too, sings "heroic song," or, as Homer puts it, songs about the famous deeds of men (*klea
andron, Od.* 8.73). Demodokos' song after the initial
feast in Odysseus' honor is briefly summarized in the
text of the poem: it is the quarrel between Odysseus
and Achilles, a parallel to the more famous quarrel
with which the *Iliad* begins. After the second, evening
feast, Demodokos (praised by Odysseus for his earlier

songs about the sufferings of the Achaians) produces the story of the Trojan horse, again briefly summarized by Homer (*Od.* 8.500ff.). Other themes that Homer mentions as likely subjects for future singers are also related, at least indirectly, to the Trojan War: Orestes' revenge for the murder of his father (*Od.* 3.204) and the evil deeds of Clytemnestra as compared to the virtuous conduct of Penelope (*Od.* 24.197ff.).

When Demodokos sings and plays his phorminx for the Phaiakian youths' dance in the public square, however, he chooses not heroic deeds but mythology.[44] This time he sings of the affair of Ares and Aphrodite and how they were caught in flagrante delicto by clever Hephaistos' net. The story, which occupies a full one hundred lines (*Od.* 8.266–366) is told in a polished form and with a charming sense of humor. The singer indeed earns the praise given him later by Odysseus, who says that he sings "in a completely well-ordered fashion" (*Od.* 8.489).

From these details about the songs of Phemios and Demodokos we can conclude that the songs sung by the professional bards for court or public entertainment had as their subjects essentially the same themes that we find in the *Iliad* and *Odyssey* themselves, namely, saga and myth. In all cases, the narrative element of the entertainment prevails, the instrumental accompaniment and even the dance being subservient to the song itself. It is the role of the bards to sing, as Penelope says, of the deeds of men and gods (*erga andron te theon te, Od.* 1.338).

Individuals also sing for their own pleasure; both Kalypso and Circe sing while they work at their looms, though we are not told what they sing about (*Od.* 5.61 and 10.221). Achilles, however, playing his phorminx by the seashore while his friend Patroklos listens in silence, sings, like Demodokos, of the "famous deeds of men" (*klea andron, Il.* 9.189). In contrast to Achilles' own peaceful mood, the famous deeds about which he sings are doubtless actions in war; the instrument on which he plays is war booty; and the envoys from Agamemnon have come to persuade him to resume his part in the war against Troy.[45]

The Lyre in Late Geometric Period Art

The counterparts of these Homeric bards and other players of the lyre appear in late Geometric vase paintings and other representations that can be assigned with confidence to the eighth century, in scenes that are more varied than those from earlier times. This visual evidence comes almost exclusively from mainland Greece—from Attica, from points along the land route from Sparta to Argos in the Peloponnesos, and

from Boeotia. It consists mainly of vase paintings, more than twenty of them, that represent lyre players; for in the second half of the eighth century mainland Greece once again produced pottery decorated with scenes showing human figures. To be sure, the silhouette style of these late Geometric vase paintings does not permit details such as the lower string fastener to be represented, and it causes the figures, objects and human beings, to be painted without overlapping in order to make their outlines intelligible. Thus, as in the earlier Cypriote paintings, instruments are often held away from the body rather than in playing position.

Since the late Geometric vase painters were still more concerned with design and emphasis on certain significant aspects than with realistic representation (as art historians have been careful to point out), it would be risky to turn to their works for information on the size of the instruments made in eighth-century Greece or on the number of strings such instruments had.[46] It seems likely that the number of strings painted in depends partly on artistic convention, partly on the width of the brush strokes and the space available.[47] Among available eighth-century representations, the largest group consists of instruments whose number of strings cannot be determined. Among those with strings clearly indicated, five strings occur somewhat more frequently than four; but there are half a dozen examples with only two or three strings.

More than half these lyres have rounded bases and arms that are straight or slightly bent inward.[48] The remainder are divided into two types, those with rounded bases but arms that curve outward, and those with bases that appear pointed or flat.[49] Most of the instruments in eighth-century representations are held vertically, but some are held tipped out somewhat, not more than about 30°. Only on Tübingen 2657 (fig. 7a) and Athens 874 are the lyres held horizontally (the players are perhaps not actually playing).

Scenes in Which the Lyre Appears

The lyre is found most frequently in scenes that show a procession (or a processional dance—it is not easy to tell the difference).[50] The participants may be men or women or both, and, especially in the case of the women, they may hold hands and carry branches between them. The women are often designated by their long skirts, the men by swords at their sides. The men sometimes carry shields (as they presumably take part in warrior dances) and sometimes they appear to be clapping. In a few scenes, we find dancing of a more vigorous kind, perhaps of the sort performed by the

athletic Phaiakian youths in the *Odyssey*: three dancers on Athens 14447 are shown jumping, their feet off
the ground; and on Copenhagen 727 (damaged section) the dancer just in front of the lyre player is making a high leap, while a pair just behind him are
engaged in a boxing match, as though to demonstrate
the association of this kind of dancing with athletics.[51]

The lyre can be found in the company of the double
auloi (Athens 291, Berlin 31573), and in three particularly interesting paintings (Athens 17497 and 18542,
Copenhagen 9367) there seem to be rattles in the
hands of the other participants (fig. 8). The latter are
the only scenes in which the performers are seated.
They appear to be taking part in a ritual: two lyre
players sit back to back in figure 8 (Athens 18542),
each facing a low table on which sits a stemmed cup
with handles. On the far side of each table sits a person
with rattles (two long objects that bulge near the middle), one held near the top, one held near the bottom
(the scenes on the other two vases are similar).

Shapes of Instruments

All but a few eighth-century representations clearly
show instruments with rounded bases, but the soundbox, arms, and crossbar of these lyres are depicted in
various ways. In most cases, the arms appear to be
either continuations of the soundbox or straight, parallel pieces set in near the corners of the soundbox.

From the Peloponnesos come four quite similar
items, three small, flat votive bronzes and a vase painting on which all the instruments represented have arms
that are straight, parallel continuations of the soundbox, with the crossbar situated a short way from the
top and protruding past the arms (fig. 9).[52] The arms
of the bronzes are wider in proportion to the soundbox
than any we have seen so far, and all have holes
pierced in them, two in each arm, separated by a diagonal strip of metal. In addition, the lyre shown in
fig. 9 has, on the soundbox, four small circles with
dots (these four circles reappear in a seventh-century
painting of the instrument, and two circles, often
painted to represent eyes, are used on later examples,
as we will see in the chapters that follow).

A plektron hanging by a cord from the arm on the
far side of the instrument is clearly represented on a
vase painted ca. 700 or a little later, Berlin Antikenmuseum 31573 (fig. 10). This instrument has arms that
may be a continuation of the soundbox but that *appear*
to bend toward each other at the top (a circumstance
also seen on two other Attic vases, Athens 291 and
14447, and one of Boeotian origin, Basel BS 406; the
size of the soundbox, however, varies greatly among

these four). The instrument on the Berlin vase also
seems to have a visible lower string fastener, a straight
horizontal line between the arms at their lower ends.
Since, if this attachment were actually placed where it
is shown, the strings would not pass over the soundbox, it is probable that some artistic license has been
used: to make it visible, the painter has moved it up
from its more likely position at the bottom of the
soundbox.

Another small group of vase paintings shows us
instruments with straight, parallel arms that seem set
into the corners of the soundbox. The clearest of these
paintings, Tübingen 2657 (fig. 7a), has a tall soundbox
leveled off at the top. The others, Athens 17497 and
Copenhagen 727 (which has two instruments), have
soundbox shapes that might be described as nearly full
crescents. Above the crossbar, the arms of the Tübingen example seem to become wider—perhaps to indicate ornamental knobs or crosspieces of the kind
found on the other two vases. These were typical Attic
decorations, apparently, for they are found on still
other Attic examples. The crossbar itself is curved in
some of these paintings, but this might best be put
down to artistic license.

The lyre in figure 7a is quite like an instrument on
a relief from Karatepe in southern Anatolia (Cilicia),
made in the late eighth century (fig. 7b).[53] This instrument has six strings, a plektron attached by a cord to
the bottom of the soundbox, and a curved lower string
fastener (like an upside-down U, also affixed at the
bottom of the soundbox). Its crossbar and arms are
straight, the latter fitted in near the upper corners of
its tall soundbox, which has a straight upper edge. This
relief, though not made by a Greek artist, comes from
an area where there was strong Greek influence. It
shows a procession of musicians at a feast of King
Asitawanda, according to Phoenician and Hittite inscriptions, and the musician with the "Greek" lyre is
followed by one with a lyre of typical Semitic shape
with rectangular soundbox, slanting crossbar, and
arms that are neither parallel nor of the same length.

A half-dozen instruments with round bases and
arms that diverge or curve *outward* have been found
on vases from mainland Greece. Three of these (Athens 313, Athens Agora P 10154, and Cambridge
M.C.A. 345), painted ca. 700 B.C. or later, may be the
first representations of the *chelys*, or lyra, with its tortoiseshell soundbox; they will be discussed in the next
chapter. Two others, Dresden 1699 (fig. 11), from
Boeotia, and Athens 874, found in Athens, seem to
show another shape: on the Dresden vase it appears
as a narrow instrument with a rim-like soundbox that
continues upward to form arms that, near the top,

curve out to meet the ends of the (curving) crossbar in an ornamental knob. It is possible that the painter, attempting to show arms that curve *forward* (as we know they did on instruments of later centuries), could only show them curving outward. This is not the impression created by Athens 874, however, although this vase (where we seem to see the lyre from the bottom) may also be an experiment with perspective. The remaining vase in this group of six, Athens 234 (fig. 12), from the Amyklaion near Sparta, has the most remarkable shape seen in any Geometric vase painting: a tall soundbox, straight-edged at the top, from which rise arms that bend sharply outward halfway up with a long tapering extension above the crossbar, and a crossbar that has small rectangular objects attached below its free ends.

One further small group of vases shows instruments that do *not* have rounded bases. Two of these, Athens 18542 (fig. 8) and Copenhagen 9367, both Attic vases, have painted on them seated figures holding instruments that might be called "heart shaped." The arms in the Athens example have at the top crosspieces of the sort mentioned above. Below the crossbar the arms first widen, then come together at the bottom in a point.[54] It seems possible that the instrument intended is the one that would become known three centuries later as the kithara, an instrument that can be more securely recognized on a sherd in Athens from the Argive Heraion (fig. 13) on which it has a *flat* base and wide soundbox that reaches up to either side, with arms inset above (all the upper part is missing). But the clearest and most detailed evidence for such an instrument comes, once more, not from a Greek source, but from another of the Karatepe reliefs, this one in Hittite-Aramaic style (fig. 14).[55] The instrument on the relief has a small, flat base; above it the soundbox broadens and continues upward to form wide arms. The crossbar is provided with decorative knobs at either end,[56] and there is a sling for the player's left wrist (not seen since Mycenaean times), a bridge over which the strings pass (not seen in any example so far mentioned), and a plektron on a cord attached to a ring in the base of the instrument. The performer stands facing a player of the double auloi, and between them are two dancers.

Aside from the triangular frame harp represented in the pre-Greek marble figurines of the Cycladic culture, the paintings, bronzes, terra-cottas, and seal stones described in this chapter create the strong impression that there were in the Aegean world, from the time of the Minoans down to the late eighth century, stringed instruments of only one basic type: lyres with parallel arms of equal length.

The Minoan evidence, the earliest of which comes from about 1600 B.C. (relatively late in the history of this colorful people of Crete), forms a consistent picture of a single type of lyre. Relative to the size of the player, it was a large instrument with a rounded base and was held in a vertical position. It had seven strings, which were struck with a plektron. The Minoan lyre is most often shown, not surprisingly, in connection with religious occasions; on the famous Hagia Triada sarcophagus, for example, it appears to be played in a funeral procession, and in other representations it is shown together with items of religious significance such as the Minoan "horns of consecration." In all cases but one, Minoan players are male; only in the Palaikastro terra-cotta group does the player appear to be female, surrounded by women who dance in a circle.

Although the archaeological evidence is limited in the case of the Mycenaeans, these earliest Greeks seem to have adopted the Minoan instrument as their own. Mycenaean representations of the lyre from the period 1550–1100 B.C., like the earlier Minoan examples, portray an instrument with a rounded base and seven strings. From Homer, whose epics reflect the traditions of the Mycenaean Bronze Age (as well as of later times), we learn that the instrument was called a phorminx, and that music making on it was referred to as kitharis. Homer also informs us of the use of sheepgut for the instrument's strings and of kollopes as tuning devices. He describes the instrument as glaphuros (curved), ligus (bright sounding), and daidaleos (ornate); the last epithet accords well with the archaeological evidence from Menidi, which includes elaborately carved ivory facings for the remains of a lyre found there. Like the Minoan lyre, the Mycenaean instrument was played in a manner that involved using a wrist sling and a plektron on a cord attached to the instrument, as the archaeological evidence clearly indicates.

Cretan, Cypriote, and mainland Greek sources suggest that an instrument of this type was used on similar occasions (that is, for religious processions and for dances) throughout the centuries of the Geometric period. The uses of the instrument as they are shown in the artistic representations of the Minoan through Geometric periods correspond in general to the scenes of musical performance that Homer describes for us, in which the phorminx is played during wedding processions and feasts, and for ritual fertility songs and the dances of young men.

The vase paintings of the late eighth century also show us such scenes, but their range is expanded. The dances can be described as processional dances, warrior dances, and athletic dances; in addition, a new kind of scene can be identified, a ritual one including a seated lyre player and a rattle (?) player. Details in these late-Geometric portrayals of the lyre are often difficult to interpret, however, especially in view of the painters' tendency to emphasize the significance of particular aspects of an object at the expense of a realistic picture of the whole. Often the number of strings cannot be determined; in other cases, only two to five strings are shown. In general, such a small number of strings seems to be the result of available space and of stylistic considerations; in all probability, the lyre continued to have seven strings, just as it had in Minoan times.

By the end of the eighth century, there is unmistakable evidence of the presence of the instruments that later received the names chelys (or lyra) and kithara. To learn more about these, we must follow their traces into the seventh century and the beginning of the Archaic period.

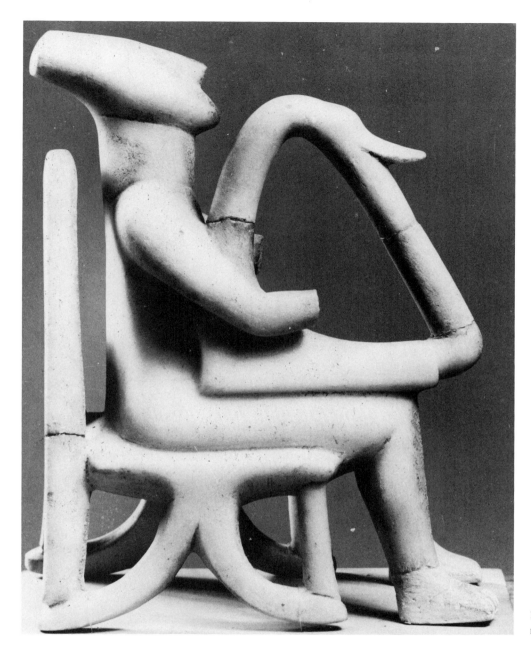

1. Athens 3908. Cycladic
marble figure of harpist.

2a. Heraklion. Hagia
Triadha sarcophagus.
Detail: musician in
procession.

2b. Khania XM 2308.
Minoan pyxis. Detail:
musician with lyre.

2c. Hagios Nikolaos.
Amphora from Sitia.
Detail: instruments.

2d. Location unknown.
Seal stone from Knossos.

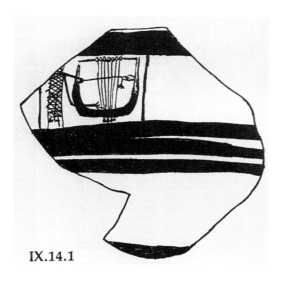

IX.14.1

3a. Nauplia. Krater
fragment from Nauplion.
Musician holding lyre.

3b. Nauplia 14.376. Vase
sherd from Tiryns.
Musician and instrument.

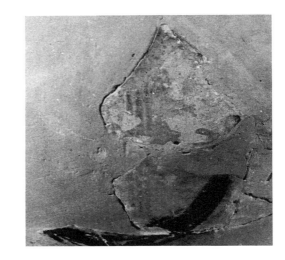

3c. Athens 9063. Kylix
fragment from Stafilos of
Skopelos. Detail:
instrument.

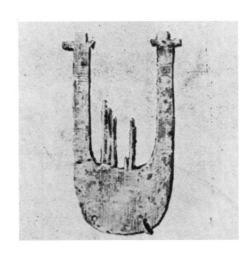

3d. Sparta. Bronze from
the Amyklaion.
Instrument.

4. Nicosia, Kouklia T. 9
no. 7. Cypriote geometric
bowl. Detail: musician
with instrument.

5a. Nicosia. Kaloriziki
amphora. Detail:
musician.

5b. Nicosia. Hubbard
amphora. Detail: musician
with lyre, dancers.

6. Heraklion 2064.
Bronze figurine of seated
musician.

7a. Tübingen 2657. Attic
geometric amphora.
Detail: dancers with
musician.

7b. Karatepe. Relief in
Assyrian-Aramaic style.
Lower register: procession
of musicians.

8. Athens 18542. Attic
geometric oinochoe.
Detail: seated musicians.

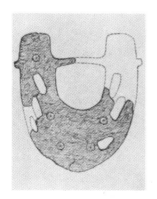

9. Tegea. Bronze from the
sanctuary of Athena Alea.
Instrument.

10. Berlin
Antikenmuseum 31573.
Proto-Attic hydria.
Procession with
musicians.

11. Dresden 1699.
Geometric kantharos.
Musician with three
female dancers.

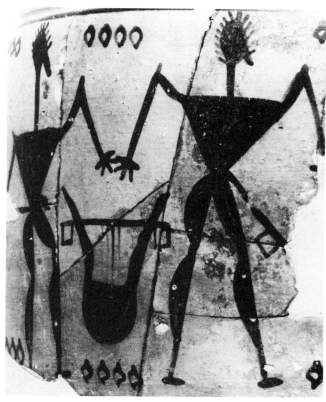

12. Athens 234. Fragment of a large pot from Sparta. Men dancing, holding hands; lyre in field.

13. Athens, sherd from the Argive Heraion. Musician in procession of men clapping hands.

14. Karatepe. Relief in Hittite-Aramaic style. Lower register: group of musicians.

The Archaic Period:
New Things and Old

The term *Archaic*, which is generally applied to the seventh and sixth centuries, describes this period from the vantage point of the heyday of Greek (and specifically Athenian) culture in the fifth century, and is perhaps misleading insofar as it suggests that the civilization of the two preceding centuries was primitive or conservative in attitude. The Archaic period was, in fact, a time of far-reaching changes. Established Greek cities founded new colonies in various parts of the Aegean and in the West; Greeks resumed or began trade with Phoenicians, Syrians, and other peoples of the Near East; coinage was introduced to Greek lands by the Lydians; and Greek visual arts of the period were profoundly influenced by oriental models.

Despite the significance of Eastern influence on Archaic Greece, the Greeks may be said to have *adapted* rather than merely borrowed Eastern ideas.[1] Though the Archaic period is rightly called an age of revolution, it was not a time of wholesale importation of Eastern art, myth, or cultural patterns at the expense of indigenous ideas or of the inheritance from the Greek past. These centuries are marked by a mixture of continuity and change, and that mixture is reflected in the history of Greek stringed instruments of this period.[2]

The Archaic age also presents us with a number of unsolved mysteries concerning the musical instruments of the Greeks. By the beginning of this period, the instruments presently known as the lyra and the kithara were already known to them; but to what extent these instruments were new inventions or borrowings from other peoples we cannot be sure. Nor is it possible to say with any certainty why the round-based phorminx gradually surrendered its place to these newer instruments. The evidence shows that these changes took place; but for the present, at least, the mysteries remain.

Nature of the Sources

Since Attic black-figured vase painting, the most significant archaeological source of evidence for Archaic-period instruments, underwent marked changes of style around 525 B.C. under the influence of the new red-figured style that had just appeared, and since the late sixth-century examples, red- and black-figured, are best grouped with the mainly red-figured vases that form the principal body of artistic evidence for the instruments of the Classical period, this chapter has been limited to a discussion of evidence that can be dated with reasonable certainty between 700 and 525 B.C.

Any assessment of the musical developments in the Archaic age must take into account not only the style, limitations, and comparative rarity of vase paintings, as well as the problems of dating all the various types of archaeological evidence, but also the many difficulties inherent in the literary evidence for the period. The spirit of the Archaic period is reflected in its literature: epic poetry and its offshoots (continuations of the old Homeric tradition) and lyric poetry, in which the voice of the individual poet is heard for the first time. Both the "old" epic poetry and the "new" lyric poetry developed side by side in the seventh and sixth centuries. From the historical point of view, a major difficulty in dealing with this literature is the lack of firm dates. Even using the best information available, we must be content to settle on approximate and often disputed dates. In addition, much of the literature is preserved only in bits and pieces—gleaned from quotations by later writers or rescued from scraps of papyrus. It is tempting to fill in our consequently incomplete understanding of the Archaic period with information from very late and possibly unreliable sources. Later Greek writers appear overly eager to assign a "first inventor" to musical (and other) innovations, and many of their works are simply uncritical compilations of traditional legends. One such essay often cited in modern studies of Greek music is the pseudo-Plutarchian *De musica*, which has been dubbed "an unintelligent source of late antiquity" and which must accordingly be used with caution.[3] In the brief survey of the authors below, some of the difficulties will be explained in more detail.

Hesiod is the earliest of the Archaic poets. Although the ancients thought him a contemporary of Homer, many scholars today regard him as belonging to a somewhat later date.[4] Born in Asia Minor, Hesiod lived and wrote in Boeotia, the territory north of Attica. There is no solid evidence that his two major works, the *Theogony* and the *Works and Days*, written in hexameters, were regarded as suitable for musical performance. Hesiod himself, in *Theogony* 30–35, says that in a moment of divine revelation the Muses appeared to him, gave him a staff (*skeptron*), and bade him "sing" (*hymnein*) about the race of gods, but we do not really know whether he is speaking in literal or metaphorical terms. In *Works and Days* 656–59 he refers more concretely to the prize tripod that he won for a victory in song (*hymnoi*) and that he dedicated to the Muses at the spot where they inspired him to "clear song" (*ligures . . . aoides*). Whether or not Hesiod himself was a forerunner of the later rhapsodes who performed epic poetry, he is the earliest poet to mention a new term for a professional musician, the *kitharistes*, perhaps the successor to the Homeric aoidos.[5]

Another early Archaic source, in which the use of the plektron is first mentioned, is the *Homeric Hymn to Apollo*. This poem, usually assigned to the seventh century, is one of a collection of hexameter hymns addressed to various deities and composed over a period of some two centuries in a style imitative of Homer.

Archilochos of Paros, one of the most vivid of the seventh-century poets, apparently wrote both epic verse on heroic subjects (nothing of which survives) and personal poetry in various meters about his own loves, hates, and adventures as a soldier on the large green island of Thasos off the coast of Thrace. He wrote during the years between 680 and 640, a period that is fixed by his reference to an eclipse of the sun.[6] In the fragments of his work a new word for a musical instrument appears—he is the first author among those preserved to us who mentions the word *lyra*.

A more shadowy figure who was perhaps a contemporary of Archilochos was the poet Terpander. Ancient sources disagree on his date, and little, if indeed anything, survives of his verse.[7] Unfortunately, most of the detailed information about Terpander's life and work comes from the author of the *De musica*, who wrote some seven hundred years later and whose reliability is questionable.[8] About all that can be said with any certainty is that he was born on the island of Lesbos, off the coast of Asia Minor, and may have gone to work as a musician in Sparta. As a conveniently remote figure, he is given the role of "inventor" of several musical "innovations" of which more will be said later.

Another musician connected with Sparta was Alkman, who can be assigned to the last half of the seventh century. Later sources sometimes give his birthplace as Lydia, but he was probably in fact a native of the district around Sparta.[9] As the fragments of his work and other evidence show, Sparta was not, at this stage, the stern military camp depicted in later accounts; on the contrary, it was a highly sophisticated cultural center that was more advanced in art and literature than Athens at the same period. Alkman appears to have written primarily choral poetry to be performed by Spartan girls on religious occasions. The surviving fragments suggest that he himself took part, as the lyre player, in the performance of these *partheneia*.[10] Alkman is also the first poet to mention a type of harp known as the *magadis*, which will be discussed in chapter 6.

Two important figures whose lives spanned the seventh and sixth centuries are Sappho and Alcaeus, both of Lesbos. The torn scraps of the poetry of Sappho (whom Plato called the tenth Muse) are sprinkled with references to stringed instruments (the lyra, *barbitos*, *pektis*, and, probably, kitharis), and in one fragment she speaks of "weaving" song upon the strings of an unnamed instrument. Since only one extant piece is without doubt a whole poem (her "Hymn to Aphrodite"), we are forced, as in the case of many of these early poets, to base our conclusions on tantalizing bits of lines whose contexts are often completely uncertain. Sappho, best known for her love poetry, and Alcaeus, who wrote political poetry as well as drinking songs and hymns, are especially significant in the history of Greek stringed instruments, for they served as links between East and West. Their poems, even in the mutilated state in which they now exist, indicate their close contact with the Lydians (on the coast of Asia Minor), from whom some important instruments may well have been borrowed or adapted for Greek culture.[11]

Amidst the activity of the lyric poets, further developments of the epic tradition still appear in the sixth century. The *Homeric Hymn to Hermes*, similar in form and style to the earlier *Hymn to Apollo* but written in a less serious vein, probably belongs to this period and is important for its description of Hermes' "invention" of the tortoiseshell lyre (*chelys-lyra*).[12]

A sixth-century poet of importance to the history of Greek lyres is Theognis of Megara (probably the Megara of mainland Greece rather than the city of the same name in Sicily). His dates, too, are uncertain, and most scholars agree that some of the poems attributed to him (all in elegiac couplets) are later interpolations.[13] Several of the poems, addressed to his fellow aristocrats on a wide range of subjects, mention lyres in connection with various types of songs.[14] One poem in the collection is particularly important for our present purposes because it contains the first extant reference to the *kithara*, a term derived from the Homeric word *kitharis*, which nevertheless now seems to designate a specific instrument rather than "string-playing" in general. The authorship of this poem is questionable, however, leaving doubt that the word *kithara* is attested in any of the surviving literature from the period before 525 B.C.

Persistence of the Term *Phorminx*

As might be expected in an era in which there is both continuity and profound change, the terminology used to designate musical instruments reflects this state of affairs. The Archaic poets use the old Homeric words (and others derived from them) as well as altogether new terms, that is, terms that do not occur in the *Iliad* or *Odyssey*.

References to the phorminx in Archaic literature occur for the most part in the *Homeric Hymns* and other poems that explicitly imitate Homer. The instrument seems to have become connected almost exclusively with Apollo and is only occasionally associated with ordinary mortal musicians. In the *Hymn to Apollo* (the earliest of the *Homeric Hymns*), only the

two Homeric names (phorminx and kitharis) are used. At his sacred precinct in rocky Pytho, Apollo plays on his "curved phorminx" (*phormingi glaphurei*) with a "golden plektron," causing the instrument to ring out with lovely sound (*h. Hom.* 3.182–85). This passage contains the earliest extant literary reference to the plektron.[15] Later in the poem Apollo plays his phorminx (the verb used is *kitharizein*) and leads a march of Cretans to Pytho while they sing a paean (*h. Hom.* 3.514–17).

In another hymn probably of equal or nearly equal antiquity, the phorminx is associated not with Apollo but with his twin sister, Artemis (*h. Hom.* 5.18–20).[16] The poet explains that the virgin Artemis is not subject to the control of Aphrodite and that her concerns are (among other things) the hunt, phorminxes, and the dance.

One of the most problematic references in literature presumed to date from the Archaic period is a two-line fragment in hexameters, tentatively attributed to Terpander by Strabo (13.618). Strabo, a geographer of the first century A.D., indicates his doubt as to their authenticity by the way he introduces the lines, saying that they are *reportedly* by Terpander.[17] He then quotes the hexameters:

> Putting aside the four-voiced song,
> we will sing you new hymns on a seven-toned phorminx.
>
> ἡμεῖς τοι τετράγηρυν ἀποστέρξαντες ἀοιδὰν
> ἑπτατόνῳ φόρμιγγι νέους κελαδήσομεν ὕμνους.

Deubner, without questioning the authenticity of the lines, took them to mean that Terpander is speaking of his "invention" of a seven-stringed instrument that superseded an earlier four-stringed one; by interpreting Geometric vase paintings literally, Deubner found evidence for the existence of a four-stringed phorminx, and wrote an influential and unfortunately misleading article in which he claimed to have proved that Terpander's introduction of a seven-stringed lyre into Greek culture was factual, not legendary.[18] Even if the lines are genuine, they need not refer to the replacement of a four-stringed instrument with a seven-stringed one; the first line refers only to "four-voiced song," which might be taken in opposition to the "new hymns" in the next line, rather than to the "seven-toned phorminx." The poet may only be saying that he is casting aside an old form of song in favor of a new one that is accompanied by the phorminx. The lines do not say that the phorminx ever had fewer than seven strings.

Another of the *Homeric Hymns* (number 4, to Hermes) for which a sixth-century date is generally thought probable, carries on the association established in the earlier hymns between Apollo and the phorminx.[19] Although the instrument described in the hymn is clearly made of a tortoise shell (unlike the "phorminx" in Geometric art), whenever it is mentioned in connection with Apollo it is called only by the Homeric names *phorminx* or *kitharis*, not, as elsewhere in the poem, *lyra* or *chelys* (tortoise). We shall return to this work shortly and for the moment note only that the association of the phorminx with Apollo helps clarify what at first appears to be the poet's hopelessly arbitrary choice of names for the instrument. When the instrument is first called a phorminx (line 64), it is at the point where the baby Hermes has just conceived a plan to steal the cattle of Apollo. The only other passage in which the instrument is given this name comes after Hermes has given the instrument over to Apollo as appeasement for the theft (line 506).

The phorminx is also linked with Apollo in another poem that imitates Homeric style, the *Shield*, a work probably of the sixth century attributed to Hesiod that describes the scenes on the shield given to Heracles by Athena.[20] In one scene, Apollo plays his "golden phorminx" and the Muses sing while the other gods dance (201–06), a picture reminiscent of Apollo's performance at the feast of the gods in *Iliad* 1.603.[21] The phorminx also provides the music for a dance in another scene on Heracles' shield, a description of a wedding procession that is clearly modeled on the wedding scene depicted on Achilles' shield in *Iliad* 18.491–96:[22]

The youths' tender mouths uttered cries
In answer to the clear-voiced syrinxes, and
    all around them broke the echo.
Girls led the lovely dance to the sound of phorminxes.
On the other side youths revelled to the aulos,
Some making merry in dance and song. . . .
                    (*Shield* 278–82)

τοὶ μὲν ὑπὸ λιγυρῶν συρίγγων ἴεσαν αὐδὴν
ἐξ ἁπαλῶν στομάτων, περὶ δέ σφισιν ἄγνυτο ἠχώ·
αἳ δ᾽ ὑπὸ φορμίγγων ἄναγον χορὸν ἱμερόεντα.
[ἔνθεν δ᾽ αὖθ᾽ ἑτέρωθε νέοι κώμαζον ὑπ᾽ αὐλοῦ.]
τοί γε μὲν αὖ παίζοντες ὑπ᾽ ὀρχηθμῷ καὶ ἀοιδῇ

In both cases, the allusion to this particular kind of lyre is dictated by the Homeric model, in which the stringed instrument in the corresponding scene is the phorminx.

The Homeric associations of the phorminx are put to good use by Theognis in a poem in which he prays that he might possess the Homeric quality of *arete* (roughly, "manliness," "excellence"):

Never may there be any other concern to me
In place of excellence and wisdom, but always
    possessing this
May I delight in the phorminx, the dance, and song,
And along with other noble men may I have a noble
    mind.
                    (Thgn. 1.789–92)

Μήποτέ μοι μελέδημα νεώτερον ἄλλο φανείη
    ἀντ᾽ ἀρετῆς σοφίης τ᾽, ἀλλὰ τόδ᾽ αἰὲν ἔχων
τερποίμην φόρμιγγι καὶ ὀρχηθμῷ καὶ ἀοιδῇ
    καὶ μετὰ τῶν ἀγαθῶν ἐσθλὸν ἔχοιμι νόον.

The word he uses for dance is *orchethmos*, an old form that is found in Homer and the *Hymn to Apollo*. For the conservative Theognis, the orchethmos and its accompanying instrument symbolize the old values of the Homeric aristocracy.[23]

The Phorminx in Archaic Art

The round-based instrument identified in chapter 1 as the phorminx is still to be seen in the art of the Archaic period, and in the seventh century it still occurs more frequently and in more locations than do the other forms of the lyre. Though most of the representations come from the Peloponnesos or from Cyprus, it is the only form of the lyre to be seen between about 675 and 600 B.C. in representations that come from Attica.

Of the most important seventh-century phorminx representations, the earliest is the late-Geometric-period vase Berlin Antikenmuseum 31573 (chap. 1, fig. 10), which probably dates from shortly after the turn of the century. Although the surface of the vase is damaged, the rounded base of the lyre can be clearly seen, as can the plektron on its cord hanging from the instrument.

But the object from the first half of the seventh century that has given rise to the most speculation is a vase fragment that comes from the excavation of the Archaic Greek settlement at Old Smyrna on the Anatolian coast (fig. 1).[24] This vase fragment shows a round-based lyre with seven strings; whether it may be classed as a phorminx remains in doubt.

Now there are, as we know, representations of seven-stringed lyres among the remains of the Minoan and Mycenaean civilizations. But since Iron Age depictions usually have only four strings, and none of them has as many as seven, this vase fragment has been taken as proof of the correctness of reports from writers of the Christian era that the legendary poet-musician Terpander "invented" the seven-stringed lyre and that he did so during the first half of the seventh century.[25]

It must be said, however, that the lyre shown on this sherd is unlike those shown on Iron Age vases in one other important respect: it is larger, so that the painter, without any unduly delicate technique, was able to paint in seven strings in the available space. The instrument is not part of a scene; it is not held by a musician whose body takes up space; it is used alone as a decorative element, so that on a sherd 15 cm high, the instrument itself is about 8⅓ cm (about 3½ in.) tall—considerably larger than the lyres found in scenes on Geometric vases. We must therefore consider once more the possibility that the lyre did not cease to be a seven-stringed instrument after the time of the Mycenaeans, but that limitations created by medium, technique, or artistic intentions prevented an accurate portrayal of the seven strings.

The instrument shown on this vase fragment from Old Smyrna has other interesting details. The bird painted just above it reminds us of the association of birds and lyres in Minoan-Mycenaean art. Like the instrument on Berlin Antikenmus. 31573, it has a plektron on a cord that is attached to the lower end of one of the arms. The crossbar is ornamented with knobs at its ends, and above the crossbar we see a series of five circles that must represent devices of some sort for securing the strings at their upper ends. A number of questions remain unanswered: why the arms are rounded instead of straight; why they bend out at such a sharp angle above the crossbar; what exactly the shape of the soundbox is meant to be; and what the x's on either side of the strings are meant to represent (if anything). If what we see here is a back view of the instrument, the horizontal line at the lower end of the strings probably represents the upper edge of the soundbox rather than the lower string fastener. One hesitates to say exactly what kind of lyre this is— it is not at all certain that it belongs to the phorminx category. (A similar lyre from the latter part of the sixth century is discussed at the end of this chapter [fig. 18]).

The second half of the seventh century provides us with several representations of the seven-stringed phorminx. The most interesting of these appears on a large (37⅜ in.), wide-mouthed amphora from the island of Melos in the Cyclades (fig. 2).[26] Here Apollo, in a chariot drawn by four winged horses, holds aloft in his left hand a round-based instrument with four circles on the front of its soundbox. Although it cannot be seen in photographs, his left hand, fingers straight, is held up behind the strings; his right grasps the plektron, which is on a red cord attached, apparently, near the base of the soundbox. The crossbar, like the one on the Old Smyrna *dinos* fragment, is furnished with

knobs or disks at the ends; it has sometimes been thought that such knobs might serve a purpose in tuning, but a consideration of the differences in tension required leads us to conclude that knobs, which on some forms of the lyre are rarely present, are likely to have been ornamental rather than useful. The crossbar also seems to be provided with what Homer called kollopes: rolls of leather around which the strings are wound to provide the friction to hold the strings tight (the wooden or bone pins through the leather, found in later examples, which aid in securing the strings, are not represented here).

An unusual feature of this painting is that Apollo does not hold the horses' reins—they are looped around the outer arm of the instrument! The free ends of the reins fall from the outer edge of the phorminx in a way that resembles the decorative fringe or "sash" often seen in later paintings.

Although this is a much more detailed painting than its predecessors, it is still not possible to form an accurate idea of the size of the instrument in relation to the performer. The painter is not particularly concerned with proportions (Apollo's right forearm, for example, is too large) and may have exaggerated or reduced the size of the instrument to suit his purposes.

Apollo's companions in this painting are his sister, the goddess Artemis, and two women who are probably Muses. Artemis, who stands before the chariot with quiver, bow, and arrow and holds a stag by its antlers, thus displays her standard attributes as goddess of the hunt, just as Apollo displays the lyre as his chief attribute. The Muses who stand behind him in the chariot are also associated with music, of course; and in later paintings we find them playing instruments similar to the one he holds here.

Two other important examples of the seven-stringed phorminx come to us from the late seventh century, one Athenian and one Corinthian.[27] Although the first of these, Athens Nat. Mus. Acr. AP 1085 (fig. 3a), is only a fragment, it shows the details of an instrument of the phorminx type: a round-based instrument with two small circles on the soundbox, on either side of the strings; a knob at the end of the crossbar; a small rectangle at the bottom of the soundbox that represents the lower string fastener; and a plektron cord, which we now find attached to this rectangular piece. Of particular interest is the bridge, a narrow rectangle protruding on either side of the strings about halfway up the soundbox. Its function was no doubt similar to that of the bridge on a modern stringed instrument: to hold the strings away from the front of the instrument and to conduct the sound to the interior of the soundbox. The scrollwork decorating the arm of the instrument calls to mind the ornamental openings in the Geometric-period bronze votive phorminx from Tegea (chap. 1). Our present example comes from the time when arm ornamentation (of a different sort, to be sure) also begins to be seen in connection with instruments of the kithara type that will be discussed later.

In this fragment we see the phorminx once again in the hand of a bearded man who apparently holds it by means of a strap across the back of the instrument, for his left-hand fingers and thumb, visible behind the strings, are straight, and, like the Apollo on the Melian amphora, he does not hold the instrument against his body.

Our remaining seven-stringed phorminx from this century, on Corinthian alabastron Syracuse 12577 (fig. 3b), adds no information about the instrument but does provide a new scene: it shows a pair of "padded dancers," one of whom holds the phorminx. Such dancers, padded front and aft, appear frequently on Corinthian vases, their burlesque dancing perhaps connected in some way with the worship of Dionysos.

The half-dozen or so remaining seventh-century representations (see n. 27) add little to what has already been presented, though their existence underlines the continued importance of the phorminx. Before passing on to sixth-century artifacts, however, let us consider for a moment a group of terra-cotta figures from Cyprus, each in the form of a standing musician carrying a phorminx. These figures, thought to have been made in the seventh and sixth centuries B.C., attract our attention, not because of the instruments themselves (for only their general shape is indicated) but because the performers and their costumes are modeled with such careful and consistent detail. In figure 4 (similar figures are housed in the Museum at Nicosia) we see one of these lyre players, whose dress proclaims him a person of some importance. He stands straight, his right hand touching the strings of his instrument, his head lifted. He wears a long robe and a high, rounded, crownlike hat; under it his hair is neatly cut to his jaw line, becoming longer toward the back. Around his neck is a high decorated collar, tied in front, and over his shoulders is a necklace with a large medallion in front, rather like a mayor's badge of office. It is tempting to believe that this is a *kitharistes*, one of the musicians of a respected class who were successors to the bards of the Homeric era (though such figures might also represent, for example, priests of Apollo).

During the period between 600 and 525 B.C., objects on which the phorminx is shown become much scarcer than objects that show the kithara or chelys-lyra. Moreover, all but two of the phorminx representations come from outlying Greek enclaves, or even from non-Greek areas. From the first half of the century, for example, we have a funerary chest (fig. 5a) found in Campania in Italy (then an Etruscan area) but possibly made by Greek artists that shows, in low relief, four male musicians, each playing a round-based, five-stringed lyre strangely similar, with its indented and curved arm shape, to the Minoan lyre.[28]

The two extant Athenian examples, on black-figured pottery, also come from the first half of the sixth century. The earlier one is a fragment of a ceramic plaque, on which part of a ritual scene is visible (fig. 5b).[29] On the left is an altar of red and white blocks on which a fire burns; on the right stands a man in a white *chiton* (robe) and red *himation* (mantle) who holds an instrument that appears to be a phorminx but is not clearly depicted in several respects: it is not absolutely certain that the base is rounded, nor is it clear whether the faintly visible horizontal line just above represents a strap across the back of the instrument, though once again the player does not hold the instrument against his body and must have some means of supporting it, since his other hand is occupied with the plektron. The plektron cord is attached to the *inside* arm of the instrument. Though for compositional reasons the painter may have shown the instrument in the player's right arm rather than his left, he has nevertheless depicted the right arm in front, rather than behind, the instrument. It is thus not possible to determine whether the painting represents a front or a back view of the instrument.[30] The lyre has small white knobs at the ends of the crossbar, as did our seventh-century examples, and faint traces of kollopes along the crossbar, but only four strings. Although this is one of the earliest known Athenian black-figured vase paintings showing the phorminx, its many doubtful details prevent us from citing it as an example of the development of the instrument of its time.

We are in a far better position when it comes to the second of our Athenian black-figured paintings, this one on *psykter* (wine cooler) Rhodes 12.200, which is painted in the manner of Lydos, an artist of the third quarter of the sixth century (fig. 6). The scene shows two nude young men facing each other and perhaps dancing, one holding a phorminx, the other a drinking horn; an old man in boots and mantle, also with a drinking horn, watches them from the left.

The performer, the youth in the center, holds his phorminx horizontally, a position rarely seen (cf. chap. 1, fig. 7a) and perhaps used only when the player was also dancing. The base of the instrument cannot actually be seen, of course, because the player holds it against himself; but the rest of its outline is not consistent with that of any member of the lyre family except the phorminx.

The painting shows us an instrument of six strings, not carefully spaced but created by means of a technique that has great potential for fine detail: incision, lines engraved in the painted surface. Using this same technique, the artist indicated the strap or sling that passes around the player's left wrist and around the outer (in this case, lower) arm of the instrument, and the rectangular bridge across the belly of the soundbox. The arms of the instrument become narrow just above the soundbox, but most of their upper length is wide again. The arms are straight and seem to lean toward each other; the lower arm has a short sash of some sort, painted red, attached near the soundbox. The crossbar shows some sign of kollopes but no knobs, and the plektron and its cord are not visible, though the performer's right hand seems to hold such an object. His left hand is visible behind the strings, fingers curved as though to pluck or grasp the strings. This painting is a particularly important one, for along with the seventh-century Melian amphora (fig. 2) and Acropolis fragment (fig. 3a), it constitutes our best evidence for the phorminx during the Archaic age and before the advent of red-figured vase painting in the last quarter of the sixth century.

From the third quarter of the sixth century we have at present only a few items from eastern Greek areas, which add little to our information on the phorminx other than the knowledge that the instrument was still known to the Greeks of Asia Minor.[31] But the last quarter of the century, with its greatly increased amounts of pottery, both red- and black-figured, and its more than half a dozen paintings of the phorminx by Athenian artists, reassures us that the instrument did not fall entirely out of use. The phorminx of this later period is discussed in chapter 6.

Kitharis and Related Words

The old Homeric noun *kitharis* and the verb *kitharizein* continue to be used throughout the Archaic period. Like *phorminx, kitharis* tends to be associated with the music of the gods, or at least with heroic figures rather than ordinary men. In the *Hymn to Apollo,* for example, the god proclaims, shortly after his birth, that the kitharis and the bow will be ever dear to him (*h. Hom.* 3.131). Later in the poem (201ff.) he plays his instrument for a dance of several goddesses while the Muses and his sister Artemis sing; he himself keeps time to his own music with a high-

stepping movement.[32] (The poet describes Apollo as wearing a "well-spun chiton," a robe that is part of the costume in which he appears, as musician, on many later vase paintings; see also fig. 4.) The music of the kitharis is also apparently spoken of by Sappho in a description of the wedding reception at Troy for Hector and Andromache; although the passage is badly fragmented, it seems to describe a scene of rejoicing as Hector and Andromache arrive in a chariot while "the sounds of the sweet-melodied aulos and the kitharis (?) were mixed together, along with the noise of krotala (castanets)."[33]

The noun *kitharis* seems to retain its Homeric associations even in literature of substantially later date than Homer. In the *Hymn to Hermes,* for example, after the tortoise-shell lyre invented by Hermes has been presented to Apollo, it is always referred to as either kitharis or phorminx, the proper Homeric names for Apollo's instrument.[34] The verb *kitharizein,* on the other hand, is found in a wider range of contexts than it had in the *Iliad* and *Odyssey,* in which, as we saw in chapter 1, it was used in reference to the playing of the phorminx. In the Archaic period, the verb clearly means "to play a stringed instrument" of any type.[35] Sometimes it is used by itself, as when the Trojan Anchises plays while wandering over a pasture where he encounters Aphrodite (in disguise), with whom he subsequently begets Aeneas (*h. Hom.* 5.80). But its wider application is demonstrated in the *Hymn to Hermes,* where it is used in connection, not with the phorminx, but with the instrument described as being made from a tortoise shell.

Kitharistes, a derivative of the Homeric term *kitharis,* appears for the first time in the Archaic period. The word first occurs in Hesiod and Alkman, where it designates a professional musician who enjoys the patronage of Apollo and the Muses and who, like the Homeric aoidos, plays at feasts and dances. This early kitharistes must be distinguished from his more familiar fifth- and fourth-century descendant of the same name, whose function was primarily to teach schoolboys how to play and sing to the lyre.

Hesiod, in his account of the Greek gods, says that kings derive their authority from Zeus but that "singer-men" (*andres aoidoi*) and *kitharistai* are under the patronage of the Muses and Apollo (*Th.* 94.96).[36] He speaks also of the therapeutic power of the Muses' gift, which enables the aoidos to cheer up a grieving man by singing of the gods and the deeds of men of former times (*Th.* 100). The association that Hesiod makes in this passage of the *Theogony* between the aoidos and the kitharistes is found again in a Hesiodic fragment which speaks of aoidoi and kitharistai who sing laments for Linos at feasts and dances.[37]

The honored position of the kitharistes in early Sparta is revealed in a short fragment from Alkman (fr. 38 *PMG*), which says, "As many as our youths are, they all praise the *kitharistes,*" by which Alkman presumably means people such as himself. The same sentiment is found in another of his fragments (41 *PMG*), which contains hints both of Sparta's early interest in military achievement and of her lesser known cultural values in the Archaic period; the poet claims that "good lyre-playing rivals iron weapons."[38]

Another kitharistes whom we know by name, of a later date than Alkman, is Arion of Lesbos (fl. 625 B.C.). Arion had a professional status at the court of Periander in Corinth during the height of that city's prosperity, in the last half of the seventh century. The great fifth-century historian, Herodotus, relates Arion's legendary rescue from mutinous sailors, during which a dolphin, charmed by his music, was supposed to have transported him back to the Greek mainland.[39] To be sure, Herodotus describes Arion as a *kitharoidos* (kitharode) rather than a kitharistes. *Kitharoidos,* which does not appear until the fifth century, combines the ideas that Hesiod had expressed with two separate words, *kitharistes* and *aoidos*; *kitharoidos* becomes the standard term among authors of the Classical period for one who sings to his own accompaniment. Arion's birth in the East (Lesbos) and subsequent career on the mainland provide yet another example of the westward movement of musical ideas and practices during the Archaic period. Although much of his achievement seems to have disappeared into the realm of legend, there can be no doubt that he was, as Herodotus says, the most famous musician of his time.

The most familiar of the terms derived from the Homeric word *kitharis* is *kithara,* which is in turn the ancestor of the names *zither* and *guitar.*[40] There is, however, no definite evidence that the word *kithara* had come into use during the period before 525 B.C. The only author of this period in whose work the word occurs is Theognis, and the particular poem in which it occurs can be almost certainly dated to about 490 B.C.:

> But you [Phoibos Apollo] keep off the insolent army of the Medes
> From this city, so that the people, in rejoicing
> When spring has come, may sacrifice famed hecatombs,
> Delighting in the kithara and in lovely merriment,
> With dances and joyful shouts of paeans around your altar.
> (Thgn. 1.775–78)

> αὐτὸς δὲ στρατὸν ὑβριστὴν Μήδων ἀπέρυκε
> τῆσδε πόλεος, ἵνα σοι λαοὶ ἐν εὐφροσύνηι
> ἦρος ἐπερχομένου κλειτὰς πέμπω σ᾽ ἑκατόμβας
> τερπόμενοι κιθάρηι κἀν ἐρατῆι θαλίηι
> παιάνων τε χοροῖσ᾽ ἰαχῆισί τε σὸν περὶ βωμόν᾽

Although scholars dispute whether or not the poem in which the passage occurs was really written by Theognis, most are agreed that the reference to the Medes must have to do with the Persian invasions of the Greek mainland. Because the Persians did not attack the mainland until 490 B.C., this passage cannot have been written much before that time.[41] The word *kithara* is thus not attested in Greek literature before approximately 490 B.C. By that time, all the kinds of lyres common in the fifth century have already appeared in the vase paintings, including the large, flat-based lyre identified, on the basis of evidence of the later fifth century, as the kithara. Although definite evidence is lacking, there is reason to assume, as we shall see in chapter 3, that this instrument, already known from visual evidence as early as the seventh century, was at first called by the old Homeric names *kitharis* and *phorminx,* and that it was not until toward the end of the fifth century that these names were supplanted by the new word, *kithara.*

Representations of the Kithara in Archaic Art

Lyres with flat bases, in various sizes and shapes, existed in both Egypt and Asia Minor long before the kithara appeared on Greek soil, and it would be arguing against common sense to hold that the Greek instrument was a complete reinvention of the flat-based lyre.[42] But aside from this one feature, its shape bears little resemblance to most of the Egyptian and Asian instruments, which tend to have asymmetrical arms.

Our first glimpses of the specifically Greek form of this instrument shape, later to be called the kithara, come from the late eighth century: the heart-shaped instruments depicted on two late-Geometric Attic vases (Athens 18542 and Copenhagen 9367, chap. 1, fig. 8); a definitely flat-based instrument seen on a vase sherd in Athens from the Argive Heraion; and a relief from Karatepe, all discussed in chapter 1. Indications of the existence of the kithara continue to be rare in the seventh century; in fact, there are only three items that can be cited: an instrument depicted on a sub-

Geometric-style krater (wine-serving bowl) from Pitane on the coast of Asia Minor near the island of Lesbos; the instrument shown on a fragment of a large pot in Orientalizing style from the island of Delos (fig. 7); and one finely engraved on a bronze back plate found at Olympia (fig. 8).

The first of these, from Pitane, dates from early in the century and presents, according to a drawing published by Ekrem Akurgal, a seven-stringed instrument with a slim, tapered soundbox and a flat base.[43] Its crossbar has knobs and kollopes, but its arms show no sign as yet of the ornamental design of the inner edges that gradually appears later, and above the crossbar the arms bend outward sharply in a way that recalls the instrument on the Old Smyrna *dinos* (festive wine bowl; fig. 1). The instrument on the sherd from Delos (fig. 7), made before the middle of the seventh century, lacks its base, which has been broken off; but what we can see closely resembles the shape of the later kithara. The arms continue, wide and straight, for some distance above the crossbar, which has knobs, and there are seven strings. The arms are decorated just below the crossbar with a white square with a dot in the center on either arm—not the ornamentation used in the later standard kithara design but a sign of the kind of elegance of construction associated with that instrument. Below this the arms curve out before they reach the soundbox, giving the instrument much the same outline as that of the later kithara. Like the latter, the instrument is held upright, by a bearded man with long hair whose hand appears behind the strings. The man, and the woman who can be seen on the right, probably represent Apollo and Artemis, not only because the two of them (and the lyre) are so often found together but because this fragment comes from the sacred island of Delos, their mythological birthplace.

Apollo, who now begins to be represented as a beardless young man, can be seen again with the kithara in the only example currently available from the second half of the seventh century, the scene engraved on the bronze back plate from a warrior's armor (fig. 8), possibly made in the Aegean islands but found in the river Alpheios at Olympia, and now in the Olympia Museum.[44] On it there are six figures. Behind Apollo are two female figures, probably goddesses in this case rather than Muses; the two intended may be Artemis and the mother of Artemis and Apollo, Leto. Facing Apollo is a bearded man in elaborate costume, probably Zeus, and behind him are two beardless men in simpler garb, who may also be deities; but none of the figures except Apollo with his kithara has any identifying attributes.

The kithara itself, seen here in back view, is remarkable because it has all the features, including the ornamentation of the inner edges of the arms, that we recognize as belonging to the kithara of the Classical period. The crossbar is furnished with knobs and seven kollopes, the latter seen above and below the crossbar, with the seven strings wrapped around them alternately above and below in a figure-eight pattern. The arms stand tall and straight above the crossbar, though they are neither as tall nor as wide as those of the kithara of later times. Below the crossbar each arm has a scroll or volute, the upper part of the elegant ornamental design of the inner edges. Just below the scroll a small point protrudes toward the strings, curving away again underneath; and farther down is a larger point, more elaborately constructed. The sling that allows the player to support the instrument with his left wrist is clearly visible. Attached to it (or formed by its free ends) is a "sash" that hangs next to the outer side of the soundbox. Next to the strings (in an unusually high position to make it visible) the player's right hand can be seen busy with the plektron, which has its cord attached to the base of the soundbox. The decorated cloth that Apollo seems to have over his shoulder reminds us of the cloth that customarily hangs down from behind the instrument in the front-view portrayals of the sixth and fifth centuries (see, for example, chap. 3, fig. 9). This cloth may have served to protect the instrument from wear and to cushion it against the player's arm and chest, and may also have provided a cover for the instrument when it was not in use. Such a cloth is not seen, even in later times, with the lyra or barbitos, and only rarely with the phorminx.

Representations of the kithara remain comparatively rare in the first half of the sixth century, though they are more often found than paintings of the phorminx. Most of the available objects come from mainland Greece, but there are individual items from the islands of Cyprus and possibly Lemnos, and from the Anatolian coast.

The most famous of the early sixth-century representations of the kithara appears on a black-figured dinos (fig. 9a, London 1971.11–11), signed by the first Athenian artist whose name is known to us, Sophilos, who worked between 580 and 570 B.C. The scene is a procession of chariots bearing gods and goddesses to the marriage of Peleus and Thetis. Apollo shares his *quadriga* (a four-horse chariot) with the god Hermes, and behind their horses walk three of the Muses (there is no doubt as to who they are in this case, for all the figures on this vase are identified by inscriptions).[45] Parts of the dinos are missing, and the top of the kithara has been lost. But enough of it remains to show that the inner edges of its arms were ornamented much as in figure 8, that it had six strings, and that there was a sling for the left wrist and a sash hanging down beside the instrument (it looks like a long fringe). As in very nearly all the examples of the kithara that we will see, the instrument is held upright. The left hand is just visible behind the strings, slanted out, while the right hand holds the plektron out just beyond the strings, near the center of the soundbox, in one of the poses frequently seen in later times. The instrument seems quite large, but its size is difficult to estimate because of the missing section.

A vase that may be approximately contemporary with the Sophilos dinos, Athens 19272 (fig. 9b), a krater that may come from the northeast Aegean island of Lemnos, shows, by contrast, a small and rather undeveloped-looking version of the kithara.[46] Although the surface of the vase is badly worn, the scene is fairly clear, as is the outline of the instrument. It is held by a man with long hair wearing a short costume that leaves his legs bare. For once the instrument is not held upright—it is tilted out at about a 45° angle. But it does not appear to be played; the man is holding it while he kneels and reaches out to receive a wreath, it seems, from an imposing (female?) figure seated on the right. A few details of the kithara (for this is clearly what it is) are visible: the arms, slender but straight in the upper section; a knob at the left end of the crossbar; faint kollopes along the crossbar; decoration along the inner edges of the arms below the crossbar (simpler, and not of the same design as that in fig. 8); the sling for the left wrist; the plektron (in the player's right hand, which also seems to reach for the wreath); and the plektron cord looped over the player's right arm. This instrument, like the one on the dinos by Sophilos, has six strings.

From the Sikyonian Treasury at Delphi there is a marble relief (fig. 9c) carved in about 560 B.C that depicts two kithara players, apparently Orpheus and perhaps Amphion, on board the ship Argo. In front of its prow are two mounted horsemen, the Dioscuri, Castor and Pollux. The scene corresponds, except for the second kithara player, to the story of Jason's quest for the golden fleece as told in the second century B.C. by Apollonios Rhodios in his *Argonautica* (1.494 and elsewhere).[47] Although the figures are extremely worn and damaged, the relief is of considerable interest for our purposes because it shows us a side view of the two kitharas. We learn with the help of this relief of the great depth of the soundbox of the kithara, and of its bulging back, over which the player's left arm must lie. The soundbox, broader at the top than at the bottom, was certainly deep enough to make this an instrument of substantial resonance.

Of the remaining objects that come from the first half of the sixth century, only one, a fragment of a black-figured vase made near the middle of the century (Athens Nat. Mus. Acr. 2203) is detailed enough and well-enough preserved to merit close attention (fig. 10).[48] The elaborateness of the costumes makes us think of a marriage celebration; the fragment includes part of a high, ornate bed on the far right, and a woman on the far left (the bride) holds out her veil. The remaining figures are two women, a child, an aulos player, and the player of the kithara.

Part of the instrument is missing, so that we cannot tell how the upper arms or ends of the crossbar might have looked—and this is especially unfortunate because the rest of the instrument is unusual, both in general outline and in the design of its ornamentation. Some aspects are familiar: the player holds the plektron just beyond the (eight) strings, about halfway up the soundbox; the plektron cord is attached to the lower string fastener, a rectangle visible at the bottom of the soundbox. Just above it, a line across the strings indicates that there is a bridge, and from behind the instrument falls the kithara "cloth" mentioned in connection with earlier examples. The line between the outer arm and the soundbox may indicate the attachment of a sash.

When we turn to the representations from the third quarter of the sixth century, we find that their number has increased markedly, partly because the kithara now appears in a number of figured scenes that are frequently painted by Athenian artists. Most of the nearly thirty available examples depict gods and goddesses, who are sometimes identified by inscriptions as well as attributes, and include Apollo as kitharode (*kitharoidos*): Apollo at the birth of Athena (fig. 11), Apollo with Artemis and/or Leto, Apollo in the procession bringing Heracles to Olympus, or Apollo accompanying a quadriga procession. In the latter, it may be a wedding procession, with figures such as Zeus and Hera or Heracles and Hebe in the chariot, but other paintings show Apollo accompanying Athena's chariot or that of Dionysos. The god with the kithara can also be seen in the company of Hermes, Athena, Dionysos, Poseidon, and Zeus in various other scenes. He is portrayed in elaborate full-length costumes made of embroidered or patterned cloth and is usually beardless to indicate his youth; but there are still some paintings in which he appears as a mature man with a beard.

In two vase paintings, London B 139 and B 260, a kithara player stands between two columns, on top of which sit cocks or (on the latter vase) sphinxes, perhaps symbols of festivals at which kithara contests took place (B 139 is a Panathenaic vase, with the figure of Athena on the reverse, also between columns surmounted by cocks). Here the players may stand for Apollo, but they may also represent contest winners (see chap. 3). There is only one scene in which we may be sure that the player is not meant to be Apollo: in a *komos* (rowdy procession) scene on a vase in Boeotian rather than Athenian style, on which nude dancers are accompanied by a kithara player who is also nude (Thebes R.50.265).

The kithara player, in all the paintings in this group, is standing or walking, holding the instrument upright or tipped only slightly away from him or toward him. His left wrist is in the sling, his left-hand fingers straight and separated, with the thumb straight out or bent over in front of the palm as though plucking the strings (the movement of the whole hand is restricted by the need to brace the instrument by means of the sling around the wrist). In this period there are not yet any paintings in which the fingers are bent or curled. The right hand, in scenes where the instrument is actually being played, holds the plektron beyond the strings or at the outer edge of the soundbox, near the bottom of the instrument or as much as halfway up the front of the soundbox, giving the impression that the player has just completed an outward sweep across the strings. No other pose that suggests playing can yet be observed.

The instruments themselves still show a considerable amount of variation in size and number of strings, and a lesser degree of variation in fittings and ornamentation. Most of them are about twice as tall as the length of the player's forearm, and anywhere from two-thirds to three-fourths as wide as they are high.[49] Most of the instruments have seven strings, but a fair number (one-third as many) clearly have only five, and a few have either six or eight or do not have visible strings.

The fittings and ornamentation shown in figure 11 may be taken as typical, though only the tips of the upper arms are white (often the upper arms are entirely white, almost certainly an indication of ivory facings), the decoration of the inner arms comes to a rather exaggerated point, and there is no visible bridge or sash. We can see the two knobs on the crossbar, the kollopes and six strings, the wrist sling, the plektron and its cord attached to the lower string fastener, and the cloth, with horizontal bands on it, hanging close against the player's mantle. The scene shows Apollo playing at the birth of Athena. The small, armed figure emerges from the head of Zeus, who sits clutching his thunderbolts; behind Apollo is the god Hermes with his winged boots, and opposite stand Eileithyia, goddess of childbirth, and Ares, god of war.

Appearance of the Terms *Lyra* and *Chelys*

There are several terms related to stringed instruments that appear for the first time in the literature of the Archaic period. An important one is the name *lyra*, which is first found among the fragments of Archilochos. Although a few etymologists have attempted to show that it is of Indo-European origin, *lyra* was probably, like most of the other names for stringed instruments, borrowed into the Greek language from some non-Indo-European tongue of the Mediterranean area.[50] Since evidence from the fifth century indicates that the word *lyra* is generic, that is, that it refers to *any* instrument of the lyre family (see chap. 4), we must remember in discussing the following references from Archaic literature that we do not always know what specific type of lyre the author has in mind.

The earliest reference to *lyra* is in a poorly preserved fragment of Archilochos that was found on a first-century B.C. inscription on Paros, the island of the poet's birth. The inscription recounts various of Archilochos' exploits, but the lines in which the lyra is mentioned appear to be introduced as the poet's own words, not those of his biographer.[51] Although the context is unclear, the lines apparently speak of efforts on the part of the Greeks to appease the rebellious Thracians (who resented Greek incursions into their territory) with gifts of gold. As part of this mission of peace, the leader of the expedition seems to have taken along with him "men who sounded well (?) the aulos and lyra," perhaps to sweeten the occasion with music.[52]

Another seventh-century reference to the lyra is to be found among the fragments attributed to Alkman (fr. 140, *PMG*), in the form *kerkolyra*. According to a Byzantine authority, this unusual word is another form of *krekolyra*, an onomatopoetic effort to imitate the sound of the instrument.[53] But it seems more likely that the first part of the word should be connected with the verb *krekein*, "to pass the shuttle across the threads," and hence by association of images (of which more will be said later) "to strike a lyre with the plektron"; *krekolyra* may simply refer to the playing of a stringed instrument.[54]

References to the lyra become increasingly common among the fragments of sixth-century authors. Stesichoros of Sicily, for example, in a traditional appeal to the Muse, says:

Come, o clear-voiced Muse, Erato, begin your
song,
Voicing to the beautiful lyra melodies about the
children of Samos.[55]

(fr. 278, *PMG*)

ἄγε Μοῦσα λίγει' ἄρξον ἀοιδᾶς †ἐρατῶν ὕμνους†
Σαμίων περὶ παίδων ἐραται φθεγγομένα λύραι.

Among the many references to instruments in the
fragments of Sappho's verse there are two that speak
of the lyra. One occurs in the form of an epithet applied to Apollo in the long fragment about the wedding reception of Hector and Andromache (44.33 LP),
in which men call upon Paeon (Apollo) "the far-
shooter and well-lyred" (*eulyros*). The other appears
in what seems to be the first line of a poem, in which
she is perhaps describing the sound of her instrument
as the poem begins (most of the line is missing, but
all the letters in the word *lyra* are clear).[56]

Three lines preserved from the opening of the
anonymous *Margites* refer to an aged bard (aoidos)
who comes to Kolophon in Ionia, lyre in hand:

An old man, a divine singer, came into
Kolophon,
A servant of the Muses and of far-shooting
Apollo,
Holding in his hand his beautiful-sounding lyra.

(fr. 1, Allen)

ἦλθέ τις εἰς Κολοφῶνα γέρων καὶ θεῖος ἀοιδός,
Μουσάων θεράπων καὶ ἐκηβόλου Ἀπόλλωνος,
φίλην ἔχων ἐν χερσὶν εὔφθογγον λύραν.

The date of the poem, a parody of heroic epic, is disputed. The language of the fragment, except for the
reference to lyra, echoes the older poets: the "divine
singer" is reminiscent of Homer, and the notion of a
singer as the servant of Apollo and the Muses recalls
Hesiod. But since Aristotle (*Po.* 4.7) regards the poem
as the mother of comedy and since the hero seems to
have been a blundering dimwit, it is reasonable to conclude that the author is a later writer who is deliberately parodying his serious predecessors, while con-
sciously or unconsciously calling the singer's instrument by the contemporary name *lyra* rather than the
Homeric name *phorminx*.[57]

The lyra is also described by this same epithet,
"beautiful-sounding" (*euphthongos*), in a couplet in
elegiac meter from the corpus attributed to Theognis.
The poet exclaims:

I rejoice in good drinking, listening to the
aulos player's tune.

I rejoice holding my beautiful-sounding lyra
in my hands.

(Thgn. 1.533–34)[58]

Χαίρω δ' εὖ πίνων καὶ ὑπ' αὐλητῆρος ἀκούων,
χαίρω δ' εὔφθογγον χερσὶ λύρην ὀχέων.

This passage has rightly raised questions about the
traditional assumption that *all* poetry in elegiac meter
was accompanied exclusively by the aulos. Theognis
seems to indicate that he might accompany his own
drinking songs in the elegiac meter with his lyra, perhaps in addition to aulos accompaniment.[59] Another
poem in the same collection, a lament on the deprivations imposed by death, also associates lyre music
and aulos playing with drinking:

No man, once the earth has covered him over
And he has gone to Erebos, the house of
Persephone,
Takes pleasure in hearing the lyra or the aulos
player
Or in raising to his lips the gifts of Dionysos.

(Thgn. 1.973–76)

Οὐδεὶς ἀνθρώπων, ὃν πρῶτ' ἐπὶ γαῖα καλύψηι
εἴς τ' Ἔρεβος καταβῆι, δώματα Περσεφόνης,
τέρπεται οὔτε λύρης οὔτ' αὐλητῆρος ἀκούων
οὔτε Διωνύσου δῶρ' ἐπαειρόμενος.

The lyra is also connected with Dionysos in the
lines of a charming Attic drinking song (*skolion*) of
uncertain, possibly late sixth-century date:

O that I might become a beautiful ivory lyra
And that beautiful youths might carry me into
Dionysos' dance.

(fr. 900, *PMG*)[60]

εἴθε λύρα καλὴ γενοίμην ἐλεφαντίνη
καί με καλοὶ παῖδες φέροιεν Διονύσιον ἐς χορόν.

It is unlikely, to be sure, that the song refers to a lyre
literally made wholly of ivory; the epithet *elephantinos*
simply shows that instruments of the Archaic age, like
those of Homer's time, might be ornamented with
ivory. This detail can be verified by reference to vase
paintings of the kithara from the third quarter of the
sixth century; a number of these have white paint on
the upper arms, on the decorative design on the inner
edges of the arms, and occasionally on the knobs;
some vases have only small touches of white on some
part of the decoration.[61]

The presumably sixth-century *Homeric Hymn to
Hermes* tells of the "invention" of the chelys-lyra by
the infant Hermes. The baby god, having stumbled
across a mountain tortoise, proceeds to make it into a
musical instrument and says (as Homer did about the
phorminx in *Od.* 8.99, 17.270–71) that it will be a

companion to the feast. The transformation of a tortoise (chelys) is described as follows (in a literal prose
translation):

> Turning it over, with a knife of grey iron he
> scooped out the marrow of the mountain tor-
> toise. . . . Then he fixed in place stalks of cane,
> cutting them in measured length, piercing the back
> of the tortoise through its shell. All around he
> stretched the hide of an ox, relying on his wits, and
> he fit the arms into place, and joined the crossbar
> to both, and stretched seven tuneful strings of
> sheep-gut. When he had built his lovely plaything,
> he picked it up and touched the strings with the
> plektron, trying out a tune.[62] The instrument re-
> sounded marvelously.
>
> (h. Hom. 4.41–54)

ἔνθ' ἀναπηλήσας γλυφάνῳ πολιοῖο σιδήρου
αἰῶν' ἐξετόρησεν ὀρεσκῴοιο χελώνης. . . .
πῆξε δ' ἄρ' ἐν μέτροισι ταμὼν δόνακας καλάμοιο
πειρήνας διὰ νῶτα διὰ ῥινοῖο χελώνης.
ἀμφὶ δὲ δέρμα τάνυσσε βοὸς πραπίδεσσιν ἑῇσι,
καὶ πήχεις ἐνέθηκ', ἐπὶ δὲ ζυγὸν ἤραρεν ἀμφοῖν,
ἑπτὰ δὲ συμφώνους ὀΐων ἐτανύσσατο χορδάς.
αὐτὰρ ἐπεὶ δὴ τεῦξε φέρων ἐρατεινὸν ἄθυρμα
πλήκτρῳ ἐπειρήτιζε κατὰ μέλος, ἡ δ' ὑπὸ χειρὸς
σμερδαλέον κονάβησε·

In addition to a soundbox made of a tortoise shell
covered with leather, other important technical features emerge from this description:

1. the *donax* (line 47), cane or reed, whose exact
   structural function is uncertain (see below);
2. the *pecheis* (line 50), or arms of the lyra;
3. the *zugon* already known from Homer (line 50),
   the crossbar or yoke across the upper ends of the
   arms, to which the upper ends of the strings
   are attached;
4. the plektron (line 53) with which the strings are
   struck (already mentioned in the earlier *Hymn
   to Apollo*);
5. seven strings (line 51) made, just as in Homer,
   of sheepgut.

Some commentators have thought that the stalks
of cane which Hermes cuts were used to form the instrument's bridge, while others argue that they might
have provided some sort of internal support (roughly
analogous to the function of the modern soundpost)
or that they somehow secured the strings at their lower
ends (like the modern tailpiece on a violin). The holes
cut symmetrically in the backs of tortoise shells (re-
constructed from fragments thought to date from the
Archaic period) in the museums at Argos and Athens
(the latter from Vassae), which may have been chelys-
lyra soundboxes, correspond nicely to the description

of Hermes piercing the tortoise shell and fixing the
pieces of cane in place, but we still cannot be certain
precisely what structural purpose the cane served.[63]
Cane can form a tough substance, especially if it
comes from the lower portions of the stalk, so that
none of the proposed suggestions can be ruled out on
the basis of unsuitability of the material.

The material for the pecheis, or arms, of the lyre
is not mentioned in the poem. Nor does the poem
provide any further details about the zugon or plektron beyond what is already known from Homer or the
Homeric Hymn to Apollo. We do, howver, have here
the earliest literary reference to the use of seven strings
(except for the probably spurious fragment of Terpander discussed above). Allen and Sikes have warned of
the dangers of trying to date the poem on the basis of
the allusion to seven strings and to their supposed "invention" by the seventh-century Terpander. As they
point out, "the writer could not have attributed the
seven strings to Hermes had not the [instrument] been
long established in that form."[64] Gods are not made
to invent *new* things but only those that tradition and
the passage of time have rendered acceptable.

In the poem, the tortoise shell lyre that Hermes
constructs is called several times simply "tortoise,"
chelone or *chelys* (the earliest use of these words to
designate an instrument), and once "lyra" (line 423),
as well as "phorminx" and "kitharis" when it is associated with Apollo. The close connection between
the word *lyra* and an instrument whose soundbox is
made of tortoise shell might be thought to be confirmed by an Archaic vase painting in which the artist
has inscribed the word *lyra* next to just such an instrument (fig. 12).[65] Later evidence indicates, however,
that the word *lyra* is generic in that it can refer to any
instrument of the lyre type; and as we have seen, it is
probable that the word carries such a meaning even in
this early period as well.

The Chelys-Lyra in the Visual Arts
of the Archaic Period

Instruments with soundboxes made of tortoise shells,
or in the shape of a tortoise shell, are first found on
three Attic Geometric- and sub-Geometric-style pots:
two *hydriai* (water jars) and a fragment of a third vase,
probably also a *hydria*, from the end of the eighth
century and the beginning of the seventh. All three
vases show essentially the same scene: on Athens 313,
the "Analatos Hydria" (fig. 13a), for example, there
is on the right a row of women in long skirts holding
hands and carrying leafy branches, while on the left
there is a row of men with branches holding hands,

and in the center, a man who holds the chelys-lyra.[66] They appear to be taking part in a stately processional dance of a ritual nature.

The chelys-lyra itself is as schematically drawn as one might expect in Geometric style. Its soundbox is more or less round (only Cambridge M.C.A. 345 gives it a more defined tortoise-shell shape), its arms are straight and angled away from each other, and the crossbar is set into them with its ends free (only on Athens 313 are there knobs on the crossbar). Two of our examples have five strings, and the strings are not indicated on the third (Athens Agora P 10154). The chelys-lyra in figure 13a has, in addition, crosspieces decorating the tops of the arms of the instrument. In this painting, in which the instrument is held tipped out at about a 45° angle, the player's left hand is visible behind the strings, but damage to the vase prevents us from seeing all of the right hand that holds the plektron.

Only one other source of seventh-century representations of the chelys-lyra is known to us at the present time. In the course of excavation of the temple of Artemis Orthia at Sparta, some half-dozen small lead votive objects, made to depict the chelys-lyra or players of the chelys-lyra, were found among the thousands of similar lead offerings unearthed in the area around the temple. Four of the objects are from the group identified as belonging to the years from 700 to 635 B.C.; the remaining two, made between 635 and 600 B.C., follow patterns from the older group.[67]

The most informative of the lead objects is one that consists of a chelys-lyra alone, without player, for here the instrument itself is large enough to offer a view not only of the tortoise-shell markings (it presents the back of the chelys), but of the remains of seven strings (fig. 13b).[68] These appear to have been fastened at the crossbar around kollopes that must have represented leather rolls with small sticks placed at right angles to the crossbar (sticks were used for this purpose, in much earlier times than this, in both Egypt and Asia Minor). The arms of this chelys-lyra curve out as they rise from the soundbox, then come closer together again at the crossbar, the shape commonly known from paintings of later periods.

Another lead figure from the early group, a player holding a chelys-lyra in front view (fig. 13c), allows us to see the rectangle with rounded corners, just above the bottom edge of the soundbox, that indicates the lower string fastener.[69]

One other class of objects from the excavation of the temple of Artemis Orthia is related to the history of the Greek lyres in general—the group of at least three ivory or bone objects, dating from the eighth to

the sixth century B.C., that may be actual plektra (fig. 13d).[70] These objects, the size and shape of small broad-bladed knives without handles, are about 3½ inches long and have from six to nine small holes in the narrow end, which also has small hook-like protrusions. It is likely that both holes and hooks were intended as means of attaching a handle, probably of leather.

In the early sixth century, vases with paintings of scenes that include the chelys-lyra once again become available, and in a surprising abundance. Corinthian influence is strong in the early part of the century: two of nine vases definitely dated before 550 B.C. are from Corinthian workshops, and several of the others, early examples of Athenian black-figured pottery, are imitations of Corinthian style and subject matter. For example, a Corinthian krater, Paris E 629 (fig. 14a), is decorated with a banquet scene, men and women reclining on couches with tables bearing food before them, and several chelys-lyres hanging on the wall behind, symbols of music to come later in the festivities.[71]

Other scenes on vases in this early sixth-century group include a wine-drinking party (fig. 14b), two paintings of processions (one also shows two sets of auloi), two paintings of the story of Theseus (Theseus fighting the Minotaur and Theseus' victory dance [fig. 14c]), a painting of a chelys-lyra player between two sirens (birds with the heads of human females [fig. 14c]), and a painting of a chelys-lyra hanging on the wall behind a bed on which lies a bearded man wearing a wreath (fig. 14e).[72] Because the body of the man in this last painting is so completely shrouded and because the chelys-lyra is present, it has been suggested that the scene depicts a poet on his death bed. Whether or not this is accepted, it seems clear that the chelys-lyra serves to some extent as a symbol, as it does in the painting with the sirens (who are themselves symbols, both of beautiful music and of death, and appear as funeral monuments now and again holding lyres).[73]

The instrument on the "siren" vase (fig. 14d) is unusual in several respects: it is much larger than the chelys-lyra ordinarily appears, it has knobs on the crossbar (an uncommon feature for the chelys-lyra), and its bridge appears above the top edge of the soundbox, probably in an effort to make visible in silhouette a detail that really belongs about halfway down the soundbox.

In the drinking-party scene on Athens Kerameikos 2869 (fig. 14b), the chelys-lyra shown is peculiar in the way it indicates the fastening of strings to the crossbar. The crossbar, with bumps along it (kollopes) is painted in black, but a fine crisscross pattern has been incised all over it, presumably to indicate the way the strings are wound on—and these were wound on thoroughly! The strings on the instrument in the banquet scene on Paris E 623, however, are more efficiently fixed in figure-eight-like patterns around the kollopes that stand at right angles to the crossbar.

Because many of these scenes show a back view of the chelys-lyra, and other paintings are too small or too damaged to show details clearly, we find only two vases with instruments on which a bridge can be seen, the "siren vase," Heidelberg 68/1 (fig. 14d), and Florence 4209, the famous "François Vase" on which Theseus' victory dance is painted (fig. 14c). Theseus, the legendary Athenian hero, seems to have acquired his association with the lyre through accounts (now lost) of this scene in which he and his companions celebrate their liberation, for even in the paintings showing him killing the Minotaur, someone stands next to him holding his chelys-lyra for him (fig. 12).

Representations of the chelys-lyra dating from about the middle of the century repeat some of the scenes already discussed: Theseus and the Minotaur (fig. 12), the partakers of a banquet, komasts (revelers) at a drinking party, and musicians accompanying a row of female dancers. But there are details that have not been seen before, and there are new scenes too. One of these, in which Nereids mourn over the body of Achilles (fig. 15a), is quite unusual, for lyres do not ordinarily appear in funeral scenes and were not customarily used, as we know, for accompanying funeral laments (see chap. 4). But the chelys-lyra is not played in this scene, it is only held by one of the Nereids. The lyre once again serves as a symbol: this time, along with the armor beneath the couch, it apparently symbolizes Achilles himself, for he is described as a lyre player in a famous scene in the *Iliad* (chap. 1). The instrument shown in this painting is remarkable in two respects: first, because it has *nine* strings, clearly incised, and second, because its chelys soundbox has such a strange shape, possibly achieved by carving the tortoise shell, since this is not likely to have been its normal shape. Notice the clear details at the joining of arm and crossbar: we can see that the crossbar sits in notches cut into the arms of the instrument (the front edge of the notch has been trimmed to a point).

Other scenes in the mid-century group are less surprising but still include features not seen earlier. On a *lekythos* (oil vase), New York 56.11.1 (fig. 15b), a row of women take part in a dignified dance (probably a wedding dance, since the main scene on this vase is a wedding procession) accompanied by a chelys-lyra player. Neither instrument nor player is unusual, but

the player is seated, the first example of a seated lyre player among the representations from the Archaic period, though we did encounter seated players in chapter 1. On Paris E 861 (fig. 15c), we find not one but four players of the chelys-lyra, bearded men with long hair wearing mantles who appear to be dancing; the second and fourth figures, with one knee lifted, certainly are. The instruments in this scene, which appear to have small cloths hanging behind the soundbox, have oddly placed lower string fasteners located more than halfway up the front of the soundbox.[74]

Semiprecious stones (cornelian, jasper, and the like) with figures cut in them (to be reproduced in relief when the stone is pressed on clay or wax) were, as we have seen in chapter 1, quite common in ancient times in the Aegean world; and various scenes showing lyres of one kind or another were among the figures cut into these seal stones. The first examples showing the chelys-lyra appear after the middle of the sixth century. On one, a nude youth runs with the chelys-lyra tucked under his arm, and what appears to be a flower in his other hand. On another, the chelys-lyra is held by an unmistakable satyr, with pointed ears, one of the first of his kind to be seen holding any of the lyres. He is accompanying a dancer. These seals, with rather ordinary-looking versions of the chelys-lyra (with little detail and only four strings, since they are less than a centimeter tall), were probably made in East Greek, Ionian workshops.[75]

Although in earlier representations the performers held the chelys-lyra upright in nearly every instance, we learn from this mid-century group of objects that chelys-lyra players do not hold their instruments upright as do kithara players. The seated players hold them tipped out at about a 45° angle from the vertical, and standing players may tip the instrument as much as 60° or even 90°.

The last group of representations of the chelys-lyra to be considered in this chapter, those painted (or carved) between the middle of the century and the advent of the red-figured style of painting in the last quarter of the century, once again contains mostly scenes that are familiar from earlier vases and other objects. But it also includes a pair of vases, New York 98.8.11 and Paris F 13, that illustrate the story of the judgment of Paris told in the *Iliad*, a subject that we have not yet seen in connection with the stringed instruments. Paris, who must serve as judge of a beauty contest between the three goddesses before him (fig. 16) has been interrupted in his solitary music making and still holds his instrument, a seven-stringed chelys-lyra with a plektron and cord painted in white (the plektron has been stuck under the strings and seems to be looped over an invisible bridge). Its soundbox is almost round and has two small circles on the front, on either side of the strings, reminiscent of the circles seen on the phorminx in figure 3a. The lower string fastener is a large rectangular fitting, and the crossbar is incised with crisscrosses to show the attachment of the strings at the top.[76]

A Corinthian painted wooden plaque (Athens 16464) in this group is of special interest, not only for its detailed sacrificial-procession scene but for its view of a chelys-lyra actually being played, in this instance by a boy in a blue mantle with a wreath on his head (fig. 17). We can see his left hand, fingers straight and spread apart, behind the strings, and the red sling around his left wrist, with the sash that hangs free from the arm of the instrument; his right hand holds the plektron. He stands holding the chelys-lyra tipped out more than 60° from the vertical. Beside him is a player of the double auloi, and in front of him are an altar, a woman bearing offerings, and a boy leading a sacrificial sheep.

In many of the representations of the chelys-lyra, from the earliest seventh-century ones through the latest group discussed here, the size of the instrument is difficult to determine, but there are enough clear examples to allow us to make at least some rough estimates. The height of the instruments in the paintings may be one to even two times the length of the player's forearm from elbow to second knuckle; the width at the widest point between the arms may be from one-half to three-quarters of the height (very few examples are larger or thinner than this). The tortoise shell from Vassae in the National Museum (late Archaic period or early fifth century), the most complete of three thought to date from this time that appear to have been used as soundboxes, is about 15 cm high and 12 cm wide.[77] This is somewhat small by the standards suggested above, even assuming that the average Greek male of the time (and the average Greek male forearm) was somewhat shorter than that of the average American male of the present time.

In a study such as this, inevitably one turns up a few examples of lyres that resist categorization. The lyre on the early seventh-century dinos from Old Smyrna (fig. 1) is one of these, tentatively placed among the phorminx examples because of its rounded base, though its arms continue the curve of the soundbox. Oxford 1892.1490 (fig. 18), a seal stone dating from the third quarter of the sixth century, offers another unusual example. One of the remarkable aspects of this scene (a boy sitting or leaning against a wall playing the lyre; an animal, possibly a goat, at his feet) is the similarity of the instrument to that on the Old

Smyrna dinos sherd: although the earlier lyre has wider upper arms and knobs on its crossbar, both lyres have curving arms that bend sharply out above the crossbar, and both seem to have shallow soundboxes.

But the instrument on the seal stone also resembles the chelys-lyra examples in some respects. In fact, the shape of the arms, curving sharply in just below the crossbar, resembles nothing so much as the long-armed version of the chelys-lyra known as the *barbitos*, an instrument that finds its way into works of art in the last quarter of the sixth century (see chap. 5). The artist who carved this seal stone probably lived on one of the eastern Aegean islands or in one of the Greek settlements on the northern coast of Asia Minor, and it is quite possible that the instrument he shows us is an East Greek version of the barbitos that predates the other representations that have come to hand.

The Barbitos in Archaic Literature

Although referred to in later Greek literature by a wide variety of authors, the barbitos, which appears for the first time in the literature of the Archaic age, is associated exclusively with the eastern Greek poets. Its connections with Terpander, Sappho, and Alcaeus, all of Lesbos, and with Anakreon, who was originally from Teos in Ionia, together with its possibly Phrygian etymology, suggest that this type of lyre had been borrowed into Greek culture by about the seventh century from some neighboring eastern people such as the Lydians or Phrygians.[78] In the period before 525, it seems to have been virtually unknown in mainland Greece.

The name *barbitos* occurs only once in the extant poetry of the Archaic age, in a fragment of Alcaeus (D 12.4 LP), in which it appears in a form peculiar to the dialect of Lesbos, *barmos*.[79] The stanza is incomplete but seems to criticize people for indulging in the idle pastime of a drinking party (in which the barmos makes sportive music) while their city is about to be devoured by political enemies. The association of this type of lyre with drinking parties is confirmed in later literature and art, where the close correspondence in the instrument's use allows a virtually certain identification of the barbitos as the long-armed, graceful, and distinctively shaped lyre discussed in further detail in chapter 5.

The association of the barbitos with the other eastern poets is known through later secondhand reports rather than from the fragments of their poems. The barbitos has the distinction of having had two different "inventors" among the Archaic poets, according to later sources. Pindar, writing in the first half of the fifth century, draws the name of Terpander out from the mists of the seventh century and claims that the Lesbian poet invented the barbitos after he heard an instrument called a pektis at banquets of the neighboring Lydians.[80] (The word *pektis* is, ironically, one of the few words of Greek origin among the names for instruments treated in this book.) Athenaeus, on the other hand, who wrote many centuries later (second century A.D.) quotes a Hellenistic historian who apparently believed that it was Anakreon who invented the barbitos.[81] Such a belief is not surprising in the light of the number of other writers who associated the instrument with Anakreon, and in the light of the fact that his arrival in Athens during the last quarter of the sixth century coincided with the sudden appearance of the barbitos in contemporary Athenian vase painting.[82] Whether or not Anakreon himself actually imported the instrument to Athens, the poet of drinking songs and the lyre for drinking parties remain firmly identified with each other even in late imitative poems such as the so-called *Anacreontea*. The popularity and significance of the barbitos in the post-Archaic period will be discussed further in chapter 5.

Archaic-Period References to the Pektis and Magadis

Primarily associated with the eastern poets, who, according to Pindar, borrowed it from the Lydians, the pektis is mentioned twice by Anakreon, once (or possibly twice) by Sappho, and once by Alcaeus. The name itself, it is generally agreed, derives from the Greek verb *pegnuein*, "to fasten," or "to fix together."[83] Why such a foreign instrument should have come to be known by a Greek name, while most of the other instruments continued to be called by foreign names, we can only guess. The occasional use of the verb *psallein* ("to pluck") in connection with the pektis suggests that it was a harp rather than a lyre.[84] The latter, as we have noted, was generally played with a plektron instead of with the bare fingers only; the action of striking the strings with the plektron is usually described by the verb *krekein,* a metaphor borrowed from the terminology of weaving. In literal usage, *krekein* describes the passing of the shuttle across the warp of a loom.

The magadis was probably a harp, since it, too, is "plucked" rather than "struck." In this case, the probability that the instrument was not a lyre is increased by the fact that (at least in later times) it apparently had twenty strings, far more than are ever depicted or described in the case of lyres.[85] Since it is thought that

the *word* magadis may be of Lydian origin, and since the *instrument* called the pektis is almost certainly of Lydian origin (see below), we may wonder if the Greeks of the Archaic age borrowed an instrument of the harp type from the Lydians, calling it sometimes by its original name, *magadis,* and sometimes by their own name, *pektis,* a term that might well have described an instrument whose sides were "fixed" together (pegnuein) to form a harp.[86] The only confirmation that the pektis and magadis were different names for the same instrument comes from Athenaeus (635e), who reports that the great music theorist of the fourth century B.C., Aristoxenos, said that the two instruments were identical. Unfortunately, there is no evidence available at present for determining the appearance or construction of harps in the Archaic age, because after the Cycladic period harps do not reappear in Greek art until the late fifth century.[87]

If the exact nature of the pektis (or magadis) is uncertain, at least the Lydian origin of the instrument is confirmed through two fifth-century sources. Pindar (fr. 125 Snell) says that Terpander heard the "twanging of the tall pektis" at banquets of the Lydians, and the historian Herodotus (1.17) describes the marching of Lydian troops to the sound of syrinx, pektis, and aulos.[88] There is also no doubt that the instrument was familiar to the Lydians' island neighbors during the Archaic age. Sappho, for example, describes something (or someone) as

> Sweeter-melodied by far than the pektis,
> More golden than gold. . . .
>
>   (fr. 156 LP)
>
> πόλυ πάκτιδος ἀδυμελεστέρα . . .
> χρύσω χρυσοτέρα . . .

Her compatriot Alcaeus also mentions the instrument in an unintelligible fragment (B4.5 LP), and another fragment from Sappho's works, probably a love poem, almost certainly contains a reference to picking up the pektis.[89] The close association of the poets of Lesbos with the instrument is further reflected in the later tradition that claimed that Sappho was its inventor.[90] It may have been Anakreon, however, who was partially responsible for introducing the pektis to the mainland Greeks, for he mentions the instrument in two separate fragments:

> I saw Simalos in the dance, holding a beautiful pektis
>
>   (fr. 386 *PMG*)
>
> Σίμαλον εἶδον ἐν χορῶι πηκτίδ' ἔχοντα καλήν.

> My meal was a mere morsel of thin cake,
> But I drained dry an amphora of wine.

Now tenderly I pluck my lovely pektis
And serenade my tender love.

(fr. 373 *PMG*)

ἠρίστησα μὲν ἰτρίου λεπτοῦ μικρὸν ἀποκλάς,
οἴνου δ' ἐξέπιον κάδον· νῦν δ' ἀβρῶς ἐρόεσσαν
ψάλλω πηκτίδα τῆι φίληι κωμάζων †παιδὶ ἀβρῆι†.

During the period from about 700 to 525 B.C., the old round-based phorminx gradually surrendered its place to the newer flat-based kithara and to the instrument made from a tortoise shell, the chelys-lyra. This period also saw the rise of new terms connected with string playing, including the words *kitharistes*, which meant a professional player similar to the Homeric aoidos, and *lyra*, which was evidently used in a generic sense to refer to any sort of instrument of the lyre family. Other new names include *magadis* and *pektis*, probably harps rather than lyres.

Although we do not know to what extent the chelys-lyra and kithara were borrowings or adaptations from other peoples, we can see that each of them had a fairly well-defined role in Greek life in the Archaic period. The kithara appears in scenes that depict the gods and is by the end of this period the constant attribute of Apollo. In scenes that depict legendary humans—Theseus, Achilles, Paris—on the other hand, and in other scenes of human life such as banquets, drinking parties, and processions, it is the chelys-lyra that is present. This difference in scenes is also reflected in the vases themselves, for the kithara generally appears only on large vases, the amphora, hydria, and krater, while the chelys-lyra also appears in scenes painted on smaller vases such as the lekythos and kylix. It is not surprising that the large and ornate kithara, which must have been considerably more difficult and expensive to construct than the simple tortoise-shell lyre, was the instrument of the gods and of professional players, and indirectly of the wealthy men who could afford to buy the pots on which it was depicted.

There is no discernible difference among the three instruments, phorminx, kithara, and chelys-lyra, as to the number of strings. From the seventh century on there are seven-stringed examples of all three types. In the sixth century there are too few examples of the phorminx to provide a pattern, but both kithara and chelys-lyra are shown most frequently with seven strings, though a surprisingly large number, some of them quite carefully painted, have five or six strings, and a very small number have eight or nine.

The *Homeric Hymn to Hermes*, which describes in detail Hermes' "invention" of the tortoise-shell lyre, mentions seven strings made of sheepgut; in addition, the poem provides us with the terms *donax* ("reed," the exact function of which remains uncertain), *pecheis* ("arms"), and *zugon* ("yoke," that is, crossbar). Of the kithara we have no such description, but the back plate from Olympia (fig. 8) and the Argo metope from Delphi (fig. 9c) provide the opportunity to observe various details of the instrument's construction, including the kollopes, knobs on the crossbar, scrolls on the arms, and a soundbox of considerable depth.

It is interesting to note that, whereas vase paintings of the chelys-lyra are relatively plentiful from the very beginning of the sixth century, it is not until after 550 B.C. or so that scenes of the kithara are frequently found (though they then become very common). This may suggest that the kithara, though long known and associated with Apollo, did not become a really standard instrument until sometime shortly before the middle of the century. However, it seems more likely that it simply reflects the fact that the scenes in which Apollo appears did not become a staple with Athenian artists until the middle of the sixth century. As for the word *kithara*, its earliest occurrence in extant literature is not until after the turn of the century in the passage attributed to Theognis and dated to about 490 B.C. The lack of evidence for the term *kithara* suggests that the old name *phorminx* may, for a time, have served for both instruments of Apollo. The role of the round-based phorminx in the Archaic period is less clear than that of the other instruments, and the scarcity of representations of it after 600 B.C. suggests that its functions were being usurped by the chelys-lyra and kithara. The large proportion of references to the phorminx in Archaic poetry that either associate it with Apollo or mention it in a context reminiscent of Homer suggests that the ceremonial uses of the round-based instrument belong more and more during the Archaic period to the realm of memory rather than current usage.

In any case, sometime in the hundred years between the middle of the seventh century and the middle of the sixth, the round-based phorminx, which had appeared as Apollo's instrument on the seventh-century amphora from Melos (fig. 2), ceased to play this role, which was given over to the kithara. It is to the kithara that we turn our attention in chapter 3, where its functions in Classical times, both in mythical scenes and portrayals of human life, will be considered.

1. Bayrakli. Dinos sherd
from Old Smyrna.
Instrument.

2. Athens 911. Amphora
from Melos. Detail:
Apollo and Muses in
chariot drawn by winged
horses.

3a. Athens, Agora AP 1085. Pinax fragment. Bearded man offering or receiving instrument.

3b. Syracuse 12577. Corinthian vase. Detail: padded dancers.

4. Athens 12210. Terracotta figure from Lapithos, Cyprus. Musician.

5a. Location unknown.
Funeral chest from
Capua. Detail: row of
musicians.

5b. Athens, Nat. Mus.
Acropolis 2523. Plaque
fragment. Musician at
altar.

6. Rhodes 12.200. Attic
black-figured (b.f.)
psykter. Komasts dancing.

7. Delos B 4260.
Fragment from the mouth
of an amphora. Apollo
and Artemis.

8. Zakynthos, priv. coll.
Bronze armor, back plate.
Detail: Apollo, gods, and
goddesses.

9a. London 1971.11-11.
Dinos by Sophilos. Detail:
Apollo and Hermes in
quadriga, Muses.

9b. Athens 19272. Large
jar, possibly from
Lemnos. Detail: musician
before seated woman.

9c. Delphi. Metope from
the Treasury of the
Sikyonians. Detail:
Orpheus and Arion.

10. Athens, Nat. Mus.
Acr. 2203. B.f. fragment.
Musician and women
before a high couch.

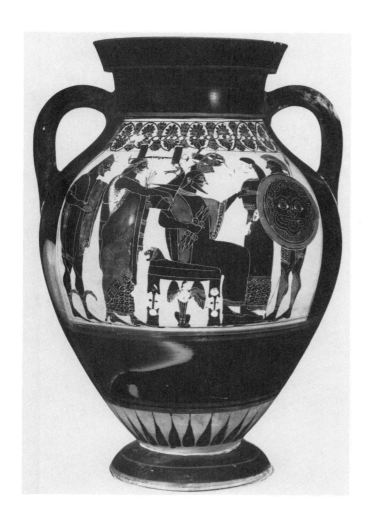

11. Boston 00.330.
Amphora, Group "E."
Birth of Athena.

12. Munich 2243. Attic
b.f. kylix. Detail: Theseus
slaying Minotaur.

13a. Athens 313. Hydria
from Analatos. Detail:
musician in procession of
men and women with
branches.

13b. Sparta, temple of
Artemis Orthia. Votive
figure in lead.
Instrument.

13c. Sparta, temple of
Artemis Orthia. Votive
figure in lead. Musician.

13d. Sparta, temple of
Artemis Orthia. Bone and
ivory plektra.

14a. Paris E 629.
Corinthian krater. Detail:
banqueters.

14b. Athens, Kerameikos
2869. Attic b.f. skyphos.
Detail: two komasts.

**14c. Florence 4209. Attic
b.f. volute krater (the
François vase). Detail:
Theseus' victory dance.**

**14d. Heidelberg 68/1.
Attic b.f. lekythos. Detail:
musician between sirens.**

**14e. New York
06.1021.26. Corinthian
b.f. plate. Poet on his
death-bed.**

15a. Paris E 643.
Corinthian hydria. Detail:
mourning Nereids.

15b. New York 56.11.1.
Attic b.f. lekythos by the
Amasis Painter. On neck,
dancers and musician.

15c. Paris E 861. B.f.
amphora. Procession of
musicians.

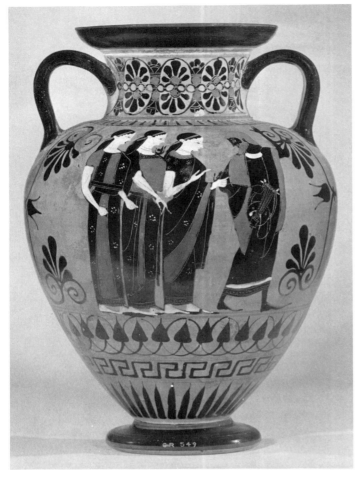

18. Oxford 1892.1490.
Cornelian scarab. Youth
tunes or plays instrument.

16. New York 98.8.11.
Attic b.f. amphora.
Judgment of Paris.

17. Athens 16464.
Corinthian plaque.
Musicians in sacrificial
procession.

CHAPTER THREE

The Kithara in Classical Athens

For the period from the late sixth century to the late fifth century, Athens becomes the focus of the study of Greek stringed instruments, since during this time Athenian literature and visual arts eclipsed those from all other parts of the Greek world both in quality and in quantity. This circumstance creates an opportunity that was not available for the investigation of the instruments of earlier periods: the opportunity to study the stringed instruments of a single city during a single century for which there is evidence so abundant that we can see the instruments themselves, their uses, and their cultural context and significance much more clearly than at any other time in the history of the ancient world.

Having said this, we must of course immediately add that this wealth of material, in many ways a joy to the cultural historian, has certain limitations and problems of interpretation. In the case of the visual evidence, for example, we cannot assume that because a particular scene was popular with the artists and their patrons, the activity shown therefore had a corresponding importance in actual Athenian life. Nor can we always understand the meaning of a scene or securely identify the participants. And finally, the apparent realism of Greek art of this period may be misleading—can we say, for instance, that two different instruments such as kithara and *krotala* (pairs of clappers) were actually sometimes played at the same time, when our only evidence for this comes from scenes depicting gods and their attendants? In the discussions that follow, it will be necessary to keep in mind the possibility of such problems and limitations.

The function of the kithara in the Classical era of Greece is most clearly revealed through the large number of Attic vase paintings in which the instrument is depicted, as well as through its presence in a few important sculptural pieces and some coins of the period. The literary references of the same period serve primarily to confirm, and in some cases to expand upon, the evidence derived from a study of the artistic representations of the instrument. The various sources of evidence indicate clearly that the kithara was primarily the professional's lyre, that it had a significant role in state religious festivals and contests, and that it was played almost exclusively by male performers. The literary references, despite their brevity in most cases, also supply such details as the types of song accompanied by the kithara, descriptions of the sound produced, and some of the materials used in the construction of the instrument.

Etymology

The name *kithara* is clearly a later form of the Homeric word *kitharis,* which, as we saw in chapter 1, occurs only rarely in the *Iliad* and *Odyssey,* where it generally designates the activity of string playing rather than a specific type of lyre. As to the origins of the words *kithara* and *kitharis,* however, we have no conclusive evidence. While most etymological dictionaries venture only so far as to state that the name was probably borrowed into Greek from some Oriental language, a few scholars have attempted to make a case for a connection with specific Indo-European or Semitic roots.

Among the proposals are *kuetuora,* "four," that is, a quadrangular-shaped instrument (which the Greek lyres were not); *quitor-,* "clear," that is, an instrument of bright sound; and *ghidh-,* "string." None of these derivations, however, has gained wide currency, nor has the proposed connection between *kithara* and the Hebrew *kinnor* ("harp") been accepted.[1]

In the absence of any strong evidence for the derivation of *kitharis/kithara* from any of these Indo-European or Semitic roots, we must agree with Strabo, who wrote (in the first century B.C.) that Greek names for musical instruments are largely of Thracian and Asian origins.[2] Strabo points out that the kithara is often referred to as "Asiatic," an epithet which is in fact sometimes applied to the instrument in the extant literature of the fifth century.[3] Although the etymology of the instrument's name must remain a mystery, at least for the time being, it seems a safe guess that the Greeks borrowed the word from one of the languages of Asia Minor.

Occurrence of the Word *Kithara*

As we have pointed out in chapter 2, the term *kithara* was a late development, occurring for the first time in Greek literature that has survived in a poem which can be dated to about 490 B.C.[4] The relative newness of the form *kithara* (versus *kitharis* or the verb *kitharizein*) is further suggested by its infrequent occurrence in the literature of the first three quarters of the fifth century. Most of the references to the kithara come from works written in the last quarter of the century, particularly the tragedies of Euripides, and from the fourth-century works of Plato and Aristotle (to be discussed in chap. 7). Pindar, writing early in the fifth century, never uses the form *kithara,* despite his frequent reference in the odes to musical instruments; he prefers instead the old Homeric word, *phorminx.*

The gap between the appearance in Archaic art of the large, ornate instrument with a flat base and the use of the name *kithara* by Greek authors to describe that instrument is initially puzzling. If we consider the relative frequency of the terms *phorminx* and *kithara* across the span of the fifth century, however, we can see that by the time the word *kithara* is in common use toward the end of the century, the word *phorminx* has almost dropped out of the literature; it was reserved primarily for mythological contexts, especially in connection with Apollo.[5] The older writers of the fifth century appear simply to have continued the practice of the Archaic poets in using the Homeric term *phorminx* as the name for Apollo's lyre; on the other hand, the vase paintings reveal that the chief instrument associated with the god was by the sixth century the large, flat-based lyre of grander proportions than the earlier phorminx. The Homeric name itself was not fully supplanted by the newer term, *kithara,* until about the time of the Peloponnesian War. Euripides, for example, in a description closely paralleled by contemporary vase paintings, speaks of Apollo making a dappled fawn dance amid pine trees to the music of his kithara.[6] Elsewhere in Euripides' plays, Apollo is often mentioned in connection with the instrument, whether it is Creusa addressing him as "lord of the seven-voiced kithara" or the chorus describing the god playing his kithara with a golden plektron.[7]

A further examination of Euripides' use of the word *kithara* reveals that in almost half the occurrences the instrument is mentioned in connection with Apollo.[8] Since Apollo, as he is shown on the vase paintings in his capacity as musician, is portrayed in about eighty percent of all such scenes as playing the large, ornate, flat-based type of lyre, we can be virtually certain that this lyre is to be identified as Apollo's special instrument, the kithara. Such an identification between name and instrument is further supported by the correspondence between the elaborate costume worn by mortal players of the instrument as it is shown on the vase paintings and as it is described in Greek literature (see the discussion of players' costumes below).

When we compare the description of the kithara below with comments in fifth-century authors about the "phorminx," we must suspect that this so-called phorminx is really the same instrument. Aristophanes, for example, describes Apollo playing on a "phorminx" inlaid with ivory (*elephantodetos*), a detail that corresponds well with the many black-figured representations mentioned above (chap. 2) of kitharas that seem to be decorated with ivory facings on the upper arms.[9] Some of the other adjectives applied to the "phorminx" in the fifth century are traditional Homeric epithets, such as *daidaleos,* "cunningly wrought," whereas others merely allude to the instrument's seven strings.[10] Occasionally the sound of the "phorminx" is described by some neutral term such as *omphe,* "voice," but other terms applied to the instrument convey loudness, such as *ayte* ("cry") and *bromios* ("thunderous"); the latter, especially, does not correspond to the adjectives that describe the sound of the Homeric phorminx.[11] The same implication of a loud volume recurs in words like *bremein* ("to thunder") and *boai* ("shouts"), applied by Pindar to the lyra, a word that he seems to use synonymously with *phorminx* (see chap. 4).[12] The early fifth-century poets Pindar and Bacchylides appear to have preferred the time-honored Homeric word or the generic term *lyra* to the relatively new name, *kithara*.

Related Terms: *Kitharizein* and *Kitharistes*

The verb *kitharizein*, which Homer had used to refer to the playing of the phorminx, has by the time of the fifth century acquired a more generalized meaning, namely, "to be knowledgeable in music," that is, educated and cultured. In most instances, the contexts of the verb suggest that the instrument in question was likely to have been not the kithara but the amateur's tortoise-shell lyra used for the musical training of schoolboys (see chap. 4).

Another related term of importance in the fifth century is the noun *kitharistes*. As we saw in chapter 2, *kitharistes* is first found in the Archaic period in the works of Hesiod and Alkman, where the term designates a professional musician dedicated to the service of Apollo and the Muses. By the last quarter of the fifth century, the term has already taken on the more concrete sense in which it is used in the fourth century by Plato and Aristotle, namely, a schoolboy's lyre instructor. In the polemic on education in Aristophanes' *Clouds*, for example, Right Logic, in reminiscing about bygone standards of strict discipline, mentions the orderly conduct of youths at their music lessons in the home of the kitharistes, a place often depicted on red-figured vases (see chap. 4).[13] It is essential to note that both these terms, *kitharizein* and *kitharistes*, although related etymologically to the word *kithara*, are often used in fifth-century literature with reference to lyres other than the kithara itself, occurring especially frequently in connection with the schoolboy's tortoise-shell lyra.

Nature of the Visual Evidence

With the exception of a few scattered coins, scarabs, and figurines, mostly non-Attic, the visual evidence of the Classical period comes from the paintings that decorate the vases made in the Athenian potters' quarter, the Kerameikos. The paintings to be examined are in both the black-figured and red-figured techniques, for black-figured pottery continued to be made in quantity until the end of the sixth century, with fewer items of generally poor quality still appearing in the first half of the fifth century. The red-figured technique, meanwhile, had appeared around 530 B.C., so that vases painted in this style are available from the beginning of the Classical period; and they continued to be made during the fourth century.

Scenes with Kithara Players

Representations of the kithara are much more common on black-figured vases than on the more abundant red-figured ones, oddly enough, and among vases that show stringed instruments, the proportion of kitharas to other instruments is much higher for the black-figured vases, though it falls dramatically among those made after 500 B.C. The black-figured vases of 525–500 B.C. reveal a fad for scenes of kithara-accompanied processions featuring a quadriga (four-horse chariot) that the red-figured vases do not share; the comparative lack of representations of the kithara on red-figured vases of the fifth century can be explained only by the widespread change in iconography at the turn of the century.

The black-figured amphora (storage jar) is the vase on which paintings of the kithara are found by far the most frequently (about a quarter of these with quadriga scenes), but the hydria is also well represented; here the quadriga scenes are more than half the total, for the hydria, a water vessel likely to have been used in marriage rituals, often has a wedding procession with quadriga decorating it. Examples of the rarely found nuptial vase called the *lebes gamikos* are painted with similar scenes.

Scenes that show performers who are clearly not gods but mortals (most of them contestants) seem to have been far more popular with the painters of red-figured vases. Among their works we also find a new kind of scene, one not represented on any black-figured vase so far found: the "libation scene," in which the god Apollo, while supporting the kithara in his left arm, holds out a *phiale*, a wide, shallow drinking dish, in his right hand. The scene often includes a woman, usually Apollo's sister, the goddess Artemis (fig. 1), who pours wine into the phiale from a pitcher and thus in some sense takes the place, perhaps, of a mortal worshiper who might offer a wine libation to Apollo.

The scene may take place at an altar, as in figure 1, emphasizing the fact that it represents a libation. Leto, the mother of Apollo and Artemis, is often present along with her children; and the god Hermes, who frequently appears in vase paintings, particularly those that show Apollo, is also sometimes present.[14] Many kinds of red-figured vases are decorated with libation scenes, not just those used for serving wine—the krater (a bowl for mixing wine and water), *oinochoe* (pitcher), and *kylix* (cup)—but also the amphora, hydria, *pelike* (a storage jar), and *lekythos* (perfumed oil jar). The kithara in these scenes is simply the chief attribute of Apollo and does not appear to have any further significance; it would probably be stretching the evidence too far to infer from the scenes that the kithara was played during formal offerings of libations to Apollo, although this may of course have been the case.

Apollo appears on a large number of vases other than those with libation scenes, alone or in the company of other gods and goddesses, such as Dionysos, Zeus, or Athena, or one or more of those mentioned above (Artemis, Leto, and Hermes); Poseidon or Ares is also occasionally present. The action in these scenes is vague; sometimes the figures are part of a procession (without quadriga), or they may simply stand facing one another, so that the special significance of the scene, if any, is not clear to us. On a number of vases Apollo plays the kithara in a scene in which Heracles (whom we meet again later in this chapter) is the chief protagonist, as in paintings of Heracles' introduction to Olympos or of his stealing Apollo's tripod from Delphi. At least one painting from the end of the Classical period includes the kithara in a version of Apollo's contest with the satyr Marsyas, who had bragged that he could play better than the god and was flayed alive for his presumption when proved wrong.[15]

Apollo is accompanied in a number of paintings by two, or sometimes four, women who wear chitons (robes) and himatia (mantles) but who have no identifying attributes. If there are two women, and either or both wear the *polos* or *stephanos* (types of crowns), we can assume that they are goddesses, probably Artemis and Leto. Lacking this means of identification, we are faced with the possibility that the two women may instead be Muses or even maenads, female followers of the god Dionysos. Maenads, often represented in scenes in which Dionysos appears (and in which Apollo is also sometimes present), are frequently shown playing the krotala. For this reason, when Apollo alone is seen with two or four otherwise unidentifiable women playing krotala, the possibility that they represent maenads rather than Muses must be considered. Except for the Sophilos vase of the early sixth century, no paintings dating from before about 425 B.C. have been found in which a kithara-playing Apollo is accompanied by women who can be securely identified as the Muses.

Apollo, or a kithara player who can usually be presumed to be Apollo, is also shown in another very large category of black-figured paintings of the kithara mentioned briefly above: quadriga scenes, paintings of formal chariot processions in which the kithara player customarily walks alongside the four horses. If the figures in the scene are provided with godly attributes, we are apt to find Hermes at the horses' heads, leading them or holding them ready to start; Apollo beside the horses on the far side, sometimes with another figure just ahead of him (Dionysos, Artemis, or another goddess); and in the chariot itself, sometimes one person (often Athena, but Dionysos, Artemis, Demeter, Apollo himself, or an unknown person may take her place), sometimes two (Peleus and Thetis, Zeus and Hera, Dionysos and Ariadne, or Athena and Heracles).[16] Only the last two pairs are easy to identify; the others are often better classed as unknown. In some paintings, none of the figures has attributes, and we might be tempted to speculate that they are mortals, were it not for the very similar arrangement of the scene to those of the gods, and the fact that a four-horse chariot is a particularly elaborate means of conveyance, even for a wedding party.

The quadriga scene most frequently painted was the "wedding" quadriga, with a man and woman in the chariot (fig. 2). The couple in the chariot in figure 2 are probably Zeus and Hera, though there are other possibilities (Peleus and Thetis, Heracles and Hebe, or even a human couple escorted by gods). Behind the chariot stands Dionysos, identified by his ivy wreath and by the vine branch that springs from his hand; alongside the horses walk Apollo and Hermes, the latter identified by his staff (the caduceus) and costume (winged boots and the traveler's short cloak and hat, the *chlamys* and *petasos*). At the horses' heads stands an unidentified woman holding the torches characteristic of wedding scenes, which show that this is a nighttime procession. This vase, like nearly half of those that show wedding scenes, is a black-figured hydria.

Second only to the wedding scenes are those quadriga scenes with Apollo playing the kithara that are part of the favorite story of the introduction of Heracles to Olympos. These usually show Heracles (with club and lion-skin mantle) standing in the chariot with his patron goddess Athena, who is identified by her helmet, spear, and *aegis* (breastplate decorated with writhing snakes).

Even among vases that offer mythological scenes, however, the kithara player is by no means *always* Apollo. In a large group of paintings, both red- and black-figured, the kithara is played by a satyr, one of the nude, bearded beings with pointed ears and horse's tail who belong to the entourage of Dionysos. The paintings may portray the satyr-musician alone or in the presence of Dionysos, sometimes along with an aulos-playing satyr; satyrs and maenads are often shown dancing in these scenes. In a few instances, the kithara player is female, a maenad or a goddess.[17]

In figure 3 Dionysos, bearded, wreathed with ivy, and holding a *kantharos* (large wine cup with handles), is seated with Ariadne in the center; before them and behind them is a satyr playing a kithara, and beyond the satyrs on either side dances an ivy-wreathed maenad with krotala; the background is filled with vine branches. On the other side of this amphora Dionysos appears again, this time riding in a quadriga, while a satyr takes the customary place of Apollo, walking along beside the horses and playing the kithara (and in place of Hermes at the horses' heads is a krotala-playing maenad seated on a satyr's shoulder). Such scenes provide little specific information about the actual use of the kithara in the cult of Dionysos, but the number of these paintings suggests that it was in fact part of certain rites connected with him.

Among paintings on black-figured vases only, there is one other, and most unexpected, mythological kithara player—Heracles.[18] He appears in this role, nearly always in the presence of his patron goddess Athena, on at least eleven vases, and five of these show him mounting a low platform such as we will see below in scenes of mortals who are taking part in kithara-playing contests (fig. 4). But Heracles does not dress like a kithara player: instead of the long robe of the musician, he wears his own traditional costume, the lion skin over his head and down his back, a short tunic, and (usually) bow and quiver on his back.[19] In figure 4, Athena, wearing helmet and aegis and carrying a spear, looks on as Heracles tunes his kithara while mounting the podium. On other vases the listeners include Hermes, Poseidon, Ares, or Iolaos. The myth illustrated by these vases (if there was one) has unfortunately been lost; but since some of the vases show scenes from other myths about Heracles on the reverse side, it seems possible that some myth concerning Heracles as kithara player did exist. Heracles, who in another story stole Apollo's Delphic tripod, may in the lost tale have stolen his instrument. The story probably had a contest element, as the vase paintings in which he stands on a platform indicate.

These vases, most of them made during the last quarter of the sixth century, may, however, simply reflect a custom of using the figure of Heracles to symbolize (and flatter?) the tyrant Peisistratos (560–527 B.C.), portraying him as strong, harmonious of spirit, and favored by Athena. The habit may have continued during the rule of his sons, Hippias and Hipparchos, from 527 to 510, and perhaps even longer, though some vase painters may have simply copied it because it was a familiar scene.[20]

Compared with the large number of paintings of mythological players of the kithara, those that show mortal performers on this instrument are few indeed, only some 15 percent of the known representations of the kithara from about 525 to 425 B.C. The majority of these are scenes that seem related, in one way or another, to kithara contests (about which more will be said below): paintings that show the performer mounting, or standing on, a platform; paintings in which the player stands between two listeners, as in figure 5; or paintings depicting a performer receiving the kithara from a Nike, a winged female personification of victory. (There is also a small group of red-figured paintings that show only the Nike bringing the kithara, not the performer.)

We know that groups of kithara players might take part in processions, especially sacrifice processions, often in the company of players of the aulos.[21] The best-known scene of this sort is the one found on panel 875 (Acropolis Museum) of the Parthenon frieze, carved between 447 and 432 B.C. The marble panel is severely damaged, but the section of the great sacrificial procession (which extended all the way around the temple) shown on it includes two kithara players walking to the left, the one behind showing the back of his instrument, and the one ahead turning back toward his companion so that we see the front of his instrument (fig. 6). Two black-figured vases from the Acropolis also depict sacrificial processions: on Acropolis 816, two kithara players, a man and a boy, walk in the company of an aulos player; and on Acropolis 2009, a woman with a basket on her head is followed by an aulos player and a player of the kithara.[22] Only fragments remain of both vases, but there is enough of 816 to show that the players wear wreaths and are dressed in ornamented himatia but no chitons, suggesting that kithara players' costumes might vary according to the occasion.

Evidence for the kithara as a provider of music for banquets is very slight: three clear scenes (two of them from mythology) and a fourth so carelessly painted that one cannot even be certain the instrument is a kithara (Paris Bibl. Nat. H 1119). One mythological scene, on Madrid 10916, shows Heracles reclining on a couch at a banquet while a bearded kitharist in chiton and himation (presumably an ordinary mortal) provides music. The second mythological scene shows the kithara being played at a *theoxenia* for the Dioscuri, a feast at which the two young gods are to be the honored guests (Plovdiv Museum 298 [fig. 7]); the Dioscuri approach a couch provided with cushions, lyres (one for each of them), two incense burners, and a table laden with food and drink, near which stands the kitharist.[23] Another clear scene, London kylix B 679, does not appear to have any mythological or religious connections—it shows a banquet scene of the usual sort, complete with couch, table of food, woman with wine pitcher, and a dog. One of the two banqueters is playing the aulos himself, and the kitharist, in chiton and himation, stands to the left of the couch. Since this is the only good example of such a scene, we cannot assume that the kithara was an instrument normally used at banquets.

The Professional Kitharode and His Costume

References to the kithara in fifth-century Greek literature clearly establish the role of the kithara as the professional's instrument—not a lyre played by an amateur for idle amusement at a drinking party or by young schoolboys or by Athenian wives entertaining one another in the women's quarters of their houses. On the contrary, the kithara, a large and rather unwieldy instrument, required the expertise that only a professional player or other highly trained musician could achieve.[24]

The most detailed as well as the earliest fifth-century description of a professional player of the kithara is to be found in Herodotus' account of the adventures of Arion of Lesbos, who earned his living at the court of Periander in Corinth in the early sixth century.[25] After a visit to Italy and Sicily, where he worked as a professional musician, Arion hired a crew of Corinthian sailors to take him and his money back to Corinth. In the midst of the journey, as Herodotus recounts the legend, the sailors mutinied, seized Arion's money, and threatened to kill him. Arion, however, persuaded them to spare his life and to let him sing for them, on the condition that he would then—of his own volition—jump overboard. Herodotus describes how Arion donned his entire professional costume, stood on the rowing benches, took up his kithara, and proceeded to render a *nomos orthios,* a particular type of melody in a high range (see chap. 7, n. 17). He then jumped into the sea, costume and all, but was miraculously rescued and carried to shore by a dolphin, which took him to Tainaron in Laconia. Upon return to Corinth, still wearing his costume (which must have been somewhat worse for the wear after the long journey from the southern Peloponnesos), he confronted the surprised sailors, who were soon convicted of their dastardly crime. Herodotus assures us that this story told by the Corinthians was corroborated by the people of Arion's native island of Lesbos, and he concludes his account with reference to a small bronze statue of a man riding on a dolphin that was erected at the spot where Arion had been brought ashore.

Romantic elements aside, the tale gives us a vivid picture of a professional court musician of international repute who traveled widely and earned considerable sums of money by singing and accompanying himself on the kithara. Such a musician, as we gather from Herodotus (1.23.6), was called a "kitharode" (*kitharoidos*), a compound word that describes the dual activity of singing and playing.[26] The emphasis in the story on the kitharode's special costume (mentioned three different times in the account) suggests an elaborate attire of the sort so often depicted in the vase paintings, in which the kithara player wears a long, flowing robe, or chiton, of richly ornamented design and an equally elaborate mantle, or himation. A literary fragment that probably dates from the early fourth century supplies the name for this special costume, the *epiporpama*, evidently so called because it was fastened at the shoulders with a *porpe*, or brooch.[27]

The vase paintings reveal that the costumes of mortal kithara players (who may be boys or men of any age) are full length and usually quite elaborate, often similar, in fact, to the costume customarily worn by Apollo (figs. 1 and 2): a long chiton decorated or (if it is white) made of pleated fabric; over this a long himation, often with a decorative pattern or bands of contrasting color; and a wreath or fillet on the head. Whereas Apollo's hair is shown long (sometimes hanging loose, sometimes bound up in a knot or roll on the back of the head, and often with curling side-locks), mortal players generally have their hair cut shorter, as in figures 8 and 9. The kitharode in figure 8, instead of the himation, wears a shorter cloak, the chlamys, which often has a dark-colored border, as in this painting. This variant of the costume is also found on occasion in paintings of Apollo. The soft leather shoes worn by the kitharode in figure 8 are rarely seen—the performers are more often barefooted.

The "real-life" scenes of kithara playing, however, show us still other possibilities. The performer in figure 5 wears no cloak or mantle at all, just his white chiton, which may be worn hanging loose or, as in this example, tied around the waist with a cord.[28] There are, among the paintings of mortal kitharists, a number of players who wear a chiton of a different sort, as shown in figure 9: a long, loose gown made from a long rectangular piece of cloth shaped, apparently, like a poncho, with an opening for the head, its side edges (with a dark border) falling over the player's arm and sewn together except for an armhole; the material seems to be gathered at the shoulder.

Kithara players who wear *only* the himation, without the chiton underneath it (a common mode of dress among Athenian men), are extremely rare and are found only in such contexts as the sacrificial processions or unusual scenes such as that of Heracles killing the Egyptian king Busiris, where the kitharist is presumably an Egyptian priest (Paris G 50). Heracles himself, as kithara player, wears his own traditional lion skin and short tunic; and the other category of mythological performers, the satyrs, wear no costume at all.

Occasions

The Kithara in Drama

The ancient playwrights, whose works were presented in Athens each year at two festivals in honor of Dionysos, the Lenaea and the Great Dionysia, were composers of music as well as of drama, for they created not only the action and dialogue of their comedies and tragedies but the song and instrumental accompaniment as well. Unfortunately none of the music of the plays has survived, with the possible exception of two short fragments of notation from Euripides' *Orestes* and *Iphigenia*.[29]

The most famous performing musician among the dramatists was Sophocles, who, according to an ancient biography, was chosen while still a mere youth to be leader of the chorus that performed at the victory celebrations after the battle at Salamis in 480 B.C. The biography also reports that Sophocles performed on the kithara for a production of his tragedy, *Thamyras*, named after the Thracian musician who foolishly challenged the Muses and lost his sight as a result.[30] Evidently Sophocles himself played the leading role, which must have required the actor to give a musical performance in the scene involving the contest with the Muses. We are further told that the famous picture collection of the Stoa Poikile in the center of Athens included a representation of Sophocles together with his kithara.

For the modern reader the emphasis on the text of the ancient plays has overshadowed the musical aspects of the performance. To the Greek audiences, a presentation of drama without music would have been unthinkable. The principal instrument in the performance of Greek drama was the aulos, as is clear both from the vase paintings and from the texts of some of the plays (particularly the comedies of Aristophanes), but the kithara and the lyra were also used on occasion to provide musical accompaniment.[31]

In addition to the evidence for Sophocles' performance on the kithara for his *Thamyras*, an amusing scene from Aristophanes' *Frogs* (1281–1308) implies that the kithara could be used to accompany choral odes in tragedy. The scene occurs during the contest

in Hades between the deceased poets, Euripides and Aeschylus. Euripides tells the judge, Dionysos, not to leave until he has heard a batch of Aeschylean choral odes based on *kitharodikoi nomoi*, or traditional types of melodies accompanied by the kithara.[32] He then launches into an absurd parody of Aeschylus' lofty style and weighty language, which he interrupts frequently with an onomatopoetic imitation of kithara accompaniment:

> *Euripides*: As the double-throned power of the
> Achaeans, the strength of Greece
> > *toplattotrat toplattotrat*
> sends the Sphinx, dog which is lord
> over ill-starred days
> > *toplattotrat toplattotrat*
> with spear and avenging hand, a
> rushing bird,
> > *toplattotrat toplattotrat*
> granting to the raging hounds winging
> o'er air to light upon
> > *toplattotrat toplattotrat*
> the forces united against Ajax
> > *toplattotrat toplattotrat*
> *Dionysos*: What's this *toplattotrat*? Did you pick
> that up from some Persian at Marathon, or where did you collect these
> rope-twisters' songs?

Eυ. ὅπως Ἀχαιῶν δίθρονον κράτος, Ἑλλάδος ἥβας,
   τοφλαττοθρατ τοφλαττοθρατ,
Σφίγγα δυσαμεριᾶν πρύτανιν κύνα, πέμπει,
   τοφλαττοθρατ τοφλαττοθρατ,
σὺν δορὶ καὶ χερὶ πράκτορι θούριος ὄρνις,
   τοφλαττοθρατ τοφλαττοθρατ,
κυρεῖν παρασχὼν ἰταμαῖς κυσὶν ἀεροφοίτοις,
   τοφλαττοθρατ τοφλαττοθρατ,
τὸ συγκλινές τ' ἐπ' Αἴαντι,
   τοφλαττοθρατ τοφλαττοθρατ.

Δι. τί τὸ 'φλαττοθρατ' τοῦτ' ἐστίν; ἐκ Μαραθῶνος ἢ
πόθεν συνέλεξας ἱμονιοστρόφου μέλη;

As the scene continues, Aeschylus defends himself by accusing Euripides of getting *his* music from brothel songs and drinking tunes, for which appropriate accompaniment can be provided not by a lyre but only by a dancing girl rattling her clackers (*ostrakoi*). The girl obligingly appears on stage just at that point, and Aeschylus proceeds to sing a parody of a Euripidean ode.

Although we must remember that we are reading a comedy and not a treatise on Greek stage practice, the imitation of kithara accompaniment certainly suggests that the kithara was strummed and that it was sometimes used in the musical accompaniment for the choral odes in Greek drama.

Victory Odes

The celebration of winners of athletic contests through the formal performance of victory odes in their honor is surely one of the most remarkable characteristics of the Greek spirit in the fifth century. The odes written in the early part of the century by the most famous of the composers of victory songs, Pindar, present modern scholars with some of the most complex problems of interpretation in all of extant Greek literature, for no Classical poet is so much the master of symbol, ambiguity, and multiple levels of meaning as Pindar.[33] Although such qualities make it difficult to connect some of his allusions to contemporary practices with actual historical fact, it is nevertheless possible to assume with reasonable certainty that the primary instrument used in the musical accompaniment of his victory odes was the kithara.

As has already been mentioned, Pindar himself never uses the word *kithara*. The term that is found most frequently in his references in the odes to stringed instruments is "phorminx"; occasionally (in similar contexts) he uses "lyra" instead, and rarely, "kitharis." He also mentions the aulos several times, occasionally in conjunction with a lyre.

Although the instrument Pindar meant to designate through the term *phorminx* is open to speculation, the function of the music it provided can be reasonably well determined. Well over half the references to lyres as accompaniment for the odes are found in the opening third of the poem and usually consist of some sort of address to the instrument. In one case (*P.* 1.1), the ode begins with the words "O golden phorminx" (*chrysea phorminx*) and goes on to speak of the instrument as giving "signs" to the dancers and singers as it strikes up the *prooemium,* or introductory section. This description, not likely to be purely symbolic in nature, suggests that Pindar's victory odes normally opened with an introduction which set the tempo for the chorus performing the song, and the poet's frequent reference to the instrument within the first third of an ode reinforces the importance of the music in giving the appropriate beat to the dancers and singers as the performance begins.[34]

The question then arises as to which instrument or instruments usually provided such accompaniment for a victory ode. As noted earlier, in four instances Pindar speaks of auloi and a stringed instrument being played in concert, so that we must assume that sometimes odes were performed with both wind and string accompaniment. In most cases, however, Pindar speaks only of a lyre, which he most frequently calls

a "phorminx." As suggested above, perhaps Pindar favors the term because of its Homeric associations; in a way the poet thinks of himself as a latter-day bard who praises famous men and their deeds, just as Demodokos sang of the exploits of the Greek heroes returning from the Trojan War.[35] The first *Olympian Ode,* in fact, contains explicit Homeric overtones in connection with the ode's instrumental accompaniment, for Pindar speaks of taking the "Dorian phorminx" down from its peg, just as Demodokos takes his instrument down from a nearby peg where the herald had hung it for him at Alkinoös' feast for Odysseus.[36]

Nothing in the text of Pindar solves absolutely the question of what Pindar's phorminx really was, but his descriptions of the instrument's thunderous sound do suggest the large resonance chamber of the kithara. There is no one standard epithet applied to Pindar's phorminx/lyra; it may be "many-voiced" or "golden," or "sweet-melodied," to name but a few of the adjectives he uses. Occasionally he refers to the instrument's seven strings, and he also mentions the use of a "golden" plektron; all these details are consonant with but not limited to the kithara.[37] But, as we have seen, the evidence of the vase paintings roughly contemporary with Pindar points to the use of the kithara as the chief instrument for formally presented songs at festivals and musical contests, so that this seems to be the instrument most likely to have been used for the accompaniment of formal choral odes.

In short, despite the undoubted importance of the instrumental accompaniment to the production of Pindar's victory odes, the poems themselves reveal very few specific details about the instruments which provided that accompaniment. Nevertheless, it can be deduced that the odes were normally accompanied by an instrument of the lyre family, probably a kithara, sometimes together with auloi, and that the music included an introduction in which the lyra set the rhythm and tempo for the chorus.

Musical Contests

The kithara was the chief instrument (besides the aulos) on which participants performed in the musical competitions held at religious festivals. Although we do not have detailed information about the musical contests at the Pythian and Olympic games (or other such national festivals) in the sixth or fifth centuries, we do know something of the preeminent local Athenian festival held every year (celebrated on a particularly grand scale every fourth year), the Panathenaia.

According to Plutarch, it was the great political and cultural leader Pericles, who sponsored a decree by which musical contests were introduced into the Panathenaic festival and who supervised the building of an auditorium in which the contestants performed. This Odeion had a pointed roof, and a comic poet of the time joked that Pericles (who was noted for his odd, pointed cranium) wore the building on his head.[38]

If Plutarch's intention here was to claim that various kinds of musical contests were first introduced into the Panathenaia in the mid-fifth century by Pericles, his account is contradicted by evidence from Panathenaic amphorae that shows that such contests were probably part of the festival before the beginning of the century.[39] Panathenaic amphorae, many inscribed with an identifying label which says that the vase is a prize from the Panathenaic contests, generally depict Athena on one side of the vase and, on the other, participants in the particular type of contest in which the recipient of the vase was victorious. In the painting of the only amphora actually known (from the inscription) to have been given (filled with oil) as a prize to a kitharode who was victorious at the Panathenaia, Leningrad 17295 (fig. 10), made about 430 B.C., the player stands on a podium in the presence of two listeners, one standing with a staff in his hand, one seated and wearing a wreath like that of the performer, a simple wreath of olive or laurel.

While it may be true that some scenes which show a kitharist standing between listeners do not represent contests, there is little doubt that the painting on the Kassel pelike (fig. 5) does indeed depict a contest of the sort held at the Panathenaia. The listeners, bearded men seated on either side of the performer, are wrapped in himatia, hold staves, and have wreaths made of long, straight branches bound about their heads. Both wreaths and staves suggest that these two men are judges, as does their formal attentiveness. But there is still more evidence, in the form of another painting by a member of the same Leagros Group of painters, in which the same figures appear.

In this second painting, on London 1926, 6–28,7 (fig. 11), there are three listeners, one of them seated, and all of them dressed as in figure 5, with staves and branches. (The kitharist, as before, wears a white chiton, though in this painting he has also a short mantle, and he too has branches bound about his head.) The important difference between figures 5 and 11 is that on the latter vase the performer steps up onto a low podium, making clear the formality of the occasion. But since the scenes on the two vases seem essentially

the same, we may assume that our figure 5 also represents a formal situation, probably a contest.

The Nike on amphora Oxford 274, who is apparently bearing a kithara to the young performer whom we find on the reverse side of the vase, flies over an altar on which a fire burns, reminding us that contests were held as part of religious festivals. A scene of a kithara-playing contest that has been found on a vase of the Panathenaic type (though without inscription) makes this even clearer, for the player, surrounded by three listening judges (one seated) who carry staves, stands next to an altar with a fire on it (Paris F 282).

In some cases, even kithara players who appear alone and without either podium or altar must be counted as contestants or victors. The kitharist who on the sixth-century amphora London B 139, for example, stands between columns with cocks atop them (just as Athena does on the other side of this Panathenaic vase without inscription) must surely be taking part in the Panathenaic festival; and the kitharist who is shown on both sides of Toronto 919.25.2, standing between columns of the same sort, is probably also a Panathenaic contestant.[40] There are also several red-figured vases of the period 490–460 B.C. on which the kitharode stands alone on one side of the vase, and the listener-judge, usually a bearded man with a staff, appears on the reverse. Figure 8 shows both sides of such a vase, Boston amphora 26.61.[41] Here the listener is a young man; but this is not surprising, since other paintings suggest that youthful contestants might be judged by young men not much older than themselves. The young judge holds his head—perhaps trying to concentrate and make a difficult decision.

In the few cases in which the kithara player is alone and there is no listener on the reverse, there is no indication of his role, unless such factors as the elaborateness of his costume or the fact that he wears a wreath are taken into account—the young kitharist who lifts his right hand to adjust his wreath on Munich 2319 looks very much like a contestant about to take his turn before the judges.[42]

From the period of the Peloponnesian War, we have the names of several competitors in musical contests, some of them, like the contemporary political figures, the butt of jokes in the plays of the comic writers of the period. For example, in a comic fragment of about 420 B.C., there is the following dialogue, which presumably concerns a musical contest of the sort held at the Panathenaia; instead of inquiring about the winners, the speaker begins at the other end:

A. Well, which kitharode turned out to be the worst?
B. Meles, the son of Peisias.
A. Who was the second worst?
B. Hold on, let me see. Oh, I know! Chairis![43]

Α φέρ' ἴδω, κιθαρῳδὸς τίς κάκιστος ἐγένετο;
Β ⟨ὁ⟩ Πεισίου Μέλης.
            Α μετὰ ⟨δὲ⟩ Μέλητα τίς;
Β ἔχ' ἀτρέμ' · ἐγῷδα· Χαῖρις.

The verbal wit of the Old Comedians even led to the coining of a superlative adjective made from the word *kitharoidos*, namely, *kitharoidotatos*—the "kith-aroediest" musician of all. In a typically earthy passage in Aristophanes' *Wasps* (1275ff.), the chorus praises Automenes for the excellence of his three sons, whose respective talents embrace a rather odd combination of expertise: performing on the kithara, performing on the stage, and performing with the tongue (one of Aristophanes' typically bawdy sexual references). The first son is described as a kitharoedic expert (*kitharoidotatos*) known to everyone. His name, not mentioned here, can be determined from another play, where the musical brother is referred to as Arignotos.[44]

The most famous of all kitharodes of the late fifth century was undoubtedly Timotheus of Miletos, who was born about 450 B.C. and who spent much of his life in Athens. A self-proclaimed revolutionary and a daring innovator, he is known to us through fragments of his poetic compositions (especially his *nomos*, the *Persae*), from a few contemporary remarks and from several later sources such as Plutarch.

In the *Persae*, a copy of which came to light in 1902 on a papyrus, Timotheus places himself third in a line of great creative musicians, following in the footsteps of Orpheus himself and the famous Terpander of Lesbos. In a puzzling passage, he claims that he has "invented kithara-playing (*kitharis*) with eleven-stroke meters and rhythms, opening up the secret, many-hymned treasure of the Muses."[45] Reports in sources dating from several centuries later indicate that this claim was somehow taken to mean that Timotheus had added four extra strings to the canonical number associated with the kithara. Such an interpretation is reflected in the story known only through writings of the Christian era that when Timotheus competed at the Spartan festival of the Karneia, the *ephor* (magistrate) in charge took a knife and cut off the four extra strings that had been added to the instrument.[46] Timotheus' own words in the *Persae*, however, include no mention at all of strings but only of meters and rhythms that involve eleven *kroumata*, or strokes. The

word *krouma* (from *krouein*, to strike) generally refers to the *sound* produced by striking the string with the plektron, not to the string itself, so that Timotheus is probably speaking of some kind of rhythmic pattern involving eleven beats rather than of the use of eleven different strings.[47]

The only other information from literary sources that sheds any light on the question of Timotheus' inventions in kithara playing comes from a fragment of Pherekrates' late fifth-century comedy, *Cheiron*, in which the character Music complains to Justice about the assaults made on her person by various musicians, among them Timotheus and his teacher, Phrynis:

> *Music*: Next Phrynis, screwing his tuning pin, turning and twisting me, ruined me utterly by having twelve *harmoniai* on five strings. . . . But Timotheus, my dearest Justice, has ruined me and worn me out the most shamefully.
> *Justice*: Who is this Timotheus?
> *Music*: A certain Milesian redhead who brought me troubles. He's outdone everyone I've mentioned, bringing strange, unmelodious ant-hills and unholy added notes and whistles; twisting me just as though I were a cabbage, he's riddled me completely with [?], and if he chances upon me somewhere as I'm walking alone, he pulls me down and undoes me with twelve strings [notes?].[48]

> Φρῦνις δ' ἴδιον στρόβιλον ἐμβαλών τινα
> κάμπτων με καὶ στρέφων ὅλην διεφθόρει
> ἐν πέντε χορδαῖς δώδεχ' ἁρμονίας ἔχων. . . .
> ὁ δὲ Τιμόθεός μ', ὦ φιλτάτη, κατορώρυχεν
> καὶ διακέκναιχ' ἄσχιστα.
>   ΔΙ. ποῖος οὑτοσί
> ⟨ὁ⟩ Τιμόθεος;
>   ΜΟ. Μιλήσιός τις πυρρίας·
> κακά μοι παρέσχεν οἷς ἅπαντας οὓς λέγω
> παρελήλυθ', ἀγαγὼν ἐκτραπέλους μυρμηκιὰς
> ἐξαρμονίους, ὑπερβολαίους τ' ἀνοσίους
> καὶ νιγλάρους, ὥσπερ τε τὰς ῥαφάνους ὅλην
> καμπῶν με κατεμέστωσε . . . .
> κἂν ἐντύχῃ πού μοι βαδιζούσῃ μόνῃ,
> ἀπέδυσε κἀνέλυσε χορδαῖς ἕνδεκα.

This fragment, with its double entendre and the risqué innuendo so characteristic of Attic comedy, is of particular importance since its author was a contemporary of Timotheus.[49] Exactly how we should interpret it is, however, problematical. The emphasis of the passage seems to be on Timotheus' twists and turns (that is, his use of embellishment and ornamentation)—his "ant-hills," extra notes, and "whistles." But does the last line mean that he achieved these effects through the use of extra strings? Because there is no evidence in the vase paintings to indicate that any form of lyre suddenly acquired five extra strings during the last decades of the fifth century, we must look for some other interpretation. A probable explanation is that *dodeka chordais* should be translated not as "twelve strings" but rather as a "dozen notes," and that the phrase is meant to continue the obscene double entendre of the passage by alluding to the "twelve positions" envisioned in the Greek version of the Kama Sutra.[50] In other words, Music is saying that Timotheus assaults her with his twists and turns and great numbers of notes, all of which result from his excessive fondness for ornamentation.

Although the picture is far from clear, Timotheus' innovations seem to have been misinterpreted by the writers of late antiquity, who, instead of stressing the musical and rhythmic complexities alluded to in the words of Pherekrates and of Timotheus himself, simply retell the story of the cutting off of the extra strings that Timotheus was supposed to have added to the kithara. The story makes a vivid and dramatic, though probably apocryphal, parable of excessive innovation curbed in the name of traditional propriety and moderation.[51]

The Technique of Kithara Playing

The kitharist, as the visual evidence shows, stands while he plays his instrument, a further indication of the formality of the occasions when the instrument is used. Among several hundred scenes with the kithara from this period, scarcely more than a dozen show a seated performer, who is always a mythological figure such as Apollo; four of them are libation scenes, in which Apollo (or, in one case, Heracles) does not actually play but holds a dish in his right hand (Heracles holds a pitcher to pour a libation to Athena).[52]

The kithara is held upright, as in figures 3 and 12, or tipped inward somewhat to rest against the player's shoulder, as in figures 2, 5, 8, and 9. The kithara is rarely tipped away from the player more than very slightly unless he is seated or not playing—when he is tuning, mounting a podium, or (if he is Apollo) accepting a libation.

The entire left hand of the player, with the left wrist in the sling that helps support the instrument, is normally visible behind the strings as the performer faces right (as he does in the great majority of paintings). The mobility of this left hand is restricted by the sling, and we must also remember that the back of the kithara is not flat, but bulging, and that the player's left forearm lies over this bulge (see chap. 2, fig. 9c), another factor to be considered when the possible left-hand techniques are discussed. The hand may be parallel to the strings, as in figure 5, or tilted to the side toward the outer arm of the kithara, as in figure 13. The palm of the left hand faces the strings, as in these two examples, or is occasionally rotated outward somewhat as in figure 9, apparently to bring the thumb into a better position to pluck the strings. The whole hand is ordinarily visible just above the upper edge of the soundbox.

In black-figured vase paintings, especially the older ones, the left hand tends to be shown with all the fingers straight and somewhat separated (figs. 2 and 12). In red-figured paintings, however, though the kinds of scenes are fewer, we see a wider variety of left-hand positions and find that the fingers may be shown in a large number of positions, close together to stretched apart, some or all of them straight or curved or bent forward from the palm or even completely curled, the thumb straight and close to or held away from the other fingers, or bent across the palm (figs. 1, 3, 5, 9, and 14 illustrate some of these possibilities).

Although it is clear enough that the players touch the strings with their left-hand fingers, we cannot use evidence of this kind to determine *which* strings are touched—tables summarizing the variety of finger positions behind the strings would be meaningless, for few vases are painted so carefully as that, and it is not likely that the painters themselves knew, or were concerned with, such fine details of kithara technique.[53] It is also not possible to tell from this evidence whether the left-hand fingers were used to stop the strings, that is, to push against them, changing their pitch by changing their effective length. It may be argued, however, that the players did *not* do this, for several reasons.

First, the arm must have been in an awkward position, lying over the bulging back of the instrument (see chap. 2, fig. 9c), and the left hand had little freedom of movement in the sling. Second, it would have been difficult, given the way the instrument was supported (by the sling and against the left side of the body), to press hard against the strings, although light pressure, producing harmonics, might conceivably have been used.[54] But most important, the points along the strings that could be reached by the restricted movement of this hand-in-the-sling are not those required for stopping the strings to change their pitch by the small amount (say, one step) that would be useful, presumably, for the purposes of either melody or accompaniment, as this would require stopping the string quite close to the crossbar or the bridge.[55] Nor are these points that can be reached sufficient for the production of more than a few harmonics (though these may be the very "ant-hills" and "whistles" alluded to in the Pherekrates fragment quoted above). It therefore seems more reasonable to assume that normally the left-hand fingers touched the strings primarily to damp certain ones (that is, to prevent them from sounding when the plektron swept over them) or to pluck them. There is considerable evidence of the latter technique among the vase paintings, which often show the tip of the thumb close to the tip of the index finger, or to one of the other fingers, as in figure 14.

The evidence indicates that the performer always holds the plektron in his right hand when playing and that he uses it in a stroke that sweeps outward across the strings, sounding all the strings that are not damped with the left-hand fingers.[56] Figures 2, 3, 5, 9, and 13 show the pose typically seen in the paintings, the right hand holding the plektron at the outer edge of the instrument or beyond, at varying heights. That this pose indicates the completion of a stroke away from, rather than the beginning of one toward, the player is suggested, at least, by the greater ease of movement possible in the former and by the rather relaxed look of the hand and arm. Other poses for the right arm, in the case of kithara players, are rare, though they are sometimes found in paintings of the other members of the lyre family, which may be presumed to use the same basic technique (see chaps. 4 and 5).[57]

The performer in figure 8 does offer us one of the few variations in right-hand position—he holds the plektron below the bridge, between the bridge and lower string fastener, a position that Otto Gombosi contended represented a technique of pressing against a string below the bridge to increase its tension and thus change its pitch.[58] The scarcity of other examples, however, and the fact that in figure 8 (the best such example) the performer is not sounding the string by plucking it, prevent us from accepting this theory. It seems far more likely that what we see here is simply the movement of bringing the plektron back to the starting point, ready to sweep outward across the strings.

The players of the kithara are rarely seen in the act of singing while they play, and no scenes have come to light in which anyone other than the kithara player is singing. Although this lack of singers and singing kitharists is certainly a matter of the conventions of painters, it is interesting to note that only two kinds of singing kitharists have been found—satyrs and mortal kitharodes—and that there are no representations at all of Apollo singing, though paintings of Apollo far outnumber those of all other kithara players combined.

The two available examples of satyr-kitharodes who are clearly singing (shown with open mouth) are both on black-figured vases, while the four paintings of mortal kitharodes singing are on red-figured or white-ground vases, mostly of later date than the satyr scenes.[59] In each of the four, the mortal kitharode stands alone, though there is a listener or Nike (on one vase, Dionysos) on the other side of the vase. The players tilt their heads back and seem to sing with gusto (see figs. 8 and 13).

Another small group of paintings allows us to see kithara players in the process of tuning their instruments. In figure 4, Heracles, while mounting a podium to play before Athena, reaches up and wraps the thumb and first two fingers of his right hand around the kollopes on the crossbar; his left hand seems to test the strings by plucking them. The fourth and fifth fingers of the right hand, at the crossbar, stand straight up, a position also seen on Hannover vase Kestner 753, in which Apollo tunes his kithara while seated on a *diphros* (stool) in the presence of Leto and Artemis. The vase Warsaw Czartoryski 11, a somewhat later, poorer vase, also has a seated Apollo (with Artemis) tuning his kithara in a similar pose.[60]

All these vases are black figured, but figure 15, though as early as the others (ca. 520 B.C.), is red figured and the only painting in this group to show a mortal performer. It shows him, moreover, in back view, giving us a rare opportunity to observe both the instrument and the tuning method from this perspective. The player, a youth in chiton and bordered chlamys, has his left wrist in the sling, his fingers and thumb straight—the pose records no visible plucking gesture. The fingers of his right hand are around the crossbar; it seems likely that the thumb is on the near side of the crossbar, as in the other paintings. The player tips the instrument out, probably to make it easier to reach the crossbar, and lifts his knee, perhaps to help steady it. These four paintings constitute conclusive evidence that the knobs at the end of the crossbar do not serve as the standard means of tuning the instrument; in fact, no examples have been found showing a player with his hand at the end of the crossbar of any type of lyre. The tuning of each string is accomplished by adjusting its kollops on the crossbar. This is probably the action given such suggestive overtones in the Pherekrates fragment (above) where Music says, "Phrynis, screwing his *strobilon* ("tuning pin") . . . ruined me utterly by having twelve *harmoniai* on five strings." In place of the word *kollops* Pherekrates uses *strobilon*, literally "ball" or "spinning top," here probably with double reference to the tuning device and to sexual intercourse.

The Sound of the Kithara

The literary references in which the kithara is mentioned by name contain only a few details about the instrument's construction and sound, so that most of our conclusions must be deduced from the evidence of the vase paintings. Euripides does provide the information that the kithara had seven strings and that it was played with a plektron, which was apparently made of animal horn.[61] In addition, he describes the sound produced by the instrument as a "cry" (enope) or "shout" (iache); in one passage, his contemporary, Aristophanes, implies (doubtless with comic distortion) that the sound of the kithara is as loud as a cock's crow.[62] Even if we allow for poetic overstatement, it appears that the kithara, in contrast to the "bright-sounding" Homeric phorminx, was thought of as producing a loud sound. It is certainly reasonable to suppose that the kithara was capable of an unusually resonant, loud volume, given its relatively large soundbox, as evident in the vase paintings, and the use of a plektron made of some hard material like horn.

The only other available evidence concerning the sound of the kithara is to be found in two onomatopoetic words that presumably imitate its music: *topla-totrat* and *trettanelo*. The repetition of the hard consonant *t* in both these words seems to suggest that the plektron stroke had a rhythmic percussive effect, or at any rate that the strumming sound produced was more like a sharply articulated striking of the strings than a gentle silvery sweep across them.[63]

Construction

The vase paintings confirm that the kithara was a seven-stringed instrument during the Classical period, at least in Athens, for though representations of kitharas with six strings turn up frequently, and some are to be found that have eight, or five, the most carefully painted vases show us seven, and only occasionally six; and approximately two-thirds of all the paintings with visible strings are of seven-stringed kitharas.

The size of the instruments can be only roughly gauged because many are only partly visible and the shape is often distorted in photographs by the curvature of the vase. Using the length of the adult player's arm from elbow to second knuckle as a convenient (if relative) unit of measure, we find that the majority of kitharas are about as wide as this unit, and nearly all the remainder are only a little wider or narrower (¾ to 1¼ times our basic unit). The height of the kithara seems to vary more than the width (though here photo distortion may be a factor). Most kitharas are from

1¼ to two times as tall as the elbow/second-knuckle unit of measure, and are normally at least high enough to extend from the player's waist to the top of his head (many extend a good bit higher). The height of a given kithara may be a little more than the width, or as much as twice the width, although most lie within the range in which the height is about 1¼ to 1½ times the width.

A tendency for the kithara to become somewhat longer in the body, foreshadowing a changed shape that becomes evident in the fourth century, is just discernible in our examples after 450 B.C., a period from which few representations of the kithara are to be found.[64]

The kithara so beautifully executed by the Berlin Painter, figure 13 (New York 56.171.38), may stand as our example of the shape of the kithara known in Classical Athens. The upper parts of the arms, above the crossbar, appear wide and tall and rectangular; the lower arms curve outward; and from them the soundbox tapers somewhat to the straight line of the flat base.

Only one side view of the kithara of this period, Bern 12409 (fig. 16), has come to light, but there are several back views of the instrument, including representations on the Parthenon frieze (fig. 6), on a coin from Delos of 525–500 B.C. (London, Knight Coll.), and on a tiny steatite scarab of the same date (fig. 17). We can consider what we see in these examples in the light of what we have found in the side views on the sixth-century relief from Delphi (chap. 2, fig. 9c). The bulging backs seen in the Delphi relief were very likely still present, though perhaps somewhat modified, in the kitharas of the Classical period; we must therefore subject the three low-relief objects mentioned above to some interpretation and assume that the instrument's back stood out more than is allowed for, at least in the coin and the Parthenon frieze.

Both the scarab (fig. 17) and the frieze show clearly that the bulge is greater at the top of the soundbox, which tapers toward the base, and that there is a slight ridge running down the center of the back (on the frieze the cloth lies just next to this ridge). From this we can assume that the bottom of the soundbox has a roughly triangular shape, as the Parthenon frieze seems to indicate.[65] The didrachm coin from Delos makes evident one feature of the general outline that can seldom be seen in paintings (though it is visible in fig. 8), since the player's wrist sling is apt to be in the way: the top of the soundbox may rise in a hump that lies just below the performer's left hand.

In a few instances, the paintings show the corner formed by the bottom and side of the soundbox, as seen in front view, as a rounded outline rather than an angle.[66] It seems possible that the painters may be confusing the characteristics of two different instruments, but it also may be that this is a rarely seen variant shape. The examples of this shape are part of scenes that have some connection with the cult of Dionysos or Heracles.

There are no archaeological remains of the kithara that would allow us to report on the material of which it was made, but there can be little doubt that the basic material was wood, sometimes decorated with ivory, amber, or small gold ornaments. There was practically no other suitable material available, and we can point to similar instruments of which remains have been found in Egypt that were of wooden construction.[67]

The arms of the kithara were made in at least two sections and set into the soundbox; the paintings often show diagonal lines across the lower arm, and lines on the soundbox below the arms that seem to indicate the joining of separate pieces (figs. 2 and 4 show the lines on the lower arms; figs. 9, 13, and 15 show the joining of lower arms and soundbox; and fig. 5 shows both types of seam). As figure 16 suggests, the arms of the kithara, like those of the other members of the lyre family discussed in chapters 4–6, are turned at an angle, and their upper sections lean forward somewhat. This figure also suggests that the belly of the kithara may not have been completely flat, but slightly arched, and that the sides of the soundbox are curved around to make a smooth transition from front to back.

Both the bridge and the lower string fastener are depicted in a variety of ways in the paintings; the bridge in particular, which may have caused problems of perspective, is portrayed in many different ways (or may not be shown at all). Its appearance varies from a thin line to a thick rectangle with "feet" showing above and below on both ends (the "feet" are sometimes indicated by small circles above and below the rectangle, sometimes by making the end of the rectangle into a cloverleaf or trefoil shape).[68]

The lower string fastener, when it is visible, also varies in size and elaborateness; the one in figure 13 is an unusually detailed example. It is not always rectangular—some examples are wider at the top, where the strings are attached, than at the bottom, where the fitting itself is presumably fastened to the base of the soundbox.

From the lower string fastener, the strings sometimes rise parallel to one another (figs. 1, 8) and sometimes fan out, as in figure 13; strings that diverge slightly, as in figure 9, are perhaps the most realistic portrayals. The way in which the strings are fixed to the crossbar of the kithara is by no means clearly shown; kollopes depicted by painters of the fifth century apparently consist of pieces of leather around the crossbar through which run small pins of wood, bone, or ivory placed at right angles to the crossbar. They are often not visible or are sketchily indicated (though they may be painted red), and the way the strings are fastened around them is rarely made evident.[69] Both figures 9 and 13 have clear kollopes (probably both of the same type, though in figure 13 they appear to be fastened on the front side of the instrument) but do not reveal how the strings are wound around them. One can occasionally see a pattern of x's along the crossbar, as on New York 21.88.73 and London E 383, suggesting that the strings were wound around the kollopes and crossbar in figure-eight patterns.

The crossbar itself, which is often depicted as wider in the center where the strings pass over it and tapering to the ends, generally appears to be placed in front of the arms, resting in grooves just above the spiral ornaments. It has knobs of some sort (a feature rarely found on other kinds of lyres) at either end, but they are often carelessly executed—figure 9 is an unusual example in which they are shown in some degree of detail.

The ornamental construction of the arms of the kithara remains basically unchanged throughout the period under consideration here; once again, figure 13 offers an excellent example of the details.[70] As in the earlier period, many of the black-figured vases show the parts of the arms above the crossbar, and sometimes the details of the inner sides of the arms as well, in white (as in figs. 2 and 12), leading us to conclude that these parts were faced with, or made of, ivory. The spiral just below the crossbar (at the base of the upper arm) is replaced in figure 8 with a large round boss; such an ornament might very well have been made of gold, at least on the most elegant instruments.

It is interesting to compare the inner-arm construction of the kithara of the Classical period, as seen in figures 9 and 13, for instance, with that of a kithara from the Archaic period, the seventh-century example on the bronze back plate from Olympia seen in chapter 2, figure 8. The two points facing inward in the early example have by the fifth century become greatly exaggerated, and there is a small support between the upper "point" and the scroll. The overall effect often makes one think of the eye (created by painting a small circle at the end of the upper protrusion) and open mouth of a bearded snake—a symbol that would be appropriate for Apollo's kithara, since it was he who slew the Python of Delphi, represented as a bearded serpent.[71] Figure 15 shows an unusual fifth-century example with three "points" on each side (the ones at the top, on the ordinary kithara, do not protrude beyond the edge of the arm).

On a number of kitharas we can see a very small, more or less rounded protrusion on the *outside* of the arm, opposite the scroll or a little lower. It appears to be nothing more than an insignificant ornament. A more obviously ornamental feature of many kitharas is the decorative band along the bottom front edge of the soundbox.

A further detail about the ornamental aspects of the kithara is revealed in a passage from one of Aristophanes' comedies in which the poet berates the audience for their unsympathetic posture toward a fellow comic poet, Cratinus, who is now past his prime:

> But now, although you see he is in his dotage, you feel no piety, even though the amber [studs] are falling out, the tension is gone, and the tunings [*harmoniai*] gape wide open. Now that he's old he wanders around, like Konnas [a music teacher], holding his crown and dying of thirst. But once his victories won him free drinks in the prytaneion and front-row seats in the theatre, right next to the priest of Dionysos.[72]

νυνὶ δ᾽ ὑμεῖς αὐτὸν ὁρῶντες παραληροῦντ᾽ οὐκ
    ἐλεεῖτε,
ἐκπιπτουσῶν τῶν ἠλέκτρων καὶ τοῦ τόνου
    οὐκέτ᾽ ἐνόντος
τῶν θ᾽ ἁρμονιῶν διαχασκουσῶν· ἀλλὰ γέρων ὢν
    περιέρρει,
ὥσπερ Κοννᾶς, στέφανον μὲν ἔχων αὖον δίψῃ
    δ᾽ ἀπολωλώς,
ὃν χρῆν διὰ τὰς προτέρας νίκας πίνειν ἐν τῷ
    πρυτανείῳ,
καὶ μὴ ληρεῖν ἀλλὰ θεᾶσθαι λιπαρὸν παρὰ τῷ
    Διονύσῳ.

Although we cannot be positive that a kithara is the type of lyre with which Cratinus is being compared, the reference to amber decorations corresponds well with the representation of kitharas in the vase paintings, in which the two small circles often shown on the instrument's soundbox seem to suggest some sort of inlaid ornaments. Furthermore, it would make better sense for a professional comedy writer to be compared with a professional's instrument (which the kithara was) rather than to a mere schoolboy's lyre, for example, which in any case does not seem to have had much decoration.

Many of the kitharas have such small circles on the soundbox, one on either side of the bridge, sometimes close to the bridge, sometimes nearer the outside edge of the soundbox, usually at about the height of the bridge, or a little above or below (see fig. 1).[73] But in several cases the circle that shows is high and usually

near the edge and resembles an eye because of its circle-within-a-circle design.[74] On Paris F 58 the circles are incised on what is presumably the back of the instrument. Circles on the soundbox, whether they are ornaments or soundholes, are found as far back as late Geometric times in connection with the phorminx and may be an inheritance from that instrument, whose functions were to a great extent taken over by the kithara.

Accoutrements

The sling with which a kithara player in the vase paintings supports the instrument against his chest is not mentioned by name in any sixth- or fifth-century sources, but according to a later (probably Byzantine) source, it was called an *aorter,* or strap, a word derived from the verb *aeirein,* "to raise up."[75]

This sling for the player's left wrist is often shown as red or decorated cloth, sometimes (in red-figured paintings) with a fringe along the lower edge. It is customarily fastened to the outside arm, either by knotting or by securing with a button or peg that is visible in some examples. A few of the later vases, however, have kitharas with slings that are attached low on the outer edge of the soundbox and run diagonally across the front to the player's hand.[76]

The accessory called here (for want of a better name) the "sash" is present on most kitharas hanging from the outside edge of the soundbox and sometimes appears to consist of the free ends of the wrist sling after it has been knotted.[77] In other paintings it seems to be separate from the sling but held by means of it—a loop of the sash often shows above the sling at the outer edge of the instrument.[78] The sash is usually quite long, extending from the sling to well below the bottom of the soundbox; but there are some that are short, little more than half the height of the soundbox. Figure 18 shows such a sash, and one, moreover, that is not fastened through the sling—it hangs from a clearly indicated peg or button halfway down the side of the soundbox.[79]

Since the sash is commonly indicated by painting or incising a number of thin lines, scholars have suggested that it represents a set of spare strings, an explanation that does seem plausible in a great many cases.[80] But there are also some difficulties with this theory—the shortness of the sash in examples such as figure 18, for example, or the fact that on some vases, both red- and black-figured, the sash is painted red (as it is in fig. 8), while the strings actually in use are incised or painted in black.[81] On the Panathenaic prize amphora, Leningrad 17295 (fig. 10), the sash, looped under the sling, is a fillet (a cloth band of the sort often worn around the head) with long fringed ends; and on London E 383 the sash, though painted in thin lines, is both short and wavy.

One of the distinguishing characteristics of the kithara is the cloth that hangs down the back of the instrument and shows beneath it as it is seen in front view. The cloth, which is rarely absent in representations of this instrument and which often has an elaborate pattern and fringed ends, is in many cases quite long and falls in several folds; sometimes, however, only a short length of it is visible below the edge of the soundbox. The pattern on the cloth is occasionally the same as that of the performer's himation, but more often it is unmistakably different from the material used for the player's garments. The cloth is customarily attached, apparently, to one of the arms of the instrument at the back; see figure 15, a back view showing the cloth fastened to the outer arm and passing under the sling.[82] But it is perhaps more commonly attached to the arm next to the player, as appears to be the case in figure 8; the bands around the base of the inner arm in figure 13 may be the cords that hold the cloth in place.[83]

Speculations concerning the purpose of the cloth, as mentioned in chapter 2, have included theories that it is a cover for the instrument when not in use, or that it may serve to protect it and cushion the player's arm when the kithara is played. The notion that it is a cover is made less plausible by the number of examples in which the cloth is long and has a rather narrow scarf-like appearance, both its ends showing below the instrument. The later the vase, the narrower the cloth is likely to be: on prize amphora Leningrad 17295 (fig. 10), ca. 430 B.C., the cloth looks almost like the two ends of a fillet, even narrower than the one in figure 1 (dated ca. 450–440 B.C.), which also shows two long sections of cloth, fringed and very narrow.[84] While the cloth may have served as a cover at some earlier stage in the development of the instrument, its function in the late fifth century, as these examples suggest, was at least in part decorative, and perhaps also practical in cushioning the player's arm against the instrument.

All the instruments of the lyre family are played by means of plektra, and all customarily have the plektron attached to the instrument by means of a cord. But whereas the cord is tied around an arm of the instrument in the case of most other lyres, the kithara normally has it fastened to the bottom of the soundbox (usually at the center, as in figure 5, but sometimes at the outer corner, perhaps to a small ring that is not

shown in the paintings) or to one of the side posts of the lower string fastener, as in figure 13.

The plektron itself is an oval, a thin piece of ivory, horn, metal, or bone, about the size of a tablespoon (see chap. 2, The Chelys-Lyra in the Visual Arts of the Archaic Period). It has a handle wrapped with cloth or leather, often with a tassel at the end, as in figure 13. The plektron, handle, tassel, and cord are frequently painted red.

When the kithara is not being played (as when the performer holds a libation phiale in his right hand, for example), the plektron may be laid over the bridge and sometimes stuck into the strings as well; Boston 94.45 (fig. 19) shows it tucked under the strings just over the lower string fastener.[85] (Both these methods provide opportunities for us to see the plektron itself better than we can when it is being used.) On Munich 2319 we see the plektron stuffed through the strings above the soundbox and wedged between the thumb and index finger of the player's *left* hand.[86] There are also several doubtful examples in which the plektron may be pushed through the knot where the sling and sash are fastened together.[87]

The Kithara with Other Instruments

Only one passage in Greek literature (Eur. *IA* 1036–39) actually mentions the kithara in combination with other instruments, the syrinx and the "Libyan lotus" (aulos?); the context, however, is a mythological reference to the marriage of Peleus and Thetis, so that we cannot be sure that the passage reveals anything of actual fifth-century practice. If the literary references of the period were the only evidence, we would have to conclude that the kithara was generally not played together with other instruments. But depictions in vase painting of the kithara and aulos in ensemble suggest that the literary evidence is deceptive in this respect. Also, if we accept the theory that Pindar's instrument was in fact the kithara, we have four references to the performance of his odes (among a total of 17) in which he specifically mentions the instrument as being played together with the aulos. (It was evidently not uncommon for a victory song to be accompanied by the kithara in combination with one or more pairs of auloi as well.)[88]

If the visual evidence is a reliable indication, the occasions at which another instrument might be combined with the kithara in actual Athenian life were very few, and the aulos is the only instrument so represented. The aulos appears with the kithara in the scenes of sacrificial processions, both in vase paintings and on the Parthenon frieze, and both are played in the one banquet scene available that appears to be taken from real life (London B 679).

But the rest of the examples of aulos and kithara show us, as in figure 12, the aulos in the hands, not of mortals, but of satyrs (or, in two instances on other vases, a maenad) in the company of Dionysos. In one of the paintings, a Return of Hephaistos to Olympos (Cambridge, Harvard 1960.236), there are satyrs playing kithara, aulos, and barbitos, the latter (common among satyrs and revelers) the long-armed relative of the chelys-lyra (see chap. 5).[89] In figure 12, kithara and aulos are joined by yet another instrument, the krotala, long pieces of bone, wood, or ivory fastened together in pairs and played roughly in the way castanets are played.

The krotala are found with the kithara more often than are the auloi, and there is reason to believe that their presence symbolizes a mythical follower of Dionysos, even when the krotala player accompanies Apollo, and neither Dionysos nor a satyr is present. The krotala are always played by women, clearly maenads in those paintings (half the available examples) that do include satyrs or Dionysos. Apollo may appear in such scenes too—in one interesting example (fig. 18) Apollo, Dionysos, and two maenads (one playing krotala) are accompanied by Hermes, who, as god of flocks, plays the shepherd's instrument, the syrinx, or reed "pan-pipes." But Apollo appears in a number of instances with two, three, or four women, at least one of whom plays the krotala, in scenes in which there are no other figures (see the discussion above concerning the identity of the women). Such scenes show that the notion of a strict dichotomy between the "Apollonian" and the "Dionysiac" is a modern fancy inspired by Nietzsche that did not occur to the Athenian vase painters.

The kithara, according to the evidence assembled here, was an instrument played by male performers for formal public occasions with some degree of religious significance. We know that there were kithara contests as part of religious festivals and that kithara players and aulos players together took part in sacrificial processions at Athens. Other religious processions in which kitharists may have taken part were the wedding processions of certain wealthy families, although the evidence is not clear as to what extent such scenes are only religious symbols rather than representations of real events.

The instrument may have played a role in the cult observances of Dionysos, for though it appears as the chief attribute of Apollo in a very great number of scenes, there is nevertheless a significant number of representations in which a satyr plays the kithara, along with the krotala and/or the aulos, before Dionysos. The instrument may also have had some role in the cult of the hero Heracles. Apart from vases that present Heracles as kitharist or show the kithara played at his apotheosis, there is a single vase on which we see a young man playing the kithara in front of a shrine to Heracles.[90]

We have some reason to believe that the kithara was occasionally heard (or used as a stage prop) in Athenian plays, which were performed in honor of Dionysos. There is only slight evidence of the kithara as a provider of music, perhaps with the aulos, at banquets (the available scenes may have only a mythological significance).

The costumes worn by players also attest to the formality and importance of the occasions when the kithara was heard. Apollo's costume, a bordered or decorated himation or chlamys over a decorated or pleated full-length chiton, is also worn by many of the mortal kitharodes; but others wear a long, loose gown with broad bands of color down the side from the arm to the hem, an equally imposing and formal garment.

The techniques available to the player of the instrument appear to have been more limited than has sometimes been conjectured (though we must keep in mind that the music was by no means necessarily rendered primitive or monotonous because of this). The player's left hand is apparently used to pluck and damp the strings and possibly to produce some harmonics; but it is not in a position to stop the strings (that is, change their basic pitch) effectively or at a useful point. The right hand sweeps the strings with the plektron, probably with an outward stroke only; perhaps the left hand plucked the strings while the plektron was being returned to its starting point. Only the strings that are not being touched with the left-hand fingers will ring clearly, so that the player can presumably command a considerable variety of sounds.

Although only half a dozen examples that show kitharodes visibly singing have been found, we have to assume that this is a matter of the painters' preference and refrain from drawing conclusions about the use of the kithara as a solo instrument on the basis of such evidence. The small group of vases that show players tuning, on the other hand, is sufficient to allow us to conclude that the strings were tuned individually by turning each kollops.

One of the great ironies of Western history is that in the midst of the most creative period in the history of Greece occurred her longest and most destructive war, the Peloponnesian War fought between Athens and Sparta (along with their respective allies) almost continuously from 431 to 404 B.C., when Athens finally fell. These turbulent final years of the fifth century brought on rapid changes in musical customs and practice, as we shall see, changes that were often later criticized by conservative figures such as Plato (of whom more will be said in chap. 7). The kithara, in somewhat changed form, continued in use after the turn of the century and into the Hellenistic (not to mention Roman) period, but the developments of the fourth century are best reserved for later discussion.

The seven-stringed kithara, large, elaborately or-namented, and provided—unlike all the other lyres—with a fringed or decorated cloth that hangs from it, was in Classical Athens both a religious symbol and a living instrument. But its uses were limited, it seems, to occasions of some religious significance; and thus, though it was certainly the most respected of stringed instruments, it was not the one chosen to accompany the more mundane events in fifth-century Athenian life. For these we must turn, in the chapters that follow, to the other members of the lyre family known to Athens in the fifth century.

1. Boston 97.370. Attic
red-figured (r.f.)
oinochoe. Detail: Apollo
and Artemis at altar.

2. Toronto 919.5.133.
Attic b.f. hydria. Detail:
Apollo as kitharist
walking beside wedding
quadriga.

3. London B 206. Attic
b.f. amphora. Detail, A:
Dionysos and Ariadne,
satyrs, maenads; B:
Dionysos in quadriga,
satyrs, maenads.

4. Munich 1575. Attic b.f.
amphora. Detail: Heracles
mounting podium.

5. Kassel T 675. Attic b.f.
pelike. Detail: kithara
contest.

6. Athens Acropolis,
Parthenon frieze, plaque
875. Kitharists.

7. Plovdiv 298. Attic r.f.
hydria. Detail: theoxenia
for the Dioscuri.

8. Boston 26.61. Attic r.f.
amphora attributed to the
Brygos Painter. Details:
side A: kitharode; side B:
listener.

9. New York 20.245. Attic
r.f. amphora attributed to
the Pan Painter. Detail:
kitharist.

10. Leningrad 17295.
Attic Panathenaic
amphora. Detail:
contestant on podium, two
judges.

11. London 1926.6–28.7.
Attic b.f. amphora.
Detail: contestant
mounting podium, three
wreathed judges.

12. London B 300. Attic
b.f. hydria. Detail:
Dionysos, satyrs, and
maenads.

13. New York 56.171.38.
Attic r.f. amphora
attributed to the Berlin
Painter. Detail: kitharode.

14. Athens Nat. Mus. Acr.
609. Attic r.f. fragment.
Kitharist.

15. Cleveland 76.89. Attic
r.f. eye kylix. Kitharist,
listeners.

16. Berne 12409. Attic
r.f. hydria. Detail: Apollo
and Artemis, libation
scene.

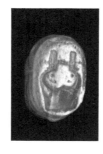

17. Cambridge Fitz. GR
18.1927. Green steatite
scarab with kithara.

18. Munich 2304. Attic
r.f. amphora. Detail:
Apollo, Hermes,
Dionysos, and women.

19. Boston 95.45. Attic
r.f. lekythos. Detail:
Apollo with phiale and
kithara.

CHAPTER FOUR

The Chelys-Lyra in Classical Athens

The "invention" of the lyra by the clever (though infantile) Hermes has already been recounted in chapter 2. This simplest, most basic, and perhaps most important of all the Greek stringed instruments, sometimes called the chelys ("tortoise"), is abundantly illustrated in Attic vase painting, where it appears in scenes both from everyday life and from the realm of mythology. Here we examine the uses of the instrument in the period after 525 and describe its appearance and construction in the fifth century on the basis of the archaeological and literary evidence.

Generic Use of *Lyra*

The common name for the instrument is lyra. Sophocles, for example, in the fragments from his satyr play, the *Ichneutai,* twice calls Hermes' instrument (made from a "dead body," that is, of the tortoise) a lyra. Whenever Aristophanes mentions instruments in connection with schoolboys and their teachers, he speaks of the lyra, which clearly corresponds to the chelys-lyra shown in such scenes on the vases.

In examining the literary references, however, we must remember that while the term *lyra* often denotes the chelys-lyra, it can also be used as a synonym for any of the lyre-type instruments, just as the derivative term *lyre* in English is applied to any member of this class of musical instruments; only if the context allows can we determine the choice of probable meaning. One passage in which *lyra* is obviously used as a synonym for another type of lyre is found in Aristophanes' comedy, *Thesmophoriazusae.*[1] In a scene in which the poet Agathon is being made fun of for his pretentious costume, the instrument that he plays is referred to first as a barbitos and then in the next line as a lyra.

In other examples, the term *lyra* seems to be used in place of the word *kithara*. We have already seen that Pindar's instrument was probably the kithara, though he never once uses that term. While he generally prefers the Homeric designation, *phorminx,* in several instances he describes the instrument that will help him praise noble winners of chariot races (and other competitions) simply as "lyra."[2] The epithets and descriptions of the "thunderous" sound of this "lyra" correspond exactly to Pindar's description of the "phorminx," and there is no reason to suppose that he is referring to two different types of lyres. This conclusion is supported by Euripides' use of *lyra* and *phorminx* as synonyms for Amphion's lyre, the music of which charmed the stones of Thebes' walls into place.[3] The same dual terminology is used by a late scholiast who seems to be summarizing the story of Amphion as it was told by fifth-century prose writers such as Pherekydes the genealogist:

> Antiope the daughter of Asopos had twin sons, Amphion and Zethus. Thebes lay nearby, still not girt with towers. . . . Amphion played upon his golden phorminx. . . . Armenidas in his first book tells how the stones, of their own accord, followed Amphion's lyra; he says that the lyra was given to Amphion by the Muses. Dioskorides says it was by Apollo, but Pherekydes in his tenth book recounts that it was the Muses.[4]

ἐν δ' ἔσαν Ἀντιόπης Ἀσω-
πίδος υἱέε δοιώ, Ἀμφίων καὶ Ζῆθος· ἀπύργωτος δ'
ἔτι Θήβη κεῖτο πέλας . . . . Ἀμφίων δ' ἐπί οἱ χρυσέηι

79

φόρμιγγι . . . ὅτι δὲ ἠκολούθησαν τῆι Ἀμφίονος
λύραι οἱ λίθοι αὐτόματοι ἱστορεῖ καὶ Ἀρμενίδας ἐν
πρώτωι (III). τὴν δὲ λύραν δοθῆναι Ἀμφίονι ὑπὸ
Μουσῶν φησί. Διοσκορίδης (III) δὲ ὑπὸ Ἀπόλλωνος. καὶ Φερεκύδης δὲ ἐν τῆι δεκάτηι (?) ἱστορεῖ ὑπὸ
Μουσῶν.

The story of Amphion does not seem to have captured
the imagination of Attic vase painters, however, and
archaeological confirmation that he was thought of as
a player of the Pindaric "phorminx," that is, the kithara, is found only in the marble relief from Delphi
(chap. 2, fig. 9c), in which the artist seems to have
represented Orpheus and Amphion as kithara players
on board the Argo.

As for the lyra mentioned occasionally in Greek
literature in connection with the Thracian singer, Thamyras, this instrument proves in the vase paintings to
be not a chelys but rather a special form of the kithara
that can be identified with Thrace (see chap. 6). In
the contest scene between Euripides and Aeschylus in
Aristophanes' *Frogs* (1281ff.), the words *lyrion* and
lyra are probably to be understood as referring to the
kithara, in the light of the reference in the passage to
kitharoedic *nomoi* (patterns). That the term *lyra* was
usually restricted to stringed instruments of the lyra
type, as opposed to harps, however, is clear from a
late-fifth-century comic fragment in which the speaker
makes a distinction between lyres and trigonoi
("three-cornered" instruments, that is, harps).[5]

The compound form *alyros* ("lyreless"), an adjective that is found frequently among the tragedians to
describe mournful tunes, dirges, and laments, occurs
in a further group of references in which the generic
sense of the term is apparent. While one cannot tell
what type of lyre is meant, it is clear enough from
these descriptions that the Greeks of the fifth century
regarded lyre accompaniment as inappropriate for
lamentations expressing deep grief. Although all the
references themselves are from mythological contexts,
the repeated notion of "lyreless laments" in connection with different situations suggests that actual practice is reflected, at least to some degree. Iphigenia
mourns her lonely state with lyreless laments, and the
distressed cry of a wood nymph pursued by Pan is
likened to a lyreless lament; in a slight variation of the
idea, the chorus sing a "lament without lyre" (*aneu
lyras . . . threnon*) for the Greek heroes at Troy; and
the servants of the Muses mourn the noble Alkestis in
"lyreless hymns."[6] Such references imply that the absence of string accompaniment heightened the mournful character of the song and that the voice alone (or
perhaps with the aulos) was thought to be more ex-

pressive of grief than a song that included a lyre part;
alyros must be taken in a generic sense to mean "without accompaniment of a lyre-type instrument."

Etymology and Terminology

Like most of the other names for stringed instruments
in the Greek language, the word *lyra* appears to be a
loanword borrowed into Greek from some other, probably non-Indo-European, language. Linguists are generally hesitant to connect the word with any known
Indo-European roots and prefer to describe it as a
term borrowed from some language of the Mediterranean area.[7]

Although Homer and Hesiod never use the word,
lyra appears frequently in later Greek literature. As
we saw in chapter 2, the earliest occurrence of the
term is in a fragment of the seventh-century Archilochos. In the sixth century it becomes increasingly common, and by the fifth century we find it appearing
relatively often in Pindar, Aeschylus, Sophocles, Euripides, and Aristophanes, that is, in all the major
poets of the Golden Age of Greece. Aristophanes supplies a variant form of the name, the diminutive *lyrion,*
and also concocts a comic compound by which he
lumps shield and lyre makers together under the name
torneuto-lyraspidopegoi, the comedy lying in the jum-
bling together of two such disparate businesses.[8] A
fragment from the poetry of Anakreon suggests that
the normal term for lyre maker was *lyropoios.*[9]

A common compound is the epithet *eulyros* ("well
lyred"), with which Apollo is often described in Greek
poetry, first by Sappho and later by Bacchylides, Aristophanes, and Euripides.[10] The instrument he plays is
occasionally described as a *lyra,* a word that the vase
paintings suggest should be interpreted in its generic
sense in this case; in the majority of the scenes on the
vases, as we have already noted, it is the kithara that
Apollo holds rather than the chelys-lyra.[11]

As for derived forms such as *lyristes* ("lyre player")
and *lyrizein* ("to play the lyre"), these are found only
in the literature of the post-Classical era.[12] Probably
no need for such terms was felt for some time because
their meanings were already included in the old words
kitharistes and *kitharizein,* which could be used with
reference to any type of lyre (see chap. 3). Several
passages in Greek literature show by their contexts
that *kitharizein* may refer to the playing of the schoolboy's chelys-lyra depicted in the vase paintings. In a
scene in a comedy by Aristophanes, for example (in
which a boy is trying to convince his juror father not
to be too hard on the family dog for having stolen a
piece of cheese), the boy argues that his father should

stop being so litigious and that the poor beast should be forgiven because, after all, he does not know how to play the lyre (kitharizein). The boy argues, in other words, that the dog is uneducated. The argument soon backfires, however, for the father then says he cannot acquit the guilty dog because he himself never learned to play the lyre, that is, that he knows only one thing, how to be a judge.[13] In another example of the use of *kitharizein* in connection with lyre playing, Damon (the great Athenian musical theorist of the fifth century mentioned several times by Plato) expressed his view of the civilizing effects of musical training by saying that education in singing and in lyre playing (kitharizein) promoted young boys' sense of courage, moderation, and justice.[14] In a further example, Herodotus reports as follows the advice of the defeated king of the Lydians, Croesus, on how to tame his rebellious people: he advises Cyrus to take away their weapons, make them wear more restrictive clothing and take up a trade, and have them teach their children to play the lyre (kitharizein) and to pluck the harp (psallein).[15]

The Chelys-Lyra in the Visual Arts

Generic Uses

Just as the word *lyra* may be substituted for the name of any member of the lyre family, so the visual image of the chelys is frequently substituted for that of the kithara and sometimes for that of one of the other lyres. In most instances the occasions portrayed are such that the chelys-lyra might actually have been used, but there is at least one kind of scene in which the kithara would be the only appropriate instrument: the quadriga procession.

The scenes of quadriga (four-horse chariot) processions are the most convincing example of this generic use of the chelys-lyra shape, for there are more than fifty vases with such scenes, nearly all of them lekythoi or other small vases, and almost all of them black-figured vases from the fifth century (fig. 1). The lekythoi, which contained grave offerings of oil, were cheaply made; since the black-figured style was out of fashion in the fifth century and had declined greatly by that time, these lekythoi and other black-figured vases showing the chelys-lyra in a quadriga procession are sketchily painted. The outline of the chelys-lyra is both easier to paint and easier (under these circumstances) to recognize than that of the kithara, but it could not be used in a scene where only the kithara would be appropriate unless the chelys-lyra was generally understood to have a symbolic or generic meaning.[16]

The kithara was the only instrument ordinarily associated with quadriga processions: the great number of large, carefully decorated vases (amphorae, hydriae, kraters, and so forth) with quadriga processions in which the kithara appears (surveyed in chap. 3) argues for this. Such large, carefully painted vases are almost completely absent from the group discussed here showing the chelys-lyra, though the scenes are essentially the same in both groups.[17]

The Interchangeability of Chelys-Lyra and Kithara

A special category of paintings of the chelys-lyra is the libation scene, in which Apollo, with lyre and phiale (drinking bowl) stands near Artemis, who holds an oinochoe (pitcher) to pour wine (fig. 2; the significance of this scene is discussed in chap. 3).[18] In most paintings of this sort, the instrument depicted is the kithara, but the scenes on just over a dozen vases in the present sample show the chelys-lyra instead. Here the substitution cannot generally be blamed on the quality of the vase: they are all red-figured vases, mostly of the larger varieties (kraters, hydriae, pelikes, and amphorae), and all but a few are reasonably well painted. The scene may be as formal as it is when the kithara is shown, the figures standing in rather stiff poses, perhaps with an altar between them; but other libation scenes show the figures in less formal poses, even seated.[19] Only a few vases in this group are done in the careless manner which suggests that the chelys-lyra was chosen because it was easier to execute and could "stand in" for another member of the lyre family. Apollo was clearly god of the chelys-lyra (given him by Hermes: see chap. 2) as well as of the kithara (as the paintings discussed below make clear) and might be portrayed with either instrument.

The chelys-lyra is Apollo's instrument in paintings on a number of other vases, both red- and black-figured, large and small, in which he is accompanied by Artemis. The painting often includes a doe or palm tree, the latter the symbol of their birth on the island of Delos. Artemis sometimes holds a bow, or occasionally a torch, as in the painting in which the pair appears with Orestes and Pylades (Bologna 660). The other gods (Hermes, Leto, Athena, and Dionysos) often present along with Artemis and the kithara-playing Apollo are also sometimes present when Apollo plays the chelys-lyra.

In two depictions of the introduction of Heracles to Olympos, Apollo officiates, not with the kithara, but with the chelys-lyra; and in another two, of the contest between Apollo and the satyr Marsyas, the stringed instrument shown is also the chelys-lyra.

Other paintings, such as that of Apollo seated in a winged tripod holding the chelys-lyra (Rome, Vatican hydria) or Apollo playing the chelys-lyra in the presence of satyrs or of Dionysos and Hermes (San Simeon 5498), also assure us that the chelys-lyra, too, is regarded as Apollo's own instrument, just as is the kithara.[20]

The chelys-lyra appears in other mythological scenes for which our survey in chapter 3 has suggested that the kithara is the instrument we might expect. Ten vases and two scarabs offer scenes of the chelys-lyra in the hands of (or at the feet of) satyrs—satyrs dancing, pursuing a woman, tuning the lyre, standing before a wine krater, or walking, sometimes in a procession (fig. 3).[21] Dionysos himself seldom appears along with lyra-playing satyrs or maenads. The latter, the female followers of Dionysos, are not nearly so rare as in the paintings of the kithara; the chelys-lyra is an instrument commonly found in female hands, while the kithara is reserved almost exclusively for males. The fact that Dionysos so seldom appears in scenes with the chelys-lyra suggests that the painters thought it more appropriate to show the kithara in paintings that include the god himself.

Another mythological figure, Heracles, whom the painters liked to portray as a player of the kithara (see chap. 3), plays the chelys-lyra on Athens 635, a black-figured *skyphos* (drinking cup). In a scene that may also be an example of the symbolic use of the chelys-lyra (in which it "stands in" for the kithara), he appears on a podium performing in the presence of Athena and Hermes, who are seated to either side.

Chelys-Lyra Interchanged with "Thamyras Kithara"

The legendary singer Orpheus is seen on red-figured paintings that provide additional instances of the interchangeability of the lyre with other instruments of the lyre family. The Orpheus story illustrated by the vase paintings is not the familiar one of his rescue of Eurydice from the Underworld, though this story may have been known in the fifth century.[22] The myth represented is the one that tells how Orpheus sang and played for the men of Thrace and roused the ire of the Thracian women (see chap. 6), who killed him. The lyre sometimes referred to as the "Thamyras kithara" (described in detail in chap. 6) is associated with Orpheus as well as Thamyras. This rather exotic member of the lyre family may be Thracian (both Orpheus and Thamyras were said to come from Thrace), but it may also be a fanciful instrument intended to look foreign, possibly an instrument created by the stage designers, since vases often show a stage version of a myth. In

any case, Orpheus, as he appears in the vase paintings, is as apt to carry the chelys-lyra as the "Thamyras kithara," giving us another example of the interchangeability of the tortoise-shell lyre with other lyre-family instruments.

On a few vases, such as Corinth C 34-365, London E 390, and New York 24.97.30, we see Orpheus singing to the Thracian men while he plays the chelys-lyra; on the last of these (fig. 4) the rest of the story is foretold, for to one side stands a Thracian woman, sickle-shaped knife in hand.[23] But most of the paintings of Orpheus with the chelys-lyra show him being slain by the Thracian women. The scene sometimes includes men in Thracian costume (including the peaked cap) mourning his death. The women, who are sometimes dressed as Thracians (with tattooed arms) and sometimes as Athenian Greeks, carry various weapons in addition to the curved knives. Orpheus himself may wear only a himation or may be dressed in Thracian style (short tunic and boots); he characteristically holds his lyre over his head as he is attacked.

The emphasis in the vase paintings on Orpheus as a player of the chelys-lyra is paralleled in the literature by a reference in Timotheus' late fifth- or early fourth-century *Persae* (221–23) that makes the Thracian musician the instrument's inventor:

> Orpheus, much versed in music,
> Son of Kalliope, was the first
>   to build the chelys.

> πρῶτος ποικιλόμουσος Ὀρ-
> φεὺς ⟨χέλ⟩υν ἐτέκνωσεν
> υἱὸς Καλλιόπα⟨ ς∪–

Timotheus' choice of the word *chelys* here (a virtually certain restoration of the text) represents a departure from the more traditional account according to which Hermes, not Orpheus, invented the tortoise-shell lyre.

The Chelys-Lyra as the Characteristic Instrument: Mythological Scenes

Although the chelys-lyra may often be interchangeable with other lyre-family instruments in mythological or legendary scenes, there are some scenes of these kinds in which the chelys-lyra seems to have been the principal lyre, the one most appropriate. When Apollo accompanies a wedding procession in which there is no quadriga—everyone on foot, for example—his instrument is the chelys-lyra. In two such scenes, Paris G 226 and London B 257, he is identified by the doe beside him. In two others he is not specifically identified: on a lebes gamikos, Athens 1172, the lyre player in the procession on the bowl is probably Apollo, for he appears again on the stand with a doe (and in the presence of Hermes); and on a kylix (cup), Berlin F 2530, he is not identified in the wedding scene but appears in a quadriga on the reverse, where Artemis carries his kithara. All four of these wedding scenes may represent the wedding of Peleus and Thetis.

The largest category of mythological scenes in which the chelys-lyra is the standard, appropriate instrument consists of representations of the Muses, who, while they may play the barbitos (chap. 5) and the phorminx ("cradle kithara," chap. 6) as well as the auloi, krotala, and *syrinx* (panpipes), are most frequently portrayed playing the chelys-lyra. Recognizable portrayals of the Muses occur only on red-figured or white-ground vases during this time. Though the vases are of all types, among them there are three examples of the pyxis, a rarely found lidded cosmetic container, suggesting that the Muses were considered an especially suitable subject for the continuous painting around such a jar. When such paintings include Apollo (as many do), usually only one or two Muses are shown (though two or three more may be painted on the reverse or interior) and the lyre is in most cases played by Apollo or is being offered to him by a Muse.[24] Some vases on which Apollo plays the chelys-lyra include Muses who also play the chelys-lyra or other instruments such as the aulos or phorminx. On the pyxis Athens 1241, Apollo plays the chelys-lyra in the company of eight Muses, two of whom have auloi, one a phorminx, and one a chelys-lyra that she is tuning. The remaining four Muses do not carry instruments, but one of them has an open scroll, an object frequently seen in paintings of the Muses.[25] They are also often shown seated on, or standing near, rocks that indicate Mount Helicon in Boeotia, on whose summit stood a sanctuary of the Muses containing a temple with their statues.

In the painting on London E 271, figure 5, in which the figures are identified by inscriptions, the two Muses Terpsichore and Melousa are accompanied, not by Apollo, but by Mousaios, a mythical singer similar to Orpheus and like Orpheus called by Plato a descendant of Selene and the Muses (*R.* 364e).[26] Mousaios is represented here as a young man in a himation wearing a laurel wreath, leaning on a laurel staff, and carrying a chelys-lyra in his left hand. If his name were not inscribed on the vase we would assume that this was Apollo, and it may be that on some of the other vases without inscription the male figure shown is sometimes intended to represent Mousaios rather than Apollo.

On several other vases still another mythological musician appears with the Muses: Thamyras, who, victorious in the Delphic contests, boasted he could win a contest even if the Muses opposed him. For his presumption they blinded the Thracian singer and made him forget his skill; on Oxford hydria 530 the "Thamyras kithara" falls from his hands as he sits blinded on the rocks, while his mother (who has tattooing on her arms, Thracian fashion) stands before him tearing her hair and a Muse with a chelys-lyra looks on. Ferrara T.127 depicts Thamyras' contest with the Muses in their sanctuary (the scene includes a tree and an altar with nine *xoana*, small, roughly carved statues of the Muses, above it). Apollo is present, standing by his tripod, to serve as judge; and the Muses, standing or sitting on the rocks with lyres, auloi, or a scroll in their hands, listen while Thamyras plays the kithara.[27]

The only male accompanying the six Muses who appear on Boston pyxis 98.887, partly illustrated in figure 6, is a cowherd who has been said by some to represent the poet Hesiod, though others say he is the poet Archilochos.[28] The Muses themselves are identified here mainly by the variety of instruments they play: chelys-lyra, two phorminxes, auloi, and syrinx. There are a few small stylized plants in the foreground and what appears to be a tree, but no altar, statues, rocks, or inscriptions to give us their names. Three of the five Muses on Paris P.P. 308, on the other hand, are named in inscriptions (Terpsichore, Kalliope, and Thalia), so that despite the fact that there are only two instruments in the painting, chelys-lyra and barbitos, and no other identifying details, they can still be recognized. It seems likely that many similar vase paintings showing groups of women playing instruments, without details such as inscriptions, rocks, or an altar and without any male figures to aid in the identification, may also have been intended to represent Muses. The ten women in Bologna 271, all of them playing instruments, are surely Muses (even if they are one more than is customary), and the three women on London E 461 must also be, for the aulos player among them sits on a rock (the chelys-lyra hangs in the background over her head).[29]

Another large category of myth-illustration in which the chelys-lyra appears consists of scenes in which Eos, winged goddess of dawn, pursues Tithonos or Kephalos (the two are difficult to distinguish), handsome youths whom the amorous goddess desired (fig. 7). The youth struggles or tries to elude her grasp; to be abducted by Eos is perhaps a metaphor for a sudden death, and the fact that Eos is sometimes much larger than Tithonos/Kephalos supports this supposition. Regardless of his degree of maturity, the youth commonly carries a chelys-lyra, not so much to label him as young (a schoolboy), perhaps, as to indicate that his abductor has surprised him in the midst of daily activities.[30]

In most of these paintings (which appear on red-figured vases of all shapes) Eos pursues the youth but has not yet caught him. In some, she grasps his arm, and on Madrid 11158 a very large Eos bears the youth away with her. There is sometimes a second, and in one case a third, youth included in the scene; we may assume that the pursued youth is then Tithonos, son of Laomedon, king of Troy, the second youth his brother Priam, and the third perhaps their companion Dardanos, for the figures on one vase, skyphos Paris Cab. Med. 846, are so identified by inscriptions.[31] On still another vase, Vienna 3700, there is a bearded man with a scepter between Eos and the two youths who is probably King Laomedon. He holds his right hand, palm out, toward the youths as though urging them to flee. The kylix is much damaged, but it can be seen that one of the youths carries a chelys-lyra.[32]

Because the sixth-century myth of Hermes' invention of the chelys-lyra, discussed in chapter 2, is already familiar, we are not surprised to find that there are a few late sixth- and early fifth-century Athenian vases that show us the instrument in Hermes' hands. An early red-figured kylix, London E 815, depicts Hermes as a bearded man wearing a cap and short tunic. He is sitting on a rock playing the chelys-lyra, and to his right are three bulls (the story of Hermes' theft of Apollo's cattle is told in the Archaic-period *Hymn to Hermes,* discussed in chap. 2). A black-figured amphora, Tarquinia 640, shows us Hermes at an altar with Athena and another woman, probably a goddess. Here we see his customary costume complete: he is a bearded man in a hat (a *pilos* with a pointed crown) and short cloak who is wearing winged boots and carrying his distinctive staff, the caduceus. In this painting he holds both lyre and caduceus in his left arm, while his right hand is extended over the altar as though to drop something on it. The interior of a red-figured cup by Makron from the early fifth century, London E 58, contains a painting of Hermes running with the chelys-lyra and looking back over his shoulder.

In the most interesting scene of this sort, on a black-figured amphora of Panathenaic shape, London B 167, ca. 510–500 B.C. (fig. 8), Hermes actually plays the lyre while leading a sacrificial procession that includes Heracles (dressed in his lion skin) and Iolaos.[33] Hermes sings as he walks along playing the chelys-lyra with a goat at his side. Behind him Heracles, playing the aulos, walks beside a bull (?), while Iolaos brings

up the rear. We see Hermes here in his role as herald and guide, escorting the hero Heracles.

The story of the invention of the lyra by Hermes and its subsequent transference to Apollo as compensation for the stolen cattle perhaps reflects the instrument's educational role (discussed below). Both gods are associated with the training and development of young men, as is suggested by such elements as the presence of herms (phallic pillars topped by a bust of Hermes) in gymnasia and by the patronage of Apollo at the athletic and cultural contests held at the pan-Hellenic Pythian Games at Delphi. In any case, Apollo's appropriation of Hermes' connections with music and the resulting emphasis instead on Hermes' role as *psychopompus,* or escorter of the souls of the dead, are aptly summarized in these words (spoken by Hermes) in a fragment from a tragedy:

> For Night bore me not to be master of the lyre
> Nor prophet, nor healer, but to be the leader
>   For the souls of the dead.[34]

> οὐ γάρ με Νὺξ ἔτικτε δεσπότην λύρας,
> οὐ μάντιν οὐδ' ἰατρόν, ἀλλὰ †θνητὸν ἅμα†
> ψυχαῖς

From the second half of the fifth century we have two representations of the Dioscuri, Castor and Pollux (Polydeukes), as players of the chelys-lyra. A Locrian relief from mid-century, London 1225, is a fragment of a scene of two horsemen, the one in the foreground holding the lyre at his side in his left hand as he rides. The identification of these horsemen as Castor and Pollux is confirmed by a later vase painting, Plovdiv 298 (chap. 3, fig. 7), where we see a theoxenia, a feast honoring the Dioscuri. A *lectisternium* has been provided for them: a table with cakes and drink, with incense burners at either end, and behind it a couch with pillows and a lyre at each end, waiting for the touch of the honored guests. Beyond columns on each side, one of the Dioscuri approaches on the left, one on the right, each leading his horse.

As in the Archaic period, there are a number of representations of the Judgment of Paris, in which Hermes leads Hera, Athena, and Aphrodite before the Trojan shepherd-prince who must judge which of them is most beautiful. This scene, found mostly on red-figured vases of various sorts, is well represented in our Classical period sample: there are nine vases portraying Paris with the chelys-lyra in his hand, a sign of his interrupted pastoral but gentlemanly music making.[35] Paris, in Classical as well as Archaic versions of this scene, is usually seated on a rock indicating Mount Ida, where he lived as a shepherd; but on Berlin Antikenmuseum 2536 (fig. 9) we see him in princely surroundings: seated in a small temple, the lyre in his left hand, a scepter in his right (he is also given a scepter in the painting on Berlin 4043).

In some paintings only Athena, of the three goddesses, is recognizable, dressed as she is in helmet and aegis. Hera carries a scepter on London E 178, on Berlin Antikenmuseum 2536 and 4043 (see above), and on London E 445; on the latter two she also wears the high, rounded crown called a polos (either Artemis or Hera may wear the stephanos, or rayed crown, as does Hera on Berlin Antikenmuseum 2536).[36] On Berlin 2291 Aphrodite is surrounded by four small figures of Eros who fly about her, and on Berlin 2536 she holds an Eros in her hand. This painting makes clear the various "bribes" the goddesses offer: Aphrodite, holding out the figure of Eros, offers him love; Athena, holding out her helmet, offers him success as a warrior; and Hera, holding out a small figure of a lion, offers him kingship.

The other legendary mortal already (chap. 2) associated with the chelys-lyra, Theseus, often seen in Attic red-figured vase painting, seems very seldom to have appeared with the lyre in these paintings. A fragment from the second half of the fifth century, Athens Agora P 18279, shows a man holding a lyre, and the arm and sword hilt of another man, presumably Theseus—the arrangement is the same as that seen in late Archaic paintings of Theseus killing the Minotaur while someone standing by holds his instrument. On calyx krater Syracuse 17427, ca. 420 B.C., he is crowned with a wreath by Athena as Poseidon watches—and then we see him again, or one of his companions, just to the right, lyre in hand, about to board ship, presumably setting out on the Cretan adventure. But no other scenes in the present sample return to the Archaic themes of Theseus with the lyre.

From the literary sources the only evidence we have for Theseus' association with the chelys-lyra is a late writer on astronomy, Hyginus (whose dates are wholly uncertain); he quotes a certain Anakreon—perhaps not the fifth-century poet but some later man of the same name—as saying that the constellation Lyra represents the lyre of Theseus, whose own constellation is placed nearby.[37] Since other late writers generally refer to this group of stars as either Lyra or Chelys, we can assume that the Greeks thought of the constellation (still known today as Lyra) as representing the tortoise-shell lyre. But whether the constellation was originally connected with Theseus cannot be determined, since the earliest extant reference to it (by Demokritos, in the mid-fifth century) mentions only that the rising of these stars at dawn is a harbinger of stormy weather.[38]

Before we turn to scenes of mortal life in which the chelys-lyra figures, there is one further lyre-playing mythological character who must be mentioned: Eros, god of love and symbol of passion and its power in human life (fig. 10). Eros can often be seen in vase paintings attending the goddess Aphrodite or looking on during wedding preparations or erotic encounters. Here we are concerned only with those paintings in which Eros himself appears as a player of the chelys-lyra. We will see him again in chapter 5 as a player of the long-armed lyre with a chelys-soundbox, the barbitos.

Although Eros appears in a considerable number of scenes in which someone else plays the chelys-lyra, it is not uncommon for him to play it himself. On several lekythoi, an *astragalos* (knucklebone-shaped ceramic object), and a scarab, a flying Eros appears alone, with the chelys-lyra and perhaps a phiale or fillet.[39] On Geneva 14986 a nude, winged Eros flies, lyre in hand, toward a woman in a decorated chiton, probably a Muse, who sits on a rock.[40] Munich 2413 offers two mythological scenes: an Eros with a lyre watching as Ge hands up the baby Erichthonios out of the ground to Athena, and on the reverse an Eros playing in the presence of Zeus. (On each side there is a second Eros as well; multiple Eros figures are quite common in Greek art.)

The Chelys-Lyra as the Characteristic Instrument: Scenes of Mortal Life

Weddings, Symposia, and Komoi. The figure of Eros is also not uncommon in scenes that otherwise are simple portrayals of human life, especially those that seem to show a bride and her attendants. A seated woman playing the barbitos (a swan or goose before her) on Syracuse 36330 (fig. 11), for example, is accompanied by two more women and a winged Eros; both Eros and a woman hold the chelys-lyra. On London E 191, the seated woman, who wears a stephanos on her head and has her feet on a footstool, is playing the aulos; on her left a young man leans forward on his staff, laying his hand on her shoulder; and on her right an Eros, holding a chelys-lyra, flies toward the couple, thus bringing to their marriage, we may presume, both harmony and desire.

The *symposium*, or drinking-party scene, is one in which the guests (usually all men) recline on couches and entertain themselves in a variety of ways, including drinking, singing, playing *kottabos* (flipping the dregs in the cup at a target), and playing the chelys-lyra or listening to the music played on it by an entertainer (the guests and entertainers sometimes also play the barbitos, aulos, or krotala). This is one of the largest categories of scenes from mortal life in which the chelys-lyra appears.[41] In a number of paintings of *symposia,* the chelys-lyra is not played but hangs on the wall behind the guests, both indicating a pastime available to the company and serving as a symbol of the pleasures of conviviality; similar scenes are known from the Archaic period (chap. 2).

The chelys-lyra seems seldom to be played by an attendant, and in the two examples now at hand, New York 07.286.47 and Canterbury, N.Z., Logie Coll. CML 6-AR 430, the attendant is a youth, whereas an attendant who plays the aulos is usually a woman (the "flute-girl" mentioned in so many translations, though the aulos is a reed pipe somewhat like an oboe). It is more common for a guest to have the lyre, although he is hardly ever actually playing it; figure 12 is a rare example in which the guest holds the lyre roughly in playing position—the guest is often simply holding the lyre, receiving it from a boy, or gesticulating with it.[42] The guests who hold the chelys-lyra may be of any age, mere boys, young men, bearded men, or white-haired elders. The same scene in which a guest holds the lyre may include a female aulos player, as on San Simeon 5614. In figure 12 the bearded man on the left has two *kylikes* (drinking cups), one held upside down. Both men wear festive wreaths and the customary garb for symposia, the mantle draped around the lower body and legs.

On one of the vases in this group, Würzburg H 5169, the scene is framed by sphinxes who face out on either end of the symposium scene, and on another, New York 07.286.47, there is a woman seated at either side of the scene, one with a branch, one with a wreath. This device of figures, usually seated women, that frame the scene, is also found among vases of another, special category not considered in the discussion above: black-figured lekythoi on which the central figure reclines on a couch (fig. 13).

Since the painting on these small vases (often used for grave offerings) is of very poor quality, it is not possible to say with great assurance what the meaning of the scene is; the best that can be done is to describe it, with its variations, and add a few conjectures as to what may have been intended. In the version most often seen (on eighteen vases), a young (beardless) man reclines on the right, and the chelys-lyra player stands or sits at his left. On either side of this central group is a figure seated on a *diphros* (stool), hair done up in a knot high on the back of his head. The faces of these two, and of the lyre player, are sometimes white, indicating that they are women; many vases, however, do not use added white, and it cannot be said

for certain that women are always intended. Vines frequently fill in the background of the scene, and there sometimes appears to be a table in front of the couch. The reclining figure may simply represent a guest at a symposium; but it seems more likely that he is Dionysos (in which case the chelys-lyra is probably once more a generic symbol for the kithara); or he may represent a deceased person with mourners seated around him (see below for a discussion of the lyre in this context).[43]

Another group of lekythoi show a *bearded* man reclining on a couch, the lyre player seated to his left, figures on ithyphallic mules to either side framing the scene, and vines trailing in the background.[44] Here the identification is more secure: the comic effect of the mules, the presence of vine branches, and the fact that the central figure is bearded, together allow us to say that this is Dionysos—and also, that if this scene were painted on a larger, more elegant vase, the instrument represented would likely be the kithara.

In addition to the sedate symposia there are scenes of a rowdier sort—komos scenes depicting more energetic revelers, who dance and drink to the music of chelys-lyra, barbitos, aulos, and krotala. (The barbitos is closely associated with such events; see chap. 5.) The komasts are generally nude or wearing only a cloak over the shoulders, and they wear wreaths of ivy or grape leaves. The participants include both young men and older, bearded men. They carry wine cups and other drinking vessels and are most frequently seen walking along with a chelys-lyra and sometimes an aulos, as in figure 14 (the lyre carried by the bearded man is not visible), apparently on their way to or from the festivities, sometimes playing and perhaps singing as they go, and in some paintings accompanied by a man carrying a torch.[45]

Other vases show komasts at a party, dancing, drinking, or playing instruments; in a few paintings we can see all of these taking place at once, as in figure 15, where the bearded dancer may be performing the *sikinnis,* a kind of satyr dance (see chap. 5). On New York cup 96.18.143 (interior) the bearded chelys-lyra player approaches the large krater in which the wine is mixed with water, and Copenhagen 3880 shows us the results of overindulgence (perhaps in wine not mixed enough): the lyre hangs on the wall while a bearded man vomits into a basin; a nude boy wearing a wreath holds his head.

Paintings in which men are dancing are usually regarded as komos scenes, whether or not they contain any wine vessels or evidence of inebriation. Usually, however, where there are no wine cups or jars the dancer is a boy or beardless young man dancing to the sound of the chelys-lyra played by another youth. Both dancer and accompanist are nude or wear only a short cloak or himation tossed carelessly over the shoulders. The gestures of the dancers are so varied as to defy categorization, and it seems quite possible that dances other than the sikinnis are depicted.

One of the scenes reveals an informal procession of female aulos player, dancer, and lyre player (Cambridge Fitz. GR 1.1950); the white flowers tucked in their headbands may indicate that it is a special occasion, perhaps a party held during a festival. Female dancers are occasionally depicted by the Athenian artists, but they perform mainly in the company of other women and are sedately dressed, though young girls wear short chitons or other costumes that leave their legs bare.[46] The (male?) lyre player on a wedding vase (nuptial *lebes*), Mykonos 970, accompanies a circle dance of fifteen women dressed in elaborate chitons. Florence 4014 (fig. 16) shows a really surprising scene: a young girl dressed as a warrior, with shield, spear, and helmet, dancing a war dance (the pyrrhic) while a woman similarly dressed stands by. A female aulos player accompanies her, while one woman with a phorminx and another with a chelys-lyra stand by; the watchers include a man and several women (this scene is discussed further in chap. 6).

Lyres and Schoolboys.. Although much of the information in Greek literature about the use of lyres in connection with the musical training of schoolboys comes from the fourth-century works of Plato and Aristotle, fifth-century sources, as well as later biographical reports about fifth-century figures, confirm the impression given by the vase paintings that instruction in lyre playing formed a basic part of Athenian elementary education, in order that the pupil might follow the Athenian custom of singing poetry to musical accompaniment.[47] Aristophanes, for example, in making fun of the greedy demagogue Kleon, tells us that when Kleon was a schoolboy he refused to tune his lyra in any manner but one—the Dorian (with a pun on *doron,* "gift," that is, "bribe"). So persistent was his annoying habit that the lyre instructor, the kitharistes, finally had him evicted from the house, or so Aristophanes claims.[48]

The sort of competence that the schoolboy was expected to acquire from his musical training is revealed in another of Aristophanes' comedies, the *Clouds,* whose chief subject is the question of how the young should be educated. The protagonist, Strepsiades, recounts an argument with his rebellious son, whom he had asked to sing to provide dinner entertainment. The request was for an old song of Simonides ("The

Ram") or something from Aeschylus, either one to be accompanied on the lyre—a request with which the son refuses to comply because he despises Simonides and Aeschylus and thinks that the whole custom of singing at dinner parties is old-fashioned. At any rate, the exchange suggests that the older generation at the end of the fifth century expected an educated person to be able to perform to the chelys-lyra, upon demand, songs from among the works of the older lyric and tragic poets. Similar expectations are indicated in a fragment from a comedy by one of Aristophanes' contemporaries, Eupolis, who describes a performance by Socrates at a party—presumably in connection with Socrates' feat of learning to play the lyra in his old age. He says that Socrates sang to lyre accompaniment a "recital piece" from Stesichoros, one of the old lyric poets of the preceding century.[49]

Later biographers of the great fifth-century political leaders Themistocles and Pericles also reveal the same expectation of basic musical competence among the educated class. According to Plutarch, one of the grounds on which Themistocles' opponents attacked him was his lack of just this sort of competence:

> Later, when [Themistocles] was jeered at in liberal and refined discourses carried on by those who thought they were educated, he was forced to defend himself vulgarly by saying that he did not know how to tune a lyra . . . , but could only, if he took a small and inglorious city, make it glorious and great.[50]

> ὅθεν ὕστερον ἐν ταῖς ἐλευθερίοις καὶ ἀστείαις λεγομέναις διατριβαῖς ὑπὸ τῶν πεπαιδεῦσθαι δοκούντων χλευαζόμενος, ἠναγκάζετο φορτικώτερον ἀμύνεσθαι, λέγων ὅτι λύραν μὲν ἁρμόσασθαι . . . οὐκ ἐπίσταιτο, πόλιν δὲ μικρὰν καὶ ἄδοξον παραλαβὼν ἔνδοξον καὶ μεγάλην ἀπεργάσασθαι.

Pericles, on the other hand, seems to have enjoyed a fine musical education under the instruction of Damon, an influential music theorist of whom Plato later spoke highly.[51] According to Plutarch, however, Damon did not confine his advice to matters of music, and as a result of his political machinations was eventually ostracized because he failed to hide his true intentions under the cover of his lyre.

The chelys-lyra is often part of school scenes and scenes in the gymnasium or palaestra as they are depicted on the vase paintings.[52] Some half dozen of the examples at hand depict actual music lessons of various sorts; and thirty-six vases show youths practicing, playing for men in the schoolroom or gymnasium, or holding the chelys-lyra while talking with men or other youths in similar places. The chelys-lyra seems especially associated with youths and young men, no doubt because it was the chief instrument they were taught to play and the one on which they were expected to demonstrate their skill.

The private lesson on the chelys-lyra, with bearded teacher on the left facing a youth on the right, both seated and holding lyres, can be seen on Schwerin KG 708 (fig. 17) and Oxford 1914.734. Both teacher and pupil are identified on the Schwerin vase (fig. 17): the inscription over the head of the bearded man names him Linos, who according to Apollodorus (2.63) was the music teacher of Heracles killed by his pupil with a blow from a lyre (the event is depicted on stamnos Boston 66.206—but Linos holds the chelys-lyra, and Heracles attacks him with a footstool). Linos is more elaborately dressed than teachers in such scenes usually are—he wears a pleated chiton, as well as a mantle draped around his legs. The student in figure 17 is Iphicles, Heracles' twin brother, who wears the usual mantle draped around his lower body. The lyre in the field between the two figures is the phorminx (the so-called cradle kithara: see chap. 6).

On Berlin kylix 2285 we see the lyre lesson taking place on the left side of the painting while a student recites an epic poem to another instructor (who holds a scroll with readable words) on the right.[53] As in figure 17, the lyre teacher sits on the left, his student on the right. Both wear mantles draped around their lower bodies and legs, both are seated on stools, facing each other, and both play lyres. In other paintings, the lyre teacher has more than one pupil: on Munich 2421 the bearded teacher Smikythos, who sits on a *klismos* (chair with back) tuning his instrument, has two students, Euthymides and Tlempolemos, on his left, though only one of them has a lyre. There are four students in the scene on London E 172, but again only the boy sitting opposite him is playing the chelys-lyra, although another boy standing behind the instructor holds one. The teacher evidently instructed only one student at a time, even though others might be present to hear what was said and played.[54]

Other paintings are more difficult to identify as music lessons or school scenes. On pelike Eleusis 626 both young man and bearded man have lyres, but the young man stands before the older one. On other vases only the seated, bearded man holds a chelys-lyra; the youth standing before him has none.[55] The seated man without a lyre on Adria B 254 appears to be a teacher sending away a student whose lesson was ill-prepared—he holds up his hand palm out toward the boy who looks back rather angrily as he hastens away, lyre in hand.

The two standing youths who hold out their lyres toward a seated bearded man without an instrument, Florence PD 272, appear to be offering them to, or asking approval of them from, their instructor (the scene on the reverse is similar, though the man stands). The standing man who hands the chelys-lyra to a boy sitting on a diphros, Athens 12462, also seems to be a teacher; but the bearded men who hold out a lyre to the boy on New York 41.162.86 and on Athens 1176 may not be; like the bearded man who stands to one side in many other scenes, they may be only watchful paidogogoi, keeping an eye on their charges.

The boys appear alone, or with only the paidogogos, in a small group of paintings in which one or more of them holds a bookroll, or scroll. A seated player of the chelys-lyra on Berlin 2549 looks up at two other boys, both with scrolls, one of whom holds a scroll open. Two other vases contain similar scenes.[56]

The "school" paintings often show one or more objects "in the field," that is, hanging on the wall behind the main figures: lyres, writing tablets, aulos bags, cups, baskets, and other bags and unidentified objects. Lyres and writing tablets appear frequently; the latter help to clarify the location of the scene, as does the bundle of writing tablets on New York 41.162.86 (see above), or on Vienna 1788, where a youth sits alone with his chelys-lyra.[57] But Warsaw 198512, on which a chelys-lyra is shown on the wall, has two young men watching a cockfight and urging on their birds, suggesting that a lyre alone in the background is not a very sure indicator of location.

The background on a number of vases includes items such as strigils, sponges, sandals, or small oil flasks (*aryballoi*), articles one might expect to see on the wall pegs at the baths or exercise ground. Usually these scenes present youths in conversation, one or two of them holding lyres but not playing.[58] The young man who sits alone on a cushioned chair with a chelys-lyra in his hand on Florence 3911 also has near him, on the wall, a sponge, strigil, and aryballos; and on his right is a Doric column. Columns, Doric and Ionic, appear on several other vases on which youths play the chelys-lyra, thereby indicating the interior of a building, perhaps the palaestra or some other part of the gymnasium or school.[59]

Men and youths together in the palaestra (sponges and strigils often on the wall) are seen playing or carrying the chelys-lyra on a number of vases, mainly kylikes. The youths are usually the lyre players, seated in most instances, with bearded men who may be taken to be suitors, that is, erasts, standing before them, often leaning on a knobby staff, as in figure 18. In this painting and several others, a man offers a rabbit as a love gift to a youth, and two scenes show a youth making a gesture of refusal of the gift or the unwanted attention.[60] Scenes of this kind may sometimes have included the figure of Eros: the fragments of kylix Florence 4219 include an Eros, a bearded man, and two youths, one with the chelys-lyra.[61] A bearded man chases a youth who raises his lyre over his head to strike at his pursuer on Cambridge Fitz. 37.26; and a fragment of a kylix, Adria Bc 47, shows a bearded man reaching out to stay a fleeing youth who holds a chelys-lyra.

The winged figure of Victory, Nike, approaches a boy or young man to symbolize his success in playing the chelys-lyra at a contest in about a dozen paintings, and appears alone, flying with lyre in hand, in another half dozen. In scenes with the contest winner, Nike may place a wreath or a fillet on his head, or hold out a lyre to him, or she may simply hold out her arms toward him in a gesture of acclaim, as in figure 19, where the boy stands on a small platform holding the chelys-lyra.[62] Sometimes the youth is in the presence of two Nike figures, or perhaps a Nike and a bearded man with a staff, evidently a judge; on Paris G 552bis the judge sits to the right of the former's podium dressed in a bordered mantle and holding a long staff.[63]

A different aspect of the contest seems to be revealed on Oxford 1916.13 (fig. 20). Here the youthful lyre player is surrounded by two women and another boy; the boy holds out a long bag to him and one woman holds out the chelys-lyra; but the other woman, who carries a pitcher, offers him a shallow bowl. Perhaps he is to make a libation before or after taking part in a contest (other vases show us a libation bowl in the hand of a Nike who also carries a lyre).[64] Just as in figure 19, there is a writing case or set of tablets hanging on the wall, probably to identify the youth as a schoolboy.

In figure 19 an altar on the left suggests that the contest takes place during a religious festival.[65] Youths holding a chelys-lyra stand or sit before an altar in a half dozen other paintings, too; but in these there is no Nike present, and we cannot be sure that these have any connection with contests. Two youths, one with the lyre, stand on either side of an altar on which a fire is burning on Toronto 365; on a hydria at Mykonos a woman with a torch stands to the left of the altar with the youthful lyre player, while a bearded man in chiton and himation carrying a long staff stands to the right of it. There are in addition four kylikes on which a single youth with chelys-lyra stands or sits next to an altar.[66]

The activities of young boys portrayed on *choes* (fat little pitchers used during the festival of Anthesteria) include lyre playing: we see a boy with a chelys-lyra approaching a large tripod on Athens 12961, and another seated on a chair playing for his dog on Athens 10452, where an aulos case can be seen hanging on the wall. Perhaps in imitation of their elders, three young boys, all crowned with wreaths and nude except for himatia over their shoulders, form a procession on Copenhagen 5377, one carrying a pitcher and a torch, one playing the chelys-lyra, and one the aulos.[67]

The chelys-lyra, on several white-ground lekythoi (painted in outline with some color), is found in the hands of a young man who stands or sits by a tombstone, as in figure 21; and on other similar white-ground lekythoi the lyre hangs in the field near the stele, again with a young man standing or sitting nearby. In most of these scenes the young man appears to represent the deceased. The objects around him and on or near the stele are of two kinds: grave offerings such as food, drink, oil, or fillets, and objects that symbolize the deceased by telling something of who he was—a shield, for example, or a lyre or a plaque showing a boxing match (all of these on Boston lekythos 01.8080). The tomb is that of a young man in all these instances; and the chelys-lyra, in this context, at least when it merely hangs in the field or lies near the stele, seems to be simply the suitable symbol for a well-educated young man.

The chelys-lyra has other meanings associated with death, however. If when we see the deceased portrayed playing the lyre, on a vase such as Athens 1950, we regard it also as a symbol of the pleasantness of Elysium and of the absence of worldly concerns, we are better able to understand the way in which sirens or harpies (birds with the head and arms of women) are associated with death. These mythical creatures who lured sailors to their death on the rocks with their singing, but whom the clever Odysseus was able to evade (his episode with the sirens is shown on Athens 1130), also appear playing the chelys-lyra on a number of lekythoi, mostly black-figured, and a few other objects.[68] Perhaps the sirens in the myth lured sailors to them by singing of the happiness (symbolized by the lyre) of those in Elysium and of their release from sorrow.

Women as Lyre Players.. Mortal women as players of the chelys-lyra have scarcely been mentioned thus far except in connection with female dancers. But it is quite evident that women did often play the lyre, though the Athenian artists did not choose to portray their pursuits nearly so frequently as those of men. It is an interesting fact that women—Muses, maenads, and mortals—are rarely portrayed as players of stringed instruments by artists using the black-figured style except perhaps in paintings on lekythoi, which, as we have seen, are not well understood. The less conservative red-figured artists, however, have left a variety of scenes in which the chelys-lyra appears in the hands of a woman. Perhaps the most interesting of these is the hydria on which the poet Sappho (identified by inscription) sits reading a scroll surrounded by three other women, one of whom holds out a lyre near her, clearly associating it with the poet (fig. 22). There is a circular fillet or wreath on the wall above her head, and the woman behind her holds her hand above Sappho's head, perhaps in a gesture of acclaim.[69] Some letters on the scroll are legible; the first word may be *theoi* ("gods").

Another group of hydriai (water jars apparently used in wedding ceremonies), to which a nuptial lebes may be added, show scenes in a bride's chambers. A common feature of these scenes is the inclusion of Eros represented as a winged youth; on Brunswick 219 another of Aphrodite's winged attendants, Himeros, who is also present (and named), ties the bride's sandal.[70] The bride is seated in the center, often with the lyre; and Eros, in most cases, flies toward her with a wreath.[71] Some of the other women present carry musical instruments (auloi, barbitoi, chelys-lyrai) or boxes (chap. 5, fig. 18). On the far right on the nuptial lebes, Athens 1171, we find a female figure with wings, perhaps the dawn goddess Eos, who also appears in a mythological wedding scene on Boston amphora 03.821.[72] Some of the furniture of the room (chest, stools) is included on London 1921.7-10.2 (chap. 5, fig. 11), and as on Brunswick 219, the scene includes a Doric column.

Several other hydriai, *pyxides,* and one or two other vases have paintings that do not appear to be bridal scenes: small groups of women playing the chelys-lyra and the barbitos or auloi. On these vases there is no Eros, though he is present in other scenes of women with the barbitos (see chap. 5); the central seated figure, if there is one, may play the auloi or barbitos. The fact that there is more than one instrument in these scenes leads to speculation that the women may be intended to be Muses. On the other hand, those without instruments may be engaged in ordinary activities such as looking in a mirror (Chicago pyxis 92.126; Athens 655) and there are no rocks or trees to identify the sanctuary of the Muses; these are clearly indoor scenes, with objects hanging on the wall. As in all the scenes we have considered, the women are dressed very sedately, in long chitons or *peploi* (robes), usually with mantles, sometimes with earrings and *sakkoi* (cloth hair coverings).

On several small vases a female lyre player appears alone, seated on a klismos or standing, but in most cases actually playing the instrument. On the wall behind there may be an *alabastron* (perfume flask); on the wall behind the seated performer on New York 06.11.29 is an aulos bag, and a bird sits at her feet. Other small vases show us two female musicians, one with chelys-lyra and one with phorminx or aulos (fig. 23). On Athens 19503 (unpublished choe) the second woman appears to have a syrinx.[73]

Miscellaneous Scenes. A number of paintings and other representations of the chelys-lyra have not been included in the discussion above, either because the scene itself is damaged or unclear or (much more frequently) because it does not contain enough details to clarify its meaning. The latter is the case, for example, with a pair of scarabs on which is carved the figure of a running youth holding a chelys-lyra and, on one stone, a flower (on the other he holds a cock).[74] But on about a dozen black-figured lekythoi, it is the scene itself (a seated lyre player between two listeners) that is unclear: the silhouette technique does not even allow us to determine whether the figures are men or women, except that in a few cases one or both of the listeners have white faces, indicating that they are women.[75]

The paintings on over a dozen red-figured vases (amphorae, several kylikes, a bell krater, and a pelike) consist of variations on the theme of two standing men (usually two young men, but occasionally an older man and a younger one), one of them holding out the lyre to the other or simply holding the lyre while conversing.[76] On several other vases the player is seated and a listener is standing by, perhaps leaning on a staff. These scenes lack sufficient details to allow us to judge who these men might be, or where; this is also true of another dozen red-figured vases (kylikes, kraters, and a stamnos) on which a man or boy holding a chelys-lyra (or extending it to another man) stands with two (in one case, three) other men. Nearly all the figures are young men without beards, the one with the lyre usually the center of the group. Although there may be objects hanging in the background (an aulos case or other bag) they are not enough to make clear the meaning of the scene.

A single youth stands or sits playing or holding a chelys-lyra on some fourteen kylikes and lekythoi, nearly all red-figured.[77] A small group of cups (and a pelike) show a lyre player walking along, alone or following a companion. The youth on Athens Nat. Mus., Akr. 311 has a basket hanging from the arm of his lyre (for similar scenes see chap. 5).[78]

The Chelys-Lyra with Other Instruments

Only about one-fifth of the representations of the chelys-lyra include a second lyre, another instrument of the lyre family, or any other kind of musical instrument; and few scenes actually show any two or more instruments played simultaneously. The aulos, as we might expect, is the most common companion of the chelys, found with it in both mythological scenes (Apollo and the Muses; Apollo and Marsyas; Dionysos and satyrs; Odysseus and the sirens; Hermes leading Heracles, fig. 8; and a procession with satyrs and centaurs) and portrayals of human situations (banquets; groups made up of women, boys, men, or combinations of these; dance scenes; informal processions; and a singing lesson, Cambridge, Fitzwilliam GR 8.1955, in which the instructor plays the aulos—the lyre, however, hangs on the wall between teacher and pupil). Procession scenes, such as the one in which Hermes leads Heracles and Iolaos (fig. 8), appear to be the most likely to show aulos and chelys-lyra actually played simultaneously; but even this most common pair of instruments are seldom seen in joint music making.[79]

Two or more chelys-lyrai can be seen in a smaller group of paintings, most of them school scenes or other representations of youths alone, with women, or with men. There are also banquet or symposium scenes with two lyres; a pair of harpies, each with a chelys-lyra; and an Apollo with two Muses, each of whom holds a lyre.

The barbitos is companion to the chelys-lyra in a dozen paintings, half of them also including auloi and most of them showing groups of women. In some cases the women represent Muses (as on Paris P. Palais 308 [chap. 5, fig. 16]), but in others they do not (on Brunswick 219, the women are named Euphemia, Kleodoxa, Kleodike, and Phanodike).[80] A woman dances and plays the krotala on Cambridge Fitzwilliam 4.1943: she is accompanied by a seated woman who plays the aulos; the other two women in the painting hold a barbitos and chelys-lyra but do not play. Lyra and barbitos also appear together in a symposium scene, Milan C 354 (the lyre is not played), and on Schwerin KG 707 in the hands of bearded men who are in the company of boys apparently at the palaestra (sponge and strigil hang on the wall); none of the instruments

(which include auloi) in the latter scene is being played.

The phorminx (see chap. 6) is present along with the chelys-lyra in over half a dozen paintings, most of them scenes of the Muses: with Apollo; with Mousaios (fig. 5, a painting that includes a harp); or with a cowherd thought to represent Hesiod or Archilochos (this painting, partly illustrated in fig. 6, includes aulos and syrinx, or panpipes—and a cow).[81] Florence 4014 (fig. 16, discussed above), on which a girl dances the phyrrhic, includes aulos, chelys-lyra, and phorminx. On Munich 2363, where a woman plays the phorminx for a dancing Eros, the lyre hangs above them on the wall. And on Oxford 1920.104 there are two women at home (mirror and pitcher hanging behind them), one seated holding a phorminx and one standing with a chelys-lyra.

The krotala (clappers; see chap. 5, fig. 13, figure on left) mentioned in passing above are seen as frequently as the phorminx and are also played by women, or at least female creatures—on Paris CA 74 there are three sirens on rocks who play auloi, lyre, and krotala. A woman plays the krotala while a siren plays the chelys-lyra on Corinth aryballos MP 116. Other vases include maenads playing krotala while another of their number, or a satyr, plays the chelys-lyra. Paris Mus. Rodin TC 232 offers an unusual scene: near an altar from which come leafy branches a woman with krotala dances, accompanied by a woman playing the chelys-lyra and a bearded man playing the auloi who must be Hermes—he wears Hermes' traditional costume with winged boots.

All the other instruments known to the Greeks—except those for signaling rather than music, the trumpet (salpinx) and horn—are also to be found on occasion with the chelys-lyra. The kithara is played at the feast for the Dioscuri on Plovdiv 298 (chap. 3, fig. 7), where a chelys-lyra for each of the heroes lies ready on each couch; a kithara played by a bearded god can be seen in a procession of three quadrigai on Paris F 232, in which a beardless Apollo with a chelys-lyra walks beside another chariot. The instrument we have called the "Thamyras kithara" (see chap. 6), which appears in several scenes in which that hero holds it in the presence of Muses who carry chelys-lyrai, must also be mentioned here, as well as the syrinx, held by a Muse on Boston pyxis 98.887, figure 6, but also played by a satyr accompanying a lyre-playing maenad on London B 353. Finally, there is the tympanon, or frame drum, held by a maenad in the presence of Dionysos while a second maenad holds a chelys-lyra (Nicosia C 430).

Performers and Costumes

Players of the chelys-lyra, as can be seen from the discussion above, may be boys or men of any age, from small children to white-haired elders. Young women—mainly Muses, maenads, Nikes, and mortal brides-to-be—are also portrayed as lyra players; but the fact that painters generally did not choose to portray small girls or elderly women does not, of course, prove that they were excluded from the art of lyre playing. The activities of women, which tended to be secluded from the view of the male population, were by and large overlooked by the artists.

There is no special costume for players of the chelys-lyra, as there is for players of the kithara. A female player, whether Muse or mortal, is always modestly dressed in the customary garb of Athenian women: a gown (chiton or *peplos*) and perhaps a mantle (himation or chlamys). The costume of the male chelys-lyra player in depictions of everyday life usually consists of himation only, wrapped about the chest and brought over the shoulder when the player is standing, or around the lower body and legs when the player is seated. Komasts (partygoers) may wear only a short cloak over their shoulders, or nothing at all. Contestants, on the other hand, may wear himatia, as does the youthful contestant shown in figure 20. Performers and their companions frequently wear wreaths, of laurel or perhaps olive; revelers sometimes wear flower wreaths. Players without wreaths often have red or purple fillets (bands of cloth) bound about their heads.

Mythological players generally appear in whatever costume is associated with them: Hermes wears a short tunic, cloak, hat, and winged boots; Apollo (at least when accompanying a quadriga and usually when receiving a libation) wears chiton, as well as himation, and (often) a laurel wreath; satyrs and Erotes are nude.[82] But as in the case of mortal men, the costumes of mythological figures seem to vary somewhat according to the formality of the occasion: when Heracles appears as a contestant playing the chelys-lyra on a podium with Hermes and Athena on either side, he wears his traditional lion skin over his head; but instead of his usual short tunic, the rest of his costume consists of long chiton and himation (Athens 635). When Apollo appears in "informal" situations (for example, among the Muses) he sometimes wears only laurel wreath and himation.[83]

Playing Techniques for the Chelys-Lyra

Whereas kithara players normally stand when they play their instruments, performers on the chelys-lyra

stand, sit, recline, or walk, as the circumstances require. The kithara player holds his instrument upright while playing (strings vertical), as a rule; but the chelys-lyra player, whose instrument is lighter and more maneuverable, may hold his instrument tipped out to a greater or lesser degree. In a majority of cases, particularly those in which the performer is standing or walking, the instrument is held with the arms tipped away from the player at about 45°, more or less. But especially in the case of seated players, the chelys is often held upright or tipped out only slightly, no more than 30°. In scenes in which the performer walks beside a quadriga (where the chelys-lyra is a substitute for the kithara, as stated above) the chelys is often held upright or only slightly tipped out, and figures such as sirens and flying Nikes or Erotes also tend to hold the instrument in this way. Walking or dancing revelers, on the other hand, as well as those reclining on couches at a party, are often shown holding the chelys at an angle of 60°–90° from the player's body, perhaps because this allows a surer or more comfortable grip on it. The angle does not appear to affect the technique with which the instrument is played.

The clear examples in which a chelys-lyra is actually being played usually show the same pose for the hands and arms that we found to be standard in representations of performing kitharists. When the right hand is in use (as it is in 111 items at hand) it holds a plektron, and in a large majority of cases (82) the hand is extended beyond the strings, strongly suggesting a just-completed outward sweep across the strings.[84] (The right hand is commonly well beyond the outer edge of the instrument, a position from which it would seem inefficient to begin an *inward* stroke.)[85]

The right hand with the plektron is held near the player's chest on only fourteen of our examples. In these, the point of the plektron is generally turned toward the player's chest, though the lyre player in the wedding scene on Berlin kylix 2530 holds the plektron point toward the strings, and several others are not clear. It appears that the more the instrument itself is tipped out, the higher the hand with the plektron is likely to be held when this pose is shown. Most of the paintings, particularly those in which the plektron tip is turned toward the player, strongly suggest a preparation for a sweep outward or downward across the strings (see fig. 24). Those that do not suggest this involve gestures that are for the most part clearly unrelated to playing.[86]

The observable positions of the left hand can be divided into two general categories: those which suggest that the player is damping the strings or producing hermonics, and those which suggest that the thumb and sometimes another finger are being used to pluck the strings.[87] The players whose left-hand position suggests lightly touching or damping the strings are mainly those whose fingers are straight or only slightly curved forward, usually somewhat separated, and on occasion tilted slightly from the wrist so that although the palm still faces the strings the fingers angle toward the outer arm of the instrument.[88] (This last might occur naturally in touching the outer strings, since the left-hand wrist, which must hold the sling taut, cannot move to the side.[89]) The possibility that the thumb, though held away from the palm, is used to pluck while the other fingers touch or damp the strings, cannot be ruled out; see figure 25.[90] This painting is of special interest because it is a back view of the lyre in which the artist has shown that the fingers of the left hand press against the strings: the fingertips are bent back.

There are about three dozen examples at hand to illustrate this pose that suggests damping, nearly half of them black-figured vases. One-third of the examples are dated before 500 B.C. and another third between 500 and 475 B.C.; nearly two-thirds of them are on vases of smaller or less carefully painted varieties. This is as we might expect: these players hold their left hands palm forward, with the fingers and thumb straight, a simple, easily stylized pose that was not difficult to represent.

Examples for the second category (left-hand positions that suggest plucking) are almost twice as numerous and rarely appear on black-figured vases or vases made before 500 B.C.; more than two-thirds of these are later than 475 B.C., and nearly one-third belong to the second half of the century; well over half of them are painted on the larger, more carefully decorated types of vases. In these examples the player bends his thumb across his palm or turns his hand to bring the thumb closer to the strings. Such poses require more detail, and it is not surprising that they are most frequently seen on larger vases in the later red-figured style, in which such detail is more easily executed. There is no reason to doubt, however, that both types of hand positions were in use throughout the period from about 525 to 400 B.C., for well-executed examples of each occur both early and late.

The point on the string touched by the fingertips (approximately one-third or one-fourth of the way along the sounding length of the string from the crossbar on those examples that can be measured) is one suitable for either damping the string (so that it no longer sounds) or touching it lightly so that harmonics will be produced. For example, a gentle touch at a point one-third of the way along the string would cause

it, when struck with the plektron, to vibrate softly at a pitch one octave and a fifth higher than the normal pitch of the string; a touch one-quarter of the way along its length would produce a sound two octaves higher. These soft sounds, along with the much louder sounds of strings allowed to vibrate at their normal pitches, would certainly have increased the range of effects the instrument could produce.

The points on the strings touched by these players would, however, be of no use for altering the pitch of the string by pressing hard against it to change its basic pitch. On an instrument of seven strings the "fixed" pitches of the tetrachords included, at least, would surely be represented, and there would be no need to raise the pitch of a string by more than a third. To raise the pitch by this amount, one would need to press hard against the string at some point closer to its upper end, and we do not see this in the vase paintings.

In order to pluck the strings, the player apparently rotated his wrist somewhat so that the palm of the hand was turned toward the outer arm of the instrument. There are only a handful of convincing examples that show the palm front, fingers straight, with the thumb bent over as though plucking (some of these suggest that the fingers are damping some of the other strings at the same time).[91] In the position portrayed in a large number of clear representations, the thumb is in front of the palm, and the other fingers are bent, some more than others, as in figure 24; the fact that the fingers angle toward the outer arm of the instrument reveals that the wrist is rotated, though the fingers also seem to damp the strings in some instances.[92]

In these examples, only the thumb is used in plucking, but in a small handful of cases (including some doubtful items), the thumb and index finger appear to be used together. In half of these, the left-hand fingers, instead of bending toward the outer instrument arm, turn slightly toward the player (that is, the palm is turned toward him rather than away): the best of these is figure 21; the thumb and index finger do not touch in this instance, nor in most of the others. Of the paintings showing thumb and index finger used to pluck while the palm is turned outward, the clearest is Florence 128, a small fragment on which two lyre players pluck in this manner (fig. 26).

When the lyre is being tuned, the player's left hand remains at the strings, often with the hand turned, thumb closest to the strings, sometimes with the fingers curved, as though testing the pitch by plucking. In figure 27, both thumb and little finger may be plucking: one string's pitch is perhaps being tested by comparing it with another.

The right hand, in the dozen and a half examples of tuning the chelys-lyra that are at hand, is invariably at the crossbar, sometimes near the middle, sometimes closer to one arm or the other, but always in the area of the kollopes. In figure 28, an early red-figured vase dated ca. 510, we see the tuning process from the other side, so that it is clear that the right-hand thumb and the first two fingers turn a single kollops. (In both figs. 27 and 28 the fourth and fifth fingers are straight; but in most examples they are allowed to curve around the crossbar.)

The chelys-lyra was clearly tuned in the same manner as was the kithara (see chap. 3), though the lyre may be held in a variety of positions while it is tuned, as the illustrations show, and the performers are often seated during the process. We do not know how frequently the chelys-lyra needed tuning or how easy or difficult the task was. What is clear is that the lyre sometimes needed on-the-spot attention: the wreathed youth in chiton and himation who stands before an altar on London E 132 must tune his lyra, as must teachers at music lessons and young men performing at symposia and in the palaestra, as well as satyrs, Muses, and Apollo himself. Whether it was only necessary to repair the accuracy of pitches that were never purposely changed, or whether certain strings were retuned to new pitches from time to time (to change *harmoniai*?), we cannot learn from evidence of this kind.

Clearly portrayed singing players of the chelys-lyra are even rarer than kitharodes among the existing examples of the vase painter's art, and singers to the aulos (found in scenes of revels and music lessons, for example) appear more frequently than singers to any of the various sorts of lyres (see chap. 8). Unless a performer has his head thrown back, as do the reveler in figure 24 and Orpheus playing the lyre and singing to the Thracian men on Berlin 3172, it is usually difficult to say whether he is singing, for he is rarely portrayed with this mouth wide open.

There is little doubt in the case of one player of the chelys-lyra, however, for though nearly all of his head is missing from the existing fragment of the painting, the artist has used another method to indicate singing: a series of meaningless letters, NN4NNN (*sic*), is painted across Athens Nat. Mus., Akr. L546 F 13, as though issuing from the performer's mouth, almost as in a modern cartoon-balloon.[93]

On Athens Agora P 18799 it is not the youthful lyre player but the bearded leader of the komos procession whose head is tilted back and whose lips are parted, although the fact that someone other than the player may sing to the lyre should come as no great surprise.[94] In a painting of a teacher and student, both with lyres, on Oxford 1914.734 the teacher's mouth is open, probably to indicate that he is singing.[95]

Construction of the Chelys-Lyra

The most detailed literary description of the construction of a chelys-lyra, as pointed out in chapter 2, is supplied by the *Homeric Hymn to Hermes*. The poem describes the instrument's soundbox formed from a tortoise shell covered with leather, the *pecheis* (arms) and *zugon* (crossbar), the *donax* (reed or cane) fixed in place by means of holes piercing the soundbox, and the use of seven gut strings and a plektron with which to strike them.[96] Fifth-century evidence for the construction of the soundbox is provided by a further description of Hermes' invention in the fragments of Sophocles' satyr play, the *Ichneutai* ("Trackers").[97] Here the chorus of satyrs is tracking down the thief who stole Apollo's cattle. They hear strange music coming from a cave, where they encounter and interview Hermes' nurse, who describes how Hermes constructed his lyre out of a dead body. The members of the chorus are surprised that so loud a sound could come from a corpse, and after several silly inquiries as to whether the dead animal is a cat, weasel, crab, or beetle, are informed that the instrument is made from a tortoise. At this point there is a short gap in the text, but the next remarks of the chorus, who immediately charge Hermes with the theft of Apollo's cattle, make clear that the nurse must have reported his wrapping of the tortoise shell with an ox-hide, just as in the earlier *Homeric Hymn*.

Only a few further details emerge from other pieces of fifth-century literature. A short fragment describes lyres as being "well-constructed" (or "well-fit together"), and another mentions the gold-covered horn of a lyre, perhaps referring to the arm of an instrument (animal horns are used for this purpose in lyres from other cultures).[98]

The question of the use of pieces of reed or cane in the construction of the lyra, suggested by the *Homeric Hymn*, arises again in connection with a passage from Aristophanes' *Frogs* (228–35). Dionysos and the chorus of frogs are exchanging insults, and the frogs point out that they are the favorites of Apollo the phorminx player, because of the reed that they raise in their lakes, which they say is used "under the lyre" (*hypolyrion*). The Alexandrian commentators and their successors puzzled over this use of reed in the construction of lyres, citing as a parallel a line from Sophocles that seems to compare something or someone to a lyre which has lost its reed.[99] In view of the evidence from the *Homeric Hymn* regarding the fixing of a measured length of reed by means of (pins through the) holes pierced in the back of the tortoise shell, it is clear that the reed mentioned by both Sophocles and Aristophanes served in a functional rather than ornamental capacity, perhaps as the bridge or as an interior brace for the arms, both of which could be said to be "under the lyre (strings)."

The height of the chelys-lyra is commonly represented in the vase paintings as about one and one-half times the length of the player's forearm, from elbow to second knuckle, but it varies from about one forearm length (only three examples are smaller) to twice this measure (only three examples are larger).[100] Even though the player's forearm is the measure, the smallest lyres are more often played by boys and youths than are the larger ones—as if the painter wished to emphasize the smallness of the child's instrument. The width of the lyre, measured between the arms at the widest point, varies less than the height, from slightly less than the forearm length to about one and a quarter times this length. In most cases the width is between one-half to three-quarters of the height of the instrument (some are narrower; none is wider), but it is very noticeable that the taller the instrument, the less its width in proportion to its height. The remains of a tortoise shell pierced with holes indicating its use as a lyre found at Vassae suggest that the lyra (or barbitos; see chap. 5) might have a soundbox as small as 15 cm high and 12 cm wide.[101]

The chelys-lyra depicted in the most carefully executed, most detailed paintings has either six or seven strings, but those with seven strings are twice as numerous, as we might expect. The category of instruments with five strings and the category of lyres with two to four strings are about the same size: each has only about half as many instruments as the six-stringed group. Instruments with eight or nine strings are rare and, like the lyres with few strings, clearly the result of carelessness. The evidence at hand indicates that throughout the fifth century, at least until the second phase of the Peloponnesian War, about 420 B.C., there are no clear representations at all of the chelys-lyra with more than nine strings.[102] The strings are usually stretched upon the lyre in such a way that they diverge to some degree, more or less, as they run to the crossbar.[103] The manner in which they are affixed will be discussed below in connection with the kollopes and lower string fastener.

The tortoise used in the construction of the chelys-lyra can be identified, on the basis of shell markings and size, as the *testudo marginata,* a species native to Greece. This land tortoise, the largest in the genus

testudo, now ranges in length from about 20 to 30 cm or more and has an average shell depth of 4 or 5 inches.[104] It is clear that the shape of the shell, as it is commonly outlined in the lyre representations, is not that of the natural tortoise shell, which does not protrude on either side as we see it in the paintings; the shell must have been cut to this shape, perhaps in imitation of the shape of the skull of an animal with lyrate horns from which the forerunenrs of the Athenian lyre were certainly made, if not in Greece very likely in countries where Greeks traveled.[105]

For another possible reason for this alteration of shape, let us in imagination turn the tortoise over. We have been considering the carapace, the domed shell over the tortoise's back. But we must also think about the plastron, the underneath shell, and the side segments of shell joining the carapace and plastron on both sides in the area between the animal's front and hind legs. If part of the plastron were left intact, or even just the side segments, and the marginal sections of the carapace were at least partly cut away above and below the side segments of the shell, the result could be a shape of the sort shown in the paintings. Such an alteration to the carapace would make its shape follow that of the plastron more closely.[106]

This shape with "ears" so familiar to Athenian painters may not have been so pervasive outside the area of the city's influence. Late sixth- and fifth-century coins and scarabs from other areas (Cyprus, Karia, Lesbos) show a rounded body, and even among the Athenian representations there are a number with round or oval soundboxes.[107]

It is of course possible that the soundbox was at times made of some other material painted to resemble a tortoise shell. But there is no reason to suppose that tortoise shells, which provided a hard, durable soundbox material, were not in good supply, even around Athens, in the fifth century, although they may have been expensive. One cup painter, on New York 07.286.47, goes so far as to use applied clay on the back of the lyre to show the bumpiness of the tortoise shell, an effort he would surely have spared himself had he been accustomed to see these marks painted on. Two side views of the lyre also attempt to depict the bumpiness of the individual carapace sections, one successfully, one not: Brussels A 1020 (fig. 23), an excellent exercise in perspective, does it well; but the painter of Vienna 697 had difficulty with the problem of perspective.[108]

The underside of the tortoise shell, which becomes the belly of the instrument, was apparently covered with thin hide, as are instruments of the lyre type in Africa today.[109] The hide, if fastened in place when damp, would draw tight for a secure fit when dried. The light-colored border that shows around the shell in back views of the instrument, as in figure 5 and 17 and many other paintings, probably represents the edges of the hide (cf. fig. 23), drawn tight with a cord and possibly also held in place by pins that may have gone through small holes in the shell, for some of the soundbox remains have small holes around the edges, and in the vase paintings small dots or short lines are sometimes painted on the "border" around the shell.[110] As for the tortoise-shell markings (representing the individual sections of the carapace), they are sometimes realistically painted, sometimes not; and the characteristic tortoise-shell pattern is not often respected.[111]

Many paintings of the front side of the lyre include the bridge (made of wood, horn, cane, bone, or other hard material) by means of which the string vibrations are transmitted to the inside of this tortoise-shell soundbox for greater volume and resonance. The bridge is normally situated somewhat below the middle of the soundbox (as in fig. 23), though there are examples with the bridge in the middle, or even higher, at the level where the arms disappear into the hide surface (fig. 24); whether it was ever actually situated this high is certainly doubtful.[112] It was seldom overlooked by the painter when the entire front of the soundbox is visible, though he might indicate it with nothing but a straight line, thick or thin, or a sort of cigar shape in black paint. A fair number of lyres have bridges that are long rectangles or other four-sided figures in black or in outline (again, thick or thin).[113]

Some of the bridges clearly have feet—supports that rest on the drumhead-like covering or pierce through it to rest on the shell itself. These may be shown as short lines drawn through the bridge at or near either end and protruding above the bridge as in figure 29 (under the strings), below it as in figures 6 and 9, or (less commonly) both above and below as in figure 30. In a few cases in which the bridge is without feet, the bridge itself is curved, with the ends turning down; and in several others, a bridge shown as a thin line has rounded dots at either end, while some narrow rectangular bridges painted in outline have heavy black outlines at the sides in lieu of feet.[114]

The lower ends of the strings are attached to a device below the bridge that, in the sketchier paintings, is often merely a straight line across the base of the soundbox. The version most often seen in more detailed paintings consists of a long line at right angles to the strings, with a short line at or near either end making a right angle and running to the lower edge of the soundbox (see figs. 6, 23, and 30). Remains of

several metal string fasteners have been recovered, and holes near the end in certain shell remains indicate that the lower ends of the metal were bent upward behind the shell and then bent inward to pass through the holes.[115] The Basel oinochoe by the Shuvalov Painter shows a back view of the chelys-lyra with vertical lines at the bottom of the soundbox where these prongs were fitted.

In front of the string fastener, the short vertical lines to the edge of the soundbox curve inward on quite a number of examples, including figure 30; sometimes the whole outline of the device is created with one continuous line that forms the upper edge, rounds the corners, and curves inward below.[116] There are also some anomalous-looking lower string fasteners, such as the one seen on the carelessly executed lyre in figure 9, a thin rectangle with what appears to be seven or eight loops above it (if these are not simply decorative, they may represent extra lengths of string below the fastening).[117]

Aside from the border around the soundbox that is occasionally present, the belly of the instrument remains without any other devices or decorations except for the small dots or circles that sometimes appear between the arm and the end of the bridge on both sides. The one on the right side is faintly visible in figure 30.[118]

The basic shape of the chelys-lyra as viewed from the side, a perspective rarely attempted in the vase paintings, is suggested in a short fragment from the fifth century. The philosopher Heraclitus, who was noted even in antiquity for his obscure manner of expression, says that "harmonia" is "stretched backward" on itself, just like the "harmonia" of the bow or the lyre. His implicit comparison between bow and lyre suggests that the lyre, too, formed an arc whose opposite ends were pulled toward each other through the tension of the strings. Seen from the side, then, the lyre must have shown a distinct curvature, a conclusion confirmed by rare attempts to depict a side view of the instrument (see figs. 7 and 23).[119]

The paintings on a great many vases make it evident that the arms of the lyre enter the soundbox from the front—that is, no holes are cut for them in the tortoise shell; they enter through the hide and are braced and secured inside.[120] The point of entry is usually quite high, just above the side bulge (if any) of the shell, though in a fair number of cases the arms enter surprisingly low, as much as halfway down the soundbox. In any case, the arms enter at an angle to the belly of the instrument, which explains why the arm of the instrument in figure 23 appears to lean forward, and if we take into account the curvature of the arms themselves, may also explain why the paint-ers, in an apparent attempt to account for this, some-times made both arms curve in the same direction, as in figure 7, or, as in figure 21, made the right arm curve more than the left.[121]

The arms, as they leave the soundbox, ordinarily curve out, in a shape reminiscent of the antelope horns from which they may once have been made.[122] Just below the crossbar they curve in again somewhat and are usually fairly straight and parallel above the cross-bar, though occasionally they curve out again at the top.[123] Their length above the crossbar varies, as the figures in this chapter reveal.

The arms are often marked with a line down the center, usually running from the height of the crossbar a little less than halfway to the soundbox, as in figures 17 (instrument on right), 6, 28 (both front and back views), 29, and 30, though sometimes shorter or longer.[124] A few instruments also have a line running from the very top down the center, part or all of the way to the crossbar.[125] We cannot be certain whether these lines are mere decorations or an attempt to sug-gest the three-dimensional shape of the arms.

The arms of the chelys-lyra are seldom ornamented further. On a handful of black-figured and white-ground vases, the arms are in white—entirely, or in some cases from the tops to a point about a third of the way down from the crossbar toward the soundbox, perhaps to indicate ivory facings.[126] Still more rarely the tips of the arms are represented as painted or carved with one or more rings, or carved to two or three points (see fig. 6).[127]

In most representations of the chelys-lyra, the out-lines of arms and crossbar are painted right across each other, as in figure 19. But more than two dozen paintings make quite clear the manner in which arms and crossbar are joined: the crossbar sits in a "notch" in each arm, represented as a curved line just over the crossbar (see fig. 29). To create this notch, the maker of the lyre found near Eleusis cut away the front half of the arm above the crossbar on the notch side and carved the notch into the top of the remaining front half (the notch is big enough because the crossbar it-self has sections cut away at these points, making it narrower).[128] This helps to explain why, in figure 23, the arm, seen from the side, looks so much thinner above the crossbar (which is not, however, visible) and why a lyre with arms done in relief in another painting (Boston 00.356 [a back view]) has much higher relief below the crossbar than above it.

In figures 12 and 28, and several other paintings, the notches are not deep enough to cover the crossbar completely.[129] Notches appear on the front (belly) side

of the instrument in nearly all cases; in figure 28, how-ever, we see them on the front of one lyre and the back of another (in other paintings with both back and front views, only the front has notches). Notches on the backs of the arms can also be seen in figure 12 and in the scene on the outside of New York 58.11.1. Paint-ings of the chelys-lyra in which the notches are not in evidence may adopt the method of indicating that the crossbar fits within the arm used in figures 15, 17 (back and front views), and in fig. 18: only the crossbar's upper line is painted across the arms. This expedient is also employed in eight other paintings, all but one of them front views of the instrument.[130]

When the outlines of the crossbar do not cross those of the arms in front view (or do cross them in back view), the crossbar appears to lie in back of the arms. We find this on five vases, as well as a drachma coin from Lesbos showing a lyre in back view, with its crossbar in relief higher than that of the arms. How-ever, three lyres on one carefully painted kylix by Douris (ca. 480 B.C.) are presented in front view, the crossbar on the front (that is, the outlines of the arms are interrupted); and three objects that use relief—a terra-cotta, a scarab (a front view), and a *stater* (large coin) from the island of Karia with a finely detailed back view—also show the crossbar on the front.[131] None of the objects mentioned includes any hint of a notch to support the crossbar.[132]

The crossbar of the chelys-lyra seldom has any dec-oration of its own. Its ends, or its whole length, are painted white in a few instances, whereas on Athens 635 they are painted red (the arms are white).[133] The lyre on London E 514 has red bands painted around the crossbar near the ends, and the instrument on Ox-ford 312 has similar bands or perhaps carved rings, while the one on Berkeley 8/4581 has horizontal lines on the crossbar that make it appear split at either end almost as far as the outside edge of the arms (the tops of the arms have similar lines). Knobs at the ends of the crossbar appear on only three vases, Athens 12282, London E 326 (a lyre of odd shape), and an unnumbered amphora from Fiesole; but four scarabs from the Greek islands display lyres with small cross-bar knobs (three of these also have small knobs at the tops of the arms).[134]

The kollopes, the leather-and-pin fittings around which the strings are wound at the crossbar, are omit-ted in many paintings of the chelys-lyra (see figs. 12, 16, 17, and 19), though in a few, the crisscross wind-ings of the strings are indicated, as on London E 815. Most of the illustrations in this chapter do reveal the presence of kollopes, however, and from these and other vases we can discover much that we would like to know about them.

We can assume that one string, one kollops was meant to be the rule, even though the painters are often careless with the number of kollopes (which disagrees with the number of strings as often as it agrees, even on completely visible examples with seven strings). The kollopes are sometimes displayed in red paint (as are those in figs. 21, 24, 28, and 29) and in a few instances in white paint.[135]

The length of the kollops pins, extending well above and below the crossbar, is often great enough to make it clear that these visible fittings, whatever the material from which they are made, do not consist only of leather wrappings around the crossbar (see figs. 21, 6, 27, and 29). This perception is supported by a number of paintings and other objects which show kollops pins that touch only one side of the crossbar (that is, lie behind it, as the viewer sees it) and in some cases have small knobs at either end, which would help prevent the strings from slipping off even if the pins are rather short.

The chelys-lyra in the hands of Mousaios, figure 5, has its kollops pins on the front side (away from the viewer), as does the one in figure 25; but the lyre of Sappho's handmaiden in figure 22 has its pins on the back (again, away from the viewer).[136] The vases on which the kollopes are painted on the viewer's side (which are much more common) show that the artists willingly portray them on either the front or the back of the instrument. Several vases, coins, and a scarab on which the kollopes are shown as small black or raised circles above and below the crossbar attest to kollops pins made of a solid material such as hardwood and provided with small knobs at either end.[137] The crisscross pattern by which the strings are wound around the kollopes is evident in figures 5 and 8, on Athens 11713, and on a Fiesole amphora, while London E 301 indicates the windings as black squares on the crossbar (the long kollops pins are behind it).[138]

Accoutrements

The plektron used by the players of the chelys-lyra is evidently the same as that wielded by the kitharists. Because there are so many scenes in which the lyre is present but not being played, however, there are many opportunities to see the whole plektron dangling from its cord unobstructed by the player's hand, as in figure 27.[139] The plektron and its cord may be painted in either black or red paint; but on several vases from the second half of the fifth century, plektron and cord are white.[140]

The head of the plektron, probably of horn, metal, bone, or ivory, is shaped like an arrowhead, the outline resembling the bowl of a spoon with a pointed tip, sometimes slim, sometimes quite wide (see fig. 4). It occasionally has a line down the center toward the point.[141] The shank apparently has a leather covering (and probably has holes drilled in it for this purpose [see the discussion of the plektron in chap. 2]). This makes a rather thick, probably somewhat flexible handle long enough to grip comfortably.[142] The end of the handle may have a tassel, as long as the head and handle together or longer (as on Hamburg 1900.164).[143] It is the tassel, made of thongs or perhaps cords, that we see falling from the right hand of Orpheus in figure 29 (he holds the plektron and the instrument's arm in the same hand).

The long cord that attaches the plektron to the instrument is also fastened at the end of the handle. Its other end is fixed, ordinarily, at or near the base of the instrument's outer arm, though we sometimes see it tied to the lower string fastener at the bottom edge of the soundbox, as is done in the case of the kithara.[144]

The player grips the handle of the plektron in such a way that his thumb and index finger touch the head of it (figs. 4, 6, 8, 17, 23, 25, and 30—the plektron is usually grasped more securely than in fig. 24). When he is not playing, he usually loops or winds the plektron cord around the arm of the lyre. But he may also tuck the plektron between the base of either arm and the soundbox (the chelys-lyra has a small crevice behind the arm, apparently), hang it over the crossbar, or tuck it just above the bridge.[145]

The sling around the player's left wrist and around the outer arm of the instrument, although actually visible in only about three dozen examples, was presumably a necessary part of the chelys-lyra player's equipment. It is usually a narrow, undecorated band of cloth, often painted in red (figs. 8, 24, 28, and 30), placed a short distance up the arm of the instrument and kept taut by the performer, since he holds the lyre up partly by this means.[146] When the lyre is not being played, the sling dangles loosely around the base of the arm.[147] It is decorated (with dots or diamond shapes) in only two scenes that have come to hand, and in both of these, it is the god Apollo who is given the kind of sling used on the kithara.[148]

The "sash" described in chapter 3 is also to be seen in representations of the chelys-lyra, though it is less often in evidence than the wrist sling. It too is painted red in a number of cases (see figs. 8, 24, and 30); only on London E 391 is it (like the plektron and cord in this painting) in white. There are some examples on which the sash appears to be made up of separate strands, as in figure 23, but whereas in some of these it is quite long, as on Oxford 312, in others it may be so short that the possibility that it represents extra strings for the instrument must be ruled out; see figure 24 and Trieste S 424.[149] The sash often appears to be made of the same material as the sling, especially when both are painted in red. In some cases both seem to be of one continuous piece, knotted to provide a sling, the free ends (which may divide toward the ends, as in figure 30) forming the sash.[150] The sash in figure 15 and other examples may be part of the sling, or it may be a separate piece, though possibly of the same material, looped through the sling and fastened to it.[151] In a few cases, the sling and sash appear to be made of a long fillet with fringe at the ends similar to the one we see worn around the head of the bearded man on the left in figure 24.[152] Since fillets are generally painted red, possibly all the representations with sling and sash in red belong in this category.

The chelys-lyra has no cloth hanging from behind it as does the kithara. Such an accoutrement can be discovered in only three vase paintings at present: in one, the chelys-lyra is played by a standing Apollo, formally dressed in chiton and himation; in each of the other two, a Nike appears in a contest-related scene.[153] It seems evident that the chelys-lyra is in some sense a stand-in for the kithara in at least one of these cases (the depiction of Apollo). In the contest scenes, the artists may have added the cloth (very long and boldly decorated on Oxford 312) to emphasize the importance and dignity of the occasion.

The chelys-lyra was both the most widely used member of the lyre family and the one whose name (*lyra*) and image were used to represent that family. Like the kithara, which it sometimes replaces, it is played by Apollo; and it is found in the hands of satyrs, maenads, Muses, and other mythological figures (Heracles, Orpheus, Tithonos, Paris, the Dioscuri, and Eros). Its invention by the god Hermes was recalled in the fifth century both by Sophocles, in the satyr play *Ichneutai*, and by several vase painters who depict Hermes holding the lyre. Nor was its connection with the hero Theseus forgotten, for at least two vase paintings recall it, as does the constellation Lyra, already known by this name in the fifth century and said by later writers to be the lyre of Theseus.

The chelys-lyra, unlike the kithara, is customarily present in many kinds of scenes of ordinary human life and was probably played by men and women of all ages. As an accompaniment for singing at the symposium and the komos, it is played by the guests themselves or one of the youths in attendance, for lyre playing was a basic part of Athenian education and the lyre is often present in school scenes. Because it was the mark of an educated man and because it symbolizes release from cares, the chelys-lyra is played by a man, probably the deceased, on lekythoi used as grave offerings. Young boys are portrayed playing the lyre, and although young girls are not, they must have learned to do so, for adult women depicted on the vases play it: the attendants of the poet Sappho, brides and bridal attendants, the accompanists of women dancing, and women taking part in quiet indoor recreation. The lyre may be found with any of the other instruments used by the Greeks for music making, but it is seldom revealed as actually being played along with another instrument, even its most frequent partner, the aulos.

Since the occasions on which the lyre is played are generally informal, lyre players, unlike kitharists, are often seated. Whereas the kithara is held upright, the chelys-lyra is usually tipped out from 30° to 90° (about 45° is most common). Whereas the playing and tuning techniques are apparently the same as those used for the kithara (though the much greater number of available examples allows us to examine these more closely here), the accoutrements of the chelys-lyra are in some respects much simpler than those of the kithara. Knobs at the end of the crossbar or a decorated cloth hanging behind the instrument are so rare among chelys representations as to suggest confusion with the kithara in the few known examples, and a "sash" attached at the base of the outer arm is also seldom seen. The lyre has the same kollopes, lower string fastener, bridge, and plektron as the kithara, but the plektron cord is attached to the base of the outer arms more often than to the base of the soundbox, as with the kithara. Though there may have been some elegantly made lyres with gold or ivory facings on the arms, the chelys-lyra was clearly a much more simply constructed instrument than the kithara with its elaborately carved arms.

The chelys-lyra was not the only instrument with a tortoise-shell soundbox known to the Athenians, who had also welcomed into their musical life its long-armed relation, the barbitos. This instrument, discussed in the next chapter, was more narrowly defined as to uses than was the chelys-lyra. Associated with satyrs and symposiasts, it was also the instrument of poets and the third of the three chief members of the lyre family in fifth-century Athens.

1. Heidelberg L 64. Attic
b.f. lekythos. Detail:
quadriga scene.

2. Oxford 535 (G. 292).
Attic r.f. lekythos. Detail:
Apollo and Artemis.

3. London B 353. Attic
b.f. oinochoe. Detail:
maenad between satyrs.

4. New York 24.97.30.
Attic r.f. bell krater.
Detail: Orpheus and
Thracians.

5. London E 271. Attic
r.f. amphora. Detail:
Mousaios, Muses.

6. Boston 98.887. Attic
white-ground (w.g.) pyxis.
Detail: Muses.

7. Hillsborough, Hearst
21. Attic r.f. kalpis.
Detail: Tithonos pursued
by Eos.

8. London B 167. Attic
b.f. amphora. Detail:
Hermes, Heracles, and
Iolaos.

9. Berlin Antikenmuseum
2536. Attic r.f. kylix.
Detail: Judgment of Paris.

10. Oxford 311
(1889.1015). Attic r.f.
lekythos. Detail: Eros
with lyre.

11. Syracuse 36330. Attic
r.f. hydria. Detail: women
and Eros.

12. London E 159. Attic
r.f. hydria. Detail: guests
at symposium.

13. Frankfurt, M.V.F. beta 304. Attic b.f. lekythos. Detail: reclining figure, attendants.

14. Cambridge, Harvard 1959.188. Attic r.f. pelike by the Pig Painter. Procession, man and boys.

15. Paris, Musée Rodin 993. Attic r.f. column krater by the Pig Painter. Detail: komasts.

16. Florence 4014. Attic
r.f. hydria. Detail: women
dancing the pyrrhic,
musicians, onlookers.

17. Schwerin KG 708.
Attic r.f. skyphos by the
Pistoxenos Painter. Detail:
Linos and Iphikles.

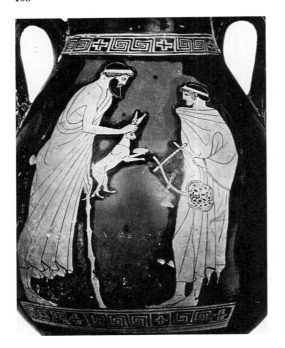

18. Athens 1413. Attic r.f.
pelike. Detail: Man
offering rabbit to youth.

19. New York 26.60.79.
Attic r.f. kylix. Interior
detail: Nike and youth.

20. Oxford 1916.13. Attic
r.f. kylix. Detail: youth
between women.

21. Vienna IV 143 (old
622). Attic w.g. lekythos.
Detail: grave scene.

22. Athens 1260. Attic r.f.
hydria. Detail: seated
woman (Sappho) reading
scroll, standing women.

23. Brussels A 1020. Attic w.g. lekythos. Detail: women with instruments.

24. Toledo 64.126. Attic r.f. kylix by the Foundry Painter. Interior: komasts.

25. Gotha 51. Attic r.f. hydria. Detail: Diomedes, youth, a Nike, Apollo.

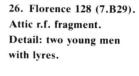

26. Florence 128 (7.B29).
Attic r.f. fragment.
Detail: two young men
with lyres.

27. Athens Agora P 43.
Attic w.g. kylix. Interior:
boy with lyre.

28. Munich 2421. Attic
r.f. hydria. Detail: teacher
and students.

29. Boston 13.202. Attic r.f. lekythos. Detail: Orpheus attacked by Thracian woman.

30. New York 07.286.78. Attic r.f. amphora. Detail: Apollo and Artemis at altar.

CHAPTER FIVE

The Barbitos in Classical Athens

The vase painters of Athens from the late sixth century through most of the fifth showed a considerable enthusiasm for another lyre with a tortoise-shell soundbox, the one that has been identified as the barbitos. The enthusiasm is understandable when we consider the uses and connotations of the instrument: the painters present the barbitos in a wide variety of scenes, nearly all of them related to the revelry of Dionysos and his troop of satyrs and maenads, or its mortal counterparts, the Athenians komos (a rowdy procession of partygoers) and symposium (drinking party).

As we saw in chapter 2, the barbitos was closely associated in the Greek mind with some of the famous lyric poets from the East, especially with Anakreon, whose arrival in Athens in the late sixth century coincided precisely with the sudden appearance of this instrument in the vase paintings. Despite its exotic status as a recent foreign importation, the barbitos is mentioned many times in Greek literature of the Classical period, often with allusions to its function as the chief instrument (beside the aulos) of the symposium.

Etymology

In discussing the Asiatic background of Greek music, the first-century B.C. geographer Strabo speaks of the influence of the Phrygians and other such peoples in connection with the kithara and aulos and includes the barbitos in a list of Greek instruments that bear foreign names. This remark, along with the lack of related words in any Indo-European language, has led to the conclusion that the instrument's name is of unknown, perhaps Phrygian, origin.[1]

Although the evidence is not conclusive, it appears that the name of this distinctive instrument first appeared in Greek in the Aeolic dialect spoken in Alcaeus' homeland of Lesbos; in this dialect the instrument was called *barmitos* (or sometimes *baromos* or *barmos*), but by the fifth century the form found in Attic literature, *barbitos*, had become standard.[2]

The relatively late entry of the instrument's name into the Greek language may account for the paucity of related terms as compared with, for example, *kitharis* and its many derivatives in use during the Archaic and Classical periods. The verb form *barbitizein* ("to play the barbitos") occurs only in two instances, and the sole compound form, *philobarbitos* ("fond of the barbitos"), is found only once in the extant literature.[3] Unlike the well-assimilated words *kitharis, phorminx,* and *lyra,* the name *barbitos* appears to have retained a certain foreign ring.

Vase Paintings of Barbitos Players

Dionysos and His Followers

Although the vase painters do not portray the barbitos as often as they do the kithara or lyra, the instrument appears on some two hundred and fifty of the vases studied, nearly all of which show its connection with Dionysos: depictions of Dionysos himself or his attendants, representations of komasts and symposiasts, and portraits of the poet Anakreon, who often appears in the context of the komos. Since amatory exploits are clearly connected with occasions of revelry, we may perhaps include portraits of Eros with a barbitos among the related scenes. A much smaller group of paintings of the barbitos, *not* related to the komos or symposium, includes other scenes of an erotic nature; portraits of other poets; depictions of the Muses; scenes of private music making by both men and women; and scenes showing the barbitos as an accompaniment to music lessons.

Although scenes of mortals taking part in the dancing and wine-drinking revelry of the komos are by far the most numerous, Dionysos and his satyrs and maenads are well represented. Dionysos, bearded, dressed in flowing chiton and himation in most cases, wreathed with ivy, and carrying a *kantharos* (wine cup with tall, exaggerated loop handles) or *rhyton* (drinking horn) and sometimes a *thyrsos* (staff topped with ivy leaves or an oversized pinecone), appears among his dancing, drinking, music-making followers in seventeen scenes in which the barbitos is found.[4] (Most of these paintings are on large red-figured wine vessels such as kraters and stamnoi.) The barbitos is generally played by a satyr, less often by a maenad (see fig. 19). Dionysos is sometimes seated, sometimes walking in a procession or standing among his ever-present followers; in one scene, on Paris G57, he dances among them, still holding his drinking horn.

One of the oldest representations, from about 525 B.C., on Frankfurt Mus. für Khw. WM 03 (fig. 1), shows Dionysos, who holds a large kantharos, seated with Ariadne and surrounded by dancing satyrs and maenads. The barbitos in this painting has arms of a peculiar shape found in very few other examples (see discussion of construction below).

In the processions, some of them torchlit, in which Dionysos appears he is generally on foot among his attendants.[5] One of these, Cambridge Harvard 1960.236 (fig. 2), depicts the Return of Hephaistos to Olympos. Hephaistos with his double ax (on the other side of this calyx krater) sits astride a mule and is followed by a satyr with a kithara; but we see Dionysos on foot, followed by a satyr with the barbitos. On New York 56.171.52, however, it is he who rides: on a donkey, holding kantharos and thyrsos, preceded by a satyr with a wineskin and followed, once again, by a satyr with a barbitos (from the arm of which hangs an aulos bag).

Satyrs and maenads dance, move in procession, flourish wine cups, and play the barbitos and aulos even more often in scenes where Dionysos does not actually appear.[6] Wine vessels are visible in most of these, as in all the Dionysos scenes, so that even where vessels are lacking, a barbitos-playing satyr conveys the idea of Dionysiac revelry.[7] The scenes themselves are painted on wine vessels (krater, amphora, and stamnos), of course, and on wine cups (kylix and skyphos) and pitchers (oinochoi).

On column krater Paris Petit Palais 326 an aulos-playing *silenus* (elderly satyr) leads an unusual procession consisting, not of other satyrs and maenads, but of Hermes, Heracles, and a man with only a folded mantle around his shoulders who carries a skyphos (Heracles' squire Iolaus?). The barbitos player is Heracles, whom we have also encountered elsewhere as a kitharist or player of the chelys-lyra (chaps. 3 and 4).[8]

The Athenian Komos

Komos scenes with the barbitos in which the participants are mortals are about twice as common as Dionysos and satyr scenes, suggesting that the barbitos appears in the hands of Dionysos' followers because of its association with the komos rather than because of any connection with the ritual of a cult of Dionysos. Specifically religious scenes in which the barbitos appears near an altar, for example, are scarcely to be found. Only five have come to light in this study: in two, a player faces an altar behind which stands a herm; the third is similar, but without the herm; and only the fourth brings together the elements of altar, barbitos, and wine drinking. The meaning of this scene is ambiguous; and there is nothing that provides a connection with Dionysos.[9] The fifth altar scene with a barbitos shows Heracles killing Busiris (Paris G 50); on the left a young man holding the instrument flees from the altar area where the murder is taking place. This event was the subject of a number of vase paintings, in some of which a lyre of one sort or another is shown. The barbitos is found only in this instance, however; and the god worshiped by Busiris, according to Herodotus, was the Egyptian equivalent, not of Dionysos, but of Zeus.[10]

The evidence for the association of barbitos with komos, on the other hand, is rich and varied. Nearly two dozen paintings include one or more dancers; a like number offer rowdy komos processions; a third, smaller group consists of scenes of general carousing and music making; and a fourth group, again including nearly two dozen paintings, shows a single komast trudging along on his way to the party or home from it. The participants, who sometimes have dogs with them, often hold wine cups or wine vessels; and their dancing and merrymaking (or progress toward the party) is often accompanied by auloi, sometimes played by a (hired) woman musician, as well as by the barbitos.

Komasts sometimes dance to the clicking of the krotala, which they themselves play, as well as to the sounds of barbitos and auloi. The steps of their dances can only be guessed at, but there are two that appear often enough in this survey to suggest typical movement patterns. In the one most often found, the dancer lifts a bent knee high, while the other leg, bearing his weight, is also bent somewhat (fig. 3). In the other, the dancer leans back, bending the leg that bears his weight and holding the other leg straight in front of him (or occasionally to the side), the foot usually touching the ground, as in figure 4, where a dancer in this pose is also playing the krotala. He holds them in the position customarily seen, one pair up and one pair down. The gestures of hands and arms (by those who do not hold krotala or wine cups) are so varied that they defy categorization, which suggests that these movements may have been left to the inspiration of the moment.

Men walking in the same direction in a file may often be identified as komasts, especially if there are women among them as aulos players or dancers, or if one or more komasts are dancing, and if some of the party carry wine cups or jars. Although there are female aulos players in nearly half our examples, women in the procession who are dancing (dressed in chiton and himation and recognizable as dancers only because of the positions of their hands and arms) are found on Gotha 2476, a black-figured vase made before 500 B.C. with depictions of the barbitos that are among the earliest found. The male figures often carry staves and wear shoes or high boots, as in another early example, figure 5, suggesting that the processions take place out of doors. There are columns, probably those of a public building, showing between the participants on a black-figured lekythos from Gela of about 510 B.C., where the barbitos player has a dog walking beside him.

When only two male figures, bearing the usual objects (staves and/or wine vessels in addition to the barbitos) and perhaps followed by a small dog, walk along in the painting, it is difficult to tell whether they are taking part in a procession of some sort or simply making their way to the celebration.[11] The two young men on Paris G 82 are apparently already celebrating, for the one in the foreground holds both a kylix and a rhyton and seems to be dancing. The two on Basel pelike 1906.301, on the other hand, may be on their way to the komos; a pitcher (chous) hangs from the arm of the barbitos, an indication that they are taking part in the festival of the Anthesteria.[12]

However, although only some half-dozen paintings show two komasts, there are two dozen on hand that are representations of a single reveler. In most of these, the context is even more ambiguous. The komast is nearly always nude except perhaps for a cloak folded like a large towel over the arms or shoulders. He wears a wreath (in a few cases, a flowered wreath) or a fillet, and, in single examples, sandals or high boots; though he often carries a walking staff, he seldom has a wine cup with him. In two paintings an aulos case hangs from the arm of the barbitos, and in two others, a large basket is similarly suspended.[13] Both these details, also seen elsewhere, strengthen the message that this is a komast taking part (or about to take part) in a celebration. In figure 6, a small pitcher, the bearded komast is evidently returning home from the party: he leans on his staff, carries his barbitos slung over his shoulder and held by the plektron cord and seems to walk with difficulty and with a somewhat glazed look in his eye. In figure 7 another komast has reached home—and is banging on the door with the butt of his staff, while a woman (his wife?) can be seen on the other side of the door, coming to open it with trepidation, fingers to lips. This scene contains a number of interesting details: the door itself, the roof tiles overhead, and the oil lamp in the woman's hand. In this painting, too, the barbitos is slung over the komast's shoulder and held by the plektron cord.

In only a small portion of the scenes of mortal komasts with the barbitos is there a group of participants at a komos whose activities do not include dancing (or processing). Here drinking is the principal occupation, and skyphoi and other drinking cups and pitchers are much in evidence. On Urbana, Ill. Krannert kylix 70–8–7 a komast lifts a large storage amphora, and a young man on Cambridge, Harvard 1959.188 is holding a very large column krater of the same sort that we see in use on New York 06.1021.188, where it sits on the floor while a young komast dips wine from it with a pitcher. The result of the drinking bout appears on Cleveland 24.197 (fig. 8): the komast leans on his staff, holding his kylix away from him, and vomits a stream of wine, while a boy stands by holding his barbitos.[14]

The women who appear among the mortal komasts are barbitos players (in one case, the player of a phorminx; see chap. 6). They are present in over a third of the examples wearing the customary feminine dress: the chiton, sometimes with himation over it, and usually a sakkos (a cloth hat) over the hair (though some have fillets or wreaths). The music is made not only by the barbitos and phorminx (Cambridge, Harvard 1959.188) but also by the aulos (New York 06.1021.188, where two sets of aulos cases are also shown hanging on the wall). The komast facing the male aulete on this New York kylix has his mouth open, singing, as does the man on Athens Acropolis 20, who stands next to a barbitos (on the wall?) holding his arm languidly behind his head.

For a discussion of the special kind of komos associated with the poet Anakreon, in which the participants dress in women's clothing, see below.

The Barbitos at Symposia

Alcaeus' identification of the barbitos with Dionysiac festivity (discussed in chap. 2) continues to be maintained in the literature of the fifth century. Here the instrument is repeatedly associated with drinking parties where the guests, reclining on couches, were entertained and entertained themselves with music—a role that is clearly borne out in the large number of Attic vase paintings showing the instrument in the hands of a reveler playing for his drinking companions. Critias, for example, in describing Anakreon, links the poet and his barbitos to dancing, drinking, and playing the kottabos game (in which the contestants aimed the dregs of their wine cups at a target poised over a small metal basin):

> Teos sent to Greece sweet Anakreon,
> Contriver of songs with tunes such as women
>   like,
> A provoker of symposia, a cozener of women,
> A rival for the aulos, fond of the barbitos,
>   sweet releaser of cares.
> Never will affection for you grow old or die,
> As long as the boy carries water mixed with wine
> In cups, handling the before-dinner drinks
>   nimbly,
> And the female dancers tend the all-night rites,
> And the disk, Daughter of Bronze, sits upon the
>   lofty tops
> Of the kottabos, ready for the drops of wine.[15]

> τὸν δὲ γυναικείων μελέων πλέξαντά ποτ' ὠιδάς
> ἡδὺν Ἀνακρείοντα Τέως εἰς Ἑλλάδ' ἀνῆγεν,
> συμποσίων ἐρέθισμα, γυναικῶν ἠπερόπευμα,
> αὐλῶν ἀντίπαλον, φιλοβάρβιτον, ἡδύν, ἄλυπον.
> οὔ ποτέ σου φιλότης γηράσεται οὐδὲ θανεῖται,
> ἔστ' ἂν ὕδωρ οἴνωι συμμειγνύμενον κυλίκεσσι
> παῖς διαπομπεύηι προπόσεις ἐπιδέξια νωμῶν,
> παννυχίδας θ' ἱερὰς θήλεις χοροὶ ἀμφιέπωσιν,
> πλάστιγξ θ' ἡ χαλκοῦ θυγάτηρ ἐπ' ἄκραισι καθίζηι
> κοττάβου ὑψηλαῖς κορυφαῖς Βρομίου ψακάδεσσιν.

Euripides, who provides the only two references to the barbitos in fifth-century tragedy, places the instrument in contexts that clearly reveal the special relationship of the barbitos to Dionysiac revelry. In his satyr play, the *Cyclops*, Euripides describes how Si-

lenus, captive of Polyphemus, hears his fellow satyrs (the mythical attendants of Dionysos) returning from pasturing the Cyclops' sheep; Silenus says that the racket reminds him of bygone days (before their unfortunate capture by Polyphemus) when they all took part in a special dance in honor of Dionysos called the sikinnis, which he says was done to the "songs of barbitoi."[16]

The special associations of the barbitos are also evident in a passage from Euripides' *Alcestis* in which Admetus declares to his wife how much he will miss her after she saves his life by dying in his stead. This is what he promises to give up as a sign of mourning:

> I will put an end to revelry and to gatherings of
>   fellow-drinkers,
> And to the garland and to the music which used
>   to occupy my house.
> Never again would I touch my barbitos,
> Nor raise up my spirits to sing to the Libyan
>   aulos.[17]

> παύσω δὲ κώμους συμποτῶν θ' ὁμιλίας
> στεφάνους τε μοῦσάν θ' ἡ κατεῖχ' ἐμοὺς δόμους.
> οὐ γάρ ποτ' οὔτ' ἂν βαρβίτου θίγοιμ' ἔτι
> οὔτ' ἂν φρέν' ἐξαίροιμι πρὸς Λίβυν λακεῖν
> αὐλόν·

Although a learned commentator on the play maintains that the word *barbitos* is here used for " 'lyre' in general," the overwhelming evidence of the vase paintings and of other literary passages compels us to conclude that Admetus is not talking about "lyre-playing" in general. Rather, he is promising to give up symposia by saying that he intends to put aside those particular instruments (the barbitos and aulos) whose special function was to accompany singing, dancing, and other revelry.[18]

A further instance of the connection between the barbitos and symposia is provided by a short fragment from Pindar in which reference is made to playing the barbitos (*barbitizein*) to calm one's spirit at a drinking party. Although again a commentator speculates that the reference is to stringed instruments in general, Pindar's choice of this rare verb and the abundant evidence for the special use of the instrument in the context of Dionysiac revelry suggest that here too we should pay attention to the specific connotations of the poet's words.[19]

The symposia represented in the vase paintings frequently include someone playing the barbitos. Unlike the ordinary chelys-lyra, which often hangs on the wall in such scenes, the barbitos is in most cases in the hands of a guest, as in figure 9. Here we see the game of kottabos being played (as it is in more than a quarter of the symposium scenes with barbitos): the bearded man on the right lifts a kylix by one handle as he prepares to swing it around and flip the few drops of wine it still contains in the direction of the tall stand located between the two couches in an attempt to hit the small bronze plate at its top. The young man just to the left of the stand peers closely at it to see what has already been scored. On his left sits a young boy looking down at one of the dogs. His headdress appears to be an imitation of rabbit ears, worn perhaps as part of an erotic initiation.

The furniture in this painting is of the sort typically found in symposium scenes: couches with striped cushions and ornately carved legs, and low tables with shelves or struts underneath (the tables are empty or hold only wine cups in almost all these paintings—dinner is over, and the food has been cleared away). Low footstools are often placed under the tables, and a large dinos supported by a tripod stands on the left on Munich 2410.[20] The guest's boots may stand underneath the couch; on London E 68 a knobby staff with a crook at the end leans against the foot of a couch. There are often various objects hanging on the wall behind the couches, such as baskets, pitchers, lyres, wreaths, aulos cases, and drinking cups.

A female aulos player in chiton and himation (and perhaps a sakkos) stands playing at the foot of a couch in six of our thirty symposium scenes.[21] Other women servants stand near the couches in two of the paintings, and on London E 68 a woman sits at the foot of one of the couches with a large kylix ready to offer to the guest. Women (hetairai) recline among the guests in three of the scenes, and two appear to include a woman holding a barbitos: on Paris F 216, a black-figured vase, the player has white-painted skin but does not seem to have female clothing or hair style and sits cross-legged; and on Berlin 4221 a person in female dress (but with the lower half of the face missing) holds a barbitos by the arm in one hand and a pair of krotala in the other.

A few symposium scenes include nude serving boys who stand between the couches with pitchers or run to serve the guests. On London E 68 (see above) a figure in a chiton, apparently a young man, holds a barbitos ready for the player (perhaps the woman seated on the end of the couch, who is nearest him), and on London E 786 a satyr hands the instrument to one of the reclining bearded men. At a symposium the barbitos is ordinarily played by one of the reclining male guests, but on Bonn 1216, 33–38, the player is a satyr who stands at the foot of a couch shared by two men, and on Ferrara 2812, T. 153, a bearded man in a himation (a guest?) stands at the foot of the couch, holding

the barbitos in his left hand and a skyphos in his right. Ahead of him is a woman playing the aulos for the reclining guest, who holds a small skyphos in one hand and a kylix raised to play kottabos in the other. On an oinochoe once Paris Market (Mikas), a young man stands playing the barbitos at the foot of a couch on which a guest playing kottabos reclines.

Eros and the Barbitos

The barbitos was associated not only with Dionysos and with wine drinking but also with Eros and with erotic love. In a group of paintings of a winged Eros alone carrying or playing the barbitos, he is portrayed as a handsome youth and perhaps represents both passionate love in the abstract and the object of the lover's affections in particular. A second group of paintings shows small Eros figures (sometimes more than one) in the company of women who play instruments; and there are a few representations in which a man approaches a woman who plays the barbitos—or has one near her—scenes that suggest erotic intention, though no Eros is present.

Eros as a winged youth with a barbitos hovers over an altar in two paintings by the Icarus Painter, Cambridge Fitz. G 150 and Berlin 2220, and although on Florence 4017 there is no altar, the flying Eros carries a phiale in his right hand as well as a barbitos in his left. Both these details suggest that the vases in question, and perhaps others in this group, may have been intended as offerings to ensure a happy outcome in some erotic venture. The Eros figures have long, curling hair bound with a fillet and wear only a folded cloak around the shoulders, or nothing at all. The Eros on Gela 67 (fig. 10) has "winged" boots (endromides). The one on Boston 27.671, an East Greek chalcedony scaraboid (ca. 500 B.C., probably the earliest object in this group), carries a wreath in his left hand and has three sets of wings—on his heels and head, as well as his back—in spite of which he appears to be running, not flying as do the Eros figures on the ten vases in this group. The feet of the Eros on Paris G 211 float about a foot above the ground (the dog walking ahead of him provides a frame of reference), and he seems to play for the benefit of the youth wrapped in a himation who stands alone on the opposite side of the vase. Eros figures are also to be found who carry only the aulos, and in the interior of Copenhagen Chr. VIII 875 there is an Eros who carries both barbitos and aulos.

When Eros appears in the company of women, it is not he but a woman seated in a chair who plays the barbitos.[22] These Eros figures are made the size of boys, and two of them may appear in the same scene.[23] All nine of the scenes of this sort at hand are found on vases from the second half of the fifth century. Five of them are hydriai; the association of the paintings with the hydria (which, as we have shown elsewhere, was almost certainly used in wedding ceremonies) and the presence of Eros in the paintings themselves together indicate that most of these scenes represent a bride and her attendants. The bride, who is seated in the center with the others facing her, is in the majority of cases the one who plays the barbitos (fig. 11).[24] In two of the paintings a crane, a large, heron-like bird— a symbol of honor and watchful protection—stands just in front of the bride facing away from her. Inscriptions on two vases allow us to know some of the women's names: Eudora and Kallipp(e) on one, Kleophonis (the bride), Kleodoxa (the barbitos player), Euphemia, Kleodike, and Phanodike on the other. On the latter vase the alter ego of Eros, Himeros ("Desire"), is also identified by inscription.[25] These bridal scenes contain from three to eight women, the larger number in scenes that go all the way around a vase. The attendants may carry boxes, a mirror, a fillet, a scroll, or a musical instrument: lyra, aulos, or phorminx (discussed in chap. 6), which appears only on Würzburg 521. In addition to the chair (klismos) on which the bride sits, the room often contains other domestic furniture in the form of one or more chests and stools.

Two paintings in which an Eros and a seated woman with a barbitos appear also include a standing young man wearing a himation. One of these, Kassel 435, seems to be a courtship scene (the Eros stands before the young woman as though arguing the young man's case with her). The other painting, on Athens 1263, appears to be a farewell scene: a young man with a spear taking leave of his mother (seated with the barbitos) and wife (standing, turned away, behind the seated woman). An Eros clings to the young man as though begging him to stay.

A red-figured kylix from about 500–490 B.C. and two reliefs from Melos show us a man and a woman alone (no Eros) in poses that suggest erotic intent. On the kylix, London E 44 (fig. 12), a woman loosens the girdle of her chiton while looking down at the man seated on a diphros who reaches out to her while still holding his staff; the barbitos lies discarded behind the woman. On terra-cotta reliefs Athens 1588 and London 622 from Melos it is the woman, dressed in chiton and himation, who is seated on a stool. She plays the barbitos, but the man standing before her reaches out and grasps the arm of the instrument as though to take it from her.

Certainly all these examples make it clear that the barbitos was an instrument associated with love, to be played for a lover, perhaps, or to be played while thinking of him, or awaiting his arrival, or making an offering to Eros to ensure the happy outcome of the meeting. If the barbitos was understood to have an erotic significance, the meaning of various portrayals of a young man with a barbitos becomes clear. The young men on Florence 3920 and Boston 13.194, both "kalos" vases (with the inscription HO PAIS KALOS, "the youth is handsome," or just KALOS), are not to be thought of as komasts but as representations of the beloved. The pose of the young man on Boston 13.194, who sits on one heel while he plays, is similar to that of the young men on three late sixth-century or early fifth-century scarabs probably from the Eastern islands or the Eastern mainland, who are shown tuning or playing the barbitos.[26] The young man walking alone on Frankfurt 409 has no *kalos* inscription; but the other side of the vase depicts a bearded man, like the young man nude except for a folded chlamys around his shoulders, walking to the left—that is, he and the young man on the other side face each other.[27]

Performers, Costumes, and Occasions

Anakreon

Ironically, the player with whom the barbitos is most closely associated, Anakreon, cannot now be connected with the instrument through his own poetry, of which we have only scanty remains. The evidence of the vase paintings (see below) and the association of the instrument with Anakreon in fifth-century (as well as later) Greek literature lead us to conclude, however, that the barbitos owed much of its popularity in Athens to the influence of this long-lived poet.

Anakreon left his birthplace (Ionia) to help found a colony in Thrace; from there he went to the island of Samos in the Aegean to serve as the music teacher for the son of the tyrant Polykrates. Finally he was summoned to Athens by Hipparchos, the younger brother of the tyrant Hippias. The two brothers, eager to carry on the program of cultural improvements begun by their father, Peisistratos, invited not only Anakreon but other poets and artists as well to join the Peisistratid court in Athens. There Anakreon remained (except for a period spent in Thessaly) until his death at a ripe old age, perhaps as late as 485. As we have already noted, Anakreon was identified with the barbitos both in fifth-century sources (such as Critias) as well as in later authors such as Athenaeus, who labels the poet as the instrument's "inventor." In addition, an epitaph written probably by a fifth-century contemporary (Simonides) speaks of Anakreon as an immortal singer who continues to sing song sweet as honey and to play the barbitos even in Hades.[28]

The role of the barbitos as the drinking man's lyre is further played out in the collection of sixty drinking songs known as the *Anacreontea*. The dates of the poems in the collection are generally uncertain and seem to vary considerably, so it is impossible to draw any conclusions from them concerning the use of the barbitos in the fifth century. The most that can be said is that they maintain the already established tradition connecting Anakreon, the barbitos, and drinking parties, and that they continue to portray the barbitos as the chief stringed instrument used for the accompaniment of Dionysiac dance and revelry.[29]

"Anakreon" in the Vase Paintings

The figures on one group of vases represent, according to Beazley, "Anakreon and his boon companions," the barbitos player being Anakreon himself.[30] The participants in figure 13 and related scenes are komasts dressed in clothing generally associated with women (long chiton with a *kolpos*—a deep overlap—at the waist, and sakkos, a cloth hat covering the hair) and/ or barbarians (earrings). Some of them carry parasols, while others may have the customary wine cups in their hands. Beazley points out that they have moustaches as well as beards (that is, the beards are not false) and that there is never any outline of a female breast; these are clearly men who wear such clothing for a particular occasion.

Three vases have been found on which a player of the barbitos is actually identified by inscription as Anakreon.[31] All three of these, unfortunately, are either badly worn or fragmentary, and on London E 18 the Anakreon figure wears only the komast's ordinary attire, a wreath and himation. But on Syracuse 26967 he wears a chiton as well, and both a *mitra* (a cloth headband) and a wreath. On Copenhagen 13365 (fig. 14), on which the name is written on the arm of the barbitos instead of in the field, the player also wears chiton and himation. Most of the painting is missing, but the fragments together indicate that it consisted of a group of men in similar costumes, wearing shoes and long, turban-like sakkoi wrapped neatly around the head—another of the several unusual kinds of headgear found in the larger group of "Anakreon" paintings.

As we have shown elsewhere, in Aristophanes' *Thesmophoriazusae* the poet Agathon is represented as wearing a costume that he himself associates with

the garb of Ionian poets such as Anakreon and Alcaeus—a costume that includes items of customary female clothing: a *krokotos* (saffron-colored robe), *strophion* (waistband), and both *kekryphalos* (= *sakkos*) and mitra.[32] Aristophanes' play concerns the celebration of a festival (the Thesmophoria) that is restricted to women participants. We meet Agathon as he is being accosted by the character Euripides, who wants Agathon to go to the festival disguised as a woman so that he can infiltrate the proceedings and defend Euripides' reputation. The reason that Agathon has been picked as the first candidate for the mission is his effeminate appearance, which is described in some detail in the play.

W. J. Slater has offered evidence to show that it was not uncommon in Greek society for men to dress as women (or women as men) for cult or ritual purposes; that such customs are associated with Dionysos and with komastic practices; and that both the vase paintings and Anakreon's description of Artemon link the poet and his friends with such practices.[33] It would be interesting to know whether their costume is part of a cult observance, as Slater suggests, or of a festival such as the Oschophoria (at which young men dressed in female clothing) or the Skirophoria, a festival apparently related to the Thesmophoria at which one of the observances may have been the carrying of a large sunshade.[34] It is of course not surprising to find Anakreon, the poet of drinking songs, at a komos; the question is, how did he come to be associated with this special komos? Since the costume is associated with the Ionian poets, we may speculate that the practices relating to it were brought to Athens from Ionia, perhaps by Anakreon himself.

In all but two of the fifteen unlabeled "Anakreon" representations presently available the figure is dressed in a fairly complete version of the costume described above.[35] In seven of these, the barbitos player appears alone, though there may be a related figure on the reverse side of the vase: on the reverse of Paris G 220, for instance, there is a similarly dressed bearded figure wearing a pleated sakkos and carrying a parasol.[36]

Three of the scenes show "Anakreon" with companions who carry parasols or wine cups. In figure 13, one of the two companions holds a kylix while the other has both a parasol and a pair of krotala; both the barbitos player and the man on his left wear earrings.[37] A fourth vase, New York 41.162.13, one of only two black-figured "Anakreon" vases, has three bearded men, each of whom plays a barbitos. They are accompanied by small figures with skin painted white (young boys?), and both the men and the children (?) wear long turbans or turban-like sakkoi. On two other red-figured vases, a single barbitos player is accompanied by one or two women who play the krotala.[38]

The headgear worn by these peculiarly dressed komasts is amazingly varied. Most of them wear a sakkos, but there are at least six different kinds, from a simple soft cloth cap over the hair (as in fig. 13) to an elaborately folded type with a topknot of hair drawn through to show at the back.[39] Only two of the "Anakreon" figures (on Paris G 220 and Syracuse 26967) wear the mitra, a headband of folded cloth similar to (but not the same as) the more customary fillet, but it is also worn by two of the "companions" on Madrid 11009.[40]

Other Poets

Besides Anakreon, two other fifth-century lyric poets are specifically linked with the barbitos, Bacchylides and his uncle, Simonides of Ceos (one of the Cyclades islands in the Aegean). Bacchylides, a highly regarded contemporary of the great Pindar, begins one of his poems with an address to the instrument:

> O barbitos, hang no longer on your peg
> Nor check your clear, seven-stringed voice;
> Come hither into my hands![41]

> Ὦ βάρβιτε, μηκέτι πάσσαλον φυλάσ[σων
> ἑπτάτονον λιγυρὰν κάππαυε γᾶρυν·
> δεῦρ' ἐς ἐμὰς χέρας·

Like Pindar, he seems to be recalling the scene in the *Odyssey* where Demodokos' instrument is taken down off its peg, but Bacchylides here and in one other poem labels his own particular instrument as the barbitos, a name never even mentioned in the extant works of Pindar.[42] Is this merely a poetic conceit in imitation of his famous predecessors, Sappho and Alcaeus, with whom the instrument was closely associated, or did Bacchylides in fact accompany his own singing with the music of the barbitos? Since we unfortunately have no vase paintings in which Bacchylides is depicted together with his lyre (as we do in the case of Sappho and Alcaeus), we cannot be certain of the answer, but the comparative rarity of the word *barbitos* (vis-à-vis *lyra* or *phorminx*), as well as its foreign overtones, suggest that the poet is at least not merely using the name *barbitos* to stand for music in general.

Bacchylides' uncle, Simonides of Ceos (ca. 556–468 B.C.), is also associated with the barbitos, although the instrument is not mentioned in any of the extant fragments of Simonides' poems. Nevertheless Theokritos, writing in the third century B.C., refers to Simonides as the divine bard (aoidos) of Ceos, who with the accompaniment of his "many-stringed" barbitos, sang the praises of kings, who, despite their great wealth, would otherwise have gone unremembered by posterity.[43] Since both Simonides and Bacchylides were from Ceos and both are connected in some way with the barbitos, we may be correct in supposing that the instrument enjoyed a popularity on the island that led to its use for the accompaniment of victory odes, encomia, and other types of songs (besides mere drinking songs) of the sort composed by the two Cean poets. Greece, after all, in antiquity as today, is formed of islands and villages of strong local customs and regional preferences, so that the use of the barbitos in Athens (from which the bulk of the evidence comes) may not necessarily correspond exactly to its use elsewhere in the Greek world.

In addition to the Anakreon portraits already discussed, the vase paintings depict the barbitos as the instrument of other poets as well. There are three portraits of Sappho as a player of the barbitos, all three of them bearing inscriptions that identify her. The earliest vase, Warsaw 142333, dates from about 500 B.C. and is decorated with a combination of incised lines and white paint ("Six's technique," used for face, arms, and feet, and the sling and plektron cord of the barbitos). Though the work is rather clumsy and careless, the name, spelled PSAPHO, is clearly inscribed. A vase, famous for its portrait of both Sappho and Alcaeus, is Munich 2416 (fig. 15), a painting from the first quarter of the fifth century in which both poets appear as players of the barbitos. The inscriptions ALKAIOS, SAPHO (*sic*) are clear, but the poets wear fifth-century Athenian dress: Sappho the chiton and himation, with a decorated fillet about her head; and Alcaeus a chiton and chlamys, with a mitra, a pleated band of cloth, about his head. Sappho appears alone again in the third portrait, the work of the Tithonos Painter from about 480 B.C., in which she is similarly dressed but wears a sakkos in place of the fillet; an aulos bag dangles from the arm of her barbitos.[44]

The Muses

Paintings of the Muses in which the barbitos appears (along with such other instruments as the lyra, aulos, and krotala) also emphasize its association with poetry. On Paris Petit Palais 308 (fig. 16) it is played by the Muse Kalliope, who is seated in the center; her name is inscribed, as are the names of two of the four other Muses in the scene, Terpsichore and Thalia (the latter holds a lyra). On two other vases the Muses are identified not by inscriptions but by the scene itself—they appear with the mythical poet/musician Thamyras in settings that indicate a precinct sacred to the Muses with trees, altar, and small female statuettes.[45] The ten women musicians, one with the barbitos, five with lyrai, and four with auloi, on Bologna 271, must also be Muses, although there is nothing else to identify them; and two scenes in which there are five women with either three or four instruments, including a barbitos, probably also represent Muses.[46]

The Barbitos at Home

There is some evidence that both men and women might while away time at home by making music with the barbitos. It is the barbitos, according to two vase paintings, that was in Aegisthos' hands when Orestes caught him unawares in a moment of relaxation and murdered him; see figure 17.[47] It may also be because the barbitos can represent quiet, personal entertainment and leisure that we see it in the hands of the bearded man on a tall grave stele dating from about 460 B.C. found in western Greece (Athens 735); here, in a context where the lyra is more commonly seen, it may symbolize either the happy pursuits of Elysium or the convivial nature of the soul who has gone to enjoy them.

But most of the glimpses of the barbitos at home involve women. The paintings of this sort that have been found resemble the bridal scenes discussed above, except that they have no Eros figures. (In a way, the bridal scenes also show the barbitos as an instrument for leisure-time music making.) Since the scenes without an Eros present only a few women (usually three, but in a few cases two or four) and seldom more than one or two instruments, it is unlikely that the women are Muses; this is also more or less ruled out by the obvious indoor locations, established by furniture, columns, and objects hanging on the wall.

The barbitos player, in all nine of the paintings of this type at hand, is seated, usually in the center of the group: on Bologna 271 where there are only two women, the one seated on the right has no instrument, but she reaches out to take the barbitos from the woman standing before her, who holds it at her side.[48] Though no instrument other than the barbitos is actually played in these scenes, one of the other women often holds a lyra or pair of auloi, and on Paris G 543 a pair of krotala hangs on the wall.[49] Four of the paintings appear on red-figured hydriai of the second half of the century; because the hydria is often associated

with weddings, it seems possible that these, too, are bridal scenes, even though no Eros figure is included; see figure 18. On another of them, Munich 6452, a crane stands before the seated woman with the barbitos, just as in two of the "bridal" paintings (see above).[50]

Music Lessons with the Barbitos

The barbitos appears in a music-lesson context only twice among all the representations now at hand.[51] In both cases it is the instructor who has the instrument; on Schwerin KG 707 the student facing him has no instrument and is presumably being taught to sing; on London E 171 the student plays the auloi and it is the instructor who sings (four small o's issue from his mouth) while accompanying himself on the barbitos. Both scenes include other students and instruments (lyrai, auloi) as well as other accoutrements (walking staves, aulos cases, and so on) and animals (dogs and, on London E 171, what appears to be a small leopard). On the latter vase a small child (?) sits on the floor behind the principal student.

Our examples show the barbitos only as an assisting instrument, used for lessons in singing and aulos playing, but it is clear that youngsters did play the barbitos: on London E 527 a small boy, accompanied by a bird and a dog with a chous tied around its neck, walks along playing a barbitos scaled to his size, and on New York 22.139.32 a youth with his dog behind him plays the instrument while a younger boy holds his staff.[52] It seems likely that one did not need special lessons in barbitos playing—the lessons with the chelys-lyra may have been sufficient for playing either instrument, since the techniques employed seem to have been the same in most respects, as will be shown below.

The role of the barbitos is well summed up in the fourth century in Aristotle's list of musical instruments that are not acceptable for educational purposes. The chief objection to the barbitos is that it is designed to give pleasure (not education), says Aristotle, to those who hear its music.[53] This instrument, perhaps more than any other, was firmly linked in the Greek mind with the pleasurable combination of wine and song.

Technique of Performance

What little is said in Greek literature about the technique of playing the instrument is found only in late sources such as Julius Pollux (2d century A.D.) and the *Anacreontea*. Pollux lists the lyra, kithara, and barbitos as instruments that are "struck" (*organa ta krouomena*), presumably with the plektron.[54] Although the plektron is not mentioned in connection with the barbitos in sixth- or fifth-century works, the author of *Anacreontea* 60.5 speaks of playing his barbitos with an ivory plektron, and the instrument as it is shown being played in the vase paintings is depicted with a plektron.

About three quarters of our barbitos players walk or stand (or, in the case of Eros, fly) while they play the instrument; a few of them are dancing. The high percentage of komos scenes, in which there are rarely any seated participants, helps to account for this, of course. Very few male barbitos players are seated while they play; men recline on couches while they play at a symposium, as we have seen, but aside from Aegisthos and the two music instructors mentioned above, the only male players who are seated are an Eros on a vase in Fiesole, three representations of youths who sit on their heels to play or tune, and a single painting of Heracles tuning his barbitos while seated on a stool (see n. 8). Women, on the other hand, who comprise almost one-fifth of the barbitos players studied, are seated in chairs in nearly half the scenes where they appear, including all but one of the "bridal" scenes and groups of women "at home," as well as two representations of the Muses.[55]

In most situations the players hold the barbitos with the soundbox tucked between forearm and side at waist level, and with the strings tipped away from the body at an angle of about 45° from the vertical, just as they do the chelys-lyra. But in many komos scenes, especially if the player appears to be dancing, the instrument is tipped out further, 60°–90° from the vertical; reclining symposiasts may also do this (the player's upper body the equivalent of the vertical in this case).

Since the positions of both right and left hands seen in paintings of barbitos players so closely resemble those in paintings of players of the lyra (analyzed in detail in chap. 4) in most respects, the hand positions of barbitos players need only be summarized here, with attention to some unusual examples.

Nearly a third of the one hundred fifty available representations in which the left hand is visible, including most of the black-figured vases, show us the player's left hand just above the soundbox, fingers straight and usually separated, as in figure 18.[56] Sometimes the thumb is bent across the palm to some extent, as if plucking one of the strings. One suspects that in practice the player's fingers curved toward the strings in order to damp them with the fingertips.[57] A still larger group (two-fifths of the total) offers what is perhaps merely a more sophisticated portrayal of

this position, with the wrist rotated to some degree toward the outer arm of the instrument, which would allow the thumb greater freedom of movement; see figures 4, 13, and 15. The fingers are ordinarily separated, rather straight but bent over from the palm somewhat to touch the strings, so that they angle toward the outer arm instead of standing parallel to the strings.

In another fifth of the examples at hand the left-hand fingers are curled over so that the nails show (though the painters do not ordinarily indicate them); see figure 3. In all but a few of these, surprisingly enough, the instrument is being played—this is not a matter of grasping the strings to secure the instrument while doing something else. Sometimes the thumb and index finger seem to be used together to pluck a string; sometimes the thumb is straight and held away from the palm, as though to be used alone.[58] On Berlin 2532 the satyr's thumb and little finger stick out as though they are being used to pluck two strings at once. In some cases the player holds the little finger alone out straight, as does the satyr on Munich 2311; but this is only a mannerism, it would seem, like holding a teacup with little finger extended.

Other left-hand positions occur in only a few instances. The index finger may be curved to meet the thumb, while the other fingers are straight or only slightly bent; or the thumb and first finger (or first and second fingers) may be straight and separated, while the other fingers are curled, as in figure 9.[59] There are also a few examples in which the wrist is rotated so as to turn the palm somewhat toward the player instead of away from him, which might be favorable for using the thumb and little finger to pluck two strings simultaneously.[60]

The barbitos player grasps the plektron in his right hand just as the player of the chelys-lyra does, and as was the case with lyra representations, the player extends his arm so that the hand with the plektron is beyond the outer arm of the instrument (as though finishing an outward sweep) in more than half the representations in which the right hand can be seen; see figures 3, 15 (Alcaeus), and 18. Although the performer sometimes is shown holding the plektron down at his side, drawn back at his waist, in his lap, or in some other position that makes it difficult to tell if he is really playing, or—if he is—how he might be using the plektron, in about a third of the clear examples the right hand holds the plektron near the chest or on or near the strings: these are the items of particular interest for investigating the question of how the plektron is used.

As figures 2 and 4 show, when the plektron is held so that its point is toward the player, it may be close to the player's chest or near the innermost string; but this hand position is rarely seen when the plektron is on or past the strings.[61] There seems little doubt that it represents the beginning of a stroke.

When the right hand is between the player's body and the strings (even with the inner arm, for example) with the plektron turned outward or when the plektron is directly in front of, or just past, the strings, however, the situation is not always so obvious. In a small number of the clearly visible right-hand examples, the possibility exists that an inward stroke is portrayed. There are eight vases that could be interpreted as representing the end of such a stroke: see figure 19.[62] It may be, of course, that what is shown is the moment before the beginning of an outward stroke, just before the performer turns the plektron head back ready to begin. Fourteen paintings might be interpreted as showing an inward sweep in progress, though an outward sweep, using only the motion of the wrist (rather than of the forearm) and perhaps touching only some of the strings, would certainly look at the end of the stroke much like what we see in these examples—plektron turned out and seen at the outermost string or just beyond.[63] In some cases there appears to be a perspective problem: the right forearm seems to be held close to the player's right side, while the barbitos is held close against his left side; the plektron may therefore not touch the strings at all but simply be in the process of being returned to the point close to the player's chest where the next outward stroke will begin.[64]

The stroke of the plektron seems normally to touch the strings at a point between the top of the soundbox and the left-hand fingertips. The strings are struck at a higher point than this in only about ten instances, including two representations on scarabs that may be intended to show the player tuning (see below). The plektron hand is at the center below the soundbox or below the top of the lower string fastener in five paintings of the barbitos; in two or three others, the plektron might be thought to touch the strings between the bridge and lower string fastener (as discussed in chap. 3), except that a fold of the player's chiton falls between plektron and strings.[65]

Tuning

The method of tuning the barbitos was the same as for the lyra, with the left hand in playing position to test the pitch by plucking the strings and the right hand at the crossbar to adjust the individual kollopes. Six vase paintings and a scarab illustrate the procedure, but only three of the paintings are careful or complete enough to show how all the right-hand fingers are used.[66] These three, however, indicate that although all the fingers may be curved around the crossbar, the second and third, or third and little fingers, may be allowed to stand out straight; apparently only the thumb and index finger are really needed to turn a kollops.

Singers to the Barbitos

Barbitos players who sing as they play are not rare at all—of about 175 clearly visible performers, 22 are certainly singing and another 14 probably are—a substantially higher percentage than among lyra or kithara players. The players in both groups are mostly komasts (including a number of "Anakreon" figures), symposiasts, or satyrs; and only three of them are women.

Five of those who are undoubtedly singing can be identified in part because the painters have shown letters issuing from their mouths. The "Anakreon" in figure 13 and the music teacher in London E 171 each have a series of four o's coming from their mouths; the komast on Erlangen 454 sings, "I am revelling to the aulos," ειμι κο[μα]ζον υπαυ[λον], possibly the opening words of a drinking song. On Paris G 30 the symposiast sings ΜΑΜΕΚΑΓΟΤΕΟ (the opening of a poem?), and on Boston 10.193 the letters the reveler sings are ΣΓΑΝΙΟΝΙΕΝ (the meaning, if any, unknown). All twenty-two of those who are clearly singing (except the player on Paris G 30, above) have their mouths open and their heads thrown back or at least raised somewhat. In the additional group of fourteen who are probably also singing, several factors prevent our being sure: the figure may be indistinct, the mouth may be only slightly open, or the head may be bent down; in a few cases, such as figure 19, the head is thrown back, and we would say that the player is singing but for the fact that the lips are closed.

The Sound of the Barbitos

While the literary references contain very little information about the tuning of the barbitos or about its construction, a scholiast on Euripides' *Alcestis* does offer one bit of useful information: in commenting upon Admetus' promise to forsake the barbitos, he explains that "the barbitos is a type of musical instrument, having strings of a rather low pitch; it is as if the name were *barymitos* ('low-stringed')."[67] This (obviously false) etymology confirms what can be conjectured from the relatively great length of the instrument's strings (as compared to the ordinary chelys-lyra), namely, that if the tension and thickness are roughly the same as in the case of the chelys-lyra, the pitch of the barbitos will be distinctly lower than the pitch of an ordinary lyra as a result of the extra length of the strings.

It might be assumed that the epithets applied to the barbitos in fifth-century literature would reveal some of the instrument's other characteristics, but these epithets appear to be conventional adjectives borrowed from the Homeric tradition and used more for their poetic effects than for their descriptive qualities. In the fifth century, Bacchylides, for example, speaks of his instrument's "clear voice" (*liguran . . . garyn*) and elsewhere describes the barbitos as "clear-sounding" (*liguachea*).[68] Both descriptions simply echo the Homeric epithet for the phorminx, *ligus* ("bright-sounding"; see chap. 1).

About all we can conclude from the literary references, then, is that the barbitos was probably a sort of tenor lyre, that it was played with the plektron, and that its sound could reasonably be described with the traditional Homeric epithets implying a bright, clear timbre.

Construction of the Barbitos

The barbitos is depicted as a seven-stringed instrument in fewer than half our representations with visible strings, a smaller number than we might expect (see figs. 2, 4, 12, 17, 19, and 21). If all the examples in which there is any doubt as to the number are weeded out (a procedure that favors the larger, better-executed works), we find that about half the instruments have seven strings; a slightly smaller number have five or six; and only a few have eight.[69] Instruments with five, six, or eight strings (see figs. 5, 6, and 20, five strings; figs. 3, 7, and 13, six strings; figs. 15 [Sappho] and 18, eight strings) appear more often on the larger, better-painted vases than on the smaller pots; seven-stringed barbitoi are more often found on the smaller vases. The seven-stringed instruments do not actually outnumber all the others together at any time between 530 and 420 B.C. except for the quarter century 500–475 B.C., when an especially large number of them appear in the komos and symposium scenes painted on drinking cups. When all these factors are considered, the possibility that the barbitos was sometimes strung with five or six strings must at least be entertained. Such instruments are well represented both early and late, the number gradually increasing between 530 and 450 B.C., and carefully painted ones are

plentiful enough to make them hard to dismiss as painters' mistakes.

The size and proportions of the barbitos, as presented by the painters, vary a good bit, but a standard size and shape can be discerned. In about half the instruments surveyed, the height is approximately twice the width between the arms at the widest point; another third are narrower, the width being as little as one-third of the height; the remaining ones are wider, as much as two-thirds of the height (though photographic distortion may make some measurements unreliable). The barbitos in figure 20 is a clear example (the only decoration on this side of the vase) of normal proportions: the arms twice as wide as the soundbox, the height 2⅓ times the width of the arms. As for size, the width between the arms is about the same as the length of the player's forearm, elbow to second knuckle, in nearly half the sample, and the height is twice this measure in over one-third of the examples.

The long arms, which diverge above the soundbox and curve inward under the crossbar, are the single most important identifying characteristic of the barbitos. Some of the vases painted in the late sixth century (mostly black-figured), however, offer examples of the barbitos that differ from this standard in one of two ways: the arms may have an undulating shape; or they turn back on themselves at the top to form a loop over which, or into which, the crossbar passes.

Four black-figured vases decorated between 520 and 500 B.C. present versions of the barbitos that have arms of a "wavy" outline. The most astonishing of these is the plate painted by Psiax, figure 21, which is sometimes considered to be the earliest of the "Anakreon" representations. Similar barbitoi on the other three vases have a less extravagant shape, with only one indentation about a third of the way down from the top.[70]

In figure 21, the arms have not only an undulating outline but are also curved out and down at the top, just under the crossbar. However, it appears that instruments were not normally depicted with both these features; of the instruments depicted around the shoulder of Paris F 314 (see n. 69), five have arms with the extra curves that do not turn out and downward at the crossbar, while at least three have arms without extra curves that do, however, turn over at the top. Figure 1 and Paris F 216 are other black-figured vases that provide evidence for the latter type (in fig. 1 the arms are barbitos-length but neither undulating nor of standard shape). Two relatively early red-figured vases show us similar instruments in which the outward curve under the crossbar becomes a loop (that is, the arm is bent around to touch itself), somewhat resembling a swan's head on New York 41.162.6; on Würzburg 4937 the loops are realistic swan's heads, complete with eyes.[71] The fitting sometimes seen just under the crossbar on the "standard" fifth-century barbitos (fig. 15) may be a reminiscence of this.

The existence of these two unusual varieties of barbitoi suggests that in the late sixth century the barbitos was indeed a newcomer to mainland Greece and that it was still viewed (and perhaps deliberately represented by the painters) as a "foreign" instrument.

The arms of these unusual barbitoi as well as those of the standard shape were probably made of wood in the late sixth and fifth centuries, though the instruments with unusually curvaceous arms certainly suggest that at one time, at least, such instruments had arms made from elegantly curved antelope horns.[72] On four vases, instruments of standard shape have lines across the arms in approximately the area where they begin to curve inward, which may indicate some kind of reinforcement at this point but may also mean that the arms are made in sections fastened together.[73]

The upper ends of the arms of the standard barbitos (as seen in fig. 20) turn toward each other beneath the fitting for the crossbar, leaving a space for the strings to pass through that sometimes seems quite wide (as in Cambridge, Harvard 1959.125) and sometimes rather narrow (fig. 20).[74] The arms themselves, in a few instances, appear to be narrowly set and straighter than usual.[75] This situation may arise from painters' efforts to present the instrument as seen from an angle rather than as seen from front or back. The remarkable painting on Brussels A 3091 (fig. 22), in which both arms of the barbitos appear to curve in the same direction, makes it clear that painters did attempt this. More important, it also confirms that the arms of the barbitos did not simply curve toward each other in the same plane as the strings—they also curve forward somewhat, with the result that the strings will stand away from the soundbox at a sharper angle than would otherwise be the case. In over a dozen paintings the arms end under the crossbar with small circles, or circles with dots in them, apparently not a decoration but a way of showing a cross section that would indeed be visible if the arms curve forward somewhat (see fig. 15).[76]

The barbitos is distinguished not only by the length and curvature of its arms but also by the attachments above the curved arm ends that hold the crossbar.[77] That these are indeed separate pieces, and not extensions of the arm, is clear enough, both from the dividing lines that are often present, and from the shape of the outer edges of the attachments, which frequently curve out at the bottom to provide reinforcement and

a larger surface in contact with the arms (see figs. 6, 12, 15, 18, 19, and 22). In some of the earlier paintings these fittings protrude above the crossbar only slightly (figs. 3–5, 12, and 13) or not at all, whereas in others, particularly those made after 450 B.C., there may be a tall rectangular piece standing above the crossbar, as in figures 19 and 20. (In this latter type the crossbar may not be affixed at the bottom but as much as halfway up this long rectangular piece, or even higher.) This extension may be wide or narrow; in some of the earlier paintings it looks wedge shaped, with the widest part at the top (fig. 5).

The inside edges of these sections are straight and nearly always parallel.[78] They are painted white in several black-figured examples such as figure 5, and on one black-figured amphora, Oxford 1885.656, Heracles tunes a barbitos with its crossbar fittings painted red. Since their purpose is ornamental as well as functional, it is not surprising that this is the part of the barbitos that is commonly provided with some decorative detail, usually in the form of two or three slits or notches in the upper ends (figs. 18 and 19) or in some cases a small cup-shaped indentation (figs. 17 and 22). In a few instances there are lines painted or carved across each piece just below the notch or indentation.[79]

Most representations of the barbitos do not reveal how the crossbar is attached to its elaborate fitting, but in more than a dozen of the paintings studied, there appear to be rounded pieces at the front of the fitting behind which the crossbar sits.[80] In another eight examples, including figures 13 and 15, the crossbar appears to sit *on* the rounded section, which perhaps has a groove into which the crossbar fits (see fig. 17).[81]

The crossbar itself is ordinarily rather narrow, and its free ends do not extend out much beyond the upright fittings in most cases; its total length is seemingly dependent upon the amount of space between the arms. In three of the available representations the crossbar has small knobs at the ends; in two others the ends are decorated with vertical or horizontal lines; and in another the entire crossbar is painted white.[82] Many of the carefully painted vases include some indication of the kollopes, often painted red, as in figure 4. In several cases the kollops pins are shown behind the crossbar or are long and narrow, as in figure 17, so that one can see that they include solid pieces (probably of wood or bone) and are not merely strips of leather wrapped around the crossbar.[83]

The soundbox of the barbitos appears to be much the same as that of the lyra. When the back is shown, the tortoise-shell markings are more or less carefully painted in, often with the plain border that we have suggested represents the overlapping of the hide that covers the front (see fig. 6 and chap. 4). In size the soundbox of the barbitos also seems similar to that of the lyra, and in some cases it actually appears to be somewhat smaller (see fig. 21). Its shape is often the same too, though the "ears," or side bulges, seen so often in paintings of the lyra seem in many cases less pronounced and quite high, producing the kind of shape seen in figures 13 and 17.[84] The arms of the barbitos enter the front of the soundbox near the top, ordinarily, at or near the top of the bulge, as the illustrations show.[85]

The bridge, and the device at the lower edge of the soundbox to which the strings are attached, are usually the only features visible on the front of the soundbox.[86] Both are depicted in ways that are already familiar from our study of the lyra. The bridge may be nothing more than a line, thick or thin; it may be a cigar shape, a long rectangle, parallelogram, or an irregular four-sided figure larger at one end than the other. It is sometimes indented at the ends in a way that suggests that it is arched, as on Athens Acropolis 20; more often, there is some indication that it has feet, usually small circles or lines above and/or below the ends (see fig. 20) or underneath the part of the bridge over which the strings pass, as on Gela 67, which also has indented ends.[87] In figure 13, the bridge's ends seem to curve down to form feet. In figure 15 the bridges of the poets' barbitoi have a series of indentations along the upper edge, apparently indicating (inaccurately) grooves for the strings, a detail also seen on New York 06.1021.188.

There is nearly as much variety of sizes and shapes for the device to which the strings are fastened at the bottom as there is for the bridge, but again the types encountered are the same as those found on the lyra. The rectangular fastener with sides that are straight or curved out toward the base as in figures 12 and 17 is most commonly found; but in some cases the fastener becomes narrower toward the base (slanted, curved, or stepped inward); and in figure 20 and Copenhagen Chr. VIII 875 the entire fastener consists of a single curved line.

The plektron and cord, wrist sling, and "sash" that are the customary accoutrements of the lyra are also the normal equipment of the barbitos. The plektron, which hangs in front of the player in figure 6, is the same sort used with the lyra. In this illustration (where the player carries the instrument by the plektron cord) we can see the head of the plektron, which is usually shaped like the back of a pointed tablespoon with a ridge running down it and a narrow "neck" (see also fig. 15). We can also see the handle, which often seems larger and more padded than it does here, covered with leather or cloth (with crosshatching on New York 06.1021.178; also fig. 19), and a tassel, which is also present in a number of paintings (see fig. 18). The cord (and sometimes the plektron, too) may be indicated in red or white paint and is a wavy line in a few cases, as though made of strands of wool. It is usually attached to the outer arm of the instrument near the soundbox (sometimes higher), but in eight paintings on hand it is attached to the bottom of the soundbox or to the string fastener (as may be the case in fig. 6). The plektron is stuck underneath the strings above the bridge in figure 20, and in figure 21 its cord is looped over the crossbar.

The player's wrist sling and the sash or tassel that often hangs from it are also similar to those seen in paintings of the lyra. The wrist sling is sometimes indicated in red paint, as in figure 4 (or white paint, on black-figured vases; on a white-ground lekythos, Athens 1792, it is in brown). It may be wide or narrow; the wider ones often have lines along them that suggest folded cloth, but none is patterned or decorated as the wrist sling of a kithara may be. In figure 21 a narrow sling can be seen hanging loose from the arm of the instrument.[88] The sling is knotted outside the outer arm of the instrument, and the sash often appears to consist of the free ends of the same piece of cloth from which the sling is made (see fig. 13; notice that the lines on the sling turn and continue down the sash). In other paintings, such as Athens 17190 and Munich 2346, it seems to be a doubled piece of folded cloth with the loop pushed through the knot of the sling; but in either case it may be long or short.

In about half the clear representations of the sash, though, it is indicated as three or four thin strands, usually rather short and done in red paint. (Figure 4 has a red sash, but it is a single long strand with both ends tied to the arm.) On Paris kylix C 14460, these separate strands are no longer than the tassel on the plektron held near them, and most of the other examples show a similar length, too short to represent extra strings.[89]

Barbitos players occasionally drape a fillet over the arm of the instrument, as have the Anakreon figure on Boston 13.199, where the fillet is long and dotted, and the player on Torino 5776. The players on both sides of Copenhagen 3880 have tied broad fillets (in bow knots!) halfway along the arm of their instruments; the player on Madrid 11122 apparently has an instrument with both a sash (of the sort that seems looped through the wrist-sling knot) and a red fillet (it is not clear where the latter is attached).[90]

Although the barbitos was evidently played in much the same way as the chelys-lyra, it probably differed from the shorter-armed instrument in having a lower pitch range, in view of the longer length of its strings (assuming comparable tension and thickness). The barbitos may thus be described as a sort of tenor lyre. It is a temptation to think that the barbitos came into favor with the Athenians either because of its association with Dionysos (whose cult had Phrygian and Lydian connections) or because it was brought to Athens by Anakreon (or through the popularity of the works of Anakreon and the other Ionian poets). Although the vase paintings do not give conclusive support to either of these notions, the evidence seems to favor the influence of Anakreon.

Dionysos and his satyrs and maenads, though they do appear among the earliest paintings (fig. 1), are rarely seen before 500 B.C. or thereabouts. In the first half of the fifth century they are the subject on about one-eighth of the vases, but it is only in the second half of the century that scenes involving the Dionysiac troop seem to have become really popular with the vase painters (more than one-third of the total). On the other hand, while the portraits of Sappho and Alcaeus and most of the "Anakreons" belong to the first half of the fifth century (half of the latter to the second quarter of the century) the *inscribed* portraits of Anakreon on London E 18 and Copenhagen 13365 belong to the last quarter of the sixth century, and the remaining inscribed portrait, Syracuse 26967, dates to about 500 B.C.[91] Two other possible Anakreons, our figure 21 and Paris G 94 (which we have not seen), also belong to the early period.

Scenes related to the komos and symposium, by contrast, account for almost three-fourths of the early barbitos representations and more than half the barbitos scenes on vases from the first quarter of the fifth century. (After about 475 B.C. the number drops off sharply, and in the second half of the century they make up less than a third of the total.) On this evidence, it seems safest to say that the Athenian use of the barbitos is best explained by its association with these social customs, which were themselves affected in the late sixth century by Ionian fashions and customs, and may have been less frequently observed in the latter half of the fifth century as the result of un-

settled political conditions and the disruptions of war. It is in this later period that pictures of the barbitos played by women or Muses, almost unknown before about 475 B.C. and infrequent before about 450 B.C., become as numerous as komos and symposium scenes, a good indication, it may be, of the potters' attempts to meet changed market conditions.

As we have seen in chapter 2, the barbitos was originally associated with the Eastern Greek lyric poets and particularly with the songs they wrote to be sung at symposia. In the fifth century its role as the chief stringed instrument of the drinking party took precedence, although the barbitos still retained its associations with specific poets from the islands and from the East. In later times, however, when the Roman poets were looking for Greek models, the barbitos once again found its chief identification as the instrument of the poets of Lesbos, Sappho and Alcaeus. Horace, for instance, hopes the Muses will offer him the barbitos of Lesbos and twice refers to his own lyre as a barbitos.[92] In Ovid's portrait of Sappho, "Sappho" explains in elegiac couplets that she must lament her lost love and that her barbitos cannot produce a song appropriately sad enough, so that she must give up her usual lyric meters for elegiac meter instead (without lyre accompaniment).[93] The barbitos, at least as a literary symbol, had come full circle and once again became the special lyre of the Aeolic poets.

But the heyday of the barbitos at Athens was undoubtedly the early fifth century, the time when it appears most frequently in vase paintings (half again as often as in the previous or following quarter-centuries), coinciding with the highest percentage of komos-symposium scenes. Its popularity seems to have grown quickly: it must have been introduced at Athens shortly before about 525 B.C., the approximate date of the earliest vase paintings; for it is only in the late sixth century that we see unusual "foreign" versions of the instrument, with arms of undulating shapes or outward curves under the crossbar.

What brought about the demise of the barbitos at the end of the fifth century? We cannot lay much stress on the scarcity of representations in the last quarter of the century, since it seems likely that the production of painted pottery in general was much curtailed at this time. But the fact remains that in our sample there are only about a dozen paintings of the barbitos from this time.

And after the end of the century—nothing. The two other prominent members of the lyre family, the kithara and the lyra (in somewhat changed forms, to be sure), continue to be depicted in fourth-century paintings and on other objects. But the barbitos is gone. Perhaps whatever place remained to it in Athenian musical life had been gradually usurped by the harps that had begun to appear in the fifth century (see chap. 6). And the very institutions with which it had formerly been most associated may have been so changed by the deprivations of war and the influence of foreign cultures that there was no longer any need for such an instrument in the transformed life of the fourth century.

1. Frankfurt, Mus. für Khw. WM 03. Attic b.f. amphora. Detail: Dionysos and Ariadne with satyrs.

2. Cambridge, Harvard 1960.236. Attic r.f. calyx krater by the Kleophrades Painter. Detail: Dionysos and satyrs.

3. Toronto 356 (919.5.21).
Attic r.f. kylix. Detail:
komasts.

4. Toledo 64.126. Attic
r.f. kylix by the Foundry
Painter. Exterior detail:
komasts.

5. New York 41.162.2.
Attic b.f. amphora.
Komasts.

6. Brussels R 255. Attic
r.f. oionochoe. Man with
barbitos slung over his
shoulder.

7. New York 37.11.19.
Attic r.f. chous. Detail:
reveler returning from
festival of Anthesteria.

8. Cleveland 24.197. Attic
r.f. column krater.
Komast and youth.

9. Milan, Coll. "H.A." C
354. Attic r.f. column
krater. Detail:
symposium.

10. Gela 67. Attic r.f.
lekythos by the Brygos
Painter. Detail: Eros with
barbitos and winged
boots.

11. London 1921.7-10.2. Attic r.f. hydria. Detail: women with lyres, crane.

12. London E 44. Attic r.f. kylix. Interior detail: woman and man, barbitos.

13. Cleveland 26.549.
Attic r.f. krater. Detail:
men in female dress
dancing and playing
barbitos and krotala.

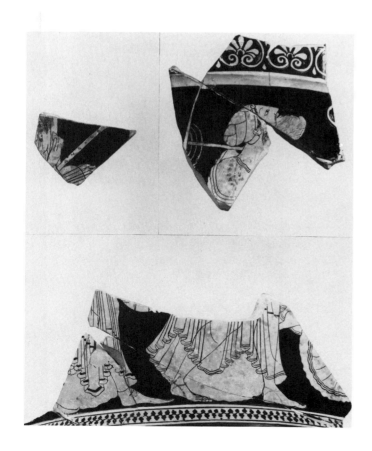

14. Copenhagen 13365.
Attic r.f. vase fragments.
Detail: men in female
dress; barbitos with
"Anakreon" inscription.

15. Munich 2416. Attic
r.f. kalathoid. Sappho and
Alcaeus.

16. Paris, Petit Palais
308. Attic r.f. hydria.
Detail: Muse.

17. Boston 63.1246. Attic r.f. calyx krater by the Dokimasia Painter. Death of Aegisthus.

18. Athens 17918. Attic r.f. hydria by the Peleus Painter. Detail: women with barbitos, chest, and lyra.

19. New York 07.286.85. Attic r.f. bell krater. Detail: Dionysos, maenads, satyr.

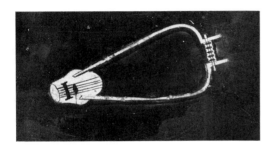

20. Munich 2404. Attic
r.f. stamnos. Detail:
barbitos.

21. Basel 421. Attic w.g.
pinax. Reveler and
musician.

22. Brussels A 3091. Attic
r.f. stamnos. Detail:
young man with barbitos.

CHAPTER SIX

Harps and Unusual Lyres
in Classical Athens

The kithara, the lyra, and the barbitos, though they were the three chief stringed instruments used by fifth-century Athenians, were not the only members of the lyre family known in Athens during this time, nor were lyres the only stringed instruments in use. The other lyres and the various kinds of harps mentioned in fifth-century literature and portrayed in art works of the time were less common than the instruments already discussed (judging by the number of citations and representations), but they were known and used by the Athenians, and each of them has a well-documented place in Athenian culture.

The Phorminx

The fourth member of the lyre family, known to us from over forty representations of the late sixth and the fifth centuries, is an instrument whose Greek lineage and association with Apollo and the Muses can be traced back at least as far as the eighth century (see chaps. 1 and 2).[1] Because its basic identifying features have not changed (rounded base, circles on the soundbox, and straight, parallel arms), this Classical-period instrument may still be referred to as the phorminx; there is no need to devise a new name (such as "cradle kithara," "Wiegenkithara") to refer to the instrument in the fifth century.[2]

Scenes

In the earliest representations of the phorminx from this period we can see evidence that the role of the instrument was gradually narrowing, as other instruments took over more and more of its functions. On vases of the late sixth century the phorminx appears only in Dionysiac scenes and komoi. Until about 500 B.C., it is still played by men, but only in the komos scenes.[3] After that time, it may still appear in komos scenes but only in the hands of women. Since women (other than goddesses) are not frequently represented in vase paintings of the last quarter of the sixth century, and recognizable Muses are generally not found in red-figured painting until after about 475 B.C., it is not surprising to find that until the turn of the century the only women who are seen to play the phorminx are maenads, whose role as followers of Dionysos gives them a place in the vase paintings. Between about 500 and 475 B.C., when Dionysiac scenes with the instrument are nearly gone and the barbitos has taken over as the primary instrument of the komos, there are almost no phorminx players at all, except for the maenad in a Dionysiac scene by Makron (once Robinson Coll.) and the women in two komos scenes. But with the increase in the number of women depicted on vases after 475 B.C. and the appearance of portraits of the Muses, representations of the phorminx are more frequent than ever, and its status, no longer as Apollo's instrument but now of the Muses alone, is abundantly confirmed.

About two-thirds of the group of paintings from the late sixth century (half a dozen paintings) are depictions of the followers of Dionysos in which maenads play the phorminx. Dionysos and his satyrs, or the satyrs alone, are included in half these scenes, and in another scene (fig. 1) the women are surrounded by vine branches with grape clusters, a clear indication that they are maenads. The two remaining paintings of women alone do not offer such clues, but like figure 1 they are found on wine pitchers (oinochoi); they wear decorated himatia and on one vase are shown dancing, one of them with krotala. There seems little doubt that these are maenads too.[4]

The only Dionysiac scene with the phorminx from the first half of the fifth century that has come to light is the kylix by Makron (Oxford, Miss.? once Robinson Coll.) on which Dionysos is accompanied by maenads playing krotala, auloi, and phorminx, but Cambridge, Harvard 1925.30.42 (fig. 8a), from after the middle of the century, testifies that the type was still known: here again is Dionysos, with an aulos-playing satyr, a maenad with a torch, and another with the phorminx.

The only other sixth-century scenes in which the phorminx is present, besides those related to Dionysos, are a small group of three komos scenes, which may be compared with a painting of a komos from before the middle of the sixth century, Rhodes 12.200 (chap. 2, fig. 6). Like this earlier work, the painting on Munich 1416 (fig. 2) includes only men. Four of the five men depicted play instruments (barbitos, phorminx, krotala, and auloi), and the one with krotala is dancing. All of them wear wreaths of some sort, three wear endromides ("winged" boots), and all but one (who is nude) wear their cloaks tied up around their waists. Each man is named by inscription: from the left, Milichos, Telokles, Mosaon, Diodoros, and Chremes. (If the central figure here represents Mousaios, the mythical poet-musician closely associated both with Apollo and with the Muses, this vase serves as a link between the earlier uses and associations of the phorminx as Apollo's instrument and its later appearance among the Muses when they begin to be represented in fifth-century art.) In a similar scene on Oxford 1919.46 two male phorminx players are joined by a woman playing the auloi, but on Los Angeles 50.8.2, a vase from the turn of the century, the women interspersed among the revelers at this large party play not only the auloi and krotala but the phorminx as well.

Only three more such scenes are to be found, all belonging to the first half of the fifth century. In these, the female player of the phorminx is at the center of the painting, with the komasts and male servants around her. One of them, Vienna 770, is of the "Anakreontic" type of komos—the two men wear sakkoi and one of them carries a parasol (see chap. 5).[5]

Representations of the Muses, which appear after 475 B.C., grow more frequent after mid-century. The presence of Apollo, dressed only in a himation and bearing lyra or laurel staff, serves to identify the women on three vases where the phorminx appears, though on Athens 1241 (fig. 6) their number (eight) and the other lyres, auloi, and open scroll they carry also indicate that they are Muses; and all three vases show some of the figures seated on rocks to indicate Mount Helicon, sacred to the Muses.[6] (This last feature alone, with the inscription "Helikon," identifies the single Muse who sits alone in fig. 7).

It is the legendary musician Thamyras (or Thamyris, according to the Homeric spelling of his name) who sits upon the rocks on Naples 3143 playing the chelys-lyra. Both the terrain and his presence in it tell us that the two women on the right, one of whom carries a phorminx, are Muses, whom Thamyras foolishly challenged (see below under Thracian Kithara). The two Muses in the company of Mousaios on London E 271 (chap. 4, fig. 2), however, are identified, as Mousaios himself is, by inscription: Terpsichora and Melousa. The phorminx, in this scene and a number of others, is hung upon the wall in the background—in this case over the head of Terpsichore—and it seems to be present simply as an identifying attribute of the Muses, for each of the three persons holds another instrument—auloi, harp, and chelys-lyra. If this is so, the phorminx suspended over the music lesson on Schwerin 708 (chap. 4, fig. 17), where Linos teaches Iphikles, the brother of Heracles, to play the lyra, may also be a symbol of the Muses' favor.

There are only six Muses on Boston 98.887 (fig. 3), and they are accompanied only by a cowherd (said to represent Hesiod or Archilochos; see *ARV*[2] 774), so that recognition depends, first, upon the number of instruments they carry (two elaborate examples of the phorminx, chelys-lyra, aulos, and syrinx), and second, on the plants and rocks that suggest a mountainous terrain. (The Muse by the same painter who stands alone playing the phorminx on Paris CA 483 is identified only by the plant growing on the left.) It is not until near the end of the century, on a Greek vase from southern Italy (Apulia), that we find nine Muses (Munich 3268). They bear among them five instruments (two sets of auloi, harp, phorminx, and chelys-lyra), an open scroll (perhaps also an attribute), and two small boxes or coffers; the only details that help to establish the location are two columns, a curling plant, and a crane.

The figures on five other vases, though they are not presented along with any of the identifying features discussed above, probably are also to be understood to be Muses. In these paintings there are only one or two women (in one case three) carrying or playing the phorminx and (when there are two or more) a chelys-lyra. Beazley calls the woman seated on a diphros on Paris CA 482 a Muse, probably because she was created by the Hesiod Painter, whose work is also seen on Boston 98.887 and Paris CA 483 (above), and despite the mirror hanging on the wall on the left, a domestic touch that might lead us to think of the woman as a mortal (on the right hangs a wreath). With this in mind, the two women in figure 5 may be considered to be Muses (a mirror hangs above the one on the left), and it seems likely that the three women on Dresden 332, where the third woman carries a small chest, are also, for such a chest can be found beside the nine Muses on Munich 3268 (above).[7]

Five other paintings with two or three women may also represent Muses, but on three of them only one of the two women has an instrument, the Stockholm "Diphilos" lekythos, Bowdoin 15.46, and Bologna 362.[8] On a fourth, both women play instruments, but there is a small Eros in the scene, Leningrad 732, as there is also on Würzburg 521, where there are three women carrying instruments—phorminx, barbitos, and auloi. Though Erotes are not unknown in portrayals of Muses (see below under Thracian Kithara), and though we are told in Plato's *Phaedrus* (259D) that lovers honor the Muse Erato, this last vase, with the barbitos player seated in the center and an open chest on the floor, the only scene of its kind known at present in which there is a phorminx, closely resembles the "bridal" scenes discussed in chapter 5.[9]

There is, however, another kind of scene in which the phorminx appears among mortal women: in it, young girls are dancing, while women play instruments to accompany them, sometimes with a man watching from the sidelines. These paintings, all but one, belong to the period after about 450 B.C., by which time the phorminx no longer appears in komos scenes. These people, then, are almost the only mortals depicted in the later paintings among whom the phorminx is to be found, and it is therefore interesting to see that in only one of the five paintings of this sort is the phorminx actually played—in two of them it hangs on the wall overheard, as in figure 4, perhaps, as is suggested above in connection with the painting of Linos, a sign that the girls have the favor of the Muses.[10]

The instrument that actually accompanies the dancers, even when the phorminx is also used, is the aulos; krotala are also in evidence, but only on Athens pyxis 14909 are they played by the dancer herself. Three or more different kinds of dances can be distinguished, mainly by the costume worn: the pyrrhic, a

dance using the motions of combat and performed bearing helmet, shield, and spear; acrobatic dances, involving somersaults and the like and performed nude; and a category of dance (or dances) of less obvious meaning, performed wearing a short chiton, as in figure 4.

The female pyrrhic dancers on Florence 4014 (see chap. 4, fig. 16) wear helmets, short chitons, and a cord around the left leg at the calf and carry spears and shields, one with the head of a woman as its device. They, and the women who play the aulos and lyra on either side of them, are named: Kleodoxa, Selinike, Dorka, and Pegasis. Farther left is a seated woman, Nikopolis; leaning on the back of her chair is a man, Kallias. Behind him stands the woman who plays the phorminx, and behind her flies a large Eros who also carries a phorminx but does not play it: perhaps these instruments at the edge of the scene serve a mainly symbolic purpose.

There is also a woman dancing the pyrrhic, with krotala for accompaniment, on Naples 81398 (fig. 8b), where all three of the categories of dances listed above are represented. This is the only vase in the group on which acrobatic dancers appear (one of the two, who has a cord tied about her left thigh, prepares to turn somersaults in and out of a hoop with swords set upright around its edge, as described in Xenophon's *Symposium* [2.11]). But the acrobats are accompanied by an aulos player, and the phorminx, held in one hand by a woman who has a pair of auloi in the other, is at the far side of the scene, nearest a pair of girls in short chitons whose dance belongs to the third category (dances of less obvious meaning).

Four of our five paintings depict girls in short chitons in a dance of this sort, and on these four, except for Naples 81398 (fig. 8b), this is the only kind of dance represented. Only on Athens 14909 does the dancer play the krotala, though on Lecce 572 they hang on the wall along with the phorminx. The elbows-out, hands-on-hip pose seen in figure 4, apparently held while swinging the upper torso from side to side, is like that on Lecce 572, although here the dancer holds her hands higher, fists clenched; the positions of legs and feet are the same in both paintings.[11] The dancers of this sort on Naples 81398, though they have one hand at the waist, extend the other arm high and straight in front of them, palm out. One of them stands on her toes, the other bends one knee to the floor. This pair of dancers is also portrayed with crown-like headdresses with thin spikes (reeds?) set in them, a costume that various scholars have associated with the Karyatid dances for Artemis Karyatis in Laconia, with the "dancing reeds" at an annual festival at Lake Tala in Lydia, or with the "basket dance" (or dance steps), the *kalathiskos* or *kalathismos*.[12]

Some, and possibly all, of the girls and women in these scenes are professional dancers. The acrobatic dancers certainly are, as Xenophon's *Symposium* (2.1–11) affirms. Since these dancers appear on Naples 81398 along with both pyrrhic dancers and what seem to be kalathiskos dancers, and since male onlookers (owners or managers?) are present on three vases watching dances of all three types (see fig. 4), there is little doubt that the costumed dancers are also professionals. (In the case of the female pyrrhic dancers there is additional evidence, for Xenophon's *Anabasis* [6.1.12] tells of an entertainment in the camp of the Greek army during which a female dancer with a shield performed the pyrrhic with great agility; she must surely be counted a professional, though we may have doubts as to how much of her living was earned in this way.) But since dancing of whatever sort was the province of the Muses, it is not surprising that the paintings allude to the Muses' favor through the presence of the phorminx.

Performance

The players of the phorminx, except on some half-dozen of the later vases, stand while they play. They hold the instrument tipped away from them 30°–45°, though in a few cases they hold it rather in the way the kithara is held (tipped out only slightly, as in fig. 2), and in a few other paintings (mostly of komos dancers) they hold the instrument almost horizontally (see chap. 2, fig. 6).

The phorminx is played as are the other members of the lyre family; the positions of both left and right hands are similar to those already noted in paintings of the other instruments. The left-hand fingers are often straight and separated, especially in the earlier paintings, sometimes with the thumb bent over the palm; the wrist is rotated in some cases and the fingers are slanted or bent as though to damp the strings with the fingertips. In three paintings the thumb is apparently being used with one of the other fingers to pluck two strings at the same time (fig. 5).[13] In half a dozen other paintings the fingers are curled forward so that the nails (theoretically) show (fig. 1), a gesture that brings thumb and forefinger or middle finger together and is perhaps a way of plucking a single string.[14]

The right hand, when actually in use, holds the plektron out beyond the outer edge of the instrument in most paintings, as we have come to expect. The stroke is in progress on several vases, either just past the strings (as in fig. 7) or in the middle of them.[15]

Florence 4014 and Oxford 225 (fig. 1) show us a stroke just beginning, and there are three anomalous representations, all by the Hesiod Painter: one of the Muses on Boston 98.887 (not the one in fig. 3) uses her right hand high on the strings, apparently to pluck them—and she has this hand through a wrist sling! On Paris CA 483 the hand is similarly located and clearly holds no plektron (it hangs by its cord looped over the arm of the phorminx); the wrist sling in this example dangles loose from the instrument. On Paris CA 482 the wrist sling lies loose in the lap of the seated Muse, who uses her right hand, it would seem, to adjust the bridge. Since these last two players are adjusting or testing their instruments, perhaps the Muse on Boston 98.887 is also testing hers—if her pose is not an invention, or a mistake, of the painter.

The phorminx is tuned as are the other members of the lyre family. We have only a single scene in which the procedure is demonstrated, and that on a Greek vase made in southern Italy (Munich 3268, Apulian), but it serves well enough to confirm this: the central Muse in this scene places her right hand at the crossbar to adjust a kollops while her left hand plucks the string to test it.

Only among the participants in the komos do we find singers to the phorminx. The two companions on either side of Mosaon (whose head is lifted but with mouth closed), figure 2, are singing, and the female player and the men on either side of her in the "Anakreontic" komos, Vienna 770, appear to be singing also. The woman who stands amid komos preparations on Cambridge, Harvard 1959.188, sings, head back somewhat and lips parted, while perhaps plucking the strings of the phorminx with her left hand (her right is underneath the soundbox). The woman who dances alone with the phorminx on Urbana, Ill. Krannert 70-8-5 (a player at a komos?), also has her head back and her lips parted.

Construction

Like the other lyres, the phorminx continues to be a seven-stringed instrument in this period: of thirty-three paintings in which its strings are visible, twenty-one provide it with seven (figs. 2, 3, 5, 7), eight show five or six (fig. 4), three have eight strings (fig. 1), and one has ten (fig. 8a). Most of the examples with more or fewer than seven strings are not very carefully painted, and there is no correlation between date and number of strings. Cambridge, Harvard 1925.30.42 (fig 8a), which shows ten strings, is an exception, however; though it is not a very late vase (it belongs to the third quarter of the century), it is a detailed, carefully painted one.

The width of the phorminx, measured at the widest part of the soundbox, is on the average approximately equal to the length of the player's forearm from elbow to knuckles, while the height is about 1⅓ times this measure. The largest examples are not wider, only taller, as much as 1½ times the elbow-knuckles unit; the smaller ones have a width of about ⅔ and a height of one unit. Like the kithara, the phorminx was no doubt constructed of wood, the more elaborate sort being decorated with ivory or gold, as in the earlier days.

The shape of the soundbox varies a good bit, as we might expect for an instrument that the painters probably did not often see. At times, as in figure 3, it resembles the waxing crescent moon, but the ends are generally elongated (fig. 1) and sometimes curved inward somewhat.[16] In the earlier representations (before about 475 B.C.) the ends are rounded as a rule (figs. 1 and 2). But squared-off ends can be seen on two late sixth-century vases, Bologna 151 and Oxford 212, and after about 450 B.C., nearly all examples are made this way (see figs. 4, 5, 7, and 8). The height of the soundbox also varies; that of the instrument on London E 185 (fig. 4) is one of the shortest examples, and the one on Lecce 572 is one of the tallest.

The soundbox of the phorminx is provided with a bridge and lower string fastener that appear to be the same as those used on other types of lyres. The bridge is usually indicated with a single line, broad or narrow, but on Paris CA 483 it is a wide parallelogram; on Schwerin 708 it has a similar shape, though smaller, with feet showing under the strings above the upper edge (see chap. 4, fig. 17).[17] On the Stockholm "Diphilos" lekythos the feet can be seen above and below the bridge. The lower string fasteners are usually simple rectangles, some longer than others, but the sides may be set in from the ends somewhat or curve out at the bottom.

Pairs of lines forming right angles, more or less, on each side of the front of the soundbox, separate the upper corners from the central and lower areas of the soundbox on nearly a third of our front-view examples (see figs. 4, 5, and 8a; in fig. 5 the corner areas are painted brown). Three early paintings (520–500 B.C.) and one made ca. 430 B.C., figure 6, appear to have a single line separating the upper corners from the rest of the soundbox (fig. 1).[18] If the testimony of the instrument in figure 6 can be accepted, the depth of the soundbox becomes shallower in its elongated corner areas; in this three-quarter view of the front of a phorminx the ends of the soundbox seem to be concave below the point where the arms are attached.[19]

Two of our paintings of the phorminx have a pair of horizontal lines all the way across the front of the soundbox just above the bridge: London E 271 (see chap. 4, fig. 5) and Bologna 362, which also has corner sections. On another three, Boston 98.887 (not visible in fig. 3), Dresden 332, and Oxford 212, the only lines showing on the front are those forming an ornamental band around the edges of the soundbox. The rest of the front views have no visible lines of any sort.

In most of the back views of the instrument there are also lines dividing the soundbox into sections the same in shape and location as those on the front: pairs of lines at right angles separate the corner sections from the rest; and there may be two horizontal lines creating a narrow band across the center of the soundbox. Most of the back views have the first of these two details; Naples Stg 274 has only the latter. Leningrad 732 and Munich ex Schoen 80 (fig. 7) have both, with the sections painted contrasting colors on the latter vase. The back of the soundbox has a decorative edging on Boston 98.887 (fig. 3) and Naples Stg 274.

The most arresting feature of the phorminx, one that instruments of this type seem to have had as early as the seventh century, is the pair of circles or eyes painted on the soundbox (see figs. 1, 3, 4, and 8a; also chap. 4, figs. 5 and 17).[20] Nearly half of all our paintings of the phorminx, both front views and back views, include "eyes" of some sort—sometimes only circles or concentric circles (the inner ones painted black), sometimes more or less realistically painted eyes (there are even eyebrows on four of the instruments).[21] When corner sections are marked off on the soundbox, the eyes are placed within these sections about as often as below them; if there are lines forming a horizontal band on the soundbox, the eye circles, if any, are within it. In more than half the paintings (all of them later than about 475 B.C.) there is some effort to make them look like eyes, semicircular or almond shaped, with a dark circle inside (in fig. 8a, each one is painted in profile, looking toward the other!).

The arms of the phorminx, straight, rectangular, rather wide, and not very long, are parallel in all but a handful of instances—in five paintings, including figure 5, they incline inward slightly (this is also seen in earlier examples; see chap. 2), and on Urbana, Ill. Krannert 70-8-5, they diverge slightly.[22] The three-quarters view of the instrument in figure 6 makes it appear that the arms are not flat but rounded, perhaps even cylindrical. This example also shows, as a simple back or front view cannot, that the arms lean forward somewhat, carrying the strings away from the soundbox at an angle, a feature of other members of the lyre family as well.[23]

In about three-quarters of all pictures of the phorminx at hand, it is clear that the arms are set above the soundbox in such a way that the instrument becomes narrower at this point: the inner edge of each arm overhangs the inner edge of the soundbox. When the corners of the soundbox are squared off, the outer edges of the arms are not flush with the outer corners but sit in from them as in figures 4, 5, 7, and 8.

On two of the black-figured vases, Oxford 225 (fig. 1) and Athens Agora P 1544, the arms are painted white, which suggests that they were sometimes faced with ivory; and there are lines across the upper ends of the arms, above the crossbar, on five or six of the instruments (figs. 3 and 6, and possibly 5).[24] But the most common, and the most striking, kind of ornamentation of the arms of the phorminx is found at their base, just over the joining of arms and soundbox, where about two-thirds of our examples have a decorative device of some sort. On a few vases this takes the form of small circles, sometimes with dots in the center, just at the lower inner corners of the arms; or of circular bosses (in gold in fig. 3) or openings (see chap. 4, fig. 17) almost as wide as the arms themselves.[25] On some of the earlier vases, and in figure 7, the shape is roughly oval with the lower end squared off (fig. 1 is also of this sort but not very clear). When the soundbox corners are squared, the inner ones impinge on the outline in question, as in figure 7.[26] But the shape most often seen, especially in examples after mid-century, is a semicircle or segment of a circle, with its straight side at the bottom, found as a rule on instruments with squared soundbox corners (see fig. 8a and chap. 4, fig. 5).

In four red-figured paintings in which the phorminx is seen against a black background, these ornamental half-circles (on Schwerin 708, chap. 4, fig. 17, full circles) are painted black, reinforcing our perception that these are openings through the arms. Cambridge, Harvard 1925.30.42 (fig. 8a) has an especially elaborate design: the inner edges of the arms do not seem to touch the inner corners of the soundbox but continue below them along the inside edge a short way, ending with small circles, a particularly convincing example of "openwork."[27] Two white-ground cup interiors, Paris CA 482 and 483, give interpretations by one painter of instruments with elegant designs that are open on the sides toward the strings, so that here too the area of actual contact between arm and soundbox seems very small.[28]

There is some evidence that arms with decorative openwork were a feature of the phorminx from very

early times (small bronze votive objects from the late Geometric period in the shape of the phorminx have pairs of holes in them at this point) and that at the joining of arm and soundbox the structure was narrower than the width of the arm, at least by the mid-sixth century (on Rhodes 12.200, chap. 2, fig. 6, there is a narrowing at this point). If this is the case, the wide arms of the phorminx were not created with greater sturdiness in mind but must have been designed for added resonance, which suggests that they were hollow and perhaps rounded to some degree (as fig. 6 seems to indicate).

The location of the crossbar is one of the identifying characteristics of the phorminx.[29] Ordinarily quite narrow and only a little longer than the distance across the arms, it is placed a short way from the top of the arms, or in eleven examples all after 475 B.C., at the very top (in most of the latter, it has no free ends at all; see figs. 4 and 8, and chap. 4, fig. 5). Only in three paintings is the crossbar provided with knobs on the ends; in one of these, Oxford 1919.46 (black-figured), both knobs and crossbar are painted white.[30] Fewer than half of our representations have any indication of kollopes, and only a few of these show them clearly and in detail (figs. 5 and 7); these few, however, indicate that these individual string-tension devices are the same for the phorminx as for the other lyres.[31]

Though in a number of paintings the player's right arm and fingers are so positioned that we can assume that the hand holds a plektron, and in a few cases the tip of the plektron is visible (in fig. 5 its shape is unusual), the shape of the plektron head can be clearly seen in only three paintings (Lecce 572, Munich 2446, Paris CA 483). The plektron hangs unused, its cord looped over the arm of the phorminx on Paris CA 483, which allows us to see that it is of the sort customarily found with other lyres, with pointed, spoon-sized head, handle, and tassel. Its cord, on Lecce 572 and Cambridge, Harvard 1959.188, is attached to the lower string fastener, at the bottom of the soundbox; on the latter vase, both plektron and cord are painted red.[32]

The wrist sling, indicated in one-third of the paintings, is simply outlined and without decoration (figs. 1, 2, and 8a), except in two white-ground paintings where it is shown in red.[33] On Paris CA 482, where it lies loose in the lap of a Muse who is adjusting her instrument, the small "button" near the outer end, which seems to fasten it when in use (and around which, perhaps, the sash is looped), is also visible.[34] There is a sash on only half a dozen of the instruments (in three of the paintings the sash is uncertain), but they are distributed from early (including Rhodes

12.200, third quarter of the sixth century) to late; the ones before about 450 B.C. resemble long tassels, whereas the later ones are more like fillets, as is the case with other lyres.[35] The phorminx has a cloth hanging from behind it only on three black-figured vases made ca. 510–490 B.C., all of them komos scenes (fig. 2, and Athens Agora P1544 and Oxford 1919.46), and on Athens 14909, a white-ground pyxis from about 440 B.C.

The Thracian (or Thamyras) Kithara

On the interior of a white-ground kylix of about 470–460 B.C., Athens 15190 (fig. 9), with the figures of Orpheus and an attacking Thracian woman, there is a lyre of unusual shape, one that is not seen earlier except on a single fragment.[36] The shapes of the upper part of the arms and the crossbar fittings resemble those of the barbitos, as Wegner has pointed out, but the arms are short for the width of the instrument, with small protuberances along them, and the crossbar has knobs.[37] Enough of the soundbox remains to reveal several interesting features: a wide, dark band along the side edge; a broad band of golden yellow across the front in the area of the bridge; two concentric circles near the end of the bridge and a flat base with a small curved indentation in the right-hand corner (and presumably on the other side too).

The Greek name for this instrument, if there was one, is unknown to us. Since the instrument is found in several scenes that involve another Thracian musician, Thamyras, who challenged the Muses and was blinded for his arrogance, Wegner suggested that it be called the Thamyras kithara. This name no longer seems entirely satisfactory, however, for in another of the paintings now known, the instrument is found in the hands of yet a third Thracian singer, Mousaios (fig. 10), and of the eighteen known representations of this instrument, only six seem closely related to Thamyras. Moreover, in one of the three paintings in which he is identified by inscription, he plays on an ordinary chelys-lyra.[38]

It would seem remarkable that Thamyras is the subject of even six of these paintings, if we did not know that early in his career Sophocles wrote a play called *Thamyras* (perhaps about 460 B.C.). As far as we can tell from the few remaining fragments, his version followed the story given briefly by Homer (*Il.* 2.594ff.): Thamyras boasted that he could best anyone in a contest, even if the Muses were against him; and they punished his hubris by blinding him, striking him dumb, and causing him to forget his skill at lyre playing. One fragment of Sophocles' play seems to refer

to the ecstasy inspired by the music of Thamyras' lyra, and in another (perhaps part of Thamyras' lament after he is blinded) the speaker apparently longs for the music of harps (*pektides*) and the lyra.[39]

Although (as was pointed out in chap. 2) later writers speak of the instrument used by Sophocles when he performed the role of Thamyras as a kithara, the vase paintings show that the lyre normally associated with this mythological figure was of a shape quite different from that of the standard kithara. Since none of the paintings that are, or may be, representations of Thamyras is earlier than about 450 B.C., and most were done by painters active around 420, it is likely that the interest in portraying this particular Thracian musician was spurred by interest in the play and the playwright.[40] Thamyras (or Sophocles as Thamyras) sits with his lyre among a relaxed and friendly-looking group of Muses in figure 11a, where he is identified by inscription. This scene suggests that early in the play, before his presumption provided the dramatic conflict, he may have been presented as the darling of the Muses (in fig. 11a and in New York 16.52 there are Erotes playing among the Muses who surround him). On the far left in the Ruvo painting (not visible in fig. 11a) stands Apollo, turned away; the woman to the left of Thamyras may be his mother, who appears in other versions.[41]

Thamyras may be preparing for his contest with the Muses on a Basel lekythos from the Meidias workshop in which he appears in Thracian costume: he sits tuning his instrument between two Muses, Klio and Erato.[42] The contest itself is clearly the subject of the scene on Ferrara T.127 (fig. 11b). Here he stands, in the formal clothing of an Athenian kitharode, holding the standard kithara (one of the Muses is playing his Thracian instrument). On the left is Apollo as judge, next to his Delphic tripod, which emphasizes the formality of the occasion. To the right of Thamyras there is a small rabbit, then a listening Muse, and finally a woman standing before an altar with hands lifted, perhaps in petition (Thamyras' mother?). Above the altar are nine statuettes, and behind it grows a tree, both indicating that this is a sanctuary of the Muses, who are also depicted with various instruments, mostly in the lower part of the painting.

Thamyras' punishment is starkly depicted on Oxford 530. His Thracian kithara falls from his hands, and his eyes are closed to indicate his blindness. His mother, tearing her hair, stands to the left, while a Muse with a chelys-lyra looks on implacably from the right.

Although the two other legendary Thracian musicians, Orpheus and Mousaios, are represented with the instrument in only one painting each, both are identified by inscription on vases painted by important Athenian artists.[43] The portrait of Mousaios, figure 10, by the Meidias Painter (the same artist who painted the inscribed portrait of Thamyras, fig. 11a) resembles the paintings of Thamyras as a favorite of the Muses: there are small Erotes about, and the attitude of the various figures, nearly all of them seated, suggest calmness and relaxation. But here, in addition to Mousaios and four Muses (Melpomene, Erato, Kalliope, and Terpsichore), we see two new groups: Aphrodite is present, along with Peitho and Harmonia as members of her retinue; and Deiope, the wife of Mousaios, sits near him with their small son, Eumolpos. The story, if any, connected with this scene is not known, but it is the earliest evidence of Mousaios as a Thracian, as well as of Eumolpos and Deiope as his son and wife.[44]

The instrument of these mythological Thracians also appears in scenes of two other sorts that are not directly related to the ones discussed above. Paintings on a group of six vases present similar versions of a contest scene: a kitharist (with a Thracian kithara) on (or mounting) a podium who is attended by one or two winged Nikes bearing fillets or prize vases, as in figure 12.[45] On this vase there is a bearded judge seated on the right with a long staff to indicate his office, but on Munich 2471 the Nike sits as judge, staff in one hand and prize hydria in the other. On the other vases there is no judge, though on Villa Giulia 5250 a woman sits on the right with a hydria beside her, and on Athens 1183 a bearded man stands on the left, leaning on his walking staff. On two vases where the Nikes bring fillets, there are no prize vases, but on both Athens 1183 and Munich 2471 there are two, and on Villa Giulia 5250, one. In the painting on Athens 1183, one of them sits on a stand near the podium.

The kitharists in these paintings appear to be boys who have not attained their full growth (except on Villa Giulia 5250 and Florence 4006), and their costumes are not specifically Thracian (that is, like those of Mousaios and Thamyras), though in figure 12 and Florence 4006 they wear chitons that reach only to mid-calf under decorated tunics, and the kitharist on Munich 2471 wears an elaborately decorated full-length gown. It is of course possible that some unknown part of the story of Thamyras (whose life, we must suppose, involved contests) is represented here; but there is nothing in the paintings to tell us so, and we may speculate that any young victor in a musical contest might be flattered to receive a vase with a painting that suggests that he is the heir of legendary musicians.

The other variety of scene not directly related to the Thracian musicians occurs only once, on New York 25.78.66 (fig. 13).[46] Here three chorus members, designated by the inscription as "singers at the Panathenaia" and costumed and masked as old satyrs, white-haired, white-bearded, and "hairy" (covered with white fleece), play instruments of the sort we have been discussing, while their aulos player looks on but does not play. It has been suggested that they are taking part in a contest of dithyrambs (songs honoring Dionysos), since there was such a contest at the Panathenaia, and since we have no reliable evidence that satyr plays were part of that festival; but there is also no evidence that the chorus for a dithyramb was costumed. In any case, whether the chorus is to perform a dithyramb or a satyr play, we have little indication of the reason why they carry these unusual instruments that have Thracian associations.[47] But for the inscription, one might speculate that the scene depicts a satyr play with the Thracian subject.[48] We are at a loss, however, to explain why the chorus for a dithyramb might carry such instruments, unless perhaps they somehow reflect the presumed Thracian-Phrygian origins of Dionysos, in whose honor the dithyramb was sung.

The players of this unusual kithara stand or sit, as the formality of the occasion requires, and they hold the instrument upright, or tipped outward slightly, just as Apollo's kithara is held. The left hand, behind the strings, seems to be used as it is with all the other lyres; and although there are only a handful of clear examples, most of them show the left hand used for plucking (figs. 10 and 13). The right hand is also in use in only a few cases, but all the stages of the stroke of the plektron are represented; the hand close to the body (fig. 13), over the strings (figs. 10 and 13 and other paintings), and beyond the strings (Florence 4006 and others). Figure 13, center figure, even offers a rare example in which the plektron may be touching a string below the bridge (see discussion of this in chap. 3). Except for the satyrs in figure 13, none of the performers appears to be singing, and only two of them (Thamyras on the Basel lekythos and the contestant on Munich 2471) are tuning the instrument, placing their fingers around the crossbar in the same manner as do players of other kinds of lyres. On the Basel lekythos Thamyras can be clearly seen using his thumb and first finger to turn a single kollops.

The painters do not agree at all on how this instrument should look, and even the same painter may give it different characteristics on different vases (see figs. 10 and 11a), so that it becomes apparent that it was an instrument that they had rarely seen (perhaps only at the theater?).[49] Its most reliable identifying characteristics are the general shape of its widely curving, rather short arms, its barbitos-like crossbar fittings, and its soundbox (broad and not very high, with a flat base). Even these features may be somewhat changed, as in figure 10, where the arm shape has been conflated with that of the standard kithara (but the shape of the short soundbox—which is wider than the arms—has not). The sparseness of the evidence makes it impossible to estimate the size of the instrument or to comment on the number of strings shown.

The arms of the instrument, in all but four cases, have small protuberances along both sides (figs. 9 and 11a) or appear segmented or tightly twisted (fig. 12), the latter type especially suggesting animal horn.[50] There are knobs on the crossbar in all but three examples. The soundbox is usually not very tall but broader at the top, and in six paintings we can see that the lower corners have an indentation, curved as in figure 13 or square cornered as on Florence 4006.[51]

In some cases, such as figure 10, however, the identification can be made partly on the basis of still other characteristics: the decorative bands, wide or narrow, around the front edge of the soundbox, at the top and sometimes along the sides and bottom (all but three examples); and the small circles on the front of the soundbox, a characteristic shared with the phorminx (all but four of the complete examples).[52] Four of the paintings exhibit in addition a broad horizontal band across the front of the soundbox, which may be painted a different color, as in figure 9.

Like the standard kithara, the Thracian kithara has a cloth hanging from behind it (all but four examples), often decorated with a characteristically Thracian zig-zag pattern (figs. 11a, 12, and 13). As with all the other lyres, the soundbox has a bridge and lower string fastener of the usual shapes, the crossbar has kollopes, and the instrument is provided with plektron, sling, and sash (all visible in fig. 13). The player on the right in figure 13 has a plektron with a clearly visible head, narrow neck, padded handle, and short "tail" where the leather of the handle is tied closed.[53] The sash itself has a pattern (but not the same pattern as the wrist sling, apparently) and a fringe in figure 10—it is clearly a narrow band of cloth (fillet).

L. Talcott and B. Philippaki, who have pointed out the difficulty with calling the instrument the "Thamyras kithara," have suggested that, because the arms so often have small protrusions along them, a more suitable name might be the "horned kithara."[54] Here too, however, there is a difficulty, for some of the instruments surveyed, among them figure 13 and Oxford 530, do not have this feature.

What is certain is that, at least to the Athenian mind, the instrument had Thracian associations (whether it was truly a Thracian instrument or only the Athenians' idea of what a Thracian lyre might look like). The conflation of the arm shape in figure 10 with that of the standard kithara makes it evident that the instrument of the Thracian musicians *was* regarded as a kind of kithara. For the time being, then, we must refer to it as the Thracian kithara and hope that some of the mysteries concerning it will be solved by future investigations.

Harps

Harps, which had been lacking in the art of the Greek world for nearly two millennia (since the time of the Cycladic harp-player figurines, ca. 2200 B.C.; see chap. 1), make their second entrance into the visual arts as well as into literature just after the middle of the fifth century.[55]

Terminology

The names of harps that are examined in this chapter occur in the literature of the period under study less frequently than names like barbitos or kithara, and the available sources do not allow us to connect a specific name with a specific instrument depicted on a given vase painting. As various types of harps and other less traditional stringed instruments became increasingly popular in the Hellenistic and Roman periods, the distinctions in terminology, along with the ever-present Greek concern with "first inventors," caught the attention of writers such as Athenaeus (second century A.D.), as well as lexicographers such as Hesychius of Alexandria (probably fifth century A.D.) and the compilers of the *Suda* (roughly tenth century A.D.). The paucity of sources from the Classical era on any one type of harp or other less common stringed instrument tempts one to rely on such very late and questionable evidence. Here, however, we include only sources that can reasonably be dated to the fourth century or earlier, with an occasional glance at slightly later authors.[56] These, together with the artistic evidence, make it clear that although harps never achieved the status of most of the other stringed instruments already discussed, they did nevertheless play an important role in Greek cultural life, particularly for women musicians, both amateur and professional.

Pektis

As we noted in chapter 2, the word *pektis* is one of the few names for Greek instruments that is Greek; it derives from the verb *pegnuein,* "to fasten." There is little doubt that it was a harp, for, in addition to the references to plucking (*psallein*) rather than "striking" (*krouein*) the instrument with a plektron, we have Plato's statement that the pektis (along with the *trigonon*) is a many-stringed instrument, in contrast to the lyre and kithara.[57] As we saw in chapter 2, it is one of the two earliest names for harps to appear in extant literature, occurring in Sappho, Alcaeus, and Anakreon. The evidence cited already (from Pindar and Herodotus) suggests that the Eastern Greeks borrowed the instrument from the neighboring Lydians; the Lydian identity of the pektis is further confirmed by a fragment from Sophocles that refers to the "harmonious tuning (*syngchordia*) of the Lydian pektis." In addition some lines from the fourth-century dithyrambic poet Telestes speak of Greeks thrumming a Lydian song on "high-pitched pektides."[58] The non-Greek aura associated with the instrument was evidently still felt well over a century after Anakreon's time, for the fourth-century Aristoxenos is quoted as calling "foreign" the pektis, magadis, trigonon, and various other instruments discussed in chapter 7.[59] Similarly, one of Aristoxenos' contemporaries describes the pektis as "boasting a foreign Muse."[60]

Much more than the various lyres, the pektis is noticeably (but not exclusively) associated in Greek literature with women players. Nevertheless, in its Lydian homeland the instrument was evidently used in masculine contexts, particularly to provide music for military marches; Alyattes, a Lydian king of the sixth century, is reported by Herodotus to have marched his troops to the music of syrinx, pektis, and auloi.[61] Furthermore, Anakreon, one of the Eastern Greeks through whom the pektis may have become known in mainland Greece, speaks of both a male dancer and a male serenader who play the instrument.[62]

The later, feminine associations of the pektis are perhaps reflected in the Hellenistic tradition that Sappho was the "first player" of the instrument. (As we saw in chap. 2, she does mention the pektis in two fragments.) In any case, nowhere in the literature of the Classical period, except for the Herodotus passage just cited, do we find mention of the use of the pektis for military purposes; instead, it is described as a woman's instrument. Diogenes of Oinomaos (of unknown date, perhaps fourth or third century B.C.), for example, provides the following vignette of Lydian and Bactrian maidens who worship the virgin goddess Artemis in a grove while they dance and play the aulos, magadis, and "triangular" pektis:

But I hear that the Lydian and Bactrian maidens
Living by the river Halys worship Artemis,
The Tmolian goddess, in a laurel-shaded grove,
Striking the magadis with motions responding
To the pluckings of the triangular pektides,
While the welcome aulos, in a Persian tune,
Sounds in concord for the dances.[63]

κλύω δὲ Λυδὰς Βακτρίας τε παρθένους
ποταμῷ παροίκους Ἅλνι Τμωλίαν θεὸν
δαφνόσκιον κατ' ἄλσος Ἄρτεμιν σέβειν
ψαλμοῖς τριγώνων πηκτίδων τ' ἀντιζύγοις
ὁλκοῖς κρεκούσας μάγαδιν, ἔνθα Περσικῷ
νόμῳ ξενωθεὶς αὐλὸς ὁμονοεῖ χοροῖς.

A scene in Aristophanes' *Thesmophoriazusae* likewise suggests that the pektis was regarded by the Greeks as an instrument played chiefly in contexts appropriate for women musicians; here the character Euripides, posing as an old lady, is described by the chorus as carrying the pektis, which we may assume is supposed to contribute to his female disguise.[64]

The literary sources are especially unrevealing of the construction and technical features of the pektis. The manufacture of the instrument is referred to in a list of various types of stringed instruments in a fragment from a fourth-century comedy called the "Lyre-Maker" (*Lyropoios*):

I used to make barbitoi, trichordoi, pektides,
Kitharas, lyres, and skindapsoi.[65]

ἐγὼ δὲ βαρβίτους, τριχόρδους, πηκτίδας,
κιθάρας, λύρας, σκινδαψὸν ἐξηρτυόμαν.

But little is said of how the instrument was made or of the technique of playing it. One fourth-century source, Sopater, is quoted as having called the pektis *dichordos;* since the interpretation "two-stringed" makes little sense in connection with an instrument of the harp type, some scholars have suggested that the term should be taken as meaning "double strung."[66] The representations of harps neither confirm nor deny the possibility of literal double stringing (two sets of strings side by side); it may be that for each string tuned at a given pitch there was another string tuned at the octave (see below on the magadis).

The instrument is further described as "triangular," "high-pitched," and "tall," but the latter two epithets do not tell us much since we do not know to what the pektis is being compared.[67] The description "triangular" confirms the identification of the pektis as a harp, as does the reference to plucking in the following fragment from a tragedy of Sophocles:

And many a Phrygian trigonos . . . [verb lacking]
And the harmonious tuning of the Lydian pektis
Sounds in accord its answering pluckings.[68]

πολὺς δὲ Φρὺξ τρίγωνος ἀντίσπαστά τε
Λυδῆς ἐφυμνεῖ πηκτίδος συγχορδία

A certain degree of complexity is implied in the banning of the pektis by Plato, who says that it is "polyharmonic" (that is, capable of being tuned according to many harmoniai), and by Aristotle, who includes it among a list of instruments that require "manual dexterity" and that are designed to give pleasure rather than edification to the listener.[69] Some suggestion of antiphonal performance may be contained in the various adjectives applied to the instrument that are compounded with *anti-* ("opposite"), such as *antispasta* in the above fragment ("answering pluckings") and *psalmon antiphthongon* ("plucking that sounds in return") in Pindar.[70]

Magadis

The magadis (probably a Lydian name, see chap. 2), like the pektis, is mentioned as early as the Archaic period by poets such as Alkman and Anakreon. The identification of the magadis as a harp or psaltery can be made on the basis of a fragment from Anakreon's poetry which indicates that it was a plucked instrument of many strings:

Holding the magadis I pluck its twenty strings;
But you, Leukaspis, are in the bloom of youth.[71]

ψάλλω δ' εἴκοσι
†χορδαῖσι μάγαδιν† ἔχων,
Ὦ Λεύκασπι, σὺ δ' ἡβᾶις.

There is little information in Greek literature about the occasions on which the magadis was played, but if Aristoxenos' view (Ath. 635e) that *magadis* and *pektis* were two names for the same instrument is correct, we can assume that the magadis, too, was associated with dancing and serenades and that it was commonly but not exclusively played by women musicians. A third-century B.C. author is quoted as having said that the magadis was popular on the island of Lesbos and that an "ancient" (presumably Archaic period) sculptor by the name of Lesbothemis had represented one of the Muses holding the instrument. Other than this reference, and Anakreon's lines about playing the instrument himself, there is no information of a literary sort about players of the magadis.[72]

In addition to the information from Anakreon that the magadis had twenty strings, we are also informed by Aristoxenos (assuming that he is correctly quoted by Athenaeus) that these were sounded by the bare fingers without the aid of a plektron.[73]

The virtuosity required to play the magadis is alluded to in the following lines from a dithyramb written perhaps about the turn of the fourth century by the minor lyric poet Telestes:

Each man hurling forth a different sound from
    the others,
Roused up the horn-voiced magadis,
Turning his hand quickly back and forth across
Five-staved joinings of the strings
Like a runner at the turning post.[74]

ἄλλος δ' ἄλλαν κλαγγὰν ἱεὶς
κερατόφωνον ἐρέθιζε μάγαδιν,
[ἐν] πενταρράβδῳ χορδᾶν ἀρθμῷ
χέρα καμψιδίαυλον ἀναστρωφῶν τάχος . . .

Several technical points are of interest here, some of which are obscured by the elaborate locutions characteristic of dithyrambic poetry. The epithet "horn-voiced" (keratophonon) has been taken by some to refer to the striking of the strings with a horn plektron.[75] It is possible, however, that the horn refers either to some structural element of the instrument itself (perhaps reinforcement for the soundbox?) or to the resemblance of the instrument's tone to that of a signal horn.[76] (We may recall that the pektis was used as an accompanying instrument for military marches, according to Herodotus, and therefore must also have had a reasonably good carrying power.) Further, the word for "sound" in the opening line (klange) normally conveys the idea of a sharp noise such as the scream of birds.

The comparison of the hand's swift motion across the strings with a runner changing direction at the turning post of the stadium race course seems to allude to the skill and virtuosity required for playing the magadis, but the description of the strings is less clear. All the evidence suggests that Athenaeus is wrong in interpreting "five-staved joinings of the strings" ([en] pentarrabdoi chordan arthmoi) as referring to a magadis with only five strings. The five staves or rods must refer instead to some structural feature in the arrangement of the strings, perhaps in five groupings of four strings each.

A further technical question about the magadis is raised by a description in Xenophon of Thracian soldiers playing ox-hide trumpets (salpinyxin omoboeiais) "in the manner of the magadis."[77] A similar analogy occurs in a fragment from an early fourth-century comic writer in which a character says, "I'll speak to you like a magadis, in both little and big sounds at once."[78] Although this could be taken to refer to soft and loud volume, later reports of the capacity of the magadis to produce octave intervals suggest that high and low pitch may be meant. In the late sources such as pseudo-Aristotle's *Problems,* the name of the instrument forms the basis of a verb, *magadizein,* which is used to mean "to sing in octaves."[79] It appears, then, that the expression "to sound like a magadis" refers to the playing or singing of a tune in octaves. Such an understanding allows a reasonable interpretation of a late fourth-century comic fragment in which the verb *magadizein* also appears:

It's a bad idea for a boy and his father and mother
To be put on the torture rack and made to sing in
    octaves [*magadizein*]
Since not one of us will even sing the same tune.[80]

πονηϱὸν υἱὸν καὶ πατέϱα καὶ μητέϱα
ἐστὶν μαγαδίζειν ἐπὶ τϱοχοῦ καθημένους·
οὐδεὶς γὰϱ ἡμῶν ταὐτὸν ᾄσεται μέλος.

The fragment seems to allude to the practice of extracting testimony from slaves under torture; the speaker claims that far from giving consistent testimony (singing in octaves, with the boy and the mother at the higher octave), these three witnesses will tell altogether different stories.

The pektis and the magadis are long-lived names in Greek literature, occurring in works dating from the Archaic through the Hellenistic periods. According to a second-century B.C. author, Apollodorus of Athens, the name *magadis* had fallen out of use by his time and had been replaced by the more general term, *psalterion,* "plucked instrument" (from *psallein,* "to pluck").[81]

Trigonon

The name *trigonon,* meaning (literally) "three-cornered," first appears in fragments from the plays of Sophocles, Pherekrates, and Eupolis in the second half of the fifth century. The obvious reference to triangular shape contained in the name, as well as the use of the name in connection with psallein, leave no doubt that the trigonon was a harp. Whether the term was applied to a particular variety of harp, as some suppose, or was merely a generic name used to describe *any* Greek harp (which were all of essentially triangular shape), we cannot tell for certain.[82] It is perhaps significant that except for the word *pektis,* *trigonon* is the only name of a Greek stringed instrument that is clearly a Greek word. Could Sophocles and his contemporaries have been using this simple descriptive

designation for various instruments that bore foreign names and were still relatively unfamiliar to Athenian (if not Eastern) Greeks? At any rate, Sophocles himself emphasizes the foreign nature of the instrument type when he speaks of the Lydian pektis sounding in concord with the Phrygian trigonon.[83] Apparently both names, despite their Greekness, were firmly associated in Sophocles' mind with the music of Asia Minor.

Information about the trigonon from literary sources is scanty, but what little there is again makes clear that harps were considered appropriate instruments for women musicians. The fullest description of its use occurs in a longer-than-average fragment from Plato the comic writer (not the more famous philosopher), whose works date from about 425–390 B.C. At the opening of the fragment a staff of servants is conversing about a dinner party, and after an interval the steward returns to the kitchen to report how the after-dinner entertainment is progressing:

The libation has already been poured, and
    they've been drinking
And singing a drinking song, and the kottabos
    game has been taken away.
Some girl playing the auloi is piping a Carian
    tune
For the drinkers, and I saw another one with her
    trigonon
Who was singing some Ionian tune to its
    accompaniment.[84]

σπονδὴ μὲν ἤδη γέγονε, καὶ πίνοντές εἰσι πόϱϱω,
καὶ σκόλιον ᾖσται, κότταβος δ' ἐξοίχεται θύϱαζε.
αὐλοὺς δ' ἔχουσά τις κοϱίσκη Καϱικὸν μέλος ⟨τι⟩
μελίζεται τοῖς συμπόταις, κἄλλην τϱίγωνον εἶδον
ἔχουσαν, ἡ δ' ᾖδεν πϱὸς αὐτὸ μέλος Ἰωνικόν τι.

The musicians referred to in this fragment probably fall into the category of hired entertainers about whom we have some specific financial information from later in the fourth century, when their wages were kept under state control (see chap. 7). There is an abundance of vase paintings that show female aulos players performing for a gathering of male symposiasts, but depictions of harpists in similar scenes are not so common.

Another comic fragment probably dating to the last quarter of the fifth century demonstrates that men also played the trigonon:

It's old-fashioned to sing the songs of Stesichoros,
    Alkman, and Simonides.
Now it's in to listen to Gnesippos, who has fashioned
Night-time songs for adulterers to sing to the
    iambuke and trigonon,
And thus to lure their ladies out.[85]

τὰ Στησιχόϱου τε καὶ Ἀλκμᾶνος Σιμωίδου τε

ᾄδειν ἀρχαῖον· ὁ δὲ Γνήσιππος ἔστ' ἀκούειν,
ὅς νυκτερίν' εὗρε μοιχοῖς ᾄσματ' ἐκκαλεῖσθαι
γυναῖκας ἔχοντας ἰαμβύκην τε καὶ τρίγωνον.

The contrast between the respectability of the old lyric
poets and the dubious purposes for which Gnesippos'
tunes are supposedly designed seems to suggest a low
status for the accompanying instruments as well, the
trigonon and the *iambuke* (probably a type of harp or
lute; see chap. 7). This is confirmed in another comic
fragment by the same poet (Eupolis), which describes
a male performer's obscene gestures in an unknown
context:

> . . . You who play the drum well
> And strum upon trigonons,
> And wiggle your ass
> And stick your legs up in the air.[86]

> . . ὃς καλῶς μὲν τυμπανίζεις
> καὶ διαψάλλεις τριγώνοις
> κἀπικινεῖ ταῖς κοχώναις
> καὶ τιθεῖς ἄνω σκέλη.

Given these associations, it is perhaps not surprising that the trigonon is specifically singled out by both
Plato and Aristotle as not being appropriate for the
ideal state they envision (see chap. 7).

Harps in the Vase Paintings

Three kinds of harps can be recognized in the vase
paintings of the latter half of the fifth century, all of a
size that sits on, or next to, the player's knee and
reaches as high as the top of the player's head, or
somewhat higher.[87] All three have a separate soundbox
and neck, jointed together; that is, they are not "bow
harps" with those two functions served by a single
curving piece, as is the case with some Egyptian harps.
Unlike the Cycladic harp, all of these have the neck
at the bottom, lying horizontally in the player's lap.

One of these harps is an "angle harp"—open,
without a post to connect the upper end of its arched
soundbox to the end of the neck below (fig. 14). The
other two types, like the Cycladic harp, are "frame
harps," with a post connecting the soundbox and neck
to make a triangular frame and strengthening the
structure so that it might have carried a higher string
tension. These frame harps would have been the ones
for which the name *trigonon* ("triangle") would have
been most appropriate. One of the frame harps has an
arched soundbox like that of the angle harp (fig. 15);
in fact, except for the presence of the post, there is in
most cases little difference between them. The second
variety (fig. 16), however, has a soundbox of a differ-

ent shape, widest in the middle (roughly spindle
shaped), angular rather than curved, and held away
from rather than against the player.[88]

Though the angle harp with arched soundbox and
no post is to be found in the earliest of the fifth-century
harp representations that has come to light (London
E 271, ca. 440 B.C.; see chap. 4, fig. 5), it is not often
seen before the fourth century. Only two other fifth-
century Athenian representations have been found,
one on a vase and one on a rock-crystal seal stone
(London 529), as well as two from southern Italy, one
on a vase (Naples 81392, fig. 14), the other a terra-
cotta relief now in Heidelberg. In all five of these representations this instrument is in the hands of a
woman: two of them are Muses (London E 271 and
Naples 81392) while another two, on Athens 15308
and the Heidelberg relief, are female entertainers who
sit at the foot of a banquet couch on which a young
man reclines.[89] These must be professional *psaltriai*
(from *psallein*, "to pluck"; *psaltria* = "one who
plucks"); we first hear of them in a fifth-century fragment of a tragedy by Ion of Chios, in which the Lydian
Queen Omphale bids her Lydian psaltriai to sing.[90] No
specific instruments are mentioned in this passage, but
since only harps are plucked—lyres are struck
(krouein)—there is no doubt that the psaltriai are
harpists.

All the players of this angle harp are seated and
hold the instrument on the knee with the soundbox
close to the body and the longest strings farthest away,
plucking its strings with their fingers—there is no plektron involved. The harpists on London E 271 and Athens 15308 tilt their heads down close to the soundbox,
as though listening closely to the notes being played.

The soundbox of this angle harp, tall and arched,
grows broader toward the top, thus permitting the
longest strings to have a large resonator. Though there
are apparently buttons or pegs of some sort along the
inner edge of the soundbox on London E 271, around
which the strings might be fixed, the painting on Naples 81392 (fig. 14) makes it clear that the adjustment
of the strings was done at the neck: here we see
rounded objects showing above and below the narrow
rod that serves as a neck, objects that resemble the
kollopes of the lyre and probably indicate a similar
manner of tuning. The number of strings indicated
varies greatly—figure 14 has only about 9; another
example has 11, another 13, and one (the smallest of
all, on the seal stone) has approximately 32!

On Naples 81392 (fig. 14) there is a separate bar
beneath the neck but not visibly connected to it that
serves as a base to keep the neck from contact with
the player's knee, thus both protecting the tuning and

improving the resonance. This feature can be discerned more often on fourth-century harps; whether it was always present (and overlooked by the painters) we cannot know.

The side of the soundbox, on Athens 15308, is ornamented with a chain of small circles and arcs. Harps of this shape, with or without post, are often given a painted decoration along the soundbox in the fourth century, and those from southern Italy are also often provided with a crest of points, as in figure 14. It is easy to imagine that such a harp might have been considered "Phrygian," since the effect resembles the designs on "Phrygian" caps (as represented by Athenian artists).

There is little doubt that the angle harp came to Greece ultimately from Mesopotamia, where similar instruments are found in both Babylonian and Assyrian representations, although the soundbox of the Greek harp is more curved than in examples from these cultures.[91] Later evidence of harps in this form comes from Cyprus, Egypt, and other parts of the Near East; it seems most likely that they came to Greece by way of Cyprus, perhaps first to the East Greek mainland and islands and later to central and western Greece. While they had been accepted (at least for some purposes) by Athenian Greeks in the latter half of the fifth century, we do not know how long they had actually been in use—whether they were newcomers, or old, well-established, but little-regarded parts of the Greek instrumentarium.

The frame harp with arched soundbox is seen even less often in the fifth century than its look-alike, the angle harp. Only one Attic representation has come to light, on Berlin Staatl. Mus. hydria 2391, dated 450–25 B.C. (fig. 15); and there are at present only two fifth-century Italiote representations of this harp available, Berlin 3291 and Munich 3268, though it is well represented on fourth-century vases from southern Italy (these early examples lack the row of points along the soundbox that is characteristic of the later Italiote harps).[92] Here too all the players are women, Muses on Berlin Staatl. Mus. 2391 (fig. 15) and Munich 3268. On Berlin 3291 we see Heracles in the company of a number of women, one of whom may be Omphale, whose Lydian psaltriai were mentioned by Ion of Chios. The players are seated except for the Muse on Berlin Staatl. Mus. 2391 (fig. 15—it is not clear how her harp is supported); she and the Muse on Munich 3268 (who tilts her head close to the soundbox) pluck the strings with both hands, the left hand reaching to the longer strings. (For further discussion of technique, see chap. 7.)

The soundbox of this harp has painted decoration along the side, and in two of the paintings it becomes wider at the top, as does that of the angle harp. But the third vase, Berlin 3291, shows a harp with a soundbox that does not become wider and that also turns up at the top in a suggestion of an S-curve, a shape seen on no other fifth- or fourth-century example. This instrument also has an upright post crudely shaped to resemble a swan (with long neck and short legs), a design executed with more grace by fourth-century Italiote painters who turn the bird into a crane (with shorter neck and longer legs; see chap. 7). Beneath its neck is a separate base apparently attached only to the soundbox and not connected to the outer end of the neck. The two other instruments do not have such a base, and none of them has an indication of how the strings are adjusted at the neck, though on Munich 3268 we can see that the strings are wound around the neck, free ends dangling. The harp on this vase, which is quite large (a head taller than the player as she holds it in her lap), has a soundbox that does not curve forward a great deal, so that the post runs diagonally from its upper end to the end of the neck. The smaller harp in figure 15, which has a more arched soundbox, has a rather thick upright post with an interesting detail at the bottom—the post appears to go through the end of the neck and extend perhaps five centimeters below it, ending in an onion-shaped ornament. Notice also the circular ornament at the joining of neck and soundbox. Fourteen strings show in this painting, with room for perhaps two more; Munich 3268 appears to have at least 13.

The representations of the other type of frame harp, the "spindle" harp (fig. 16), belong mostly to the fifth century, and none of them was made in Italy.[93] Of eight fifth-century examples, four are by a single painter, the "Washing Painter." All the vase paintings can be dated ca. 430–420 B.C., and the other items belong to the late fifth century or to the end of the century.[94]

This harp differs from the others in several important respects. In addition to the post that completes its triangular frame, it has a soundbox that is "spindle" shaped, that is, widest at the midpoint and tapering at both ends; the instrument is generally held with the soundbox away from the player, and in the majority of cases the longest strings are the ones closest to the player.

The Muse Melpomene plays this harp on New York 37.11.23, figure 16, and an unidentified Muse carries it on Ferrara T.127, figure 11b (these scenes, the first with Mousaios and the second with Thamyras, are discussed above under Thracian Kithara). But all four paintings by the Washing Painter are scenes of wedding preparations, showing a bride and the women attending her; in three of them, it is the bride herself who plays the harp. Only on seal stones (London 563; Leningrad, unnumbered) is the harp played by a young man, who may represent Dionysos, for on the later stone he sits on a panther skin.

The players of this frame spindle harp, like those who play the other varieties, are usually seated, but they stand on Athens 14791 and Ferrara T.127 (fig. 11b), neither of which shows how the harp is supported when the player stands. On the latter vase the harpist may have her left forearm underneath the base and play only with her right hand; the vase is cracked and very worn in this area. This player also has the spindle-shaped soundbox next to her body, so that the strings are reversed—longest strings the farthest away, as with the arched angle and frame harps—a way of holding it seen only on one other example, seal stone London 563, where the player is seated. In most cases, the players pluck the strings with the fingers of both hands, with the post tucked against the left shoulder and the harp supported on the left thigh.[95] Since the representations are few and several of them are damaged, the details of technique and the difference in technique (if any) created by string lengths that run opposite to those of the angle harp cannot be assessed. In general, this harp appears to have been played in much the same manner as were the others.

The handful of artists who have left us representations of this frame harp with spindle-shaped soundbox either did not see the instrument often, did not observe it carefully, or were acquainted with a great variety of harps of this general shape. Or perhaps they created apparent differences through their experiments with the use of perspective. Whereas three of the harps by the Washing Painter (all but Würzburg H 4455) have a post and neck of about the same length, the post is as much as a third again longer than the neck in the rest of the fifth-century examples. The Washing Painter shows us harps with post and neck forming a right angle; the rest of the artists make the angle somewhat less.[96]

There is no consistency whatever as to the angle at which the strings are stretched: on Ferrara T.127 (fig. 11b) and New York 16.73, they run approximately at right angles to the neck and parallel to the post; on the seal stones they are still all parallel to the post, but the post is not at a right angle. On New York 07.286.35 and 37.11.23 (fig. 16) they seem to fan out from the post. But the oddest of all string arrangements is to be seen on Athens 14791 and Würzburg H 4455 (fig. 17), two vases on which the Washing Painter

has made the strings, all parallel, run from the soundbox into both the neck and the post! While this seems an unlikely arrangement, it does have the advantage that the longest strings run from the center of the soundbox, where it is deepest and has the most resonating capacity.

The Washing Painter's harps have about twenty strings, except for New York 16.73 (fourteen).[97] Only on New York 37.11.23 (fig. 16) and on the Attic grave relief (see n. 92) can we see how the strings are adjusted: in figure 16 a series of small black dots on either side of the neck indicates the kollopes. A separate base rod underneath the neck, protecting the tuning and improving resonance, is (as in the case of the other harps) seldom seen in fifth-century representations. Only the grave relief and seal stone London 563, as well as the later Leningrad seal stone, have it.

The spindle-shaped soundbox, which is quite narrow in figure 16 and on seal stone London 563, appears wider in the other examples and tapers to a point (which overruns the meeting with the post) only at the top of the Washing Painter's works; the lower end, which stops where it joins the neck, does not taper quite so much. This painter seems to try to indicate the three-dimensional shape of the soundbox: except on New York 07.286.35, there is a curved contour line that touches the outer edge of the soundbox at the center, the widest part, and ends at the inner edge, above and below, halfway between the middle and the ends, as though to suggest that the soundbox bulges on the sides and is deeper in the center, especially at the inner side.

In figure 16 and on all the harps by the Washing Painter except New York 16.73, the soundbox is decorated with dots (studs of some sort) that run along the edges and contour lines and sometimes form patterns that are repeated down the middle; there may even be a line of dots along the post. The harp on New York 16.73, however, has only a plain border of double lines along the edges and contour lines of the soundbox, and along the rather broad post. On Ferrara T.127 (fig. 11b) the only decoration consists of lines of small zigzags that run horizontally across the soundbox from top to bottom; on seal stone London 563 the instrument has no decoration except for a three-pronged crown-like ornament at the top, where post and soundbox meet.

Since frame harps in this form (with spindle-shaped soundbox) have not been found in other Near Eastern cultures, it may be assumed that this particular version of the frame harp is Aegean in origin. Though it appears only in the late fifth century, it may, of course, have been in use (in Athens, at least, evidently only among women) for decades or even centuries before that time. But when we first encounter it, its day was already coming to a close, for it is scarcely seen in the fourth century. It may be that the place of this apparently indigenous instrument was gradually usurped by the imported or adapted foreign harps, the angle harp and frame harp with arched soundbox. Two small details are perhaps worth noting in this regard: first, that there are no professional psaltriai among the players of spindle harps that we now know, whereas there are several among the players of the arched angle and frame harps; and second, that in two cases we see the spindle harp reversed so that it is held in the same manner as the angle harp, suggesting that this method was beginning to win favor, which may in the end have helped the arched angle and frame harps to prevail.

Since there are all together fewer than a dozen and a half fifth-century representations of these three kinds of harps, it is not surprising that we have no examples that show the harp being tuned and that we do not find any singers to the harp, although it is seen in the company of other instruments (all the lyres, auloi, and tympanon) thanks mainly to the paintings of the Muses, who play all these instruments. It is clear that in the late fifth century the harps, like the phorminx, were almost exclusively women's instruments, which helps to explain why they are so seldom seen; why they do not appear on coins or in sculpture (except for one relief) or on any other objects except for the small group of vases and a seal stone; why there is no first inventor reported in the literature, as there is for many instruments (though a woman, Sappho, was proposed in Hellenistic times as the first player); and why there is no god for whom the harp serves as attribute (though in the fourth century there is certainly an association with Aphrodite; see chap. 7).

An Eleven-stringed Harp?

As we have seen in chapter 3, one of the most vexing questions about the construction and technique of playing instruments of the lyre type in the fifth century concerns the literary references of the last part of the century that raise the possibility of increased numbers of strings. We concluded that at least as far as Timotheus was concerned, his innovations were in all probability matters of style and technique, and not of the addition of strings to the kithara, a development for which there is no evidence in the vase paintings. The vase paintings do, however, point to a sudden popularity of harps in Athens during the last part of the century and suggest that *these* were the instruments

that elicited references to "many-stringed" or "many-noted" instruments.

The chief evidence from the fifth century that remains to be considered is a four-line elegiac fragment by Ion of Chios that probably belongs to the third quarter of the century (Ion died sometime shortly before 421). The possibility does not seem to have been suggested that the "eleven-stringed lyra" (*hendeka-chorde lyra*) to which Ion refers was not a lyre at all, but rather one of the harps. The text of the two couplets may be literally translated as follows:

Eleven-stringed lyre, having a flight of ten steps
    to the concordant three-road meeting of *harmonia,*
Formerly the Greeks all plucked you, seven-toned,
    through fourths,
    raising up a meagre music.[98]

Ἐνδεκάχορδε λύρα, δεκαβάμονα τάξιν ἔχοισα
    εἰς συμφωνούσας ἁρμονίας τριόδους,
πρὶν μέν σ' ἑπτάτονον ψάλλον διὰ τέσσαρα πάντες
    Ἕλληνες σπανίαν μοῦσαν ἀειράμενοι. . . .

The lack of any eleven-stringed lyres among the archaeological evidence, together with the firm distinction that Plato maintains between lyres and "many-stringed" harps (see chap. 7), suggests that we should abandon the notion that Ion is speaking of a freakish kithara or chelys-lyra. If instead we grant Ion some poetic license in his use of terminology and assume that "lyra" means "stringed instrument" and remember that *lyropoios,* "lyre-maker," can refer to one who makes harps, the rest of the fragment, especially the second line, whose interpretation has caused great difficulty, begins to make reasonable sense.[99]

The "three-road meeting of *harmonia,*" we suggest, may refer to the tuning of the instrument's eleven strings in three tetrachords (the tetrachord, a group of four contiguous descending notes spanning the interval of a perfect fourth, formed the basis of the Greek musical system; for example, edcb agfe [e]dcb.) The proposal that a harp is meant explains the use in the third line of the verb *psallein,* which is almost always used elsewhere with reference to "plucking" instruments of the harp type, as opposed to "striking" (*krouein* or *paiein*) instruments of the lyre type.[100]

Although the matter of Ion's *hendekachorde lyra* cannot be resolved beyond a doubt, the above interpretation does fit the archaeological evidence. While an occasional experiment with one or two additional lyre strings may have been tried, there is no good reason to connect Ion's "lyre" with the stories in later writers like Plutarch, Cicero, and Boethius claiming that during the fifth century Athenian lyres suddenly sprouted excessive numbers of extra strings which were then unceremoniously chopped off by stern officials at Spartan musical contests.[101] Artemon, a first-century B.C. source quoted by Athenaeus, in fact gives a version of the excessive strings story in which the instrument Timotheus supposedly played at Sparta was not a lyre at all, but the magadis, an instrument said to have twenty strings. Such stories, none of which is earlier than the first century B.C., are better explained as legends that reflect the sudden popularity of instruments such as the harp in Athens during the late fifth and early fourth centuries. Although all these stories must be viewed as dubious at best (the report in Boethius, for example, quotes a "Spartan edict" about Timotheus that is of doubtful origin), Arte-

mon's reference to a magadis may at least point in the direction of whatever grain of historical truth is concealed in them.[102]

By the beginning of the fourth century, most of the instruments discussed in this chapter—phorminx, Thracian kithara, and frame spindle harp—had disappeared or were just about to disappear. Only the arched angle and frame harps persist in the later period. In chapter 7, where the other stringed instruments of fourth-century Greece, the kithara and lyra, along with a new, rectangular member of the lyre family, are discussed, these two arched forms of the harp are considered further.

1. Oxford 225 (1879.159).
Attic b.f. oinochoe.
Maenads.

2. Munich 1416. Attic b.f.
amphora. Detail:
Komasts.

3. Boston 98.887. Attic w.g. pyxis. Muses.

4. London E 185. Attic r.f. hydria. Detail: girls dancing while man and woman look on.

5. Oxford 1920.104 (266).
Attic w.g. lekythos.
Detail: women with
instruments.

6. Athens 1241. Attic r.f.
pyxis. Detail: Muses on
Mt. Helicon.

7. Munich ex Schoen 80.
Attic w.g. lekythos.
Detail: Muse on Mt.
Helicon.

8a. Cambridge, Harvard
1925.30.42. Attic r.f.
stamnos. Dionysos,
maenads, and satyr.

8b. Naples 81398 (H
3232). Attic r.f. hydria.
Details: female dancers
and musicians.

9. Athens 15190. Attic
w.g. kylix fragment.
Detail: Orpheus attacked
by Thracian woman.

10. New York 37.11.23.
Attic r.f. pelike. Mousaios
and Muses.

11a. Ruvo, Jatta Coll.
1538. Attic r.f. aryballos.
Thamyras and Muses.

Detail: Muses with harp
and Thracian kithara.

11b. Ferrara T. 127, inv.
3033. Attic r.f. volute
krater.

12. Athens 1469. Attic r.f.
pelike. Detail: contestant,
judge, and Nike.

13. New York 25.78.66.
Attic r.f. bell krater.
Detail: satyr chorus.

14. Naples 81392.
Lucanian r.f. pelike.
Detail: Muse with harp.

15. Berlin, Staatl. Mus.
2391. Attic r.f. hydria.
Detail: Muse.

16. New York 37.11.23.
Attic r.f. pelike. Detail:
Muses.

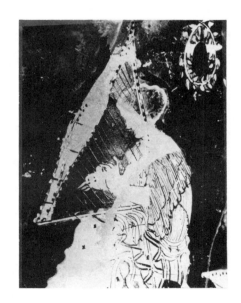

17. Würzburg H 4455 (L.
541). Attic r.f. pyxis.
Detail: woman with harp.

CHAPTER SEVEN

Late Classical and Early Hellenistic Stringed Instruments

All our information about the stringed instruments of late fifth- and fourth-century Greece, both from literary sources and from the visual arts, reflects changes in customs concerning music and in attitudes toward it; and these, in their turn, reflect the great changes that had taken place in the society at large.

From this age of the great philosophers, whose works often include a critique of musical customs and innovations, we have direct information about music and musical instruments of a sort that is not available for earlier periods. Although in many respects the phenomena described by Plato and Aristotle anticipate the Hellenistic period and represent significant changes in the old styles and practices, the fourth century, especially from 400 to 350 b.c., can also be viewed as a consolidation of some of the developments of the late fifth century that we have already considered, including a greater emphasis on virtuoso technique and the increasing use of complex rhythms and a variety of different tunings.[1]

In Athenian visual arts instruments were less often portrayed in the fourth century than in earlier times, and as a result of altered artistic styles and techniques there was also less interest in realism and careful detail. Since much of the visual evidence for stringed instruments comes from south Italian vase paintings, it becomes important to distinguish, whenever possible, the instruments shown in these paintings from the ones on Athenian vases.

The kithara (referred to below as the "standard kithara" to differentiate it from several later forms of the instrument), though it is well represented in fourth-century art, particularly in south Italian vase paintings (fig. 2a), is no longer found in fourth-century Athenian vase paintings (in which it had already become rather uncommon in the late fifth century); it is present only on a few marble reliefs from Attica. There are about a dozen other objects, primarily terracotta statuettes and engraved gems from Cyprus and other parts of eastern and northern Greece, on which it also appears.

Another form of the kithara, barely foreshadowed in a few late fifth-century paintings, becomes more evident in the fourth century and in later Hellenistic times: a kithara with a longer body, somewhat narrower for its length than the standard kithara, with simplified ornamentation of the inner sides of the arms, or sometimes none at all (figs. 5 and 6). The fourth-century representations of the instrument, few in number, appear on Athenian vases and on a Thessalian marble relief (Athens 1380) as well as on vases from the Greek cities of Apulia, Sicily, and Campania.

In these Greek areas of southern Italy, in the second half of the fourth century, a new member of the lyre family makes its appearance on red-figured pottery. This instrument (figs. 7–9), seen from the front, has straight arms, crossbar knobs, and a soundbox that is often a squarish rectangle or hexagon. Since it has been found in some twenty-four fourth-century Italiote examples, and only one from Attica, we have provisionally referred to it below as the Italiote kithara. It is rarely seen after the end of the fourth century.

After the first decade of the fourth century, the chelys-lyra (figs. 10–12), like the standard kithara, no longer appears in Athenian vase paintings (with one exception), though it is well represented on vases of the period between 420 and 390 B.C. Thereafter it is seen only on several grave monuments now in Athens and Thessaloniki, the odd terra-cotta, coin, or engraved gem from mainland Greece or Rhodes, and at the end of the century as a decorative device on a few fragments of "West Slope" pottery, a type first discovered in excavating the west slope of the Akropolis. In southern Italy, on the other hand, the chelys-lyra continues to appear in scenes on red-figured vases throughout the century, though not quite as frequently as the kithara.

Harps are more plentiful in the Greek world in the fourth century than in the fifth, though they are still less abundant than either the standard kithara or lyra. The harps known to the Greeks in Italy are clearly distinguishable from those painted by artists in mainland Greece: only the painters of Italiote vases give us examples of the open, arched harp (without a post, fig. 16); and their frame harps are highly decorated, the posts often carved to resemble a bird (crane) and the upper edge of the soundbox bristling with a row of points (fig. 17). Neither of these features is present in the small handful of Attic paintings of the frame harp, although the soundbox (very narrow in most Attic examples) and post may be decorated with painted scrollwork.

Instruments of the lute family, which first appear in Greek lands in the late fourth century, can be seen in only a small handful of representations of widely scattered origin (terra-cottas and a marble relief) before 300 B.C. Two types can be discerned, however, one an instrument with an almond-shaped soundbox (fig. 19), the other a lute with a larger, more rectangular soundbox (fig. 18).

Literary Sources

Since the major literary sources of information about stringed instruments are primarily philosophical in nature (Plato, Xenophon, and Aristotle), it is not surprising that fully one-third of the fourth-century references to the instruments are found in the context of various philosophical analogies. Some of these are informative, but others serve only to point out that the philosophers regarded musical knowledge as common enough among their followers to be helpful in the drawing of a particular analogy. For example, when Xenophon's Socrates points out that just as a man who has learned to play the lyre can be called a kitharistes even when he is not playing, so also a man who has learned the art of generalship can still be called a general even if he is not reelected *strategos*, we learn more of Socrates' fondness for homely comparisons than we do about musical terminology.[2]

A further characteristic of these philosophically oriented sources is their overriding concern with the presumed ethical effects of music and musical training on the citizens of the *polis*. It may have been Damon, Perikles' music teacher and political adviser, who first posited a relationship between musical custom and the laws of the state; Socrates, as he is depicted in Plato's *Republic* (424c), acknowledges a debt to Damon when he says, "By no means can the types (*tropoi*) of music be disturbed without also disturbing the great laws (*nomoi*) of the *polis*, as Damon says and I agree." Besides developing the notion of a connection between musical changes and political changes, Damon seems to have anticipated Plato and Aristotle in assuming that musical training exerts influence on a person's character. According to a first-century B.C. source, Damon said that "in singing and playing the lyre a boy ought properly to reveal not only courage and moderation but also justice."[3] The subject of musical ethos in Greek thought requires a separate treatment (such as that of Anderson), and here we shall only touch on the matter when the instruments themselves or the manner of playing them are involved.

Uses: Education

The works of Xenophon, Plato, and Aristotle reinforce earlier sources regarding the importance of music in the Athenian schoolboy's curriculum. According to Plato, the proper subjects of an aristocratic education are letters (*grammata*), lyre playing (kitharizein), and wrestling (*palaiein*).[4] In his description of the ideal educational system envisioned in his utopia, he suggests that a pupil should study literature for three years between the ages of 10 and 13, and the lyre for another three-year period between the ages of 13 and 16.[5] Such exact prescriptions in the context of proposing an ideal curriculum imply that in practice no such clearly defined scheme was followed.[6]

The standard term for lyre teacher in the fourth century is *kitharistes*, a word that originally referred to a professional minstrel of the sort mentioned in the literature of the Archaic period (see chap. 2). Plato mentions a particular kitharistes by name, Konnos, son of Metrobios, who, Socrates says, is still trying to teach him to play the lyre despite the pupil's advanced age; Socrates claims to be afraid that his young fellow-students will call Konnos an "old-geezer-teacher" (*gerontodidaskalos*).[7] The instruction, offered at the teacher's home, evidently consisted of training in rhythm and the various harmoniai and in singing lyric poetry to the accompaniment of *kitharismata*, which must have been rhythmic or melodic patterns that could be played on the lyre.[8] In Plato's view, the goal of all this training is to instill *sophrosyne* ("moderation") in the young pupil; he wants the lyre teachers to concern themselves more with the development of their students' character than with technical expertise in performance.[9]

The need for careful training and supervision of the novice lyre player on the part of the kitharistes is suggested in an analogy in which inexperienced lyre players who damage their instruments are compared to an inexperienced manager of estates who may ruin the house on which he is practicing his skills.[10] Of the actual procedures followed in teaching the instrument, however, the ancient sources provide no details, and we can only conjecture that simple drills in rhythm and various pitch patterns were followed by more complex training in singing lyric poetry to one's own accompaniment.

Uses: Entertainment and Festivals

The members of the lyre family continued to be used in connection with entertainment and public performance in much the same way as in the preceding century. Xenophon, for example, mentions a youth who plays the lyre (in concert with the aulos) while he sings and dances for the guests at a symposium.[11] Aristotle twice relates a parable about an anonymous king and the kitharode whom he employed to entertain at his court; the king promised that the better the kitharode played, the more he would pay him, but when the man tried to collect his money, the king said he had already paid for the pleasure he had received by the pleasure he had given in making such promises![12]

Musical contests are frequently mentioned in fourth-century literature. Plato thought them an important enough part of the responsibilities of the polis to include rules and regulations for the setting up of such competitions in his ideal state. According to his recommendations, all solo performers (including rhapsodes, kitharodes, and auletes) should be judged by one set of judges, while choral performers should be judged by a different set.[13] Elsewhere he makes a distinction between kithara-playing alone (*kitharisis*) and kithara-playing to accompany one's own singing (*kitharodia*), both of which are distinguished from rhapsodizing (*rhapsodia*), in which the emphasis was on the recitation of epic poetry, apparently with little or no musical accompaniment.[14] As always, Plato is concerned that such competitions should exist for the purpose of improving the audience, and not merely to give them pleasure and gratification; as a bad example of a competitor he singles out in particular one Kinesias, son of Meles, a composer of dithyrambs (lyric poems in honor of Dionysos) who lived in the last half of the fifth century and first decade of the fourth:

> Or do you think that Kinesias, son of Meles, gives any thought as to how he might say something by which his listeners would be improved, or only what is likely to give gratification to the throng of spectators?[15]

$$\mathring{\eta} \; \mathring{\eta}\gamma\tilde{\eta}$$
τι φροντίζειν Κινησίαν τὸν Μέλητος, ὅπως ἐρεῖ τι τοιοῦτον ὅθεν ἂν οἱ ἀκούοντες βελτίους γίγνοιντο, ἢ ὅτι μέλλει χαριεῖσθαι τῷ ὄχλῳ τῶν θεατῶν;

A substantial part of the repertory of such contestants doubtless consisted of *nomoi*, of which Timotheus' *Persae* is a surviving example (though lacking the musical notation). We have already mentioned kitharoedic nomoi in connection with the famous kitharode of the court of Periander in Corinth, Arion, whose dolphin call was supposed to have been a *nomos orthios*, or "high-pitched" nomos (chap. 3). Plato makes clear that in earlier days songs could be distinctly classified as hymns, threnoi ("dirges"), paeans, dithyrambs, and nomoi, but that in his own day the distinctions were becoming blurred (much to his dissatisfaction).[16] What the special characteristics of nomoi may once have been, however, is uncertain, because apart from Plato's mention of a prooemium ("prelude") as part of a kitharoedic nomos and the references in fifth- and fourth-century literature to the nomos orthios, there is little contemporary information about this particular type of song.[17] Eventually the term probably came to mean any melody suitable for performance with the kithara (with which the term was most clearly associated, even in the fifth and fourth centuries), as in a satirical reference from the Roman period to an overly zealous—albeit deceased—kitharode who was buried together with twelve kitharas and twenty-five boxes of nomoi, with which he now plagues everyone in Hades just as he had formerly plagued the living.[18]

Technique and Terminology

A new development found among fourth-century writers, particularly Plato, is the conception of lyre playing not so much as a gift from the gods (as it is viewed, for example, by Homer or Hesiod) as merely a type of skill or technical capacity (*techne*) analogous to horseriding or generalship.[19] Plato seems to regard musical accomplishment not as the privilege of a select few but rather as a useful skill that can be acquired by virtually anyone who receives proper training, a view that fits logically with his overriding interest in the educative value of rhythm and melody. This matter-of-fact attitude leads to increased discussion in the fourth century as to which instruments, styles, and techniques are most useful for the purpose of instructing the citizens of the polis.

The reactionary remarks of Plato regarding new developments in the technique of kithara playing (discussed further below) reveal that traditional distinctions among styles and genres had broken down by the fourth century. Plato is especially critical of the tendency of kithara music to imitate aulos music, as his comments in the *Laws* suggest:

> Later, as time passed, there came into being as leaders of tasteless disorderliness certain poets, who, though naturally possessing the qualities of a poet, were ignorant as to the just and lawful element of the Muse. They were like Bacchants and were possessed by pleasure in a greater degree than was necessary, mixing together dirges with hymns and paeans with dithyrambs, imitating aulos [accompanied] songs in songs to the kithara, and confusing everything with everything else.[20]

> μετά δὲ ταῦτα,
> προϊόντος τοῦ χρόνου, ἄρχοντες μὲν τῆς ἀμούσου παρανομίας ποιηταὶ ἐγίγνοντο φύσει μὲν ποιητικοί, ἀγνώμονες δὲ περὶ τὸ δίκαιον τῆς Μούσης καὶ τὸ νόμιμον, βακχεύοντες καὶ μᾶλλον τοῦ δέοντος κατεχόμενοι ὑφ' ἡδονῆς, κεραννύντες δὲ θρήνους τε ὕμνοις καὶ παίωνας διθυράμβοις, καὶ αὐλῳδίας δὴ ταῖς κιθαρῳδίαις μιμούμενοι, καὶ πάντα εἰς πάντα συνάγοντες.

On the basis of a passage in the *Republic* (399C, discussed below), we can deduce that what Plato objects to most about the aulos is its capacity to produce a large number of pitches so that it can encompass a wide range of different harmoniai, each distinguished from the other by a different arrangement of notes within the compass of an octave. In Plato's view, however, of all these various harmoniai (the so-called modes), only the Dorian and Phrygian can inspire the qualities appropriate to a citizen of the ideal state; hence he deplores any instrument that can easily produce more pitches than those necessary for the two approved harmoniai.[21] In the *Republic* he therefore criticizes all instruments that are characterized by

what he calls *panharmonia* and *polychordia*, among which he brands the aulos as the worst offender.

Plato's reference to polychordia (literally, "many-stringedness") in connection with a wind instrument raises the question as to exactly what he meant the term to imply. Since the literal meaning is inappropriate as far as the aulos (which has no strings at all) is concerned, we can assume that the word is intended here as a synonym for *polyharmonia*. Such a conclusion is confirmed by Plato's use elsewhere of the word *chorde* ("string") with reference to the aulos; the context here (*Philebus* 56A) is a theoretical discussion as to what would happen if the elements of arithmetic and measurement were removed from what would in modern parlance he called the arts and sciences:

> *Socrates*: There would be left only conjecture about these matters and the exercise of one's perceptions through trial and error, using the powers of guesswork which many call "skill"—guesswork that reaches its culmination through practice and hard work.
> *Protarchos*: Quite true.
> *Socrates*: Is not musical skill, first of all, full of this—fitting together harmonious sounds not so much by measuring as by guesswork based on practice—and the entire art of aulos-playing, seeking through guesswork the measure of each pitch (chorde) produced, so that the uncertainty involved is great, the certainty small?

> ΣΩ. Τὸ γοῦν μετὰ ταῦτ' εἰκάζειν λείποιτ' ἂν καὶ τὰς αἰσθήσεις καταμελετᾶν ἐμπειρίᾳ καί τινι τριβῇ, ταῖς τῆς στοχαστικῆς προσχρωμένους δυνάμεσιν ἃς πολλοὶ τέχνας ἐπονομάζουσι, μελέτῃ καὶ πόνῳ τὴν ῥώμην ἀπειργασμένας.
> ΠΡΩ. Ἀναγκαιότατα λέγεις.   ΣΩ. Οὐκοῦν μεστὴ μέν που μουσικὴ πρῶτον, τὸ σύμφωνον ἁρμόττουσα οὐ μέτρῳ ἀλλὰ μελέτης στοχασμῷ, καὶ σύμπασα αὐτῆς αὐλητική, τὸ μέτρον ἑκάστης χορδῆς τῷ στοχάζεσθαι φερομένης θηρεύουσα, ὥστε πολὺ μεμειγμένον ἔχειν τὸ μὴ σαφές, σμικρὸν δὲ τὸ βέβαιον.

Clearly, when Plato speaks of measuring each "string" on the aulos by means of educated guesswork, he refers simply to "note" and "pitch." Like *chorde*, then, the term *polychordia* seems also to carry a double sense: the literal meaning, "many-stringedness," and the transferred meaning implying the capacity to produce a large number of different pitches.

With Plato's comments on polychordia in mind, we are in a position to interpret the fragmentary report in a fourth-century philosopher-historian that one Stratonikos was the first to introduce polychordia into kithara playing.[22] The author probably means that

Stratonikos made use of frequent changes from one harmonia to another, presumably by retuning, not by literally introducing more strings to the instrument; the archaeological evidence does not allow us to entertain the notion (derived largely from late and unreliable reports; see chap. 3) that the lyre-type instruments had large numbers of extra strings added to them during the period under study. Stratonikos, who lived in Athens during the period 400–350 B.C., was a professional virtuoso kitharist noted for his witty sayings. He is reported also to have been the first kitharist to take on students of music theory and to establish a definite pattern for its study and analysis. Whether or not Stratonikos actually was the source of these various innovations, his biography suggests that polychordia was becoming a characteristic of kithara playing in the first half of the fourth century.

In addition to the use of frequent transitions from one harmonia to another, the new style apparently also involved an emphasis on virtuoso speed and smoothness of which Plato also disapproved, particularly in connection with kithara music without singing. Plato berates "bare" kithara playing (*psile kitharisis*) and its excessive displays of virtuoso technique and imitations of animal-like sounds:

> They see all this confusion, and still the poets tear rhythm and form from the tune, putting bare words into meter, but leaving the tune and rhythm without words, and availing themselves of bare kithara and aulos playing; in this sort of music it is extremely difficult to understand the intent of the rhythm and music, since they are divorced from words, and to know of what worthy models they are imitations. One ought to realize that this sort of music appeals only to country-bumpkins, insofar as it is excessively fond of speed, flashiness, and animal-like noise, with the result that aulos playing and kithara playing are used independently of dance and song; but the use of either alone amounts to Museless sleight of hand.[23]

> τοῦτά γε γὰρ
> ὁρῶσι πάντα κυκώμενα, καὶ ἔτι διασπῶσιν οἱ ποιηταὶ ῥυθμὸν μὲν καὶ σχήματα μέλους χωρίς, λόγους ψιλοὺς εἰς μέτρα τιθέντες, μέλος δ' αὖ καὶ ῥυθμὸν ἄνευ ῥημάτων, ψιλῇ κιθαρίσει τε καὶ αὐλήσει προσχρώμενοι, ἐν οἷς δὴ παγχάλεπον ἄνευ λόγου γιγνόμενον ῥυθμόν τε καὶ ἁρμονίαν γιγνώσκειν ὅτι τε βούλεται καὶ ὅτῳ ἔοικε τῶν ἀξιολόγων μιμημάτων· ἀλλὰ ὑπολαβεῖν ἀναγκαῖον ὅτι τὸ τοιοῦτόν γε πολλῆς ἀγροικίας μεστὸν πᾶν, ὁπόσον τάχους τε καὶ ἀπταισίας καὶ φωνῆς θηριώδους σφόδρα φίλον ὥστ' αὐλήσει γε χρῆσθαι καὶ κιθαρίσει πλὴν ὅσον ὑπὸ ὄρχησίν τε καὶ ᾠδήν, ψιλῷ δ' ἑκατέρῳ πᾶσά τις ἀμουσία καὶ θαυματουργία γίγνοιτ' ἂν τῆς χρήσεως.

Plato thus advocates the use of the kithara only as an accompanying instrument for the voice or for dance. Elsewhere he specifies (*Laws* 812D) that the lyre accompaniment should avoid excessively close or wide spacing of notes, excessive speed or slowness and high or low pitches; and any overly elaborate embroideries (*poikilmata*) in the rhythms.[24] Plato's strong objections to such characteristics (which he feels are innately wrong, not to mention impractical for citizen musicians) imply that technically complex rhythmic elaborations were in fact the vogue in fourth-century styles of performance, no doubt trademarks of virtuoso players such as Stratonikos. Plato does not comment directly on the exact relationship that he advocates between the sung tune and the accompaniment. In the same passage in the *Laws*, he speaks of the desirability of having the sounds of the song accompanied by lyre sounds that are *proschorda*, literally, "with the string," or "with the note." This has usually been interpreted as meaning "in unison," but if our analysis of lyre technique is correct and the player did not in fact pick out a melody but rather strummed across several strings in succession (perhaps damping some of them), then Plato's remarks would more logically refer to some kind of rhythmic correspondence rather than any correspondence in pitch; he may mean simply that the player should stick to providing a rhythmic foundation for the song and should not indulge in a kind of percussive obbligato.[25]

The subject of tuning is mentioned on several occasions in Plato's works, usually by way of illustrating a philosophical concept such as Socrates' notion that he would rather have his lyre be out of tune (*anarmostein*) than experience internal discord within himself.[26] The standard verb used of tuning is *harmottein* (literally, "to fit together," the verb from which *harmonia* is derived); the tightening of the strings is called *epitasis* (from *epiteinein*, "to stretch"), and the loosening *anesis* (from *anienai*, "to release").[27] In one instance, in a discussion in which the speakers are criticizing people who waste time measuring one sound against another and claiming that they can detect very small differences in pitch, Socrates sarcastically compares their twisting of the strings on the kollopes to the stretching of a victim on a torture rack:

> You are referring to those noble fellows who cause their strings trouble and put them to torture, twisting them upon the kollopes.[28]

> Σὺ μέν, ἦν δ' ἐγώ, τοὺς χρηστοὺς λέγεις τοὺς ταῖς χορδαῖς πράγματα παρέχοντας καὶ βασανίζοντας, ἐπὶ τῶν κολλόπων στρεβλοῦντας·

As this reference shows, the basic method of stringing and tuning the instruments in the fourth century had changed little since the time of Homer. The same passage also mentions the problem of unresponsive and overly responsive strings, which we may assume were still made of gut.

One small but useful piece of information regarding the technique of playing the lyre is contained in the distinction between the verbs for striking (*krouein*) the instrument's strings with the plektron and plucking them (*psallein*), a practice that, as we have seen, is reflected in the many vase paintings in which the player's hand is shown in a plucking position. Although the verb *krouein* is much more common than *psallein* in connection with instruments of the lyre type, occasional plucking of the strings with the left hand must have been used to add variety to the kinds of sounds that could be produced. The two techniques are mentioned in a passage from Plato, in which the point is being made that parents prevent their children from doing certain things, not because of their youth but because of their ignorance:

> *Socrates*: And if, as I think, you take up your lyre, neither your father nor your mother prevents you from tightening or loosening any of the strings you wish, or from plucking them and striking them with the plektron. Or do they prevent you?
> *Lysis*: No, certainly not.[29]

> καὶ ἐπειδάν, ὡς ἐγῷμαι,
> τὴν λύραν λάβῃς, οὐ διακωλύουσί σε οὔτε ὁ πατὴρ
> οὔτε ἡ μήτηρ ἐπιτεῖναί τε καὶ ἀνεῖναι ἣν ἂν βούλῃ
> τῶν χορδῶν, καὶ ψῆλαι καὶ κρούειν τῷ πλήκτρῳ.
> ἢ διακωλύουσιν;—Οὐ δῆτα.

New Terminology

While the basic terminology used in connection with the stringed instruments remains the same, the available vocabulary is expanded slightly through the addition in the fourth-century authors of adjectives formed from nouns, such as *kitharistikos*, "related to the kithara," and *kitharoidikos*, "related to singing to the kithara" (and, in slightly later Greek, *lyrikos*, "related to the lyre"). These may, in turn, be used to create new abstract nouns, as for example, *kitharistike* [*techne*], "the art of kithara playing." These new words reflect a general tendency of the Greek language in the fourth century to develop an increased supply of words that express concepts and abstractions rather than objects. Unlike the old word *kitharis* (which, we may recall, Homer generally uses to mean lyre playing but once for the instrument itself), *kitharistike* always refers to the concept or art of kithara playing, never

to the physical reality of a particular kithara or to a specific instance of playing. Thus Aristotle, for example, can speak of kitharistike as a form of imitation (*mimesis*) of reality, along with tragedy, epic, comedy, dithyramb, and aulos playing; or Plato can talk of the goal of kitharistike in contests as the giving of pleasure.[30] In a sense the development of such abstract nouns is parallel to the increased interest among fourth-century writers in the abstract notion of *mousike*, with a resulting lessened emphasis on the details of particular instruments.[31]

Another phenomenon that appears in the language for the first time in the fourth century is the metaphorical use of terms related to instruments. Skythinos of Teos (as quoted by Plutarch), writing ca. 400 B.C., speaks of Apollo as having the sun as a "plektron" with which to sweep across the "lyre" of the universe.[32] Although such metaphors are found in later Greek (and Roman) poetry, they do not occur in Homer or in the poets of the Archaic and Classical eras when the names connected with the instruments do not seem to lend themselves to metaphorical expression.

Instruments in the Art of the Fourth Century

Although the production and quality of painted vases diminished in Greece proper during the fourth century, at the same time wares from the Greek cities of southern Italy, especially Apulia, became established, at first painted with scenes derived from Athenian models but, as time went on, more often decorated with more indigenous themes.

Four of the instruments familiar to a fifth-century Athenian—the barbitos, the phorminx, the "Thracian" kithara, and the frame harp with spindle-shaped soundbox—are no longer to be found in Athenian art of the fourth century. The barbitos (which had all but disappeared even before the end of the fifth century and which is never mentioned by Plato) surfaces again briefly in Italian (Apulian and Etruscan) art of the fourth century but only in fewer than a dozen examples, all of them dating before mid-century.[33] A few faint rumors of the phorminx persist in Etruscan and Lucanian art of the fourth century; but the only representations that are at all convincing appear on a cornelian pendant of the mid-fourth century (from Athens), London 564, and an Etruscan *askos* (flask) from late in the century, London G 151.[34] Two Italian paintings of the Thracian kithara, both from the first half of the fourth century, are known to us, one a Death of Orpheus (in which Orpheus wears Thracian dress), Heidelberg 26.90, and another, much less certain, on Berkeley 8.997, where Apollo sits tuning the instrument.[35]

The Standard Kithara in the Fourth Century

Although the kithara of standard fifth-century shape is still to be found in a handful of Attic and Boeotian vase paintings made between about 420 and 390 B.C., by the end of that time it had disappeared from such paintings, and only the longer-bodied "Hellenistic" form of the instrument is still sometimes seen in them. The standard fifth-century form of the kithara is still depicted in fourth-century Italiote vase paintings but is present in the rest of the Greek world only on marble reliefs, statues, terra-cottas, gem stones, and coins. These objects indicate that, except in the Italiote sphere (which we will discuss separately later), the standard kithara was regarded almost exclusively as the property of Apollo in the fourth century, and it is possible that kitharas in this form were no longer being made.

The Apollo whom we see in contest with the satyr Marsyas in two Attic paintings from the period 420–390 B.C. is represented on a scaraboid of the first half of the fourth century and on a famous relief from Mantinea (fig. 1) of ca. 330–320 B.C. (which also depicts other instruments of interest to us).[36] The familiar group of Apollo, Leto, and Artemis, still to be seen on at least one Athenian and one Boeotian krater of the late fifth century, is rare thereafter; a marble relief votive plaque from the late fourth century in the form of a shrine containing the three figures is preserved at Athens (Athens 3917).[37] The theme of Apollo among the twelve gods, seen on New York krater 27.122.8 (ca. 420 B.C.), still finds expression in the first half of the fourth century on a round altar, Athens 1731, with relief figures of the gods (Apollo seated) around it. Apollo alone, his laurel tree behind him, plays the kithara on a small cup from the late fifth century, Athens 12740, a figure reminiscent of various terra-cottas of the fourth century from Athens, Olynthos, and Rhodes, standing male figures holding the kithara, all (though some are headless) presumably representing Apollo.[38]

Rites associated with Dionysos appear to be represented on several vases from the end of the fifth century: on a fragmentary pelike at Barcelona, where actors in a play are shown (satyrs, woman with mask, figure with thyrsos), Apollo sits near his tripod with the kithara; on Würzburg H 5708 a figure dressed as a kitharist (possibly a satyr) tunes up to play at a symposium (the guests seem to be Dionysos and Hephai-stos); and on a small skyphos, Athens 12266, a young man wearing a himation holds a thyrsos while another, nude, holds the kithara. But this theme is not continued among the objects from the fourth century.

A woman with the kithara, a rare sight, is clearly shown on a garnet ring stone, Oxford 60, from the first half of the fourth century.[39] On a marble grave relief of ca. 350 B.C., Kavala 228, the deceased (male) is shown seated with a kithara, while on a gold ring from the first quarter of the century at Leningrad, the instrument is played by a grotesque figure with a woman's head, arms, and upper torso attached to a locust body with a scorpion's tail ending in a griffin head.[40]

Although Italiote vase paintings also frequently depict Apollo, in these his place is sometimes taken by Orpheus (fig. 3), who appears here for the first time as a customary bearer of the standard kithara. The kithara is almost never seen in these paintings except in the hands of these two; only one painting has come to hand that seems to portray a mortal kitharist, a contestant to whom a Nike is bringing a wreath.[41] Since this scene seems borrowed from Athenian vases, we are left with a strong suspicion that the standard kithara was not actually used by the Greeks in Italy in the fourth century but only copied from older art works brought from Greece or known to emigré painters.

The contest of Apollo and Marsyas is the subject of eight Italiote paintings in which Apollo's instrument is the standard kithara (fig. 2a).[42] In seven of these it is Apollo's turn to perform, usually with a rather dejected Marsyas looking on; but on Brussels R227 Marsyas is already bound to a tree, and Apollo approaches him with the flaying knife; the kithara sits on the ground between them.[43] Apollo sits among other deities in the upper zone of three Apulian vases that depict mythological scenes in their lower zones: the Madness of Lykurgos on London F 271, the name-vase of the Lykurgos Painter (where Lyssa—madness—appears in the upper zone next to Apollo); Achilles and Penthesilea on Adolphseck 178; and perhaps the story of King Minos on a fragmentary krater from The Hague 2572.[44]

It is useful to bear in mind when discussing Italiote paintings that a large part of the Apulian vases (which constitute the greater part of those studied in this chapter), and very likely of the Lucanian, Campanian, and Sicilian vases as well, were made for funerary purposes—especially those that are very large, expensive, and elegantly painted. According to H. R. W. Smith, the scenes on a number of these vases reflect the beliefs of the Italian (Messapian) neighbors of the Greeks that couples separated by death would be reunited in Elysium, and that those who had died unmarried would be given ideal partners in the afterlife in rites supervised by Dionysos and Aphrodite with the assistance of Apollo or Orpheus.[45] The view that marriage and remarriage rites are portrayed, while controversial, seems for our purposes a satisfactory explanation of the scenes that include Orpheus, as well as certain of those that depict Apollo; and we will return to it a number of times elsewhere in this chapter.

On Apulian krater Bari 6270 (fig. 2b), where Apollo sits playing the kithara to the upper right of the temple-like grave monument (*naiskos*) of a young warrior, there are a number of objects related to marriage ceremonies: Hermes, lower left, leans against a laver on a pedestal; Aphrodite (?), upper left, has cakes and the ladder-like object (often taken to be a musical instrument, but probably in fact a handloom, or perhaps an abacus) that frequently appears in marriage scenes; and there are phiales and a krater below the temple.[46] The kithara on Apulian vase Taranto 8129, though it is held by Aphrodite (the presence of Eros and Pan, as well as a swan and certain objects—tympanum, phiale, wreath—attest that it is she), symbolizes Apollo's part in marriage rites.[47]

In contrast with these scenes of marriage rites, there are two bell kraters, Paestan (fig. 2c, a Salerno vase by the painter Asteas) and Apulian (Naples 3370), that present Apollo as a comic character in a phlyax play.[48] The two figures on the Paestan vase are identified: Phrynix, who holds the kithara (and according to Webster wears an Apollo mask) may be the fifth-century musician who had the dubious distinction of being denounced by "Musica" in Pherekrates' *Cheiron* (see chap. 3) and of quarreling, like Timotheus, with the Spartan ephors who were supposed to have cut away his instrument's extra strings. Although Plutarch, some centuries after the fact, may have been misinformed about the cause of the quarrel (since evidence for a lyre with more than seven strings is quite sparse), a "Phrynis and the Spartan ephors" story may have been the subject of a fourth-century phlyax play; the second figure, Pyronides, may represent an ephor. On the Apulian vase the laurel-wreathed actor with the kithara also plays Apollo, for there is a tripod and laurel tree; the second figure is not identified.

The instrument of Orpheus, as we see him on about a dozen Apulian vases found so far, is also the standard kithara. In these paintings his role, except in two or three cases, is not that of the rescuer of Eurydice but apparently that of the author of the "Orphic" texts attributed to him; he appears in these underworld scenes as a guarantor that the prescribed purification rites have been performed. On Munich 3297 (fig. 3) he stands in his elaborate kitharist's costume, with a "Phrygian" cap, to the left of the small palace of Persephone and Hades; behind him to the left is a reunited family—man, wife, and small son. The rest of the scene contains many mythological figures in Hades, among them Heracles restraining Cerberus (bottom center) and at the upper left the wife and sons whom Heracles murdered—a family that will never be reunited.[49] Most of the same mythological figures, including Heracles with Cerberus, and Heracles' wife and sons, are painted in the same positions on Karlsruhe B4; Orpheus again stands to the left of the temple, but behind him are two Furies—the mortal couple seem to be the two to the right of the temple, urged forward by Aphrodite (?). On a third volute krater of this kind, Naples 3222, where all the mythological figures mentioned above are identified by inscription, there are no mortals on this side of the vase (though there are on the reverse). Here Hades and Persephone themselves appear to be the focus of attention: both (for once) are seated on a low dais within the palace, and they have at least two objects, the garnished phiale that Persephone holds out and the tympanum suspended overhead, that are associated with marriage rites.[50]

Orpheus plays the kithara in two other scenes where the symbolism of purification rites for marriage is even more in evidence, on Milan 270 and Bari 873, scenes in which he is also once more among other Thracians (so identified by their clothing, including their Phrygian caps), though the significance of this has not yet been discovered.[51] On the Milan vase, Aphrodite and Eros are above him; and to his right, with a Thracian warrior leaning against it, is a large laver on a pedestal, with a conch shell for dipping out water. There is a similar laver on Bari 873, with a nude male leaning against it holding a phiale; behind him one of the Thracians stands ready with the conch shell to pour water over him, and in front of him is an incense burner, a symbol of Aphrodite. Orpheus, seated, and two more Thracians, one holding a horse's bridle, look on. (In the zone below, friends or relatives bring to the grave stele offerings that are also part of the marriage paraphernalia.) Orpheus stands in the naiskos of an elderly deceased warrior on Basel S40; even here the dipping pan and garnished phiale (and, on the reverse, tympanum and flower chain) held by the relatives and friends suggest marriage rites.[52]

Eurydice is probably the woman who stands near Orpheus on two vases, Naples Stg 709 and a fragment from the Fenicia Collection (location unknown).[53] In the former, similar to the great underworld scenes (though here Persephone and Hades have no palace), Orpheus lays his hand on the arm of the woman, who stands to his left, while an Eros hovers at his shoulder. In the other, more doubtful painting, Orpheus stands in his usual place by the palace; slightly above and to the left a winged woman, whose name, partly lost, may be read]IKA, begins to open a door. Can this be Eurydice, as Harrison suggests in *Themis*, ascending without Orpheus?[54]

On Apulian vase Basel S34 there is a kithara of an unusual sort. Here Apollo sits in the upper zone with Artemis, Aphrodite, and Eros (the mythological scene below includes Skythes, Rhodope, Heracles, and Antiope) playing an instrument with a body somewhat longer (with a light-colored stripe down each side) and arms less curved than usual; its most peculiar feature, however, is the outward curve of the arms just below the crossbar, forming "swans' heads" similar to those seen on some early examples of the barbitos (chap. 5). The "swans' heads" also appear in three other paintings, on kitharas more in the standard shape, though like Basel S34 they have no inner-arm decoration: on Naples Stg 11, Apollo is seated with such a kithara above and to the left of the small temple in which Persephone stands before a youthful Hades; and on two other vases the swan's-head kithara symbolizes Apollo's part in the rites of otherworldly marriage, though he himself is not present. On Kassel T.723 it hangs above the marriage of Paris and Helen, and on the upper zone of Basel S29 (fig. 4) it sits between Dionysos and Aphrodite, the gods chiefly involved in Elysian marriages, who are attended by a satyr and a maenad (in the zone below are three women with a great deal of nuptial paraphernalia). All four vases with swan's-head kitharas were made in Italy ca. 350 B.C. or somewhat later.[55]

As far as one is able to tell from this rather small collection of Greek and Italiote representations (a number of them by no means clear), the kithara continued to be held and played in the fourth century as it was in the fifth. There are no obvious examples of singing to the kithara, and only one painting, on an Attic krater of ca. 400 B.C., that depicts the tuning of the kithara (Würzburg H 5708). The method is the familiar one, the right hand at the crossbar to turn the kollopes, the left hand ready to test the pitch.

Some of the clearest and most detailed representations of the instrument itself are found on fourth-century coins, from Macedonia (Chalcidian League, Bottiasi, Olynthos), Megara, Zacynthus, the Aegean islands (Delos, Lesbos), Asia Minor (Troas, Colophon), and North Africa (Cyrene). Though some of these were made from stamps that were mere recast-

ings of late fifth-century stamp designs, it is interesting to see, first, that all the kitharas are of the standard shape (the long-bodied kithara on a coin from Mytilene [London, Anson no. 333], which he dates to 350–250 B.C., may well be third century); and second, that none of the ones with countable strings has more than seven.[56] It may be objected, as we have done elsewhere in this study, that on small objects such as coins, fewer strings may be indicated because the space is limited. But the situation does not change greatly if all the other fourth-century representations are considered: while quite a number of them (mainly reliefs and terracottas) do not have sufficient detail to allow strings to be counted, over three-quarters of those with strings indicated have no more than seven strings (some have six or five). Only five instruments (one of them of the "swan's-head" type) that have more than seven have been located: two of these have eight, one eight or nine, one has ten, and one eleven strings.[57]

Although there are considerable variations in size and shape among the fourth-century representations of the standard kithara, it does not seem likely that they reflect differences between actual instruments in use at the time; at least in the case of the Italiote vase painters, they may result from interpretations by individual artists of an instrument seen rarely (if at all) and copied from depictions on imported Attic vases. Fine details such as section lines and circles on the soundbox appear rarely or not at all (the instrument is often entirely in white on Italiote vases), but the small bumps or knobs on the outside edges of the arms just below the crossbar are still present on some of the Chalcidian League coins, in Italiote paintings (fig. 3), and on marble relief Athens 1731.[58]

The scaraboid in Leningrad, Boardman no. 601, and the coins of the Chalcidian League give us opportunities to see the bridge and the lower string fastener slightly raised from the soundbox surface. These fittings have not changed, nor has the crossbar or its kollopes and knobs, except on Mantinea relief (fig. 1), where the "knobs" are disks set well in from the ends of the crossbar, and on The Hague 2572, where there are two disks on each side, the smaller one to the inside. The kollopes are presented in interesting detail on Sydney frag. 51.37: they form thick loops around the front of the crossbar and have a straight piece behind it, as in the collar-and-pin device described in chapter 3. The accoutrements of the kithara—sling, sash, cloth, and plektron—also are unchanged. The sling in some cases runs diagonally down to the outer edge of the soundbox, as in some late fifth-century examples, and the cloth now ordinarily consists of two long narrow strips (or one strip folded at the top) with fringe at the ends (see figs. 2 and 3).[59]

Aside from the "swan's-head" variant of the standard kithara, there are two observable differences in the fourth-century depictions that seem significant. First, the upper part of each arm (above the crossbar) is now often quite abbreviated, and sometimes widens at the top, as on Munich 3297 (fig. 3) and Basel S40 as well as on "swan's head" example Basel S29 (fig. 4) and Kassel T.723, where the effect is like a knob at the top. Second, the inner-arm decoration, while it is sometimes of the elaborate three-pointed variety seen on the Mantinea relief (fig. 1), may at times be simplified to a single point, as on Athens relief 1731, or two points high and close together as on Leningrad 988 and (elongated) on The Hague 2572; and the instruments on Apulian krater Ruvo J 494 and a Sicilian krater in Lentini have, like the "swan's head" type, no such decorative work at all.[60]

After the end of the fourth century, the standard kithara is seldom found in any part of the Greek world, although its shape is still found for a while on a few coins from Megara and Asia Minor. The instrument (much damaged) on a third-century limestone statue from Cyprus (Toronto 958.61.325) appears to be a standard kithara, as does the one on a fragment of a Hellenistic stele at Athens (Svoronos 482). A second-century B.C. relief from the Acropolis, Athens 1966, shows Apollo with a kithara (back view) that lacks only inner-arm decoration; it is in a deliberately Archaic style, however, as is the marble relief of the Augustan period (27 B.C.–A.D. 14), Cleveland 30.522, an excellent, detailed representation of the kithara that has a thick crossbar resting atop the lower arms— the very short upper arms rise behind it.

From Italy there are late-first-century B.C. examples on Arretine ware, but these have no upper arms, or almost none, and the inner-arm decoration has been reduced to a single point (New York 08.258.37 and 19.192.20). A first-century A.D. wall painting from Herculaneum (London 26) depicts a couple sitting together, the woman with a small kithara of eight (?) strings that has very short upper arms that flare, and an inverse point sinking into the center top of the soundbox. It seems likely that this, like the rest of the instruments in this small post-fourth-century group, is a depiction of an ancient instrument seldom (or never) seen by the artist except on art works of earlier centuries. The long-bodied Hellenistic kithara (discussed below), more commonly seen on objects of the Hellenistic and Roman periods, was probably the only kithara generally known after about 300 B.C.

The Hellenistic Kithara

Though the elongated kithara (see fig. 5), somewhat narrower for its length than the standard kithara, is not often found in fourth-century representations, the first hints of its development can already be seen in the instruments on several late fifth-century vases (see chap. 3); and it continues to appear after 300 B.C. (when depictions of all instruments become still less frequent) in various versions, all the way down to the second century A.D.

The myth of Apollo and Marsyas is the subject of the paintings on all three of the fourth-century Attic vases on which this form of the kithara appears; Apollo plays, wreathed and gowned as a contestant, on the two red-figured vases, San Simeon 9941 and Leningrad St. 1795. On the third vase, Naples 2991 (polychrome relief ware), the scene is the flaying of Marsyas. Here Apollo stands to the right looking on while a Muse seated behind him calmly tunes Apollo's kithara.

A Muse holds Apollo's kithara on one of three Italiote vases that depict this form of the instrument, Campanian kylix Vienna 217. The scene is in the interior: Apollo seated to the right, wreathed, with his laurel staff, while the Muse stands before him with the kithara and plektron. The other two Italiote vases do not show Apollo. On Apulian vase, Leningrad St. 498, a rather typical afterlife scene containing a number of marriage-rite symbols, Orpheus (wearing his Phrygian cap) stands with kithara before Hades and serves as guarantor of the lady with matron's fan behind him (on the far right is Aphrodite, who with her incense burner before her, is seated with a parasol beside a large laver on a pedestal). The remaining piece, a *lekanis* (dish) lid from Sicily now at Palermo, has only an odd outline sketch of a long kithara, which is used to fill the space around the woman's head that forms the main design.

Aside from the few vases described above, there is only one other fourth-century object with a scene in which this "Hellenistic" kithara appears: a marble votive relief from Thessaly, Athens 1380, which depicts Apollo, Leto, and Artemis.

Since all these scenes are the same as those in which the standard kithara is found, making it clear that this instrument is nothing more than a modernized version of the standard kithara, we are not surprised to find that it is held, played, and tuned just as is the standard kithara. The performers hold the instrument upright and stand to play; the woman seated with it on Naples 2991 is tuning, right hand at kollopes, left hand testing the strings in the usual manner.

The small amount of evidence indicates that both hands are used to play in the manner common to all Greek lyres, except that in two of the three examples of the right hand in use, the plektron sweeps the strings above the top of the soundbox (Leningrad St. 1795, San Simeon 9941).[61]

The details of the construction of this instrument as it existed in the fourth century are difficult to pin down, since our few depictions of it were not executed with great care and some of them have been damaged. The clearest representation is not from a scene at all but from a jasper scaraboid on which the instrument itself is the only design (fig. 5). This may be taken as a representative example, though every other depiction differs in at least one respect. The most common difference is in the inner-arm decoration, confined to a small area close to the crossbar in about half our examples, completely absent in two cases, and very small in another. The arms are longer above the crossbar in half the representations and usually somewhat thicker, but only two examples lack the knobs that flare out at the top in figure 5. The crossbar has its knobs set in from the ends in three cases, and on Vienna 217 it appears to have no free ends or knobs at all. The curve of the arms is the same as, or similar to, the one shown in figure 5 in most cases, but the sides are straighter on Naples 2991 and Athens 1380, and on the diagrammatic Palermo lid figure the curve ends abruptly above a long, rectangular soundbox. More than half the available examples do have a longer soundbox than in our illustration, a foretaste of the even longer form the instrument was to acquire in one of its later Hellenistic-period manifestations. That the base of the instrument is triangular (or rather pentangular, with a point at center back) has been indicated by the artist of Leningrad St. 1795, who has let the bottom show as though the instrument were tipped back.

The number of strings this kithara had in the fourth century cannot be ascertained. Vienna 217 has six; our illustration shows seven; the silver coin from Lesbos with an elongated kithara (London, Anson 333) has eight; Naples 2991 has perhaps eight; and the instrument sketched on the Palermo lid has nine (with six kollopes). None of the others has strings indicated. The situation is much the same for representations from the Hellenistic and Roman periods.

After the fourth century, the instrument seems to have continued to change gradually, losing its upper arms (so that the crossbar sometimes sits atop the arms) and becoming less curved along the sides (losing the "hip") and longer in the soundbox, which tapers inward at the sides and is narrowest at the bottom.

The small votive bronze from the third-century Antikythera shipwreck, in the Athens Museum, is an example of this changed shape (fig. 6). The instrument also loses the rest of its inner-arm ornamentation in most cases, though this is occasionally still present, usually in a much simplified form. In a few examples the soundbox (and thereby the whole instrument) is very elongated (Athens 1485, of 119 B.C.; London 2191, 150–120 B.C.; Argos 339, Hellenistic). Two Roman copies of Hellenistic Greek statues of Apollo (London 1380, first century A.D.; Nicosia, from Salamis, second century A.D.) show, as does figure 6, that the instrument curved from top to bottom. These very late examples also have a deep box the full width of the soundbox at the bottom front to serve as the lower string fastener; strings fastened to its outer edge would have run to the crossbar at a considerable distance from the player's left hand, making any theory of pitch changes involving the left hand still less tenable. Throughout its history, the instrument continues to be closely associated with Apollo, who is the player in nearly all the identifiable depictions.

The Italiote Kithara

A kithara with parallel arms that do not curve out to the sides and a straight-sided, often rectangular soundbox is found in the fourth century almost exclusively in Italiote vase paintings. This kithara, which first appears ca. 360 B.C., is not seen until somewhat later, and then only on rare occasions, in other parts of the Greek world.

On Apulian vases, which account for most of the fourth-century examples, this "Italiote" kithara generally appears along with other objects that have been identified as symbols of marriage rites (see above), but it does not seem to be associated with Apollo. It lies near the feet of a young man who is apparently being instructed and prepared for the rites under the supervision of Aphrodite (Naples 2867), and it lies between Aphrodite and Eros, who are part of a purification scene at a laver on a pedestal (Richmond, Va. 80.162). It hangs above another young gentleman who has reached a later stage, perhaps, and is about to be presented to Persephone and Hades (Leningrad St. 426); it is played by the young man who has doffed his wreath and seated himself beside his bride on a pelike in the Chamay Collection in Geneva (while Aphrodite rides overhead in a chariot pulled by Erotes); and on four pelikes, Boston 10.234, Naples 3224, San Simeon 5609 (fig. 7), and Torino 4149 (fig. 8), it is played by or (on the Boston vase) lies near a young man seated on his marriage couch.[62] His bride sits beside him on the Boston and Torino vases; on the Naples and San Simeon vases the woman seated nearby, with matron's fan (San Simeon) or wreath and small chest (Naples), may be the bride or the goddess. The young man on these last two vases might be thought to be Apollo were it not for the plethora of marriage symbols surrounding him: Eros, a laver on a pedestal, two chests, the strange ladder-like object (possibly a handloom or abacus), the swan (associated with Aphrodite as well as with Apollo), Persephone's whirligig torch (?), and perhaps the fruit-bearing tree, all on San Simeon 5609; all but the laver and torch also appear on Naples 3224, which has in addition wreaths, fillets, and a swag of flowers.

Two Campanian vases on which the Italiote kithara appears (in the hands of a seated young man attended by two women), Ann Arbor 28809 and Naples 808, have been thought to represent Apollo or a victorious kitharode. But here again there are unmistakable symbols, particularly the incense burner (associated with Aphrodite) that stands behind the player on both vases, as well as the panther skin spread over the stool on which the player sits, which calls to mind the other deity associated with these rites, Dionysos. Other small items, on one vase or the other, reinforce the symbolism: swan (or crane) on the player's knee, elaborate basket of food, sprays of leaves, fillets, flowers, and grape cluster.

The Italiote kithara may turn up in mythological scenes, however. On Apulian vases, where one side, or one major scene, may be mythological while the rest portrays the afterlife, we find it in several contexts: it lies at Aphrodite's feet as she and Eros look down on the pursuit of Ganymede by Apollo (disguised as a swan) on a Noble Coll. *situla* (cylindrical pot) in Maplewood, New Jersey; Dionysos plays it in the upper corner of a scene devoted to the story of Hypsipyle and the Seven against Thebes on Naples 3255; and it appears in two paintings of Niobe mourning, once lying below the naiskos in which Niobe stands (Naples 3246), once in the hands of an attending woman (Taranto 8935). In the first two of these, since Aphrodite and Dionysos belong as much to the marriage-rite scene on the other side of the vase as to the mythological one, the presence of the instrument is easily understood, especially since on Naples 3255 funeral rites for Hypsipyle's young charge Archemoros are portrayed. In the paintings of Niobe, various objects that might be brought to a tomb and that have been identified as symbols of the marriage ceremony—boxes, baskets, wreaths, mirror, fan, as well as kithara—are depicted, and we may speculate that these are being brought as funeral gifts for Niobe's children,

who were destroyed by Apollo and Artemis as punishment for Niobe's hubris; the scenes on the reverse sides do not contradict this interpretation.

Outside Apulian-Campanian circles, the Italiote version of the kithara had more conventional associations in the late fourth century. On the lid of a Sicilian lekanis, Lipari 749A (ca. 340–330 B.C.), it is held by Apollo, who is seated near an *omphalos* (round stone representing the navel of the earth), has a phiale in his right hand, and is accompanied by Artemis (who holds a torch and has an arm around a large hound) and a drum-bearing satyr. Our only certain fourth-century representation from Greece proper, a marble slab from Mantinea that formed part of the base for a sculpture group of Apollo, Artemis, and Leto (fig. 9), depicts this rectangularly shaped kithara in the hands of one of the Muses watching the contest of Apollo and Marsyas. (On a Hellenistic marble relief from the second century B.C. depicting the Apotheosis of Homer, London 2191, this kithara is again held by a Muse.)

The Italiote kithara appears in quite a different context on a second Sicilian vase. On Leningrad 2079, ca. 340–300 B.C., we see a drunken Heracles with two maenads (one of whom holds an aulos, while the other has an oversize version of the Italiote kithara) who try to distract the satyr (?) leaning over a gate pouring water on Heracles as he lies happily on the ground on his lion skin, his club beside him. This theme of wine and music is echoed somewhat later in the paintings on three Gnathian vases, Naples 80987, Naples 80084, and Warsaw 138485. The first of these is decorated only with the kithara, a krater, and a pair of crisscrossed auloi surrounded by grape clusters and leaves, and the second is similar, with crisscrossed auloi, harp (see below), and rectangular kithara framed in the same fashion. On the third vase an actor representing Heracles (he is seated on an animal skin and wears a sort of double mask) sits playing the Italiote kithara in an arbor with grape clusters and leaves overhead. These tantalizing glimpses of a connection between this instrument, Heracles, and wine drinking are all we can bring forward at present to mark this aspect of the associations of the Italiote kithara (cf. the discussion of Heracles in chap. 3).[63]

Eros joins the list of players of this instrument on two later Hellenistic terra-cottas, Boston 97.300 (from Euboea) and a terra-cotta at Samothrace, thus bringing us around again to the associations with love and marriage found earlier on the Apulian vases. These Erotes, along with a few other unidentifiable terra-cotta figures, and a Muse on London 2191, mentioned above, carry the only later Hellenistic examples of the Italiote kithara now at hand.[64]

This instrument, like the standard kithara, is held upright when it is played; but it may not always have been played with a plektron. The evidence is very sketchy: only two vases show the left hand in use, Apulian pelike Torino 4149 (fig. 8; the vase has two examples) and Gnathian krater Warsaw 138485. Two of the players on these vases appear to pluck with both hands (their hands are open, with fingers and thumbs separated and curved), while the woman playing on Torino 4149 (whose left hand is not visible) may use her right hand to pluck. The seated man on Campanian krater Naples 808 may hold a plektron, but he is gesturing, not playing; a Santangelo Coll. terra-cotta in Naples showing a seated woman with the Italiote kithara shows the instrument played with a plektron. When the right hand plucks, it may be below the upper edge of the soundbox (fig. 8) or up near the crossbar (Warsaw 138485).

The left hand, sometimes in playing position even when the right hand is not, can be clearly seen on two other vases in addition to the three just mentioned, Leningrad 2079 and Ann Arbor 28809. All but one of this group of five portray the left hand in plucking position, thumb and index finger, or thumb and little finger, brought close together, or, in one case, thumb bent in front of palm, with other fingers straight. On the Ann Arbor vase the thumb and fingers are all extended straight and separate, in the position that may indicate damping.

The player tunes his Italiote kithara on two vases, Apulian pelikes Naples 3224 and Geneva, Chamay Coll. In both of these he places his right hand over the crossbar, while his left hand, in playing position, tests the strings—the typical tuning technique already frequently observed in fifth-century examples. When playing, the performers, both women and men, are in most cases seated. None of them sings while playing (as far as can be discerned), nor does anyone else in the vicinity.

Because the examples are comparatively few and the variants many, the Italiote kithara is somewhat difficult to describe. The arms of the instrument usually seem to be quite narrow and straight, though a few objects make it clear, by making both arms appear to curve in the same direction (see fig. 7), that they do curve *forward*. (This effect is also slightly visible in fig. 9.) The arms often extend downward all along the sides of the soundbox, according to a number of paintings such as figure 7. They are also often provided with ornaments just below and/or sometimes just above, the crossbar, small disks, knobs, or crosspieces, some-

times two or three (a few have many) on a side, painted white if the instrument itself is in white (often the case) and resembling crossbar "knobs" (fig. 8).

The crossbar, which may or may not have knobs, is attached a short way down from the upper end of the arms (it is at the top in fig. 9 and on the Chamay Coll. pelike in Geneva). The kollopes that secure the strings at the upper end appear to be the same as those used with other members of the lyre family. The information about the number of strings is inconclusive: they are indicated in only 16 of 30 examples, 2 with five strings (or kollopes), 4 with six strings, 6 with seven strings, and 4 with nine strings (one vase, Torino 4149, accounts for one seven-stringed and one nine-stringed example).

The body of the instrument is in some cases simply a squarish rectangle, as in figure 7, but more than half the items available indicate that the upper edge of the soundbox rises to a point at the center (see fig. 9). In five of the paintings the lower edge of the front of the soundbox also seems to come to a point, making a shape that looks hexagonal (Naples 808 is a good example). But evidence from the two marble reliefs, figure 9 and London 2191, corrects this impression, reassuring us that the lower front edge is straight and that what the painters attempt to show in these cases is the triangular base, with a point at the center back. Figure 9 indicates these features clearly, while the second-century London 2191, a back view, confirms that this instrument, like the standard kithara, has a humped back with a rounded ridge running down the center.

Such details as bridge and lower string fastener are rarely indicated; the bridge can be seen only on Sicilian lekanis Lipari 749A (as a line) and Gnathian krater Naples 80084 (as a wide black rectangle); and the lower string fastener is visible in only just over half a dozen examples, including two from the Hellenistic period, in the shape of a long rectangle, in outline or relief.[65] None of the representations shows a wrist sling, and only two players, as noted above, seem to be holding a plektron (Naples 808 and a Naples Santangelo Coll. terra-cotta). None of the Italiote kitharas has a cloth hanging from behind it (the billow of cloth behind the one on Leningrad 2079 is part of the maenad's cloak), and only five have sashes: two long, ribbon-like strands on Ann Arbor 28809 (in white), Bari, Lagioia Coll. (white), Taranto 8935, and Lipari 749A; and two white ribbons, a bit wider and attached to the wrong arm, on Leningrad 2079.

Seen directly from the front, the Italiote kithara with its straight arms and almost square soundbox front looks like a long rectangle. Its size, like its other features, varies a good bit. The instrument in figure 7 is one of the smaller examples, while Leningrad 2079 has the largest, reaching from the player's mid-thigh to the top of her head. The width also varies, from ¼ to ¾ of the height (most often between ⅓ and ½ of the height). Like the standard kithara and its descendants, this instrument must have been constructed mainly of wood. Since in a number of cases it is painted white, we may speculate that the actual instruments were also painted or perhaps made from wood of a light color.[66]

The Chelys-Lyra in the Fourth Century

Images of the chelys-lyra grow comparatively scarce in the fourth century, though they are still better represented among the stringed instruments than are the harps. Two-thirds of the fifty or so representations of the fourth-century chelys-lyra assembled for this study were made in Greece or East Greek areas, the rest (consisting of vase paintings only) in southern Italy. Most of them are vase paintings, for only a few terracottas, coins, gem stones, and marbles of the fourth century include recognizable images of the chelys-lyra. This dependence on vases gives rise to an odd chronological distribution, for most of the vases from Greece were made before 390 B.C., while nearly all those of southern Italy (from which we have only vase paintings) were made after about 375 B.C.

The scenes on vases from Greece in which the chelys-lyra appears follow for the most part themes familiar from the late fifth century: Dionysos with Ariadne, satyrs, and maenads; Apollo and Marsyas or Apollo and Artemis; and banquet or symposium scenes, processions, and single figures before a tripod (a boy, a Nike, or a person seated). The scene of a girl dancing, seen on Athens 1187 (ca. 410), where her accompaniment is the aulos (the lyra hangs on the wall), is echoed in a later vase made for a wedding ceremony, on which three young women dance while a fourth plays the lyra (Athens 12894). Less familiar themes include a lyre-playing Eros astride a dolphin, the Meidias Painter's Aphrodite and her attendants at the wedding of Demonassa and Phaon (a mortal to whom she gave irresistible charm), figure 10, and two marble sirens with lyres from the Kerameikos cemetery at Athens (fig. 11).[67] These sirens, along with grave monuments on which the deceased is portrayed playing the chelys-lyra, show the continued association of the instrument with ideas of death and afterlife.[68] To the representations of Apollo must be added the Meleagros Painter's scene of Apollo's arrival on Delos

seated on a swan, and a later painting (ca. 370 B.C.) that shows him riding a griffin.[69]

Some of the scenes on Italiote vases are borrowed from Greek models, in idea if not in actual composition. An Italiote vase from the late fifth century has a painting of nine Muses, and others ca. 400 B.C. show Apollo and Artemis, or Dionysos (?) riding a camel surrounded by men and women in eastern dress playing frame drums and lyres.[70] The main group of Italiote vases, beginning ca. 375 B.C., also continues various representations of Apollo (alone, with other gods, with the Muses, or competing with Marsyas), banquet or symposium scenes (still found on relief ware of the first century B.C.), and Dionysiac celebrations. Here too we find Apollo arriving on a swan, and (on the reverse of the same vase) a dolphin bearing a lyre player (Arion, Taras, or Apollo); and sirens can be seen, in a scene that shows Odysseus tied to the mast of his ship to resist their song.[71]

Brides attended by women and Erotes (fig. 16) also appear on these Italiote vases in scenes similar to those on a number of fifth-century Athenian vases. But since south Italian vases were made as funerary ware, H. R. W. Smith's contention that their scenes indicate a belief in marriage and remarriage in the afterlife, discussed above in the section on the standard kithara, must be recalled once more. There are four vases that appear to show the preparations of the bridegroom, attended by Aphrodite.[72] These scenes usually have a seated central male figure (the groom) and may include Aphrodite, Eros, Pan (who provides water for Aphrodite's rites), and various of the objects that may also be found in brides' scenes: mirrors, *situlae,* wreaths, phiales, round covered baskets, and musical instruments (the brides also have fillets, balls, fans, and the ladder-like object discussed above, probably an abacus or handloom). The significance of the god Pan in this context may carry over to a Campanian vase on which we see only two figures: Pan confronting a woman who sits on a rock playing the lyre.[73] That the chelys-lyra also has a funerary meaning, as on the Attic stelae, perhaps as a symbol of the pleasure of the afterlife, is made clear by several paintings that show the deceased as a statue in a temple-like grave monument (naiskos).[74] The lyre may hang from the rafters of the naiskos or be held either by the deceased, or, on a funerary vase of a comic poet (fig. 12), by a youth who perhaps represents his slave.

In Greek vase paintings of the end of the fifth century and the first decade of the fourth, the chelys-lyra appears along with krotala and frame drums in Dionysiac scenes, and sometimes with the standard kithara and auloi in depictions of the story of Apollo and

Marsyas; in the late fifth century it is still paired (though not played) with the aulos in a painting of a girl in (Thracian?) costume dancing, and played with the aulos in a procession of revelers—with the aulos case attached to the arm of the lyra, as in earlier paintings.[75]

Italian vases include frame drums, but not krotala, in Dionysiac scenes along with the chelys-lyra and continue the custom of including the lyra along with standard kithara and aulos in paintings of Apollo and Marsyas. Following traditions of earlier decades of the fifth century at Athens, a late fifth-century Italian vase portrays the Muses with chelys-lyra, trigonon, phorminx, and auloi, while a vase from the main group (375–325 B.C.) brings together lyra and standard kithara in a painting of Apollo and two Muses. Aulos and chelys-lyra, often seen together in Athenian banquet or symposium scenes in the fifth century, also appear in such a scene in this group. Finally, the lyra takes its place along with the harp, or harp and auloi, in scenes in which brides are made ready for their otherworldly marriages (see fig. 16).[76]

Players of the chelys-lyra on Attic vases made before 390 B.C. are, as earlier in the fifth century, nearly all male (boys, young men, or mature men, mythological or mortal) and without any special costume; they wear only a mantle or are nude, perhaps with a folded cloak over arms or shoulders.[77] The few women who hold or play the lyre in both Greek and Italian paintings before 390 B.C. are modestly dressed mythological figures in chiton or *peplos* (Artemis, Ariadne, a Nike, the Muses) except on a lebes stand of 400–390 B.C., Athens 12894, which depicts a female lyre player and three dancing women, all in the same unusual costume: they are nude to the waist, with straps crisscrossed back and front, and wear skirts that come only to their knees. According to Metzger, the dance is the *kalathiskos* (literally, "basket dance"); the vase shape is one associated with weddings.[78]

Female players of the chelys-lyra are better represented on the Italiote vases of ca. 375–325 B.C., thanks to the wedding-preparation scenes in which the instrument is held by brides or female attendants. The costumes of both men and women remain the same as in the earlier period, with exceptions of two kinds: first, in two of the Italiote paintings, the young men (in one case a groom-to-be, in the other his attendant) wear high boots and short, decorated tunics, a common local style of dress not restricted to musicians and seen in a number of paintings from southern Italy at this time.[79] A second kind of exception comes from the eastern edge of the Greek world in the form of small fourth-century terra-cotta votive figures from

Rhodes—standing, youthful male musicians draped in mantles wearing high round hats, a headdress reminiscent of the Archaic terra-cotta musicians from Cyprus discussed in chapter 2.

Chelys-lyra players in fourth-century representations, whether they are male or female, may stand or sit as the circumstances require. No examples have come to hand that show them tuning, and only on Berlin 2402 does there appear to be a singer to the lyra, a satyr who sits on the foot of Dionysos' couch singing and playing. The manner in which the lyra was held when played had clearly not changed since its days in fifth-century Athens; it is still supported by the left arm and wrist, the wrist holding taut a band that passes around the outer arm of the instrument, which is tipped away from the player somewhat (there are the usual variations from upright to 90°). The left-hand fingers show the same variety of positions for damping or plucking the strings noted earlier and common to all members of the lyre family; the right hand is not often seen in action in the fourth-century paintings and sculptures located for this study, but it wields the plektron with the familiar gestures, with two notable early fourth-century exceptions, both of them Greek: in the courtship of Phaon and Demonassa by the Meidias Painter (fig. 10), lyre-playing Phaon holds his plektron against the strings in a way that might be interpreted as drawing the plektron toward him or perhaps plucking individual strings with it; and the woman who accompanies the dancers on Athens 12894 holds her right forearm at shoulder level, wrist arched, sweeping the strings with the plektron at the point where her left-hand fingertips will also touch them.

The fourth-century evidence for the chelys-lyra, though it does not permit conclusions of the sort that must be based on a large number of carefully painted examples, does offer individual paintings and other objects that should be considered in forming a general picture of the instrument throughout its history.

A good estimate of the size of the chelys-lyra, or at least of one appropriate for a boy to play, can be made from measurements taken from a large stele found at Potidaea (Thessaloniki 2465). The height of the chelys-lyra here is slightly more than one and a third times the length of the boy's forearm (elbow to first knuckles); and it is half as wide as it is tall. Among the eastern and mainland Greek fourth-century examples, there is none with more than seven strings, though three to six strings may be found, since there are a number of small objects and carelessly painted vases. The Italiote examples yield a similar picture, except that three paintings more or less certainly show eight strings (see fig. 12).[80]

Most of the fourth-century representations indicate both soundboxes and arms of the familiar shape, though lyres of anomalous shapes appear more frequently in the fourth century than in the earlier periods (especially in view of the smaller size of the total available sample), nearly all of them in paintings or on seal stones that are of non-Attic manufacture.[81] There are still mainland Greek efforts to show that the arms slant forward from the soundbox. Two turn-of-the-century Athenian painters have left three-quarter views of the chelys-lyra with arms either curving to the left or with one nearly straight and one curving left (see fig. 10).[82] The reality behind these attempts at perspective is apparent when one examines the large sepulchral sculpture of a siren from the Kerameikos cemetery at Athens, dated ca. 350 B.C. (fig. 11): the siren's left hand, even though the fingers are gone, reaches over the top of the chelys soundbox quite a distance in what must have been the gesture of damping the strings; the length of the hand and the missing fingers suggest how far the strings slanted away from the soundbox.

The chelys pattern on the back of the lyra, and its border, can be seen in both Attic and Italiote paintings of the fourth century, in relief on the lyra of the marble siren (fig. 11), and on fourth-century terra-cottas from Tiryns and Rhodes.[83] The way in which the arms fit into the front of the soundbox, suggested in figure 10, can be ascertained from the shaped opening left in the soundbox of the marble siren in figure 11, though a similar siren with a less detailed instrument (Athens 775) shows only a small hole pierced through the upper edge of the shell: in sculpture as in painting the artist does not trouble himself with the details of instrument construction unless it serves his purpose.

The bridge of the lyra continues to be represented as a black line, thick (fig. 10) or thin (sometimes wider at one end), or as an outlined rectangle. The gem cutter who made the cornelian ring stone London, Walters cat. 1153, made the bridge stand in considerably higher relief than the soundbox on which it sits. The feet of the bridge are not customarily shown in the paintings, which are often sketchy or inept, but they can still be found at the end of the century on "West Slope" ware: on fragments of two phiales decorated with lyres and rhytons, bridges with feet are painted in red against white soundboxes.[84] The lower string fastener is also very seldom indicated, and then only as a straight line, or at the most, a line with short lines joining its ends to the lower edge of the soundbox (as in fig. 10).[85]

Kollopes are often shown in fourth-century paintings from both Attica and Italy, and all through the

century there are examples (fig. 10) that clearly show the long, individual kollops pins extending above and below the crossbar.[86] As in the fifth century a small handful of chelys-lyra representations have crossbars that end in knobs.[87] There are almost no other decorative touches; even lines down the arms, as in figure 10, or across the tops of the arms are rare.[88]

Clear views of the plektron are scarcely to be found in the fourth century; all the paintings in which it is really visible are Attic and dated between 420 and 390 B.C. Marble siren Athens 775 (similar to the one in fig. 11), who, though her chelys-lyra is not carefully detailed, holds a well-sculpted plektron against her breast, is thus of special importance. She gives us a three-dimensional view of a plektron much like the one in figure 10 and so allows us to see in particular the thick, rounded plektron handle, which we might otherwise have taken to be flat.[89] The tassel of the plektron, barely indicated in figure 10, is clearly shown in detail only on New York 49.11.2, a Boeotian black-figured oinochoe of the late fifth century. In this painting the plektron cord is attached to and looped over the arm of the instrument that a boy is lifting down from its peg on the wall.

Both wrist sling and sash are also seldom seen in the fourth century, and for the few examples we must turn this time to south Italian vase paintings. Three on which wrist slings are indicated are Munich 3268 (late fifth century), Rome, Vatican T 11, and Toronto 410, though on the latter (Apollo seated on a swan) the sling is loose and the instrument is unsupported. (One suspects that the painter had not often seen a chelys-lyra, and perhaps had never seen one actually played.) On these same vases and on Mannheim, Reiss Cg 315, a sash is also present, shown as a long, wide fillet, doubled through the sling on the latter vase and on Vatican T 11. It is shown as a bow knot of the sling on Toronto 410 (swan side) and as a few short string-like strands on Munich 3268.

Materials Used in Construction of Lyres

The fourth-century literary sources add a few pieces of information to our meager knowledge of the construction of instruments of the lyre type. Plato, for example, in referring to *keratinois plektrois* ("plectra made of horn"), confirms what could only be conjectured from a line in Euripides regarding the material used to manufacture plektra.[90] Plektra may also have sometimes been made of wood (or perhaps with a wooden handle?), if the mention of an ivory lyre and a *plektron xylinon* ("wooden") on a late-fifth- or early-fourth-century inscription recording the inventory of items housed in the Parthenon refers to a playable instrument rather than a votive model.[91] Aristotle, although he does not mention the material used, compares plektra with shuttles, an especially significant analogy when one takes into account the resemblance in form of both these spoon-shaped objects as they are shown in the vase paintings, not to mention their analogous function in "striking" the strings of the lyre or the warp of the loom, either of which activities can be described by the same verb in Greek, *krouein*.[92]

Plato mentions the lyre maker (lyropoios) several times in various analogies; for example, he has Socrates contend that the user of an object is best qualified to supervise the making of that object, just as the user of lyre maker's work, that is, the kitharistes, knows best whether the product is well made or not.[93] Plato also provides a particularly helpful reference to a "lyra" that mentions the use of wood (*xyla*) as the major component of the instrument besides the strings. In the passage in question one of the speakers with whom Socrates converses on the final day of his life raises doubts about Socrates' arguments that the soul survives the destruction of the body. He says that if it is true that the soul is a harmonia, will that harmonia survive the destruction of the body any more than the harmonia of a lyra would survive the breaking of the instrument and the cutting of its strings? Yet according to Socrates' theory, he goes on, the harmonia of the broken instrument would still exist somewhere, at least until the wood and the strings rotted away.[94] There seems little doubt that the instrument the speaker is envisioning is the kithara, since the soundboxes of the other likely candidates (the chelys-lyra and the barbitos) are shown in the vase paintings to have been made chiefly of tortoiseshell (which does not decay), not wood; the point of the analogy—the existence of harmonia for at least the life span of the components of the broken instrument—would be lost if the speaker referred to any sort of lyre other than one made primarily of perishable materials.

Fourth-Century Harps

Whereas nearly all fifth-century representations of harps are Attic in origin, in the fourth century over two-thirds of them come from southern Italy, and the few that do come from Greece proper differ from those seen in Italiote paintings. Moreover, the scenes in which harps are included are generally not the same for these groups, though they share some elements, and both show a preponderance of female players.

In three of the nine available Attic and East Greek representations, a woman (Ariadne or a maenad)

plays the harp in the presence of Dionysos, while a satyr plays for him on a fourth; and the young man seated on an animal skin playing the harp on an unnumbered Leningrad scaraboid may be Dionysos himself.[95] The banquet scene on Attic krater Naples 2202, with its wine vessels, Erotes, and three pairs of lovers (one of the women holds the harp), contains objects that symbolize both Dionysos and Aphrodite (the latter, with Eros on her lap playing the harp, appears on Jena 390). The women on Leningrad B3128, one of whom has the harp, are probably Muses (and the standing man with a lyre between them, Apollo), while the player on Boston 01.8101, an Attic polychrome molded wine pitcher, is a siren.

Otherworldly or mythological courtship and marriage scenes, by contrast, are the subject of nearly all the Italiote paintings that include harps: of twenty-four studied, all but one or two (Stockholm 12 and perhaps the Basel Priv. Coll. skyphoid pyxis) seem to belong to this category. Two are mythological wedding or courtship scenes: Helen and Menelaus, with an Eros and harp player on Boston 00.360 (fig. 13); Heracles and Omphale (?) among women on Berlin 3291. On New York L63.21.6 (fig. 14) a woman harpist sits at the foot of a couch on which a young man reclines. The krater in his hand, the satyr with thyrsos who stands behind him, and the young man's mask that hangs above him on the wall, all indicate that this is Dionysos. The maenad on the left, however, bears not only a thyrsos but a *thymiaterion* (incense burner), an attribute in these paintings of Aphrodite; and in the scene on the reverse a woman holding a chest and a fillet stands between young men bearing wreaths, all part of the customary wedding paraphernalia.

Among the paintings of the main group all stages in the process of otherworldly courtship and marriage are represented. On a pelike at Paris a deceased woman is painted seated in her naiskos playing the harp while two female friends or relatives stand around her with objects she will need for the rites to be performed: fan, fillet, and small chest. Courtships in progress can be observed on two vases where a woman sits with a harp and a man stands before her, wreath in hand and one foot up on a low object; both scenes include Erotes and objects such as mirrors and phiales (fig. 15).[96]

The part of the proceedings most frequently depicted is the bride's preparation for the wedding. The bride herself usually sits playing the harp while the attendants around her, male and female, bring the necessary items (fillets, fans, wreaths, mirrors, the loom- or abacus-like object, and so on). On Copenhagen Chr. VIII 316 (fig. 16) a group of women dance and play the aulos and harp in the upper zone on the vase while the bride is arrayed in the lower zone, where the figures around her include Aphrodite with a swan, two Erotes, a fawn, and four attendants, three female and one male, carrying fan, perfume bottle, wreaths, mirror, and chest (in the upper zone are fillet, "abacus," sluicing pan, and another mirror and fan); her husband-to-be is similarly attended on the reverse side.[97]

Four of the scenes include a large laver on a pedestal for the ritual bath, and in two of these the harpist officiating is Orpheus, the great authority on purification rites, who is identified by his Phrygian cap (fig. 17). He seems to fill his musicianly role in connection with the groom's preparations rather than the bride's, though in the case of Paris Bibl. Nat. 1047, it is not clear for whom the bath is intended.[98]

The harp is part of the other stages of the groom's preparations for the ritual in two paintings. In Herbig's IV-2b, 4, he himself plays it—he, Orpheus, and the young man playing for a woman reading a scroll on the Basel skyphoid pyxis are the only males among the Italiote harp players. On Naples 2867 a female harpist looks on while three other women and an Eros attend the groom; wreaths hang above, and a lyre and the loom- or abacus-like object lie about on the ground. Finally, on one vase we see the couple sitting together on a couch surrounded by women with boxes, parasol, ball, sluicing pan, mirror, and harp, while the ubiquitous Eros brings a wreath; a swan preens itself among the women, and the ladder-like abacus lies on the ground.[99]

A harp appears with another instrument only once among the Athenian examples: a Dionysiac scene in which a maenad plays the tympanum (frame drum). In the wedding preparation scenes on Italiote vases the harp appears with the Italiote kithara or chelys-lyra, and with aulos.[100]

All the fourth-century players of the harp are seated, except for the woman who stands with her left foot on a column drum to lift her knee so that the harp can rest on it (fig. 13), and the siren (Boston 01.8101) whose harp is perhaps magically supported and whose knees would not, in any case, be suitable. The harp ordinarily rests on the player's left knee (in paintings similar to fig. 15 it seems held against the side of the thigh, but this would be unlikely since it would restrict the movement of the left arm and hand). But it sits beside the player on Cambridge Mus. Class. Arch. UP 143 and two other Italiote vases; it sits on the ground as does the player, at an angle of more than 90° from her legs, on Los Angeles 50.8.25; and on Heidelberg 26.86 the harp is turned away at the same angle, but

the player is seated on a folding stool, and the harp has no visible support.

Though the players are often shown with only the left hand at the strings, simply supporting the harp or idly plucking the strings, nearly a dozen fourth-century harpists with both hands engaged have been located. From these we learn that the players are regularly portrayed with the left hand touching the farther strings, the right hand the nearer ones; that is, the left hand playing the longer, lower pitched strings, the right hand the shorter, higher pitched ones (the players of arched harps on fifth-century vases are also depicted with left hands advanced).[101] Since the harp sits on the player's left thigh, the left hand can indeed reach the farthest strings somewhat more easily than can the right hand. The paintings may thus simply reflect a convention that, except when the course of the music makes it inconvenient, the farthest strings are to be plucked and damped with the left hand.

Right hand and left hand perform the same functions, both plucking and damping the strings, in both fifth- and fourth-century representations. The paintings that show both hands clearly in use are too few to do more than suggest the details of technique, but what evidence there is suggests that thumb and fingers may pluck together (to sound a single string or two at once) or alternately, the choice of finger depending on the distance between the required strings.

Of the three varieties of harp known to the Greeks in the fifth century—the angle harp (open, no post) with arched soundbox, the frame harp (with post) with arched soundbox, and the frame harp with spindle-shaped soundbox—only the first two are still often seen in the fourth century, mainly in Italiote examples (the angle harp is seen only on Italiote vases). The third variety, the Athenian spindle harp, was apparently a rather short-lived phenomenon. The isolated examples of fourth-century harps that resemble it suggest that it was no longer in common use (if indeed it ever had been); the best example, the unnumbered scaraboid at Leningrad (Boardman 600: its post and longest strings closest to the player, as with the spindle harps; its soundbox, away from him, deepest in the center), has a much narrower soundbox altogether than the fifth-century spindle harps.[102]

The angle harp, with its arched soundbox unsupported by a post, is encountered less often than the frame harp; but it did not cease to exist after the fourth century and, despite the lack of non-Italiote fourth-century examples, was known throughout the Greek world, as later depictions from Nauplia, Nicosia, Kerch, and Tarentum attest.[103] The fourth-century examples we do possess appear to be of two slightly different varieties, one (perhaps the more common) with a rather slim soundbox (fig. 16) that may be decorated along the sides but lacks the row of points along the upper edge that we see in the second sort, which also has a deeper soundbox. The first type without points corresponds to the arched angle harps most often seen in fifth-century examples (chap. 4, fig. 5) though the fourth-century soundboxes seem narrower; the second type, with points, is elusive both before and after 400 B.C., Naples 81392 (chap. 6, fig. 14) standing as the only known fifth-century example, Stockholm 12 (a dubious painting in other respects; see above) as possibly the only later one.[104] Where strings can be counted, these harps have between 10 and 12 (the Stockholm krater, again an anomaly, shows 15 or 16); some of them are provided with a separate base underneath the neck that protects the tuning arrangements, and some are not.[105]

Frame harps with arched soundboxes are present in both Attic and Italiote paintings, but the Attic examples are scarce and so can yield little solid information. Of the five available examples, four are instruments with very narrow soundboxes, decorated or plain. Of these only one, Athens 14901, has a clearly separate base beneath the neck where the strings are attached.[106]

The remaining fourth-century Attic representation, on Jena 390, is also a harp with an arched soundbox but a much deeper one than those above and similar to the soundboxes of the fifth-century arched frame harps Berlin Staatl. Mus. 2391 (Attic, chap. 6, fig. 15) and Munich 3268 (Italiote). Like them, it has a decorative design painted on the side of the soundbox, and no separate base for the harp to rest on—the neck, with kollopes and string windings, must also serve as the base. (All Greek harps may of course in actuality have had either separate bases or some arrangement such as tuning pegs along the side of the neck, so that the tuning could not accidentally be altered by the pressure of the harp against the leg.)

The arched frame harps of Italiote fourth-century vases also resemble Jena 390 and its fifth-century relatives, but they are decorated in ways that the Attic harps are not. One group has a row of points along the upper edge of the soundbox such as we have also seen on Italiote angle harps, and a second group has not only the row of points but also a post ornamented with the figure of a waterbird, a crane, or a design in the shape of such a bird.

The instruments in the first group have a post that is straight and unadorned except, in some cases, for a small turned bobbin- or spool-shaped ornament near the top (see fig. 15; part of the post is missing where

the painting is damaged).[107] The soundbox may have a painted design along its sides as well as points along its top, as we see on New York L63.21.6 (fig. 14), which also has a small figure of a bird at the front edge, like the figurehead on a ship's prow.[108] The strings in this example are secured to the neck with kollopes, and there is no separate base; but on Los Angeles 50.8.25, where the kollopes are also visible, there is a separate base below the neck, and both are joined to the post.[109] The instrument on the Basel skyphoid pyxis has eleven strings; figure 15 seems to have nine strings, figure 14 has eleven kollopes (not all the strings show), and Toronto 926.19.7 seems to have ten strings; they are not visible in reproductions of the two other vases in this group.

The second group, with a bird or bird-like shape built into the post of the instrument, is particularly interesting in view of the Greek penchant throughout their history for making parts of their stringed instruments resemble birds' heads. This largest group of fourth-century harps is evenly divided between those with the figure of a bird on the post, and those that have only a design that resembles a bird. Ruvo 1554 (fig. 17) is an example of the former type, Boston 00.360 (fig. 13) one of the latter sort.[110]

The waterbird represented has long legs as well as a long neck in all the paintings for which reproductions are presently available except one, suggesting that the bird intended is the crane rather than the swan, and distressing all who, because of the swan's association with both Apollo and Aphrodite, might confidently have expected to find the latter bird. Since the exception, Berlin 3291, is much earlier than the rest (late fifth century), since its harp has a soundbox of unusual shape lacking the row of points that all the others have, and since its bird is the most awkwardly shaped of those found, it offers little support for the view that the fourth-century harp bird is meant to represent a swan.

The soundbox of this harp is shaped and decorated like that of the previous group without a bird on the post, and the arrangements for fastening the strings to the neck show the same range of possibilities observed above. In figure 17 we see the kollopes on the neck and the separate base below it; both neck and base have disk-shaped ornaments at the outer ends.[111] Naples 3218 appears to have the same arrangement but without the separate base. In figure 13, the row of circles along the neck suggests side tuning pegs, which would eliminate the need for a separate base.[112] The harps in this group are ten or eleven stringed; two examples that are not completely clear also seem to show ten or eleven strings.

Harpists and Harps in Fourth-Century Literature

The phenomenon of women harp players that we have observed in the vase paintings was evidently widespread enough that a need was felt for a term to designate a female performer: *psaltria*, literally, "one who plucks." The term had first occurred in the second half of the fifth century in a fragment from one of the tragedies of Ion of Chios, in which the Lydian queen Omphale bids Lydian psaltriai to sing and play.[113] No specific instrument is mentioned in the two-line fragment, but the Lydian context suggests the magadis.

Early in the fourth century the term *psaltriai* is used by Plato to refer to specialized professional entertainers at symposia, along with auletrides (female aulos players) and *orchestrides* (female dancers). Socrates claims that only the uneducated need the "voice" of such musicians to make up for their inability to use their own voices for intelligent conversation during a drinking party; true gentlemen require no such distractions.[114]

A good deal more information about such entertainers is found in a discussion of the Athenian government that is dated to about 325, the *Athenaion Politeia.* The anonymous author, in explaining the role of a board of ten city controllers (astynomoi, a term now used in modern Greece to refer to the police), includes among their duties the supervision of psaltriai, auletrides, and kitharistriai:

> They oversee the women harpists, aulos players, and lyre players in order to keep them from earning more than two-drachma fees, and if several people want to get the same entertainer they cast lots and hire her out to whoever wins.[115]

> καὶ τάς τε αὐλητρίδας καὶ τὰς ψαλτρίας καὶ τὰς κιθαριστρίας οὗτοι σκοποῦσιν ὅπως μὴ πλείονος ἢ δυεῖν δραχμαῖς μισθωθήσονται, κἂν πλείους τὴν αὐτὴν σπουδάσωσι λαβεῖν οὗτοι δια-κληροῦσι καὶ τῷ λαχόντι μισθοῦσιν.

These details reveal that, at least during the fourth century, the profession of symposium entertainer in Athens was highly specialized and carefully regulated. Had the legal restrictions on earnings not existed, it might have offered good prospects for the best professional performers, who, as the regulation implies, could have commanded higher fees than the two drachmas permitted by law.[116] One drachma was the standard daily wage for an ordinary laborer at the end of the fifth century, and with the effects of inflation, the sum of two drachmas was perhaps about its equivalent three-quarters of a century later.[117] Thus it appears that the psaltriai and the other women musicians were capable of earning something resembling an average daily wage.

The cost of hiring psaltriai and auletrides is also the subject of a comic fragment from Menander from about the same period. Here, however, the precise costs are obscured through comic exaggeration, in which the speaker claims one gets from the gods only what one gives; he himself can afford to offer only a little ten-drachma sheep, whereas it costs hardly short of a talent (six thousand drachmas) to pay for the wine, eels, cheese, honey, perfume, auletrides, and psaltriai one needs to give a symposium.[118]

Some of the more foreign names for harps, such as *magadis,* appear to have fallen out of use during the Hellenistic period and to have been replaced by the general designation, *psalterion,* or "plucked instrument." It is under this term that we find the sole reference in Greek literature of the period in question to the material used in the construction of harps. Theophrastus, Aristotle's successor and an expert in the natural sciences, reports that the wood of the oak tree (prinos, either holm oak or kermes oak) was used for the "crossbars" of the lyra and the psalterion; presumably in the case of the latter instrument, the neck of the harp is meant.[119]

Another name that may designate a harp, or possibly one of the lutes described below, is *sambyke* (or, in a variant spelling, *iambyke*), yet another of the many instrument names borrowed from some unknown Near Eastern source.[120] Although neither form appears in extant literature earlier than the last quarter of the fifth century, Aristotle includes the sambyke in a list of "old" instruments that should be thrown out, along with the pektis, barbitos, trigonon, and something he calls a *heptagonon* (otherwise unknown).[121] Aside from the Eupolis fragment cited in chapter 6 regarding the use of the instrument (together with the trigonon) to serenade women, along with Aristotle's condemnation of it, Greek literature of the fourth century and earlier provides no information about the sambyke. There is no evidence from earlier periods to support the third-century claim by Euphorion that the instrument was used by the Parthians and the Troglodytes (of Ethiopia) and that it had four strings.[122] The use of the same word in later Greek to indicate a type of siege machine raises more questions than it answers, and we are left with only a guess that this instrument was probably either a lute or another of the several varieties of harps seen in the late fifth- and fourth-century vase paintings.

A follower of Aristotle also mentions an instrument called a *phoinikion,* a name that seems to be a diminutive of the phoinix mentioned by Herodotus (see chap. 6) but that does not itself occur until the fourth century; whether this instrument was a lyre or harp, we cannot tell.[123]

Lute-Family Instruments

The last instruments to be discussed in this study, the lutes, first come into view in the late fourth century on Greek terra-cottas and an important marble relief from Mantinea (fig. 18).[124] They seem to appear in many parts of the Greek world—southern Italy, the Peloponnesos, Egypt, Cyprus—almost simultaneously, and to have burst upon the scene about the time of Alexander's Persian campaigns in the late 330s. The Asiatic origins of these instruments are not disputed, though the particular area from which they were brought into Greece is not certain. Lutes may have come to Greek lands as a result of Alexander's conquests, though Higgins and Winnington-Ingram argue for a somewhat earlier date for their introduction; a large part of the evidence, though mostly later than the fourth century, comes from Alexandria, suggesting that they may have been imported from Egypt, where lutes had long been in use.

The scene on the three Mantinea reliefs in Athens (see also figs. 1 and 9) may suggest a connection between the instruments displayed and the Persian campaigns, though the date of the reliefs is still in question, and neither the choice of instruments nor the way in which they are depicted helps to resolve the problem of date directly.[125] The reliefs sheathed a base that according to Pausanias supported statues of Apollo, Leto, and Artemis. On one slab Apollo and Marsyas are shown contesting while a servant holds the flaying knife, and on the other two are six of the Muses (the fourth side with the remaining three Muses is missing). One of the Muses holds an Italiote kithara—the only non-Italiote representation of this instrument that has been found for which a fourth-century date is reasonably secure. On another slab a Muse plays the lute, and the only other instruments are Apollo's kithara and Marsyas' auloi. Whatever instruments, if any, there may have been on the fourth side, it seems possible that the instruments on the reliefs suggest the extent of the Greek world, from southern Italy in the west (represented by the Italiote kithara) to Egypt and Asia Minor in the south and east (represented by the lute). If we consider the strength of Macedonian sympathies in fourth-century Arcadia, a likely time for this political allegory, if such it is, would certainly be the years when Alexander was bringing large amounts of Persian territory under Greek control. An allegory of this sort would also

explain the depiction of such "exotic" instruments in Mantinea, a city known for its musical conservatism.[126]

Only three of the other representations of the lute listed by Higgins and Winnington-Ingram can be dated with some security to the late fourth century: a gilded terra-cotta relief from Tarentum (Munich 8702, made as a coffin appliqué), and two figurines of the Tanagra type: standing women playing the lute, one from Egypt, Alexandria 9033, and London 1919.6–20.7 (fig. 19), thought to come from Cyprus. The lute held by the seated woman on the terra-cotta from Tarentum, like that on the Mantinea relief, is of the sort identified by Higgins and Winnington-Ingram as type A: the distinction between neck and soundbox is clear; the front of the soundbox is roughly rectangular but with sloping shoulders; and the base, as seen on the Mantinea relief, is triangular, suggesting that this lute has a ridge like that of the kithara running down its back.[127] Like the lutes of type B (see below), it may have a rectangular bridge (seen only on later examples) and like them is played, at least most of the time, with a plektron. The players of both types clearly stop the strings against the neck with their left-hand fingers to change their pitch. Neither type has any indication of how the strings are fastened or tuned at the end of the neck. The examples of type A that have been located come from Greece or southern Italy (only one other is known, a small terra-cotta Eros from Euboea, probably of later date than the other two).

The lutes held by the Tanagra figures (fig. 19) belong to the same authors' type B, which includes all the other examples that have been found: a narrow, teardrop-shaped instrument, with a small soundbox tapering into the neck without any demarcation. The figure from Alexandria and some of the later examples have a small knob at the lower end of the soundbox; the instrument in figure 19 appears to have a small opening (like the rose-hole on a Renaissance lute) in the center of the belly. All the type B examples except one come from Egypt, Cyprus, or the coast of Asia Minor (Myrina).[128]

Greek literature provides us with two names that we may associate with lutes, the *skindapsos* (a four-stringed instrument) and the *pandoura* (a three-stringed instrument). The small number of strings and the fact that neither term appears in extant literature earlier than the fourth century—the very time when lutes first appear in Greek art—suggest that both the skindapsos and pandoura referred to instruments of the lute type; *pandoura* and *tanbur,* words that come from a common root, are names for the long-necked lute found today from the Balkans to the Middle East. Like the majority of names used by the Greeks to designate stringed instruments, both *skindapsos* and *pandoura* are of uncertain Near Eastern origins; although the name *skindapsos* disappeared into obscurity, *pandoura* eventually became the Latin *pandura*, from which modern words such as "bandurria" and "mandoline" are derived.[129]

As we have already seen in chapter 6, the skindapsos is mentioned in a list of instruments in a fourth-century comic fragment in which the speaker says he has manufactured it along with barbitoi, pektides, kitharas, lyres, and *trichordoi* ("three-strings," presumably also referring to some kind of lute). One other fourth-century source refers to a woman player of a four-stringed skindapsos.[130] The pandoura is not mentioned in the extant literature until the third century, and then only briefly by a geographer who lists mangrove (a type of tropical tree) as the wood used for making the instrument.[131] A Hellenistic source of uncertain date describes the skindapsos as being made of *promalos,* a kind of tree (probably willow) noted for the suppleness of its wood.[132]

Reaction against Developments of the Fourth Century

Although Greece had always been receptive to the introduction of new instruments from the East (as in the case of the barbitos, for example), the wide variety of stringed instruments in use in the fourth century produced a reactionary attitude, at least on the part of Plato and Aristotle, who advocated the elimination of instruments thought unnecessary or harmful. Such an attitude is first apparent in Plato, who recommends the banishment of the trigonon and the pektis and other "many-stringed" instruments from the ideal state envisioned in the *Republic*:

— "Well then," said I [Socrates], "We will not want *polychordia* or *panharmonia* in our songs and melodies."
— "No, I don't think so," he said.
— "Then we will not support makers of trigona and pektides and all the other instruments that are many-stringed (*polychordia*) and capable of many *harmoniai* (*polyharmonia*)."
— "So it appears."
— "What about this? Will you receive makers or players of auloi into the city? Or isn't this the most "many-stringed" instrument of all, and aren't the [other] "pan-harmonic" instruments an imitation of the aulos?"
— "Yes, clearly," he said.
— "You have left, then," said I, "the lyra and the kithara, and they are useful for the city."

Οὐκ ἄρα, ἦν δ' ἐγώ, πολυχορδίας γε οὐδὲ παναρμονίου ἡμῖν δεήσει ἐν ταῖς ᾠδαῖς τε καὶ μέλεσιν.

Οὔ μοι, ἔφη, φαίνεται.

Τριγώνων ἄρα καὶ πηκτίδων καὶ πάντων ὀργάνων ὅσα πολύχορδα καὶ πολυαρμόνια, δημιουργοὺς οὐ θρέψομεν.

Οὐ φαινόμεθα.

Τί δέ; αὐλοποιοὺς ἢ αὐλητὰς παραδέξῃ εἰς τὴν πόλιν; ἢ οὐ τοῦτο πολυχορδότατον, καὶ αὐτὰ τὰ παναρμόνια αὐλοῦ τυγχάνει ὄντα μίμημα;

Δῆλα δή, ἦ δ' ὅς.

Λύρα δή σοι, ἦν δ' ἐγώ, καὶ κιθάρα λείπεται [καὶ] κατὰ πόλιν χρήσιμα·

Only the schoolboy's lyra and the kithara are to be allowed in Plato's ideal state, along with the shepherd's panpipes, or syrinx.[133]

Aristotle goes even further in banning instruments from the ideal community, for he disapproves not only of Plato's blacklisted instruments but also of the kithara, which he regards as unsuitable for educational purposes because it requires too much technical expertise.[134] In the same passage he reports (with approval) the decline in popularity of other "old" instruments such as the pektis, the barbitos, the heptagonon, the trigonon, and the sambyke, and all such instruments requiring manual dexterity—at least among people capable of judging which kinds of music lead toward virtue (*arete*) and which do not. Although it is impossible to confirm this statement through the evidence of the vase paintings (since we cannot, for example, assign specific names to the various types of harps represented), the visual evidence does suggest that the barbitos, at least, lost the wide popularity it had enjoyed throughout the fifth century. It is an instrument that Plato never even mentioned, and, as we noted above, it is completely lacking in fourth-century Athenian art.

Plato's remarks about players and the audience for whom they performed suggest that by the fourth century the old festivals and their musical competitions were dominated by a few virtuoso kithara players who catered to the public's demand for what Plato considered showy displays of technique. He states that the contemporary decline in the Athenian democracy is reflected in the parallel decline in the habits of audiences at competitions. Whereas in the old days educated people listened to the music in silence and children were kept in line through the application of a paddle, now the audience responds with yelling and applause to displays of brilliance, virtuoso tricks, and exciting rhythms.[135] Despite Plato's tendency toward conservatism and even anachronism in musical taste (as Henderson puts it, "he talked of the innovations of thirty years ago and called them modern"), it is clear that the rise of virtuoso players in the late fifth century led to fundamental changes in the relationship between performer and audience by the time of the fourth century.[136] Plato may complain of "New-Music" performers active at the end of the preceding century (as, for example, Meles and his son Kinesias), but his remarks about the audience seem to describe a well-established relationship of "stars" and "fans" that could have developed only over the course of several decades after such virtuoso players had begun to appear.[137] Plato's suspicion of professional performers is well summed up in the words about Orpheus that he puts into the mouth of Phaedrus in one of the speeches on love in the *Symposium*. In contrast to the brave spirit of Alcestis, who out of love for her husband was willing to die in his place, Orpheus' mission to the Underworld to retrieve Eurydice through the charm of his singing was a cowardly act:

> They sent Orpheus son of Oeagrus back from Hades with his mission unaccomplished, having shown him a mere phantom of the woman for whom he came, but not giving him the real person; for he seemed to them to be soft, inasmuch as he was a kitharode, and not to have been daring enough to die for love (as Alcestis had), but to have contrived to enter Hades without losing his life.[138]

> Ὀρφέα δὲ τὸν Οἰάγρου
> ἀτελῆ ἀπέπεμψαν ἐξ Ἅιδου, φάσμα δείξαντες τῆς γυ-
> ναικὸς ἐφ' ἣν ἧκεν, αὐτὴν δὲ οὐ δόντες, ὅτι μαλθακ-
> ίζεσθαι ἐδόκει, ἅτε ὢν κιθαρῳδός, καὶ οὐ τολμᾶν
> ἕνεκα τοῦ ἔρωτος ἀποθνῄσκειν ὥσπερ Ἄλκηστις,
> ἀλλὰ διαμηχανᾶσθαι ζῶν εἰσιέναι εἰς Ἅιδου.

Orpheus, the musician par excellence in the eyes of earlier writers, has become a symbol of the decadence that Plato attributed to the class of professional virtuoso performers against whom, in his deeply ingrained conservatism, he felt scornful resentment.

The fourth-century evidence for the kithara suggests that this instrument was being used less often than formerly. In Athens it may have gradually become the province of professional virtuosi who devised new tunings for it and new techniques involving "many-notedness" (*polychordia*) and complex rhythms. Although its classical shape, seen on only a few Athenian marbles and no Attic paintings after 390 B.C., is still present on Italiote fourth-century vases, it is found only in the hands of mythological figures,

which leads us to suspect that the instrument may have been seldom actually used, or perhaps not used at all, by the Italiote Greeks. (The swan's head variant, on the other hand, though rarely found, may be a genuine Italiote form of the kithara.) The shape of the standard kithara seems to have changed gradually over the course of the century from 420 to 320 B.C. to produce the long-bodied instrument identified above as the Hellenistic kithara.

The rectangular lyre that makes its first appearance in southern Italy in the fourth century, which we have called the Italiote kithara, was probably an instrument actually used in, and perhaps indigenous to, that area, despite the funerary nature of the vases on which it is seen and the otherworldly character of the scenes painted on them. It is not an image borrowed from the Athenian painters, and it appears mainly in the hands of mortals—deceased, to be sure—rather than mythological figures. Nor is it particularly associated with Apollo: though one of the Muses holds it on the Mantinea reliefs, in Italy it has been found in Apollo's presence on only one vase. A few terra-cottas and a marble relief survive to testify to the continued existence of this instrument as late as the second century B.C.

It is difficult to assess the use of the chelys-lyra in the fourth century because there are almost no Attic vases with scenes that include it after about 390, and virtually all the evidence of mortal lyre playing from later in the century is funerary in nature. But in view of the later fourth-century pottery that uses the chelys-lyra as a decorative design (along with dogs, rhytons, and ivy leaves) it seems reasonably safe to suppose that the lyra remained an instrument for general-purpose and amateur music making throughout the fourth century, though perhaps not as widely used or taught as in the fifth century. It seems to have survived into late Hellenistic and even Roman times in perhaps several somewhat changed forms.

When the lute family of instruments first makes an appearance near the end of the fourth century, two distinctly different types are represented; but only one of them seems to survive into later times. Evidence for the teardrop-shaped type B lute (see above) becomes stronger in the late Hellenistic period, but the more rectangular type A, of which we have only three examples, has not been found after the mid-third century.

Both angle harps and frame harps flourished in southern Italy in the fourth century, according to the evidence of a sizable group of scenes of otherworldly courtship, and were apparently associated to some extent with the goddess Aphrodite. In Athens, where the chief association was perhaps with Dionysos, on the other hand, only the frame harp (principally a variety with a narrow, arched soundbox) continued to be used in the fourth century. Italiote frame harps, which have an arched soundbox of considerable depth, are frequently found to have posts in the shape of a long-legged water bird, presumably a crane. (The use of the water-bird motif calls to mind the swans' heads that decorate certain Italiote representations of the standard kithara, as well as a small group of fifth-century Attic barbitoi, at least some of the lyres of the Minoan-Mycenaean period, and, in schematic form, the harps of the Cycladic period.)

Angle harps with arched soundboxes continue to appear in the late Hellenistic period. Although the survival of the particular varieties of frame harps known in the fourth century has not been established, several new varieties seem to have become current. The Italiote frame harp with a crane-shaped post has not been found, but we do have a later harp that uses the water-bird motif in a different way. It is held by a seated woman on Naples terra-cotta 113347 from Tarentum (fig. 20).

The post of this instrument is plain, but the soundbox (mostly hidden by the player) is apparently in the shape of the body of a swan, with the bird's long neck curving over so that its beak lies along the top of the post. The resemblance of this instrument to the one that appears at the beginning of this study (chap. 1, fig. 1), the Cycladic harp of ca. 2200 B.C. with its beak-shaped ornament curving out just below the top of the post, is amazing, especially in view of the almost complete absence of archaeological evidence for harps in nearly all the intervening centuries. But it is gratifying to end this study of Greek stringed instruments with one so like the one with which we began, for we could scarcely ask for a better symbol for the continuity of Greek musical culture through the vicissitudes of nearly two thousand years.

1. Athens 215. Marble relief. Detail: Apollo with kithara.

2a. Ruvo 1500. Apulian r.f. pelike. Detail: Apollo, Marsyas, and Muses.

2b. Bari 6270. Apulian
r.f. volute krater. Details:
statue of young man in
naiskos, Apollo.

2c. Salerno, Museo
Provinciale. Paestan r.f.
bell krater by Asteas.
Detail: Phrynis and
Pyronides.

3. Munich 3297. Apulian
r.f. volute krater. Detail:
Orpheus, Hades,
Persephone.

4. Basel S 29. Apulian r.f.
amphora. Detail, upper
zone: Dionysos (?),
Aphrodite (?), satyr and
maenad.

5. Oxford 1921.1236.
Jasper scaraboid.

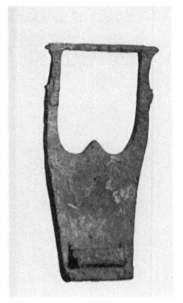

6. Athens 15104. Bronze
from Antikythera.

7. San Simeon 5609.
Apulian r.f. pelike. Detail:
youth seated on couch,
women.

8. Torino 4149. Apulian
r.f. pelike. Detail:
wedding scene.

9. Athens 217. Marble
relief. Detail: Muse with
lyre.

10. Florence 81947. Attic
r.f. hydria. Detail: Phaon
and Demonassa.

11. Athens 774. Marble
sculpture of sepulchral
siren with lyre.

12. Madrid 11223.
Apulian r.f. amphora by
the Iliupersis Painter.
Detail: grave monument of
comic poet.

14. New York L63.21.6.
Apulian r.f. calyx krater.
Maenad, harpist,
reclining man, satyr.

13. Boston 00.360.
Apulian r.f. alabastron.
Menelaos, Helen, Eros,
and harpist.

15. Naples 81953.
Apulian r.f. amphora.
Detail: seated harpist and
man with strigil.

16. Copenhagen Chr.
VIII 316. Apulian r.f.
pelike. Detail: woman
dancing, women with
harp and auloi.

17. Ruvo 1554. Apulian r.f. oinochoe. Seated harpist and attendant.

18. Athens 216. Marble relief. Detail: Muse playing lute.

20. Naples 113347. Terra-cotta figurine of seated woman with harp.

19. London 1919.6-20.7.
Terra-cotta figurine.
Woman with lute.

CHAPTER EIGHT

Questions and Conclusions

The literature and visual arts of ancient Greece have left us a record of the stringed instruments of that civilization that, while often ambiguous, is consistent in many respects and seldom misleading as far as we can tell, at least when there is a quantity of evidence that can be studied in detail. The combination of evidence from both literary and visual sources, while often difficult, sometimes produces remarkably conclusive results; a case in point is the association of the barbitos with Anakreon by means of poetic references and the association of the long-armed lyre with the same poet by means of inscribed paintings, thus confirming the identity of instrument name and shape (see chap. 5). If these two types of evidence are to fit together in a satisfactory way, however, the literary works in question must be translated with great care, with the names of instruments and of complex musical concepts such as *harmonia* left untranslated. The casual reader of a translation of Plato's *Republic* 399C, to take one very obvious example, may fail to understand the idea of "many-stringedness" if modern names for the instruments are substituted by the translator. In advising as to which instruments are appropriate for the ideal state, Plato says, "We will not have *trigona* or *pektides* or other instruments of many strings and *harmoniai*. . . . The *lyra* and *kithara* are left, however, and they are useful for the city." In the translation by W. H. D. Rouse, not only is *harmonia* misleadingly translated as "keys," but the first pair of instruments becomes "psalteries and gitterns," the second pair "lyre and harp"—thus putting one "many-stringed" instrument in each pair and destroying the sense of the passage.

Gaps in the Evidence

As abundant as the evidence is, especially for Athens in the Classical period, we must not forget that there are gaps in the knowledge it hands down to us. Instruments not used at Athens (and perhaps one or two that were) may have escaped our net, and many instruments of earlier ages may be entirely unknown to us. Certain of these lurk just at the edge of our vision, barely seen and not understood. Examples might include the triangular object held by a figure on a Geometric vase, perhaps the only representation of a harp to appear in Greek areas other than Cyprus (a crossroads where many cultures met) during the long period between the Cycladic harpists and those represented in fifth-century Athenian vases; the lyre on a sixth-century Etruscan box lid with arms curved in a way that resembles the Minoan lyre; and various lyres on Attic vases that are anomalous in some respect and resist categorization among the Athenian instruments.[1]

There are a number of areas in which new archaeological finds that shed light on the history of particular instruments would be most welcome. It seems unlikely that there were no harps in mainland Greece between the time of the Cycladic civilization and the Classical period at Athens, and evidence to prove their existence may still be unearthed. Objects discovered in the last decade have aided our understanding of "Minoan" and "Mycenaean" lyres, and new items might help us learn whether a distinction between these two is justified and, if it is, what the relationship between them was. The mysteries surrounding the or-

igin and development of the kithara might also be un-
raveled if enough archaeological evidence of the eighth
century and earlier could be unearthed; the objects
now available might then seem less ambiguous and
difficult to interpret (see chap. 1; fig. 7 and perhaps
fig. 4; and chap. 2, figs 7 and 8). The discovery of an
unmistakable kithara of mainland-Greek origin earlier
than the Argive Heraion fragment at Athens (chap. 1)
would also change the nature of the debate about foreign influences during the Archaic period.

Other research problems might also seem more
soluble in the light of expanded evidence: the reasons,
for example, why the phorminx underwent a change
of role in the course of the seventh century, so that
while we see it as Apollo's instrument on the Melos
amphora (chap. 2, fig. 2), it is replaced by the kithara
on a seventh-century vase fragment from Delos and a
bronze back plate from Olympia (chap. 2, figs. 7 and
8). (If we were to assume that the word *phorminx*
formerly covered both instruments, the question
would be why Apollo ceases to play the *round-based*
phorminx.)

Another complex of questions that would be a re-
warding area for further research concerns both the
presence of birds near instruments in the representations and the use of bird-shaped devices in the construction of instruments. The latter, seen on Cycladic
harps, Minoan lyres, Athenian paintings of barbitoi,
and kitharas and harps in fourth-century Italiote representations, clearly indicates an idea important to the
Greeks from the earliest times. The gap in time between early and late examples is of course quite large,
but not so large in the case of birds *near* instruments;
for here, after the Minoan-Mycenaean frescoes, we
can call to witness the vase fragment from Old Smyrna
(chap. 2, fig. 1) before passing on to the examples
from Athenian vase paintings such as the Delphi
Apollo cup (Dephi 8140) or New Yok 06.11.29 (both
discussed in chap. 4).

The Lyre's Music

The sophisticated metrical rhythmic systems of the ancient Greeks and their subtle and highly developed
pitch systems are well known to us, though their use
in the tuning and playing of actual instruments is im-
perfectly understood, to say the least. But there can
be no doubt that the techniques and patterns of lyre
playing—which used these systems and were a basic
part of the musical expression of the culture—were
also sophisticated, despite the kinds of limitations we
have pointed out (that is, that the right hand does not
pluck the strings or perform any maneuver designed

to change their pitch; that the left hand is restrained
in its movements by the wrist sling and also does not
press against the strings to change their pitch).

It seems evident that the rhythmic aspect of the
music of the lyre was of great importance—more importance, one might contend, than any melodic function it might have. The sweep of the plektron across
the strings must have produced an almost drum-like
effect, creating a rhythmic framework that could not
be ignored. It is interesting to remember in this connection that elegies, laments, and expressions of
mourning of all sorts are said to be *alyros*, lyreless,
perhaps for this very reason: the steady strokes would
interfere with the free ululations of grief, and the emphatic beats may have carried an inappropriate association with dancing (Artemis is said to love
"phorminxes and dancing and wild cries," *h.Hom.*
5.18–20).

The fact that the plektron sweeps (strums) the
strings, sounding several nearly simultaneously, should
not lead us to assume that the resulting sounds were
used as modern Europeans and Americans would expect, that is, in a series of accompanying chord
changes. The Greeks have transmitted to us no system
of simultaneous pitches. Like many non-European cultures, they seem to have emphasized highly developed
rhythmic and melodic systems instead. This is *not* to
say that it did not matter which strings were struck or
how those strings were tuned: the outer notes of a
tetrachord and perhaps the note(s) an octave above,
for example, might have been considered suitable for
drone-like reiteration in the strumming; and the note
of the melody being sung at the same moment may
have been included also.

The sound made as the plektron swept the strings
did vary: the left hand touched certain strings, damping them so that they would not ring out; but there is
no reason to suppose that it was always the same
strings that were damped. For one thing we do see on
the vases a variety of finger positions that do not seem
to be used in plucking; and for another, some change
would be necessary if the note being sung, whatever
it might be at the moment, were always to be included
in the strum. Further variety would result if the strings
were touched in such a way as to produce harmonics,
though these were probably such as would mainly du-
plicate in a higher octave pitches being sounded normally: octave, octave plus fifth, double octave, and
possibly double octave plus third (see discussion of
hand position and harmonics in chap. 4).

Between the strokes of the plektron, as the vase
painters show us, the left hand plucked individual
strings, most often with the thumb but sometimes with

another finger. We also see the thumb and another finger used together to pluck one string (perhaps for a more emphatic sound); and occasionally it appears that the thumb and another finger pluck two different strings, though whether sequentially or simultaneously, we cannot tell.

Whether, in addition to damping strings, the left hand played all the notes of the melody sung (or, indeed, whether all the notes of the melody were available on the lyre) we also do not know. It may be worthwhile to consider in this connection, however, whether the finger-plucked notes, having less éclat than those struck with the bone or ivory plektron, were apt to have been the primary focus of attention.

The question of whether the lyre played, or could play, the same melody that was sung or played on the aulos, though unanswered, is one that has a bearing on another question of significance: Was the lyre able to make music alone, without singer or aulos player? And if so, when and to what extent was this done? The references to "bare" kithara playing (*psile kitharisis*) are complaints (see Plato, *Laws* 699e), and their rarity suggests that it was an experimental oddity rather than a common practice.

It is true that lyre players are not frequently depicted singing in an obvious way (head thrown back, mouth open). Singing barbitos players are found somewhat more often than others, perhaps because their singing is of a lusty sort that can be adequately portrayed only with these large gestures. If it is true, as Wegner indicates, that singers to the aulos are shown more commonly than singers to the lyre, however, this may simply be a matter of necessity.[2] A lyre player may have his hands full, as it were, but he can still sing and can be assumed to be singing; the aulete cannot sing, and there is no assumption that anyone is singing unless the painter shows it to be so. We suggest that lyre players can be assumed to be either singing or about to sing, and that the painters portray them with heads thrown back and mouths open only when they wish to represent, shall we say, god-sent enthusiasm.

The Mythological Tradition

The importance of the various lyres in Greek culture during the millennium between the Bronze Age and the end of the Classical period is nowhere better illustrated than in the number of mythological figures whose stories are associated with music. Besides Apollo, the Muses, and the satyrs, all of whom are closely connected with the stringed instruments, there are several other musicians about whom there are stories that suggest the significance of lyric song, including Thamyras, challenger of the Muses, Orpheus, charmer of men and beasts, and Amphion, mover of stones. Even Heracles, the single most often represented mythological hero in Attic vase painting and a figure noted primarily for his superhuman defeats of noxious monsters and fierce animals, is shown in a curious group of black-figured vase paintings as a kitharist mounting a podium to take part in a musical contest. Though the scene may have been encouraged in sixth-century B.C. Athens by the propagandists for the Peisistratids (whom Heracles may symbolize in this context), it may also reflect a lost story in which the club-toting, lion-skin-clad hero entered a musical competition, perhaps in connection with the rivalry between himself and his half-brother Apollo. At any rate, to the Greeks it was apparently not an outrageous incongruity to behold the equivalent of a modern-day professional athlete playing the cello in an international competition. From the heroic Heracles as musical competitor to the warrior Achilles as amateur lyre player, all these mythological musicians, together with their legendary counterparts such as Arion and Terpander, demonstrate the preeminence of the lyre-type instruments in the development of Greek musical tradition.

Names of the Instruments

Although exact lines of influence have not been traced, it is apparent that the stringed instruments of the Greeks were largely derived from those of their Near Eastern neighbors, especially those bordering on the Greek communities in Asia Minor. Ancient writers like Strabo were evidently aware that nearly all the names of the instruments are of non-Indo-European origins, a conclusion confirmed by modern etymological studies. The only exception are two names for harps, the *pektis* and the *trigonon,* both of which are clearly Greek.

Various circumstances complicate our efforts both to correlate the names for instruments that are reported in ancient Greek literature with the representations in Greek art, and to use these two forms of evidence to determine the date when an instrument was introduced. In some cases we have names for instruments but no representations with which the names can be even tentatively linked, for example, sambyke, *phoenix, klepsiambos, skindapsos,* and *enneachordon,* all mentioned in a fragment attributed to Aristoxenus.[3] For other instruments we have paintings but no name, as in the case of the instrument we have called the Thracian kithara, or at least none that can be securely applied, as in the case of the arched harp. The names of some of the instruments appear long before their representations: Alkman of Sparta and Sappho of Lesbos provide us with the names *magadis* and *pektis* before the end of the seventh century, but harps to which these names might be applied do not appear until after 450 B.C.; their contemporary Alcaeus also mentions the barbitos, not seen until after about 525 B.C.

The kithara, on the other hand, is clearly represented by the end of the eighth century (and may have been intended in even earlier representations); but the name *kithara* is not found until the early fifth century, the likely date for the lines attributed to Theognis of Megara that mention it. The possible explanations for this are: first, that the name had an earlier form, *kitharis,* a word that appears in Homer; second, that this instrument could formerly be indicated with the term *phorminx,* no verbal distinction being made between these two forms of the lyre, a hypothesis supported by the evident interchangeability of terms in Archaic literature and in Pindar; and third, that the kithara was always called by this name, but that early evidence is lacking.

Roles of Individual Instruments

The literature and the vase paintings bear ample witness to the generally well-defined roles that the stringed instruments acquired within specifically Greek social customs. Perhaps the most sharply delineated role is assigned to the barbitos, the elongated tenor lyre that functioned as the chief stringed instrument associated with Dionysos—the god himself and his attendants, the maenads and satyrs—or with celebrants taking part in processions (*komoi*) or drinking parties (*symposia*). Not surprisingly, the barbitos also has close associations with Eros, who sometimes appears in the vase paintings playing the instrument himself or hovering over a group of women in the women's quarters, one of whom (sometimes a bride-to-be) performs for the others.

Also clearly defined is the role of the large, ornate kithara, which seems to have taken over the function of the early-period phorminx as the chief instrument of Apollo. Certainly the close connections between the kithara and the god of music himself reflects the prestigious status of the instrument, which was played on formal occasions sponsored by the state; these included religious processions such as the one held during the annual Panathenaic festival, musical contests held during such festivals, victory songs sung in honor of winners of athletic events at Pan-Hellenic festivals,

and the dramatic performances that formed the central part of the Lenaia and the Great Dionysia, celebrated in Athens in the months of Gamelion (January) and Elaphebolion (March). In all cases the performers are men—again a reflection of the high status of the kithara in a culture that with few exceptions restricted the role and activities of women. Despite the close associations of the instrument with Apollo, the very fact that it was used as accompaniment in the dramatic festivals of Dionysos and appears in the vase paintings in the hands of Dionysos' attendants reminds us not to draw too Nietzschean a distinction between barbitos and kithara; the kithara enjoyed a higher status than the barbitos, but it was hardly the exclusive property of Apollo, nor was it a symbol of the rational as opposed to the emotional.

The tortoiseshell lyra, the instrument whose invention the mythmakers assigned to the enterprising infant Hermes, serves a wide variety of purposes as the stringed instrument simplest both to play and to manufacture. It is the instrument most often represented in scenes of the Muses, although they often play other kinds of instruments as well. It is also played by women at home—a bride and her attendants, for example—but even more commonly it is associated with boys and young men, whether in myth (Apollo, Hermes, Tithonos, Paris, and others) or in real life (school scenes, gymnasia, contests, and symposia). As the stringed instrument taught to boys at school by the kitharistes, and to girls at home (by their relatives or servants, presumably), it was the means of acquiring skills that could then be adapted to the kithara and other lyres.

Not all instruments have such well-defined roles as those of the barbitos, kithara, and chelys-lyra. In the case of the phorminx, the lyre of rounded base that appears in Greek art work from the earliest times and continues unchanged in basic shape down into the fifth century B.C., the function of the instrument appears to narrow over the course of the centuries. In earlier art, it is associated not only with Apollo and the Muses but also with dancing, processions, and various kinds of rituals, but by the late sixth century it appears only in Dionysiac scenes, and finally in the fifth century only in scenes of the Muses and of women, chiefly women or girls dancing.

The evidence for the use of harps in Greek lands is sporadic and scanty both in art and in literature. Although harps were used in the Cycladic culture of the third millennium B.C., they disappear until the mention of the pektis and magadis by poets from East Greece in the sixth century B.C. and of the trigonon during the late fifth century. Only during this latter period do representations of harps again appear in Attic vase paintings, and these connect the instruments primarily with women players, both amateur and professional.

Lyre Shapes

Although the literary evidence provides only limited information about the materials used in the making of the stringed instruments (such as horn for plektra and sheep-gut for strings), several common misconceptions about the construction of the instruments can be corrected through the use of comparative information from literary sources, vase paintings, and three-dimensional representations such as those in sculpture and coins. One such misconception involves the notion of the chelys-lyra as similar to a straight chair-back ornament of the sort found in eighteenth-century furniture. But as the philosopher Heraclitus suggests (in his comparison of a lyre and a bow; see chap. 4, n. 119) and as a few side views of the lyre confirm, the instrument was in fact curved from top to bottom, so that seen from the side the chelys-lyra would describe an arc, not a straight line. Even in frontal reconstructions of the lyre one occasionally finds basic errors in the understanding of how the instrument was put together. The Loeb translation of the *Imagines* of Philostratus, a sophist of the second and third centuries A.D. who describes a painting of Amphion charming the stones of Thebes into place with his lyre playing, includes as a frontispiece a drawing of the instrument in which the strings are stretched over the *back* of the tortoiseshell soundbox in a manner quite unconducive to the production of sound.

Another misconception can be seen in some modern reconstructions of the concert kithara in which the soundbox is assumed to be rather shallow and of uniform depth. But as the coins and sculpture reveal, the back of the soundbox bulges out in a hump which gradually tapers down toward the base, so that the base describes not so much a rectangle as a triangle. Since the size and shape of an instrument affect not only its sound but also the playing technique used, it is important to correct misunderstandings based on the limited perspective attempted by the vase painters, who generally show the instruments only in front view.

The Strings of the Lyres

The number of strings of the lyre-type instruments, from Minoan lyres before the eleventh century B.C. down to the kithara, chelys-lyra, and barbitos of the fifth and fourth centuries B.C., probably remained constant. As detailed studies reported in these pages have affirmed, lyres of almost any period may be depicted with fewer than seven strings or as many as eight or nine; the number shown on any particular example is influenced by the material (bronzes and terra-cottas tend to show few strings), the space available (seal stones generally have few), and the carelessness or interest in realism of the individual artist. But although some depictions show one or two more than, and some fewer than, seven strings, seven seems to have been the canonical number for the entire period in question. As we have seen, the limitations imposed by the technique and style of Geometric and Archaic art have led to misinterpretations that erroneously assume that a painter is portraying literally instruments that actually had four strings. The confusion has been compounded by Deubner's influential interpretation of the lines attributed to Terpander in which the poet refers to the "seven-toned phorminx" as opposed to the old "four-voiced song." There is little reason to believe that these lines, first reported by Strabo in the first century A.D. and later cited by the theorist Kleonides, even if they are by the seventh-century Terpander, describe a sudden increase in number of strings.[4] Similarly, the stories in which Christian-era writers attribute to Timotheus the adding of still more strings in the late fifth century seem to be nothing more than misinterpretations several centuries after the fact that were based on erroneous understanding of Timotheus' own poetry and of attacks against him in contemporary comic writers. Variations of a minor sort probably occurred, but in essence the seven-stringed lyre remained seven stringed from before the days of the Trojan War to the time of Alexander the Great and probably beyond.

The Greeks did, of course, have "many-stringed" instruments—the various kinds of harps that they called trigonon, pektis, and magadis—and it may have been sudden popularity of these instruments (with twenty strings or more) during the late fifth century that led to the legends of added numbers of strings in the case of the lyra or kithara.

The instruments of least importance in Greek culture, harps and lutes, have become the more important instruments in the West. Although the kithara has left its name in words like *gittern, guitar,* and *zither,* all of these are in fact instruments of the lute of psaltery types. Indeed, instruments of the lyre type survive, as plucked instruments, only in certain areas of Asia and East Africa. Yet the Minoan and Greek versions of the lyre were once thriving participants in a musical culture that extended over a period of nearly two millennia, and as such deserve to be studied in close detail as the data about them slowly increase with the publication of more works of art in which they are depicted. New archaeological finds, perhaps models or parts of actual instruments, may also add to the store of information. In any case, the material available at present is sufficient not only to correct the misunderstandings mentioned above but also to contradict certain popular assumptions about these instruments, such as the notions that they had a "weak voice" or were "primitive and insecure" in their tuning.[5] Pindar's lyre was "well strung" and "deftly wrought," capable of both soft singing and "thunder-ous" sound; "bright-sounding" and "glorious," it is addressed in his first *Pythian Ode* with these words:

Golden phorminx, joint possession of Apollo and the
    violet-haired Muses, you whom the
    steps hear in the merry dance,
The singers obey your notes
    when your vibrating strings are struck
To begin the choir-leading prooemium.[6]

Χρυσέα φόρμιγξ, Ἀπόλλωνος καὶ ἰοπλοκάμων
σύνδικον Μοισᾶν κτέανον· τᾶς ἀκούει
    μὲν βάσις ἀγλαΐας ἀρχά,
πείθονται δ᾽ ἀοιδοὶ σάμασιν
ἀγησιχόρων ὁπόταν προοιμίων
    ἀμβολὰς τεύχῃς ἐλελιζομένα.

Objects Mentioned

See Introduction for method of citing museums and volumes of the
Corpus Vasorum Antiquorum (*CVA*).

CHAPTER ONE

Athens Agora P 10154. Wegner *MT* cat. 7; *BCH* 61
(1937), 447, pl. 35b.

Athens 234, from the Amyklaion, Sparta. Fig. 12; Aign V/
5, p. 86; Wegner, *MT* cat. 20; Wegner, *Griechenland*, pl.
27, no. 4.

Athens 291, from the Acropolis. Wegner, *MT* cat. 23, pl.
IVc.

Athens 313, from Analatos. Aign V/15, pp. 95–96; Wegner, *MT* cat. 25.

Athens 784. Aign V/14, p. 95; Wegner, *MT* cat. 27.

Athens 874, from Athens. Aign pl. 4; Wegner, *MT* cat.
31; *CVA* 2, pl. 10.

Athens 9063. Kylix fragment from Skopelos. Fig. 3c; Platon, *Kretika Chronika* 3 (1949), 552.

Athens 1972, from Menidi, ivory facings with plektron.
Aign V/2, p. 82; Wegner, *MT* cat. 37/38; Platon, *Charisterion eis A.K. Orlandon* III pll. 70 and 71a.

Athens 3908, from Keros. Fig. 1; Aign I/1, p. 30; Wegner,
MT cat. 39; Thimme, *Art and Culture of the Cyclades*,
fig. 39, p. 69.

Athens 8833 from Naxos. Wegner, *MT* cat. 41; *Archaiologikon Deltion* 17, pt. A (Athens, 1967), p. 148, pll. 79–
80.

Athens 14447, from Anavyssos. Wegner, *MT* cat. 43, pl.
IIIa.

Athens 17497, from Attica. Aign V/11, p. 92; Wegner, *MT*
cat. 45, pl. IIa; *CVA* 2, pl. 56, 1–4.

Athens 18542, from Attica. Fig. 8; Aign V/9 a and b,
p. 91; Wegner, *MT* cat. 46; Coldstream, 71–72.

Athens, unnumbered sherd from the Argive Heraion. Fig.
13; Aign V/13, p. 94; Wegner, *MT* cat. 51; C. Waldstein, *The Argive Heraion* 2 (1905), pl. 51, 7.

Athens (?), plektra and fragments from Mycenae. Platon,
Charisterion eis A.K. Orlandon III, pl. 71b.

Basel BS 406, from Boeotia. Wegner, *MT* cat. 61, pl. IIIb.

Berlin Antikenmuseum 31573, from Aigina. Fig. 10; Aign
V/17, p. 97; Wegner, *MT* cat. 69; *CVA* 1, pl. 47, 2.

Cambridge Mus. Class. Arch. 345, from Attica. Wegner,
MT cat. 72, pl. 2b.

Copenhagen 727, from Athens. Aign V/8 a and b, p. 90;
Wegner, *MT* cat. 99, pl. VI a and b; *CVA* 2, pll. 73, 5,
and 74, 3 and 6.

Copenhagen 9367, from Attica. Aign V/10, p. 91; Wegner,
MT cat. 101.

Copenhagen 12433, from Exochi, Rhodes. Wegner, *MT*
cat. 103; *Acta Archaeologica* 28 (1957), 26ff., fig. 57.

Delos, 7th-century vase sherd. See chap. 2, fig. 7.

Dresden 1699, from Boeotia. Fig. 11; Aign V/16, p. 97;
Wegner, *MT* cat. 74; Wegner, *Musikleben* 136, fig. 20/3.

Hagia Nikolaos, amphora from Sitia. Fig. 2c; Platon,
Charisterion eis A.K. Orlandon III, p. 214, fig. 4.

Heraklion 2064, bronze figure. Fig. 6; Aign II/16, p. 56;
Wegner, *MT* cat. 90; Wegner, *Griechenland*, pl. 25, 1.

Heraklion, Hagia Triada fresco. Aign II/10, p. 43; Wegner, *MT* cat. 82; Long, Studies in Mediterranean Archaeology 41 (1974), pl. 17, fig. 43.

Heraklion, Hagia Triada sarcophagus. Fig. 2a; Aign II/11,
p. 44; Wegner, *MT* cat. 81; von Matt, *Ancient Crete,*
p. 138.

Heraklion, Knossos seal stone. In Aign II/8, p. 41; Xanthoudides, *EA* 1907, 177, pl. 8, fig. 111; *EA* 1913, 100,
pl. 2, fig. 111.

Heraklion, Palaikastro terra-cotta group. Aign II/12,
p. 46; Wegner, *MT* cat. 80; von Matt, *Ancient Crete,*
pl. 202.

Karatepe, relief. Lower excavation, by "Master A." Fig.
14; Aign
A/6a, p. 175.

Karatepe, relief. Upper excavation, by "Master B." Fig.
7b; Aign
A/5, p. 174.

Karlsruhe B 863 and B 864 from Thera. Aign I/2 and I/3,
p. 31; Wegner, *MT* cat. 98 and 97; Thimme, *Art and
Culture of the Cyclades*, color pl. 4, p. 202, and pll. 254–
55, pp. 300–01.

Khania 2308, from Kalamion. Fig. 2b; Long, *Studies in Mediterranean Archaeology* 41 (1974), pl. 18, fig. 48.

Khora, Pylos fresco. Aign V/1, p. 80; Wegner, *MT* cat. 136; Lang, *The Palace of Nestor at Pylos,* 2, color pl. A.

Location unknown, Knossos bead seals. In Aign II/1 and II/3, pp. 35–37; Wegner, *MT,* U 77–78, nos. 83 and 84. See Evans, *Scripta Minoa* I, 192, and pl. III, fig. 64a.

Location unknown, Knossos seal stone. Fig. 2d; Evans, *Palace of Minos* IV, 151.

Locations unknown, seal stones from Rhodes or Euboea. Porada, *The Aegean and the Near East: Studies Presented to Hetty Goldman,* 185–211.

Location unknown, Swiss private collection, Cycladic figures. Thimme, *Art and Culture of the Cyclades,* fig. 77, p. 89.

Location unknown, cylinder seal from Tarsus. Aign A/2, p. 142, fig. 86.

London E 270, 5th-century vase. *ARV²* 183 and 1632.

London 1920.12-20.1, Cypriote bronze stand.

London 1946.10-17.1, Cypriote bronze stand.

London 134306, cylinder seal from Anatolia. Joan Rimmer, *Ancient Musical Instruments of Western Asia in the Department of Western Asiatic Antiquities,* p. 28, fig. 6 and pl. VIIIa.

Meggido, Israel, rock drawing. Aign, pp. 118–20.

Nauplia 14.376, vase fragment from Tiryns. Fig. 3b; Vermuele and Karageorghis, *Mycenaean Pictorial Vase Painting,* pl. XI, 69.

Nauplia, krater fragment from Nauplion. Fig. 3a; Vermuele and Karageorghis, *Mycenaean Pictorial Vase Painting,* pl. IX, 14.1.

New York 47.100.1. Aign I/4, p. 33, discussed as a forgery; Thimme, *Art and Culture of the Cyclades,* pll. 253a and b, pp. 298–99.

Nicosia, Hubbard amphora. Fig 5b; Aign III/5, p. 63; Wegner, *MT* cat. 120; Dikaios, *BSA* 37 (1936–37), pl. 8.

Nicosia, Kaloriziki amphora. Fig 5a; Aign III/4, p. 62; Wegner, *MT* cat. 121; Dikaios, *BSA* 37 (1936–37), p. 71, fig. 7.

Nicosia, Kouklia T. 9, no. 7. Fig. 4; Karageorghis, *Mycenaean Art from Cyprus,* pl. 16, 1.

Oxford CS 170, 1938.793, from Heraklion. Aign, pp. 349–50.

Sparta, Laconian-Geometric vase sherd. Aign V/4, p. 85; Wegner, *MT* cat. 148.

Sparta, bronze votive lyre from the Amyklaion. Fig. 3d; Aign V/3, p. 84; Wegner, *MT* cat. 139; Guillemin and Duchesne, *L'Antiquité classique* 4 (1935), pl. 7, no. 28.

Tegea, votive bronzes. Fig. 9; Wegner, *MT* cat. 151–53; Dugas, *BCH* 45 (1921), 394 no. 210, figs. 39, 47; and Rhomaios, *EA* 1952, 26ff., fig. 20a.

Tübingen 2657. Fig. 7a; Aign V/7, p. 89; Wegner, *MT* cat. 156; *CVA* 44, pl. 2116, 2.

CHAPTER TWO

Argos A56 U 14 Tortus 2, fragments of tortoise shell from a lyre.

Athens Nat. Mus. Acr. 2203. Fig. 10; Graef–Langlotz I, pl. 93.

Athens Agora AP 1085. Fig 3a; Aign V/23, p. 103; *ABV* 6, 23; *Para* 5, 28; *Hesperia,* 1938, pp. 160ff. and pl. 1.

Athens Agora P 10154. *BCH* 61 (1937), pl. 35.

Athens Kerameikos 2869. Fig. 14b.

Athens 313, the Analatos Hydria. Fig. 13; Aign V/15, pp. 95–96.

Athens 784, Geometric period vase. Aign V/14, p. 95.

Athens 911, Melian amphora. Fig. 2; Aign V/20, p. 100; Arias and Hirmer, *A History of Greek Vase Painting,* pll. 22–23 and text pp. 29–30.

Athens 5708, Boeotian terra-cotta.

Athens 12210, terra-cotta figure from Cyprus. Fig. 4.

Athens 16464, Corinthian plaque. Fig. 17; Charbonneaux, Martin, and Villard, *Archaic Greek Art,* 312, pl. 357.

Athens 18542, late Geometric-period vase. See chap. 1.

Athens 19272, krater from northeast Aegean. Fig. 9b; Wegner, *MT* cat. 47.

Athens Nat. Mus. 2523. Fig. 5; Wegner, *MT* cat. 12; Aign V/25, p. 232; Graef–Langlotz I, pl. 104.

Athens, unnumbered Corinthian aryballos from Perachora.

Athens 0.76.9, fragments of tortoise shell for a lyre, from Vassae. *Archaiologikon Deltion* 32, pt. A (Athens 1977), 220ff. and pll. 77–78.

Athens, vase sherd from the Argive Heraion. See chap. 1.

Ayia Irini, Cyprus, steatite seal stones 2123, 2180. Aign III/11–12, pp. 71–72.

Bayrakli, Old Smyrna dinos sherd. Fig. 1; J. M. Cook, *JHS* 71 (1951), 248, fig. 8.

Berlin Antikenmuseum 31573, late Geometric period. See chap. 1, fig. 10.

Boston 00.330. Fig. 11; *CVA* 14, pl. 627, 1 and 3.

Boston 23.595, seal stone. Boardman, *Greek Gems,* pl. 304.

Cambridge Mus. Class. Arch. 345. Wegner, *MT* pl. U II b, cat. 72.

Copenhagen 3241. *CVA* 3, pl. 104, 2b.

Copenhagen 9367, late Geometric-period vase. See chap. 1, fig. 7.

Copenhagen 13536. *CVA* 8, pll. 322, 1a, and 323, 1a; *ABV* 714.

Copenhagen, Ny Carlsberg Glyptotek, stone siren from Kyzikos, Turkey. Ekrem Akurgal, *Die Kunst Anatoliens von Homer bis Alexander,* p. 265, fig. 228.

Cyprus, silver cup. Aign III/8, p. 67.

Delos B 4260. Fig. 7.

Delphi, marble relief from Sikyonian Treasury. Fig. 9c; also in Wegner, *Griechenland,* p. 58 and pl. 31.

Florence 4209. Fig 14c; *ABV* 76, 1; *Para* 29; Karl Schefold, *Myth and Legend in Early Greek Art,* p. 62, fig. 18.

Heidelberg Univ. 68/1. *CVA* 31, pl. 1506, 2 and 3. Fig. 14d.

Istanbul, relief from Xanthos in Lykia. Ekrem Akurgal, *Die Kunst Anatoliens von Homer bis Alexander,* p. 135, fig. 86.

Karatepe, relief. See chap. 1.

Kassel T. 448. *CVA* 1, pl. 1694, nos. 1 and 2.

Lindos, Rhodes, marble figures 1712, 1716, 1717, 1820. Blinkenberg and Kinch, *Lindos* I, pt. 2, pll. 70 and 76.

Location unknown, band kylix once Basel *Auction* 18, 1958, no. 85 (H. A. Cahn), privately owned. In Erika Simon, *Die Götter der Griechen,* p. 193, pl. 176.

Location unknown, bronze votive kithara. Aign V/37, p. 240.

Location unknown, Etruscan funerary chest from Campania. Fig. 5a; Aign E/1, p. 187.

Location unknown, vase from Pitane. Drawing in Akurgal, *The Art of Greece,* 211, fig. 155.

London B 46. *ABV* 91, 5.

London B 139. *CVA* 1, pl. 5, 3a and b; *ABV* 139; *Para* 57.

London B 260. *CVA* 5, pl. 64, 2a and b.

London 88.2-8.10, fragment of an East Greek pot from Tel Defenneh, Egypt. *CVA* 13, pl. 604, no. 16; drawing, pl. 598, no. 9.

London 1971.11-11. Fig. 9a; *Para* 19.16 bis; Boardman, *ABFV* 24; Paul Zanker, *Wandel der Hermesgestalt in der Attischen Vasenmalerei,* pl. 3, no. 1.

London 459, seal stone. Boardman, *Greek Gems,* pl. 316.

Munich 1472. *CVA* 7, pl. 1564, 1; *ABV* 143.

Munich 2243. Fig. 12; *ABV* 163; Boardman, *ABFV* pl. 116, 2.

New York 06.1021.26. Fig. 14e; *AJA* 63 (1959), 353–54 and pl. 89.

New York 06.1021.47.

New York 14.105.10.

New York 17.230.14. *CVA* 16, pl. 744, 1, and pl. 747, 2.

New York 41.162.184. *CVA* 8, pl. 384, 1b; *ABV* 305; *Para* 132.

New York 56.11.1. Fig. 15b; Met. Museum Bulletin 15 (1956), 54–55.

New York 98.8.11. Fig. 16. G. M. A. Richter, *Handbook of Greek Art,* (1967), p. 59, no. 40, pl. 40a.

Nicosia, limestone votive statuette.

Olympia 11327, bronze relief. Aign V/21, p. 101.

Olympia, bronze cup. Aign S/7, p. 161.

Olympia, bronze shield-strap plate. Aign V/36, p. 239.

Oxford 1892.1490. Fig. 18; Boardman, *Archaic Greek Gems,* no. 180, p. 77, pl. 12.

Paris CA 3329. *CVA* 26, pl. 1156, 3.

Paris E 623. *CVA* 19, pl. 833, 1 and 3; *ABV* 83; *Para* 31.

Paris E 629. Fig 14a; Charbonneaux, Martin, and Villard, *Archaic Greek Art,* p. 43, pl. 46.

Paris E 643. Fig. 15a; *Archaic Greek Art,* p. 74, pl. 79.

Paris E 861. Fig. 15c; *CVA* 1, pl. 36, 12; *Para* 33.

Paris F 13. *CVA* 4, pl. 148.

Philadelphia Univ. Mus. L 64.180. *Museum Journal* 4 (1913), 141 and pl. 151.

Philadelphia Univ. Mus. MS 4841. *Museum Journal* 4 (1913), 142 and p. 152.

Rhodes 12.200. Fig. 6; *ABV* 115; *CVA* 9, pl. 451, 2.

Sparta, ivory or bone plektra. Fig. 13d; R. M. Dawkins, *The Sanctuary of Artemis Orthia at Sparta,* pl. 166, no. 5, and 167, pt. A.

Sparta, lead figures. Aign V/33–34, p. 236. R. M. Dawkins, *Sanctuary,* pl. 189 no. 7.

Sparta, lead votive objects. Figs. 13b and 13c; R. M. Dawkins, *Sanctuary,* pll. 180, no. 19; 183, nos. 18–20; 189, nos. 10, 11.

Syracuse 12577. Fig. 3b; Aign V/24, p. 231. Payne, *Necrocorinthia,* 119, fig. 44A.

Taranto 117234. Heide Mommsen, *Der Affecter,* pl. 58 B.

Tegea, Geometric-period bronze votive phorminx. See chap. 1.

Thebes R.50.265. *BSA* 14, pl. 10ff. and pp. 260–61.

Zakynthos, priv. coll., bronze back plate (armor) from Olympia. Fig. 8; Wegner, *Griechenland,* 44 and pl. 20.

CHAPTER THREE

Altenburg 202. *CVA* 17, pl. 817.

Athens Acropolis 816. Graef and Langlotz, *Die antiken Vasen von der Akropolis zu Athen* ser. I, pl. 49, no. 816.

Athens Acropolis 836a. Graef and Langlotz, *Die antiken Vasen von der Akropolis* ser. I, pl. 56, no. 836a.

Athens Acropolis, Parthenon plaque 875. Fig. 6.

Athens Acropolis 2009. Graef and Langlotz, *Die antiken Vasen von der Akropolis* ser. I, pl. 89, no. 2009.

Athens Nat. Mus. Acr. 609. Fig. 14. *ARV²* 190.

Athens 1626. *ARV²* 663.

Austin, University of Texas 1980.63. H. A. Shapiro, ed., *Greek Vases from Southern Collections,* no. 9, p. 33.

Berlin 1846. *CVA* 45, pl. 2175.

Berlin 1869. *CVA* 45, pl. 2181.

Berlin 1966.1. *CVA* 45, pl. 2176.

Berne 12409. Fig. 16; *ARV²* 1212, 5; Adrienne Lezzi-Hafter, *Der Schuwalow-Maler,* pl. 133f.

Bologna 228. *ARV²* 511; *CVA* 5, pll. 238 and 239.

Bologna 276. *ARV²* 569; *CVA* 27, pl. 1211, 1 and 3.

Bonn 72. *ARV²* 250; *CVA* 1, pl. 18, 1–5.

Boston 26.61. Fig. 8. Caskey and Beazley, *Attic Vase Paintings in the Museum of Fine Arts, Boston,* pl. 8 and fig. 19.

Boston 95.45. Fig. 19; Caskey and Beazley, *Attic Vase Paintings,* pl. 46, no. 88.

Boston 96.719. *ARV²* 1107.

Boston 97.370. Fig. 1. Caskey and Beazley, *Attic Vase Paintings,* supp. pl. 15, no. 105.

Brussels A 200. *ABV* 392; *CVA* 3, pl. 117, 1b.

Brussels A 3089. *CVA* 3, pl. 120, 2a.

Brussels R 240. *CVA* 2, pl. 58, 5b.

Bucharest 03207. *CVA* 1, pl. 32, 1.

Cambridge, Fitzwilliam X, 13.

Cambridge, Fitzwilliam GR 18.1927, scarab. Fig. 17.

Cambridge, Harvard 1960.236. *ARV²* 185. See chap. 5, fig. 2.

Canterbury, N.Z., University, Logie Coll. 3/53. Trendall, *Greek Vases in the Logie Collection,* pl. 30.

Cincinnati, Univ. Classics Library, kalyx krater. *ARV²* 215, 10.

Cleveland 76.89. Fig. 15. *Bulletin of the Cleveland Museum of Art* (February 1977), p. 43.

Ferrara VP T.55. *CVA* 37, pl. 1680, 4.

Ferrara 2893. *ARV²* 1038 and 1679; *Spina*, pll. 89–92.

Fiesole, black-figured amphora. *CVA* 57, pl. 2524.

Frankfurt STV 4. *CVA* 30, pl. 1437; *ABV* 430, 23.

Gotha 36. *CVA* 24, pl. 1154, 1.

Hannover 1964.9. *CVA* 34, pll. 1641, 2, and 1643, 1.

Hannover 1965.30. *CVA* 34, pll. 1650–51.

Hannover Kestner 753. *ABV* 392; *CVA* 34, pll. 1641, 3 and 1644, 2.

Kassel T. 675. Fig. 5; *Para* 167, 223bis. *CVA* 35, pl. 1704, 1.

Leiden PC 2. *CVA* 3, pl. 101.

Leiden PC 3. *ABV* 372, 164; *CVA* 3, pl. 124.

Leiden PC 41. *CVA* 4, pl. 167.

Leningrad 612. *ARV²* 198; *Para* 510; A. Peredolskaya, pl. 29.

Leningrad 614. *ARV²* 288; *Para* 511; A. Peredolskaya, pl. 41.

Leningrad 17295. Fig. 10; *ABV* 410. *L'Antiquité classique* 5, pl. 37, 1.

London B 139. *CVA* 1, pl. 5, 3a, b; *ABV* 139; *Para* 57. See chap. 2.

London B 202. *ABV* 284; *CVA* 4, pl. 162, 1a and b.

London B 206. Fig. 3; *ABV* 369; *CVA* 5, pl. 191, 1a and b.

London B 258. *ABV* 402; *CVA* 5, pl. 208, 4a and b.

London B 262. *ABV* 321; *CVA* 5, pl. 213, 2a.

London B 300. Fig. 12; *ABV* 324, 694. Boardman, *Athenian Black Figure Vases*, pl. 222.

London B 460. *ABV* 212, 1; *CVA* 2, pl. 80, 2a and b.

London B 679.

London E 265. *ARV²* 1594. *CVA* 3, pl. 173, 1.

London E 383. *ARV²* 630, 25; drawing in Beazley, *ARFV* in American Museums, p. 156.

London E 444. *ARV²* 208; *CVA* 4, pl. 141, 4.

London 1926, 6-28, 7. Fig. 11; *ABV* 375; *CVA* 5, pl. 206, 4.

London, Brit. Mus., Knight Coll. Didrachm from Delos. G. K. Jenkins, *Ancient Greek Coins*, pp. 34–35.

Madrid 10916. *ABV* 508; *CVA* 1, pll. 39, 3b, and 40, 2.

Montpelier 130. *ARV²* 197, 10; *JHS* 42 (1922), 75, fig. 3.

Munich 1575. Fig. 4; *ABV* 256; *CVA* 37, pll. 1781, and 1782.

Munich 2304. Fig. 18; *ARV²* 220; *CVA* 12, pl. 557, 2.

Munich 2319. *ARV²* 198 and 1633; *CVA* 20, pll. 925 and 926, 8.

Naples 192. Beazley, *Pan Painter*, pl. 17, 3.

New York 20.245. Fig. 9; *ARV²* 552, 30; *AJA* 27 (1923), 278, fig. 15.

New York 21.88.73. Richter and Hall, *RFAV*, pl. 125; *ARV²* 1029.

New York 25.78.66. *ARV²* 1172, 1685; Richter and Hall, *RFAV*, pl. 155. See chap. 6, fig. 13.

New York 53.224. *Met. Mus. of Art Bulletin*, new ser. 21, p. 8, pl. 8.

New York 56.171.38. Fig. 13. Charbonneaux, Martin, and Villard, *Archaic Greek Art*, pl. 389.

New York 57.12.8.

New York 67.44.1. *CVA* 16, pl. 762, 1.

Oxford G.240. *ABV* 484, 9; *CVA* 14, pl. 637, 1.

Oxford 274. *CVA* 3, pl. 107; *ARV²* 203.

Oxford 1911.630. *CVA* 3, pl. 19, 6.

Oxford 1965.116. *ABV* 273; *CVA* 14, pl. 625.

Oxford 1965.119. *ABV* 261; *CVA* 14, pl. 652.

Paris Bibl. Nat. H 1119. *ABV* 552; *CVA* 10, pl. 465.

Paris E 669. Karl Schefold, *Götter- und Heldensagen der Griechen in der spätarchäischen Kunst*, p. 80, pl. 91.

Paris E 861. *Para* 33; *CVA* 1, pl. 36, 12.

Paris F 58. *ABV* 312; *CVA* 5, pl. 196, 9.

Paris F 282. *CVA* 8, pl. 358.

Paris F 297. *ABV* 333; *CVA* 9, pl. 410, 9.

Paris G 50. *ARV²* 188 and 1632; *CVA* 9, pl. 431.

Paris, Petit Palais 304. *CVA* 15, pl. 647, 1.

Philadelphia, Univ. of Pa. MS 5399. *ARV²* 6.

Plovdiv 298. Fig. 7; *ARV²* 1187, 36; Van Hoorn, *Choes and Anthesteria*, pl. 241, and text note 114.

Rome, Vatican kylix by Douris. *ARV²* 437, no. 116; *AJA* (1962), pl. 78, 7.

Rome, Villa Giulia 15730. *ABV* 373; *CVA* 3, pl. 103, 1.

Syracuse 17427. *ARV²* 1184, 4; *CVA* 17, pl. 824, 5.

Syracuse 45911. *ARV²* 1053, 32; *CVA* 17, pll. 829, 1, and 830, 1 and 2.

Tarquinia 678. *CVA* 25, pl. 1137, 1 and 3.

Tarquinia 681. *CVA* 25, pl. 1143, 3.

Tarquinia RC 2800. *CVA* 26, pl. 1181, 5.

Tarquinia RC 8262. *ABV* 258; *Para* 138; *CVA* 26, pl. 1189, 1.

Toledo 56.70. *CVA* 17, pl. 803, 1.

Toronto 919.5.133. Fig. 2. Robinson, Harcum, and Iliffe, *A Catalogue of the Greek Vases in the Royal Ontario Museum of Archeology, Toronto*, pl. 32.

Toronto 919.25.2. Robinson, Harcum, and Iliffe, *Cat. of Greek Vases in the R.O.M.*, pl. 43.

Trieste S 405. *ABV* 350, 695; *CVA* 43, pl. 1911, 3.

Vienna 415. *ARV²* 591; *CVA* 3, pl. 101, 1.

Vienna 698. *ARV²* 432; *CVA* 2, pl. 59, 2.

Vienna 3739. *CVA* 3, pl. 140, 1 and 2.

Warsaw, Czartoryski 11. *CVA* 1, pl. 13, 2b.

Warsaw, Czartoryski 34. *ARV²* 646; *CVA* 1, pl. 22, 2c.

Würzburg 216. *ABV* 383, 13; Langlotz, *Griechische Vasen in Würzburg*, pl. 50.

Würzburg 222. *ABV* 405; Langlotz, *Griechische Vasen in Würzburg*, pl. 50.

Würzburg 308. *ABV* 267. Simon, *Die Götter der Griechen*, pl. 104.

Zakynthos, priv. coll., bronze back plate. See chap. 2, fig. 8.

CHAPTER FOUR

Adolphseck 68. *ARV²* 1207; *CVA* 11, pl. 521, 1–2.

Adria B 254. *ARV²* 411; *CVA* 28, pl. 1259.

Adria B 330. *CVA* 28, pl. 1261, 6.

Adria B 534. *CVA* 28, pl. 1267, 7.

Adria B 809. *ARV²* 357; *CVA* 28, pl. 1254, 4.

Adria Bc 47. *ARV²* 803; *CVA* 28, pl. 1285.

Ann Arbor, Univ. of Mich. 2601. *CVA* 3, pl. 100.

Athens Agora P 43. Fig. 27; *ARV²* 1578.

Athens Agora P 7246. *ARV²* 962.

Athens Agora P 18279. *ARV²* 1030. *Hesperia* 17 (1948), pl. 67, 4, and p. 188.

Athens Agora P 18292.

Athens Agora P 18799. *Hesperia* 17 (1948), pl. 67, 1, and p. 187.

Athens Acropolis NA 57Aa 696.

Athens Kerameikos Gr. 131, P 28, 1116.

Athens 635.

Athens 655. *ABV* 562.

Athens 1130. *Para* 217; *ABV* 476.

Athens 1134.

Athens 1171. *ARV²* 1179.

Athens 1172. *ARV²* 585.

Athens 1176. *ARV²* 287; *CVA* 1, pll. 30 and 31.

Athens 1230. *ARV²* 782.

Athens 1241. *CVA* 2 pll. 76 and 77. See chap. 6, fig. 6.

Athens 1259.

Athens 1260. Fig. 22; *ARV²* 1060; *Para* 445.

Athens 1300. *ARV²* 535.

Athens 1413. Fig. 18. *ARV²* 285; *CVA* 1, pl. 31.

Athens 1418. *ARV²* 1104; *CVA* 2, pl. 88, 1–3.

Athens 1467. *ARV²* 1084.

Athens 1546. Van Hoorn, *Choes*, 65, no. 44, pl. 502.

Athens 1809. *ARV²* 689.

Athens 1950. *ARV²* 1242; *Para* 468; *CVA* 1, pl. 43.

Athens 1982. *ARV²* 751.

Athens 10452. *ARV²* 779.

Athens 11713.

Athens 12282.

Athens 12462. *ARV²* 959.

Athens 12803. *ARV²* 452; *CVA* 1, pl. 32.

Athens 12961. *ARV²* 1282.

Athens 17539. *ARV²* 1255.

Athens 17918. *ARV²* 1040, 19. See chap. 5, fig. 18.

Athens 18599. *ARV²* 699; *Para* 407.

Athens 19296. *Para* 149.

Athens 19503, unpublished choe.

Athens, Nat. Mus. Acropolis Coll. 311. *ARV²* 478. Graef–Langlotz, pl. 19.

Athens, Nat. Mus. Acropolis Coll. 546. Graef-Langlotz, text v. 2, p. 49, on inscription.

Basel, oinochoe by the Shuvalov Painter. Adrienne Lezzi-Hafter, *Der Schuwalow-Maler* (Mainz: Verlag Philipp von Zabern, 1976), 2, pl. 180.

Berkeley 8/930. *ARV²* 839; *CVA* 5, pl. 218, 4b.

Berkeley 8/4581. *ARV²* 974; *CVA* 5, pl. 222.

Berlin 2278. *ARV²* 21; *CVA* 21, pll. 978, 2, and 979, 4.

Berlin 2285. *ARV²* 431; *CVA* 21, pll. 1006 and 1007.

Berlin 2291. *ARV²* 459; *CVA* 21, pll. 1013 and 1014.

Berlin 2530. *ARV²* 831; *CVA* 22, pl. 1030.

Berlin Antikenmuseum 2536. Fig. 9; *ARV²* 1287; *CVA* 22, pll. 1046 and 1047.

Berlin 2547. *ARV²* 606; *CVA* 22, pl. 1038.

Berlin 2549. *CVA* 21, pl. 1022, 3 and 7.

Berlin 3172. *ARV²* 1103; Wegner, *Musikleben*, pl. 21.

Berlin 3359. *ARV²* 267; *CVA* 21, pl. 1003.

Berlin 4043. *ARV²* 833; *CVA* 22, pl. 1066, 2.

Berlin 4059. *CVA* 22, pl. 1036.

Berlin 11.863.66, scarab. Boardman, *Archaic Greek Gems*, pl. 24, no. 335, and p. 110.

Bologna 271. *CVA* 33, pll. 1492, 2, and 1493, 1–4; *ARV²* 825.

Bologna 292. *ARV²* 1116; *CVA* 27, pll. 1231, 1b, and 1234, 3a.

Bologna 301. *ARV²* 1184; *CVA* 27, pll. 1237, 3, and 1238, 2.

Bologna 361. *ARV²* 65; *CVA* 5, pl. 198, 3.

Bologna 660. *CVA* 5, pl. 246, 1.

Boston scarabs. Boardman, *Greek Gems*, nos. 304, 333, and 351.

Boston 00.347. Caskey and Beazley, pl. 61, no. 109.

Boston 00.356. *ARV²* 741; Caskey and Beazley, pl. 15, no. 36.

Boston 01.8080. *ARV²* 1231. Fairbanks, *Athenian Lekythoi*, 6, pl. 6.

Boston 03.816. Caskey and Beazley, pl. 44, no. 83.

Boston 03.821. *ARV²* 1186. Caskey and Beazley, pl. 102, no. 170, and text v. 3, supp. pl. 27.

Boston 13.202. Fig. 29. Caskey and Beazley, pll. 22 and 26, no. 49.

Boston 61.1233. *CJ* 59 (1964), 204, figs. 13–14.

Boston 66.206. *Para* 356; *AJA* 70 (1966), pl. 6, fig. 18.

Boston 90.156. Caskey and Beazley, pl. 57, no. 107.

Boston 98.734, cornelian scarab. Boardman, *Archaic Greek Gems*, pl. 23, no. 334, and p. 110.

Boston 98.887. Fig. 6; *ARV²* 774; *Para* 416. See also chap. 6, fig. 3.

Brunswick 219. *ARV²* 1037; *CVA* 4, pll. 169 and 170.

Brussels A 1020. Fig. 23; *ARV²* 743; *CVA* 1, pl. 42, 4.

Cambridge, Fitzwilliam GR 1.1950. *ARV²* 1115.

Cambridge, Fitzwilliam GR 8.1955. *ARV²* 648.

Cambridge, Fitzwilliam GR 22.1937. *CVA* 11, pl. 519.

Cambridge, Fitzwilliam G. 73. *ARV²* 1287; *CVA* 6, pl. 265, 2a and b.

Cambridge, Fitzwilliam 4.1943. *ARV²* 935.

Cambridge, Fitzwilliam 37.26. *ARV²* 506; *CVA* 11, pl. 521.

Cambridge, Lewes House, 6th-century green jasper scarab. Boardman, *Greek Gems*, no. 416.

Cambridge, Harvard column krater. *ARV²* 275; *CVA* 1, pl. 12, 1.

Cambridge, Harvard 1895.248. *ARV²* 803, *CVA* 8, pl. 352.

Cambridge, Harvard 1927.30.21. *CVA* 1, pl. 4, 9.

Cambridge, Harvard 1959.188. Fig. 14; *ARV²* 566.

Canterbury, N.Z. Logie CML 6-AR 430. Trendall, *Greek Vases in the Logie Collection*, pl. 26.

Chapel Hill, kylix. *ARV*² 1655.

Chicago 89.95.

Chicago 92.126.

Cleveland 30.104. *CVA* 15, pll. 703–04.

Copenhagen Chr. VIII 519. *CVA* 4, pl. 160, 10.

Copenhagen Chr. VIII 991. *CVA* 3, pl. 113, 4.

Copenhagen 3634. *ARV*² 293; *CVA* 3, pl. 134, 1a and c.

Copenhagen 3878. *ARV*² 479; *CVA* 3, pl. 141.

Copenhagen 3880. *ARV*² 373; *CVA* 3, pl. 144, 1a.

Copenhagen 5377. *ARV*² 1277; *CVA* 4, pl. 159, 6a and b.

Corinth C 34-365. *Hesperia* 6 (1937), 262, fig. 4.

Corinth MP 116, aryballos.

Delphi 8140. Basil Petracos, *Delphi* (Athens: Hesperus Editions, 1971), cover.

Eleusis 470. *ABV* 335?

Eleusis 626.

Eleusis, black-figured lekythos.

Ferrara T. 127. *ARV*² 1171; *CVA* 37, pl. 1656; *Spina*, pl. 108. See chap. 6, fig. 11b.

Ferrara T. 293. *ARV*² 733, n. 1. *Spina*, pl. 98.

Ferrara T. 563. *ARV*² 1286; *Spina*, pl. 113.

Fiesole, amphora. *CVA* 57, pl. 2533.

Florence PD 267. *ARV*² 920; *CVA* 30, pl. 1377.

Florence PD 272. *ARV*² 834; *CVA* 30, pl. 1375.

Florence 128 (7.B29). Fig. 26; *CVA* 8, pl. 382; *ARV*² 205.

Florence 3911. *ARV*² 389; *CVA* 30, pl. 1366.

Florence 3933. *ARV*² 929; *CVA* 13, pl. 655.

Florence 3946. *ARV*² 792; *CVA* 30, pl. 1371.

Florence 4014. Fig. 16; *ARV*² 1060; *CVA* 13, pl. 643.

Florence 4219. *ARV*² 809; *CVA* 38, pl. 1699, 3.

Florence 74355. *ARV*² 1290; *CVA* 38, pl. 1724, 1–2.

Florence 81268. *ARV*² 568; *CVA* 13, pl. 628.

Florence 91288. *CVA* 38, pl. 1706.

Frankfurt 304. *CVA* 30, pl. 1440, 1–3.

Frankfurt Mus. für V. F. 6 304. Fig. 13; *CVA* 30, pl. 1441, 3.

Gela 112/B. *ARV*² 423; *CVA* 54, pll. 2402, 3, and 2403, 2.

Geneva 14986. *ARV*² 1290; *Para* 473; *CVA* 1, pll. 9 nd 10.

Geneva 14987. *ARV*² 1019; *CVA* 1, pl. 20, 2.

Genoa 1216. *ARV*² 1048; *CVA* 19, pl. 914.

Gotha 51. Fig. 25; *ARV*² 1028; *CVA* 29, pll. 1387–89.

The Hague, Scheurleer 623. *CVA* 2, pl. 82, 4 and 6.

Hamburg 1900.164. *ARV*² 880.

Hannover 1961.24. *CVA* 34, pl. 1677.

Heidelberg Univ. L 64. Fig. 1; *CVA* 31, pl. 1513, 2 and 3.

Hillsborough, Hearst 17. *ARV*² 310. I. K. Raubitschek, *The Hearst Hillsborough Vases*, 64–65.

Hillsborough, Hearst 21. Fig. 7; I. K. Raubitschek, *The Hearst Hillsborough Vases*, 75–76.

Karlsruhe B 777. *CVA* 7, pl. 308, 6, and 309, 2–3.

Kassel T. 429. *ARV*² 904; *CVA* 35, pl. 1718.

Kassel T. 436. *ARV*² 626; *CVA* 35, pll. 1717 and 1720.

Kavala A 1789.

Laon 371059. *ARV*² 627; *CVA* 20, pl. 917.

Lecce 573. *ARV*² 262; *CVA* 4, pl. 153.

Leningrad, The Hermitage, unlabeled kylix.

Lindos, Rhodes 2355, terra-cotta (standing young man with lyre). Blinkenberg, *Lindos, les petits objets* 2, no. 2355, pl. 110.

London B 167. Fig. 8; *ABV* 382; *CVA* 4, pl. 154.

London B 171.

London B 257. *ABV* 401; *CVA* 5, pl. 208, 3.

London B 353. Fig. 3; *ABV* 535; *CVA* 8, pl. 356, 5.

London B 651.

London E 58. *ARV*² 467.

London E 132.

London E 149. *ARV*² 1301; *CVA* 5, pl. 223.

London E 159. Fig. 12; *ARV*² 24; *CVA* 7, pl. 322.

London E 171. *ARV*² 579; *CVA* 7, pl. 326, 2.

London E 172. *ARV*² 565; *CVA* 7, pl. 307, 2.

London E 177. *CVA* 7, pl. 331.

London E 178. *ARV*² 503; *CVA* 7, pl. 331.

London E 191. *ARV*² 1119; *CVA* 8, pl. 361.

London E 214. *ARV*² 1082; *CVA* 8, pl. 364. 6.

London E 271. Fig. 5; *ARV*² 1039; *Para* 398, 443; *CVA* 4, pl. 176.

London E 274. *ARV*² 604; *CVA* 4, pl. 178.

London E 301. *ARV*² 647.

London E 326. *ARV*² 534.

London E 330. *ARV*² 842; *CVA* 7, pl. 313, 3a.

London E 341. *ARV*² 668; *CVA* 7, pl. 318.

London E 381.

London E 390. *ARV*² 1148.

London E 391. *ARV*² 1136.

London E 400. *ARV*² 1176.

London E 445. *ARV*² 217; *CVA* 4, pl. 186.

London E 454. *CVA* 4, pl. 189, 1b.

London E 455. *CVA* 4, pl. 189, 2b.

London E 456. *CVA* 4, pl. 189, 3b.

London E 461. *ARV*² 601.

London E 514. *ARV*² 210.

London E 525. *ARV*² 754; Van Hoorn, *Choes*, pl. 196, cat. no. 629.

London E 542. *ARV*² 853.

London E 787. *ARV*² 870; *CVA* 5, pl. 233, 2.

London E 815. *ARV*² 125.

London 1916.6-10.501, fragments of a lyre.

London 1920.3-15.1.

London 1920.6-13.2. *ARV*² 1190.

London 1921.7-10.2. *ARV*² 1060; *CVA* 8, pl. 358. See chap. 5, fig. 11.

London 459, cornelian pseudo-scarab. Boardman, *Greek Gems*, no. 316.

London 1225, Locrian relief.

London, drachma from Pordosilene. Anson pt. 6, pl. 5, no. 351.

London, tetradrachm from Abdera. Anson pt. 6, pl. 3, no. 192.

London, stater from Kalymna, 6th century. Jenkins, *Ancient Greek Coins*, pp. 30 and 32.

Los Angeles 48.25. *CVA* 18, pl. 870.

Madrid 11158. *ARV*² 649; *CVA* 2, pl. 71, 2.

Madrid 11268. *ARV²* 473; *CVA* 2, pl. 58, 4a.

Mainz 91. *CVA* 15, pl. 739, 2 and 4; *Para* 289.

Milan C 354. *CVA* 51, pll. 2275, 1, and 2276, 1. See chap. 5, fig. 9.

Munich 2306. *CVA* 12, pll. 560 and 563.

Munich 2323. *ARV²* 571; *CVA* 20, pl. 928.

Munich 2363. *ARV²* 853; *CVA* 6, pll. 272, 1, and 274, 1.

Munich 2413. *ARV²* 495; *CVA* 20, pll. 967, 969, and 970.

Munich 2421. Fig. 28; *ARV²* 23; *CVA* 20, pll. 937 and 938.

Munich 3268 (Apulian). Arias and Hirmer, pll. 236–37.

Mykonos 970. *ARV²* 261. *Ecole Française d'Athènes* 21, *Délos,* pll. 5–7.

Mykonos, hydria fragments. *ARV²* 572, 86; *Ecole Française d'Athènes* 21, *Délos,* pl. 26, 62.

Naples, Roman copy of relief, 5th century, Orpheus with Eurydice and Hermes (?). *Hesperia* 33 (1964), pl. 12d and pp. 76ff.

New York L 68.142.15. *Bulletin of the Met. Mus. of Art* 27 (1968–69), cover, frontispiece.

New York L 1970.32.6.

New York 06.11.29. *ARV²* 777. G. M. A. Richter and M. J. Milne, *Shapes and Names,* fig. 99.

New York 07.286.47. *ARV²* 175 and 1631; G. M. A. Richter and L. F. Hall, *RFAV,* pl. 10.

New York 07.286.78. Fig. 30; *ARV²* 227; Richter and Hall, *RFAV,* pl. 21.

New York 08.258.5, bronze figure. G. M. A. Richter, *Handbook of the Greek Collection,* pl. 48c and p. 67.

New York 08.258.57. Richter and Hall, *RFAV,* pl. 56.

New York 12.236.2. *ARV²* 989; Richter and Hall, *RFAV,* pl. 117.

New York 16.52. *ARV²* 1321; Richter and Hall, *RFAV,* pl. 160.

New York 22.139.72. *ARV²* 781; Richter and Hall, *RFAV,* pl. 107.

New York 23.160.54. *ARV²* 441; Richter and Hall, *RFAV,* pl. 64.

New York 24.97.30. Fig. 4; *ARV²* 1079; Richter, *Handbook of the Greek Collection,* pl. 82c.

New York 25.189.2. *ARV²* 988; Richter and Hall, *RFAV,* pl. 120.

New York 26.60.79. Fig. 19; *ARV²* 891; Richter and Hall, *RFAV,* pl. 81.

New York 28.167. *ARV²* 890; Richter and Hall, *RFAV,* pll. 76, 178.

New York 40.11.22. *ARV²* 965; *Bulletin of the Met. Mus. of Art* 36, 123.

New York 41.162.33. *ARV²* 834; *CVA* 1, pl. 50.

New York 41.162.86. *ARV²* 564; *CVA* 8, pl. 405.

New York 41.162.155. *ARV²* 502 and 1656; *CVA* 1, pl. 38.

New York 41.162.169. *CVA* 8, pl. 408, 1.

New York 52.11.4. *ARV²* 437; *Bulletin of the Met. Mus. of Art* (1952–53) 101.

New York 57.12.12. *Para* 234.

New York 58.11.1. *ARV²* 835.

New York 63.11.4. *Para* 158.

New York 96.18.76. Richter and Hall, *RFAV,* pl. 78.

New York 96.18.143.

New York, cornelian scaraboid from Cyprus. Richter, *Cat. of Engraved Gems,* (1956), no. 41. Boardman, *Greek Gems,* no. 359.

Nicosia C 430. *Proceedings of the British Academy* (Athens) 33, 3ff.

Once Northampton, Castle Ashby 67. *ARV²* 1193; *CVA* 15, pl. 698.

Once Northampton, Castle Ashby 74. *ARV²* 1186; *CVA* 15, pl. 706.

Oxford 1914.734. *ARV²* 362; *CVA* 3, pl. 123, 4.

Oxford 1916.13. Fig. 20; *ARV²* 1259; *CVA* 3, pll. 96 and 103.

Oxford 1920.104(266). *ARV²* 1000. P. Gardner, *Catalogue of the Greek Vases in the Ashmolean Museum* (1893), 21; pl. 20, 1. See chap. 6, fig. 5.

Oxford 1929.4. *ARV²* 410; *CVA* 9, pl. 416, 7.

Oxford 1965.118. *ABV* 335; *CVA* 14, pl. 649–50.

Oxford 1965.125. *Para* 295; *CVA* 14, pl. 631, 4.

Oxford 311 (1889.1015). Fig. 10; *CVA* 3, pl. 131, 1.

Oxford 312. *CVA* 3, pl. 125.

Oxford 530. *CVA* 3, pl. 124; *ARV²* 1061.

Oxford 535 (G. 292). Fig. 2; *CVA* 3, pl. 127.

Oxford, Miss. Once Robinson Coll. *ARV²* 238; *CVA* 6, pl. 267.

Palermo 97. *CVA* 50, pl. 2217.

Paris B 115, terra-cotta. Seated man playing lyre. *Cat. raisonné des figurines et reliefs* I (1954).

Paris Cab. Méd. 846. *ARV²* 1050; Caskey and Beazley, *Attic Vase Paintings,* text vol. 2, p. 37.

Paris CA 74. *Para* 285; *CVA* 26, pl. 1155, 1.

Paris F 232. *ABV* 281; *CVA* 5, pl. 210, 4–7.

Paris F 309. *CVA* 2, pl. 76, 3.

Paris G 17. *ARV²* 62; *CVA* 17, pl. 760, 3.

Paris G 162. *ARV²* 186; *CVA* 2, pl. 83, 8.

Paris G 226. *ARV²* 250; *CVA* 9, pl. 423, 4 and 9.

Paris G 436. *ARV²* 1014; *CVA* 12, pl. 517.

Paris G 486. *ARV²* 1163; *CVA* 8, pl. 373, 9.

Paris G 552 bis. *CVA* 12, pl. 520, 8.

Paris M 2847, scaraboid.

Paris, Musée Rodin TC 232. *CVA* 16, pl. 707, 3–4.

Paris, Musée Rodin 993. Fig. 15; *ARV²* 564; *CVA* 16, pl. 710, 1.

Paris, Petit Palais 308. *ARV²* 1040; *CVA* 15, pl. 657, 4–8. See chap. 5, fig. 16.

Paris, Petit Palais 319. *ARV²* 1112 and 1703; *CVA* 15, pl. 658.

Philadelphia, Univ. of Pa. 30-33-130.

Plovdiv 298. *ARV²* 1187. Van Hoorn, *Choes,* pl. 241 and note 114.

Rhodes 12887. *ARV²* 1116; *CVA* 10, pl. 506, 4.

Rome Mus. Capit. 122. *ABV* 536; *CVA* 36, pl. 1632, 4.

Rome, Vatican 432. *ABV* 154; *Para* 64, 48; Semni Karouzou, *The Amasis Painter,* pl. 41.

Rome, Vatican, hydria. *ARV²* 209, 166. Erika Simon, *Die Götter der Griechen,* p. 140, pl. 133.

Rome Villa Giulia 3584. *ARV²* 1028; *CVA* 1, pl. 27, 2.

San Simeon 5498.

San Simeon 5614.

Schwerin KG 706. *ARV*² 618; *CVA* [DDR] 1, pll. 35 and 37.

Schwerin KG 707. *CVA* [DDR] 1, pl. 23; *ARV*² 565, 41.

Schwerin KG 708. Fig. 17; *ARV*² 863; *CVA* [DDR] 1, pll. 24 and 26.

Sèvres 2038. *ARV*² 697; *CVA* 13, pl. 547, 7.

Syracuse 17427. *ARV*² 1184; *CVA* 17, pl. 824, 4.

Syracuse 23794. *ARV*² 1144; *CVA* 17, pl. 825, 1.

Syracuse 36330. Fig. 11; *ARV*² 1062; *CVA* 17, pl. 839, 1 and 2.

Taranto 54384. *ARV*² 553; *CVA* 35, pl. 1577.

Tarquinia 640. *CVA* 26, pl. 1180, 5.

Thessaloniki, black-figured squat lekythos.

Toledo 64.126. Fig. 24; *CVA* 17, pl. 836, 1. See chap. 5, fig. 4.

Toronto 365. *ARV*² 565; Robinson, Harcum, and Iliffe, *Cat. of Greek Vases in the R.O.M.,* pl. 64.

Trieste S 424. *ARV*² 217; *CVA* 43, pl. 1915.

Tübingen S/10 1630b, Boeotian. *CVA* 36, pl. 1773, 7.

Vienna IV, 143. Fig. 21. Karl Schefold, *The Art of Classical Greece,* pl. 34.

Vienna 697. *ARV*² 1075; *CVA* 3, pl. 115, 1 and 2.

Vienna 947. *ARV*² 567; *CVA* 2, pl. 91, 1–2.

Vienna 1093. *ARV*² 357; *CVA* 2, pl. 76.

Vienna 1788. *ARV*² 787; *CVA* 1, pl. 16, 1–3.

Vienna 3700. *ARV*² 882; *CVA* 1, pl. 19.

Vienna 3733. *CVA* 3, pl. 114; *ARV*² 1067.

Warsaw 198512. *CVA* 6, pll. 264 and 266; *ARV*² 1682.

Warsaw, once Goluchow 23. *CVA* 1, pl. 14, 4.

Warsaw, once Goluchow 64. *ARV*² 982; *CVA* 1, pl. 40.

Washington 136373. *ARV*² 781; *AJA* 52 (1948), pl. 37, pp. 424–25.

Wuppertal, private coll. Heydt Museum, *Antike Kunst aus Wuppertaler Privatbesitz,* no. 49.

Würzburg H 5169. *ABV* 195; *Para* 80; *CVA* 39, pl. 1925, 1 and 2.

CHAPTER FIVE

Adolphseck 56. *ARV*² 253–54; *CVA* 11, pl. 518, 3–4.

Adolphseck 74. *ARV*² 371; *CVA* 11, pl. 522.

Adria Bc.45. *ARV*² 176; *CVA* 28, pl. 1251, 4.

Adria B 248. *CVA* 28, pl. 1280, 1b.

Adria B 317. *CVA* 28, pl. 1250, 5.

Adria B 318. *ARV*² 469; *CVA* 28, pl. 1267, 5.

Altenburg 301. *ARV*² 1046; *CVA* 18, pl. 846–47.

Athens Agora P 42, 85-81. *ARV*² 415.

Athens Agora P 7242. *ARV*² 566.

Athens Agora P 12960. *ARV*² 779.

Athens Agora P 24115. *ARV*² 176; *Hesperia* 24 (1955), pl. 33d.

Athens Acropolis 20. *ARV*² 385, 229; Graef and Langlotz, *Die antiken Vasen von der Akropolis,* ser. 2, pl. 1.

Athens Acropolis 229. *ARV*² 1626; Graef and Langlotz, *Die antiken Vasen von der Akropolis,* ser. 2, pl. 12.

Athens Acropolis 372. *ARV*² 820; Graef and Langlotz, *Die antiken Vasen von der Akropolis,* ser. 2, pl. 23.

Athens Kerameikos HS 89.

Athens 735. Stele from Vonitsa.

Athens 1263. *ARV*² 1324.

Athens 1792. *ARV*² 686.

Athens 2022. *ARV*² 729.

Athens 12777.

Athens 15372.

Athens 15881, Melian relief.

Athens 17190.

Athens 17918. Fig. 18; *ARV*² 1040, 19.

Bari 4395. Van Hoorn, *Choes,* pl. 408.

Bari, column krater.

Basel 1906.301. *ARV*² 174; Van Hoorn, *Choes,* 32–33 and pl. 109.

Basel 421. Fig. 21; *Para* 128; *ARV*² 294, 21; G. M. A. Richter, *ARFV: A Survey,* fig. 36.

Bayrakli. Old Smyrna dinos sherd. See chap. 2, fig. 1.

Berlin Sa 481. *ARV*² 1262; *CVA* 22, pl. 1037, 3.

Berlin 2220. *ARV*² 697.

Berlin 2309. *ARV*² 373; *CVA* 21, pl. 998, 3.

Berlin 2351.

Berlin 2532. *ARV*² 1253; *CVA* 22, pl. 1041, 1.

Berlin 4221. *ARV*² 61; *CVA* 21, pl. 983, 3.

Bologna C 100. *ARV*² 508; *CVA* 5, pl. 220.

Bologna 106. *CVA* 5, pll. 246, 4 and 247, 1.

Bologna 271. *ARV*² 825; *CVA* 33, pll. 1492–93.

Bologna 308. *ARV*² 1029; *CVA* 27, pll. 1243–44.

Bologna 396. *ARV*² 801; *CVA* 33, pl. 1489.

Bonn 1216, 33–38.198. *CVA* 1, pl. 33, 2.

Boston 01.8078. *ARV*² 790; Caskey and Beazley, *Attic Vase Paintings in the Museum of Fine Arts, Boston,* pl. 20, 45.

Boston 10.193. *ARV*² 1567; Caskey and Beazley, *Attic Vase Paintings,* pl. 71, 136.

Boston 13.194. *ARV*² 447; Caskey and Beazley, pl. 84, 2.

Boston 13.197. *ARV*² 630; Caskey and Beazley, pl. 18, 40.

Boston 13.199. *Para* 393; Caskey and Beazley, pl. 51, 99.

Boston 27.671, East Greek chalcedony scaraboid. Boardman, *Archaic Greek Gems,* pl. 11, 172; p. 73.

Boston 27.760, sardonyx scarab. Boardman, *Archaic Greek Gems,* pl. 19, 279; p. 99.

Boston 63.1246. Fig. 17; *Para* 373; *AJA* 70 (1966), pl. 4.

Boston 91.227. *Para* 343; *AJA* 70 (1966), pl. 8.

Boston 95.27. *ARV*² 325; Caskey and Beazley, pl. 41, 79.

Brunswick 219. *ARV*² 1037; *CVA* 4, pl. 169.

Brussels A 1652; *ABV* 387; *CVA* 3, pl. 119, 5.

Brussels A 3091. Fig. 22; *ARV*² 1144; *CVA* 3, pl. 128, 2.

Brussels A 3094. *ARV*² 842; *CVA* 3, pl. 129, 3b.

Brussels R 255. Fig. 6; *ARV*² 670; *CVA* 2, pl. 74, 1.

Bryn Mawr P-192. *CVA* 13, pl. 585, 3.

Bucharest 03231. *ARV*² 1296, nos. 3, 26; *CVA* 1, pl. 32.

Cambridge, Fitzwilliam GR 19.1937. *CVA* 11, pl. 517.

Cambridge, Fitzwilliam G 150. *ARV*² 697.

Cambridge, Fitzwilliam 4.1943. *ARV*² 935.

Cambridge, Harvard 1959.125. *ARV*² 566; *CVA* 6, pl. 271.

Cambridge, Harvard 1959.188. *ARV*² 566. See chap. 4, fig. 14.

Cambridge, Harvard 1960.236. Fig. 2; *ARV*² 185.

Cleveland 24197. Fig. 8; *ARV*² 564; *CVA* 15, pll. 707–08.

Cleveland 26.549. Fig. 13; *ARV*² 379; *CVA* 15, pl. 706.

Compiegne 1065. *ABV* 388; *CVA* 3, pl. 108, 1.

Copenhagen ABc 1021. *ARV*² 1035; *CVA* 4, pl. 148.

Copenhagen 596. *ARV*² 610; *CVA* 4, pl. 155.

Copenhagen Chr. VIII 875. *CVA* 3, pl. 146, 1.

Copenhagen 3632. *CVA* 6, pl. 236, 1.

Copenhagen 3635. *CVA* 6, pl. 236, 3.

Copenhagen 3880. *ARV*² 373; *CVA* 3, pll. 143–44.

Copenhagen 13365. Fig. 14; *ARV*² 185, 32; *CVA* 8, pl. 336, 1.

Erlangen 454. *ARV*² 339.

Ferrara T. 127 (inv. 3033). *ARV*² 1171; *CVA* 37, pl. 1656; *Spina*, pl. 108. See chap. 6, fig. 11b.

Ferrara 2812, T 153. *ARV*² 290; *CVA* 37, pl. 1679, 3.

Fiesole, unnumbered. *CVA* 57, pl. 2555.

Florence B 324. *ARV*² 1258; *CVA* 8, pl. 397, 324. Leipzig T727 is a part of this vase; see below.

Florence 3920. *ARV*² 341; *CVA* 30, pl. 1360.

Florence 3987. *CVA* 13, pl. 617, 1.

Florence 4017. *ARV*² 655; *CVA* 13, pl. 613, 1.

Florence, Campanian kylix. *CVA* 8, pl. 389, 226–27.

Florence, kylix fragments. *CVA* 8, pl. 379, 40.

Frankfurt Mus. für Khw. WM 03. Fig. 1; *Para* 140; *CVA* 25, pl. 1205, 1.

Frankfurt 409. *ARV*² 202; *CVA* 30, pl. 1460, 3.

Gela 67. Fig. 10; *ARV*² 384; *CVA* 54, pl. 2403, 3.

Gela 126/B, lekythos. *CVA* 54, pl. 2392, 3.

Gotha 53. *ARV*² 1049; *CVA* 29, pl. 1386.

Gotha 2476. *Para* 168; *ABV* 384; *CVA* 24, pl. 1162.

The Hague, Scheurleer 623. *CVA* 2, pl. 82, 4.

Kassel 435. *ARV*² 1083, 1; *CVA* 35, pl. 1715, 3.

Leipzig T 727. Van Hoorn, *Choes*, fig. 365. Florence B 324 is a part of the same vase; see above.

Location unknown, once Paris Market (Mikas), oinochoe. *ARV*² 544.

Location unknown, once Robinson Coll., oinochoe. *CVA* 7, pl. 306, 1.

London E 18. *ARV*² 62–63. Schefold, *Die Bildnisse der antiken Dichter, Redner und Denker* (Basel, n.d.), 51, fig. 1.

London E 44. Fig. 12; *ARV*² 318; Charbonneaux and Villard, *Archaic Greek Art*, pl. 394.

London E 64. *ARV*² 455.

London E 68. *Para* 365 and 367; *ARV*² 371; G. M. A. Richter, *Furniture of the Greeks*, fig. 332.

London E 171. *ARV*² 579; *CVA* 7, pl. 326, 2.

London E 266. *ARV*² 198; *CVA* 4, pl. 173.

London E 308. *ARV*² 673; *CVA* 7, pl. 305, 2a.

London E 314. *CVA* 7, pl. 307, 2a.

London E 527. Van Hoorn, *Choes*, pl. 96 and cat. no. 631.

London E 767. *ARV*² 31; *CVA* 8, pl. 379.

London E 786. *ARV*² 1537; *CVA* 5, pl. 232, 1.

London 27.760, sardonyx scarab. Boardman, *Archaic Greek Gems*, pl. XIX, no. 279.

London 493, cornelian scaraboid. Boardman, *Archaic Greek Gems*, IX, no. 133.

London 622, terra-cotta relief from Melos.

London 1921, 7–10, 2. Fig. 11; *ARV*² 1060; *CVA* 8, pl. 358.

London 1946.11-8.1, cornelian scarab. Boardman, *Archaic Greek Gems*, pl. XI, no. 163.

London, Boeotian red-figured cup. *AM* 65, 1940, pl. 3.

London, coin from Teos, 4th century. British Mus. Anson cat. 363.

Madrid 11009. *CVA* 2, pll. 63 and 65.

Madrid 11122. *ARV*² 564; *CVA* 2, pl. 66, 2.

Madrid 11268. *ARV*² 473; *CVA* 2, pl. 61, 2.

Maplewood, N.J., Noble Coll. calyx krater. *ARV*² 1078, 7. *Ancient Art from New York Private Collections*, pl. 85.

Milan 842. *CVA* 31, pl. 1395, 2.

Milan Coll. "H.A." C 354. Fig. 9; *CVA* 51, pl. 2275, 1.

Munich 1416. *ABV* 367; *CVA* 3, pl. 144. See chap. 6, fig. 2.

Munich 2311. *ARV*² 197; *CVA* 12, pll. 571 and 573.

Munich 2317. *ARV*² 226; *CVA* 20, pll. 926–27.

Munich 2339. *ARV*² 637; *CVA* 6, pll. 249 and 252.

Munich 2346. *ARV*² 565; *CVA* 6, pl. 266, 2.

Munich 2404. Fig. 20; *CVA* 20, pl. 959.

Munich 2410. *ARV*² 1069; *CVA* 20, pl. 966, 3.

Munich 2416. Fig. 15; *Para* 367; *ARV*² 385; G. M. A. Richter, *Greek Portraits*, 1, fig. 252.

Munich 2424. *ARV*² 129; *CVA* 20, pl. 943, 1.

Munich 6452. *ARV*² 787; *CVA* 20, pl. 946, 2, 10.

New York 06.1021.178. *ARV*² 1077; Richter and Hall, *RFAV*, pl. 112.

New York 06.1021.188. *ARV*² 413; Richter and Hall, *RFAV*, pl. 45.

New York 07.286.85. Fig. 19; *ARV*² 632; Richter and Hall, *RFAV*, pl. 109.

New York 09.221.41. *ARV*² 646; Richter and Hall, *RFAV*, pll. 32 and 169.

New York 16.52. *ARV*² 1321; Richter and Hall, *RFAV*, pl. 160.

New York 22.139.32. *ARV*² 210; Richter and Hall, *RFAV*, pll. 17, 177.

New York 37.11.19. Fig. 7; Van Hoorn, *Choes*, pl. 117.

New York 41.162.6. *ARV*² 456; *CVA* 8, pl. 397. 2.

New York 41.162.7. *CVA* 8, pl. 406, 3.

New York 41.162.13. *ABV* 538; *CVA* 1, pl. 27, 8.

New York 56.171.52. *ARV*² 1051; *Bulletin of the Metropolitan Museum of Art* 15 (1957), 178, 1.

New York 41.162.2. Fig. 5; *CVA* 1, pl. 23.

Oxford G.265. *ARV*² 63; *CVA* 3, pl. 97.

Oxford 1885.656. *ABV* 484; *CVA* 14, pl. 638, 3.

Oxford 1892.1490, cornelian scarab. See chap. 2.

Oxford 1965.106. *ARV*² 646.

Oxford 1966.704. *ARV*² 1060; *Para* 445; Beazley, *Ashmole Catalog*, pl. 38, 262.

Paestum, tomb painting. Gisela M. A. Richter, *Perspective in Greek and Roman Art*, pl. 109.

Palermo V 666. *ARV²* 211; *CVA* 14, pl. 676.

Paris AM 1064bis. *ARV²* 508; *CVA* 12, pl. 517, 8.

Paris C 14460.

Paris F 207. *CVA* 4, pl. 159, 4.

Paris F 216. *ABV* 389; *CVA* 5, pl. 205, 1, and p. 22, notes for pl. 39.

Paris F 314. *Para* 170; *ABV* 388; *CVA* 2, pl. 78.

Paris G 4bis. *ARV²* 125; *CVA* 28, pl. 1279, 1.

Paris G 30. *ARV²* 15; *CVA* 8, pl. 366, 4.

Paris G 50. *ARV²* 188; *CVA* 9, pl. 431.

Paris G 57. *ARV²* 188; *CVA* 12, pl. 514, 5.

Paris G 82. *ARV²* 98; *CVA* 28, pl. 1283, 1.

Paris G 94. *ARV²* 134.

Paris G 139–140. *ARV²* 120; *CVA* 28, pl. 1272, 2.

Paris G 174. *ARV²* 205–06; *CVA* 2, pl. 82, 2.

Paris G 211. *ARV²* 653; *CVA* 9, pl. 418, 3–4.

Paris G 220. *ARV²* 280; *CVA* 9, pl. 421, 3.

Paris G 369. *ARV²* 577; *CVA* 4, pl. 170.

Paris G 422. *ARV²* 1019; *CVA* 5, pl. 222, 6.

Paris G 543. *ARV²* 1059; *CVA* 12, pl. 523, 2.

Paris S 1335. *ARV²* 83; *CVA* 17, pl. 767, 3.

Paris, Petit Palais 308. Fig. 16; *ARV²* 1040; *CVA* 15, pl. 657, 5–6.

Paris, Petit Palais 326. *CVA* 15, pl. 661, 5.

Rhodes 13.129. *ARV²* 564; *CVA* Italy 9, pl. 455.

Rhodes 13.210. *ABV* 344; *CVA* Italy 9, pl. 446, 5.

Rome, Mus. Cap. 56. *Para* 167; *CVA* 36, pl. 1631, 2.

Rome, Mus. Cap. 176. *CVA* 39, pl. 1754.

San Simeon 5630.

Schwerin KG 707. *ARV²* 565, 41; *CVA* [DDR] 1; pl. 23, 2.

Syracuse 23794. *ARV²* 1144; *CVA* 17, pl. 825, 1.

Syracuse 26967. *ARV²* 36; Schefold, *Die Bildnisse der antiken Dichter* 51, fig. 3.

Syracuse 36330. *ARV²* 1062; *CVA* 17, pl. 839. See chap. 4, fig. 29.

Toledo 64.126. Fig. 4; *CVA* 17, pl. 836, 1.

Torino 5776. *ABV* 214, 50; *CVA* 40, pl. 1786.

Toronto 356 (919.5.21). Fig. 3; *ARV²* 464.

Urbana, Ill. Krannert 70-8-7, kylix.

Vienna 823. *ARV²* 781; *CVA* 2, pl. 98, 3.

Vienna 1104. *ARV²* 1078; *CVA* 3, pl. 107.

Vienna 1777. *CVA* 1, pl. 3, 1.

Vienna 3693. *CVA* 1, pl. 3, 3.

Warsaw 142333. *Para* 246; *ARV²* 300; *CVA* 1, pl. 16, 3.

Warsaw 142465. *ARV²* 1019; *CVA* 1, pl. 26.

Warsaw, Czartoryski 77. *ARV²* 1253; *CVA* 1, pl. 38b.

Wuppertal, private coll. Heydt Museum, *Antike Kunst aus Wuppertaler Privatbesitz*, no. 49.

Würzburg 521. *ARV²* 1046. Wegner, *Musikleben*, pl. 20.

Würzburg 4937. *ARV²* 871, 95; *CVA* 46, pl. 2219.

Chapter Six

Athens Agora P 1544. *ABV* 518. *Hesperia* 15 (1949), 290, pl. 39.

Athens Agora, Pnyx P 139. *Hesperia* suppl. 10, 49–50, pl. 19, no. 213.

Athens 911. See chap. 2, fig. 2.

Athens 1183. *ARV²* 1123.

Athens 1241. Fig. 6; *CVA* 2, pl. 77.

Athens 1469. Fig. 12; *ARV²* 1084.

Athens 14628.

Athens 14791. *ARV²* 1126.

Athens 14909. *Revue Archeologique*, ser. 6, vol. 35 (1950), 40–75, figs. 8 and 12.

Athens 15190. Fig. 9; *ARV²* 860; formerly Acropolis 439.

Athens 15308. *ARV²* 1249.

Athens, unnumbered pyxis. *Para* 479, 91bis.

Basel, P. Von der Mühll, lekythos from the Meidias workshop. Schefold, *Meisterwerke griechischer Kunst*, pp. 232–33, no. 287.

Berlin Staatl. Mus. 2391. Fig. 15; Herbig, *AM* 54 (1929), 171, fig. 3, no. I-10.

Berlin 3291. Herbig, *AM* 54 (1929), Beilage 56, pp. 168–69.

Bologna 151. *Para* 113; *ARV²* 4; *CVA* 33, pl. 1470, 5.

Bologna 362. *ARV²* 1000.

Boston 27.669, cornelian scarab. Boardman, *Archaic Greek Gems*, pl. 13, 211; p. 82.

Boston 98.887. Fig. 3; *Para* 416; *ARV²* 774. Caskey and Beazley, *Attic Vase Paintings*, pl. 15, fig. 37.

Bowdoin 15.46. *ARV²* 857–58.

Cambridge, Harvard 1925.30.42. Fig. 8a; *ARV²* 1048; *CVA* 1, pl. 16.

Cambridge, Harvard 1959.188. *ARV²* 566, 8.

Copenhagen 7776. *ABV* 1199; *CVA* 4, pl. 166, 4.

Dresden 332. *ARV²* 1206. Adrienne Lezzi-Hafter, *Der Schuwalow-Maler*, pl. 82 c and d.

Ferrara T. 127 (inv. 3033). Fig. 11b; *ARV²* 1171; *CVA* 37, pl. 1656; Aurigemma, *Scavi di Spina*, pll. 2–15; *Spina*, pl. 108.

Florence 4006. *ARV²* 1062; *CVA* 13, pl. 640, 3.

Florence 4014. *ARV²* 1060; *CVA* 13, pl. 643. See chap. 4, fig. 16.

Florence, unnumbered frag. *CVA* 8, pl. 388, 239.

Heidelberg E 34, Etruscan pyxis. *CVA* 23, pl. 1096, 2.

Heidelberg 26.90. *CVA* 23, pl. 1109, 3.

Heidelberg, terra-cotta relief. *Münchener Jahrbuch* 3 (1926), 267, pl. 8.

Jena 390. See chap. 7.

Lecce 572. *Para* 389; *ARV²* 564; *CVA* 4, pl. 154.

Leningrad B 3128. *Otchët*, 1903, p. 165, fig. 322.

Leningrad 711. *ARV²* 1123; *Österreichisches Archäologisches Institut* (Vienna) *Jahreshefte* 8 (1905), 39, fig. 7.

Leningrad 732. *Para* 516; *ARV²* 857. Anna A. Peredolskaya, *Krasnofigurnye atticheskie vazy*, pl. 129.

Leningrad 798. *Para* 513; *ARV²* 574, 4. Peredolskaya, *Krasnofigurnye atticheskie vazy*, pl. 73.

Leningrad, lekanis lid. Talcott and Philippaki, *Hesperia* suppl. 10, p. 50.

Leningrad, seal stone. Boardman, *Greek Gems*, no. 600.

CHAPTER SEVEN

Athens 12254. *ARV*² 1426–27.

Athens 12266. *AM* 65 (1940), pl. 15, fig. 2, p. 16.

Athens 12740.

Athens 12894. Metzger, *BCH* 66–67 (1942–43), 234, pl. 13.

Athens 14791. *ARV*² 1126.

Athens 14901. Boháč, *Kerčské vázy*, pl. 17.

Athens 15104, votive bronze. Fig. 6. Svoronos, *Das Athener Nationalmuseum*, p. 38; pl. 9, no. 5.

Athens, Hellenistic stele. Svoronos no. 482, pl. 255 and p. 681.

Barcelona, pelike fragment. *CVA* 3, pl. 131, 1a.

Bari 873. Smith, *Funerary Symbolism*, pl. 23.

Bari 3720. Trendall and Cambitoglou, *RFVA*, pl. 364, 1, and p. 927.

Bari 6270. Fig. 2b; Trendall and Cambitoglou, *RFVA*, pl. 154, 3–5.

Bari, Lagioia Coll. Trendall and Cambitoglou, *RFVA*, pl. 386, 3, and p. 985, 272.

Bari, Perrone Coll. 14. Trendall and Cambitoglou, *RFVA*, pl. 190, 3, and p. 523.

Basel, private coll., skyphoid pyxis. Beck, *Album of Greek Education*, pl. 72.

Basel S 29. Fig. 4; Schmidt, Trendall, and Cambitoglou, pl. 8.

Basel S 34. Schmidt, Trendall, and Cambitoglou, pl. 26.

Basel S 40. Schmidt, Trendall, and Cambitoglou, pl. 11.

Berkeley 8.935. Beazley, *Etruscan Vase Painting*, p. 107, pl. 25, 1.

Berkeley 8.997. Beazley, *Etruscan Vase Painting*, 84–85, pl. 15, 11.

Berlin Staatl. Mus. 2391. See chap. 6, fig. 15.

Berlin 2402. Boháč, *Kerčské vázy*, pl. 2; *ARV*² 1152.

Berlin 3291. Herbig, "Griechische Harfen," *AM* 54 (1929), Beilage 56, pp. 168–69.

Berlin 4532. Trendall, *Paestan Pottery*, pl. 24b.

Bonn 98. Cambitoglou and Trendall, *ARFVP*, p. 50, no. 2, pl. 29.

Bonn 100. Trendall and Cambitoglou, *RFVA*, pl. 150, 1; p. 417, no. 14.

Boston 00.360. Fig. 13; Caskey and Beazley, II, 44.

Boston 01.8101. *Trojan War in Greek Art*, 1965 Mus. F. A. Calendar, fig. 49a.

Boston 01.8255. Van Hoorn, *Choes*, fig. 112 and p. 113, no. 380.

Boston 10.206. *ARV*² 1324; Van Hoorn, *Choes*, fig. 154 and p. 113, no. 386.

Boston 10.234. Trendall and Cambitoglou, *RFVA*, pl. 183, 4, and p. 513.

Boston 13.207. Comstock and Vermeule, *Greek, Etruscan and Roman Bronzes*, p. 268, pl. 387.

Boston 28.108. *ARV*² 1340, 2.

Boston 61.112. 1962 Boston F. A. Calendar, fig. for July.

Boston 97.300, Hellenistic terra-cotta from Euboea.

Brussels R 227. *CVA* 2, pl. 88, 7a.

Brusuglio, private coll., 9. Trendall and Cambitoglou, *RFVA*, pl. 183, 2, and p. 510.

Cambridge, Fitzwilliam GR 147.1899, 160.1899, 161.1899. *ARV*² 1333; *CVA* 11, pl. 506.

Cambridge, Mus. Class. Arch. UP 143.

Cleveland 28.601. Trendall and Cambitoglou, *RFVA*, pl. 306, 1, and p. 819.

Cleveland 30.522, marble relief, Augustan period.

Copenhagen Chr. VIII 316. Fig. 16; *CVA* 6, pl. 264, 1a and c.

Copenhagen 3757. Trendall, *LCS* 2, pl. 149, 4, and 1, p. 184.

Eleusis, marble relief of two figures, one a bearded man with lyre.

Ferrara T. 406. *ARV*² 1452.

Florence 81947. Fig. 10; *ARV*² 1312; *CVA* 13, pll. 648–49.

Geneva, Chamay Coll. pelike. Trendall and Cambitoglou, *RFVA*, pl. 156, 1, and p. 426.

The Hague 2572. *CVA* 2, pl. 90, 1.

Heidelberg E 96. *CVA* 23, pl. 1103, 4.

Heidelberg 26.86. *CVA* 23, pl. 1111, 1.

Heidelberg 26.90. *CVA* 23, pl. 1109, 3.

Jena 390. *ARV*² 1511; Herbig, fig. 9, p. 182. Hahlund, *Vasen um Meidias*, pl. 2c.

Karlsruhe B 4. *CVA* 8, pl. 361.

Kassel T. 723. *CVA* 38, pl. 1874, 1.

Kavala 228, marble grave relief.

Leipzig Univ. T-716. Herbig, IV-2b, no. 2, p. 183.

Leningrad B 3128. *Otchët*, 1903, p. 165, fig. 322.

Leningrad St. 355. Macchioro, "I ceramisti," p. 293, fig. 20b.

Leningrad St. 426. Pensa, *Rappresentazioni*, pl. 9.

Leningrad St. 498. Pensa, *Rappresentazioni*, pl. 12.

Leningrad St. 1795. Boháč, *Kerčské vázy*, pl. 26.

Leningrad 875 EE. Winter, *Typen* II, 96, 4.

Leningrad 878 S, terra-cotta. Winter, *Typen* II, 95, 4.

Leningrad 988. See Leningrad St. 355.

Leningrad 2079. Trendall, *LCS*, pl. 237, 2, and p. 604.

Leningrad, gold ring. Boardman, *Greek Gems*, no. 721.

Leningrad, burnt scaraboid. Boardman, *Greek Gems*, no. 600.

Leningrad, burnt scarabold. Boardman, *Greek Gems*, no. 601.

Lentini, Sicilian krater. Trendall, *LCS*, pl. 228, 3, and p. 589.

Lindos, Rhodes 2355, 2918, 2919, terra-cotta figures of musicians. Blinkenberg, *Lindos* I, 2, pll. 110 and 135.

Lipari 749A. Smith, *Funerary Symbolism*, pl. 22a–c; Trendall, *LCS*, p. 635.

Location unknown, once Basel Market. Trendall and Cambitoglou, *RFVA*, pl. 185, 1, and p. 513.

Location unknown, once Berlin, Adolf Hitler, column krater. Trendall and Cambitoglou, *ARFVP of the Plain Style*, p. 35, pl. 12.

Location unknown, Fenicia fragment. Pensa, *Rappresentazioni* 47, fig. 8.

Location unknown, Lucanian oinochoe. Mayo, *The Art of South Italy: Vases from Magna Graecia*, p. 69.

Location unknown, once New New York, Kevorkian 71. Trendall, *LCS*, pl. 146, 1, and p. 380, cat. 3/125.

Location unknown, once Northampton 74, krater. *ARV²* 1186, 21; *CVA* 15, pl. 706, 1.

Location unknown, once Roman Market, alabastron. Trendall and Cambitoglou, *RFVA*, pl. 232, 7, and p. 606.

Location unknown. Herbig, IV-2b, no. 4, p. 184.

Location unknown, pelike. Herbig, IV-2b, no. 5, p. 184.

London C 352, Cypriote half-length statue.

London E 129. *ARV²* 1414; Metzger, *Representations* I, 115, no. 11; II, pl. 11, 2.

London E 228. Boháč, *Kerčské vázy*, pl. 8; Metzger, *Representations* II, pl. 11, 4. *CVA* 8, pl. 368, 3.

London E 502. *ARV²* 1156, 10.

London E 695, Lucanian squat lekythos.

London F 270. Pensa. *Rappresentazioni*, pl. 16; fig. 9, p. 49.

London F 271. Trendall and Cambitoglou, *RFVA*, pl. 147, 1, and pp. 415–16.

London F 309. Higgins and Winnington-Ingram, *JHS* 85 (1965), 69 (no photo).

London F 399. Higgins and Winnington-Ingram, *JHS* 85 (1965), 69 (no photo).

London G 21, Campanian squat lekythos. Trendall, *South Italian Vase Painting*, pl. 16c.

London G 151, Etruscan askos. E. A. Zervoudaki, *AM* 93 (1968), 1–88, pl. 28.

London R 1068, ring. Boardman, *Greek Gems*, no. 781.

London 26, wall painting from Herculaneum.

London 564, cornelian pendant. Boardman, *Greek Gems*, no. 615.

London 1153. Boardman, *Greek Gems*, no. 605.

London 1380, Roman copy of Hellenistic statue of Apollo.

London 1917.7-25.2. *ARV²* 1410; Metzger, *Representations* I, 171, no. 26; and II, pl. 24.

London 1919.6–20.7, Tanagra figure. Fig. 19.

London 1968.11-29.1, terra-cotta from Egypt.

London 2191, Hellenistic marble relief. *E.A.A.* I, 542 (upper zone).

London, coin from Mytilene. Anson cat. 333.

London, coin from Teos. Anson cat. 363.

London, cornelian ring stone. Walters cat. 1153. Boardman, *Greek Gems*, no. 605.

Los Angeles 50.8.25. *CVA* 18, pl. 883, 2.

Madrid 11034. Trendall, *LCS*, pl. 49, 3; cat. no. 511.

Madrid 11078. Trendall and Cambitoglou, *RFVA* 93, pl. 32, 1–2.

Madrid 11223. Fig. 12; Trendall and Webster, *Illustrations*, pl. IV, 7b; Trendall and Cambitoglou, *RFVA*, p. 196.

Malibu 77 AE 13. Trendall and Cambitoglou, *RFVA*, pl. 323, 3, and p. 863.

Mannheim, Reiss Cg 143. *CVA* 13, pl. 630, 1–2.

Mannheim, Reiss Cg 315. *CVA* 13, pl. 627, 5–6.

Maplewood, N.J. Noble Coll., situla. Trendall and Cambitoglou, *RFVA*, pl. 143, 6, and p. 405.

Melbourne 90/5. Trendall, *Phlyax Vases*, pl. 13a, no. 195.

Milan ST 6873. Trendall and Cambitoglou, *RFVA*, pl. 148, 1, and p. 416, no. 6.

Milan 270. Smith, *Funerary Symbolism*, pl. 12.

Munich 3268. Arias and Hirmer, *History of Greek Vase Painting*, pll. 236–37. See chap. 6.

Munich 3297. Fig. 3; Trendall and Cambitoglou, *RFVA*, pl. 194, 1, and p. 533.

Munich 8702, 1–7, set of gilded terra-cotta reliefs from Tarentum. *AA*, 1954, 286–88, fig. 19.

Naples 808 (82659). Trendall, *LCS*, pl. 202, 1, and p. 516.

Naples 1984. Kossatz-Diessmann, *Dramen des Aischylos auf westgriechischen Vasen*, pl. 19.

Naples 2202. Metzger, *Representations* I, 363, and II, pl. 48.

Naples 2867. Macchioro, "I ceramisti," p. 279, fig. 8a; Herbig, IV-2a, no. 6, p. 182.

Naples 2991, polychrome relief ware. Zervoudaki, *AM* 93 (1968), 19, pll. 12–13.

Naples 3218. Herbig, IV-2a, no. 3, p. 183; fig. 10.

Naples 3222. Trendall and Cambitoglou, *RFVA*, pl. 160, and pp. 430–31.

Naples 3224. Macchioro, "I ceramisti," p. 288, fig. 14a.

Naples 3240. *ARV²* 1336; Metzger, *Representations* I, 115, no. 9; II, pl. 11, 1.

Naples 3246. Kossatz-Diessmann, pl. 9b.

Naples 3255. Smith, *Funerary Symbolism*, fig. 9.

Naples 3370. Trendall, *Phlyax Vases*, pl. 4b, no. 49.

Naples Stg 11. Trendall and Cambitoglou, *RFVA*, p. 424, no. 54 (no plate); Pensa, *Rappresentazioni*, pl. 7.

Naples Stg 574. Trendall and Cambitoglou, *RFVA*, pl. 139, 4a and b, and p. 398.

Naples Stg 699. Herbig IV-1, no. 4, p. 181, fig. 7.

Naples Stg 709. Trendall and Cambitoglou, *RFVA*, pl. 196, 1, and p. 533.

Naples 80084, Gnathian ware. Wegner, *Griechenland*, fig. 70, p. 111; *CVA* 24, pl. 1113, 1 and 3.

Naples 80987, Gnathian ware. *CVA* 24, pl. 1115, 1.

Naples 81392. See chap. 6, fig. 14.

Naples 81953. Fig. 15; Wegner, *Griechenland*, fig. 68, p. 109.

Naples 82110 (1762). Macchioro, "I ceramisti," p. 292, fig. 19.

Naples 85873. Trendall, *LCS*, pl. 178, 1; cat. 4/70.

Naples 112855, Gnathian. *CVA* 24, pl. 1117, 5.

Naples 113347, terra-cotta from Tarentum. Fig. 20; Winter, *Typen* II, 138, 6, from Levi, *Le terrecotte figurate de Museo Nazionale di Napoli*, 202, fig. 46.

Naples 113349. Winter, *Typen* II, 138, 7.

Naples, Lucanian oinochoe. Macchioro, "I ceramisti," 282, fig. 9a–b.

Naples, private coll., 23. Trendall and Cambitoglou, *RFVA*, pl. 205, 5, and p. 543.

Naples, private coll., 352. Trendall and Cambitoglou, *RFVA*, pl. 184, 1, and p. 511.

Naples, Santangelo Coll. terra-cotta. Winter, *Typen* II, 138, no. 10.

Nauplia, plaque from Tiryns.

Nauplia, unnumbered Hellenistic oinochoe.

New York L63.21.6. Fig. 14; Trendall and Cambitoglou, *RFVA*, pl. 67, and p. 212, no. 152.

New York 07.286.35. *ARV²* 1126; Richter, *RFAV,* pll. 146 and 174.

New York 08.258.37 and 19.192.20. Arretine ware. *CVA* 9, pll. 421, 427, and 451.

New York 11.210.3. Trendall and Cambitoglou, *RFVA*, pl. 174, 2, and p. 489.

New York 17.46.2. Trendall and Cambitoglou, *RFVA*, pl. 187, 2, and p. 518.

New York 19.192.16 and 19.192.18, Arretine relief ware. *CVA* 9, pll. 421, 2a, and 425, 1b.

New York 19.192.31, relief ware. *CVA* 9, pl. 452, 4.

New York 20.196. Trendall, *Early South Italian Vase Painting,* pl. 30 and p. 20.

New York 27.122.8. *ARV²* 1171, Richter and Hall, *RFAV,* pl. 154.

New York 31.11.10. *ABV* 154, 688.

New York 37.11.23. *Para* 477; *ARV²* 1313; *AJA* 43 (1939), 4. See chap. 6, figs. 10 and 16.

New York 49.11.2. Met. Mus. *Bulletin* n.s. 8, no. 3, p. 95.

Nicosia XVI, 77. terra-cotta.

Nicosia, XVI, 90a and 90b, terra-cotta figures.

Nicosia, Roman copy of Hellenistic statue of Apollo from Salamis.

Oxford 60, garnet ring stone. G. M. A. Richter, *Engraved Gems of the Greeks, Etruscans, and Romans,* no. 250.

Oxford 1917.54. Beazley *EVP,* pl. 13a, 1.

Oxford 1921.1236, jasper scaraboid. Fig. 5; Boardman, *Greek Gems,* no. 614.

Oxford 1945.2. Van Hoorn, *Choes,* pl. 370, cat. 797, p. 165.

Palermo, lekanis lid. Trendall, *LCS,* pl. 250, 5, and p. 636.

Paris Bibl Nat. 1047. Drawing in Lenormant and de Witte, *Elite des monuments ceramographiques* II, pl. 88.

Paris Cab. Méd, 483. Trendall, *LCS,* pl. 152, 5; cat. no. 3/249.

Paris Cab. Méd. 1048.

Paris Cab. Méd. 1048. Trendall and Cambitoglou, *RFVA,* pl. 307, 3, and p. 821. Herbig, IV-2b, no. 6, p. 184.

Paris CA 574.

Paris G 516. *ARV²* 1189; *CVA* 8, pl. 380, 5; Immerwahr, *Studies Ullman* I, fig. 11.

Paris H 261 and H 292, relief ware. *CVA* 15, pl. 993, 1 and 3.

Paris K 121. *Gli Indigini nella pittura italiota,* pl. 32.

Paris K 526. Trendall, *LCS,* II pl. 72, 4, cat no. 923.

Paris K 570. Trendall, *Paestan Pottery,* pl. 11c; fig. 23 and p. 42, no. 3.

Paris, pelike. Herbig, IV-1, no. 2, p. 180.

Paris, terra-cotta from Kyrenaika (Benghazi, Libya). Winter, *Typen* I, 225, 9; Herbig, I, no. 5, p. 170.

Paris, terra-cotta. Froehner, *Terres cuites d'Asie de la collection Greau,* pl. 110, 2, p. 85.

Parma C 101. *CVA* 46, pl. 2047, 2.

Richmond, Va. 80.162. Mayo, *The Art of South Italy: Vases from Magna Graecia,* pp. 128–30.

Richmond, Va. 81.55. Mayo, *The Art of South Italy: Vases from Magna Graecia,* pp. 133–36.

Rome, Vatican T 11. Trendall, *Vasi italioti ed etruschi a figure rosse,* pl. 30, i.

Ruvo J 494. Kossatz-Diessmann, *Dramen,* pl. 7a.

Ruvo 1500. Fig. 2a; Trendall and Cambitoglou, *RFVA,* pl. 142, 5, and pp. 403–04.

Ruvo 1554. Fig. 17; Smith, *Funerary Symbolism,* fig. 13; Herbig, IV-2b, no. 1, p. 183.

Salerno, Paestan krater by Asteas. Fig. 2c; Trendall and Webster, *Illustrations,* pl. IV, 31.

Samothrace, terra-cotta figures. Higgins, *Greek Terracottas,* pl. 48, E.

San Simeon 5609. Fig. 7; Trendall and Cambitoglou, *RFVA,* p. 341.

San Simeon 9941. *ARV²* 1477; Tillyard, *The Hope Vases,* pl. 27, no. 169.

Sparta 468, votive relief.

Stockholm 2. *ARV²* 1470; Inghirami, *Monumenti etruschi* 5, pl. 45.

Stockholm 12. Trendall, *LCS,* pl. 36, 4; cat. no. 394.

Sydney 51.37. Cambitoglou and Trendall, *ARFVP of the Plain Style,* pl. 3 and p. 11.

Syracuse 17427. *ARV²* 1184, 4; *CVA* 17, pll. 824–25.

Taranto 8129. *Enciclopedia Classica,* sec. 3, v. 11, pt. 5 (1963), pl. 164.

Taranto 8925. Trendall and Cambitoglou, *RFVA,* pl. 182, 1, and p. 506.

Taranto 8935. Schmidt, Trendall and Cambitoglou, pl. 33a.

Taranto, amphora. Trendall and Cambitoglou, *RFVA,* pl. 284, 1, and p. 763, 293.

Thessaloniki VII, 190, terra-cotta.

Thessaloniki XIV, 222, terra-cotta.

Thessaloniki 2465, stele from Potidaea.

Torino 4129. *CVA* 32, pl. 1440, 1.

Torino 4149. Fig. 8; *CVA* 23, pl. 1443, 3.

Toronto 410. Robinson, Harcum, and Iliffe, *Catalogue* II, pl. 78.

Toronto 456 (926.19.7), lekanis lid. Robinson, Harcum, and Iliffe, II, pl. 83.

Toronto 958.61.325, limestone statue from Cyprus.

Trieste S 401. Trendall and Cambitoglou, *RFVA* p. 320, no. 26; *Gli Indigini nella pittura italiota,* pl. 34.

Trieste 1695. Trendall, *LCS,* pl. 11, no. 6, cat. 134.

Vienna 202. *ARV²* 1523; *CVA* 1, pl. 30, 1.

Vienna 217. Trendall, *LCS,* pl. 146, 4, and p. 383.

Warsaw (Goluchow) 125. *CVA* 1, pl. 49, 4b.

Warsaw 138485, Gnathian ware. *CVA* 9, pl. 392, 4.

Würzburg H 4455 (L.541). *ARV²* 1133; *CVA* 46, pl. 2236, 8. See chap. 6, fig. 17.

Würzburg H 5708. *CVA* 46, pl. 2244.

York, City Art Gallery 19. Trendall and Cambitoglou, *ARFVP of the Plain Style,* p. 44, pl. 22.

Notes

Introduction

1. The term *harp* is used to designate any instrument with strings of graduated length that are attached at one end to a soundbox and at the other end to a neck that extends from one end of that soundbox. A *lyre* is an instrument with strings of (roughly) equal length, attached above to a crossbar that is supported by two arms, and below to the lower end of a soundbox; a "lute" also has strings of equal length, but the strings pass from the soundbox over a neck and are attached at the far end of the neck. For more specific definitions of these instrument types, see Sibyl Marcuse, *Musical Instruments,* articles "harp," "lyre," and "lute."

2. Helmut Huchzermeyer, *Aulos und Kithara in der griechischen Musik bis zum Ausgang der Klassichen Zeit.*

3. David H. Fischer, *Historians' Fallacies,* 109–10.

4. A recent anthology containing English translations of selections pertaining to music from Homer, Hesiod, the *Homeric Hymns,* Greek lyric, tragedy, comedy, and other sources, is Andrew Barker, *Greek Musical Writings, Volume 1: The Musician and His Art.* A recent compilation of vase paintings showing musical instruments of all types is Daniel Paquette, *L'instrument de musique dans la céramique de la Grèce antique.*

5. The standard reference works for Greek vases, which make up the bulk of the art objects cited, are the volumes by Sir John Beazley, *ABV, ARV²,* and *Para,* which also provide the names of museums.

Chapter 1: Homer and Before

1. Athens 3908 from Keros, Athens 8833 from Naxos, Karlsruhe B 863 and B 864 from Thera, New York 47.100.1 of unknown provenance, and two figures of unknown provenance in a Swiss private collection, location unknown. According to Jürgen Thimme, *Art and Culture of the Cyclades,* 494–96, fragments of other figures of this type have been found in the excavations on Naxos.

2. Aign, 113–14. A rock drawing 300–1400 years earlier than the Cycladic harpists from Megiddo (Israel) is, if correctly interpreted by Aign (118–20), possibly a related instrument. The statement in *The New Grove Dictionary of Music and Musicians*

(London: Macmillan, 1980), vol. 8, p. 193, to the effect that the Cycladic instruments are asymmetrical lyres, is misleading.

3. Aign, 349–50, has suggested that a hieroglyphic sign on a green steatite bead seal of ca. 1850–1700 B.C. (Oxford CS 170, 1938.793) from Heraklion, Crete, represents a stringed instrument, perhaps a harp; that this instrument has at the top a bird beak similar to that on the Cycladic harp from Keros; and that this establishes a relationship between the two instruments and the musical cultures to which they belong. But because the hieroglyph cannot be securely identified as either a harp or a lyre (instruments that almost certainly developed independently) or even as a musical instrument, it cannot be accepted as evidence.

According to fn. 5 in Arthur Evans, *The Palace of Minos at Knossos,* II, 835, the side of the Knossos bead seal with the "lyre" shown in fig. 550b was accidentally inserted with views of another seal in vol. I, 277, fig. 207. The Knossos items (present location unknown) listed by Aign, 35–36, as II/1 and II/2, and by Wegner, *MT,* U 77–78, as nos. 83 and 85, are therefore the same object; and Evans' figs. 550a and 551 (Aign II/3 and II/4, Wegner, nos. 84 and 86) also represent the same object, as Evans makes clear in his *Scripta Minoa* I, 192, and pl. III, fig. 64a. If these examples, which are after all very small, have a meaning connected with stringed instruments, there is no reason to expect them to portray such instruments in a very realistic way.

4. See also the lyre on a vase fragment from Nauplia (fig. 3a), discussed below under Mycenaean Lyres.

5. The Knossos seal stone listed by Aign, II/8, p. 41. (Heraklion Mus. 143?) is not clear; it is not generally agreed that the female figure on it holds a lyre. Stephanos A. Xanthoudides describes the stone without mentioning an instrument. The alabaster fragments presumed to be small bits of a lyre, described by Platon, are not extensive enough to be securely identified and so cannot contribute to our understanding of Minoan instruments. The same must also be said of the fragments described by Marcelle Duchesne-Guillemin, "Restitution d'une harpe minoenne et problème de la ΣAMBYKH," who discusses ivory fragments from a (probably Mycenaean) tomb at Zafer Papoura near Knossos, which she identifies as the remains of the soundbox of a harp. (Egyptian lyres of this

219

period that have been preserved are made of wood; cf. Lisa Manniche, *Ancient Egyptian Musical Instruments*, 81–83.)

6. The latter shape is also to be seen on the Knossos seal stone (fig. 2d) and, less certainly, on the amphora from Sitia (fig. 2c). On the Kalamion pyxis (fig. 2b) the soundbox appears to have small "handles" protruding from the outer edge just below the arms, and the seal stone gives a similar impression, since the arms are set in somewhat from the ends of the soundbox.

7. The heads have red masks on the Pylos fresco, and on one side the beak seems clear. But scholars have perhaps been misled about the clarity of these details by Piet de Jong's reproduction. See Mabel L. Lang, *The Palace of Nestor*, 2:79–80, and pll. 27, 125, 126 (the reproduction), and color plate A (actual fragments).

8. The flower that appears above the right arm of the instrument on the Hagia Triada fresco may or may not be an ornamental part of the instrument itself. On the pyxis and on the seal stone the arms end at the crossbar, whereas on the amphora from Sitia they are so fantastically elongated that perhaps another interpretation is in order: the painter may have meant these black lines, extending from the crossbar up to a black band around the neck of the vase, to show a means of suspending the two instruments (which are shown without performers or scene).

9. A similar curved lower string fastener is to be seen on a kylix (cup) from Skopelos (fig. 3c, see Mycenaean Lyres below). On the amphora from Sitia, the upper edge of the soundbox rises to a tall point in the center. Whether this is an attempt to show soundbox shape, the string-fastening device, or merely fanciful creativeness cannot be ascertained.

10. Long, *Ayia Triadha Sarcophagus*, 36.

11. Ibid., 74.

12. There is at present no sign that either the Minoans or the Mycenaeans used harps, although they must have known of such instruments, which were common enough among the Egyptians and the peoples of the Middle East and were known in Cyprus (Cypriote bronze stands London 1920.12-20.1 and 1946.10-17.1 depict an angle and an arched harp). But as Bernard Aign has pointed out, instruments are not items of trade; they are unlikely to travel unless the musician travels too; and they so often exist in close connection with religious practices that they do not pass easily from one culture to another unless the cultures themselves have mingled (Aign, 111–12).

13. From Parry's 1928 doctoral thesis, reprinted in Adam Parry, ed., *The Making of Homeric Verse*, 9. Although Parry's definition of formula has since been broadened, his work still forms the basis for our present understanding of how the poems were composed. For an example of a much expanded notion of formula, see Michael Nagler, *Spontaneity and Tradition*.

14. The formula is *phorminga ligeian* (or *phormingi ligeiei*), "bright-sounding phorminx," which occurs a total of 9 times in the poems, always in the final 2½ feet of a verse (*Il.* 9.186 and 18.569; *Od.* 8.67, 105, 254, 261, 537, 22.332, 23.133). Parry's investigations were expanded (and carried on after his death by Albert B. Lord and James Notopoulos) to include a study of formulaic composition as practiced by modern Yugoslav bards, who accompany their heroic song on a bowed, one-stringed instrument called a *gusle*.

15. The following are representative exponents of the composite theory: H. L. Lorimer, *Homer and the Monuments*; Emily T. Vermeule, *Greece in the Bronze Age*; A. M. Snodgrass, "An Historical Homeric Society?"; J. V. Luce, *Homer and the Heroic Age*. See, contra, M. I. Finley, *Early Greece*, who rejects the notion that the poems are a reflection of the Mycenaean world.

16. We have virtually no concrete information regarding how, when, or for whom the *Iliad* and *Odyssey* themselves were performed. According to sources from later times, recitations of Homer at the Panathenaic festival in Athens were instituted in the 6th century (Kirk, 306–07, summarizes the evidence). These recitations were given by rhapsodes, whose name means "stitchers-together of songs" (*rhaptein oidas*). It is often assumed that these rhapsodes used no musical accompaniment, since some 5th-c. vase paintings (e.g., London E 270 [ARV² 183, 1632]) show the reciter holding not a lyre but a staff. For a study of the origin and meaning of the name *rhapsode* (which was falsely connected with *rhabdos*, "staff"), see Harald Patzer, "ΡΑΨΩΙΔΟΣ"; on rhapsodes in general, see Kirk, 312ff. There is not enough evidence about rhapsodes before the time of Plato to allow any firm conclusions about the nature of their recitals; and of performances of the epics before the 6th century we know literally nothing. We can only suppose that earlier audiences heard the poems (perhaps in installments?) at festive occasions similar to those described in the epics themselves. See Denys Page, *The Homeric Odyssey*, 75–76, who summarizes the details·of our ignorance on the subject of early performances of Homer. It requires some 20 hours to recite the *Iliad*, so that most scholars assume that performances were spread out over a period of three or more days.

17. Eustathius 1586.45.

18. On the proposed connection with Sanskrit, see Boisacq, 1035, and the counterarguments referred to in Frisk, 1036–37. An even more unlikely suggestion (based on Hesychius) is offered by L. Radermacher, "Der homerische Hermes hymnus," 73, who connects phorminx with the Latin *formica* ("ant") and says the instrument was probably so called because it had an ant-like appearance. We seem to have here cases of entomology rather then etymology.

19. Strabo, *Geog.* 9.17, says that most Greek names for instruments are either Thracian or Asiatic in origin.

20. Frisk, 850–51. Others have tried to show a connection between *kitharis* and the Hebrew *kinnor* (see bibliography in Abert, "Saiteninstrumente," col. 1761). See also chap. 3, Etymology.

21. Regarding the meaning of *kitharis*, an incorrect definition is given by Alfred Sendry, *Music in the Social and Religious Life of Antiquity*, 292: "The technique of playing a stringed instrument was called, by Homer, kitharis." The only word in Homer that could possibly mean "technique" of playing is *kitharistus*, which occurs only once (Il. 2.600), when the Muses are said to have caused Thamyris to forget "the art of lyre playing."

22. The verb *phormizein* is rare in Homer (and in later authors as well), occurring only in *Od.* 1.155, 4.18, and 8.266 and in a bracketed phrase in *Il.* 18.605.

23. On the meaning of *demioergos*, see T. B. L. Webster, *From Mycenae to Homer*, 131; Kirk, 278; and Schadewaldt, 69. The word *demos* in its earlier form (*damos*) occurs in Linear B tablets from Pylos and is taken by John Chadwick, *The Mycenaean World*, 76–77, to refer collectively to the people of a given administrative district.

24. See Schadewaldt, 70.

25. In view of the archaeological evidence from Homer's own time as well as from the Bronze Age (see below) which proves that the plektron was used, one must avoid categorical statements such as that of K. Schneider, "Plectrum": "Homer does not yet know of the plectrum. His *phorminx* and *kitharis* were played with the fingers."

26. Eustathius 1915.7–10. His fanciful etymology seems to have caused some tc suppose that the *kollopes* were literally sticky or gluey and that the process of stringing the phorminx must have been quite a messy operation; in fact, the roughness of the leather itself was probably sufficient for the purpose.

27. Ar., fr. 646 (Edmonds).

28. W. B. Stanford, ed., *The Odyssey of Homer*, vol. 2, p. 369, favors Düntzer's emendation, which would render the text as ῥηι-δίως ἐτάνυσσε νέην περὶ κόλλοπι χορδήν.

29. Wegner, *MT* 2, states categorically that the adjective *glaphure* means the instrument had a hole on one side and a vaulted shape on the other. He concludes that this can refer only to a soundbox and that the phorminx was therefore a stringed instrument, a fact which would have been much easier to prove by merely noting that Homer says the phorminx has strings! On side views of the instruments, see M. Maas, "On the Shape of the Ancient Greek Lyre."

30. Huchzermeyer, 28. Wegner, *MT* 2, seems unaware of Huchzermeyer's convincing argument and says the phorminx had a "laute Stimme." Abert, "Saiteninstrumente," also apparently takes *ligus* to mean loud or raucous, for he says that the description is not consonant with the dignified ethos associated with the later kithara. On the positive connotations of *ligus* in Homer (and the Homeric Hymns) see also M. Kaimio, "Music in the Homeric Hymn to Hermes," 33.

31. Compare the Minoan instrument on the Hagia Nikolaos amphora from Sitia (fig. 2c). The instrument on Tiryns fragment Nauplia 14.376, more crudely painted (fig. 3b), has arms with double curves and only three strings.

32. Near the base of the instrument, on either side, are two small holes, one with a small metal ring through it.

33. The reconstruction is surely inaccurate in a number of respects; in particular, the rectangular relief that now forms its base is not likely to have been part of the instrument. There is no corroborative evidence to indicate the existence of a lyre of such a shape.

34. Platon, "Minoiki Lyra," 221. Platon's proposed new reconstruction of the first Menidi lyre, however, still incorporates the rectangular griffin relief as its base.

35. The soundbox shown in the vase painting from Skopelos (fig. 3c), however, is narrow, resembling that of the Minoan lyre shown on the Hagia Triada sarcophagus (fig. 2a).

36. Vassos Karageorghis, *Mycenaean Art from Cyprus*, 5.

37. Other panels on the interior of this vase show birds, a palm tree, and a human figure with a mouflon (a wild sheep with curved horns).

38. A much taller lyre is represented on a 12th-c. B.C. Cypriote bronze pot stand: the scene on one side of the stand shows three musicians, an aulos player, a player of an angle harp of Near Eastern type, and a seated player who holds what appears to be a lyre with a round base and straight arms, tall enough to reach from the player's lap to the top of his head. The player faces left and holds the instrument in his right arm instead of his left (London 1946.10-17.1).

39. London 134306. Another cylinder seal (location unknown) tentatively dated ca. 1000 B.C., from Tarsus in southern Anatolia, shows a round-based, nearly symmetrical lyre with curves rather than zigzags in the arm construction, rather reminiscent of Minoan pyxis Khania 2368 (fig. 2b). Both Anatolian seals show instruments held horizontally, a position not often encountered in Greek representations.

40. Porphyrios Dikaios, *A Guide to the Cyprus Museum*, 78.

41. The word *paieon* is probably of considerable antiquity, since it is apparently mentioned in one of the Linear B tablets from Knossos, on which it is included in a list of several Olympian deities (Athena, Poseidon, and Enualios, or Ares); cf. Chadwick, *Mycenaean World*, 88–89, and George Huxley, "Cretan *Paiawones*." For a thorough analysis of the god Paian ("Healer") and his relationship

to Apollo, as well as of the various functions of the paean itself, see A. Fairbanks, *A Study of the Greek Paean*.

42. See James George Frazer, *The Golden Bough*, pt. V, vol. 1, pp. 216, and 257–58. He discusses a Phoenician song sung at the vintage that the Greeks called by the name *Linos* or *Ailinos*, probably mistaking what was merely a cry of lamentation (*ai lanu*, "woe to us") as a proper name.

43. We know from Proclus' summary (in his *Chrestomathia*) that included in the 7th-6th-c. "epic cycle" was an epic in five books on the *Nostoi*, or returns, of the Greeks as they made their way home after the war. Phemios' theme, the return of the Achaians (*nostos Achaion*), thus appears to have enjoyed wide popularity.

44. Besides this scene (*Od.* 1.153ff., *Od.* 4.18, and *Il.* 18.494ff.) there is one other reference in Homer to the phorminx accompanying dance, but the phrase is generally regarded as interpolated (*Il.* 18.605).

45. Schadewaldt, 65, provides a sensitive discussion of the dramatic contrasts of this memorable scene.

46. As Martin Robertson, *A History of Greek Art*, vol. 1, p. 19, puts it, one of the characteristics of Geometric drawing is "the tendency to put down each part separately, as though the artist were referring to an itemised list in his mind rather than drawing the whole he sees." See also John Coldstream, *Greek Geometric Pottery*, 28, and Martin Robertson, *Greek Painting*, 37.

47. For opposing views, see Ludwig Deubner, "Die viersaitige Leier"; Wegner, *MT* 9; and Aign, 221.

48. Vases: Athens 291, Athens 14447, Athens 17497, Basel BS 406, Berlin Antikenmuseum 31573, Copenhagen 727, Sparta unnumbered, Tübingen 2657, bronzes from Tegea.

49. Vase paintings of instruments with rounded bases, arms curving outward: Athens Agora P 10154, Athens 234 (fig. 12), Athens 874, Cambridge Mus. Class. Arch. 345, Dresden 1699 (fig. 11).

Instruments with flat or pointed bases: Athens 18542 (fig. 8), Athens unnumbered, from the Argive Heraion (fig. 13), Copenhagen 9367, Copenhagen 12433.

There is also one vase painting, Athens 784, on which there is a figure holding what appears to be a frame harp, but its shape cannot be equated with either the Cycladic harps or Greek harps of the 5th and 4th centuries.

50. Athens 291, 313, 874, and the sherd from the Argive Heraion (fig. 13); Athens Agora P 10154; Basel BS 406; Berlin 31573; Cambridge Mus. Class. Arch. 345; Copenhagen 727 (undamaged section); Dresden 1699 (fig. 11); Tübingen 2657 (fig. 7a).

51. The scenes on the two Laconian vases from Sparta and the Amyklaion are difficult to categorize. The vase from the Amyklaion (Athens 234, fig. 12) shows three dancers with lyres in the field between them. Their dance is not a leaping dance, but it does not seem to be a procession either. The vase sherd from Sparta, which shows two figures on either side of a lyre, each holding it by one arm, is quite unlike any other scene. It reminds one of later paintings of Artemis and Apollo with a kithara between them—there is a 7th-c. sherd from Delos (now in the Delos Museum) that seems to be another early version of such a scene (see chap. 2, fig. 7).

52. Tegea Museum, two votive bronzes from the sanctuary of Athena Alea (one shown in fig. 9) and one from the sanctuary of Artemis Krakeatis; Sparta Museum, Laconian-Geometric sherd. All the soundboxes of the bronze lyres are fairly tall, though they vary somewhat, while that of the instrument on the vase in this group is rim like, no wider than the arms themselves (the ring *below* the soundbox in this painting is very likely meant to be the plektron cord).

53. Upper excavation, relief by "Master B" (fig. 7b). Four musicians in procession: an aulos player, two lyre players, tympanon (frame drum) player (Assyrian-Aramaic style).

54. The instrument on the vase from Exochi (Copenhagen 12433) also has a pointed base, with a lower string fastener painted above the soundbox (see the remarks on Berlin Antikenmuseum 31573 above) and arms that first diverge and then come closer together nearer the top (the crossbar and all above have been obliterated). It is possible that these vases show an instrument related to that on the Cypriote Kaloriziki amphora át Nicosia (fig. 5a), two centuries earlier.

55. Lower excavation, relief by "Master A" (fig. 14): aulos player, kithara player, and two dancers.

56. Crossbar knobs or crosspieces, also found in several of the vase paintings mentioned above (Athens 313 and 874, Dresden 1699 [fig. 11]), cannot have been used for tuning, as Aign, 213, has clearly demonstrated; the whole tuning cannot be transposed by turning the crossbar.

Chapter 2: The Archaic Period

1. Cf. T. J. Dunbabin, *The Greeks and their Eastern Neighbors,* 25: "The Greeks learnt much from the Phoenicians and other Semitic people, but made it their own."

2. On the continuity in patterns of Greek culture from Mycenaean times on, see Chester Starr, *The Origins of Greek Civilization, 1100–650 B.C.,* 6 et passim.

3. Isobel Henderson, "Ancient Greek Music," 1:379, an excellent survey of Greek music. See also D. A. Campbell, "Flutes and Elegiac Couplets," 68: "Assertions in late historians, geographers and lexicographers are of extremely doubtful value to the history of early music." On the "first inventor" as a *topos* in Greek literature, see Adolf Kleingünther, "ΠΡΩΤΟΣ ΈΥΡΕΤΗΣ."

4. Herodotus (2.53.1) says both Homer and Hesiod lived four hundred years before his own time, i.e., ca. 850 B.C. For the argument by which Hesiod's floruit is dated to 725–700 B.C., see George L. Huxley, *Greek Epic Poetry from Eumelos to Panyassis,* 124–25. M. L. West, ed., *Hesiod: Theogony,* 46–47, argues that Hesiod's poems (ca. 730–690) predate those of Homer slightly.

5. According to a late source, Hesiod was excluded from taking part in a Pythian musical contest because he did not accompany himself on the lyre (Pausanias 10.7.3). Yet if he in fact appeared at such a contest, he must have regarded his poetry as belonging to a musical genre. Hesiod himself, fr. 357 (Merkelbach and West), says that he and Homer were the first to "stitch together song" "ῥαψαντες ἀοιδήν), and Plato uses the verb ῥαψῳδεῖν of both Homer and Hesiod (*R.* 600D).

6. On the epic side of Archilochos' output, see James A. Notopoulos, "Archilochus, the Aoidos." For an assignment of Archilochos to an earlier date (ca. 740–ca. 670), see Alan Blakeway, "The Date of Archilochus." He identifies the eclipse which Archilochos mentions as the one that occurred on Thasos on 14 March 711 B.C. rather than the eclipse on Paros of 6 April 648 B.C. Most scholars now prefer the latter date.

7. In Athenaeus 14.635e (quoting Hellanikos) it is reported that Terpander was summoned to Sparta during the twenty-sixth Olympiad (676–73). The *Marmor Parium* (49) mentions him in connection with the year 644–43. Ps.-Plutarch, *de mus.* 1132e, quoting Glaucus of Rhegium (ca. 400 B.C.), says Terpander was older than Archilochos. As Albin Lesky, *A History of Greek Literature,* 129, points out, "The few surviving fragments under Terpander's name, even if genuine, teach us very little."

8. Of twelve passages from ancient sources cited in Walther Vetter, "Terpandros," half are from *De Musica* and the rest from Athenaeus, Pollux, and the *Suda.*

9. See Douglas Gerber, *Euterpe,* 83, and D. A. Campbell, *Greek Lyric Poetry,* 193.

10. The evidence is collected by Thomas Rosenmeyer, "Alcman's *Partheneion* I Reconsidered," 338.

11. Huchzermeyer 41 points out the close relationship between Lesbos and Lydia, as reflected in the fragments of Sappho and Alcaeus.

12. The date of the *Hymn to Hermes* is widely disputed. T. W. Allen, W. R. Halliday, and E. E. Sikes, eds., *The Homeric Hymns,* 276, think it "not later than the seventh century," while Ludwig Radermacher, "Der Homerische Hermeshymnus," 216, 222, regards it (on the basis of the characterization of Hermes) as contemporary with Old Comedy (i.e., 6th century). More recent scholarship generally places the poem in the last part of the 6th century; cf. S. C. Shelmerdine, "The Homeric Hymn to Hermes."

13. Theognis' year of birth may be placed tentatively at ca. 580 B.C. on the assumption that the statement by the *Suda* that he was γεγονώς in the fifty-ninth Olympiad (544/3–541/0) refers to his *floruit,* not his birth. See E. Rohde, "Γέγονε in den Biographica des Suidas." If these dates are accepted, Theognis would had to have been virtually a centenarian in order to have made some of the allusions, in the collection of poems attributed to him, to impending Persian invasions, which did not begin until 490.

14. It is often assumed that because Theognis' poems were in the elegiac meter, they were accompanied by the aulos and never by the lyre. See, contra, Campbell, "Flutes and Elegiac Couplets." An annoying aspect of this otherwise excellent article is the casual attitude toward the name of the instrument. He states (p. 63, n. 3) that he ought to call the instrument an aulos, since it is not in fact a flute, but that he has chosen instead an English word which has "many of the correct associations." Unfortunately, the incorrect associations with respect to sound, sound production, appearance, and use far outweigh any "correct" ones.

15. The *Suda* (s.v. Σαπφώ) ascribes the invention of the plektron to Sappho. Although the word is never mentioned in Homer, archaeological evidence shows that the plektron was known in both Mycenaean and Geometric times (see chap. 1), so that we must regard the story of Sappho's "invention" as but another of the musical "firsts" which were passed on in Greek legend. See chap 1, n. 25.

16. For the date of this hymn to Aphrodite, see Allen et al., *Homeric Hymns,* cvi, 350–51.

17. Strabo's doubts are shared by modern writers. Huchzermeyer 43 regards the lines as spurious, as does Ulrich von Wilamowitz-Möllendorff, *Timotheus,* 64, n. 1; and B. A. von Groningen, "A propos de Terpandre," does not include this fragment among the two that he considers authentic. See, contra, A. R. Burn, *The Lyric Age of Greece,* 229: "There is no reason to doubt his real existence or authorship of a few lines, of much charm, preserved in quotation."

18. L. Deubner, "Die viersaitige Leier," (a small slip has led to a more amusing version of the title in Albin Lesky, *A History of Greek Literature,* 128, no. 3, where the article is referred to as "Die einsaitige Leier"). See also Deubner, "Terpander und die siebensaitige Leier."

19. Another example in a late hymn is found in *h.Hom.* 21.3–4, a short hymn to Apollo, in which an *aoidos* plays his bright-sounding phorminx (*phorminga ligeian*) and sings of Apollo.

20. R. M. Cook, "The Date of the Hesiodic Shield," shows that where the author of the *Shield* is not just borrowing from Ho-

mer, his descriptions are based on Archaic art from the decade 580–70 B.C.

21. The strong connection between Apollo and the phorminx is borne out in a recently published fragment of a lyric poem of unknown (but probably Archaic) date and author. In lines 3 and 4 of the fragment, the only words that can be made out are *phorminx*, *Phoebus* (Apollo), and *Delos*, the island of Apollo's birth; Adespota 442a.3–4, D. Page, *Supplementum Lyricis Graecis*.

22. See chap. 1.

23. The phorminx is also mentioned, together with the aulos, in Thgn. 1.761 (in the context of a prayer to Zeus and Apollo to protect the city), but the authenticity of the passage is doubtful in view of the reference (in 764) to war with the Medes (see n. 41).

24. George M. A. Hanfmann, "Ionia, Leader or Follower?" fig. 5 and p. 16; bibliography, p. 33, n. 86 (Hanfmann assumes that the Mycenaean lyre was eight-stringed and that the dinos offers the earliest representation of the seven-stringed lyre).

25. Strabo 13.618; Ath. 635 E. Terpander's role is discussed later in the present chapter. Compare Ekrem Akurgal, *Die Kunst Anatoliens von Homer bis Alexander*, pp. 14–15.

26. Athens 911.

27. Athens Agora AP 1085 (fig. 3a); Syracuse 12577 (fig. 3b). Other 7th-c. items: a bronze cup from Olympia with six strings, "Cypro-Phoenician" work; a silver cup from Cyprus with no strings visible; steatite seal stones from Ayia Irini, Cyprus, nos. 2123 and 2180, showing three strings; a bronze relief, Olympia 11327, with four strings; and lead figurines from Sparta showing four strings.

28. Location unknown. Four marble figurines from Lindos, Rhodes, but in Cypriot style, dated before 550 B.C. by Blinkenberg, hold instruments that appear to be of the phorminx type: Lindos 1712, 1716, 1717, and 1820 (the latter is a creature with bearded human head and fish body who is holding a red-painted instrument with a soundbox rounded at the bottom but also having lower corners.

29. Athens National Museum Acr. 2523.

30. But see Aign, 232.

31. A statue from Kyzikos of a siren holding a phorminx (Copenhagen, Ny Carlsberg Glyptotek) shows a diagonal strap across the back of the instrument for the player's left arm; a badly damaged relief from Xanthos in Lykia (now in Istanbul) shows a phorminx with eight strings and fantastically ornamented arms filling the whole space on either side of the strings. A fragment of an East Greek pot found in Tel Defenneh, Egypt (London 88.2.-8.10) shows satyrs palying aulos and phorminx over a large wine bowl.

32. The verb used of Apollo's musical performance is *engkitharizein*, "to play a stringed instrument *for* someone." Just before this passage, his arrival on Olympus causes the gods to anticipate the delight of "kitharis and song" (188). A similar scene, but without dance, is described in ps.-Hesiod, *Shield* 202ff., where Apollo on Olympus plays (*kitharizein*) on his golden phorminx and the Muses sing.

33. Fr. 44 (LP). The name for the second instrument is not actually in the text, which has a gap with room for a word of seven letters. Editors have proposed either *magadis* (see below, Archaic-Period References to the Pektis and Magadis) or *kitharis* (the Greek spelling of which [κίθαρις] also has only seven letters); in view of the poem's epic subject matter, meter, and diction, *kitharis* is probably to be preferred. Sappho's contemporary, Alcaeus, also mentions both *kitharis* and *kitharizein,* but the contexts cannot be determined (fr. B 9.15 and B 6ᴮ.3, LP).

34. Kitharis: *h.Hom.* 4.499, 509 (and 510, *kitharizein*), and 515; phorminx: 506.

35. *h.Hom.* 4.17 (*engkitharizein*); 4.423, 425. 433, 455, and 476 (*kitharizein*).

36. These lines are echoed verbatim in one of the late Homeric Hymns (*h.Hom.* 25.2–4).

37. Fr. 305 (Merkelbach and West). In fr. 306, Linos himself is described as a *kitharistes,* either by the source for the fragment (Clement of Alexandria) or by Hesiod.

38. The Greek for "good lyre-playing" is *to kalos kitharisden* (= *kitharizein*).

39. Hdt. 1.23–24. See also chap. 3. The story of Arion is widely told in later accounts as well, most of which seem to be derived from Herodotus (see O. Crusius, "Arion"). Herodotus also claims that Arion invented the dithyramb, or choral song in honor of Dionysus, and that he produced dithyrambs is Corinth. The word *dithyramb*, however, is found as early as Archilochos, fr. 120 (West), mid-7th century.

40. Sibyl Marcuse, *Musical Instruments: A Comprehensive Dictionary*, s.v. "guitar" and "zither."

41. The name for the instrument in this passage appears in its Ionic form, *kithare;* the more familiar *kithara* is the form used in the Attic dialect. On the date of the passage, see E. L. Highbarger, "Theognis and the Persian Wars," who argues that it must refer to events of the spring of 490 B.C. He claims (110) that Theognis could have written the poem and cites other examples of longevity. B. A. van Groningen, ed., *Théognis: Le premier livre*, 302, agrees that the poem must be dated to the period of the Persian wars but does not accept the attribution to Theognis. Jean Carrière, *Théognis: Poèmes élégiaques,* 121, prefers to date the poem to 479 (the time of Mardonius' invasion of the Megarid) and says Theognis cannot have been the author. See also n. 13.

42. For further information on non-Greek lyres see Lisa Manniche, *Ancient Egyptian Musical Instruments;* Wilhelm Stauder, *Die Harfen und Leiern Vorderasiens in babylonischer und assyrischer Zeit;* and Max Wegner, *Die Musikinstrumente des alten Orients.*

43. Location unknown, unpublished vase. The two narrow protrusions shown by Akurgal on either side of the soundbox are possibly a mistake; one of these protrusions may be the plektron cord (a mistake of this sort was made in the second illustration on the page, in drawing the instrument from the Old Smyrna dinos fragment with two plektron cords, one on either side).

44. For a convenient summary of bibliography, see Miriam Ervin, "Newsletter from Greece"; see also Roland Hampe and Erika Simon, *The Birth of Greek Art,* pp. 127–28 and pll. 195–96. Another object from this period, the figure of a kneeling youth published by Dieter Ohly, "Zur Rekonstruktion des samischen Geräts mit dem Elfenbeinjüngling," may, as Ohly theorizes, have been part of the decoration of a lyre, perhaps a kithara; but no part of the instrument has survived.

45. A photograph of this section of the painting appears in Zanker, *Wandel der Hermesgestalt,* but the instrument does not show up clearly.

46. The authors are indebted to Shirley Schwarz for help in estimating the date of this unpublished vase.

47. The term used for the instrument in this passage is *kitharis.*

48. Other items from the first half of the 6th century: large limestone votive statuette, Nicosia Museum, ca. 560–550 B.C., damaged but useful for left-hand detail, size of instrument, costume of player (which resembles fig. 4); bronze shield-strap plate from Olympia, very damaged (instrument not as clear as drawing makes it seem); bronze votive kithara described by Aign, location unknown, possibly from Asia Minor, placed by him at the beginning of the 6th century.

49. There are examples as small as 1⅓ and as large as 2¼ times as tall as the length of the player's forearm, and anywhere from ½ to almost equally as wide as they are high.

50. Chantraine 651 gives the etymology as "unknown" and says that the term is perhaps a borrowed one. Frisk 146 concludes that it is a loanword from the Mediterranean area but cites several attempts to prove that it is Indo-European. Boisacq 592 believes it can be connected with I. E. *lu-, *leu-.

51. Fr. 93a.5 (West). This fragment was evidently overlooked by Huchzermeyer in 1931 even though it had been published some thirty years earlier; he says (p. 38) that Archilochos makes no mention of stringed instruments. Despite variations in the reading of the fragment among different editors, all are agreed on the words αὐλὸν καὶ λύρην in line 5.

52. Reading Diehl's suggested ἄνδρας/εὔφ/ωγοῦντας; in his text he prints ἄνδρας [-]ω/λοῦγτας (so also Tarditi). West prints ἄνδρας ..(.) ωλεῦγτας. See M. Treu, Archilochos, 212, whose general interpretation of the fragment is followed here. Archilochos himself is described (in the 3d century B.C.) as a poet who sang verses to the accompaniment of the lyra (Theoc. Ep. 21.6).

53. Zonaras 1190, and cf. Et. Mag. 506.18. Other onomatopoeic renderings of the sound of various types of lyres include tenella (Archilochos 324 [West, under spuria]); threttanelo (Ar. Pl. 290); and tophlattothrat (Ar. Ra. 1285ff.).

54. Cf. Sappho fr. 99.4 (LP): χορδαισιδιακρεκην, which would appear to refer to "weaving" a song on the strings of an instrument. See J. M. Snyder, "The Web of Song: Weaving Imagery in Homer and the Lyric Poets," CJ 76 (1981), 193–96.

55. If the correction Ἐρατώ, νόμους (Meineke) for †ἐρατῶν ὕμνους† is right, there seems to be a kind of pun on the name of the Muse, Ἐρατώ, and the epithet for the lyra, ἐρατᾷ.

56. Cf. Denys Page, ed., Sappho and Alcaeus, 117.

57. On the subtlety with which the poet separates himself from the Homeric tradition (versus the blunt criticism of Xenophanes, for example), see H. Langerbeck, "Margites: Versuch einer Beschreibung und Rekonstruktion," 58–59. It is perhaps significant that the lyra is mentioned in the jarring line of iambics (following the two verses of heroic hexameters); just as we have begun to think of the poet as a follower of Homer (the divine singer of the opening line?), he suddenly introduces the non-Homeric meter and instrument name. In the space of the three opening lines, the poet both compliments Homer (as the source, it appears, of the ensuing story) and at the same time announces his own independence and innovation. The date is disputed by modern scholars. A Byzantine source claims that Archilochos ascribed the Margites to Homer, which would mean that the poem was known as early as the 7th century. On doubts about the validity of such a claim, see J. A. Davison, "Quotations and Allusions in Early Greek Literature." See, contra, G. L. Huxley, Greek Epic Poetry, 176, who believes that the Margites "may well have been composed by an epic poet of Homer's time."

58. Reading the MSS ἀκούων rather than Pierson's ἀείδων.

59. See Campbell, "Flutes and Elegiac Couplets." Van Groningen, Théognis, p. 212, suggests that the lyre is probably the barbitos, the instrument preferred by drinkers (see chap. 5). Since lyra can be used as a generic term, at least in 5th-c. authors, this may well be the case.

60. Campbell, Greek Lyric Poetry, 449, dates the collection of skolia to the late 6th through 5th centuries; he believes (452) that this poem may allude to the performance of a dithyramb. One further late 6th/early 5th-c. reference is a possible allusion to an instrument maker in Anakreon fr. 387, PMG: "I asked the lyre-maker Strattis if he would wear his hair long," reading λυροποιὸν (Hephaestion) rather than μυροποιὸν (Pollux).

61. Examples include Philadelphia Univ. Mus. L 64.180 and MS 4841; Munich 1472; Copenhagen 3241; London B 139; New York 06.1021.47, 14.105.10, and 17.230.14. See also chap. 3, figs. 2 and 12.

62. Accepting the emendation μέλος (not the MSS μέρος) in order to match the MSS reading in 419 and 501. In line 418, just before the repeated line and a half, we learn the further detail (not a surprising one) that the instrument was held in the left hand. For a different chronology of Hermes' deeds, cf. S. Ichn. (see chap. 4).

63. Cf. Allen and Sikes, Homeric Hymns, 286–87. Radermacher 71 argues that there was a separate reed (cane) fastener for each of the seven strings. Hesychius (s.v. δόνακα ὑπολύριον), in commenting on Ar. Ra. 233, says that in former days cane (instead of horn) was "placed under" or "placed at the foot of" lyres. Thphr. HP 1.6.10 comments on the strength of cane, particularly that cut from the lower part of the stalk. Sophocles, fr. 36 Pearson (see chap. 4), speaks of something snapped like a lyra without its cane, but the fragment provides no information as to the specific function of the donax (reed). Abert, "Saiteninstrumente," col. 1761, interprets the cane as being used for the lower string fastener, and seems to have no doubts that the statements by later commentators about the substitution of horn also refer to the lower string fastener. On the fragments of shell from Argos and Vassae, see below, p. 39 and n. 77; see also chap. 4.

64. Allen and Sikes, 275. Cf. also Albert Gemoll, Die Homerischen Hymnen, 193, who argues that the seven-stringed instrument must predate Terpander.

65. John Boardman, ABFV, pl. 116.2. Other early references to the chelys as a lyre include Sappho's address to her "god-like chelys" (fr. 118, LP) and her mention of a "clear-sounding chelys, fond of song" (φιλάοιδον λίγυραν χελύνναν, fr. 58.12, LP). In addition, Alcaeus, fr. 736.2, LP, mentions a sea-chelys, which may or may not refer to an instrument.

66. On Athens Agora P 10154 there seems to have been only one man on the left; those behind him are probably women. On Cambridge Mus. Class. Arch. 345, both groups are women.

67. R. M. Dawkins, ed., The Sanctuary of Artemis Orthia at Sparta, pl. 189, nos. 10, 11.

68. Ibid., pl. 180, no. 19.

69. Ibid., pl. 183, no. 19. Numbers 18 and 20 are back views. In 19 and 20, the free ends of arms and crossbar may have been broken off, or the figures may have been made without them to avoid small protruding pieces likely to be broken off.

70. Ibid., pl. 166, no. 5, and 167, part A.

71. The same scene, with many of the same details, also appears on a krater from an Attic workshop, Paris E 623.

72. In order of reference: Athens Kerameikos 2869 (fig. 14b); Athens Nat. Mus. unnumbered Corinthian aryballos from Perachora; band kylix, location unknown; Copenhagen 13536; Florence 4209 (fig. 14c); Heidelberg Univ. 68/1 (fig. 14d); New York 06.1021.26 (fig. 14e).

73. A similar scene with the lyre player between two sphinxes occurs in the third quarter of the century on a roughly painted Boeotian lekanis, Kassel T. 448.

74. The photograph of Paris E 861 (fig. 15c), CVA 1, pl. 36, 12, appears to be reversed. A lyre similar to the ones on Paris E 861 appears on a vase painted about the same time, London B 46. A small Boeotian terra-cotta of a standing chelys-lyra player (Athens 5708) also exhibits a high position for the string fastener. (The player is nude except for a headdress similar to that of the Cyprus figurines. His chelys-lyra has knobs on the crossbar and no free ends for the arms, as is common in the case of bronze or terra-cotta figures.)

75. Boston 23.595 and London 459.

76. Neat crisscrosses can also be seen on the crossbar on New York 41.162.184, a scene with a seated performer accompanying dancing komasts, bearded nude males with ivy wreaths on their heads (another scene of wine drinking and revelry). On Paris F 13, the second judgment of Paris scene (on both sides of the vase), the chelys-lyra is painted with arms attached at the *sides* of a small oval soundbox; this may be a chelys of an odd variety, the painter's attempt at perspective, or simply a chelys-lyra painted by an unobservant artist. See also Paris CA 3329, a mid-century vase with a similarly shaped instrument. Another oddly shaped example appears in a "Theseus and the Minotaur" scene on a vase by the Affecter (Taranto 117234). In one of the two similar scenes on this vase, a bystander holds Theseus' chelys-lyra: an instrument with a soundbox shaped like the waxing moon—the curve of its upper edge, between the two arms, parallels the bottom of the soundbox.

77. Panayiotis Phaklaris, "ΧΕΛΥΣ," 220ff. and pll. 77, 78. See also chap. 4.

78. Strabo 10.3.17 discusses the Asiatic sources of Greek music in general and mentions "barbitos" as an example of a foreign name. Both Frisk vol. 1, 220, and Chantraine 165 agree that the name is a foreign word of perhaps Phrygian origin. On the erroneous derivation of *barbitos* from the Sanskrit *bharbi* ("to pluck") given by F. Behn, *Musikleben im Altertum und frühen Mittelalter,* 87, see J. M. Snyder, "The Barbitos in the Classical Period," 332, n. 5. See also below, chap. 5, Etymology.

79. On this and another variant (*baromos*), see Snyder, "Barbitos," 332.

80. Pindar fr. 125, Snell.

81. Ath. 4.175d.

82. Ath. 4.182f. quotes another authority who says that Anakreon (as well as Sappho) mentioned the barbitos (= Sappho fr. 176, LP). Critias fr. 8D describes Anakreon as a "lover of the barbitos," and an elegiac poem attributed to Simonides (126, Diehl) says that Anakreon did not lay down his barbitos even in death (see Snyder, "Barbitos," 333–34). For a discussion of several vase paintings identified by Beazley as showing Anakreon (usually with the barbitos), cf. J. M. Snyder, "Aristophanes' Agathon as Anacreon."

83. Frisk, vol. 2, 525–26; Chantraine, 894–95.

84. For *psallein,* cf. Anakreon fr. 373, *PMG,* and Pindar fr. 125, Snell (*psalmon . . . paktidos,* "the twanging of the pektis"); the noun *psalmos,* "twanging" or "plucking," is used elsewhere for the twanging of a bowstring (Eur. *Ion* 173).

85. Anakreon fr. 374, *PMG.* The reading of the text varies among different editors, but all seem to agree that the verb used is *psallein* and that the magadis is described as having twenty strings. Alkman fr. 101, *PMG,* also mentions the magadis, but the three-word fragment is otherwise uninformative. These are the only occurrences of the word in Archaic literature.

86. On the etymology of magadis, cf. Frisk, vol. 2, 154, and Chantraine, 655. On the impact of Lydian influence on the eastern Greeks in general, see Dunbabin, *Greeks and their Eastern Neighbors,* 62–63.

87. A single vase painting of the Geometric period, Athens Nat. Mus. 784, may show a harpist and his instrument.

88. A mythological version of the Lydian origin of the pektis is reflected in a story told by Ath. 14.625e (quoting Telestes of Selinus), who says that the Lydians and Phrygians who came to Greece with Pelops (after whom the Peloponnesos was named) played the aulos and the pektis.

89. Fr. 22.11, LP. The first two letters of the instrument's name are missing, but the editors suggest the restored reading πᾱ] κτιν.

90. Ath. 14.635e (quoting Menaechmus of Sicyon).

Chapter 3: The Kithara in Classical Athens

1. See W. Merlingen, review of *Etudes Pélasgiques* by A. J. van Windekens; D. A. Hester, "Pelasgian," 356–57; Chantraine 530; Frisk 850–51.

2. Strabo, *Geog.* 9.17.

3. Eur. *Hyps.* 64.101 (Bond) and *Cyc.* 443–44; cf. also Ps. Plut. *de mus.* 3 and Ar. *Th.* 120. One "Asian" language with which the word *kithara* has been tenuously connected is Avestan (Old Persian), an Indo-European tongue in which the word *sihtar* (modern Hindu *sitar*) designates a three-stringed instrument (see F. Kluge, *Etymologisches Wörterbuch der deutschen Sprache,* 886). Although linguists have clearly established that initial *k* sounds in Proto-Indo-European remained plosives in the western branches of Indo-European and became sibilants in the eastern branches (the so-called centum-satem phenomenon), the form *sihtar* is so much later than *kitharis* that the two words cannot be cited as certain examples of this phenomenon; the word *sihtar,* in its earlier forms, may not have begun with a sibilant.

4. See p. 31.

5. In the literature from the first half of the 5th century (including Pindar, Bacchylides, and Aeschylus) there are 22 references to the word *phorminx* or its compounds, but only 6 from the second half (S. fr. 16 [Pearson]; Eur. *Ph.* 823, *Ion* 164, *Hel.* 172; Ar. *Av.* 219, *Th.* 327).

6. Eur. *Al.* 583.

7. Eur. *Ion* 882 and *H.F.* 350. Cf. also *IT* 1237, *Ion* 905, and *IA* 1037 (a reference to the music at the wedding of Peleus and Thetis). In *Hyps.* fr. 1.4 (Bond), the kithara is linked indirectly with Apollo via the Muses. Just as Apollo is closely associated with the kithara, so his polar opposite, Ares the war god, is described in Greek drama as *akitharis* (A. *Supp.* 681), "not sharing in lyre-playing," and *achoros,* "not sharing in the dance." The same sentiment is expressed in nonmythological terms by Bacchylides (14.13, Snell), who says that the "phorminx" and the dance have no place in the context of war.

8. The kithara is associated with Apollo in Eur. *Ion* 882 and 905, *IT* 1237, *Alc.* 583, and *HF* 350. Of the many references in Euripides to *lyra* (or to compound words formed from *lyra*), only four have to do with Apollo: *IT* 1129, *Med.* 424, *Alc.* 570, and fr. 480 (Nauck). No other names for lyres are mentioned by Euripides in connection with Apollo except for phorminx, in imitation of Homer (*Ion* 164).

9. Ar. *Av.* 219.

10. For *daidaleos,* see Pi. *P.* 4.296 (cf. *Il.* 9.187); another adjective that Pindar uses for the "phorminx," *liguspharagos* ("high crackling," fr. 140a.61, Snell) is based on the common Homeric epithet *ligus* (see p. 7). Epithets referring to the strings include *heptaktupos* ("seven-toned," Pi. *P.* 2.70), *heptaglossos* ("seven-tongued," Pi. *N.* 5.24), and less directly, *poikilogarys* ("many-voiced," Pi. *O.* 3.8). Another epithet applied by 5th-c. authors to the phorminx is *chryseos* ("golden," Ar. *Th.* 327; Pherekydes, *FGrH,* fr. 141 A).

11. Cf. Pi. fr. 140a.61 (Snell) and *N.* 9.8.

12. B. *Epin.* 14.13 and Pi. *P.* 10.39. Similar language is found in a fragment (*PMG* 948) attributed to Kydidos of Hermione (a kitharode): "some far-reaching cry [*boama*] of the lyra."

13. Ar. *Nu.* 963–66.

14. Leto has no distinctive attributes; if Artemis is represented with her attributes (bow, quiver), however, a second woman in the painting may be assumed to be Leto. One libation scene has been found in which both Zeus and Apollo are present; each of them holds a phiale, and a goddess holds a pitcher (London E 444).

15. Syracuse Museo Arch. Naz. 17427. See also John D. Beazley, *Etruscan Vase-Painting*, 75–76.

16. There are a number of scenes with an unidentified woman alone in the chariot. The woman is sometimes taken to represent Artemis or Ariadne (as bride of Dionysos). There is a single example in which the woman in the chariot is identified as Demeter (Würzburg 308), one in which a youth in the chariot is escorted by Dionysos, Apollo, Athena, and Hermes (Tarquinia RC 8262), and one in which Apollo himself mounts the quadriga while Artemis waits to hand the kithara up to him (Paris F 297).

17. On Berlin 1966.1 (black figured), three satyrs with three kitharas (part of the chorus of a satyr play?) walk to the right. The kithara player is a maenad on Rome, Villa Giulia 15730, and London B 202. Paintings of the kithara in female hands can be explained in other instances by the presence of Apollo; the woman (Artemis?) holds or carries the instrument for him. But see Berlin 1846, where Athena plays the kithara in the company of Dionysos, and Berlin 1869, on which a female kitharist accompanies the quadriga of Poseidon and Amphitrite.

18. There are also several paintings in which a mortal (presumably) plays the kithara in the presence of Heracles: Paris G50 (Heracles killing Busiris); Madrid 10916 (a bearded kitharist at a banquet where Heracles reclines on a couch); and Bucharest 03207 (boy playing kithara before a shrine of Heracles). A judgment of Paris scene is found on Brussels A 3089, and in this single instance, Paris' instrument is the kithara, not (as in the Archaic period representations) the chelys.

19. In a late black-figured painting by the workshop of the Athena Painter, Heracles and Athena sit facing each other, Heracles' club on the ground behind him (Altenburg 202). This is one of the rare scenes of a seated kithara player; there are a few others in which Apollo is the player. Heracles' club is also shown on Oxford G.240.

20. John Boardman, "Herakles, Peisistratos and Eleusis"; see especially pp. 10–11 on Heracles *mousikos*. See also Boardman, *ABFV*, 221.

21. Three vases depict a row of players of stringed instruments: Paris E 861, four players of the chelys (discussed in chap. 2); New York 25.78.66, three "woolly satyrs" playing "Thracian" kitharas (see chap. 6, fig. 13); and Berlin inv. 1966.1, three satyrs playing standard kitharas (see n. 17). According to information received from the Paris Bibliothèque Nationale, however, their vase numbered AVH 3392, which shows three kithara players in procession, is no longer considered authentic.

22. N.Y. 57.12.8 consists of several fragments of a lebes gamikos (wedding vase) on which a (wedding) procession that included two kithara players was painted.

23. This vase is especially interesting because it appears to depict a real-life religious custom. It is the only painting that has come to hand in which the couch is empty, i.e., shown as it would actually be at such an event.

24. Arist. *Pol.* 1341A labels the kithara an *organon technikon,* a "technical" instrument, i.e., one requiring the technique of a professional player.

25. Hdt. 1.23–24. In Herodotus' dialect, the term is *kithare.*

26. Another early occurrence of *kitharoidos* is in a comic fragment of about 430 B.C.; cf. Cantharus fr. 1 (Edmonds). The term *kitharist,* on the other hand, is used for a kithara player who may or may not be singing.

27. Pl. Com fr. 10 (Edmonds, vol. 1, p. 492), in which the speaker asks for his kithara and his *epiporpama.* Poll. 10.190 defines the latter as *kitharoidou skeue,* the costume of the kitharode.

28. The youth who plays the kithara before a shrine to Heracles, Bucharest 03207, ca. 430 B.C., wears a decorated and bordered sleeveless chiton.

29. Cf. E. G. Turner, "Two Unrecognized Ptolemaic Papyri," and D. D. Feaver, "The Musical Setting of Euripides' *Orestes.*" On the *Iphigenia* fragment (P. Leid. Inv. 510), see Thomas J. Mathiesen, "New Fragments of Ancient Greek Music"; the fragment was first published by D. Jourdan-Hemmerdinger, "Un nouveau papyrus musical d'Euripide."

30. On Sophocles' musical talents, see the anonymous *Vita,* secs. 3 and 5. Although the date of the biography is not known, its sources include reliable scholars such as Aristoxenus (4th century) and Ister (3d century). Cf. also Ath. 1.20F, and Karl Rupprecht, "Sophocles als Kitharistes." On the other hand, ancient biographies often contain much that is obvious fiction; see Mary R. Lefkowitz, *The Lives of the Greek Poets,* 75–87.

31. For a more detailed discussion, see J. M. Snyder, "*Aulos* and *Kithara* on the Greek Stage." Cf. also A. W. Pickard-Cambridge, *Dramatic Festivals of Athens²,* 257–62, and Flora R. Levin, "Music in Ancient Greek Drama."

32. Ps.-Plutarch, *de mus.* 3 (1132D) lists the names of the various kitharodic *nomoi* as follows: Boeotian, Aeolian, Trochaic, Oxys, Cepion, Terpandrean, and Tetraoidion. All these were apparently solo songs. A processional song, in which the kithara accompanied a chorus of singers, was called a *prosodion* (cf. Paus. 4.33.3 and Poll. 4.64). See also Abert, "*Kitharoidia,*" col. 531, and W. Vetter, "Nomos." See also chap. 7, n. 17.

33. On the general dangers of interpreting Pindar, see Mary R. Lefkowitz, *The Victory Ode,* 2, and Douglas Gerber, *Pindar's Olympian One.*

34. As R. W. B. Burton, *Pindar's Pythian Odes,* 91, notes with regard to *P.*1: "[The] impression of unity, clear enough even to us who can only read the poem, must have been much more vivid to those who heard it performed, because the lyre of the opening verses, the symbol of music and what music stands for in this ode, was visible and audible throughout as the unifying instrument." For a detailed study of the performance aspects of Pindar's odes in the light of their dance component, see William Mullen, *Choreia: Pindar and Dance.*

35. See p. 4. The word *lyra,* which occurs eight times in the odes (all but two of which are connected with performance of songs), is not found in any contexts significantly different from those in which *phorminx* occurs, and the adjectives used with either name are similar.

36. There has been much scholarly debate on the significance of the epithet "Dorian." Ulrich von Wilamowitz-Möllendorff, *Pindaros,* 233, thought that it referred to the particular type of lyre used as opposed to the mode of the song in question, for the mode, as he points out, is elsewhere (line 101) called Aeolian. For a different view, see Lefkowitz, *Victory Ode,* 80, who follows the scholiast in taking the adjective to refer to the type of song involved. It may be, however, that Pindar intends no special technical meaning; he is writing the ode for Hieron of Syracuse, a Corinthian colony in a generally Dorian island, and he may simply be acknowledging Sicily's Dorian way of life.

37. *N.* 5.24, *P.* 2.70–71.

38. Plu. *Per.* 13.5–6.

39. See chap. 2 on representations of contestants with the kithara, and J. A. Davison, "Notes on the Panathenaea," 42. Davison suggests (p. 41) that Pericles may have reinstituted contests that had been allowed to lapse for a time.

By the 4th century the victorious competitors at the Panathenaia were no longer awarded an amphora of highly prized olive oil but received instead a more readily convertible reward in the form of gold and silver (Arist. *Ath. Pol.* 60.3 and *IG* ii–iii.² 2311).

40. Würzburg 222 has, on one side, a kithara player standing between columns with cocks, but the obverse shows Dionysos and a maenad on a donkey.

41. Other examples include New York 20.245 and 56.171.38 (figs. 9 and 13).

42. Other kitharists standing alone, with no listener on reverse: London E 265, a young man in a bordered chiton; and Tarquinia RC 2800, a bald, bearded kitharist in a bordered chiton and himation.

43. Pherekrates fr. 6 (Edmonds).

44. Ar. *Eq.* 1278. For the superlative adjective *kitharoidotatos,* cf. also Eupolis fr. 293 (Edmonds).

45. Timotheus fr. 15, 229–33 (Page, *PMG*). Earlier in the poem (203–06) he speaks (perhaps even more obscurely) of the "newly-built Muse of the golden kitharis" (*chryseokitharin . . . mousan neoteuche*).

46. Plu. *Moralia* 238D (and cf. Plu. *Agis* 10.4; *Moralia* 84A) and Paus. 3.12.10.

47. Huchzermeyer 63–64 seems to ignore the wording of the Greek by citing this passage as proof that Timotheus' instrument was the "eleven-stringed kithara." So also Abert, "Saiteninstrumente," col. 1763. For the use of the *kroumata* of a lyre in connection with setting the rhythm for dancers, cf. Ar. *Th.* 120ff.

48. Fr. 144B (Edmonds, vol. 1, pp. 262–65), lines 8–10, 19–28. The translation is based on the Ms readings rather than the emendations that attempt to make the numbers correspond to the later accounts of Timotheus' and others' supposed additions of extra strings. The play is dated variously to 418 or 410 B.C.

49. For a detailed discussion of the double entendre in the passage, see E. K. Borthwick, "Notes on the Plutarch *De Musica* and the *Cheiron* of Pherecrates." The fragment is dated by Ingemar Düring, "Studies in Musical Terminology in 5th Century Literature," 177, to about 410 B.C.

50. Düring, 181–82, compares Ar. *Ra.* 1129, where the character Euripides speaks of Aeschylus' mistakes as being "more than twelve," or as we would say, "dozens." For *chorde* as "note" rather than "string," cf. Pl. *Phlb.* 56A, where the term is used in connection with the aulos. As Düring says, "the historical development of the kithara . . . has nothing to do with the expression *dodeka chordais* in this fragment." For the probable obscene double entendre, see Borthwick, "Notes," 68–69.

51. Increased complexity is attributed also to Lysander of Sicyon, whose dates are uncertain but who may have been a contemporary of Timotheus. The 4th-c. Philochorus of Athens (quoted in Ath. 637F) reports as follows: "[Lysander] was the first kithara-player to establish the practice of 'bare' kithara-playing [*psilokitharistike*], stretching the strings tight and making [the instrument's] voice rich and full—indeed making string-music like aulos-music, a practice first used by Epigonos [6th century] and his followers. Discarding the simplicity common among kitharists, he was the first to play well-colored modifications, as well as to perform on *iambi*, the *magadis,* and the so-called *syrigmos;* he alone could substitute one instrument for another of those at hand, and having increased the size of his presentation, was the first to establish a chorus around himself." This passage must be treated with caution, for it attributes a suspiciously large number of "firsts" to Lysander, and its language is open to debate on several points; the most serious dispute centers on the phrase *ten enaulon kitharisin,* which some take to mean that Lysander combined wind- and string-music rather than that he altered the latter so that its sound more closely resembled the former; see von Jan and Graf.

52. Heracles: Leiden PC 41.

53. The contention that the left-hand fingers did touch the strings is supported not only by the vase paintings but also by the remains of the Parthenon frieze, Acropolis plaque 875. The left hand of the figure on the left was visible; the fingers are now missing above the lowest joint, but enough remains to show that they angled forward toward the strings.

54. Harmonics are soft tones at least an octave higher than the fundamental pitch produced by the string. They are created by touching the string lightly at a point along its length such that the string will be caused to vibrate, not as one unit, but as several equal shorter units which will sound a higher pitch.

55. Shortening the vibrating length of a string gives it a higher pitch. If the pitch desired is only, say, a step or half-step higher than the pitch of the open string, the string must be shortened by only a small amount; that is, its effective length must be shortened by pressing it firmly close to one end or the other.

56. The plektron is not always visible, but when it is not, the position of the right hand and fingers suggests its presence.

57. Cambridge, Harvard 1960.236, shows a satyr who holds his plektron up near his face, wrist rotated so that the plektron is near his nose, in a position that could indicate either the beginning of a stroke outward or the completion of one inward.

58. Otto Gombosi, *Tonarten und Stimmungen der Antiken Musik,* 118–120. Of the 20 examples (not 21, as two refer to the same vase) cited by Gombosi, only a few—not more than 4—actually show the plektron held between bridge and lower string fastener by a person in the act of playing the instrument. One of these is Boston 26.61 (fig. 8).

59. Satyrs: Tarquinia 678 and Frankfort, STV 4. Kitharodes: New York 56.171.38 (fig. 13), Boston 26.61 (fig. 8), London E 265, Univ. of Canterbury, N.Z. Logie Coll. 3/53, and Leningrad 614.

60. See also Leiden PC 3. Artemis, who holds the kithara for Apollo in the scene on Paris F 297, has her right hand around the crossbar in "tuning" position; her left hand, however, is not in the sling but underneath the soundbox.

61. Eur. *Ion* 881ff., *heptaphthongou,* "seven-toned." The same passage speaks of the "cry of the kithara, which rings out the Muses' lovely-sounding hymns amidst/by means of the rustic, lifeless horns." The reference to horns has been interpreted as meaning either the "horns" formed by the lyre's arms or the horn used as material for a soundboard. The former is unlikely, since in the case of the kithara the arms are not horn-shaped, and the latter is not supported by any other evidence from the Classical period. A third possibility is that the phrase *agraulois kerasin en apsychois* refers to the means by which the kithara is made to ring out, i.e., the plektron (for similar instrumental datives with *en,* cf. Hom. *Il.* 7.429, S. *Ph.* 60, and so on). The point would be that the horn-plektron, though itself "lifeless," can bring the instrument to life; the use of the plural, "horns," is, however, troublesome if the plektron is meant.

62. Eur. *Ion* 882; *IA* 1039. Ar. *Ec.* 737–41.

63. *Toplattotrat* occurs repeatedly in Ar. *Ra.* 1281–1308, where Euripides parodies Aeschylus' choral odes; *trettanelo* is from the scholiast on Ar. *Pl.* 290, who says that Aristophanes is imitating the tragedian Philoxenus' use of the onomatopoetic word to describe the Cyclops Polyphemus *kitharizonta* ("playing the kithara" or "playing the lyre"). Both words are here transliterated in such a way as to reproduce the actual sound of the Greek as accurately as modern theory allows. For later evidence connecting the sound of the letter *tau* with the sound of stringed instruments, see Aristides Quintilianus 2.14 (Thomas J. Mathiesen, trans., *On Music,* by Aristides Quintilianus, 143).

64. The kitharas on New York 21.88.73, Syracuse 45911, and Ferrara 2893 all show this characteristic elongation of the bottom of the soundbox. They are dated between 450 and 420 B.C.

65. Martha Maas, "Back Views of the Ancient Greek Kithara," 175 and pl. 19a.

66. Examples: London B 258 and B 460.

67. Curt Sachs, *Die Musikinstrumente des Alten Ägyptens*, pll. 6–8; Lise Manniche, *Ancient Egyptian Musical Instruments*, 81–83.

68. The bridge of the kithara on Plovdiv 298 (fig. 7) is a rectangle (without "feet") on which lines are drawn to indicate a prism-like shape. The bridge is not always at right angles to the strings— it may tilt up on the right side, as on Cambridge, Harvard 1960.236, leading us to speculate that the strings on the right side in this instance may have been ones of higher pitch, since they are effectively somewhat shorter. The (possibly late) Greek term for bridge seems to have been *magas* (or, in the diminutive form, *magadion*); cf. Luc. *DDeor.* 7.4, and Hsch., s.v. *magas*. See also Michaelides, *Music of Ancient Greece,* 196.

Leningrad 612, in the place where the bridge should be, has a peculiar large dark circle with smaller circles inside it. An excellent detailed representation of the lower string fastener is found on the instrument on a Fiesole black-figured amphora, CVA 57, pl. 2524. The (possibly late) Greek terms for the lower string fastener include *bater* and *chordotonos;* cf. Michaelides, *Music of Ancient Greece,* 51.

69. The instrument shown on Vienna 415 has long "pin"-shaped kollopes showing above and below the crossbar, which also widens at the center.

70. Ferrara 2893, dated ca. 430–420 B.C., lacks the scroll part of the ornament; but other vases of late date, such as Syracuse 17427 and Syracuse 45911, still have it.

71. The serpent (or "dragon") effect is especially marked in the case of the kithara on a red-figured lebes stand, Cambridge, Fitzwilliam Mus. X 13; another example is Paris, Petit Palais 304. Representations of the Python are rare and of poor quality; but the serpents/dragons encountered by Jason (who is being regurgitated by one on the Vatican kylix by Douris) and by Kadmos (who fights two smaller ones on Paris E 669) will serve well enough to illustrate the similarity.

72. Ar. *Eq.* 531–36. Although the ancient scholiast on this passage interpreted the metaphorical description of Cratinus' senility as being based on the image of a decrepit bed, recent commentators have noted the much more likely metaphor of a lyre whose decorations are falling out and whose strings can no longer be properly tuned. See W. W. Merry, ed., *Aristophanes' Equites,* 36, and J. van Leeuwen, ed., *Aristophanis Equites,* 101. Some erroneously take the amber as referring not to amber studs but to amber "pegs" (kollopes), as does H. Blümner, *Technologie und Terminologie der Gewerbe und Künste bei Griechen und Römern,* vol. 2, p. 384, n. 2; but the evidence suggests that even in post-Homeric times the kollopes were not "pegs" in the modern sense of the word, and that they were normally made of leather and wood (see p. 64).

73. Other examples: (circles near edge of soundbox) Trieste S 405, Ferrara VP T.55; (circles near bridge) Bologna 228; Brussels R 240; Gotha 36; (circles midway between bridge and edge) Oxford 1965.119.

74. See London B 262, New York 67.44.1, Tarquinia 681, Hannover 1964.9, and Hannover 1965.30. Boston 96.719 also has a circle in the upper corner marked off by the section lines, as does Leiden PC 2.

75. Sch. *Il.* 15.256; the scholiast derives the Homeric epithet of Apollo (*chrysaor*) from the name for the strap of the kithara (*aorter*).

76. See Bologna Pell. 276, dated ca. 465; Warsaw, Czar. 34, dated 475–50 B.C.; and Syracuse 45911, dated 450–20 B.C.

77. London E 383 is an example.

78. On Paris F 297 there is no loop, but the painting is interesting because (a) the sling hangs loose (it is not being used), and (b) the sash, apparently of different material, hangs from it at its "button" fastener.

79. Other examples of the separate peg: fig. 4 and Brussels A 200.

80. L. D. Caskey and J. D. Beazley, *Attic Vase Paintings in the Museum of Fine Arts, Boston,* text vol. 2, p. 42.

81. Other examples: (red figured) Cincinnati, Univ. Classics Library, kalyx krater; (black figured) Toledo 56.70; Oxford 1965.116. In the notes for Munich 2319 it is suggested that the sash represents a narrow case that contains the extra strings, an explanation that would at least account for the fact that the sash is sometimes painted red.

82. The cloth shown on Warsaw, Czar. 34, also seems to be fastened under the sling. Paris F 297 is apparently a back view with the cloth hanging at the outer arm but on the front instead of the back of the kithara. The arrangement shown on Austin, Univ. of Texas 1980.63 (red-figured lekythos, ca. 470 B.C.), also appears to be an exception; here the diamond-patterned cloth, shown in back view, is draped over Nike's left wrist, not attached to the instrument.

83. Similarly, on Philadelphia, Univ. of Pa. MS 5399, the cloth seems to be draped over the arm of the instrument nearest the player (the authors have inspected the vase), and on Munich 2319 the cloth hangs from behind the left side of the instrument.

84. Other examples: Athens 1626; Bonn 72; Ferrara VP T.55; Vienna 415.

85. Plektron over the bridge: New York 53.224; Vienna 698; Naples 192. Plektron over lower string fastener: Boston 95.45. An actual plektron made of bronze in the Badisches Landesmuseum, Karlsruhe, is discussed by Dieter Metzler, "Ein griechisches Plektron."

86. This method of holding the plektron is also found in a painting on a red-figured kalyx krater now in the Univ. of Cincinnati Classics Library (manner of the Berlin Painter, ca. 500–475 B.C.).

87. On Vienna 3739 the plektron cord is looped over the right (outer) arm of the instrument from the front; the plektron can be seen behind the outside edge of the arm.

88. Huchzermeyer 47 overgeneralizes when he claims that the "phorminx" was usually played simultaneously with auloi, according to Pindar. In fact, Pindar mentions them together in only six instances, of which the following four are references to the actual performance of the odes: *O.* 3.8, 7.12, and 10.93; *N.* 9.8.

89. In the scene of Heracles killing Busiris before an alter (Paris G 50), discussed above, there is a player of the barbitos as well as a kithara player; since the scene is supposed to take place in Egypt, perhaps we should consider anomalies of costume and instruments as deliberately introduced barbarous details to indicate foreignness.

90. Bucharest 03207, dated ca. 430 B.C.

Chapter 4: The Chelys-Lyra in Classical Athens

1. Ar. *Th.* 136–41.

2. Pi. *N.* 3.12, 10.21, and 11.7; *P.* 8.31; *O.* 2.47; 6.97, and 10.93. Cf. also *P.* 10.39, in which reference is made to the "shouts" (*boai*) of lyres in the land of the Hyperboreans.

3. Eur. *Ph.* 822–25.

4. Pherekydes, fr. 41a (*FGrH*).

5. Pherekrates, fr. 42 (Edmonds). But see the discussion in chap. 6 on Ion of Chios for an exception.

6. Eur. *I. T.* 143–47; Eur. *Hel.* 184–90; A. *A.* 988–94; and Eur. *Alc.* 445–47. Cf. also S. fr. 849 (Pearson) and *OC* 1220–23; Eur. *Ph.* 1026–31 and *Alc.* 430–31.

7. Cf. Frisk, 146, and Chantraine, 651. See, contra, Boisacq, 592, who derives the name from I.E. *lu-, *leu-d (as in Latin *laus, laudis*).

8. Ar. *Ra.* 1304 and *Av.* 491. A fragment from one of Aristophanes' comedies (671, Oxford) mentions a particular lyre maker by name, one Eudoxos, on whose lyre someone is playing a twittering, simpleminded tune.

9. Fr. 387 (*PMG*). The reading of *lyropoios,* however, is doubtful. Kritias fr. 67 (Diels and Kranz) mentions the term *chordopoles,* or "dealer in music strings."

10. Sapph. 44.33 (L-P); B. 20B (Snell); Ar. *Th.* 969; Eur. *Alc.* 570; fr. 480 (Nauck). Cf. also Ar. *Th.* 315 (*chrysolyra,* "golden lyred").

11. For "lyra" in connection with Apollo, see e.g., Pi. fr. 215a.9 (Snell); Eur.*IT* 1129 and *Med.* 424. Cf. also Stesich. fr. 278 (*PMG*) for the association of "lyra" with the Muses.

12. A rare compound is *antilyros* ("responsive to the lyre"), as in S. *Tr.* 643.

13. Ar. *V.* 957ff. For similar uses of *kitharizein,* cf. also Ar. *Nu.* 1353–58 and Phryn. Com. fr. 2 (Edmonds).

14. Phld. *Mus.* 1.13.

15. Hdt. 1.155.4.

16. There are some small indications that the artist, though painting the outlines of a chelys-lyra, was really thinking in terms of the kithara: the lyre in a quadriga scene on Athens 12282 is provided with knobs, almost unknown on the chelys-lyra; and on Warsaw, once Goluchow 23, in a crudely painted quadriga scene, the upper arms of the lyre above the crossbar are long and rectangular, and the outline of the instrument is similar to that of the kithara.

17. There are seven large paintings of the chelys-lyra in quadriga processions, four black-figured (two amphoras, a krater, and a stand), Oxford 1965.118, Paris F 232, Paris F 309, and Eleusis 470, and three red-figured (two amphoras and a krater), Munich 2306, Athens Acropolis NA 57Aa 696, and Cleveland 30.104. On the Munich vase Apollo rides in the chariot, and the lyra tucked under his arm takes up less room than would the large kithara. On Paris F 232 there are three wedding quadrigas, one with no instrument, one with a kithara (played by a bearded man), and one with the chelys-lyra and a youthful player. The figures in the small paintings are difficult to identify, but Hermes, Athena, Dionysos, and satyrs can be recognized in some of them. Apollo is presumably the lyre player, though the exaggerated bun (*krobylos*) on the back of the head that this style produces has sometimes led writers to say that the figure is female. Several vases present a lyre player with white-painted arms and face, the conventional indication that the player is female. Another unusual detail is the presence of a figure seated on a *diphros* (stool) usually at the horses' heads, a feature rarely found in the quadriga processions on large vases, and in the chelys-lyra group, only on lekythoi and a single cup. Both the white-painted flesh and the seated figure are found on funerary vases on which the figures have no identifying characteristics.

18. On Bologna 292 Artemis holds the phiale and Apollo carries only a staff (a youth to his left carries the chelys-lyra). Behind Artemis on the right is Leto, seated, it appears, on a rock. Beazley suggests the youth is Mousaios, but he does not give a sufficient reason.

19. There are a number of paintings of Apollo alone, or single figures that can be assumed to be Apollo, holding the chelys-lyra in the left arm and a phiale in the right hand, an abbreviated version of the libation scene. Apollo is often seated, as in the white-ground plate Delphi 8140. The standing woman on Athens 1300 holds both a chelys-lyra and a phiale and may represent Artemis, though she is alone.

20. The two examples of Heracles' introduction in the present sample are Trieste S 424 and Berlin 2278. The paintings of Apollo and Marsyas are Bologna 301 and London 1920.6-13.2.

On a hydria by Polygnotos, Gotha 51, Apollo stands to the right of an altar with the chelys-lyra; a man identified as Diomedes (a Greek who fought in the Trojan War) stands with a youth at the left; and above the altar flies a Nike.

21. The two scarabs, both in the Boston Mus. of Fine Arts, are pll. 304 and 351 in Boardman, *Greek Gems.*

22. A Roman relief at Naples, said to be a copy of a Greek relief from the 5th century B.C., portrays Orpheus with Eurydice and Hermes: Evelyn B. Harrison, "Hesperides and Heroes," pl. 12d and pp. 76ff.

23. The sickle-shaped knives of the Thracian women suggest that this story has its origin in a fertility myth. The story also suggests that Orpheus (said to have foresworn women after the loss of Eurydice) was killed for alienating the affections of the Thracian men (see chap. 6). The painting on Ferrara T. 563, if indeed it is of Orpheus, seems to show him with a woman's breast, apparently to suggest effeminacy. The figure is in the clothes of a Thracian man (short chiton and boots) and is seated on a rock, as Orpheus often is portrayed. Across from him is a winged Eros, a branch in his right hand and what appears to be an extinguished torch in his left.

24. There are exceptions: On Vienna 697 and Boston 00.356 it is a Muse who has the chelys-lyra, and on Schwerin KG 706 and Adolphseck 68 both Apollo and a Muse have a chelys-lyra.

25. Others are Ferrara T. 127, Hannover 1961.24, and Cambridge Fitz. G. 73. Henry R. Immerwahr, "Book Rolls on Attic Vases," includes sixteen vases that show Muses holding scrolls.

26. Traditional names of the Muses are provided by Hesiod *Th.* 25ff., but they were not individually assigned to specific arts until Roman times. In this painting Terpsichore plays a harp, and there is a "late phorminx" suspended on the wall above and behind her; for discussion of these instruments see chap. 6.

27. For the instrument usually played by Thamyras, and associated with him, see chap. 6. On a much damaged late 5th-c. vase (New York 16.52) the central facts of the story are not in evidence: we see only a young man playing the lyre surrounded, with no hint of conflict, by seven of the Muses, playing lyres and krotala, and two Erotes. There are a tree to indicate the out-of-doors and an altar, a platform with three small female statues. Perhaps there was a version of the story in which Thamyras was said to have been at one time a favorite of the Muses, as he seems in this painting.

28. J. Caskey and J. D. Beazley, *Attic Vase Paintings in the Museum of Fine Arts, Boston,* 1:36. See *ARV*[2] 774 for other opinions.

29. The three women on the B side of Vienna 697 are Muses, though only one has an instrument, the chelys-lyra, for the A side of this bell-krater shows Apollo with two lyre- and aulos-playing Muses. Other vases of the late 5th and early 4th centuries show Muses with the chelys-lyra, among them The Hague, Scheurleer 623, and Munich 3268, an Apulian volute krater.

30. On the difficulty of exact identification of the youth in many cases, see Sophia Kaempf-Dimitriadou, *Die Liebe der Götter in der attischen Kunst des 5. Jahrhunderts V. Chr.,* 16–21, 81–93. Some

Eos–Tithonos scenes do not include a lyre. The association of the chelys-lyra with schoolboys is discussed below.

On *rhyton* London E 787 there are two Eos figures pursuing one youth. Since the youth is fleeing, there seems no need to reinterpret the winged figures as Nikes. On Cambridge GR 22.1937 it is Eos who holds out the lyre toward Tithonos as she pursues him; he prepares to strike her with a small branch.

31. Caskey and Beazley, *Attic Vase Paintings*, text vol. 2, p. 37. The second youth is included on Chicago 89.95, Genoa 1216 (where he wears "hunter" costume), and on Hearst Hillsborough 21.

32. There is another bearded man on the far left, behind Eos. The scene is nearly the same on the other side of this vase: here the bearded man with a scepter stands between the youths, both of whom have lyres, and there is a third youth (Dardanos?) fleeing on the left behind Eos, in the place of the second bearded man.

33. The same scene, differing only in small details, appears on both sides of the vase.

34. Adesp. 405 (Nauck, *TGF*).

35. Paris is also portrayed without the lyre in some paintings of this scene. On London E 330 Hermes alone approaches Paris—there are no goddesses included in the scene.

36. On Berlin 4043 both Aphrodite and Hera carry apples, which therefore cannot serve as attribute for either (nor can one of them represent the "Apple of Discord"). There is also a Nike in this scene; she does not reveal the winner (Aphrodite), however, for she stands next to Hera. Hera also carries an apple on London E 178. On London E 445 Artemis carries a flower.

37. Hyg. *Astr.* 2.2. See W. Gundel, "Lyra," *RE* vol. 13, pt. 2, cols. 2489–90.

38. Diels 2.143.9.

39. Lekythoi Oxford 311, Athens 1809 and 18599; astragalos New York 40.11.22; scarab from Boston, no. 333, in Boardman, *Greek Gems*. For a comprehensive survey of Eros figures in vase painting, see Adolf Greifenhagen, *Griechische Eroten*.

40. The same scene appears on the interior of kylix Florence 74355.

41. There are sometimes tables alongside the couches in these paintings, but there is no food on them—it is after dinner and time for wine and entertainment.

42. On New York kantharos 63.11.4 the chelys-lyra is actually being played by an elderly guest with long white hair (and a red beard!). The scene includes an entertainer playing the aulos.

43. The framing figures on Copenhagen Chr. VIII 991 are not seated; they are walking away to either side and looking back at the scene.

44. On skyphos Cambridge, Harvard 1927.30.21, the central figure is seated, not reclining on a couch, and the scene is framed by walking, draped figures. On a small squat lekythos at Thessaloniki there are no figures other than that of the bearded man who reclines on a couch; the lyre (painted in white) hangs above him, as it does in some symposium scenes on larger vases.

45. Mainz 91 is another example.

46. A girl in a knee-length chiton (bound in at the waist) and headband dances (elbows out, hands close to waist) on an unlabeled kylix in the Hermitage, Leningrad (photograph by J. M. Snyder). A chelys-lyra lies on the ground at her right.

A woman with krotala dances to the accompaniment of a woman playing the auloi on Cambridge, Fitzwilliam 4.1943, while a seated woman with the barbitos and another standing with the chelys-lyra hold their instruments without playing. On Munich 2363 the chelys-lyra hangs on the wall while a woman plays the "cradle kithara" for a dancing Eros (see chap. 6).

47. The Romans were aware of this practice. Cicero (*Sen.* 8.26) makes his character Cato say that although he learned Greek late in life, he was unable to emulate Socrates' old-age feat of learning to play the lyre so as to be able to accompany his singing.

48. Ar. *Eq.* 985–96.

49. Fr. 361 (Edmonds). See also n. 47.

50. Plu. *Them.* 2.4.

51. Plu. *Per.* 4.1–2; Pl. *R.* 4.424C. On Damon, see Anderson 74–81.

52. All the school and palaestra scenes (some forty vases in all) are painted on red-figured vases, with the exception of Boston 61.1233, a late 6th-c. black-figured skyphos, possibly made in Sicily.

53. The words may be translated "My Muse, by the smooth-flowing Skamandros I begin to sing. . . ." This fragment appears in Diehl's *Anthologia Lyrica* as Stesich. fr. 26. See Immerwahr, "Book Rolls," 19: "The boy seems to be reciting, the teacher checking."

54. There is no evidence of singing in the scenes discussed above, but on Cambridge, Fitzwilliam GR 8.1955 a youth sings (head raised, mouth open) while a bearded instructor sits playing the aulos. (There is a chelys-lyra hanging in the field.)

Several of these paintings have a second bearded man standing or sitting to one side; he is taken to be a *paidogogos*, a slave or freedman who accompanies a boy to school to protect him and see that he attends as he should. The paidogogos on London E 172 (see above) holds the chain of a young panther as he waits on the far left; on Munich 2421 he is named (Demetrios) with the words ναί ζῶν, i.e., "drawn from life."

On Philadelphia, Univ. of Pa. 30-33-130, a black-figured kylix, two figures, each with a lyre, are seated facing each other between palmettes. The figures may be women (the hair is done up in a knot on the back of the head); the silhouette technique does not permit identification.

55. On black-figured skyphos Boston 61.1233, the boy is nude and holds a *strigil* and *aryballos* (skin scraper and oil flask).

56. London E 525 and Washington 136373.

57. The tablets with a stylus, suspended in the background on *stamnos* (storage jar) London E 454, reverse side, where three youths, one with chelys-lyra in his hand, stand conversing, similarly identify the location as a school. Two other *stamnoi*, London E 455 and E 456, have similar scenes on the reverse but without the tablets in the background; and a considerable number of other large vases also have this rather simple scene, which, even without the tablets, may be tentatively designated as a "school" scene.

58. New York 58.11.1 is a good example. Others: Paris G 486, Cambridge, Harvard column krater, Laon 371059, Berkeley 8/930, Athens 1259, Chapel Hill kylix (lyre under handle), Copenhagen 3634.

59. Columns can also be seen in similar scenes on New York 41.162.33, Athens L 546, Oxford 1929.4, Sèvres 2038, and Athens 1418.

60. Other vases showing a rabbit being offered: New York L 68.142.15, Frankfurt 304, and Madrid 11268. Gesture of refusal: New York 52.11.4, Madrid 11268. On courtship and love gifts, see K. J. Dover, *Greek Homosexuality*, 91–100.

61. The youth with lyre faces right in one fragment, the Eros left in another; the Eros does not appear to pursue either youth. The two figures on a ceramic "bobbin," New York 28.167, are regarded as Zephyros and Hyakinthos by both Beazley and Richter, who note that the hair of the winged "Zephyros" figure is straight ("wild"). But the two figures are remarkably alike, apart from the wings and (partly) straight hair of the one on the left; both wear crown-like circlets, higher in the front, on their heads. It seems quite

possible that the youth on the right (with a chelys-lyra) is being seized by Eros (perhaps as a result of his lyre playing).

62. The youth on Paris G 552 bis stands on a two-step platform, and the object between the two figures on London E 542 may also be a platform.

On Munich 2323 one of the two Nikes (the one presenting the wreath) is not winged; she may, of course, represent a mortal woman, perhaps the boy's mother.

The woman who holds out the lyre to the youth on London E 542 also does not have wings, nor does the woman making a gesture of acclaim on Rome, Vatican 432, a black-figured oinochoe by Amasis (see further discussion of this vase [n. 63]).

63. The bearded judge stands on Geneva 14987; on Florence 74355 the figure in himation with staff (head missing) may also be the judge. The wreathed, bearded man seated on a diphros holding staff and flower on Rome, Vatican 432, may be a judge; though the scene looks domestic at first glance, the woman gesticulating behind the lyre player may be a goddess (a small fawn or kid stands near her), ivy branches surround the young man's lyre, and the youth in short chlamys with spear, a dog (probably—the head is damaged) beside him, may be the judge's attendant.

The young (beardless) man in a himation who stands leaning on his staff on Geneva 14986 does not appear to be a judge.

The scene on Athens 17539, much damaged, shows three youths: one whom a Nike approaches, perhaps presenting a fillet; another with a lyre; and a third without lyre.

64. There is a similar scene, but including an aulos player, on the reverse of this vase. Nike bearing phiale: Gela 112/13 and Taranto 54384.

65. Another custom that may have been followed in connection with contests is the dedication of votive objects at a sanctuary. The class of small terra-cotta figures from Rhodes of a standing young man with a lyre were perhaps made for this purpose, as was the small bronze, New York 08.258.5, a standing, bearded man in a chiton who plays the chelys-lyra and bears the inscription, in Attic alphabet and dialect, "Dolichos dedicated me."

66. On New York L 1970.32.6 a youth holding a lyre at his side holds out a *phorbeia* (aulos player's cheek strap) over the altar. The youth on London E 132 stands tuning his lyre, and on New York 22.139.72 the boy sits on a stool before the altar while playing; a long bag hangs on the wall next to him. On Athens Agora P 7246 the youth is also seated, but the lyre hangs on the wall, and he is wrapped in his himation.

67. Other choes with similar scenes: Athens 1546, Athens 1230, and Copenhagen Chr. VIII 519.

68. Several vase paintings seem related to the sailors-and-sirens myth: Paris CA 74 shows three sirens on rocks playing lyre, auloi, and krotala; there is a small dolphin in the field (two other vases also show harpies on rocks). Two vases by the Athena Painter, London B 651 and London 1920.3–15.1, show sirens on low platforms. In some instances there are human figures on either side of the siren. The representations found include a scaraboid, Paris M 2847, engraved with the figure of a siren holding a chelys-lyra with a flattened (?) base. It belongs to the second half of the 5th century.

69. Two of the three standing women are also named: Nikopolis and Kallis. The former appears on another hydria (both are by painters in the Group of Polygnotos), Florence 4014, discussed above (see women dancers). For another painting of Sappho with the chelys-lyra, see N. Kunisch, ed., *Antike Kunst aus Wuppertaler Privatbesitz*, no. 49.

70. On Brunswick 219 some of the women are named too: the bride is Kleophonis, and the other women are Kleodoxa, Euphemia, Kleodike, and Phanodike.

71. Scenes in which the bride plays a harp are more common, especially on lebetes. See chap. 6.

72. According to Beazley (*ARV²* 1179) there is a winged figure on both sides of the scene; he therefore calls them Nikes.

73. On Florence 3933 the second woman has no instrument but holds out a circular fillet to the lyre player.

On London E 326 a woman holds out both chelys-lyra and auloi; the second figure is a youth. A seated woman plays the lyre, feet on a small stool, while a man leaning on a staff with a small bag in his hand listens on Rhodes 12887.

74. London 459 and Cambridge, Fitzwilliam (no number), nos. 316 and 416 in Boardman, *Greek Gems*. Several vases also depict a running youth with a chelys-lyra: Bologna 361, Paris G 17, and Adria B 809.

75. On a black-figured lekythos in the Eleusis Museum there is only one listener, with a white face. On New York 57.12.12 the player stands between two seated figures, "Apollo and two seated goddesses."

76. In two examples a young man with the lyre and a woman are shown together: red-figured skyphos frag., Tübingen S/10 1630b, and Athens Kerameikos Gr. 131, P 28, 1116, a white-ground lekythos.

77. A bearded man in himation and headband with a single "point" in front carries a chelys-lyra and looks back on kantharos Warsaw, once Goluchow 64. The scene may be related to the one on the reverse side, where a youth holds out an aryballos.

78. On a white-ground eyecup a man with the chelys-lyra and a woman with auloi sit between the eyes; a (palm?) tree between them suggests Apollo and Artemis: Karlsruhe B 777. In a small yet heterogeneous group of red-figured cups we find two youths, both with a lyre or one with lyre and the other with auloi. In most of these scenes there are other figures as well, other youths or women; the women on New York 23.160.54 have flowers, a perfume vase, and a fillet.

79. Aulos and chelys-lyra account for almost half the scenes with another instrument present, nearly a tenth of all chelys-lyra representations. In addition, there are a number of paintings in which, though no aulos is visible, an aulos bag hangs on the wall or dangles from the lyre player's wrist or the arm of his instrument.

80. The Muses, with barbitos, auloi, and five chelys-lyrai, fill the space surrounding Thamyras (who plays the kithara) and Apollo on a vase discussed earlier, Ferrara T. 127.

81. The harp in London E 271 is discussed in chap. 6.

82. Orpheus is sometimes portrayed wearing laurel wreath and himation, sometimes wearing "Thracian" costume (short tunic and high boots), as on Boston 90.156.

83. On vases painted near the end of the 5th century we occasionally see a nude Apollo, and there are some "formal" scenes (such as libation scenes) from this time in which he wears only the himation.

84. The plektron itself is not always clearly visible, but when it is not, the fingers of the right hand are bunched as they are in holding the plektron, and the hand and wrist form the same angle seen when the plektron is visible.

85. There are, however, rare examples in which the hand is quite close to the strings on the side away from the player; these might be interpreted as showing the beginning of a stroke inward, though we do not consider it likely: Vienna 1788; New York 22.139.72.

86. There are also 15 vases at hand on which the performer holds the plektron at the center of the instrument, on or near the strings. In at least one-third of these either the strings or the player's hand is not clearly shown; in others, a fold of cloth or (in the case

of seated players) the performer's thigh comes between the plektron and the instrument. There are only five instances in which the plektron touches the strings, and none of these allows us to reach a conclusion about the direction of the stroke or affords any evidence that the plektron is plucking one string at a time. In one further case, the plektron is shown just to the right of the strings, and low—near the lower ends of the strings on the outer side (London B 167, fig. 8). But in no case is the plektron shown on the strings below the bridge, in the position suggested by Gombosi as a way of changing the pitch of the strings by pressing the plektron against them (see chap. 3).

87. There are also a number of examples in which the left-hand fingers, tightly curled, appear to grasp the strings. In about a dozen cases the lyre is definitely not being played: the player may have a libation dish in his right hand (as in Delphi 8140) or may hold the plektron down by his side (as in Brussels A 1020, fig. 23). In a few other cases his right hand is near some point in the usual line of stroke-and-return, but the player appears to meditate or to give his attention to something else, so that perhaps no actual playing is in progress; his left hand may be grasping the strings or perhaps absentmindedly plucking them with the thumb (see fig. 4 [New York 24.97.30]; London E 178; and Hamburg Inv. 1900.164).

88. A small number of vases that show a player who is not actually playing, i.e., whose right hand is not being used for this purpose, have been considered in reaching these conclusions, since the left hand maintains the same positions observable among players who *are* fully engaged. Vases on which the player's thumb is not actually visible have also been considered here if the other fingers are straight. The core of this group consists of over a dozen chronologically well-distributed vases showing a performer whose left-hand thumb is visible and whose right hand uses the plektron to play.

89. Left hand tilted: Vienna 947; once Northampton, Castle Ashby 67. A more doubtful example: New York 06.1129, on which the hand is very tilted; both the thumb and third finger may be plucking the strings.

90. Another example is Trieste S 424, on which the player's thumb is quite separate from the fingers and somewhat bent back; the fingers themselves are curved somewhat toward the *inner* arm. On Hillsborough Hearst 17 the player's thumb is out, but the fingers curve forward: similar positions are rarely found elsewhere except when the player is tuning (and presumably plucking two strings at once with thumb and little finger to test their pitches). See also once Northampton, Castle Ashby 74, where the little finger is extended straight to the side.

Good red-figured examples of the left hand with fingers and thumb quite straight and separated are Mykonos 970 and a Rome, Vatican hydria.

91. Good black-figured examples include Oxford 1965.125 and Oxford 1965.118; the "teacher" on Berlin 2285 is a good example in red figure, as is the "student" on Oxford 1914.734.

In New York 22.139.72 the player plucks with his thumb while his other left-hand fingers are curled; New York 96.18.143 is another example. New York 41.162.169 shows us a woman whose left-hand fingers are bent straight forward to touch the strings of her lyre; her thumb is bent over her palm but appears not to pluck the strings.

92. A good example is Paris G 226, a back view. Another back view, Ferrara T.293, shows two fingers and three more bent than four and five, presumably to allow them to damp strings that lie closer when the wrist is rotated. The straight index finger shown in Paris Musée Rodin 993 clearly does not take part in damping, though the other fingers appear to; in Syracuse 23794 it is difficult to say which fingers might take part—the index, fourth, and fifth

fingers are bent stiffly from the first knuckle (the palm) while the third finger curves forward.

93. A similar example (a series of o's) is found among the players of the barbitos (see chap. 5), on London E 171; the o's are not visible on the *CVA* photograph.

94. Singers to the chelys-lyra may be included among groups of partygoers on two other vases: Rome Mus. Capit. 122 is painted too crudely to make it certain that the player sings; and Rome Villa Giulia 3584 is too damaged, though it does seem likely that the player is singing.

95. The youths who play before the altar on New York 22.139.72 and Toronto 365 have their lips slightly parted, and on London E 390 Orpheus, playing his lyre while seated on a rock, appears to sing for the Thracian men.

96. The chelys-lyra is also identified by Eur. *HF* 683 as having seven strings.

97. Lines 252ff. in D. L. Page, ed., *Select Papyri*, vol. 3.

98. S. fr. 238 and fr. 244 (Pearson). Pearson's comment that *pektai lyrai* is a periphrasis for *pektides* is questionable. On animal horns, cf. Hdt. 4.192.1 on the Libyans' use of antelope horns in the construction of lyres.

99. The relevant comments are collected by A. C. Pearson, ed., *The Fragments of Sophocles*, vol. 1, pp. 27–28. None of the commentators mentions the important description in the *Homeric Hymn to Hermes*. Instead, they generally conclude that horn is the contemporary replacement for reed but without mention of its exact placement or function; the only hint of location is contained in their common view that the material is "placed under" the lyre. Do they mean that horn was used as reinforcement for the soundbox? Or are they referring to something placed under the strings, i.e., a bridge to support them?

100. Of 246 instruments that can be measured in this way, 64 are one (or slightly less) to 1¼ as tall as the forearm measure; 117 are from about 1⅓ to 1⅔ of this measure; and 65 are from about 1¾ to 2 times this length.

In some cases, the conditions under which items were studied (photographic distortion, vases locked in display cases, and so forth) have made measurements of great exactness impossible.

101. Similar remains at Arta measure 16.6 by 13.1 cm, and those at Argos are 17.5 cm high: Panayiotis Phaklaris, "ΧΕΛΥΣ." (The surprisingly small dimensions of these shells, which belonged to lyres found in graves or in the refuse from offerings at temples of Apollo, are perhaps accounted for if the instruments were made to be grave or temple offerings.) In the vase paintings, the width of the soundbox is normally the same as, or only slightly less than, the width between the arms.

102. Of 386 instruments with strings that can be counted, 53 have two or four strings; 42 have five; 92 have six; 180 have seven; 14 have eight; and 5 have nine strings. Instruments with two to four strings and those with five strings appear mainly on lekythoi and similar vases that are generally small and poorly painted.

103. For examples of the extremes, see black-figured amphora San Simeon 5498 (parallel strings) and red-figured hydria Athens 1176 (widely diverging).

104. The depth of the chelys-lyra's soundbox can be seen in figs. 7 and 23. For assistance in identifying the *testudo marginata*, the authors wish to thank John Condit and George Dalrymple, Department of Zoology, Ohio State University.

105. See the discussion of the shape of the arms below. On a 5th-c. cornelian scarab, probably from Ionia (Boston 98.734), a youth tunes a lyre that appears to be made of the skull and horns of an antelope or gazelle. See also n. 98.

106. For a discussion of the way in which the bridge and cara-pace might have been used to brace the arms of the lyre and a more detailed discussion of the construction and reconstruction of the chelys-lyra, see Helen Dalby Roberts, "Ancient Greek Stringed Instruments, 700–200 B.C.," 37–128.

107. Rounded shapes: London, Kalymnian stater, late 6th century; London, drachma from Pordosilene, after ca. 450 B.C.; Cambridge, Lewes House, green jasper scarab, late 6th century; New York, cornelian scaraboid from Cyprus, early 5th century.

Several particularly squashed-looking examples on Athenian vases such as London B 171 may be yet another experiment with perspective, though one cannot rule out the possibility that the natural oval of the tortoise shell was sometimes used sideways, with an arm fitted at each end, or that some other soundbox material is depicted.

108. Some of the terra-cottas in the class of Lindos 2355 (a young man standing holding a lyre) indicate the individual shell "bumps" (laminae) with rounded, raised sections, as does a Karian stater with a lyre in back view (see n. 111). A coin with a whole tortoise on it shows this feature in the same way. For the view that the soundbox was often of wood, see Phaklaris, "ΧΕΛΥΣ," pp. 230–31; but lyrai elephantinai (IG I² 276.15) is surely a generic use—the instruments meant were probably ivory-decorated kitharas. No evidence has come to light to show that the lyra might be made of wood and decorated with tortoise-shell laminae (Wegner, Musikleben, p. 37–38).

109. On a white-ground vase, Boston 01.8080, the belly of the instrument and the strings are painted in a golden yellow. For an account of a method of fixing the hide in place used in an experimental reconstruction, see Helen Roberts, "Reconstructing the Greek Tortoise-shell Lyre," especially pp. 309–10.

110. Holes in edges of shell remains: Phaklaris, "ΧΕΛΥΣ," pp. 222–25. Short lines or dots on border: London E 58, Florence 3946, London E 191, London E 178, and Adria B 254.

On several vases the shell has a border painted with tortoise-shell markings, as if these were the marginal laminae, though the shape of the shell is not the natural shape: Adria B 534; Athens 1418.

Some paintings show no border at all: London E 159, London E 445, and Munich 2421. The chelys markings on the latter are unusually fanciful (see fig. 21), resembling maeanders.

On a few front views of the chelys-lyra a border can also be seen: New York 28.167, Vienna 3700, and Chicago 89.95, for example; the last also has small black dots along the border. If this is not a mistake, it may represent a narrow band of hide fastened over the edge for greater strength.

111. On a stater in London, late 6th century, from Kalymna (island of Karia in the eastern Aegean), the back of a chelys-lyra is represented, with realistic pattern of raised laminae. The shape of the shell itself is round, except for an irregularity at the bottom.

On the reverse side of a drachma from Pordosilene (Lesbos) dated after ca. 450 B.C. (London) is a chelys-lyra without shell markings, but with a raised border.

112. The painter might simply be trying to make the bridge visible when much of the soundbox is obscured, or to paint the instrument from an unusual angle (he might also, of course, be careless or unobservant). Other examples: fig. 9; Ann Arbor, Univ. of Mich. 2601; Athens 1809. Bridge at the middle of soundbox: Laon 371059; Munich 2323; Cambridge, Fitzwilliam GR 22.1937; New York 28.167.

113. An unusual bridge, in both size and shape, serves the lyre on Gela 112/13. It is almost as wide as the soundbox, its ends slope upward, and its upper edge has a series of five bumps. These, how-

ever, do not coincide in any regular way with the strings passing over them.

114. Examples of curved bridges: Taranto 54384, Plovdiv 298 (lyre on left), and Florence 3933 (a thick bridge). Dots or heavy outlines at ends: Munich 2323, Adria B 330, and Berlin 3359. Some bridges are wider at one end, as on Athens 1809, perhaps also as a way of indicating that they have feet.

115. Phaklaris, "ΧΕΛΥΣ," pp. 228–30.

116. Rounded corners: Gela 112/13; Taranto 54384, and Vienna 3733. In a few instances the lower string fastener is represented as a single curve, the ends of which touch the lower edge of the soundbox: vases New York 12.236.2 and 25.189.2, both by the Meletos Painter; Kassel vase T.436; and a scarab, probably East Greek, Berlin 11.863.66. All these are dated to the second quarter of the 5th century.

117. The other curious examples are unusual only in the shapes of the sides or the placement of the device itself. Sides of lower string fastener, unusual shapes: on London E 341 the lines are straight but slant inward; on Paris G 436 the curved side-lines join the long top line not at its ends but well in toward the center; on Oxford 312 the visible side is in two parts—first a short, straight line perpendicular to the top line and below this a line that curves inward. On London E 214 each side is shown as three short lines at right angles to one another and the long top line, going down, inward, and down again and making the device quite narrow at the edge of the soundbox.

In a few cases, the string fastener is placed higher than usual, its sides not touching the lower edge of the soundbox, but all these are carelessly painted vases: Athens 1809, low but not touching edge; Athens 1982, middle of soundbox; Athens 635 and London E 326, near top of soundbox. The reason for these, visual or practical, is not at all evident.

118. Other examples: Munich 2323, New York 41.162.86, Florence 81268, and London E 172.

119. Fr. 51 (no. 212, Kirk and Raven). The exact reading is uncertain; many favor palintonos ("stretched backward") but others defend palintropos ("turning back"), as G. Vlastos, "On Heraclitus." See also J. M. Snyder, "The Harmonia of Bow and Lyre in Heraclitus Fr. 51 (DK)."

See also Adesp. 951 (PMG), a fragment quoted by Aristotle, in which a bow is compared to a "stringless phorminx." This also suggests a parallel in the shape of bows and instruments of the lyre type. The diagrams in Phaklaris, "ΧΕΛΥΣ," figs. 8 and 10, and the reconstruction in the British Museum do not take the curvature into account.

120. The hide shows a few wrinkles where the arms enter on Ann Arbor, Univ. of Mich. 2601. For a detailed discussion of the way in which the arms might have been braced and fastened within the soundbox, see Roberts, "Ancient Greek Stringed Instruments, 700–200 B.C.," 43–44, 76.

121. Other examples: arms curve in same direction on Athens 1241; The Hague, Scheuleer 623; Plovdiv 298. Arms curve in same direction only at top: Ferrara T.563; London 1920.6–13.2. Outer arm curves more: Berlin 4059.

122. See n. 98.

123. Some examples: Chicago 89.95, New York 07.286.47, Copenhagen 3878, and Boston 61.1233 (possibly made in Selinunte, a Sicilian colony).

124. In a few cases the lines begin slightly above the crossbar, run down through the "notch" that holds the crossbar (discussed below), and continue for a short distance below it; this may be nothing more than carelessness. See Hamburg 1900.164; Gela 112/13.

On Berlin 2291, on the other hand, the lines begin some distance *below* the crossbar, at the inner edge of the arm, curve gradually to the center, and run down the center to the soundbox. The lines running down from the crossbar on New York 58.11.1 end in a pair of horizontal rings on each arm.

125. Short line from top: Oxford 312 and Berkeley 8/4581. Line that joins with line below crossbar: Florence 3946, Cambridge, Harvard 1895.248. London E 274 has lines only from the top to the crossbar, none below. Once Northampton, Castle Ashby 67 has lines from the top to the crossbar, and lines on the lower part of one arm, resembling those on Berlin 2291 (see n. 124).

126. Arms in white: Delphi 8140; Athens 12282; Tarquinia 640 (paint worn away; Kavala A 1789. Arms in white to point below crossbar: Würzburg H 5169, Athens 635, Athens 1982. On Athens Agora P 43 (fig. 20), the arms are white only above the crossbar; on Rome, Vatican 432, they are white only below the crossbar, for a short distance. On Boston 00.356 the arms were done in gilded relief; some traces of gold remain on the left arm.

127. Rings around tips of arms: London E 177; Oxford 312; Berlin 2291; Oxford, Miss., once Robinson Coll.; Florence 81268. On Berlin 2547 the tips of the arms appear to be carved to two points. On a scarab at Cambridge (Lewes House) a youth runs with a lyre that has round knobs at the tops of the arms.

128. Fragments, possibly 5th century B.C., assembled by British Mus., London 1916.6-10.501. The crossbar has apparently warped, twisting it so that it cannot be placed in both notches. It seems likely that this is a child's instrument, as its height is only approximately 45 cm (the original shell survived only in small fragments). In the present reconstruction, which does not attempt to show that the arms would have tilted forward, the arm notches are at the back, though the evidence of the paintings suggests they were more commonly at the front, despite the loss of structural strength this might involve.

129. Other examples: Athens Acropolis NA 57Aa696; Mykonos 970; Hamburg 1900.164. In a few examples it appears that the artist did not understand the purpose of the notch. It is painted too low (below the crossbar) on Berkeley 8/4581; Cambridge, Harvard 1895.248; and Boston 00.347. On a vase once Northampton, Castle Ashby 67, the curved line of the notch is above the crossbar—but there is a curved line on the crossbar too, and the outlines of the crossbar are painted across those of the arms.

130. Back view: Los Angeles 48.25. Front views: New York 12.236.2 and New York 25.189.2 (these two by the same painter); New York 22.139.72; New York 41.162.86; Athens 1176; Taranto 54384; Lecce 573.

131. Crossbar on back: Athens 1241 (the Muse's chelys-lyra, with crossbar unusually high); Paris G 162; Florence 81268; Athens 12803; Vienna 1093; London, drachma from Pordosilene, Lesbos, after 450 B.C.

Crossbar on front: Berlin 2285 (Douris); Paris terra-cotta B 115; cornelian scarab Berlin 11.863.66, possibly Ionian; London, Kalymnian stater, ca. 520 B.C.

132. The lyre on Paris G 162 (see n. 131) has a broad crossbar behind the arms and apparently attached to them with rings. The lyre has several other odd features: the crossbar is fixed very high; the arms are almost barbitos shaped; the strings run parallel to one another; and the area of the crossbar where they are attached is broadened at the lower side (though the strings are not attached at the lower edge).

133. White ends of crossbar: Rome, Vatican 432; Boston 61.1233; London B 167. Whole crossbar white: Kavala A 1789; Athens 1982.

134. New York, Met. Mus. Cat. (1956) no. 41, cornelian scaraboid from Cyprus; Berlin 11.863.66, cornelian scarab, possibly Ionian; Boston 98.734, cornelian scarab. Crossbar knobs only: London 459, cornelian pseudo-scarab. All these are dated between 525 and 450 B.C.

Phaklaris, "ΧΕΛΥΣ," p. 228, indicates that the crossbar had holes for the fixing of the kollopes; but there does not seem to be any solid evidence for this, and it is unlikely in that this would prevent the kollopes from being adjusted to tune the strings.

135. Kollopes in white: Delphi 8140; London E 400.

136. On Munich 2413 two Erotes hold the chelys-lyra, one front view, one back; but in both cases the kollopes are on the side away from the viewer.

137. Berlin 2278; Ferrara T.563; London, 5th-c. tetradrachm from Abdera, Thrace; London, late 6th-c. stater from Kalymna, island of Karia; early 5th-c. cornelian scarab (Boston 98.734, which has raised circles only above the crossbar).

138. For further discussion of the nature and use of kollopes, see chap. 3 and Roberts, "Ancient Greek Stringed Instruments, 700–200 B.C.," 60–66.

139. Other unobstructed views of plektron: New York 28.167, New York 96.18.76, Copenhagen 3878, Vienna 3700, Florence PD 267, and Florence 91288.

140. Athens 1467; London E 391.

141. Examples: Paris, Petit Palais 319; London E 149; Oxford 312.

142. However, the carefully painted plektron that hangs from its cord on New York L68.142.15 appears not to have any handle.

143. The tassel is to be seen in at least sixteen representations. In addition to those already mentioned, all those cited under unobstructed views of the plektron (n. 139) have tassels, as well as Athens 18599; Athens Nat. Mus., Acropolis 311 and 546; New York 08.258.57, 12.236.2, and 41.162.33; Warsaw, once Goluchow 64; and Paris G 436.

144. A clear example of cord attached to lower string fastener: New York 28.167. There are almost a dozen examples altogether. The cord is, in rare instances, shown attached to the inner, rather than the outer arm: Cambridge, Fitzwilliam GR.22.1937; Athens 1467.

145. A good example showing plektron looped over arm: New York 28.167. Plektron tucked behind arm: Boston 03.816, Athens 17918. Hung over crossbar: Athens 1467. Tucked above bridge: Cambridge, Fitzwilliam GR.8.1955; London E 341.

146. On Delphi 8140, a white-ground plate, the sling is painted brown; the two examples on Laon 371059 are painted in white. On Berlin 2530 the sling runs diagonally from the player's wrist to the base of the instrument arm.

147. The sling hangs loose on Schwerin KG 708 (side with Heracles and Gerapso); London E 191; Adria B 330; Florence 3911; New York L 68.142.15 and 41.162.155; Laon 371059, and Rome, Vatican 432. Three other vase paintings show something attached to the outer arm, but whether it is a sling is not certain: Adria B 254, Kassel T.429, and Oxford 1929.4.

On a cornelian scaraboid New York *Met. Mus. Cat.* (1965) no. 41, the strip of cloth (?) that hangs from the instrument is attached to the inner arm and thus would not serve as a sling.

148. London E 177; Trieste S 424. On the latter vase, a very short sash is attached to the sling by means of a kind of button or ring—again, a detail seen elsewhere only on the kithara.

149. Long, separate strands: London E 177. Medium length: Vienna 1788; Tarquinia 640. Uncertain length (medium or long), sash looped through sling: vase fragment Athens Agora P 18292.

150. Other examples that seem to be in one piece: Athens, Nat. Mus., Acropolis 546; Cambridge, Fitzwilliam GR.1.1950; Athens 19296; Oxford 1920.104. The last of these shows a sling that is a thin cord hanging loose from the arm; the free ends of the cord below the knot are the only "sash." The sash on Paris G 226, which is in red and barely visible, is definitely *not* made of the same material as the sling.

151. Other examples: Berlin 2530; London E 172; London E 191; Paris, Petit Palais 319; Bologna 292.

152. Athens 1172; Athens 1134; once Northampton, Castle Ashby 67; and a Fiesole amphora. Fragments of a hydria in Mykonos show the ends of what appears to be a fillet hanging from the outer arm of a chelys-lyra. The fillet that is tied to the *inner* arm of the lyre on Athens 19503, however, serves no functional purpose. Palermo 97 has a red sash in two pieces like the ends of a fillet; the sling is not visible.

153. Apollo with Dionysos, Hermes, and a goddess: Athens 1134. A Nike carries the lyre on Oxford 312; and on Paris G 552bis, a representation made doubtful in several respects by damage and restoration, the lyre with cloth is held by an ephebe standing on a platform and being crowned with a fillet by a Nike.

Chapter 5: The Barbitos in Classical Athens

1. Str. 10.3.17. Cf. Frisk, vol. 1, p. 220; Chantraine, vol. 1, p. 165; and Snyder, "Barbitos," 331–33.

2. Snyder, "Barbitos," 332–33.

3. *Barbitizein* occurs only in fragments (Ar. fr. 752 and Pi. fr. 132 [Turyn], 124 d [Snell]); *philobarbitos* occurs in Critias 8.4 (Diehl).

4. Late in the 5th century Dionysos is sometimes portrayed wearing a short chiton, as on Bologna 106. In fig. 19, New York 07.286.85, dated ca. 450, he is nude, with only a himation over one shoulder. On both vases he wears *endromides,* high boots with flaps at the top. On an early 5th-c. vase, Cambridge, Harvard 1960.236 (fig. 2), he wears panther skin, chlamys, and shoes.

5. The scene that goes all the way around the exterior of kylix New York 41.162.6 shows Dionysos mounting a quadriga, perhaps for a race, for there is a young man mounting a second chariot. Both are surrounded by maenads and satyrs (two of them playing barbitoi); Dionysos still holds his wine cup.

One quadriga scene, on Paris F 207, on which a man and woman mount the chariot, is taken as a representation of Dionysos and Ariadne, apparently because the musician accompanying them is female and because the shape of the arms of her instrument is that of the barbitos.

6. Of the six satyr scenes in which the participants are clearly dancing, two are of interest for the portrayal of maenads dancing with hands covered by sleeves: Berlin 2532 and Warsaw, Czar. 77.

In a very fragmentary scene on Florence B 324, one of two women is identified as [Tr]agoidia; the other plays the barbitos; a satyr and a child satyr are also visible (other fragments of the same vase: Leipzig T 527).

7. Of seven scenes in which a single barbitos-carrying satyr appears, three show him also carrying a wineskin or pitcher: Munich 2424, Paris G 174, and Oxford 1965.106. A fourth scene does not include a wine vessel, but the vase has one, held by another satyr, on the reverse (New York 09.221.41); and a fifth, a Campanian kylix in Florence, may well have had wine vessels in the satyr scene on the exterior, now destroyed. Only two vases, Munich 2311 and Munich 2404 (fig. 20), have no wine vessels. The former has one satyr with barbitos on each side; the latter has, on one side, a satyr who

reaches out for the barbitos—which is on the other side (in the field)!

8. On Oxford 1885.656 he tunes a barbitos in the presence of Athena, who is seated on a diphros. For similar scenes with kithara or lyra, see chaps. 3 and 4.

9. Athens Agora P 42, 85–81. The altar is under the handle of this kylix and seems to belong more to the figures to the right (fragmentary, one with shield and greaves) than to those on the left (women pouring wine for two men, barbitos player walking away left).

Altar with herm: Madrid 11122; Athens pelike 17190. Altar without herm: Milan 842.

10. Hdt. 2.45. There is also a kithara in the scene on Paris G 50.

11. A similar difficulty exists with Oxford G.265, on which three nude youths run to the right, the last one holding a barbitos by the arm.

12. Basel pelike 1906.301.

13. Aulos bag attached to arm: Munich 2339; London E 314. Basket attached to arm: Adria B 318; Madrid 11268.

14. Large baskets, of the sort sometimes suspended from the arm of the barbitos, are to be seen here too: on Bologna 396, carried in this way by a komast perhaps just arriving at the scene of the festivity; and on New York 06.1021.188, hanging on the walls.

15. Critias 8 (Diehl).

16. Eur. *Cyc.* 37–40. This passage provides us with the earliest *literary* reference to the use of the barbitos as accompaniment for dance (the play is usually dated to shortly before 438 B.C.).

17. Eur. *Alc.* 343–47.

18. A. M. Dale, *Euripides' Alcestis,* 78.

19. Pi. fr. 132 (Turyn) = fr. 124d (Snell); cf. n. 3. B. A. van Groningen, *Pindare au banquet,* 110, while noting that the barbitos was a distinctive type of lyre, nevertheless maintains that Pindar is thinking of music in general; yet the illustration chosen for his book contradicts this assumption, for it depicts a symposium scene with barbitos and aulos (red-figured kylix by the Ashby Painter, London E 64).

20. Ten of the symposium scenes contain no furniture—the guests recline against cushions on the floor (or apparently on the floor). In every case these paintings occupy a restricted space and so may be abbreviations—the neck of a rhyton (3), kantharos (1), or amphora (1); the shoulder zone of a stamnos (1); the exterior of a kylix (2); or the tondo area of a kylix interior (1). The largest space is the side zone on a stamnos (Compiegne 1065), but it too would have required very small figures if the high couches had been included.

21. On a seventh vase, Paris F 314, the aulos players recline among the guests; but this is a painting in a restricted space, the shoulder of a stamnos.

On Paris F 216 there are two women and two men playing auloi, according to *CVA* 5, p. 22, notes for pl. 39. Only one aulete, a woman, is visible in the photographs. The visible standing males are nude and bearded.

22. The Eros who runs toward the women on Syracuse 36330 carries a lyra, but the seated woman plays the barbitos. The Eros on Athens Kerameikos HS 89 plays the auloi.

23. Brunswick 219, Altenburg 301, and Bucharest 03231.

24. On London 1921, 7-10,2 (fig. 11) the seated woman in the center plays the lyra; the player of the barbitos sits facing her on the right. On Brunswick 219 the bride probably does not play an instrument (the vase is very damaged); Himeros is lacing her shoe, and female players of barbitos, lyra, and auloi appear elsewhere in the scene.

25. Cranes on: London 1921, 7-10,2 (fig. 11) and Syracuse 36330. Inscriptions: Altenburg 301 and Brunswick 219.

26. London 493, cornelian scaraboid; London 1946.11-8.1, cornelian scarab; Boston 27.760, sardonyx scarab. On Boston 27.760 the young man leans against the wall, knees bent.

27. The painting on Athens 2022, which has no inscription and no other figure to support this interpretation of the meaning of the barbitos, may nevertheless properly belong in this category. The youth who walks holding out the barbitos on this vase, however, is draped in his cloak, not nude as in the other examples.

28. Simon. 126 (Diehl); Lesky, *History of Greek Literature*, 188, points out that the authenticity of most of the epigrams attributed to Simonides cannot be confirmed.

29. The barbitos is mentioned in nos. 2, 15, 23, 42, 43, and 60.

30. Caskey and Beazley, *Attic Vase Paintings*, text vol. 2, 55–61, esp. 57. See also Keith De Vries, "East Meets West at Dinner," who argues on the basis of the Apadana friezes of Persepolis that the costume should be taken as Lydian in origin and that Anakreon might have adopted the fashion while at the court of Polykrates on Samos.

31. Copenhagen 13365 (fig. 14, the Curtius Krater); London E 18; Syracuse 26967. The Copenhagen vase includes symbols indicating the sounds produced by the singer; see H. R. Immerwahr, "Inscriptions on the Anacreon Krater in Copenhagen."

32. J. M. Snyder, "Aristophanes' Agathon as Anakreon."

33. W. J. Slater, "Artemon and Anacreon: No Text without Context."

34. H. W. Parke, *Festivals of the Athenians*, 77, 82–88, 156–62. It may also be a feature of a special komos held during the Thesmophoria (a women's festival dedicated to Demeter at which verbal abuse similar to that mentioned by Slater was practiced).

35. Two of the representations show "Anakreon" figures who wear no chiton: on Paris G 4bis a bearded man wears high boots, a himation, and an elaborate sakkos; a basket hangs from the arm of his barbitos. Vienna 1777 has a similarly dressed figure; he has no boots, however, and there is a flowered wreath around his turban.

Four of the twenty-three "Anakreon" paintings that have been identified to date have not been available for this study. They are described by Beazley in Caskey and Beazley, *Attic Vase Paintings*, text vol. 2, pp. 55–61, who does not indicate whether the lyre carried is a barbitos: Berlin 2351, no. 14 in his list; Athens Agora P 7242, his no. 7; a column krater at Bari, his no. 26; and Paris G 94, a red-figured cup mentioned without number on p. 61.

36. Other vases in this group are Munich 2317; London E 308; Florence 3987; Adolphseck 56; Boston 13.199; and Cambridge, Harvard 1959.125.

37. The other two vases of this type are Madrid 11009, on which four men, including the barbitos player, carry parasols (one also has a skyphos); and Adria B.248, of which only enough fragments remain to show two bearded heads in sakkoi, the arms of a barbitos, and part of a skyphos.

38. Rome, Mus. Capit. 176 and Rhodes 13.129, both pelikai.

39. One wonders whether the name *kekryphalos* might apply only to certain of these more elaborate varieties. Madrid 11009 provides examples of five of the types of pleated sakkoi, with and without hair drawn through, and two of the figures wear the mitra looped in the characteristic way.

40. The mitra, worn more commonly by men (victors and symposiasts) than the sakkos, appears in the portrait of Alcaeus, fig. 15, and is worn by a symposiast on Berlin 4221.

A wreath may be added to either mitra or sakkos; the man on the right in fig. 13 has a flowered wreath over his sakkos; the barbitos player on Syracuse 26967 wears both wreath and mitra.

41. B. 20 B.1–4. For the reference to the peg cf. Pi. *O*. 1.17–18 (and Hom. *Od*. 8.67).

42. B. 20 C.1–2. Pindar does, of course, use the verb form *barbitizein* (see nn. 3 and 19).

43. Theoc. 16.42–47.

44. Wuppertal, private collection.

45. New York 16.52, a late 5th-c. vase, and Ferrara T.127, also from the last quarter of the century.

46. Cambridge, Fitz. 4.1943 (barbitos, aulos, krotala, lyra) and The Hague, Scheurleer 623 (barbitos and two lyrai).

47. See J. M. Snyder, "Aegisthos and the Barbitos." The two vases were painted by different artists ca. 475–460. The second vase is Boston 91.227.

48. A fragment of a kylix interior, Berlin Sa 481, shows a standing woman with barbitos at her side in her left hand and a staff in her right. Before her stands a woman with a wreath.

There are also three vases on hand with the figure of a single woman walking and playing the barbitos. These are almost entirely without details that might provide a context: the woman on Athens 1792 (who wears both a wreath and a sakkos) has a dog with her; the one on New York 41.162.7 has an aulos case hanging from the arm of her barbitos; and the woman on an oinochoe once Robinson Coll. has no details other than her costume, which is like that of the other two (sakkos, chiton, himation, and sandals), to assist us. The figure on a fourth vase, Paris AM 1064 bis, is much damaged; the head is wreathed but does not include sakkos.

49. On Syracuse 23794 the woman on the left holds a lyra in playing position, but her right arm is at her side, and the plektron dangles free on its cord attached to the arm of the lyra.

50. The other hydriai are Oxford 1966.704 and Gotha 53. On pelike Copenhagen 596 there is a fawn between the two women.

51. A third painting that might be thought to belong to this category, Torino 5776, is doubtful on two counts: first, it is not certain that the instrument is a barbitos, though the shape of the arm suggests it; if it is, it is one of the earliest representations of the instrument (ca. 525 B.C.). Second, the meaning of the scene is not clear, as both the nude bearded man with barbitos and the two nude youths on either side of him are standing, and neither youth has an instrument. The bearded man with a staff who sits wrapped in a decorated himation on the right resembles a judge more than a paidogogos.

However, even if the scene is accepted as a music lesson, the conclusions stated here will not be altered, as neither youth holds a barbitos.

52. London E 527.

53. Arist. *Pol*. 1341a–b.

54. Pollux I, p. 218, 23 (Bethe).

55. Komos scenes, mortal and Dionysiac, provide the majority of the standing or walking female players. The others are the portraits of Sappho, two paintings of Muses, three of a single woman walking, and one "bridal scene."

56. The hand is higher, i.e., part of the forearm is visible on London E 767 and also on Paris S 1335, where the fingers are curled, thumb across palm.

57. See, e.g., the back view of the barbitos on Vienna 1104, where the player's hand is upright, palm toward the strings, but with the fingers curved toward them.

58. Boston 13.197 is a good example of thumb and index finger apparently used together to pluck; of the examples of the thumb

used alone, Bologna C.100 and London E 266 are among the more convincing.

59. Index and thumb curved together, other fingers straight: New York 07.286.85 (fig. 19) and terra-cotta Athens 15881. Index and thumb straight, others curled: London E 171; Palermo V 666, and (indistinctly) Athens Acropolis 372. Thumb and first two fingers straight, others curled: fig. 9 and (indistinctly) Copenhagen ABc 1021.

60. Bologna 308, Copenhagen 3635, and (indistinct) Florence, kylix fragments.

61. The players on both sides of Gotha 2476, however, hold the plektron at the outer arm and bend the right wrist up, pointing the plektron (not actually visible) back toward the player in an awkward-looking gesture not seen elsewhere.

On Madrid 11009 the player's hand, wrist bent up, appears to place the plektron on the strings between bridge and lower string fastener. It may be, however, that a fold of his chiton falls between plektron and strings.

On three vases, Adria Bc.45, Athens Agora P 24115, and Athens Acropolis 229, all early red-figured vases, the player's right hand, plektron turned toward him, is shown on the strings at a very high point, almost at the crossbar in the first two examples. The thumb of the plektron hand appears to pluck the innermost string on Acropolis 229.

62. The others are New York 56.171.52; Boston 13.197; London E 266; Copenhagen 3635; The Hague, Scheurleer 623; Vienna 823; and Munich 2339.

63. Bonn 1216, 33–38.198 and Copenhagen 596 are among the most interesting examples.

64. See Bologna 396, Brussels A 3094, Adria B 317, and Rhodes 13.210.

65. Chiton between plektron and strings: Adolphseck 74 and Cleveland 26549 (fig. 13). See also Madrid 11009 (n. 61).

66. The three best examples are Munich 2317; Oxford 1885,656; and Paris G 543. The other examples are Athens Acropolis 372; Bryn Mawr P-192; London, Boeotian red-figured cup ca. 475 B.C. (*AM* 65, 1940, pl. 3); and sardonyx scarab Boston 27.760.

Two other scarabs show the player's right hand as a fist close under the crossbar; these may also be intended to indicate tuning: cornelian scaraboid London 493 and cornelian scarab London 1946.11-8.1.

67. *Scholia in Euripidem* (Schwartz), *Alc.* 345. Against the claim of certain modern scholars that the barbitos was tuned one octave lower than the pektis, see Snyder, "Barbitos," 335–36.

68. B. 20 B.2 and 20 C.1. Aristophanes, on the other hand, describes the barbitos as producing a chirping sound (*lalein, Th.* 138).

69. The percentages are not improved for the seven-stringed barbitos when the less certain examples are included: seven strings, 44%; five and six strings, 50%.

70. Paris F 314, Brussels A 1652, and Rome Mus. Cap. 56.

71. A 4th-c. coin from Teos (London, Anson Cat. 363) shows a barbitos with arms that curve out at the top, below the crossbar. Another red-figured example: Vienna 1777. On San Simeon 5630, on which the top of each arm curves out and down, and on Vienna 3693, on which the tops form swan's head loops, the crossbar fits *into* the curved portion rather than above it. On San Simeon 5630 the crossbar had knobs out beyond the curving arm ends!

72. On a white-ground lekythos, Athens 12777, the arms are painted golden yellow; on Melian relief Athens 15881 they were originally painted red.

73. Paris G 422 and G 369, London E 171, and Adria B.318.

74. In a few cases the tips of the arms seem to curve downward somewhat, like a heart shape with the center missing: see Berlin Sa 481 and Athens 15372.

75. Copenhagen 3635; Athens 1263.

76. But the circles are also evident on fig. 6, Brussels R255, which is a back view.

77. Two Campanian examples illustrate an instrument without a crossbar attachment. The arms come together to form a shape like a snowshoe, and the strings are attached directly to this: Florence, Campanian kylix, and a tomb painting from Paestum. The former example has five strings, the latter seven; the latter example also has clear kollopes.

78. On Oxford 1892.1490, an East Greek cornelian scarab, possibly dated earlier than 525 B.C. and perhaps the earliest, or one of the earliest representations of the barbitos (if that is what it is), the sections above the crossbar bend sharply outward in a way reminiscent of the lyre on the 7th-c. dinos sherd from Old Smyrna (Bayrakli, chap. 2, fig. 1). Both these objects are discussed in chap. 2.

79. On a sardonyx scarab of the early 5th century from near Anaktorion, Boston 27.760, the tops of the upper pieces have, on one side, a knob, and on the other side, a notch of the usual sort.

80. Cleveland 24.197 and New York 22.139.32 are among the best painted of these.

81. Bologna 308 is of this sort, but the rounded sections are at the back (it is a back view). On Brussels R 255 (fig. 6) the fitting has a vertical line from the top to two-thirds of the way down. It seems to be a split in which the crossbar is held.

82. Knobs: Erlangen 454, Florence 3987, and cornelian scaraboid London 493. Two lines around tip of arm: Munich 2317. Line running in from tip a short way (as though the ends are split): Berlin 2309. white paint: Athens 12777.

83. Other examples: Boston 01.8078; Boston 13.194; and Copenhagen 3632 (a Lucanian vase), which also has x's on the crossbar to indicate the strings wrapped around it.

84. In the back view on Berlin 2532 the shape is approximately that of the natural tortoise shell (without "ears"). Four other back views show soundboxes that seem especially long and narrow, although they do have slight bulges along the sides: Warsaw 142465; Basel 1906,301; Paris G 139-140; and Bologna 308.

The soundbox shown on the chalcedony scaraboid Boston 27.671, on the other hand, is wide and almond shaped, perhaps an attempt to show the soundbox from an unusual angle.

85. On Cambridge, Fitz. GR 19.1937 the arms appear to taper and to enter the soundbox close together, nearly at its center. There are three lines across the soundbox between them, but no other body detail.

86. The front of the soundbox rarely has a border, as on Munich 2424 and Cambridge, Harvard 1959.125. The small circles sometimes seen on the belly of the lyra are to be found in the case of the barbitos only on the reverse of Munich 2317; only one circle shows.

87. Other bridges with some indication of feet: Munich 2424; Cambridge, Harvard 1959.125; Munich 2311; Boston 95.27; Athens Agora P 12960; and New York 16.52, a vase from the end of the century.

88. When the instrument is not held in playing position, it may be difficult to tell whether a short piece of cloth attached to the base of the arm is the wrist sling or a short decorative sash. This is the case with Paris F 314, Athens Acropolis 20, and London E 68 (on which it is attached to the wrong arm).

89. In Paris AM 1064bis and Munich 2317, the strands are long enough, especially on the latter instrument, to be strings.

90. The player on Bari 4395 also has fastened a long narrow fillet halfway up the arm of the barbitos. In two paintings it is not clear whether what we see is a sash or a fillet. On a Maplewood, Noble Coll. calyx krater, it is where a sash should be but looks somewhat like a fillet; on Munich 1416 (see chap. 6, fig. 2) it hangs behind the instrument (not played and held vertically), below the inner arm.

On Copenhagen 3635, a Lucanian vase, the satyr player has a large cloth with a border (a chlamys?) perhaps thrown over his left forearm, which holds the barbitos. This is the only thing at all resembling the cloth of the kithara to be seen among the barbitos examples.

91. Caskey and Beazley, *Attic Vase Paintings,* 57–58, 61. (Our fig. 21 is Beazley's no. 1, p. 58). As far as has been determined at present, there are no representations with the characteristic arm shape of the barbitos earlier than the last quarter of the 6th century from *anywhere,* except for the scarab mentioned above (n. 78) and in chap. 2, Oxford 1892.1490 (which may be only a few years earlier).

92. Hor. *C.* 1.1.34, 1.32.4, and 3.26.4.

93. Ov. *Her.* 15.8.

Chapter 6: Harps and Unusual Lyres in Classical Athens

1. The evidence for the continuity of the instrument type into the Classical period has been assembled by M. Maas, "The Phorminx in Classical Greece." To the list of vases there (pp. 54–55) should be added the following items:

Second half, 6th century: Oxford 1919.46; Los Angeles 50.8.2.

First half, 5th century: Oxford 225 (fig. 1); Athens Agora P 1544; Paris CA 483; Leningrad 798.

Second half, 5th century: Naples 3143; Dresden 332; and Naples Stg 274.

There is, in addition, a cornelian scarab, Boston 27.669, and an Etruscan pyxis, Heidelberg E 34, both late 6th century; see n. 3. Leningrad 732 and Copenhagen 7776 have now been confirmed as belonging to the list; possible further additions are a column krater (location unknown) by the Pig Painter and a lekythos (location unknown) by the Klügmann Painter.

2. See discussion above (chap. 3) on Pindar's use of the word *phorminx.* For the term *cradle kithara* see M. Maas, "Phorminx," and Wegner, *Musikleben,* pp. 30–31.

3. Male performers: Munich 1416; Oxford 1919.46. See also Rhodes 12.200, dated before 550 B.C. (chap. 2, fig. 6).

On a late 6th-c. cornelian scarab, Boston 27.669, a nude male runs with a cock in one hand and a round-based lyre in the other. There is a late 6th-c. Etruscan vase, Heidelberg E 34, on which a satyr plays an instrument of this general type.

4. The three women on Rome Mus. Cap. 259 are described as "maenads dancing" by Beazley; the similar single figure on Munich 2446 is probably also a maenad. The other vases in this late 6th-c. group are Bologna 151; Oxford 212; and Philadelphia, Univ. Mus. 2462.

5. The others are Cambridge, Harvard 1959.188, and Athens Agora P 1544. The woman who stands alone on Urbana, Ill. Krannert 70-8-5 (ca. 475 B.C.) resembles the musicians on these other vases; but she might also be a muse or a maenad.

6. The others are Munich 2362 and Tarquinia 684. On Leningrad 798 the figures, according to Beazley, represent Apollo and a Muse (with the phorminx, Artemis, and Hermes).

7. The other two vases are Naples Stg 274 and Copenhagen 7776.

8. Beazley (*ARV*² 857–58) regards the women on both Bowdoin 15.46 and Leningrad 732 as possibly Muses.

9. On Munich 2363 a woman plays the phorminx while a small Eros dances. A chelys-lyra hangs behind and above them; there are no other figures.

10. The phorminx is played on Florence 4014. The second vase on which it hangs on the wall is Lecce 572.

11. Lillian B. Lawler called attention to this arm gesture in "Dancing with the Elbows."

12. Lillian B. Lawler, *The Dance of the Ancient Greek Theatre,* 39–41.

13. The other vases are Paris CA 482 and Leningrad 732.

14. Others are Rhodes 12.200, Oxford 1919.46, Paris CA 483, Vienna 770, and Florence 4014.

15. Just past the strings: Urbana, Ill. Krannert 70-8-5. Middle of strings: Munich 2363. Two other vases, back views, leave the position of the right hand uncertain: Leningrad 732 and Naples Stg 274.

16. Rome Mus. Cap. 259 (identified as a phorminx partly because of its high crossbar), Cambridge, Harvard 1959.188, and Tarquinia 684 have corners that are very elongated; the latter two also have the most inward curve.

The elongation and inward curve suggest that the phorminx shape was influenced (at least in the painters' minds) in some cases by that of the kithara. Some further evidence of this is found on London E 38 (Heracles killing Busiris), where the instrument has inner-arm decorations resembling those of the kithara; the instrument on a vase made in S. Italy (Lucania, ca. 380–60 B.C.), Stockholm 12, is similar but with crossbar knobs and cloth.

On two vases dated before 500 B.C. there seems to be scrollwork on the elongated, rounded tips: Munich 2446 and Los Angeles 50.8.2.

17. On Schwerin KG 708 there is what appears to be a brace across the instrument between the corners of the soundbox. Since this is found on no other instrument, it is not clear what the painter had in mind—perhaps it is simply a mistake.

18. The other two are Los Angeles 50.8.2 and Munich 2446.

19. The misshapen left side of the instrument on Vienna 770 may also be an effort to portray a concavity at this point.

20. On Bologna 151, a late 6th-c. back view, there are two sets of very small circles, one set inside the corner sections and one set below. For a 7th-c. example with two sets of circles on the front, see Athens 911 (chap. 2, fig. 2).

21. On late 6th-c. cornelian scarab Boston 27.669, the phorminx has two raised circles on what appears to be the back of the soundbox. Eyebrows: Paris CA 482; Munich 2362; Urbana, Ill. Krannert 70-8-5; and Cambridge, Harvard 1959.188.

22. The others with arms inclining inward slightly: the Stockholm "Diphilos" lekythos, Leningrad 732, Munich 3268, and Oxford 212.

On Dresden 332 the arms are somewhat longer than usual. On Cambridge, Harvard 1925.30.42 (fig. 8), and Lecce 572 they are unusually short (the soundbox corners on the former are very elongated, and on the latter the soundbox itself is very tall).

The arms on Munich 2446 are unusually wide; and on this vase and on Los Angeles 50.8.2, the arms have an extension at the bottom that appears to run all the way around the upper edge of the soundbox.

23. M. Maas, "On the Shape of the Ancient Greek Lyre."

24. Also Oxford 212 and 1919.46 (lines in white) and Paris CA 483. On London E 185 (fig. 4) the elongated ends of the soundbox have bands of white across them.

25. Small circles: Oxford 1919.46; Urbana, Ill. Krannert 70-8-5; and Lecce 572. Large circles also on Copenhagen 7776.

26. Others are Bologna 151 and Oxford 212.

27. The other two vases are Würzburg 521 and London E 271 (chap. 4, fig. 2). Another opinion on this detail is expressed by Bo Lawergren, "The Cylinder Kithara in Etruria, Greece, and Anatolia."

28. On Paris CA 483 the upper part of each circle, above the opening, has small crosspieces, making the design even more elaborate.

29. It is this that makes the instrument on the Rome, Vatican amphora by the Kleophrades Painter (early 5th century) difficult to classify: its crossbar sits at the bottom of the arms. The arms incline inward slightly and are not set in from the edges of the soundbox. Since the scene is a komos and the instrument is carried at a 90° angle and has no arm decoration, it can hardly be a kithara. Since its soundbox is not chelys shaped, the lyra and barbitos are ruled out. On the other hand, the elongated and inward-curved corner extensions are not unlike those on Los Angeles 50.8.2 or Cambridge, Harvard 1959.188, both paintings of the phorminx.

30. The others: Copenhagen 7776 and Naples 81398.

31. Other clear examples: Paris CA 482 and 483, Vienna 770, and Munich 2362.

32. The plektron cord can also be seen on Oxford 1919.46, Munich 2446, Athens Agora P 1544, and Naples 3143, but it is not clear in these examples where it is attached.

33. On Paris CA 483 the sling (not in use) hangs loose around the outer arm of the instrument. On Boston 98.887 (not shown in fig. 3) one Muse, who seems to test her phorminx, has a sling around her *right* wrist. It is an odd fact that none of the players whose instrument is seen in back view has a wrist sling.

34. This interpretation corrects the one mentioned in M. Maas, "Phorminx," p. 44, n. 21.

35. Boston 98.887, Dresden 332, Florence 4014, Lecce 572, Munich 2446, and Rhodes 12.200 (chap. 2, fig. 6). Uncertain: Athens Agora P 1544, Munich 2363, and Paris CA 483.

36. Florence, unnumbered frag. of a large vase. According to L. Talcott and B. Philippaki, "Figured Pottery," pp. 49–50, it is late Archaic, i.e., ca. 500–475 B.C., somewhat older than the Orpheus cup. The arm that shows appears to be made of a variety of horn that has a spiral twist; the soundbox has a narrow band with dots around the edge, and there is a bridge, sling, and sash.

37. Wegner, *Musikleben*, 45.

38. Rome, Vatican 16549. A similar painting without inscription is Naples 3143; both are by the Phiale Painter. On a third vase, a bearded man in Thracian dress sits on a rock (?) with two women on each side of him (none of the women has identifying attributes). The instrument he plays appears to be a standard kithara like those in chap. 3; we have seen only a drawing: Leningrad 711.

39. S. fr. 245 (Pearson): "I was seized by the Muse-maddened . . . and I am captivated by the lyra and the *nomoi* with which Thamyras makes wonderful music." S. fr. 241 (Pearson): "For the songs resounding from the *pektides* are gone, and the lyra. . . ."

40. Trendall and Webster, *Illustrations of Greek Drama*, 69.

41. On a lekanis lid in the Hermitage Museum, Leningrad, a player of this instrument stands near an altar, with a seated female aulos player behind him, and five women in clothing of different styles dancing toward him while holding hands. The word *kale* ("beautiful") is repeated between the dancers. It seems likely that the women are Muses and the player is Thamyras. (This piece is listed in Talcott and Philippaki, "Figured Pottery," p. 50.)

42. All the figures are identified by inscriptions.

43. Orpheus, in Thracian costume, also appears on an Apulian vase of ca. 370 B.C., Heidelberg 26.90, brandishing an instrument that resembles a Thracian kithara in its arm shape, crossbar knobs, and circles on the soundbox.

44. Gisela M. A. Richter, "A Pelike by the Meidias Painter," 4.

45. The others are Athens 1183; Florence 4006; Munich 2471, a late vase (ca. 400 B.C.); Rome, Villa Giulia 5250, where there are two women rather than two Nikes; and Rome, Vatican, Sala VII, case N, no. 18. We have not seen the latter vase, listed by Talcott and Philippaki as having an instrument of this shape with arms of horn, and described by Beazley as "Citharode with Nikai."

46. On Athens 14628 (from the end of the century?) a satyr plays what appears to be an ordinary chelys-lyra, except that its arms have, on the inside edges, curving, roughly triangular protrusions, two on each side, that are reminiscent of those on some of the Thracian kitharas (see fig. 11), though these are much larger.

47. M. Wegner, *Musikleben*, 46, asks whether this instrument may not be the "Asiatic kitharis" mentioned by the satyrs in Euripides' *Cyclops* 443ff., but there does not seem to be any strong reason to think so.

48. We do have evidence that a chorus might be represented playing identical lyres or kitharas: see chaps. 2 and 3.

49. Since none of the representations is a back view, nothing can be said of the depth of the soundbox or the shape of the back.

50. Two vase fragments, clearly instruments of the type in question, show the "tightly twisted" effect. Both also have decorative bands around the top and side of the front of the soundbox. The Florence fragment is discussed above (n. 36); Athens Agora Pnyx P 139 has in addition a band across the soundbox and an eye circle, as well as a dotted sling and one knob showing.

The instrument held by Thamyras on the Basel lekythos has arms that loop outward under the crossbar and are made to represent swans' necks and heads, like those on certain early paintings of the barbitos (see chap. 5) and those on a group of kitharas in 4th-c. Italian vase paintings (chap. 7).

51. On a Greek milky chalcedony scaraboid dated 450–400 B.C. (Paris, Cab. des Méd. 1513ᵗᵉʳ = M2847) a siren plays an instrument with an arm- and body-shape resembling that of the instruments discussed here and having a soundbox with a large rectangular indentation in the lower corner.

52. No examples in which the circles have been changed into eyes have come to hand.

53. The plektron and its handle are clearly the same as that used for playing other lyres. The plektron cord is visible only on Rome, Villa Giulia 5250; there is no tassel visible in any of the examples.

54. "Figured Pottery," p. 50.

55. Most of the known representations of harps have been assembled by M. Wegner, *Musikleben*, 203–05, and by Reinhard Herbig, "Griechische Harfen," pll. 7–8, supplementary pll. 55–58.

56. For citations of most of the late (as well as earlier) sources, see the appropriate entries in Michaelides, *Music of Ancient Greece*. Many of the references to harps and other stringed instruments in the earlier sources that seem most reliable are preserved for us by Athenaeus. Whereas his own interpretations may be dubious at times, his quotations are thought to be reasonably accurate; see K. Zepernick, "Die Exzerpte des Athenaeus in den Dipnosophisten und ihre Glaubwürdigkeit."

57. Pl. *R.* 399C; see chap. 7.

58. S. fr. 412 (Pearson); Ath. 625e.

59. Ath. 182f.

60. Sopater, quoted in Ath. 183b.

61. Hdt. 1.17. The pektis is also mentioned in a nearly unintelligible fragment from Sophocles' *Thamyras* (fr. 241, Pearson), but the player cannot be ascertained.

62. See chap. 2, Archaic-Period References to the Pektis and Magadis.

63. Ath. 636a. On Diogenes of Oinomaos, see *RE* 5, col. 737 (no. 36); despite the use of *krekein* ("to strike") in connection with *magadis* here, elsewhere the verb generally associated with this instrument is *psallein* ("to pluck").

64. Ar. *Th.* 1217; they use the plural, but it seems unlikely that we are to imagine Euripides carting around two or three instruments.

65. Ath. 183b. The play is by Anaxilas, most of whose comedies date to the 350s and 340s. Note that the *lyropoios* here, as one might expect from the generic sense of *lyra*, is a manufacturer of all kinds of stringed instruments.

66. Daremberg and Saglio, s.v. "Lyra," vol. 3, pp. 1449–50; W. Vetter, "Magadis." Both sources claim that the instrument must have had a tuning device that allowed simultaneous octaves to be played, but there is no evidence for this assumption.

67. Diog. Ath., quoted in Ath. 636a; Telestes, quoted in Ath. 625c; Pi. fr. 125 (Snell).

68. S. fr. 412 (Pearson). The word for "answering twangings" is ἀντίσπαστα, from σπάω, "to draw," "to pull." Pearson takes the word to mean "doubly-twanged," referring to two sets of strings each in a different octave; but his interpretation seems to stretch the meaning of the word.

69. Pl. *R.* 399C; Arist. *Pol.* 1341ᵃ40.

70. Pi. fr. 125 (Snell). Cf. ἀντιζύγοις ὁλκοῖς as applied to the magadis in Diog. Ath. (Ath. 636a) and ψαλμοῖσιν ἀντίσπαστ' (no instrument name mentioned) in Phrynichus fr. 11 (Snell).

71. Anakreon fr. 374 (Page); cf. Alkman fr. 101 (Page).

72. Euph. quoted in Ath. 635a. The instrument is also mentioned (in the plural) in an unintelligible fragment from Sophocles' *Thamyras* (fr. 238, Pearson).

73. Ath. 635b.

74. Ath. 637a.

75. See C. B. Gulick, trans., *Athenaeus: The Deipnosophists*, vol. 6, p. 437, n. h.

76. The latter is suggested by Vetter, "Magadis." In connection with the former, see chap. 2, n. 63, on the use of horn as a substitute for reed in the construction of lyres. There is evidence that the term *magadis* could also refer to a type of aulos; see Michaelides, *Music of Ancient Greece*, 195–96 and below, n. 81.

77. X. *An.* 7.3.32.

78. Anaxandrides, quoted in Ath. 634e.

79. Ps.-Arist. *Pr.* 19.18. See also Phillis of Delos (quoted in Ath. 636b), whose date is unknown but who seems to have been relying on Aristoxenos for the information that the magadis was used to accompany songs sung in octaves (see M. Wegner, "Phillis," *RE* vol. 19, pt. 2, col. 2430).

80. Theophilus, quoted in Ath. 635a.

81. Apollodorus of Athens, quoted in Ath. 636f. One further reference to the magadis that should be mentioned is in Ion of Chios fr. 23 (Snell): Λυδός τε μάγαδις αὐλὸς ἡγείσθω βοῆς, "Let the Lydian magadis-aulos lead the cry." Athenaeus (634c and cf. 634e) takes this to mean that the term *magadis* could refer also to a type of aulos.

82. Daremberg and Saglio, s.v. "Lyra," 1448, think that the term *trigonon* was restricted to the small triangular harp popular on Roman reliefs, an explanation that does not seem to take account of the term's much earlier appearance.

83. S. fr. 412 (Pearson).

84. Pl. Com. fr. 69.10–14 (Edmonds).

85. Eupolis fr. 139 (Edmonds). For a discussion of *iambuke* and related terms, see chap. 7.

86. Eupolis fr. 77 (Edmonds). Another, less informative comic fragment of the same period (Pherekrates, fr. 42, Edmonds) is a request by one of the characters to throw out "trigonons and lyres."

87. Some differences in shape within each of the groups may be caused by the painters' use of perspective. This factor is difficult to assess when there are so few examples available.

88. We have not classified the harps on two vases listed by Beazley, as we have not seen them: Athens unnumbered pyxis with Thamyras and Muses, Mousaios seated playing harp, and Apollo; and Syracuse 35812, a seated woman playing a harp.

The harp with a poet on Apulian vase Munich 3268 is like the angle harps discussed below in that it is played by a Muse, has the same shape (except for the post), is held and played in the same manner, and has a decorated soundbox. It has approximately 13 strings. Harps of this type are discussed in chap. 7.

89. The fifth representation, seal stone London 529, shows a woman sitting on a straight-backed chair playing the harp.

90. Ion fr. 22 (Snell); quoted in Ath. 634c.

91. Wilhelm Stauder, *Die Harfen und Leiern Vorderasiens in babylonischer und assyrischer Zeit*, 39–50, 58–60, 69–70, and figs. 25, 26, 41, 42, 62, and 64.

92. Attic: Berlin Staatl. Mus. 2391. The 4th-c. evidence yields only one more really comparable Attic example, Jena 390; other 4th-c. Attic harps have much narrower soundboxes. See chap. 7. Italiote: Berlin 3291; Munich 3268.

93. There are at present eight 5th-c. examples. A seal stone in Leningrad with a doubtful example belongs to the early 4th century.

Fourth-century Attic vases Leningrad B 3128 and Stockholm 2 may preserve other examples; the available photographs are not clear enough to allow a determination.

94. By the Washing Painter: Athens 14791; New York 07.286.35 and 16.73; Würzburg H 4455. All of these are nuptial lebetes except Würzburg H 4455, a pyxis.

Other vases: New York 37.11.23 (fig. 16, by the Meidias Painter) and Ferrara T.127 (by Polion).

Other items: cornelian bead seal stone, London 563, late 5th century; Attic grave relief (siren with harp), location unknown, ca. 400 B.C. The latter is a crudely executed and somewhat doubtful example.

95. The standing harpist on Athens 14791 holds the harp diagonally somehow, the top to the left of her head, the lower corner under her right arm.

96. On New York 07.286.35 the post appears to be bowed out somewhat.

97. On the Leningrad seal stone there seem to be 15 or 16 strings; on Ferrara T.127 about 11 or 12, and the same number on seal stone London 563.

98. The translation is of the text in Diehl, fr. 6. For a convenient summary of earlier interpretations of the lines, see Flora R. Levin, "The Hendecachord of Ion of Chios."

99. On *lyropoios*, see n. 65.

100. For *paiein*, see A. fr. 174 (Lloyd-Jones) = fr. 314 (Nauck).

101. Plu. *Aegis* 11.2; *Moralia* 84A; 220C; 238D. Cic. *Leg.* 2.39; Boëth. *Mus.* 1.1 (cf. also Paus. 3.12.10). Paul Maas, "Timotheus,"

col. 1334, labels these and other later reports as for the most part "phantastisch."

102. Artemon, quoted in Ath. 636e. On the Spartan edict, see U. von Wilamowitz-Möllendorff, *Timotheos*, 70.

Chapter 7: Late Classical and Early Hellenistic Stringed Instruments

1. See C. Schneider, *Kulturgeschichte des Hellenismus*, vol. 2, p. 635.

2. X. *Mem.* 3.1.4.

3. Phld. *Mus.* 3.77.13–17 (p. 55, Kemke). The translation is that of Anderson, *Ethos*, 79. For the influence of Damon on Plato, see E. Moutsopoulos, *La musique dans l'oeuvre de Platon*, 96, and Anderson, 74–81.

4. Pl. *Thg.* 122E; *Clit.* 407C; cf. *Alc.* 1.106E and 107A.

5. Pl. *Lg.* 809E.

6. F. A. G. Beck, *Greek Education, 450–350 B.C.*, 81, points out that Pl. *Prt.* 325–26 seems to suggest that letters, music, and gymnastics were normally studied concurrently.

7. Pl. *Euthd.* 272C; cf. *Mx.* 236A.

8. Pl. *Prt.* 326B. A good discussion of the harmoniai may be found in Isobel Henderson. "The Growth of Ancient Greek Music."

9. See Pl. *Prt.* 312B on the kind of nontechnical training suitable for a liberal arts education, and 325E on parents' concern regarding their children's instruction in behavior.

10. X. *Oec.* 2.13.

11. X. *Sym.* 2.1, 3.1. The dramatic date of the work (422 B.C.) is much earlier than the date at which it was actually written, but the detail with which Xenophon describes the entertainment suggests his own familiarity with the practice.

12. Arist. *EE* 1243b24 and *EN* 1164a15.

13. Pl. *Lg.* 764D.

14. Pl. *Ion* 533B. On rhapsody cf. H. Patzer, "ΡΑΨΩΙΔΟΣ." In addition to treating rhapsody as the concern of professionals like Ion of Ephesus, Plato also mentions it in connection with amateur recitals at festivals such as the Apaturia, at which he says boys sang the works of various poets, including Solon (*Ti.* 21B).

15. Pl. *Grg.* 501E. He further claims that the kitharode Meles, the father of Kinesias, is a prime example of someone who not only did not look to the educative value of music but whose playing actually pained his audience. On Kinesias, see also Ar. *Ra.* 153 and *Nu.* 333, 448, as well as Pherecr. fr. 144B (Edmonds, *Fragments of Attic Comedy*, vol. 1, pp. 262–65).

16. *Lg.* 700B. Plato seems to have been intrigued with the double sense of *nomos* as "musical order" and as "law," particularly because he advocates strict government regulation of music (*Lg.* 799E; cf. *R.* 424C on the effect of musical changes on the nomoi of the polis; see Literary Sources above).

17. See T. J. Fleming, "The Musical Nomos in Aeschylus' *Oresteia*," for a summary of the characteristics of the nomos as they are described by Proclus, Pollux, ps.-Plutarch, and others. Ps.-Arist. *Pr.* 19.15 says that nomoi were not arranged in the usual strophe-antistrophe form, and were therefore suited not so much to the citizen chorus (who needed the regularity of form) as to the individual professional artist. See also H. Grieser, "Nomos: Ein Beitrag zur griechischen Musikgeschichte."

18. Lucillius, *Anth. Pal.* 11.133.

19. Pl. *Ion* 540D-E.

20. Pl. *Lg.* 700D. Huchzermeyer, 73–74, rightly points out that this "opposition" between lyre and aulos has been greatly exaggerated in modern criticism, and that it was not until the time of Socrates that prominent philosophers began to attack the influence of aulos music.

21. On Plato's views on the various harmoniai, see Anderson, *Ethos,* 72–73.

22. Phainias, quoted in Ath. 352C. For the biographical details concerning Stratonikos, see Paul Maas, "Stratonikos," and E. K. Borthwick, "Some Problems in Musical Terminology."

23. Pl. *Lg.* 669E.

24. Cf. also *Lg.* 810B for Plato's view that rhythm and harmonia are essential parts of poetic composition; it follows that anything which tends to obscure those basic elements is unacceptable to Plato.

25. For the "unison" interpretation, see Liddell, Scott, and Jones, *Greek-English Lexicon*, s.v. πρόσχορδος; also Anderson, *Ethos*, 96. Ps.-Plu. *De mus.* 1133B may be correct in describing the older style (advocated by Plato) as involving a fixed kind of rhythm and a fixed harmonia during the course of a particular song, as opposed to the frequent changes allowed in the newer style.

26. Pl. *Grg.* 482B.

27. Cf. Pl. *Tht.* 144E; *Plt.* 349E; *Ly.* 209B.

28. Pl. *R.* 531B.

29. Pl. *Ly.* 209B.

30. Arist. *Po.* 1447a15; Pl. *Grg.* 501E.

31. Further examples of new words developed from existing words include *kitharisma* ("that which is played on the kithara") and *kitharisis*, another word for "kithara playing."

32. Plu. *De Pyth. or.* 16.

33. Apulian: Altamura 2; Madrid 11078; Trieste S401; Bonn 98; column krater once Berlin, Adolf Hitler; York, City Art Gallery 19. Lucanian: Trieste 1695. Etruscan: Berkeley 8.935; Heidelberg E96; Parma C101.

34. Doubtful examples: Naples H1984 (with inner-arm decoration and an added rectangular base); Paris K526 (a lyra?); Boston 13.207 (a kithara?), Etruscan; ring, London R1068 (a lyra?); an unnumbered Naples oinochoe (a crescent soundbox with finger-length protrusions along the outer edge).

35. Heidelberg 26.90; Berkeley 8.997.

36. Vases: Syracuse 17427 and Boston 28.108. Scaraboid from Leningrad in Boardman, *Greek Gems*, no. 601.

37. Athenian krater: London E502; Boeotian krater: Athens 1385. On a votive relief of ca. 400 B.C., Sparta 468, Apollo and Artemis appear in the familiar libation scene. A marble relief of ca. 27 B.C.–A.D. 14, Cleveland 30.522, in archaizing neo-Attic style, presents a libation scene; but the figures are Apollo kitharoidos and a Nike pouring the libation.

38. Terra-cottas: Athens Kerameikos HS 264; Thessaloniki VII, 190, and XIV, 222; Lindos, Rhodes 2917.

There are also a number of Hellenistic statues and reliefs, and Roman copies of Hellenistic statues, of Apollo Kitharoidos (London 1380 and Nicosia, statue from Salamis), but the instruments included are no longer of the old 5th-c. type.

39. The women portrayed in a Cypriote terra-cotta (Nicosia XVI, 77) and a small Cypriote half-length statue (London C352) may also play the standard kithara; their instruments are too damaged for this to be certain.

40. Boardman, *Greek Gems*, no. 721.

41. Madrid 11034; the painting seems to be a Lucanian copy of ca. 380–360 B.C. from an Athenian model.

An early Lucanian squat lekythos, London E695 (ca. 400 B.C.) seems to have a Dionysiac scene, with a central bearded figure (Dionysos?) riding a camel, and attendants playing kithara and tympana. A satyr plays the kithara on an alabastron of ca. 340–320 B.C.

(once Roman Market). On Taranto 8129 a seated woman (Aphrodite) holds the kithara (see text below).

42. In two further paintings the instrument is of uncertain type: on a Paestan lekanis lid, Paris K570, the instrument's undecorated arms are thin and the crossbar has no knobs; on Apulian-Campanian lekythos Warsaw (Goluchow) 125 the long, lyre-like arms have no visible crossbar.

43. The other vases are Naples Stg 574; Ruvo 1500; Copenhagen 3757; Naples 1762 (82110); Leningrad 355; an early 4th-c. Lucanian oinochoe of unknown location; and Melbourne 90/5, an Apulian vase with a scene that includes two comic (*phlyax*) characters.

On a Campanian bell krater once New York, Kevorkian 71, there is no Marsyas, but Apollo sits with the kithara between two Muses.

44. Other fragments offer Apollo with scepter-bearing Zeus and a Nike bringing a fillet (Boston 61.112); Apollo in elaborate costume reaching out toward another figure, New York 20.196; and a head, presumably Apollo, Sydney 51.37.

45. H. R. W. Smith, *Funerary Symbolism in Apulian Vase-Painting*.

46. Apollo, his kithara near him, observes a young couple driving away in a quadriga on Richmond, Va. 8.55, where the loom/abacus is also present. On the handloom, see Sarah Pomeroy, "Supplementary Notes on Erinna," 19. For the argument that the ladder-like object is a musical instrument, see Eva Keuls, "The Apulian 'Xylophone': A Mysterious Musical Instrument Identified," 476–77 and pl. 66, fig. 2.

47. Apollo is part of a purification scene on Taranto 8925.

48. See A. D. Trendall and T. B. L. Webster, *Illustrations*, pl. IV, 31; A. D. Trendall, "Phlyax Vases," pl. 46, no. 49.

49. Smith, *Funerary Symbolism*, pl. 1a and p. 43, has pointed this out.

50. Orpheus appears before Hades on several other vases: Bari, Perrone Coll. 14; an amphora at Taranto; and Malibu 77 AE 13.

51. See Smith, *Funerary Symbolism*, pll. 12, 23.

52. This Orpheus and the one on Milan 270 stand on tiptoe as though dancing.

53. According to Trendall and Cambitoglou, the seated youth in Thracian costume on Naples, private coll. 352 (*RFVA*, pl. 184, 1, and p. 511), is not Orpheus but Paris, and the woman whom Aphrodite takes by the wrist to lead her toward him is Helen. The youth does not wear the long robe that Orpheus customarily wears in these paintings, but the kithara lying behind him and the Eros with a wreath above him (often seen above Orpheus) allow us to at least speculate that the couple may be Orpheus and Eurydice.

54. Below him and left a seated woman has the name ΔIKA; Harrison believes this name is whole, and there does not seem to be room for more than one additional letter; cf. Jane Ellen Harrison, *Themis*, 521–23.

55. Other swan's-head instruments: a 4th-c. barbitos on a coin from Teos (London, Anson 363); a lyra on an Etruscan stamnos ca. 400–350 B.C., Oxford 1917.54; and a kithara later than the 4th century held by a figure in terra-cotta in W. Froehner, *Terres cuites d'Asie de la collection Greau*, pl. 110, 2, p. 85. See also F. Winter, *Die antiken Terrakotten III: Die Typen der figürlichen Terrakotten II*, pp. 138–141.

56. L. Anson, *Numismata Graeca*, pt. 6, pll. 4–8. The coin of Mytilene mentioned (Anson no. 333) has eight strings.

57. 8: Kassel T. 723, Munich 3297. 8 or 9: Milan 270. 10: frag. from Fenicia Coll., location unknown (if the drawing reprinted in Pensa, *Rappresentazioni*, p. 47, fig. 8, is correct). 11: Naples 82110.

58. The soundbox sections are indicated on Adolphseck 178 and perhaps also on Naples 82110. The small protrusions are also seen on Ruvo 1500 (fig. 2a), Madrid 11034, and Karlsruhe B4.

59. Diagonal sling: Madrid 11034, Karlsruhe B4, Copenhagen 3757, Boston 61.112. Others with cloth in two strips: Copenhagen 3757, Karlsruhe B4, Milan 270, Munich 3297, Naples 82110, and Naples 3222; others have none or are not clear.

Madrid 11034 has an "old style" cloth, another indication that this is a copy of a scene from an Attic vase of earlier date. The "swan's-head" examples have no sling, sash, or cloth.

60. Apollo is the player in both: seated in the upper zone with Hermes and Athena, above the Danaids, on Ruvo J 494; again with Hermes attending a bride on the Lentini vase.

61. The painter of Leningrad St. 498 did not understand the purpose of the left-hand wrist sling, for he drapes it slackly, diagonally across the soundbox.

62. Other examples of marriage rites: seated couples on New York 11.210.3, Bari 3720, and Bari, Lagioia Coll.; seated man or woman with attendants in preparation scenes on Brusuglio private coll. 9, vase once Basel Market, and New York 17.46.2.

63. On Athens Acropolis 56 NAK 232 (late 4th century?) one of the few non-Italian representations, a seated woman plays the Italiote kithara in a scene of women and Erotes moving about an altar and a large krater, with grape clusters in the background.

64. Other terra-cottas (except the Samothrace Eros and Boston 97.300) in Wintèr, *Typen II*, 138–40.

65. Boston 10.234 (dots on lower string fastener), Geneva, Chamay Coll. pelike, Lipari 749A, Torino 4149, Leningrad terracotta 878S, Nauplia oinochoe without number, and Bari, Lagioia Coll.

66. On Boston 10.234 the soundbox is white and the arms are gold. Two further examples of the Italiote kithara on Apulian vases London F 309 and F 399, which have not been seen by the authors, are reported in R. A. Higgins and R. P. Winnington-Ingram, "Lute-Players in Greek Art," 69.

67. Oxford 1945.2; Florence 81947; Athens 774 and 775, dated after 350 B.C. For a phorminx-playing siren from Asia Minor, see chap. 6.

68. Thessaloniki 2465; Eleusis Mus. marble relief of two figures, one a bearded man who holds a lyre.

69. London 1917.7-25.2 and Vienna 202.

70. Munich 3268, Amsterdam 2579, and London E695.

71. Toronto 410 and Berlin 4532.

72. Brides: Copenhagen, Chr. VIII 316; Cambridge, Mus. Class. Arch. UP 143. Grooms: London F270; a Naples oinochoe; Rome, Vatican T 11; Mannheim, Reiss Mus. Cg 143.

73. Paris, Cab. Med. 483.

74. Bonn 100; Mannheim, Reiss Mus. Cg 315; Madrid 11223.

75. Athens 1187; krater once Northampton 74.

76. Muses: Munich 3268; krater once New York, Kevorkian 71. Muses also appear in the Apollo/Marsyas scenes where lyra, kithara, and auloi are found. Symposium: Naples 85873. Brides: Cambridge, Mus. Class. Arch. UP 143; Copenhagen Chr. VIII 316.

77. On one of the few early Italiote vases, London E695, a bearded man in Eastern dress, with cap and zigzag-decorated boots plays the lyra (?) while walking with a similarly dressed man riding a camel (Dionysos?).

78. Henri Metzger, "Lebes gamikos a figures rouges du Musée National d'Athènes," p. 234 and pl. 13.

79. Mannheim Reiss Cg 143; Rome, Vatican T 11.

80. Copenhagen Chr. VIII 316 (eight kollopes), Madrid 11223, Naples 85873.

81. The most common variant, seen on several Italiote vases and a ring stone of mainland or East Greek origin, is a soundbox that looks squashed—usually an oval lengthwise between the arms, though on the ring stone there are squared corners: Bonn 100, Paris K 121, Toronto 410, Naples 112855 (Gnathian), cornelian ring stone London 1153. The lyre on Paris K 121 also has straight, diverging arms, and its crossbar is at their top.

The soundboxes seem crescent shaped (with squared ends) or half-ring shaped on Italian relief ware of the 3d–2d centuries B.C., e.g., Paris H 261, H 292, and 1st century A.D.: New York 19.192.31 (with chelys pattern on the front!). The lyre on Mannheim Cg 143 appears to have been carelessly repainted at some time; it may actually have been an Italiote kithara.

82. Florence 81947; Paris G 516.

83. Attic vases Boston 10.206; London E 129; Naples 3240. Marble siren Athens 774 (a similar siren, Athens 775, shows the border only). Terra-cottas: Nauplia, plaque from Tiryns; Rhodes 2355, 2918, 2919. Italiote vases: Munich 3268 (see above); Paris K 570. The chelys pattern can be seen in 1st-c. B.C. Arretine relief ware examples: New York 08.258.37, 19.192.16, and 19.192.18.

84. Ring stone dated ca. 375–325 B.C. West slope ware: Athens Acropolis 1177 and Athens Agora P 7888.

85. Attic examples, all from the turn of the century (ca. 420–390 B.C.): Athens 1187; Berlin 2402; Florence 81947; Cambridge, Fitzwilliam GR 147, 160, 161.1899. Italiote: Cambridge, Mus. Class. Arch. UP 143; London F 270.

86. Some good examples: Attic: Florence 81947, krater once Northampton 74; London E129; Athens Agora P 7888; Athens Acropolis 1177. Italiote: Amsterdam 2579, Milan ST. 6873, and Toronto 410.

87. Attic: Athens 12254, Boston 01.8255, Vienna 202. Italiote: krater formerly New York, Kevorkian 71.

88. Lines on arms: Attic, Florence 81947; Italiote, Amsterdam 2579. Lines across tops of arms: Paris, Cab. Méd. 483.

89. For an earlier example see chap. 6, fig. 13 and n. 53. Vases with clear views of the plektron dated between 420 and 390 B.C.: Berlin 2402, Florence 81947, New York 49.11.2, krater once Northampton 74.

90. Pl. *Lg.* 794E. See chap. 3, nn. 7 and 62.

91. *IG* ed. min. II/III, 1388 Z.80.

92. For a good illustration of the shuttle, see the black-figured lekythos attributed to the Amasis Painter, New York 31.11.10. Further discussion of the analogies in Greek literature between weaving and playing the lyre may be found in J. M. Snyder, "The Web of Song: Weaving Imagery in Homer and the Lyric Poets." On the loom itself and problems in terminology, see Grace M. Crowfoot, "Of the Warp-Weighted Loom."

93. Pl. *Cra.* 390B. See also *Euthd.* 289B–D.

94. Pl. *Phd.* 85E–86B.

95. Athens 14901, Ferrara T.406, Stockholm 2. Satyr: London E 228.

96. Woman in naiskos: Paris, pelike. Courtship: Naples 81953, Toronto 456, and possibly Naples 3218.

97. On three vases with small areas for scene painting, a woman playing the harp appears alone. Various elements (thymiaterion, grape cluster and flowers, or on the reverse, Eros, swan, and fawn) suggest that this is Aphrodite. Women are almost invariably modestly dressed, but two of these figures (the third has not been seen) are nude to the waist: Heidelberg 26.86, Los Angeles 50.8.25, and Leipzig Univ. T-716.

98. Lavers also on Naples, private coll. 23 and Paris, Cab. Méd. 1049.

99. Groom and attendants: vase of unknown shape and location (Herbig IV-2b no. 4, p. 184); Naples 2867. Couple: Torino 4129.

There are no harp-playing sirens from the western Greek world, but a Paris terra-cotta from Kyrenaika (Benghazi, Libya) of a monkey that plays the harp may be of the late 4th century.

100. Attic: London E228. Italiote vases: Copenhagen Chr. VIII 316, Cambridge, Mus. Class. Arch. UP 143, Naples 2867. On Stockholm 12 (Apollo between two Muses) the open arched harp and a standard kithara (but with rounded base) appear together. On a Gnathian krater (late 4th century), Naples 80084, the same instruments—aulos, harp, Italiote kithara—are used as decoration. On Stockholm 12 Apollo holds an instrument that is a conflation of kithara and phorminx, while a Muse plays the harp.

101. This was noticed long ago; Wegner, *Musikleben,* 47, quotes Abert to this effect and agrees. The only 4th-c. exceptions occur on Stockholm 12, where the player's extended right hand holds a plektron (!) also seen on Paris Cab. Méd. 1048, and on London E228, where the satyr playing is seen not from the right but from the left front, making the right-hand position hard to judge.

The unnumbered Leningrad scaraboid, Boardman, *Greek Gems,* no. 600, shows the instrument held with the longest strings nearest the player, but the left hand still reaches to the farther (in this case, shorter) strings. Among the similar 5th-c. spindle harps, the player's left hand is on the shorter strings in Athens 14791, the longer ones on New York 37.11.23; on New York 07.286.35 and Würzburg H 4455, both hands are at the same place.

Only on Naples 81392 (5th-c. Italiote) does the player of an arched harp have her right hand advanced, but it appears to be damping, not plucking. For 5th-c. references, see chap. 6.

102. This example has a separate base underneath the neck to which the strings are attached. The harps on Leningrad B 3128 and Stockholm 2 (no satisfactory reproductions available) may be of the same kind; Stockholm 2 may show an instrument with a separate base.

103. Nauplia, unnumbered Hellenistic-period oinochoe, buff with red, black, and white; Nicosia, Cyprus, terra-cotta figures XVI, 90a and 90b; Leningrad 875 EE; and Naples 113349 from Taranto.

104. It is not certain to which of these groups the Paris vase mentioned by Herbig should belong (IV-1, 2, p. 180); he seems to say that it has the row of points, since of his four examples "with or (less often) without rows of points," two of the remaining three lack them.

105. 10–12 strings: Copenhagen Chr. VIII 316, Naples Stg 699, Paris Bibl. Nat. de Ridder 1047.

Arched angle harps, separate base: Paris pelike, Naples Stg 699, Paris Bibl. Nat. de Ridder 1047.

No separate base, or uncertain: Copenhagen Chr. VIII 316, Paris terra-cotta from Kyrenaika, Stockholm 12, Torino 4129.

106. Items in this group: London E228, Athens 14901, Boston 01.8101, Naples 2202. The row of small circles along the neck on London E228 suggests side tuning pegs around which the strings are affixed rather than around the neck. On Naples 2202 the 12 strings are carelessly drawn so that they run from the neck to the post.

107. See also Naples 2867.

108. Toronto 926.19.7 also seems to have a bird, or perhaps an animal's head, at the front of the soundbox.

109. Toronto 926.19.7 does not have a separate base; Naples 2867 and 81953 (fig. 15) are not completely clear.

110. Others with figure of bird: Cleveland 28.601 and Naples, private coll. 23, both excellent examples with kollopes and separate bases as well as long-legged cranes; Berlin 3291 (late 5th century);

Naples 80084; Leipzig Univ. T-716; a vase of unknown location and shape, Herbig's IV-2b, 4, p. 184 (no reproductions of the last two now available).

Others with design resembling shape of bird: Naples 3218 (close resemblance); Cambridge, Mus. Class. Arch. UP 143 (lower half of instrument only); Paris Cab. Méd. 1048; pelike of unknown location (Herbig, IV-2b, 5, p. 184 [no reproduction available]).

111. Berlin 3291 (late 5th century) also has a separate base, and the presence of one is suggested on Naples 80084 (350–300 B.C.).

112. Cambridge, Mus. Class. Arch. UP 143 and Heidelberg 26/86 show harps with wide necks similar to that of Boston 00.360 (fig. 13). Heidelberg 26/86 is damaged, but the harp's post may have been bird shaped, as the remaining lower part of the post curves outward.

113. Ion fr. 22 (Snell), quoted in Ath. 634E.

114. Pl. *Prt.* 347D.

115. Ps.-Arist. *Ath.* 50.

116. As Chester Starr, "An Evening with the Flute Girls," 406, points out, this passage "is the *only* evidence for the fixing of wages at Athens." For a survey of several woman musicians of the 4th century, see Sarah Pomeroy, "Technikai kai Mousikai."

117. H. Michell, *The Economics of Ancient Greece*, 131, 165.

118. Men. fr. 319.1–6.

119. Thphr. *HP* 5.7.6.

120. Frisk, vol. 2, p. 674; Chantraine, 986.

121. Arist. *Pol.* 1341a40. A 3d-c. B.C. historian, Neanthes, thought that the sambyke was the invention of Ibykos (6th century); see Ath. 637B.

122. Ath. 633F.

123. Ps.-Arist. *Pr.* 19.14. The context is the author's query as to why the voice when singing an octave apart from the accompaniment of the *phoinikion* is often perceived as being in unison with the instrument. Michaelides, *Music of Ancient Greece*, 250, classifies phoinix and phoinikion as harps (but on what evidence?).

124. R. A. Higgins and R. P. Winnington-Ingram, "Lute-Players in Greek Art," have assembled a group of representations that includes ten terra-cottas dated 330–200 B.C., plus the Mantinea relief, Athens 216. An additional terra-cotta from Memphis is of later date, according to the authors; and on a Campanian squat lekythos (London G 21), dated by Trendall ca. 20 B.C. (*Early South Italian Vase Painting*, pl. 16c), a woman "is apparently playing a musical instrument, which can only be a lute." However, though the woman's arms are positioned as though she were playing the lute, she may hold only a fillet, or a tablet seen edge-on.

An additional terra-cotta not listed is London 1968.11-29.1, from Egypt, a figure of a boy playing a lute dated ca. 250 B.C.

125. Pausanias 8.9.1 attributes the work to Praxiteles, who worked from about 370 to "not more than some ten years after 343"; see A. W. Lawrence, *Greek and Roman Sculpture*, 188. This attribution is accepted by Margarete Bieber, *The Sculpture of the Hellenistic Age*, 22.

126. Ps.-Plu. *De mus.* 1142F; Phld. *Mus.* 11.77 fr. 9 (p. 10, Kemke).

127. Higgins and Winnington-Ingram, "Lute Players in Greek Art," 65.

128. The exception, Paris CA 574, is said to come from Tanagra, but this may be open to question.

129. Chantraine, 855, 1019. On *pandoura* see also Emilia Masson, *Récherches sur les plus anciens emprunts sémitiques en grec*, 90–91.

130. Matron, quoted in Ath. 183A.

131. Pythagoras, quoted in Ath. 184A.

132. Theopompos of Colophon, quoted in Ath. 183B.

133. Pl. *R.* 399C–D. Translations of the names for instruments can render this passage hopelessly garbled; cf. Rouse, who translates the many-stringed pektis as "gittern" (a guitar-like instrument with few strings) and the seven-stringed kithara as "harp" (which usually has many strings). The passage is sometimes misinterpreted as referring literally to an increase in the number of strings, as in Pierre M. Schuhl, "Platon et la musique de son temps"; he quotes Robin's translation, which reads, "Nous n'aurons donc pas besoin, pour les chants et la melodie, de multiplier le nombre de cordes, ni non plus d'embrasser la totalité des harmonies?" See above on the use of *polychordia* as a synonym for *polyharmonia*.

134. Arist. *Pol.* 1341a21.

135. Pl. *Lg.* 700C. In later times, the pressures of changing customs in connection with musical competitions are reflected in a 3d-c. A.D. papyrus from Karanis that prescribes the rules of conduct for auletes and kitharists; cf. Orsamus Pearl, "Rules for Musical Contests."

136. See Henderson, "Growth of Ancient Greek Music," 12.

137. Pl. *Grg.* 501E–502A.

138. Pl. *Symp.* 179D.

Chapter 8: Questions and Conclusions

1. Possible harp: Athens 784 (Aign 95, V/14). The 6th-c. lyre with arms like those of the Minoan lyre, on a funerary chest from Campania, is discussed in Aign 187, E/1.

2. Wegner, *Griechenland*, 65, 71, 94, with pll. 36 and 42.

3. Ath. 182f.

4. Kleonides *Eisagoge* 3.67.

5. Peter Gammond, *Musical Instruments in Color*, 13.

6. Pi. *N.* 10.21–22; *P.* 4.294–297; *N.* 9.7–9; fr. 140a.61 (Snell); *P.* 1.1–4.

Bibliography

Abert, H. "Kitharoidia." *Paulys Real-Encyclopädie*. Vol. 11, part 1 (1921), columns 530–34.

——. "Saiteninstrumente." *Paulys Real-Encyclopädie*. Series 2, vol. 1, part 2 (1920), columns 1760ff.

AA *Acta Archaeologica.*

Aign Aign, Bernhard. "Die Geschichte der Musikinstrumente des Ägäischen Raumes bis um 700 vor Christus." Diss. J. W. Goethe-Universität, 1963. Frankfurt am Main.

Akurgal, Ekrem. *The Art of Greece: Its Origins in the Mediterranean and Near East.* Trans. Wayne Dynes. New York: Crown, 1968.

——. *Die Kunst Anatoliens von Homer bis Alexander.* Berlin: de Gruyter, 1961.

Spina Alfieri, Nereo, and Paulo Arias. *Spina: Die neuentdeckte Etruskerstadt und die griechischen Vasen ihrer Gräber.* Munich: Hirmer, 1958.

Allen, T. W.; W. R. Halliday; and E. E. Sikes, eds. *The Homeric Hymns.* Oxford: Clarendon Press, 1936.

AJA *American Journal of Archaeology.*

Anderson, Warren D. *Ethos and Education in Greek Music.* Cambridge: Harvard Univ. Press, 1966.

——. "Hymns That Are Lords of the Lyre." *Classical Journal* 49 (1954), 211–15.

——. "What Song the Sirens Sang: Problems and Conjectures in Ancient Greek Music." *Research Chronical of the Royal Musical Association* 15 (1979), 1–16.

Angel, J. Lawrence. "Skeletal Material from Attica." *Hesperia* 14 (1945), 279–331.

BSA *Annual of the British School at Athens.*

Anoyianakis, Phoibos. *Greek Folk Musical Instruments.* New Rochelle, N.Y.: Caratzas, 1979.

Anson, L. *Numismata Graeca: Greek Coin-Types Classified for Immediate Identification.* Part VI. London: Kegan Paul, Trench, Trübner and Co., 1916.

L'Antiquité classique.

Archaiologikon Deltion.

Arias, Paolo, and Max Hirmer. *A History of Greek Vase Painting.* Trans. B. B. Shefton. London: Thames & Hudson, 1962.

AM *Athenische Mitteilungen.* (= *Mitteilungen des Deutschen Archäologischer Instituts, Athenische Abteilung*).

Aurigemma, Salvatore. *Scavi di Spina.* Rome: Bretschneider, 1960.

Barbour, J. Murray. "The Principles of Greek Notation." *Journal of the American Musicological Society* 13 (1960), 1–17.

Barker, Andrew. *Greek Musical Writings,* Volume 1: *The Musician and his Art.* Cambridge: Cambridge Univ. Press, 1984.

——. "Innovations of Lysander the Kitharist." *Classical Quarterly* 32 (1982), 266–69.

ABV Beazley, John D. *Attic Black-Figure Vase-Painters.* Oxford: Clarendon Press, 1956.

ARV² ——. *Attic Red-Figure Vase-Painters.* 2d edition. 3 vols. Oxford: Clarendon Press, 1963.

——. *Attic Red-Figured Vases in American Museums.* Cambridge: Harvard Univ. Press, 1918.

————. "Citharoedus." *Journal of Hellenic Studies* 42 (1922), 70–98.

EVP ————. *Etruscan Vase-Painting.* Oxford: Clarendon Press, 1947.

————. "Hymn to Hermes." *American Journal of Archaeology* 52 (1948), 336–40.

————. *The Pan Painter.* Mainz: P. von Zabern, 1974.

Para ————. *Paralipomena.* Oxford: Clarendon Press, 1971.

Beck, Frederick A. G. *Album of Greek Education.* Sydney: Cheiron Press, 1975.

————. *Greek Education, 450–350 B.C.* New York: Barnes and Noble, 1964.

Behn, F. *Musikleben im Altertum und frühen Mittelalter.* Stuttgart: Hiersemann, 1954.

Berkowitz, Lucille. "An Index of Musical Terminology in Homer, The Cycle, and the Hymns." M.A. thesis, Ohio State Univ., 1961.

Bethe, Erich, ed. *Pollucis Onomasticon.* 3 vols. Leipzig: Teubner, 1900–37.

Bieber, Margarete. *The Sculpture of the Hellenistic Age.* New York: Columbia Univ. Press, 1961.

Blakeway, Alan. "The Date of Archilochus." *Greek Poetry and Life: Essays Presented to Gilbert Murray.* Oxford: Clarendon Press, 1936, pp. 34–55.

Blinkenberg, Christian S. *Lindos: Fouilles et recherches, 1902–14.* 2 vols. (Vol. 2: *Les Petits Objets.*) Berlin: de Gruyter, 1931.

Blümel, Carl. *Der Hermes eines Praxiteles.* Baden-Baden: W. Klein, 1948.

Blümner, H. *Technologie und Terminologie der Gewerbe und Künste bei Griechen und Römern.* 4 vols. Leipzig: Teubner, 1875–87; rpt. Hildesheim: G. Olms, 1969.

ABFV Boardman, John. *Archaic Greek Gems: Schools and Artists in the Sixth and Early Fifth Centuries B.C.* Evanston, Ill.: Northwestern Univ. Press, 1968.

————. *Athenian Black Figure Vases.* London: Thames & Hudson, 1974.

Greek ————. *Greek Gems and Finger Rings.* New
Gems York: H. N. Abrams, 1970.

————. "Herakles, Peisistratos and Eleusis." *Journal of Hellenic Studies* 95 (1975), 1–12.

————. "Some Attic Fragments: Pot, Plaque, and Dithyramb." *Journal of Hellenic Studies* 76 (1956), 18–25.

Boehme, Robert. *Orpheus: Der Sänger und seine Zeit.* Bern and Munich: A. Francke, 1970.

Boháč, Jiří M. *Kerčské vázy se zřetelem k památkám v československých sbírkách.* Prague: Československé akademie věd, 1958.

Boisacq Boisacq, Emile. *Dictionnaire étymologique de la langue grecque.* Heidelberg: Carl Winter, 1950.

Borthwick, E. K. "ΚΑΤΑΛΗΨΙΣ: A Neglected Technical Term in Greek Music." *Classical Quarterly* 11 (1959), 23–29.

————. "Notes on the Plutarch *De Musica* and the *Cheiron* of Pherecrates." *Hermes* 96 (1968), 60–73.

————. "Some Problems in Musical Terminology." *Classical Quarterly* 17 (1967), 145–57.

Bothmer, Dietrich von. *Ancient Art from New York Private Collections.* New York: Metropolitan Museum, 1961.

Bragard, Roger, and F. de Hen. *Musical Instruments in Art and History.* New York: Viking, 1968.

Brommer, Frank. *Herakles: Die Zwölf Taten des Helden in antiker Kunst und Literatur.* Munster-Cologne: Böhlau, 1953.

————. *Satyrspiele.* Berlin: de Gruyter, 1959.

————. *Vasenlisten zur griechischen Heldensage.* 3d edition. Marburg: N. G. Elwert, 1973.

BCH *Bulletin de Correspondance Hellénique.*
Bulletin of the Cleveland Museum of Art.

Burn, A. R. *The Lyric Age of Greece.* London: Edward Arnold, 1960.

Burton, R. W. B. *Pindar's Pythian Odes.* Oxford: Oxford Univ. Press, 1962.

Buschor, Ernst. *Die Musen des Jenseits.* Munich: Bruckmann, 1944.

ARFVP Cambitoglou, Alexander, and Trendall, A. D. *Apulian Red-Figured Vase-Painters of the Plain Style.* Archaeological Institute of America, 1961.

Campbell, D. A. "Flutes and Elegiac Couplets." *Journal of Hellenic Studies* 84 (1964), 63–68.

————, ed. *Greek Lyric Poetry.* New York: St. Martin's Press, 1967.

Carrière, Jean. *Théognis: Poèmes élégiaques.* Paris: Belles Lettres, 1948.

Caskey, L. D., and J. D. Beazley. *Attic Vase Paintings in the Museum of Fine Arts, Boston.* 3 vols. Oxford: Oxford Univ. Press, 1931–54.

Catalogue raisonné des figurines et reliefs en terre-cuite grecs, étrusques et romains. Compiled by Simone Mollard-Besques. Musée National du Louvre. Paris: Editions des Musées Nationaux, 1954–.

Chadwick, John. *The Mycenaean World.* Cambridge: Cambridge Univ. Press, 1976.

Chailley, Jacque. *La musique grecque antique.* Paris: Belles Lettres, 1979.

Chantraine Chantraine, Pierre. *Dictionnaire étymologique de la langue grecque.* Paris: Klincksieck, 1974.

Charbonneaux, Jean; Roland Martin; and François Villard. *Archaic Greek Art, 620–480 B.C.* London: Thames & Hudson, 1971.

Classical Journal.

Coldstream, John. *Greek Geometric Pottery.* London: Methuen, 1968.

Comstock, Mary; Alice Graves; Emily Vermeule; and Cornelius Vermeule. *The Trojan War in Greek Art.* Boston: Museum of Fine Arts, 1965.

Comstock, Mary, and Cornelius Vermeule. *Greek, Etruscan and Roman Bronzes in the Museum of Fine Arts, Boston.* Greenwich, Conn.: New York Graphic Society, 1971.

Cook, R. M. "The Date of the Hesiodic Shield." *Classical Quarterly* 31 (1937), 204–14.

———. *Greek Painted Pottery.* London: Methuen, 1960.

CVA *Corpus Vasorum Antiquorum.* Union académique internationale. Issued in portfolios.

Crowfoot, Grace M. "Of the Warp-Weighted Loom." *Annual of the British School at Athens* 37 (1936), 36–47.

Crusius, O. "Arion." *Paulys Real-Encyclopädie.* Vol. 2, columns 836–41.

Dale, A. M., ed. *Euripides' Alcestis.* Oxford: Oxford Univ. Press, 1966.

Daremberg Daremberg, Charles V., and Edmond Saglio,
and eds. *Dictionnaire des antiquités grecques et*
Saglio *romaines, d'après les textes et les monuments.* Paris: Hachette, 1877–1919.

Davison, J. A. "Notes on the Panathenaea." *Journal of Hellenic Studies* 78 (1958), 23–42.

———. "Peisistratus and Homer." *Transactions of the American Philological Association* 86 (1955), 1–21.

———. "Quotations and Allusions in Early Greek Literature." *Eranos* 53 (1956), 125–40.

Dawkins, R. M., ed. *The Sanctuary of Artemis Orthia at Sparta.* London: Macmillan, 1929.

Deubner, Ludwig. *Attische Feste.* Berlin: Akademie Verlag, 1956.

———. "Terpander und die siebensaitige Leier," *Philologische Wochenschrift* 50 (1930), 1566–67.

———. "Die Viersaitige Leier." *Athenische Mitteilungen* 54 (1929), 194–200.

Diels, Hermann, and Walther Kranz, eds. *Die Fragmente der Vorsokratiker.* 3 vols. Berlin: Weidmann, 1969.

Dikaios, Porphyrios. *A Guide to the Cyprus Museum.* [3d revised edition]. Nicosia: C. Nicolaou and Sons, 1961.

Dover, K. J. *Greek Homosexuality.* Cambridge: Harvard Univ. Press, 1978.

Drachmann, A. B., ed. *Scholia vetera in Pindari carmina.* 1903; rpt. Amsterdam: Hakkert, 1964.

Duchesne-Guillemin, Marcelle. "Restitution d'une harpe minoenne et problème de la ΣΑΜΒΥΚΗ." *L'Antiquité Classique* 37 (1968), 5–19.

———. "Survivance orientale dans la designation des cordes de la lyre en Grece?" *Syria* 44 (1967), 233–46.

Düring, Ingemar. "Greek Music: Its Fundamental Features and Its Significance." *Journal of World History* 3 (1956), 302–29.

———. "Studies in Musical Terminology in 5th Century Literature." *Eranos* 43 (1945), 176–97.

Dugas, Charles. "Héraclès Mousicos." *Revue des Etudes Grecques* 57 (1944), 61–70.

Dunbabin, T. J. *The Greeks and their Eastern Neighbors.* London: Society for the Promotion of Hellenic Studies, 1957.

Duysinx, François. "Homère et les instruments de musique." *Didaskalikon* 38 (1977), 17–22.

Ecole Française d'Athènes, Exploration Archeologique de Delos.

Edmonds, John M. *The Fragments of Attic Comedy.* 4 vols. Leiden: E. J. Brill, 1957–61.

Enciclopedia Classica. Enciclopedia Classica, section 3, vol. 11, part 5, *Storia della ceramica,* by Paolo E. Arias. Rome: Istituto della Enciclopedia Italiana, 1963.

EAA *Enciclopedia dell' Arte Antica.* Rome: Istituto della Enciclopedia Italiana, 1958–66.

EA *Ephēmeris Archaiologikē.*

Ervin, Miriam. "Newsletter from Greece." *American Journal of Archaeology* 74 (1970), 263–64.

Evans, Sir Arthur. *The Palace of Minos at Knossos.* 4 vols. London: Macmillan, 1921–35.

———. *Scripta Minoa: The Written Documents of Minoan Crete.* 2 vols. Oxford: Clarendon Press, 1909.

Fairbanks, Arthur. *Athenian Lekythoi, With Outline Drawing in Glaze Varnish on a White Ground.* New York: Macmillan, 1907.

————. *A Study of the Greek Paean.* Cornell Studies in Classical Philology, no. 12. New York: Macmillan, 1900.

Fairclough, H. Rushton. "The Connection between Music and Poetry in Early Greek Literature." In *Studies in Honor of Basil L. Gildersleeve.* Baltimore: Johns Hopkins Univ. Press, 1902. Pp. 205–27.

Feaver, D. D. "The Musical Setting of Euripides' *Orestes.*" *American Journal of Philology* 81 (1960), 1–15.

Finley, M. I. *Early Greece: The Bronze and Archaic Ages.* London: Chatto & Windus, 1970.

Fischer, David H. *Historians' Fallacies.* New York: Harper & Row, 1970.

Fleming, T. J. "The Musical Nomos in Aeschylus' *Oresteia.*" *Classical Journal* 72 (1977), 222–33.

Frazer, James George. *The Golden Bough.* 3d edition. 12 vols. London: Macmillan, 1913–15.

Frisk Frisk, Hjalmar. *Griechisches Etymologisches Wörterbuch.* 3 vols. Heidelberg: Carl Winter, 1954–70.

Froehner, Wilhelm. *Terres cuites d'Asie de la collection J. Greau.* Vol. 2 of *Terres cuites d'Asie Mineure.* Paris: H. Hoffmann, 1881–86.

Gammond, Peter. *Musical Instruments in Color.* New York: Macmillan, 1975.

Gardner, Percy. *Catalogue of the Greek Vases in the Ashmolean Museum.* Oxford: Clarendon Press, 1913.

Gemoll, Albert, ed. *Die homerischen Hymnen.* Leipzig: Teubner, 1886.

Gerber, Douglas, ed. *Euterpe.* Amsterdam: Hakkert, 1970.

————. *Pindar's Olympian One: A Commentary.* Toronto: *Phoenix* supplement 15, 1982.

————. "Studies in Greek Lyric Poetry: 1967–1975." *Classical World* 70 (1976), 65–157.

————. "Survey of Publications of Greek Lyric Poetry." *Classical World* 61 (1968), 265–79, 317–30, 373–85.

Gombosi, Otto. "Key, Mode, Species." *Journal of the American Musicological Society* 4 (1951), 20–26.

————. "The Melody of Pindar's Golden Lyre." *Musical Quarterly* 26 (1940), 381–92.

————. *Tonarten und Stimmungen der Antiken Musik.* Copenhagen: Ejnar Munksgaard, 1939.

Graef– Graef, B., and E. Langlotz. *Die antiken Va-
Langlotz sen von der Akropolis zu Athen.* 4 vols. Berlin: de Gruyter, 1925–33.

Greifenhagen, Adolf. *Griechische Eroten.* Berlin: de Gruyter, 1957.

Grieser, H. "Nomos: Ein Beitrag zur griechischen Musikgeschichte." Ph.D. diss. Heidelberg, 1937.

Groningen, B. A. van. "A propos de Terpandre." *Mnemosyne* 8 (1955), 177–91.

————. *Pindare au banquet: Les fragments des scolies.* Leiden: A. W. Sythoff, 1960.

————. *Théognis: Le premier livre.* Amsterdam: North Holland, 1966.

Guillemin, Marcelle, and Jacques Duchesne. "Sur l'origine asiatique de la cithare grecque." *L'Antiquité classique* 4 (1935), 117–24.

Gulick, C. B., trans. *Athenaeus: The Deipnosophists.* 7 vols. Cambridge: Harvard Univ. Press, 1959.

Gundel, W. "Lyra." *Paulys Real-Encyclopädie.* Vol. 13, part 2, columns 2489–90.

Hahlund, Walter. *Vasen um Meidias.* Mainz: P. von Zabern, 1976.

Hainsworth, John B. *The Flexibility of the Homeric Formula.* Oxford: Clarendon Press, 1968.

Haldane, J. A. "Musical Instruments in Greek Worship," *Greece and Rome* 13 (1966), 98–107.

————. "Musical Themes and Imagery in Aeschylus." *Journal of Hellenic Studies* 85 (1965), 33–41.

Hampe, Roland, and Erika Simon. *The Birth of Greek Art.* New York: Oxford Univ. Press, 1981.

Hanfmann, George M. A. "Ionia, Leader or Follower?" *Harvard Studies in Classical Philology* 61 (1953), 1–37.

Harrison, Evelyn B. "Hesperides and Heroes: A Note on the Three-Figure Reliefs." *Hesperia* 33 (1964), 76–82 and plates 11—14.

Harrison, Jane Ellen. *Themis.* 1927; rpt. Cleveland: World, 1962.

Henderson, Isobel. "Ancient Greek Music." *New Oxford History of Music.* Vol. 1. London: Oxford Univ. Press, 1966, pp. 336–97.

————. "The Growth of Ancient Greek Music." *Music Review* 4 (1943), 4–13.

Herbig, Reinhard. "Griechische Harfen." *Mitteilungen des Deutschen Archäologischer Instituts, Athenische Abteilung* 54 (1929), 164–93.

Hesperia.

Hester, D. A. "Pelasgian." *Lingua* 13 (1965), 335–84.

Higgins, R. A. *Greek Terracottas.* London: Methuen, 1967.

Higgins, R. A., and R. P. Winnington-Ingram. "Lute-Players in Greek Art." *Journal of Hellenic Studies* 85 (1965), 62–71.

Highbarger, E. L. "Theognis and the Persian Wars." *Transactions of the American Philological Association* 68 (1937), 88–111.

Hoorn, G. van. *Choes and Anthesteria.* Leiden: E. J. Brill, 1951.

Huchzermeyer Huchzermeyer, Helmut. *Aulos und Kithara in der griechischen Musik bis zum Ausgang der klassischen Zeit.* Emsdetten: H. and J. Lechte, 1931.

Huxley, George L. "Cretan *Paiawones.*" *Greek, Roman, and Byzantine Studies* 16 (1975), 119–24.

———. *Greek Epic Poetry from Eumelos to Panyassis.* Cambridge: Harvard Univ. Press, 1969.

———. "A Note on the Seven-Stringed Lyre." *Journal of Hellenic Studies* 90 (1970), 196–97.

Immerwahr, Henry R. "Book Rolls on Attic Vases." In *Classical, Mediaeval and Renaissance Studies in Honor of Berthold Louis Ullman.* Ed. Charles Henderson, Jr. Rome: Edizioni di Storia e Letteratura, 1964, pp. 17–48.

———. "Inscriptions on the Anacreon Krater in Copenhagen." *American Journal of Archaeology* 69 (1965), 152–54.

Inghirami, Francesco. *Monumenti etruschi o di etrusco nome, disegnati, incisi, illustrati e pubblicati dal cavaliere Francesco Inghirami.* 6 vols. Fiesone: Poligrafa fiesolana, 1821–26.

Jan, Karl von. "Die griechischen Saiteninstrumente." *Programm des Gymnasiums Saargemund.* Leipzig: Teubner, 1882.

———. "Die Musikinstrumente der Griechen und Römer." *Festgaben zum 25 jährigen Jubiläum des Gymnasiums und Realgymnasiums zu Landsberg a. W. dargebracht von ehemaligen Lehrern und Schülern.* Landsberg an der Warthe: F. Schoeffer, 1885, pp. 24–30.

Jan, Karl von, and Ernst Graf. "Epigonos." *Paulys Real-Encyclopädie.* Vol. 6 (1909), column 69.

Jenkins, G. Kenneth. *Ancient Greek Coins.* New York: G. P. Putnam's Sons, 1972.

Jourdan-Hemmerdinger, D. "Un nouveau papyrus musical d'Euripide." *Comptes rendus des séances de l'Acad. des Inscriptions et Belle-Lettres,* 1973, pp. 292–99.

JHS Journal of Hellenic Studies.

Kaempf-Dimitriadou, Sophia. *Die Liebe der Götter in der attischen Kunst des 5. Jahrhunderts V. Chr.* Bern: Francke, 1979.

Kaimio, M. "Music in the Homeric Hymn to Hermes." *Arctos* 8 (1974), 29–42.

Karageorghis, Vassos. *Mycenaean Art from Cyprus.* Nicosia: C. Nicolaou and Sons, 1968.

Karouzou, Semni. *The Amasis Painter.* Oxford: Clarendon Press, 1956.

Kemp, J. A. "Professional Musicians in Ancient Greece." *Greece and Rome* 13 (1966), 213–22.

Keuls, Eva. "The Apulian 'Xylophone': A Mysterious Musical Instrument Identified." *American Journal of Archaeology* 83 (1979), 476–77.

Kirk Kirk, G. S. *The Songs of Homer.* Cambridge: Cambridge Univ. Press, 1962.

Kirkwood, G. M. "A Survey of Recent Publications Concerning Classical Greek Lyric Poetry." *Classical Weekly* 47 (1953–54), 33–42, 49–54.

Kleingünther, Adolf. "ΠΡΩΤΟΣ ΕΥΡΕΤΗΣ: Untersuchungen zur Geschichte einer Fragestellung." *Philologus* suppl. 26, vol. 1 (1933), 1–155.

Kluge, F. *Etymologisches Wörterbuch der deutschen Sprache.* Berlin: de Gruyter, 1967.

Knitterscheid, Emil. "Musikinstrumente auf antiken Münzen." *Mitteilungen für Münzsammler* 6. Frankfurt am Main: Hamburger, 1929, pp. 310–15.

Koller, Hermann. *Musik und Dichtung im alten Griechenland.* Bern: Francke, 1963.

Kossatz-Diessmann, Anneliese. *Dramen des Aischylos auf westgriechischen Vasen.* Mainz: P. von Zabern, 1978.

Kretika Chronika.

Kunisch, Norbert, ed. *Antike Kunst aus Wuppertaler Privatbesitz.* Wuppertal: Heydt Museum, 1971.

Landels, J. G. "Fragments of Auloi Found in the Athenian Agora." *Hesperia* 33 (1964), 393–400.

———. "Ship-shape and *Sambuka*-fashion." *Journal of Hellenic Studies* 86 (1966), 69–77.

Lang, Mabel L. *The Palace of Nestor at Pylos,* vol. 2. Ed. Carl W. Blegen and Marion Rawson. 2 vols. Princeton: Princeton Univ. Press, 1966–69.

Langerbeck, H. "*Margites:* Versuch einer Beschreibung und Rekonstruktion." *Harvard Studies in Classical Philology* 63 (1958), 33–63.

Langlotz, Ernst. *Griechische Vasen in Würzburg.* Munich: J. B. Obernetter, 1932.

Lawergren, Bo. "The Cylinder Kithara in Etruria, Greece, and Anatolia." *Imago Musicae* 1 (1984), 147–74.

Lawler, Lillian B. *The Dance in Ancient Greece.* Middletown, Conn.: Wesleyan Univ. Press, 1965.

———. *The Dance of the Ancient Greek Theatre.* Iowa City: Univ. of Iowa Press, 1964.

———. "Dancing with the Elbows." *Classical Journal* 38 (1942), 161–63.

Lawrence, A. W. *Greek and Roman Sculpture.* London: J. Cape, 1972.

Leeuwen, J. van, ed. *Aristophanis Equites.* Leiden: Sijthoff, 1968.

Lefkowitz, Mary R. *The Lives of the Greek Poets.* Baltimore: Johns Hopkins Univ. Press, 1981.

———. *The Victory Ode: An Introduction.* Park Ridge, N.J.: Noyes Press, 1976.

Lenormant, Charles, and J. de Witte. *Elite des monuments céramographiques.* Paris: Leleux, 1844–61.

Lesky, Albin. *A History of Greek Literature.* New York: Thomas Crowell, 1966.

Levi, Alda. *Le terrecotte figurate de Museo nazionale di Napoli.* Naples: Vallecchi, 1926.

Levin, Flora R. *The Harmonics of Nicomachus and the Pythagorean Tradition.* University Park, Pa.: American Philological Association, 1975.

———. "The Hendecachord of Ion of Chios." *Transactions of the American Philological Association* 92 (1961), 295–307.

———. "Music in Ancient Greek Drama." In *Oedipus Rex: A Mirror for Greek Drama.* Ed. Albert Cook. Belmont, Calif.: Wadsworth, 1963, pp. 4–8.

Lezzi-Hafter, Adrienne. *Der Schuwalow-Maler.* 2 vols. Mainz: P. von Zabern, 1976.

Liddell, Henry George; Robert Scott; and Henry Stuart Jones, ed. *A Greek-English Lexicon.* Oxford: Clarendon Press, 1966.

Lippman, E. A. *Musical Thought in Ancient Greece.* New York: Columbia Univ. Press, 1964.

Lippold, Georg. *Griechische Porträtstatuen.* Munich: Bruckmann, 1912.

LP Lobel, E., and D. Page. *Poetarum Lesbiorum Fragmenta.* Oxford: Clarendon Press, 1955.

Lohmann, J. *Musike und Logos.* Stuttgart: Musikwissenschaftliche Verlags-Gesellschaft, 1970.

Long, Charlotte R. *The Ayia Triadha Sarcophagus. A Study of Late Minoan and Mycenaean Funerary Practises and Beliefs.* Studies in Mediterranean Archaeology, vol. 41. Göteborg: Paul Åströms, 1974.

Lord, Albert B. *The Singer of Tales.* Cambridge: Harvard Univ. Press, 1960.

Lorimer, H. L. *Homer and the Monuments.* London: Macmillan, 1950.

Luce, J. V. *Homer and the Heroic Age.* London: Thames & Hudson, 1975.

Maas, Martha. "Back Views of the Ancient Greek Kithara." *Journal of Hellenic Studies* 95 (1975), 175 and pl. 19a.

———. "On the Shape of the Ancient Greek Lyre." *Galpin Society Journal* 27 (1974), 113–18.

———. "The Phorminx in Classical Greece." *Journal of the American Musical Instrument Society* 2 (1976), 34–55.

Maas, Paul. "Stratonikos." *Paulys Real-Encyclopädie.* Series 2, vol. 4, part 1 (1932), columns 326–27.

———. "Timotheus." *Paulys Real-Encyclopädie.* Series 2, vol. 6, part 2 (1937), columns 1331–37.

Macchioro, Vittorio. "I ceramisti di Armento in Lucania." *Jahrbuch des Deutschen Archäologischen Instituts* 27 (1912).

Manniche, Lisa. *Ancient Egyptian Musical Instruments,* Münchner Ägyptologische Studien 34. Munich: Deutscher Kunstverlag, 1975.

Marcuse, Sibyl. *Musical Instruments: A Comprehensive Dictionary.* New York: Doubleday, 1964.

Marx, Friedrich. "Musik aus der griechischen Tragödie." *Rheinisches Museum* 82 (1933), 230–46.

Masson, Emilia. *Récherches sur les plus anciens emprunts sémitiques en grec.* Paris: Librairie C. Klincksieck, 1967.

Mathiesen, Thomas J. *A Bibliography of Sources for the Study of Ancient Greek Music.* Hackensack, N.J.: J. Boonin, 1974.

———. "New Fragments of Ancient Greek Music." *Acta Musicologica* 53 (1981), 14–32.

———, trans. *On Music,* by Aristides Quintilianus. New Haven: Yale Univ. Press, 1983.

―――. "Problems of Terminology in Ancient Greek Theory: ʿAPMONIA." In *Festival Essays for Pauline Alderman*. Ed. Burton L. Karson. Provo, Utah: Brigham Young Univ. Press, 1976.

Matt, Leonard von, and Stylianos Alexiou. *Ancient Crete*. New York: Praeger, 1968.

Mayo, Margaret E., ed. *The Art of South Italy: Vases from Magna Graecia*. Catalog of Exhibition. Richmond, Va.: Museum of Fine Arts, 1982.

Megaw, J. V. S. "The Earliest Musical Instruments in Europe." *Archaeology* 21 (1968), 124–32.

Merkelbach, R., and M. L. West, eds., *Fragmenta Hesiodea*. Oxford: Oxford Univ. Press, 1967.

Merlingen, W. Review of *Etudes Pélasgiques*, by A. J. van Windekens. *Kratylos* 6 (1961), 173.

Merry, W. W., ed. *Aristophanes' Equites*. Oxford: Clarendon Press, 1895.

Metzger, Henri. "Lebes gamikos a figures rouges du Musée National d'Athènes." *Bulletin de Correspondance Hellénique* 66–67 (1942–43), 228–47.

―――. *Les représentations dans la céramique attique du IVe siècle*. Bibliothèque des écoles françaises d'Athènes et de Rome, no. 172. 2 vols. Paris: E. de Boccard, 1951.

Metzler, Dieter. "Ein griechisches Plektron." *Archiv für Musikwissenschaft* 28 (1971), 147–50.

Michaelides, Solon. *The Music of Ancient Greece, An Encyclopaedia*. London: Faber & Faber, 1978.

Michell, H. *The Economics of Ancient Greece*. New York: Macmillan, 1940.

Mommsen, Heide. *Der Affecter*. 2 vols. Mainz: P. von Zabern, 1975.

Mountford, James F. "The Music of Pindar's 'Golden Lyre.'" *Classical Philology* 31 (1936), 120–36.

Moutsopoulos, E. *La musique dans l'oeuvre de Platon*. Paris: Presses Universitaires de France, 1959.

Münchener Jahrbuch.

Mullen, William. *Choreia: Pindar and Dance*. Princeton: Princeton Univ. Press, 1982.

Nagler, Michael. *Spontaneity and Tradition: A Study in the Oral Art of Homer*. Berkeley: Univ. of California Press, 1974.

Neubecker, Annemarie J. *Altgriechische Musik: Eine Einführung*. Darmstadt: Wissenschaftliche Buchgesellschaft, 1977.

New York Metropolitan Museum Bulletin.

Notopoulos, James A. "Archilochus, the Aoidos." *Transactions of the American Philological Association* 97 (1966), 311–15.

Österreichisches Archäologisches Institut, Jahreshefte.

Ohly, Dieter. "Zur Rekonstruktion des samischen Geräts mit dem Elfenbeinjüngling." *Athenische Mitteilungen* 74 (1959), 48–56.

Otchët Imperatorskoĭ Arkheologicheskoĭ Kommissii.

Otto, Walter F. *Die Musen und der göttliche Ursprung des Singens und Sagens*. Düsseldorf: E. Diederich, 1955.

Page, Denys. *The Homeric Odyssey*. Oxford: Clarendon Press, 1955.

PMG ―――, ed. *Poetae Melici Graeci*. Oxford: Clarendon Press, 1962.

―――, ed. *Sappho and Alcaeus*. Oxford: Clarendon Press, 1959.

―――, ed. *Select Papyri*. 3 vols. Cambridge: Harvard Univ. Press, 1962.

―――, ed. *Supplementum Lyricis Graecis*, Oxford: Clarendon Press, 1974.

Paquette, Daniel. *L'Instrument de musique dans la céramique de la Grèce antique*. Paris: Diffusion de Boccard, 1984.

Parke, H. W. *Festivals of the Athenians*. London: Thames & Hudson, 1977.

Parry, Adam, ed. *The Making of Homeric Verse: The Collected Papers of Milman Parry*. Oxford: Clarendon Press, 1971.

Patzer, Harald. "ΡΑΨΩΙΔΟΣ." *Hermes* 80 (1952), 314–25.

Payne, Humfry. *Necrocorinthia: A Study of Corinthian Art in the Archaic Period*. Oxford: Clarendon Press, 1931. College Park, Md.: McGrath, 1971.

Pearl, Orsamus. "Rules for Musical Contests." *Illinois Classical Studies* 3 (1978), 132–38.

Pearson, A. C., ed. *The Fragments of Sophocles*. 3 vols. Cambridge: Cambridge Univ. Press, 1917.

Pensa, Marina. *Rappresentazioni dell' oltretomba nella ceramica apula*. Rome: Bretschneider, 1977.

Peredolskaya, Anna. *Krasnofigurnye atticheskie vazy v Ermitazhe*. Leningrad: Sovetsky Khudozhnik, 1967.

Petracos, Basil. *Delphi*. Athens: Hesperus Editions, 1971.

Pfulh, Ernst. *Malerie und Zeichnung der Griechen*. Munich: F. Bruckmann, 1923.

Phaklaris, Panayiotis. "ΧΕΛΥΣ." *Archaiologikon Deltion* 32, pt. A (1977), 218–23.

Philadelphia Museum Journal.

Pickard-Cambridge, A. W. *Dramatic Festivals of Athens*. Oxford: Oxford Univ. Press, 1968.

Platon, Nikolaos. "Minoiki Lyra." *Charisterion eis A. K. Orlandon*, III, 208–26. Athens: Bibliothēkē tēs en Athēnais Archaiologikēs Hetaireias, no. 54, 1965.

Pomeroy, Sarah. "Supplementary Notes on Erinna." *Zeitschrift für Papyrologie und Epigraphik* 32 (1978), 17–22.

———. "Technikai kai Mousikai: The Education of Women in the Fourth Century and in the Hellenistic Period." *American Journal of Ancient History* 2 (1977), 51–68.

Porada, Edith. "A Lyre Player from Tarsus and his Relations." In *The Aegean and the Near East: Studies Presented to Hetty Goldman*. Ed. Saul S. Weinberg. Locust Valley, N.Y.: J. J. Augustin, 1956.

Proceedings of the British Academy

Prudhommeau, Germaine. *La danse grecque antique*. 2 vols. Paris: Editions du Centre National de la Recherche Scientifique, 1965.

Radermacher, L. "Der homerische Hermeshymnus." *Sitzungsberichte, Akademie der Wissenschaften in Wien*. Vol. 213, no. 1. Vienna and Leipzig: Hölder-Pichler-Tempsky, 1931.

Raubitschek, Isabelle K. *The Hearst Hillsborough Vases*. Mainz: P. von Zabern, 1969.

Reinach, T. "Lyra." In *Dictionnaire des antiquités grecques et romaines, d'après les textes et les monuments*. Ed. Charles Daremberg and Edmond Saglio. Vol. 3, part 2, pp. 1437–51. Paris: Hachette, 1877–1919.

Revue Archéologique.

ARFV Richter, Gisela M. A. *Attic Red-Figured Vases: A Survey*. New Haven: Yale Univ. Press, 1946.

———. *Catalogue of Engraved Gems*. Rome: Bretschneider, 1956.

———. *Engraved Gems of the Greeks, Etruscans, and Romans*. London: Phaidon, 1968.

———. *The Furniture of the Greeks, Etruscans, and Romans*. London: Phaidon, 1966.

———. *Handbook of Greek Art*. 5th edition. London: Phaidon, 1967.

———. *Handbook of the Classical Collection*. New York: Gilliss Press, 1922.

———. "A Pelike by the Meidias Painter." *American Journal of Archaeology* 43 (1939), 1–9.

———. *Perspective in Greek and Roman Art*. London: Phaidon, 1970.

———. *The Portraits of the Greeks*. London: Phaidon, 1965.

———, and Lindsley F. Hall. *Red-Figured Athenian Vases in the Metropolitan Museum of Art*. New Haven: Yale Univ. Press, 1936.

Richter, Gisela M. A., and Marjorie J. Milne. *Shapes and Names of Athenian Vases*. New York: Metropolitan Museum of Art, 1935.

Richter, Lukas. "Instrumentalbegleitung zur attischen Tragödie." *Das Altertum* 24 (1978), 150–59.

———. "Musikalische Aspekte der attischen Tragödienchöre." *Beiträge zur Musikwissenschaft* 14 (1972), 247–98.

Rimmer, Joan. *Ancient Musical Instruments of Western Asia in the Department of Western Asiatic Antiquities*. London: British Museum, 1969.

Robert, C. "Diogenes Oinomaios." *Paulys Real-Encyclopädie*. Vol. 5 (1903), column 737.

Roberts, Helen Dalby. "Ancient Greek Stringed Instruments, 700–200 B.C." Ph.D. diss. Univ. of Reading, 1974.

———. "Reconstructing the Greek Tortoise-shell Lyre." *World Archaeology* 12 (1981), 303–12.

———. "The Technique of Playing Ancient Greek Instruments of the Lyre Type." In *Music and Civilization*. Ed. T. C. Mitchell. *British Museum Yearbook* 4 (1980), 43–76.

Robertson, Martin. *A History of Greek Art*. 2 vols. Cambridge: Cambridge Univ. Press, 1975.

Robinson, David M.; Cornelia G. Harcum; and J. H. Iliffe. *A Catalogue of the Greek Vases in the Royal Ontario Museum of Archeology, Toronto*. 2 vols. Toronto: Univ. of Toronto Press, 1930.

Roebuck, Carl, ed. *The Muses at Work: Arts, Crafts, and Professions in Ancient Greece and Rome*. Cambridge, Mass.: MIT Press, 1969.

Rohde, E. "Γέγονε in den Biographica des Suidas." *Rheinisches Museum* 33 (1878), 161–220.

Roscher, Wilhelm Heinrich, ed. *Ausführliches Lexicon der griechischen und römischen Mythologie*. Leipzig: Teubner, 1885–1937.

Rosenmeyer, Thomas. "Alcman's *Partheneion* I Reconsidered." *Greek, Roman, and Byzantine Studies* 7 (1966), 321–59.

Rupprecht, Karl. "Sophocles als Kitharistes." *Philologus* 76 (1920), 213–15.

Sachs, Curt. *The History of Musical Instruments.* New York: W. W. Norton,
1940.

———. *Die Musikinstrumente des Alten
Ägyptens.* Berlin: Verlag von Karl Curtius, 1921.

———. *The Rise of Music in the Ancient
World.* New York: W. W. Norton, 1943.

Schadewaldt Schadewaldt, Wolfgang. *Von Homers Welt
und Werk.* Leipzig: Koehler and Amelang,
1944.

Schefold, Karl. *The Art of Classical Greece.*
Trans. J. R. Foster. New York: Crown,
1966.

———. *Die Bildnisse der antiken Dichter,
Redner und Denker.* Basel: B. Schwabe,
n.d.

———. *Götter- und Heldensagen der
Griechen in der spätarchäischen Kunst.*
Munich: Hirmer, 1978.

———. *Meisterwerke griechischer Kunst.*
Basel: B. Schwabe, 1960.

———. *Myth and Legend in Early Greek
Art.* Trans. Audrey Hicks. New York: H.
N. Abrams, 1966.

Schlesinger, Kathleen. *The Greek Aulos.*
London, 1939. Rpt. Groningen: Bouma,
1970.

Schmidt, Margot; A. D. Trendall; and Alexander Cambitoglou. *Eine Gruppe apu-
lischer Grabvasen in Basel.* Basel:
Archäologischer Verlag, 1976.

Schneider, Carl. *Kulturgeschichte des Hellenismus.* 2 vols. Munich: C. H. Beck,
1969.

Schneider, K. "Plectrum." *Paulys Real-Encyclopädie.* Series 2, vol. 21, part 1, column
187–89.

Schoeller, Felix M. *Darstellungen des Orpheus in der Antike.* Freiburg, 1969.

Schuhl, Pierre M. "Platon et la musique de
son temps." *Revue internationale de philo-
sophie* 9 (1955), 276–87.

Schwartz, Eduard, ed. *Scholia in Euripidem.*
Berlin: G. Reimer, 1887–91.

Sendry, Alfred. *Music in the Social and Religious Life of Antiquity.* Rutherford, N.J.:
Fairleigh Dickinson Univ. Press, 1974.

Shapiro, H. A., ed. *Greek Vases from
Southern Collections.* New Orleans: New
Orleans Museum of Art, 1981.

Shelmerdine, S. C. "The Homeric Hymn to
Hermes." Ph.D. diss. Univ. of Michigan,
1981.

Simon, Erika. *Die Götter der Griechen.* Munich: Hirmer, 1969.

Slater, W. J. "Artemon and Anacreon: No
Text without Context." *Phoenix* 32 (1978),
185–94.

Smith, H. R. W. *Funerary Symbolism in
Apulian Vase-Painting.* Berkeley: Univ. of
California Press, 1976.

Snodgrass, A. M. "An Historical Homeric
Society?" *Journal of Hellenic Studies* 94
(1974), 114–25.

Snyder, J. M. "Aegisthos and the Barbitos."
American Journal of Archaeology 80
(1976), 189–90.

———. "Aristophanes' Agathon as Anacreon." *Hermes* 102 (1974), 244–46.

———. "*Aulos* and *Kithara* on the Greek
Stage." In *Panathenaia: Studies in Athe-
nian Life and Thought in the Classical
Age.* Ed. T. Gregory and A. Podlecki.
Lawrence, Kans.: Coronado Press, 1979,
pp. 75–95.

———. "The Barbitos in the Classical
Period." *Classical Journal* 67 (1972),
331–40.

———. "The *Harmonia* of Bow and Lyre in
Heraclitus Fr. 51 (DK)." *Phronesis* 29
(1984), 91–95.

———. "The Web of Song: Weaving Imagery in Homer and the Lyric Poets." *Classical Journal* 76 (1981), 193–96.

Solomon, Jon. "*Ekbole* and *Eklusis* in the
Musical Treatise of Bacchius." *Symbolae
Osloenses* 55 (1980), 111–26.

———. "*Orestes* 344–45: Colometry and
Music." *Greek, Roman, and Byzantine
Studies* 18 (1977), 71–83.

Spina Spina. See Alfieri, Nereo, and Paulo Arias.

Stanford, W. B., ed. *The Odyssey of Homer.*
London: Macmillan, 1965.

Starr, Chester. "An Evening with the Flute
Girls." *La Parola del Passato* 183 (1978),
401–10.

———. *The Origins of Greek Civilization,
1100–650 B.C.* New York: Knopf, 1961.

Stauder, Wilhelm. *Die Harfen und Leiern
Vorderasiens in babylonischer und assy-
rischer Zeit.* Frankfurt: Bildstelle der J. W.
Goethe Universität, 1961.

Svoronos, Ioannes N. *Das Athener Nationalmuseum.* Athens: Beck and Barth, 1908–
37.

Talcott, Lucy, and Barbara Philippaki. "Figured Pottery." In *Small Objects from the
Pnyx: II. Hesperia* supplement 10. Princeton: American School of Classical Studies,
1956, pp. 1–77.

Thimme, Jürgen, ed. *Art and Culture of the
Cyclades: Handbook of an Ancient Civilization.* Karlsruhe: C. F. Müller, 1977.

Tillyard, Eustace M. W. *The Hope Vases.* Cambridge: Cambridge Univ. Press, 1923.

Trendall, A. D. *Early South Italian Vase-Painting.* Mainz: P. von Zabern, 1974.

———. *Gli Indigini nella pittura italiota.* Taranto, 1971.

———. *Greek Vases in the Logie Collection.* Christchurch, N.Z.: Univ. of Canterbury, 1971.

———. *Paestan Pottery.* Rome: British School at Rome, 1936.

———. "Phlyax Vases." University of London, *Bulletin of the Institute of Classical Studies,* supplement 19, 1967.

LCS ———. *The Red-Figured Vases of Lucania, Campania, and Sicily.* 2 vols. Oxford: Clarendon Press, 1967.

———. *South Italian Vase Painting.* London: British Museum, 1966.

———. *Vasi italioti ed etruschi a figure rosse.* (Monumenti, musei e gallerie pontificie. Vasi antichi dipinti del Vaticano). Citta del Vaticano, 1953–55.

RFVA Trendall, A. D., and Alexander Cambitoglou. *The Red-Figured Vases of Apulia.* Oxford: Clarendon Press, 1978.

Trendall, A. D., and T. B. L. Webster. *Illustrations of Greek Drama.* London: Phaidon, 1971.

Treu, M., ed. *Archilochos.* Munich: Ernst Heimeran, 1959.

Turner, E. G. "Two Unrecognized Ptolemaic Papyri." *Journal of Hellenic Studies* 76 (1956), 95–98.

Vermeule, Cornelius. "Eleven Greek Vases in Boston." *Classical Journal* 59 (1964), 193–207.

———. "Vases and Terracottas in Boston: Recent Acquisitions." *Classical Journal* 64 (1968), 49–67.

Vermeule, Emily T. *Greece in the Bronze Age.* Chicago: Univ. of Chicago Press, 1964.

———, and Vassos Karageorghis. *Mycenaean Pictorial Vase Painting.* Cambridge, Mass.: Harvard Univ. Press, 1982.

Vetter, W. "Magadis." *Paulys Real-Encyclopädie,* vol. 14, part 1 (1928), columns 288–91.

———. "Die Musik im platonischen Staate." *Neue Jahrbücher* 11 (1935), 306–20.

———. "Nomos." *Paulys Real-Encyclopädie.* Vol. 33 (1936), columns 840–43.

———. "Terpandros." *Paulys Real-Encyclopädie.* Series 2, vol. 5, part 1 (1934), columns 785–86.

Vlastos, G. "On Heraclitus." *American Journal of Philology* 76 (1955), 348–51.

Vries, Keith De. "East Meets West at Dinner." *Expedition* 15.4 (1973), 32–39.

Wace, A. J. B., and F. H. Stubbings, ed. *A Companion to Homer.* New York: Macmillan, 1962.

Waldstein, Charles, et al. *The Argive Heraion.* 2 vols. Boston, 1902–05.

Webster, T. B. L. *From Mycenae to Homer.* New York: Norton, 1964.

———. "Greek Archaeology and Literature." *Lustrum* 6 (1961), 5–37; 11 (1966), 5–32; 15 (1970), 5–35.

———. "Monuments Illustrating Tragedy and Satyr Play." University of London, *Bulletin of the Institute of Classical Studies,* supplement 20, 1967.

Wegner, M. "Phillis." *Paulys Real-Encyclopädie.* Vol. 19, part 2,, column 2430.

Griechenland Wegner, Max. *Griechenland.* In *Musikgeschichte in Bildern.* Vol. 2, part 4. Ed. H. Besseler and M. Schneider. Leipzig: Deutscher Verlag für Musik, n.d.

———. *Die Musikinstrumente des alten Orients.* Orbis Antiquus 2. Münster: Aschendorff, 1950.

Musikleben ———. *Das Musikleben der Griechen.* Berlin: de Gruyter, 1949.

MT ———. *Musik und Tanz.* Archaeologia Homerica, Vol. 3, chapter U. Göttingen: Vandenhoeck and Ruprecht, 1968.

West, M. L., ed. *Hesiod: Theogony.* Oxford: Clarendon Press, 1966.

———. "Note on a Note." *Journal of Hellenic Studies* 91 (1971), 143.

———. "The Singing of Homer and the Modes of Early Greek Music." *Journal of Hellenic Studies* 101 (1981), 113–29.

Wilamowitz-Möllendorff, Ulrich von. *Pindaros.* Berlin: Weidmann, 1922.

———. *Timotheos: Die Perser.* Leipzig: Hinrichs, 1903.

Winnington-Ingram, R. P. "Ancient Greek Music, 1932–1957." *Lustrum* 3 (1958), 6–57; 259–60.

———. "Greece I (Ancient)." In *The New Grove Dictionary of Music and Musicians.* 20 vols. Ed. Stanley Sadie. London: Macmillan, 1980. Vol. 7, pp. 659–72.

———. "The Pentatonic Tuning of the Greek Lyre: A Theory Examined." *Classical Quarterly* 6 (1956), 169–86.

Winnington-Ingram, R. P., and J. F. Mountford. "Music." In *Oxford Classical Dictionary.* 2d edition. Oxford: Clarendon Press, 1970, pp. 705–13.

Winter, F. *Die antiken Terrakotten III: Die Typen der figürlichen Terrakotten II.* Berlin: Verlag von W. Spemann, 1903.

Winternitz, Emanuel. *Musical Instruments and their Symbolism in Western Art.* London: Faber & Faber, 1967.

———. "The Survival of the Kithara and the Evolution of the English Cittern: A Study in Morphology." *Journal of the Warburg and Courtauld Institute* 24 (1961), 222–29.

Zanker, Paul. *Wandel der Hermesgestalt in der attischen Vasenmalerei.* Bonn: R. Habelt, 1965.

Zepernick, K. "Die Exzerpte des Athenaeus in den Dipnosophisten und ihre Glaubwürdigkeit." *Philologus* 77 (1921), 311–63.

Index

An entry that begins with an italicized, lowercased word refers to discussions of the word itself; under "*kithara*," for example, are listed discussions of the word *kithara*; in contrast, the entry "Kithara" cites discussions of the instrument.

Achilles, 4, 5, 6, 11, 38, 41, 201
Acrobatic dances, 141, 142
Aeschylus, 80, 225n5
Afterlife: and chelys-lyra, 89, 178
Alcaeus, 25, 26, 223n33, 224n65; and barbitos, 39, 116, 120, 127, 202; and harps, 40, 148
Alcestis (Euripides), 116, 123
Alkman, 25, 30, 31, 34, 55, 149, 202
alyros, 80
Amphion, 33, 79–80, 201
Amphitrite, 226n17
Amphorae, 55, 61, 81, 114, 229n17
Anabasis (Xenophon), 142
Anacreontea, 40, 119, 122
Anakreon, 80, 140; and barbitos, 39, 113, 116, 118–20, 127, 225n82, 236n30, 236n35, 236n37; and harps, 40–41, 148, 149
Anatolia, 1, 9, 12, 13, 221n39, 221n53
Anaxilas, 148
Angle harps, 151, 152, 154, 182–83, 187, 188
Anthesteria festival, 89, 115
antilyros, 229n12
Antiope, 173
Aoidoi, 5–6, 10–11, 30, 31
aorter, 67, 228n75
Apaturia festival, 241n14
Aphrodite, 84, 85, 146, 172, 230n36; and harps, 154, 181, 182, 243n97; and kithara, 172–76 passim, 242n41; and chelys-lyra, 178
Apollo, 200, 201, 226n16, 231n83; and lyre, 5, 10, 35, 36, 229n11; and phorminx, 26–30 passim, 54, 139, 140, 222n19, 223n21, 238n6; and

kithara, 32, 33–34, 41, 54–58 passim, 63, 64, 69, 80, 171–74 passim, 202, 221n51, 225nn7–8, 226nn16–17, 241n38, 242nn43–44, 46, 60; and kitharistes, 55; in libation scenes, 55, 225n14, 241n37; and chelys-lyra, 81–84 passim, 91, 92, 178, 179, 229nn17–20, 24, 242n76; and Thracian kithara, 145, 171; presented as comic character, 172; and Hellenistic kithara, 174, 175; and Italiote kithara, 175, 176; with harp, 181, 240n88; and lute, 185
Apollodorus of Athens, 150
Apollonios Rhodios, 33
Archaic period: sources on, 24–26; phorminx in, 26–30, 41; kithara in, 30–34; lyre in, 34–35; chelys-lyra in, 35–39; barbitos in, 39–40; harps in, 40–41
Archemoros, 176
Archilochos of Paros, 83, 222n6, 223n39, 224nn51–52, 57; and *lyra*, 25, 34, 80
Ares, 56, 57, 225n7
Argonautica (Apollonios Rhodios), 33
Ariadne: pictured with Apollo, 56; pictured with Dionysos, 57, 114, 178, 179, 181, 226n16, 235n5
Arion of Lesbos, 31, 58, 167, 178, 201, 223n39
Aristophanes, 55, 67, 87, 94–95, 148; on phorminx, 54, 59, 62, 65; use of *lyra*, 79, 80, 229n8; on barbitos, 119, 237n68
Aristotle: references to kithara, 54, 226n24; on music and education, 87; on barbitos, 121;

on harps, 149, 151; on music, 166, 167, 170; on musical instruments, 181, 184, 186
Aristoxenos, 40, 148, 149, 201
Arms: on Minoan lyre, 2; on Mycenean lyre, 8; on post-Mycenean lyre, 9; in late Geometric art, 11, 12, 13, 221n52, 222n54; on phorminx, 28–29, 30, 143–44, 238n22; on kithara, 32–35 passim, 54, 65, 66; on chelys-lyra, 36, 37, 38, 96–97, 180, 233nn120–21, 243n81; on barbitos, 124–25, 237nn71, 74, 77–78; on Thracian kithara, 145, 147, 239n50; on 4th-c. kithara, 174; on Hellenistic kithara, 175; on Italiote kithara, 177, 242n66
Artemis, 85, 225n14, 230n36; and phorminx, 26; pictured with Apollo, 28, 32, 56, 64, 81, 83, 171–79 passim, 185, 226nn16–17, 227n60, 241n37; in libation scenes, 55, 81, 229nn18–19
Artemon, 155
"Asiatic kithara," 239n47
Asteas, 172
Athena, 61, 84–85, 226nn16–17; pictured with Apollo, 56, 81; pictured with Heracles, 57, 226n19, 235n8; pictured with chelys-lyra, 82, 229n17; in Italiote paintings, 242n60
Athenaeus, 40, 118, 147, 149, 155, 239n56
Athenaion Politeia, 184
Athena Painter, workshop of, 226n19
Athens, 53. *See also individual instruments by name*
Auletrides, 5, 184

Aulos, 201; played by women, 5, 85, 86, 90, 115, 117, 140, 141, 230n46, 235n21; in Homer, 10; and lyre in late Geometric art, 12, 13; in Archaic period, 30, 33, 34, 35, 39, 222n14, 223nn23, 31; played by satyrs, 56; and kithara, 57, 58, 68–69, 176; and drama, 59; mentioned by Pindar, 68; and musical contests, 69; and laments, 80, 229n29; and chelys-lyra, 85, 89, 91, 178, 179, 230n42, 231nn78–80; and drinking, 114, 115; and phorminx, 140, 141; and harps, 148, 154, 182, 243n100; comments of philosophers on, 168, 169, 241n20; and lutes, 185

Bacchylides, 55, 80, 120, 124, 225nn5, 7
Banquet scenes: and chelys-lyra, 41, 178, 179; and kithara, 57–58, 69; and harps, 181
barbitizein, 113, 116, 235n3
barbitos, 39, 113, 120, 225n78
Barbitos, 127–28, 184, 186, 201, 228n89, 230n46; and Sappho, 25, 39, 120, 127; in Archaic literature, 39–40, 224n59; and chelys-lyra, 86, 90, 91, 231n80; vase paintings of, 113–21 passim; literary references to, 116, 119, 120; and Anakreon, 118–20; and poets, 120; used at home, 120; music lessons with, 121; and phorminx, 140, 141; in 4th-c. paintings, 170, 242n55; role of, 202. *See also under subject headings*

257